READING WITH THE GRAIN OF SCRIPTURE

READING *with the* GRAIN *of* SCRIPTURE

RICHARD B. HAYS

William B. Eerdmans Publishing Company
Grand Rapids, Michigan

Wm. B. Eerdmans Publishing Co.
4035 Park East Court SE, Grand Rapids, Michigan 49546
www.eerdmans.com

Published 2020
Printed in the United States of America

26 25 24 23 22 21 20 1 2 3 4 5 6 7

ISBN 978-0-8028-7845-8

Library of Congress Cataloging-in-Publication Data

Names: Hays, Richard B., author.
Title: Reading with the grain of scripture / Richard B. Hays.
Description: Grand Rapids, Michigan : William B. Eerdmans Publishing Company, 2020. | Includes bibliographical references and index. | Summary: "A collection of Richard Hays's most significant essays from the last twenty-five years"—Provided by publisher.
Identifiers: LCCN 2020017024 | ISBN 9780802878458 (hardcover)
Subjects: LCSH: Bible. New Testament—Theology. | Bible. New Testament—Criticism, interpretation, etc. | Bible—Hermeneutics.
Classification: LCC BS2361.3 .H39 2020 | DDC 225.6—dc23
LC record available at https://lccn.loc.gov/2020017024

To my students and colleagues at Duke University, 1991–2018, in gratitude for long-running conversations about reading with the grain of Scripture.

ὁ μὲν θερισμὸς πολύς, οἱ δὲ ἐργάται ὀλίγοι·
δεήθητε οὖν τοῦ κυρίου τοῦ θερισμοῦ
ὅπως ἐργάτας ἐκβάλῃ εἰς τὸν θερισμὸν αὐτοῦ.
(Luke 10:2)

Contents

Abbreviations

AB	Anchor Bible
ABR	*Australian Biblical Review*
ABRL	Anchor Bible Reference Library
AnBib	Analecta Biblica
ANF	*Ante-Nicene Fathers*
ANTC	Abingdon New Testament Commentaries
BDAG	Danker, Frederick W., Walter Bauer, William F. Arndt, and F. Wilbur Gingrich. *Greek-English Lexicon of the New Testament and Other Early Christian Literature.* 3rd ed. Chicago: University of Chicago Press, 2000
BDF	Blass, Friedrich, Albert Debrunner, and Robert W. Funk. *A Greek Grammar of the New Testament and Other Early Christian Literature.* Chicago: University of Chicago Press, 1961
BGBE	Beiträge zur Geschichte der biblischen Exegese
BHT	Beiträge zur historischen Theologie
BNTC	Black's New Testament Commentaries
BZ	*Biblische Zeitschrift*
BZNW	Beihefte zur Zeitschrift für die neutestamentliche Wissenschaft
CBET	Contributions to Biblical Exegesis and Theology
CBQ	*Catholic Biblical Quarterly*
CJT	*Canadian Journal of Theology*
CRBR	*Critical Review of Books in Religion*
EKKNT	Evangelisch-katholischer Kommentar zum Neuen Testament
EvT	*Evangelische Theologie*
ExpTim	*Expository Times*
FC	Fathers of the Church

FRLANT	Forschungen zur Religion und Literatur des Alten und Neuen Testaments
HBT	*Horizons in Biblical Theology*
HNTC	Harper's New Testament Commentaries
HThKNT	Herders Theologischer Kommentar zum Neuen Testament
HTR	*Harvard Theological Review*
HUCA	*Hebrew Union College Annual*
IBC	Interpretation: A Bible Commentary for Teaching and Preaching
ICC	International Critical Commentary
Int	*Interpretation*
JBL	*Journal of Biblical Literature*
JSNT	*Journal for the Study of the New Testament*
JSNTSup	Journal for the Study of the New Testament Supplement Series
JSOT	*Journal for the Study of the Old Testament*
JTC	*Journal for Theology and the Church*
JTI	*Journal of Theological Interpretation*
LCC	Library of Christian Classics
LNTS	The Library of New Testament Studies
NIB	*The New Interpreter's Bible.* Edited by Leander E. Keck. 12 vols. Nashville: Abingdon, 1994–2004
NovT	*Novum Testamentum*
NovTSup	Supplements to Novum Testamentum
NT	New Testament
NTAbh	Neutestamentliche Abhandlungen
NTS	*New Testament Studies*
OT	Old Testament
ProEccl	*Pro Ecclesia*
RB	*Revue biblique*
SBL	Society of Biblical Literature
SBLDS	Society of Biblical Literature Dissertation Series
SBLMS	Society of Biblical Literature Monograph Series
SBT	Studies in Biblical Theology
SJT	*Scottish Journal of Theology*
SNTS	Studiorum Novi Testamenti Societas
SNTSMS	Society for New Testament Studies Monograph Series
SSEJC	Studies in Scripture in Early Judaism and Christianity

TPINTC	TPI New Testament Commentaries
TU	*Texte und Untersuchungen*
TWNT	*Theologische Wörterbuch zum Neuen Testament.* Edited by Gerhard Kittel and Gerhard Friedrich. Stuttgart, 1932–1979
TynBul	*Tyndale Bulletin*
WBC	Word Biblical Commentary
WMANT	Wissenschaftliche Monographien zum Alten und Neuen Testament
WUNT	Wissenschaftliche Untersuchungen zum Neuen Testament
ZNT	*Zeitschrift für Neues Testament*
ZNW	*Zeitschrift für die neutestamentliche Wissenschaft und die Kunde der älteren Kirche*
ZTK	*Zeitschrift für Theologie und Kirche*

Introduction

Gathering the Wheat

In the Gospel of Matthew, Jesus tells a parable about a landowner who finds that his field has unexpectedly produced a mixture of wheat and weeds. His workers ask whether they should pull out the weeds, but the owner decides to let them grow together with the wheat until the time of harvest, when the reapers will be instructed as follows: "Collect the weeds first and bind them in bundles to be burned, but gather the wheat into my barn" (Matt 13:30b).

When I retired from the faculty of Duke Divinity School in the summer of 2018, I began the formidable task of weeding out multiple file cabinets full of correspondence, notes, manuscripts, and such. Much of it needed to be gathered into bundles—not to be burned, but to be consigned to the shredder for recycling. But as I sorted through this *corpus mixtum* of materials, it gradually occurred to me that amidst all the weeds, there were some stalks of wheat worth harvesting. The present volume of collected essays represents my attempt, at the end of a long career of teaching and writing, to harvest some of the wheat and gather it into the barn.[1]

The essays selected for inclusion in this collection span a period of twenty-five years, though the majority of them appeared in print since 2008. The pieces chosen here, all but one previously published, were singled out from the others in my file cabinets because they represent major themes of my work; they stake out positions I have taken on key controverted issues in the field of New Testament studies.[2] More importantly, all these essays illustrate, in one

1. I am of course aware that my analogical application of the parable differs from the eschatological interpretation given in Matthew's Gospel (Matt 13:36–43). Parables are open-ended invitations to the imagination.

2. A previous volume of collected essays gathered up a number of my earlier essays on Paul: Richard B. Hays, *The Conversion of the Imagination: Paul as Interpreter of Israel's Scripture* (Grand Rapids: Eerdmans, 2005). All the essays in that volume were originally

way or another, how I have sought to carry out scholarly work as an aspect of discipleship—as a process of faith seeking exegetical clarity.

If it is true that in Christ God was reconciling the world to himself, and if it is true that Jesus was raised from the dead on the third day, it follows that all our reading and thinking must be reshaped by those truths. For the past forty years I have been seeking to learn how to read closely and faithfully the testimonies of the early authors who wrote about these world-shaking events. The essays gathered here are the fruit of my effort to listen carefully to their testimony-bearing texts.

The Organization of the Collection

The present volume is organized into five thematically grouped parts.

Part 1 offers a set of four essays that reflect broadly on the task of interpretation. In various ways, these pieces address the unity and diversity of the narratives of Scripture; the hermeneutical perspective of the interpreter; the implications of the resurrection for our work of reading; and the figural relationship between the Old Testament and the New.

Part 2 gathers up four essays addressing the problem of knowing the historical figure of Jesus. The first three of these are critical reviews of widely read books that approach this question from very different angles; the last represents my own preliminary attempt to sketch out a constructive picture of the historical person Jesus of Nazareth.

Part 3 encompasses seven essays on Paul the apostle. As the titles of these pieces indicate, the first six take up particular theological issues that are foregrounded in Paul's thought: the identity of Jesus, the saving significance of his death, the apocalyptic inbreaking of new creation, the role of the Holy Spirit, the shape of Paul's gospel in Romans, and the eschatological destiny of Israel. The last essay in part 3 attempts to reframe the relationship between Paul's own writings and the portrayal of his preaching in the Acts of the Apostles.

Part 4, then, moves to address a broader range of issues in New Testament theology. The six essays in this section cast a net more broadly across the New Testament canon. They explore the Christology of the book of Revelation, the problem of supersessionism in the Letter to the Hebrews, the character of Pauline anthropology, the understanding of law in the Acts of the Apostles,

published before the year 2000. Only one essay from that volume ("A Hermeneutic of Trust") has been included in the present book.

the impact of rereading Romans through the third article of the Nicene Creed, and the theological problem of long-deferred eschatological hope.

The conclusion, subtitled "A Hermeneutic of Trust," returns to explore once again the posture from which all our reading should be performed; this piece interrogates the corrosive hermeneutic of suspicion that has characterized much late modern interpretation. The epilogue, "A Dark Fruition," is the valedictory lecture I gave to the community of Duke Divinity School on the occasion of my retirement; it is an exercise in looking backwards and summing up some important things I have learned over the span of my academic career.

Diversity and Coherence in the Collection

The essays gathered here differ in genre because they were written for various occasions and diverse audiences. Some originated as public lectures, some as papers at academic conferences, some as reviews of books, some as journal articles, and some as invited contributions to edited volumes of essays on a particular topic. I therefore must ask readers of the present volume for their indulgence in adjusting their readerly expectations to the tone and character of each essay.

Nonetheless, I do believe that the essays in this collection, though disparate in origin, reflect an underlying coherence of thought. As I read backwards over my own work, I would identify at least six recurrent themes that are woven throughout these essays:

1. The importance of narrative as the "glue" that holds the Bible together.
2. The retrospectively discerned figural coherence between the Old Testament and the New.
3. The centrality of the resurrection of Jesus.
4. The hope for new creation and God's eschatological transformation of the world.
5. The importance of standing in trusting humility before the text.
6. The importance of reading Scripture within and for the community of faith: the ἐκκλησία τοῦ θεοῦ.

The seeds of these ideas were germinating in my writing from the beginning of my scholarly career, but they have grown to mature fruition only in the past ten years, during which my thinking has developed and deepened. I hope that readers of this book will be able to follow that development and see how, at the end of the day, these themes converge and complement one another.

Some Notes on the Production of the Collection

All of the essays included in this volume have been given new titles that seek to suggest how they fit together as part of a larger intellectual project. The essays themselves, however, have undergone only minor revision and editing. In general, I have not attempted to update footnotes and bibliographical references. In a few places, I have added references to particularly significant works published more recently, but there are only a small number of such additions. To provide more thorough bibliographical updating would have been a comprehensive task that might have delayed publication indefinitely.

Readers should therefore see each of the individual essays as a word written for its time and occasion. To take one example, chapter 21 ("Eschatology: 'Why Do You Stand Looking Up into Heaven?'") addresses the popular eschatological speculations that arose around the turn of the millennium in the year 2000. To cite another instance, chapter 5 ("Rebranding Jesus and the Pitfalls of Entrepreneurial Criticism") was a sharply critical review of the momentary sensation caused by the publication of the work of the Jesus Seminar in the early 1990s; even though that particular cultural phenomenon has faded from view, the issues it raised concerning method in the study of the historical Jesus are perennial. Or, to give a third example, the epilogue ("A Dark Fruition") is a very personal parting word addressed to the community where I taught and served for twenty-seven years. No attempt has been made in any of these cases to revise the essays to remove their situational particularity.

Nor have I sought to remove all repetitions. Readers may find a few points that appear in more than one of the essays; I have left these in place because each one is an integral part of the argument in the context where it originally appeared. Similarly, a couple of the essays in this volume contain a few paragraphs of material that was later taken up into my books *Reading Backwards* and *Echoes of Scripture in the Gospels*. In this case, some readers may be interested to see the context in which I first developed my interpretations before they were woven into the larger fabric of my books.[3]

Unless otherwise indicated, translations of biblical texts throughout all the essays are either my own or taken from the New Revised Standard Version. For the most part, I have not flagged the places where my translations differ slightly from the NRSV. To do so would simply clutter up the text; readers who

3. Seeing this relation between earlier essay and later book content is perhaps loosely analogous to hearing how the Beatles' *Esher Demos* prefigure the more fully produced versions of the songs that eventually appeared on the *White Album*. (Let the reader understand.)

are interested can check the Greek or Hebrew texts to see the underlying basis for my translation choices.

One other stylistic feature of these essays may require explanation: wherever the NT uses the word νόμος to refer to the Torah, or to Israel's Scripture more generally, I have chosen to capitalize the English translation "Law" in order to distinguish this term from other meanings of "law." For example, the lowercase spelling is used in expressions such as "Roman law" or "the law of sin," but the uppercase in instances such as Rom 3:19: "Now we know that whatever the Law says, it speaks to those who are under the Law."

The compilation of this collection of essays has proven to be a lengthy and complicated task. I am deeply in the debt of all those who contributed to the process.

First of all, I am greatly indebted to Carey Newman, who shared the initial vision for this book and brainstormed creatively with me to figure out how to process the kernels of raw wheat into a loaf of bread. Without his collaborative guidance, this book could not have assumed its present shape.

I am also grateful to Jenny Hunt, Cade Jarrell, and Anna Lam for their careful labors in pulling together the material that is contained between these covers and assisting with the preliminary editorial work. Their task was especially challenging because the essays presented here were previously published in various venues with divergent stylistic conventions.

My thanks and appreciation go also to James Ernest, editor-in-chief at Eerdmans, for reading the manuscript with a careful eye and graciously accepting it for publication, to Ellen Vosburg for her thorough copyediting, and to Jenny Hoffman, senior project editor, who oversaw the final editing and production of the book. They, along with all the Eerdmans staff, have made the publication process go smoothly.

Finally, I want to offer a word of gratitude to my students at Yale (1981–1991) and Duke (1991–2018), and also to my faculty colleagues at both of these institutions. It was a privilege and a joy to engage in a long-running conversation, over a period of thirty-seven years, with these friends and students about how to read Scripture well. Their insights, criticisms, and wisdom have made me a better reader—and, I hope, a better man.

Counsel to the Reader

One of the key developmental tasks of late life is to look back over one's career and think integratively about it, asking how it has held together and how it has mattered. For that reason, the work of gathering in the harvest of these essays has been a rewarding project for me. I hope that this volume may also be of some use and benefit to readers. But I offer a preliminary word of advice to those readers who decide to enter this great barn of a book, with sheaves stacked all around. Heed the admonition that the Nun's Priest in Chaucer's *Canterbury Tales* offered to his hearers at the end of his tale: "Taketh the fruit, and lat the chaf be stille."[4]

4. Geoffrey Chaucer, "The Nun's Priest's Tale," l. 623, in *Chaucer's Poetry: An Anthology for the Modern Reader*, ed. E. T. Donaldson (New York: Ronald Press, 1958).

Part 1

INTERPRETATION

1

Narrative Interpretation and the Quest for Theological Unity

> It is of the very nature of narratives to subsume variations that outside their narrational context are contradictions.
>
> George Lindbeck[1]

The Problem of Diverse Voices in Scripture

The question of unity within the diversity of Christian Scripture is an ancient problem.[2] Its roots lie in the formative period of the second and third centuries, when fateful decisions were taking shape about the scope and content of the body of writings that should be regarded as authoritative by the emergent Christian church. Should the Law and the Prophets be read as Scripture by Christians? If so, how was the church to construe their coherence with the story of Jesus Christ, despite Marcion's vigorous assertion of their theological incompatibility with the Gospel? Or, to take another problem, did the Gospel of John really belong alongside Matthew, Mark, and Luke as an authoritative testimony to the truth about Jesus, despite its obvious material differences from the other three and its disturbing dualistic tendencies? Was Irenaeus's argument for including John within a fourfold Gospel witness persuasive against gnostic readings of the Fourth Gospel? Irenaeus claimed that the (notoriously elusive) Rule of Faith gave him both a lens through which to discern the unity of the fourfold Gospel and a criterion for the exclusion of other gospels that conflicted with this norm. Even after the fourfold Gospel canon was firmly

1. George Lindbeck, "The Story-Shaped Church: Critical Exegesis and Theological Interpretation," in *Scriptural Authority and Narrative Interpretation*, ed. Garrett Green (Philadelphia: Fortress, 1987), 169.

2. This essay was originally a paper delivered in the Theological Hermeneutics of Christian Scripture Group at the Annual Meeting of the Society of Biblical Literature, Washington, DC, November 18, 2006.

settled,[3] conversations about the proper extent of the collection that the church came to call its canon persisted well into the fourth century—and these conversations turned, in part, on the question of the *theological* coherence of various disputed writings such as the book of Revelation with the apostolic message attested by other writings already deemed authoritative in the community.

So the problem of "unity and diversity in the Bible" is not a new problem in modernity. It would, however, be fair to observe that in antiquity the operative assumption of all parties was that Scripture *should* be read as a unified witness to the truth; the debates turned on the question of how to draw the boundaries of the operative canon so as to safeguard its material unity. Even in the Reformation era, Luther's well-known denigration of the Epistle of James[4] illustrates the same tendency: rather than seeking to demonstrate James's coherence with Paul, Luther sought to relegate it effectually to deuterocanonical status. He made this drastic hermeneutical move in order to protect his conviction that Paul and the Gospels consistently bear witness to a unified message: they proclaim Christ in a way that he believed James did not.

In post-Enlightenment biblical criticism, the framing of the problem shifted. Near the end of the eighteenth century, Johann Philipp Gabler articulated the governing assumption of the age: the timeless theological truths of the Bible come to us buried like nuggets of gold in the dross of historically contingent writings, or—as Gabler's contemporary Thomas Jefferson put it with greater rhetorical flair—like diamonds in a dunghill.[5] The role of the critic is to refine the raw material of the Bible and to cull out the precious conceptual abstractions that are the real stuff of theology proper. It is not a matter of deciding which individual writings are reliable witnesses to the truth; rather, it is a matter of discerning a conceptual unity that lies somewhere beneath the surface of the diverse texts. Gabler was confident that historical criticism could excavate pure truths that would lend themselves to the dogmatician's construction of a coherent universal theology.

As the work of historical criticism proceeded, however, the Enlightenment's serene confidence about discovering unified universal truth in the Bible re-

3. Cf. Graham N. Stanton, *Jesus and Gospel* (Cambridge: Cambridge University Press, 2004), 63–91.

4. Martin Luther, *Prefaces to the New Testament*, in *Luther's Works*, vol. 35, ed. E. Theodore Bachmann (Philadelphia: Fortress, 1960), 362.

5. John Sandys-Wunsch and Laurence Eldredge, "J. P. Gabler and the Distinction between Biblical and Dogmatic Theology: Translation, Commentary, and Discussion of His Originality," *SJT* 33 (1980): 133–58, esp. 138; *The Jefferson Bible: The Life and Morals of Jesus of Nazareth* (Boston: Beacon, 2001), 17.

ceded. One cumulative effect of historical-critical work throughout the nineteenth and twentieth centuries was to undermine assumptions about the unity of the Bible's witness. This development had at least four facets:

(1) Historical critics exposed seams and sources within individual texts, claiming to discern multiple and even conflicting perspectives behind and within a single witness. One thinks, for example, of Bultmann's hypothesis that an ecclesiastical redactor had injected fragments of apocalyptic eschatology into the Fourth Gospel precisely to contravene John's own radically existential message.[6] Or, to cite a more widely accepted hypothesis, many critics have suggested that the Gospels of Matthew and Luke have incorporated a hypothetical Q source that saw no saving significance in Jesus's death.[7]

(2) The historical approach tended to highlight the situationally contingent character of individual biblical writings. The Pauline Letters, for example, according to many critics, could no longer be read as expressions of a consistent theology; rather, they were ad hoc responses to various local problems, and one should not expect them to hang together conceptually.[8]

(3) Critical attention to the original historical settings of the biblical writings also generated numerous theories about early Christianity as an arena of conflict between rival theologies and practices. The apparent *Auseinandersetzung* between the Pauline Letters and the Letter of James was only the tip of the iceberg; what we see through critical examination of the NT, it is alleged, is a collision of conflicting ideologies vying for power. Of course, one thinks here of the massively influential constructions of F. C. Baur.[9] One of the most powerful *theological* articulations of this viewpoint was Ernst Käsemann's blistering polemic in 1963 against the World Council of Churches for sponsoring a modernized version of Lukan *Heilsgeschichte* that threatened to engulf and negate the lordship of Christ over the church.[10] According to Käsemann, the

6. Rudolf Bultmann, *Das Evangelium des Johannes* (Göttingen: Vandenhoeck & Ruprecht, 1950), 98.

7. James M. Robinson, "History of Q Research," in *The Critical Edition of* Q, ed. James M. Robinson, Paul Hoffman, and John S. Kloppenborg (Minneapolis: Fortress, 2000), esp. xxxviii–xlvii.

8. In the SBL Pauline Theology Group of the 1980s, J. Christiaan Beker's attempt to find within the contingency of the letters a coherent apocalyptic message was decidedly the minority view.

9. F. C. Baur, "Die Christuspartei in der korinthinischen Gemeinde, der Gegensatz des petrinischen und paulinischen Christenthums in der ältesten Kirche," *Tübinger Zeitschrift für Theologie* 5 (1831): 61–206.

10. Ernst Käsemann, "Unity and Diversity in New Testament Ecclesiology," *NovT* 6 (1963): 290–97; subsequently published as "Unity and Multiplicity in New Testament Ec-

Pauline kerygma of the crucified Christ was the nonnegotiable critical norm that must stand in irreconcilable conflict with all ecclesial triumphalism, even if that triumphalism should appear within the NT itself. (Notice the formal similarity to Luther's assessment of James.) In our own time, we have seen several variants of this hermeneutical move, replacing the doctrine of justification with theological perspectives based on gender or ethnicity as the critical norm for championing some NT voices against others.[11]

(4) Finally, historical criticism has highlighted the distance of the Bible from our world and our categories of interpretation. This created a new kind of hermeneutical problem. Prior to modernity, theologians saw themselves living within the symbolic world of Scripture and therefore understood the church's confessional tradition as nothing other than the organic explication of the Bible's coherent message. With the rise of historical consciousness in modernity, the contingent character of that confessional tradition became more readily visible; consequently, many critics came to see the church's dogma not as a faithful interpretation of the Bible but as an alien imposition upon it, an anachronistic harmonization of the pluralism of these ancient texts. One outcome of this trajectory of thought has been a newly heightened interest in the history of interpretation, not in order to illuminate the theological meaning of the Bible's witness, but rather to trace its diverse social effects. In his 2004 presidential address to the Studiorum Novi Testamenti Societas (SNTS) in Barcelona, Wayne Meeks argued that we should give up the effort to find "normative" meanings in texts. The student of the NT should now instead seek to trace the "formative" effects of the NT, i.e., its influence on the formation of culture. "We should start," Meeks writes, "by erasing from our vocabulary the terms 'biblical theology' and, even more urgently, 'New Testament theology.'" Why? Because these terms "claim textual and historical warrants" for normative and unifying propositions that are actually nothing other than contingent products of the interests of later interpretative communities.[12]

---

clesiology," in *New Testament Questions of Today,* trans. W. J. Montague and W. F. Bunge (London: SCM; Philadelphia: Fortress, 1969 [1965]), 252–59. Käsemann's position had already been substantially articulated in a 1951 lecture, published in English translation as "The Canon of the New Testament and the Unity of the Church," in *Essays on New Testament Themes*, SBT 41 (London: SCM, 1964), 95–107.

11. E.g., Elisabeth Schüssler Fiorenza, *In Memory of Her: A Feminist Theological Reconstruction of Christian Origins* (New York: Crossroad, 1983).

12. Wayne A. Meeks, "Why Study the New Testament?," *NTS* 51 (2005): 155–70, esp. 167–68. Meeks's position aligns closely with the programmatic views of William Wrede, "The Task and Methods of 'New Testament Theology,'" in *The Nature of New Testament*

In the face of these developments, it has become increasingly difficult to talk about the unity of Scripture. Under the impact of historical criticism, the Bible seems to fall apart into a diversity—or even a cacophony—of disparate voices.

Narrative Interpretation to the Rescue of Scripture's Unity?

During the past generation, however, we have also witnessed an explosion of interest in literary approaches to the Bible, often with a particular focus on narrative interpretation. The widespread appeal of such approaches has almost surely had something to do with an underlying hope that they might help us recover the unity of Scripture, or at least the unity of individual Scriptural texts.

Powerful impetus was given to this literary turn by the work of Hans Frei, whose paradigm-changing book *The Eclipse of Biblical Narrative* devastatingly documented the literary tone-deafness of eighteenth- and nineteenth-century biblical hermeneutics, particularly in Germany. Frei showed that criticism during this era, by focusing almost exclusively on reconstructing a history of events and sources behind the texts, had forfeited theology's traditional capacity to read the Bible as a narrative text whose meaning was imbedded precisely in its way of telling the story.

> By speaking of the narrative shape of these accounts [i.e., Genesis and the Gospels], I suggest that what they are about and how they make sense are functions of the depiction or narrative rendering of the events constituting them—including their being rendered, at least partially, by the device of chronological sequence. The claim, for example, that the gospel story is about Jesus of Nazareth as the Messiah means that it narrates the way his status came to be enacted.[13]

Theology: The Contribution of William Wrede and Adolf Schlatter, ed. Robert Morgan, SBT 2/25 (London: SCM, 1973); recently championed once again by Heikki Räisänen, *Beyond New Testament Theology: A Story and a Programme*, 2nd ed. (London: SCM, 2001). Meeks's new version of *Religionsgeschichte*, however, is concerned not only with the religion of the ancient communities that produced the text but also with the religion of later communities of interpreters.

13. Hans W. Frei, *The Eclipse of Biblical Narrative: A Study in Eighteenth and Nineteenth Century Hermeneutics* (New Haven: Yale University Press, 1974), 13.

Frei followed up his critique of earlier criticism by publishing his own constructive proposal in a slender but influential volume entitled *The Identity of Jesus Christ*, which sought to show how "The New Testament Depiction of Jesus Christ" narrates his enacted, self-manifested identity.[14] One striking feature of Frei's account, which focuses particularly on the passion and resurrection narratives, is that he pays no attention to the differences between the four distinct canonical Gospels. Without reflecting explicitly on the problem of their diversity, he seems to treat them as complementary witnesses to a single unified story, a story that coherently bears witness to the identity of Jesus and actually mediates his presence to the reader. Of course, in treating the Gospels in this manner, Frei is faithfully following the precedent of the classic "Western Christian" hermeneutics that he was seeking to recover. Thus, Frei's work provided both a theoretical justification for the practice of narrative hermeneutics and an encouragement to believe that such a practice might assist in the retrieval of the unity of the scriptural witness.

The great difficulty, however, is that Frei—oddly—paid so little attention to the actual narrative particularity of the *individual* Gospel narratives. Not surprisingly, as narrative-critical studies of the Gospels proliferated in the wake of Frei's work, most of them were less theologically synthetic; instead, they tended to highlight the unity of each individual Gospel narrative and its distinctness from the others. Rather than drawing on a confessional construal of canonical unity, they employed narratological methods to study the evangelists' uses of emplotment, characterization, point of view, and other narrative devices.[15]

But the claim that a literary approach could recover the unity even of the individual biblical writings soon came to be seen as suspect. As Stephen Moore has tellingly argued, the interpretative methods that were fashionable among biblical literary critics in the 1970s and 1980s were heavily indebted to the school of New Criticism, which had characteristically sought to read literary works as self-contained, well-wrought artifacts; however, this critical perspective had already by that time fallen out of favor with cutting-edge critics in the field of literary studies, who—under the influence of theorists such as Derrida and Foucault—were more interested in *deconstructing* literary texts by expos-

14. Hans W. Frei, *The Identity of Jesus Christ: The Hermeneutical Bases of Dogmatic Theology* (Philadelphia: Fortress, 1975), esp. 86–152.

15. E.g., David Rhoads and Donald Michie, *Mark as Story: An Introduction to the Narrative of a Gospel* (Philadelphia: Fortress, 1982); Jack Dean Kingsbury, *Matthew as Story* (Philadelphia: Fortress, 1982); and R. Alan Culpepper, *Anatomy of the Fourth Gospel: A Study in Literary Design* (Philadelphia: Fortress, 1986).

ing their internal fault lines and concealed political agendas.[16] And one of the most brilliant literary readings of a Gospel text produced during that era was Frank Kermode's *The Genesis of Secrecy*, which explicated the Gospel of Mark as a narrative encoding of the indeterminacy of narrative interpretation. According to Kermode's analysis, the message of Mark is that the messages of all narratives are dark, elusive, and fragmentary, always luring the reader to strive after a closure that the narrative itself resists.[17] Between Frei's *The Identity of Jesus Christ* and Kermode's *The Genesis of Secrecy*, published only four years apart in the late 1970s, a great conceptual chasm was fixed so that no one could cross from one side to the other.

But even in less theoretically radical versions of literary criticism, the problem of *canonical* unity remains a vexing and perhaps insuperable one. The more one attends to the individual integrity of the various tellings of the story of Jesus, the more difficult it is to see how they can be construed as expressing a theological unity. If Mark's Jesus dies crying, "My God, why have you forsaken me?" (Mark 15:34), and John's Jesus goes to his death in the serene confidence that he remains in control of events, that he has power to lay his life down and take it up again (John 10:17–18), are we not in the presence of two radically different stories that lead to dramatically different Christologies and theologies of atonement?[18] Rather than recovering the theological unity of Scripture, then, a literary reading of biblical narratives may actually exacerbate the problem by more clearly delineating the diversity of the voices in the Bible. By contrast, at least some versions of historical criticism sought to reconstruct one Jesus of history behind the texts and to show how the various canonical witnesses stood within some sort of coherent diachronic process of the development of tradition.[19] If the Bible presents us with a collection of different textually encoded Jesuses, what is to prevent the skeptical reader from concluding that they are all purely fictional and incommensurate with one another? Brevard Childs incisively describes the theological problem here:

16. Stephen D. Moore, *Literary Criticism and the Gospels: The Theoretical Challenge* (New Haven: Yale University Press, 1989).

17. Frank Kermode, *The Genesis of Secrecy: On the Interpretation of Narrative* (Cambridge: Harvard University Press, 1979).

18. For a recent engagement with such questions by a collaborative team of biblical scholars and theologians, see Beverly Roberts Gaventa and Richard B. Hays, eds., *Seeking the Identity of Jesus: A Pilgrimage* (Grand Rapids: Eerdmans, 2008).

19. See, e.g., Peter Stuhlmacher, *Biblische Theologie des Neuen Testaments*, 2 vols. (Göttingen: Vandenhoeck & Ruprecht, 1992–1999).

> It has become increasingly evident that narrative theology, as often practised, can also propagate a fully secular, non-theological reading of the Bible. The threat lies in divorcing the Bible when seen as literature from its theological reality to which scripture bears witness. . . . The effect is to render the biblical text mute for theology and to deconstruct its tradition in a way equally destructive as the nineteenth-century historicists.[20]

The key loophole in this apparently fatal diagnosis is, of course, the phrase "narrative theology, *as often practised*." This leaves open, at least in principle, the possibility of another sort of narrative criticism that might serve a different master, a narrative criticism that would not divorce biblical narrative from the reality to which it bears witness.[21] What might such a narrative criticism look like, and what are its possibilities and limitations?

A Proposal: Scripture as Coherent Dramatic Narrative

In light of this brief survey of the inability of both historical and literary methods to articulate a basis for perceiving the unity of the Bible, the first thing to be said is that *method is not the answer*. The notion that we can devise a methodology to guarantee a unified interpretation of the Bible is one more technological illusion of modernity. If Scripture bears some sort of coherence, that is not because of the secondary methods that are employed to read it, but because of its substance. Christian Scripture is unified only insofar as it reaffirms Israel's *Shema* by bearing witness to one God: the God of Abraham, Isaac, and Jacob and the God and Father of Jesus Christ. In this respect, Childs is quite right to insist that any synthetic attempt to grasp the unity of the Bible must deal with the "theological reality to which scripture bears witness."

This theological claim, however, can hardly end the discussion because of the complexity of the text(s) with which we are dealing. Even an elementary acquaintance with the contents of the Christian Bible shows that it is a multilayered collection of texts composed by many human authors in different locations in the ancient Near East and the ancient Mediterranean world, across

20. Brevard S. Childs, *Biblical Theology of the Old and New Testaments: Theological Reflection on the Christian Bible* (Minneapolis: Fortress, 1992), 723.

21. As rightly observed by Craig G. Bartholomew and Mike W. Goheen, "Story and Biblical Theology," in *Out of Egypt: Biblical Theology and Biblical Interpretation*, ed. Craig G. Bartholomew et al., Scripture and Hermeneutics Series 5 (Grand Rapids: Zondervan, 2004), 144–71, esp. 162–65.

the timespan of a millennium. How then could its testimony about God possibly be a unified theological whole?

This question was confronted directly by the fifteen scholars who participated for four years in an ongoing interdisciplinary research group called the Scripture Project, at the Center of Theological Inquiry in Princeton. The answer that they gave, corporately, is found in the book entitled *The Art of Reading Scripture* as Thesis 2 of nine programmatic theses that summarize the hermeneutical consensus reached by the group over the four years of their common labors:

> Scripture is rightly understood in light of the church's rule of faith as a coherent dramatic narrative. Though the Bible contains the voices of many different witnesses, the canon of Scripture finds its unity in the overarching story of the work of the triune God. While the Bible contains many tensions, digressions, and subplots, the biblical texts cohere because the one God acts in them and speaks through them: God is the author of Scripture's unity for the sake of the church's faithful proclamation and action.[22]

This densely packed statement, metaphorically describing Scripture as "a coherent dramatic narrative," requires explication and reflection.

How does a dramatic narrative work? It will contain numerous voices, diverse characters, and many discrete scenes. It will unfold across time, and its words and images will gather denser significations as the plot develops. Consequently, its meaning can be grasped only when the totality of the action is considered from its endpoint. No one supposes that every character who speaks in a drama must represent the playwright's own point of view. For example, if we read the speeches of Polonius in *Hamlet* and think we are meant to accept everything he says, we are singularly bad readers of Shakespeare. Indeed, even the speeches of the hero do not necessarily articulate the full meaning of the play. On the contrary, the play's meaning comes to the audience through a complex interplay of character, speech, and action. The complexity of viewpoints in a drama is not necessarily a sign of incoherence; it may be instead a sign of the drama's depth of engagement with human life. The more complex the drama, the more is required of the audience by way of patient, mature, reflective reception. All of this is directly pertinent to our consideration of the problem of the unity of the Bible.

22. Ellen F. Davis and Richard B. Hays, eds., *The Art of Reading Scripture* (Grand Rapids: Eerdmans, 2003), 1.

According to Thesis 2 of the Scripture Project, God is involved in the biblical drama in three interwoven ways: first, God is the *author* of the drama; second, God is the *chief actor* in the drama, the one about whom the story is told, the one who moves the action of the play forward; and third—and here the metaphor starts to reach its limitations—God is actually *working through* the drama to transform the audience. As the play unfolds, members of the audience gradually realize that they cannot be neutral spectators; they are drawn into the action of the drama, and they have an urgent stake in its outcome.[23] Thus, according to the proposal of the Scripture Project group, the unity of the Bible is grounded in the ongoing action of the one God who is both its central character and its ultimate author. Because God is one, Scripture turns out to be coherent. That is what is meant by the claim that "God is the author of Scripture's unity": the Bible's many human characters, and even the human authors of the individual biblical writings, are taken up into the complex dramatic design of the one from whom are all things and for whom we exist.

Thus, if we fail to find unity in Scripture it may be because the unity we are looking for is too simple; our criteria for coherence are too flat and literalistic. We are like the sophomore who grumbles, "Why can't Shakespeare just say what he means?" But even more fundamentally, we may fail to find unity in the Bible because we are looking for it in too narrow a textual field. We are looking for coherence at the level of the conceptual articulations of the individual authors such as Isaiah, Mark, and John, who are themselves—in terms of the metaphor of the overarching dramatic narrative—only characters in the play, albeit very important characters. Instead, the unity we seek must be discerned through the texture and structure of the whole divinely scripted performance. It is this totality that bears witness to the identity of the God rendered in the dramatic narrative.

The multivocality of the dramatic narrative is an integral part of its communicative strategy. Richard Bauckham's splendid essay on "Reading Scripture as a Coherent Story" in *The Art of Reading Scripture* sketches an account of how this might work. Drawing on Gérard Genette's distinction between story and narrative,[24] he notes that a single underlying story can be narrated in various ways. The narration is a performance that may not follow precisely a linear chronological order of events; it may selectively tell some parts of the story while omitting others. Most significantly for our purposes,

23. For a much more fully worked-out theological proposal along similar lines, see now Kevin J. Vanhoozer, *The Drama of Doctrine: A Canonical-Linguistic Approach to Christian Theology* (Louisville: Westminster John Knox, 2005).

24. Gérard Genette, *Narrative Discourse Revisited* (Oxford: Blackwell, 1980), 13.

> it may recount some events a number of times—from different points of view (whether of characters or narrators), from different temporal junctions within the story, conveying different information, highlighting different aspects of significance. This important distinction between story and narrative may help us to see that the plurality of narratives in Scripture . . . is not in principle an obstacle to seeking in the Bible a single coherent story, which all the narratives together tell and each partially tells.[25]

This description, so far as it goes, challenges us to become more complex and interesting readers, alert to the Bible's literary nuance and complexity. Yet, such an account could still fall afoul of Childs's protest against clever aesthetic renderings that fail to reckon with the Bible's witness-bearing function. One might give an elegant account of the Bible's unity as a literary masterpiece while sidestepping its truth claims. (For an example of this sort of reading, consider Northrop Frye's learned book *The Great Code.*[26]) In order to move beyond this point, we must take cognizance of Bauckham's further claim about the hermeneutical significance of the plurality of witnesses within the NT canon:

> While the telling of a story can be true, it can never be adequate to or exhaustive of the reality it renders. In this case, the fact that versions and interpretations multiply—especially in the case of the story of Jesus—is testimony to the importance of not reducing his reality to the limitation of a single rendering. The existence of the four Gospels, not to mention commentary in the apostolic letters, keeps readers aware that Jesus is neither captured in the text nor existent only as a textual construction but that he had and has his own reality to which the texts witness.[27]

With this affirmation, we begin to see how we might practice a sort of narrative criticism that recognizes the *witness-bearing function* of the text while at the same time attending to the *multidimensional literary character* of the dramatic narrative in which its testimony is embodied.

But I have so far omitted reference to one final key element of the Scripture Project's Thesis 2. The understanding of Scripture as a coherent dramatic narrative is rightly to be done "*in light of the church's rule of faith*." In other words,

25. Richard Bauckham, "Reading Scripture as a Coherent Story," in Davis and Hays, *Art of Reading Scripture*, 43.

26. Northrop Frye, *The Great Code: The Bible and Literature* (New York: Harcourt Brace Jovanovich, 1982).

27. Bauckham, "Coherent Story," 44.

the Bible's coherence cannot simply be read off the surface of the text as though it were self-evident to any impartial reader. (The empirical evidence of our library shelves, with their many learned books on hermeneutics, will suffice to show that it is not so!) On the contrary, the skilled exegete must come to the text with the hermeneutical guidance of the distilled wisdom of a historically grounded interpretative community, the church. Why is this so? Because the Christian Bible is already narratively shaped, in the very act of its collection and preservation by the church in order to remember and proclaim the gospel. As Robert Jenson declares, "Outside the community with this purpose, binding these particular documents into one volume would be pointless. Outside the community with this purpose there is no reason to treat all and only these documents as making any kind of whole or to read any of them as part of a whole."[28] The Bible has the sort of unity it has because it has been gathered and ordered by the community of faith to serve as a standard (*kanōn*) for the church's identity and preaching. That is why the reductive canon of Marcion was deemed inadequate: it failed to tell truly the story of God's creation of the world and election of Israel.

As this example suggests, the Rule of Faith has a narrative character to it, as Paul Blowers has persuasively argued.[29] Whatever else we might think is meant by "rule of faith," it at least encompasses the storyline embedded in the early ecumenical creeds and in the two-testament structure of the Christian canon. "The Great Church committed itself not to a universally invariable statement of faith but to variable local tellings of a *particular* story that aspired to universal significance."[30] It is important to insist, however, that this story is not artificially superimposed upon the documents collected in the Bible; rather, it emerges precisely out of the attentive reading of those very documents. It is a distillation of a pattern of narrative meaning found in the biblical texts themselves.[31] This sort of patterned narrative sense is described by Frye, following Aristotle, as the *dianoia* of the tale.[32]

28. Robert W. Jenson, "Scripture's Authority in the Church," in Davis and Hays, *Art of Reading Scripture*, 27–28.

29. Paul M. Blowers, "The *Regula Fidei* and the Narrative Character of Early Christian Faith," *ProEccl* 6 (1997): 199–228.

30. Blowers, "*Regula Fidei*," 208.

31. For excellent examples, see Bauckham, "Coherent Story," 38–42. On the dialectical relation between the Rule of Faith and the canon, see James L. Kugel and Rowan A. Greer, *Early Biblical Interpretation* (Philadelphia: Westminster John Knox, 1986), 155–76.

32. Northrop Frye, *Anatomy of Criticism* (Princeton: Princeton University Press, 1957), 77–79.

The implications of this last point for our present inquiry are great. Just as, on the one hand, a general theory of narratology is an inadequate tool to discern the *unity* of the Bible, so, on the other hand, a static, propositionally formulated orthodoxy is equally inadequate to grasp the living narrative character of the Bible's witness. All attempts to speak meaningfully about the unity of the Bible must grapple in detail with *close readings of actual biblical texts*. The failure to do this was the fatal flaw in Frei's thoughtful attempt to delineate the identity of Jesus Christ: his attempt to describe the way in which the Gospels render the identity and presence of Jesus tended to hover at the level of generalizing summary. We never find out, for example, how he would deal with the apparent tensions between the Markan and Johannine passion narratives, or even with the apparent divergence between Mark and Luke on the final words of Jesus on the cross (Mark 15:34: "My God, my God, why have you forsaken me?"; Luke 23:46: "Father, into your hands I commend my spirit"). It is precisely at this level of interpretation that the real work of biblical theology must be done.

If so, then the *practice of narrative criticism—understood as close reading—is necessary, though not in itself sufficient, to articulate the elusive unity of the biblical witness*. In a recent review essay on major European efforts to write a theology of the NT, C. Kavin Rowe remarks on their persistent inattention to narrative as a way of addressing the classic problem of the unity and diversity of these writings. This inattention, Rowe observes, "is particularly regrettable, since narrative has the inherent structural ability to exhibit considerable diversity and discontinuity within the unity and continuity of one story. . . . As a medium for New Testament Theology, narrative seems well suited to the task."[33] I agree emphatically with this judgment. But we cannot be content merely to state such a claim at the formal level; it must be demonstrated through actual readings of texts. It will be the task of the final part of this essay to sketch one brief example of the sort of thing I have in mind.

The Narrative Enactment of Faithfulness: A Preliminary Probe

It is often supposed that Paul, Matthew, John, and the Letter to the Hebrews represent significantly divergent theological perspectives. Paul's assertion of

33. C. Kavin Rowe, "New Testament Theology: The Revival of a Discipline: A Review of Recent Contributions to the Field," *JBL* 125 (2006): 409. Cf. the quotation from George Lindbeck appended as an epigraph to the present essay.

justification by faith and Spirit-led freedom from the Law seems sharply juxtaposed to Matthew's insistence on fulfillment of the Law and the necessity of radical obedience to the teachings of Jesus. The Fourth Gospel's strikingly otherworldly Christology, along with its pervasive apparently anti-Jewish polemic,[34] give it the appearance of a sectarian document theologically dissonant with the Synoptic Gospels. And the Letter to the Hebrews has seemed to many interpreters to stand theologically apart from all the rest of the NT, not only in its distinctive portrayal of Jesus as the High Priest but also in its purportedly dualistic, quasi-Platonist soteriology.

As it happens, I think that several of the characterizations and contrasts I have just sketched are distorting caricatures. But my present purpose is not to undertake a rebuttal to such accounts. Rather, without denying the very real differences of theological vocabulary and sensibility manifest in these different writings, I want to suggest that attention to the *story* of Jesus in these four authors will demonstrate a surprising coherence in their theological understanding of the soteriological purpose and effect of his death. Specifically, all four authors narrate Jesus' death on the cross as an act of radical faithfulness to God's redemptive purpose; further, in each of the four authors, this act of faithfulness provides in turn a normative paradigm for the ongoing narratively shaped identity of all who trust in Jesus and find themselves reconciled to God through him.

A full demonstration of this sweeping claim is impossible in short compass. What follows will be only a preliminary probe intended to gesture toward the sort of narrative interpretation that might—if more fully explored—suggest a way to imagine the unity of the Scriptural witness.

We begin in an unlikely place, with the Letter to the Hebrews. Of course, this "word of exhortation" (Heb 13:22) does not belong to the literary genre of narrative. But it does refer to and summarize key moments in the story of Jesus. At a climactic moment of the letter's argument, readers are urged to look to "Jesus τὸν τῆς πίστεως ἀρχηγὸν καὶ τελειωτήν, who for the sake of the joy that was set before him endured the cross, disregarding its shame, and has taken his seat at the right hand of the throne of God" (12:2). This concise summary reminds readers of the kerygmatic passion and resurrection story. The Jesus of the Letter to the Hebrews is the preexistent Son of God of whom it can be said, "the heavens are the work of your hands" (1:10); nonetheless, he

34. For a nuanced corrective to the impression of anti-Jewish tendencies in John's Gospel, however, see now the important work of Christopher M. Blumhofer, *The Gospel of John and the Future of Israel*, SNTSMS 177 (Cambridge: Cambridge University Press, 2020).

became a flesh-and-blood human being (2:14–18) who, despite suffering the agonizing prospect of death, "learned obedience through what he suffered" (5:8) and was finally vindicated through resurrection from the dead (13:20) and exaltation to God's right hand. He thereby destroyed the devil's power and set humanity free from lifelong slavery to the fear of death (2:14–15); further, he prepared the way for us to enter into the presence of God (10:19–22). Thus, the character of Jesus supremely embodies faithful obedience to God; this is what it means to call him "pioneer and perfecter of faith." His πίστις—his faithfulness—is soteriologically efficacious for human beings who would otherwise be enslaved and alienated from God.

At the same time, his faithfulness provides a model for the readers, who are called to "lay aside every weight and the sin that clings so closely" and to "run with perseverance the race that is set before us, looking to Jesus." As they look to him, they receive this further word of encouragement: "Consider him who endured such hostility against himself from sinners [note again the allusion to the passion narrative], so that you may not grow weary or lose heart" (12:1–3). As a final point of narrative interpretation, we may note that Jesus's enactment of faithfulness did not occur in a historical vacuum; rather, it was the climactic act of faithfulness played out before a great gallery of witnesses from Israel's whole long story, from Abel to Abraham to Moses to Rahab to the prophets (ch. 11 as a whole). For the reader of Hebrews, to look to Jesus is to embrace this epic story as one's own and to carry the story forward by going outside the camp and bearing the same abuse that these witnesses, especially Jesus, endured, looking as they did to the eschatological future (13:13).

This condensed summary of Hebrews' account of the character of Jesus illustrates the way in which a discursive, didactic text can encapsulate narrational summaries that make sense only in the context of a larger story. Hebrews requires the reader to recall an already-known story about Israel and about Jesus, and it provides crucial indications of how the story should be interpreted, as well as a clear invitation to the readers to enter the unfolding drama by patterning their own lives after the story's protagonist.

When we turn to the letters of Paul, we find a very similar pattern of argumentation, evoking the story of Jesus's obedience in a way that simultaneously declares its soteriological effects and invites readers into living conformity with that story.[35] Like Hebrews, Paul portrays Jesus as the preexistent Son of God who was the agent of creation (1 Cor 8:6). He was sent by God into the

35. For a summary account, see Richard B. Hays, "The Story of God's Son: The Identity of Jesus in the Letters of Paul," in Gaventa and Hays, *Seeking the Identity of Jesus*, 180–99

world to redeem those who were in bondage to sin and death (Rom 8:3–4). He accomplished this mission through an act of loving self-sacrifice by giving himself for us, even though we were in a state of alienation from God (Gal 2:20; Rom 5:8). Thus, his death can be described as an act of self-emptying obedience "to the point of death—even death on a cross" (Phil 2:7–8). This obedience stands in typological antithesis to Adam's disobedience, but as a result of Jesus's obedient death, God's life-giving power, grace, and righteousness now overflow to us (Rom 5:12–21). As I have repeatedly contended, it is precisely this pattern of Jesus's gracious self-giving death that is evoked by Paul's use of the phrase πίστις Ἰησοῦ Χριστοῦ.[36] But the narrative pattern I am describing here is abundantly attested in Paul's writings regardless of how one interprets that particular phrase.

God raised Jesus from the dead; consequently, he is the firstfruits of the new creation in which we hope ultimately to share (1 Cor 15:20–23). He is also exalted to the right hand of God, where he intercedes for us (Rom 8:34). This whole narrative pattern is concisely sketched in the so-called Philippians Hymn (Phil 2:6–11), and its soteriological implications are developed repeatedly throughout Paul's letters. As in the case of Hebrews, however, Paul sees the story as unfinished in the present; the final eschatological triumph of Christ's lordship will be accomplished only at the end, the resurrection of the dead, when death will be at last vanquished (1 Cor 15:23–28).

Like Hebrews, Paul seeks to locate the story of Jesus within the larger frame of Israel's story. This story was adumbrated beforehand through the prophets in holy Scripture, and the decisive kerygmatic events of Jesus's death, burial, and resurrection took place "according to the Scriptures" (see Rom 1:2; 1 Cor 15:3–5). Further, the future redemptive outworking of the story will mysteriously include the salvation of "all Israel" (Rom 11:26–27). In the meantime, those who have received the good news of Christ are summoned to find their own lives in the present conformed to the self-sacrificial pattern of Jesus's action and so to "fulfill the law of Christ" (Rom 15:1–3; Gal 6:2; Phil 2:1–13). As Stephen Fowl has shown, the dramatic christological passages in Paul provide a template and summons for believers to live their lives in conformity with his story.[37]

(chapter 9 in the present volume); see also "Christ Died for the Ungodly: Narrative Soteriology in Paul?," *HBT* 26 (2004): 48–68 (chapter 10 in the present volume).

36. Richard B. Hays, *The Faith of Jesus Christ: The Narrative Substructure of Paul's Theology in Galatians 3:1–4:11*, 2nd ed., The Biblical Resource Series (Grand Rapids: Eerdmans, 2002 [1983]).

37. Stephen E. Fowl, *The Story of Christ in the Ethics of Paul: An Analysis of the Function of*

We have now observed that Hebrews and Paul, while using very different language and images, are telling a story that is recognizably the same. But in what sense does that story correspond to what we find in the Gospels? We turn next to the Gospel of Matthew.

To be sure, Matthew includes numerous major narrative elements that are not present at all in Paul and in Hebrews, including sustained portrayals of Jesus as a teacher and healer. My claim must be carefully stated: I am not arguing that attention to narrative will dissolve or harmonize all differences between the NT witnesses; rather, I am suggesting that narrative analysis will help us see how the differing portrayals of the figure of Jesus in the various texts converge and cohere as distinct witnesses to the same underlying story. And indeed, we will see that Matthew, no less than Hebrews and Paul, narrates the death of Jesus as his act of obedient faithfulness to God.[38]

Although Matthew makes no overt claim concerning Jesus's preexistence,[39] the evangelist makes it clear that Jesus is sent by God on a mission to "save his people from their sins" (Matt 1:21) and that he represents in their midst nothing less than the presence of God ("Emmanuel," 1:23). He enters into fundamental identification with Israel, as Matthew artfully suggests in the brief narrative episode of the flight into Egypt, in typological fulfillment of Hos 11:1, "Out of Egypt I have called my son" (Matt 2:13–15). In this narrative context, the reader quickly perceives Jesus's symbolic assumption of Israel's role as God's son (Exod 4:22–23). This hint is confirmed in the account of his baptism by John; despite needing no repentance, he undergoes baptism in order to "fulfill all righteousness" as Israel's representative—a point reconfirmed when a voice from heaven reaffirms his identity as God's Son (Matt 3:13–17). In the immediately ensuing temptation in the wilderness, Jesus defeats the devil by three times quoting Deuteronomy, climaxing in the decisive citation of the *Shema*, thus showing what it means to "worship the Lord your God and serve only him" (Matt 4:10, quoting Deut 6:13). Here he declares his uncompromising allegiance to Israel's God, enacting the full obedience that Israel

the Hymnic Material, JSNTSup 36 (Sheffield: JSOT Press, 1990). See now also Michael Gorman, *Cruciformity: Paul's Narrative Spirituality of the Cross* (Grand Rapids: Eerdmans, 2001).

38. For a reading that highlights the importance of this narrative motif in Matthew, see esp. R. W. L. Moberly, *The Bible, Theology, and Faith: A Study of Abraham and Jesus* (Cambridge: Cambridge University Press, 2000), 184–224.

39. The implicit identification of Jesus with the figure of divine Wisdom (esp. in Matt 11:28–30 [cf. Sir 51:23]) may hint at the possibility of his preexistent status, but it is only a hint, not an assertion.

was always meant to offer. In other words, he takes upon himself the role and destiny of obedient Israel.

These same themes come to the surface of the narrative again near the end of the story, as Jesus prays at Gethsemane. Though in his grief he wishes that the cup of suffering might pass from him, he once again aligns his will with God's and prays, "your will be done" (Matt 26:36–46), knowing that his submission will lead to his death. Indeed, in the immediately preceding account of his final meal with the disciples, he had already employed the symbol of the cup to represent his own bloody death as a sign of "my blood of the covenant, which is poured out for many for the forgiveness of sins" (26:27–28). The phrasing of this tradition not only echoes the language attending the initiation of the Sinai covenant (Exod 24:8) but indicates clearly that for Matthew—as we have already seen in both Hebrews and Paul—Jesus's death is a self-offering for the sake of redeeming others. To save his people from their sins, he must give up his own life. And so he goes to the cross as an act of self-sacrificial obedience.

It is also noteworthy that in Matthew, Jesus is not only an authoritative moral teacher; he also *models* the radical obedience to God demanded by his teaching. In the passion narrative, by refusing to resort to force to defend himself against enemies, he paradigmatically exemplifies his own teaching of turning the other cheek and nonviolent love of enemies. Indeed, a strong case can be made that Jesus comprehensively exemplifies the attributes that are pronounced blessed in the Beatitudes, up to and including being persecuted for righteousness' sake. I offer for purposes of illustration a single example. Jesus's blessing on the gentle ones (πραεῖς, Matt 5:5) directly echoes Ps 37:11 (36:11 LXX): "The gentle ones (πραεῖς) will inherit the land." With that OT promise displayed prominently in the third sentence of the Sermon on the Mount, we are then shown its meaning in specific terms by Jesus's own story. In Matt 11:29, Jesus calls his hearers to follow his way: "Take my yoke upon you, and learn from me; for I am gentle (πραΰς) and humble in heart."[40] And when he rides into Jerusalem, Matthew reminds us that Zechariah prophesied the event: "Look, your king is coming to you, gentle (πραΰς), and mounted on a donkey, and on a colt, the foal of a donkey" (21:5, quoting Zech 9:9). It cannot be accidental that Matthew thus narratively links the prophetic depiction of the gentle king with Jesus's own self-description in a passage that calls his followers to "learn from" him (Matt 11:29). One thing they are supposed

40. This passage probably echoes Sir 51:25–28, though the word πραΰς does not appear there.

to learn is to embody in their own obedient discipleship (5:7) the gentleness that Jesus definitively displayed. To take on the "yoke" of Jesus's teaching is to adopt his way of life. And he himself is the gentle one who inherits the earth and therefore commands his disciples to be like him.

I have traced this line of reasoning at some length in order to emphasize that Matthew's narrative does in fact present Jesus's story as a paradigm for obedience that is meant to be followed. And the paradigm looks strikingly like the pattern of self-emptying lowliness that we saw in Phil 2. Jesus does not merely issue imperious commands that are to be obeyed, but he himself embodies the meekness and mercy that are to characterize his followers. Thus, when the risen and vindicated Jesus declares after the resurrection that now all authority in heaven and on earth has been given to him, he instructs his disciples to teach others to "obey everything that I have commanded you" (Matt 28:18–20)—and those commandments can be epitomized in sayings such as these: "The greatest among you will be your servant. All who exalt themselves will be humbled, and all who humble themselves will be exalted" (23:11–12). Thus, according to Matthew, the narrative pattern of discipleship is to be homologous with the narrative pattern of Jesus's own meek and obedient identity.

In light of such readings, it will not be difficult to see how the Gospel of John, despite its remarkably different imagery and theological idiom, gives yet another expression of the story pattern we have identified in the three major NT witnesses we have already considered. Indeed, John, the master dramatist, composes one powerful scene that encapsulates all I have been trying to say: the footwashing scene in John 13.[41] Jesus, the incarnate Word, knowing that he has been sent into the world by God, removes his clothing and takes the form of a servant, washing the feet of his disciples. This action is both a parable of his own obedient servanthood and impending death for the sake of his followers and, at the same time, an example that they are to follow. Despite the exalted ontological claims made for Jesus in the Fourth Gospel, the text insists that he is radically obedient to the Father. To take just one representative example out of many possible instances, consider Jesus's words in John 5:30: "I can do nothing on my own. As I hear, I judge; and my judgment is just, because I seek not to do my own will but the will of the one who sent me." And the Father's sending of the Son into the world to serve and suffer prefigures the Son's sending of the disciples: "As the Father has sent me, so I send you" (20:21b;

41. On this passage see Marianne Meye Thompson, "'His Own Received Him Not': Jesus Washes the Feet of His Disciples," in Davis and Hays, *Art of Reading Scripture*, 258–76.

cf. 17:18). I need hardly belabor the parallels with the texts we have discussed above. Once again, we see the pattern of self-emptying obedience to God that leads Jesus both to the cross and to vindication through the resurrection; once again, we see that discipleship entails assuming the vocation of recapitulating this christologically formed pattern in the life of the community, for the sake of making the love of God present to others.

This is the sort of narrative analysis that holds at least the possibility of recovering the theological unity of Scripture. The very different surface details of the various biblical texts, their distinctive styles, even their attention to different moments in God's story, do not stand as barriers to discerning the underlying coherence of the story we have described here.

Someone might protest that the patterns I have described are too general to be meaningful or useful, either for narrative analysis or for theology. But I do not believe such a charge would be accurate. Consider this experiment: try to find the narrative pattern of self-giving cruciform obedience in the Gospel of Thomas or the Gospel of Judas. The futility of the attempt will immediately drive home what Irenaeus meant when he charged the heretics with disregarding the Rule of Faith and rearranging the traditions about Jesus into a false and disordered picture.[42] As Irenaeus knew well, the truth of the gospel cannot be abstracted from the story in which it comes to us, and the coherence of Christian Scripture depends upon that story.

42. Irenaeus of Lyons, *Against the Heresies* 1.8.1, trans. Dominic J. Unger, Ancient Christian Writers (New York: Paulist, 1992).

2

Reading Scripture with Eyes of Faith

"Can You See Anything?" Seeking Restored Vision

The title of this essay recalls and celebrates the work of Paul Minear, the extraordinary biblical theologian, who reached his one hundredth birthday in 2006. It has now been exactly sixty years since Minear, who taught NT for many years at Yale Divinity School, published a challenging programmatic book entitled *Eyes of Faith: A Study in the Biblical Point of View*.[1] At the heart of Minear's work lies one luminous insight: what we ordinarily take to be "real" is in fact a distorted picture of the world, and it is only the revelatory power of God's word that casts a true light on the landscape of human experience and, at the same time, heals our capacity to *see*.

Minear prefaces his work with an epigraph from William Blake that describes the eyes, the human organs of vision, as "dim windows":

> This Life's dim windows of the Soul
> Distorts the Heavens from Pole to Pole
> And leads you to Believe a Lie
> When you see with, not thro' the Eye

1. Paul S. Minear, *Eyes of Faith: A Study in the Biblical Point of View* (Philadelphia: Westminster, 1946). Minear explains that his intent in this work is "not to construct a Biblical theology, but to provide a preface for such theology by charting its context of presuppositions, those axiomatic attitudes and convictions that lie so deep that they are taken for granted" (1–2). That is to say, he is offering a prolegomenon that outlines the epistemological preconditions for composing a biblical theology.

An earlier version of this essay was presented as a main paper at a conference on "Preaching, Teaching, and Living the Bible," sponsored by the Center for Catholic and Evangelical Theology, at Duke Divinity School, May 23, 2006.

One could take Blake's verse as an invitation to embrace Gnosticism or perhaps Plato's allegory of the cave—an invitation, that is, to renounce sensory experience in favor of some ethereal realm of ideas. Minear, however, has something quite different in mind. When he speaks of what we see through "eyes of faith," he refers to the very concrete and radically disturbing vision of embodied reality offered us by the biblical narrators and by the prophets and apostles. In this vision of the world, the truth about human life is given only in Scripture—that is to say, only through the mysterious working of God in the election of Israel and the death and resurrection of Jesus. It is no accident, then, that the epigraph to the final chapter of Minear's book is drawn not from Blake but from Karl Barth's commentary on Romans; Minear's approach to biblical theology is deeply shaped by Barth's radical call for all our perceptions to be interrogated and reshaped by the Word of God as disclosed in Jesus Christ.[2]

The image of "eyes of faith" as the epistemological precondition for grasping the surprising truth about the real world serves well as an entry point to our reflections about biblical hermeneutics and "theological exegesis." Minear's visual imagery might well remind us of a distinctive story in Mark's Gospel, in which Jesus performs a peculiar two-stage healing of a blind man at Bethsaida (Mark 8:22–26).[3] After putting saliva on the blind man's eyes and laying hands on him, Jesus asks, "Can you see anything?" The man replies, "I can see people, but they look like trees, walking around." Then, Mark tells us, Jesus laid hands a second time on the man's eyes, "and he looked intently" (interestingly, the verb is διαβλέπω—in light of Blake's poem, I am tempted to translate it "he looked *through* the eyes") and "his sight was restored, and he saw everything clearly." I fear that, most of the time, even if we have been touched by Jesus, when we biblical scholars look at the text of Scripture, we see trees walking. (Or perhaps in some cases, we see trees chopped down, split, and stacked into piles of firewood.) It is my devout hope, however, that we are entering a new historical moment in which we will again be touched by Jesus so as to find our sight clarified.

2. For Minear's later assessment of Barth's significance, see his essay "Barth's Commentary on the Romans, 1922–1972, or Karl Barth vs. the Exegetes," in *Footnotes to a Theology: The Karl Barth Colloquium of 1972*, ed. H. Martin Rumscheidt (Waterloo, ON: Corporation for the Publication of Academic Studies in Religion in Canada, 1974), 8–29.

3. Interestingly, nowhere in his book does Minear refer to this story.

Blurry Vision, Diverging Roads

The clarification of sight mentioned above is urgently necessary, for the past two centuries of critical study of the Bible have brought us to a fork in the road, and we need to be able to read the road signs before us. The Finnish NT scholar Heikki Räisänen describes the diverging paths as follows:

> Biblical scholars will soon find themselves at a crossroads. Will they remain guardians of cherished confessional traditions, anxious to provide modern man with whatever normative guidance they still manage to squeeze out of the sacred texts? Or will they follow those pioneering theologians fearlessly reflecting on the biblical material from a truly ecumenical, global point of view?[4]

With the choice so described, it is not hard to see where Räisänen's own sympathies lie. He is convinced that "the absolutizing interpretation given by the early Christians to the 'Christ event'" was "somewhat exaggerated"[5] and that the duty of "serious scholarship" is to render a purely historical account of the biblical texts. As a result, the older project of "NT theology" should be replaced by two different projects: (1) the writing of "a history of early Christian thought" from a dispassionate neutral perspective;[6] and (2) a critical reflection on the NT and its history of influence, from a philosophical perspective informed by modern awareness of religious pluralism.[7] Räisänen bemoans the fact that for more than a hundred years the truly historical project of NT interpretation was sidetracked by the influence of confessional neo-orthodox theology because of the influence of Barth and Bultmann. But now at last in the bright new world come of age, NT scholarship can be liberated to move forward to a purely historical interpretation (following the fearless pioneers who approach the Bible from a "global point of view," whatever that might mean) and to leave behind the constraints of dogma. If all this sounds eerily reminiscent of the nineteenth century, that is because it is.

4. Heikki Räisänen, *Beyond New Testament Theology*, 2nd ed. (London: SCM, 2000 [1990]), 209.

5. Räisänen, *Beyond New Testament Theology*, 202.

6. This was, of course, already proposed incisively by William Wrede in 1897. Räisänen explicitly describes his own constructive proposals as a return to the critical program of Wrede and the *religionsgeschichtliche Schule*.

7. Räisänen, *Beyond New Testament Theology*, 8 et passim.

At least in Räisänen's case, he clearly recognizes the nineteenth-century intellectual sources of his proposal, and he understands that he is making a revisionary proposal "against the grain" of a long tradition of significant theological inquiry. But alas, it is not always so among members of the biblical guild, especially in the United States. Whereas a generation ago it was widely accepted that there could be a fruitful synthesis of historical and theological inquiry in biblical studies, this claim is increasingly challenged by some insistent voices that seek to exclude any sort of explicitly religious or theological perspective from a place at the table in scholarly study of the Bible. In the spring of 2006, an article was posted on the Society of Biblical Literature website by Michael V. Fox, a professor of Hebrew Bible at the University of Wisconsin. In this essay, Fox forcefully argues that "faith-based study" has no place in biblical scholarship: "Faith-based study . . . can dip into Bible scholarship for its own purposes, but cannot contribute to it." Fox continues with the following disdainful remarks: "Trained scholars quickly learn to recognize which authors and publications are governed by faith and tend to set them aside, not out of prejudice but out of an awareness that they are irrelevant to the scholarly enterprise. Sometimes it is worthwhile to go through a faith-motivated publication and pick out the wheat from the chaff, but time is limited."[8]

Lest it be thought that Räisänen and Fox represent marginal, idiosyncratic perspectives, I place in evidence the presidential address given by Wayne Meeks in Barcelona at the 2004 meeting of the Studiorum Novi Testamenti Societas, the major international society of NT scholars. In this lecture, entitled "Why Study the New Testament?" Meeks contends that the traditional theological approach to interpretation has a baleful effect because it seeks to find "normative" meanings in texts. The student of the NT should now instead seek to trace the "formative" effects of the NT—that is, its influence on the formation of culture. Meeks does concede that biblical scholars may continue to speak to "the whole unruly assortment of faith communities for whom the documents we are interested in are construed as part of sacred scripture." He even generously remarks that there is "no reason to be embarrassed about the proprietary claim that *these groups* make on *us*."[9] Still, our "largest audience" is "the *non-Christian* majority of the world," and addressing that audience is

8. Michael V. Fox, "Bible Scholarship and Faith-Based Study: My View," *SBL Forum* 4.2, February 2006, http://www.sbl-site.org/publications/Article.aspx?ArticleId=490.

9. Wayne A. Meeks, "Why Study the New Testament?," *NTS* 51 (2005): 167, emphasis added. The firm distinction between "these groups" and "us" eloquently discloses the author's hermeneutical location.

"the most exciting and certainly the most important challenge we will face in the present century."[10]

The fantasy that the vast non-Christian world will have more than a slight passing interest in the scholarly deliberations of the SNTS is perhaps a forgivable foible of a superb scholar who has carved out a distinguished career at Yale in a secular department of religious studies. What is of more concern, however, is that Meeks's desiderata for the future trajectory of NT scholarship include not only the challenge to address the non-Christian world but also the assertion that NT scholars should abandon their role as teachers of the church. He puts his case like this: "We should start by erasing from our vocabulary the terms 'biblical theology' and, even more urgently, 'New Testament theology.' Whatever positive contributions these concepts may have made in the conversation since Gabler, we have come to a time when they can only blinker understanding." This is so because these terms "smuggle in a cognitivist model of religion"[11] and because they "claim textual and historical warrants" for normative propositions that are actually contingent products of the interests of later interpretive communities. And finally, Meeks declares, "'biblical theology' has functioned ideologically in the attempt to secure our own positions in the theological hierarchy, as the teachers of the teachers of the church. We have not done very well in that role, and we should give it up."[12]

If that is the view from the chair of the SNTS presidency, how does the future of biblical scholarship look from lower down the academic pecking order? I take you back now to an even more recent posting on the SBL website, this time an article by Hector Avalos of Iowa State University, entitled "The Ideology of the Society of Biblical Literature and the Demise of an Academic Profession."[13] Avalos sweepingly describes "the ever-growing irrelevance of biblical studies in academia" and opines that "keeping biblical scholars employed, despite their irrelevance to anyone outside of faith communities, is the main mission of the SBL." This is, however, a doomed enterprise, because "the

10. Meeks, "Why Study the New Testament?," 168–69, emphasis original.

11. Here, as in Räisänen, we see the continuing influence of the *religiongeschichtliche Schule*, which sought to give priority to the lived experience of religious communities over expressions of thought and doctrine. In view of the actual importance of "cognitive" teaching in Christian communities in history, the dichotomy may be less than illuminating for the study of the NT and early Christianity.

12. Meeks, "Why Study the New Testament?," 167–68.

13. Hector Avalos, "The Ideology of the Society of Biblical Literature and the Demise of an Academic Profession," *SBL Forum* 4.4, April 2006, http://www.sbl-site.org/publications/Article.aspx?ArticleId=520.

Bible has no intrinsic value or merit. Its value is a social construct, and the SBL is the agent of an elite class that wishes to retain its own value and employment by fostering the idea that biblical studies should matter." Avalos goes on, "in the interest of self-disclosure," to describe himself as a "secular humanist" and to admit that even though he loves studying the Bible (a surprising statement not corroborated by anything else in his essay), "my conscience is increasingly telling me to do something more beneficial for humanity." Given the opinions expressed in Avalos's essay, this is probably a wise vocational discernment.

Here is the point I am leading to. There is an important sense in which Avalos is correct: the intense academic study of the Bible really is not important outside of faith communities. Once one starts down the fork in the road to which Räisänen, Fox, and Meeks beckon the scholarly guild, one ultimately, inevitably, arrives at the dead end portrayed in Avalos's gloomy postcard from Ames, Iowa. Once one has arrived at this destination, the very project of studying something called the Bible becomes intellectually incoherent. As Robert Jenson has incisively remarked, "outside the church, no such entity as the Christian Bible has any reason to exist." The Bible is a collection of documents gathered by and for the church to aid in preserving and proclaiming the church's message. Therefore, "the question, after all, is not whether churchly reading of Scripture is justified; the question is, what could possibly justify any other?"[14]

Precisely because the dead-end character of secularistic study of the Bible has become increasingly apparent, many thoughtful interpreters have begun to explore the other fork in the road. I am happy to say that the past ten years have witnessed an extraordinary resurgence of interest in theological exegesis of Scripture and that several fascinating new projects are in the early stages of development. One noteworthy component of many of these initiatives has been a sustained effort to recover a sympathetic understanding of the church's ancient traditions of scriptural interpretation.[15] A great deal of scholarly en-

14. Robert W. Jenson, "Scripture's Authority in the Church," in *The Art of Reading Scripture*, ed. Ellen F. Davis and Richard B. Hays (Grand Rapids: Eerdmans, 2003), 27, 29.

15. As examples of the growing interest in theological exegesis, I would draw attention particularly to the work of scholars such as Brevard Childs, Stephen Fowl, Francis Watson, N. T. Wright, Luke Timothy Johnson, Christopher Seitz, R. W. L. Moberly, Ellen Davis, Douglas Harink, Karl Donfried, and Markus Bockmuehl. Noteworthy also are programmatic initiatives such as the Scripture Project at the Center of Theological Inquiry in Princeton and the Scripture and Hermeneutics Seminar in the UK. One barometer of this resurgence of theological exegesis is the growing number of significant journals, commentary series, and other publication initiatives that are serving as conduits for these fresh

ergy is now being poured into theological exegesis. The initial results of these efforts are, not surprisingly, mixed in quality, but there are many encouraging signs that theological exegesis can produce readings that are nuanced in their attention to textual detail and simultaneously—*mirabile dictu*—nourishing for the church.

It is, however, not always clear exactly what is meant by the catchall term *theological exegesis*. Someone might suggest that theological exegesis is like pornography: we do not know how to define it, but we know it when we see it. Perhaps it would be wise to leave it at that. But I think, on the contrary, that there may be value in offering some identifying characterization of the sort of exegesis that we are seeking to encourage and recover. There is a certain value in naming the goals we seek. In the remainder of this essay, then, I want to offer two things: (1) a brief description of the character of theological exegesis as I understand it and (2) an example of my own recent attempts to read Scripture with eyes of faith.

What Is "Theological Exegesis"?

What makes exegesis "theological"? Theological exegesis is not a "method." It is not a set of discrete procedures that could be set alongside, say, textual criticism or redaction criticism. Rather, theological exegesis is a complex *practice*,[16]

streams of thought; see, for example, *Pro Ecclesia*, *Journal for Theological Interpretation*, *Ex Auditu*, *Horizons in Biblical Theology*, the Brazos Theological Commentary on the Bible, the Two Horizons Commentary, the (older) Interpretation Commentaries series, Baker Academic's new series Studies in Theological Interpretation, the *Dictionary of Theological Interpretation of the Bible*, The Ancient Christian Commentary on Scripture, and The Church's Bible. For some particularly useful entry points to the current discussion, see Ellen F. Davis and Richard B. Hays, eds., *The Art of Reading Scripture* (Grand Rapids: Eerdmans, 2003); Stephen E. Fowl, ed., *The Theological Interpretation of Scripture: Classic and Contemporary Readings* (Oxford: Blackwell, 1997); Brevard S. Childs, *The Struggle to Understand Isaiah as Christian Scripture* (Grand Rapids: Eerdmans, 2004); R. R. Reno, "Biblical Theology and Theological Exegesis," in *Out of Egypt: Biblical Theology and Biblical Interpretation*, ed. Craig Bartholomew et al., Scripture and Hermeneutics Series 5 (Grand Rapids: Zondervan, 2004), 385–408; Markus Bockmuehl, *Seeing the Word: Refocusing New Testament Study*, Studies in Theological Interpretation (Grand Rapids: Baker Academic, 2006).

16. In the sense defined by Alasdair MacIntyre: "By a practice I am going to mean any coherent and complex form of socially established co-operative human activity through which goods internal to that form of activity are realised in the course of trying to achieve those standards of excellence which are appropriate to, and partially definitive of, that form of activity, with the result that human powers to achieve excellence, and human conceptions

a way of approaching Scripture with eyes of faith and seeking to understand it within the community of faith. What are the salient identifying marks of this practice? I propose *twelve* identifying marks.

(1) Theological exegesis is *a practice of and for the church.* We lavish our attention on the biblical texts because these texts have been passed on to us by the church's tradition as the distinctive and irreplaceable testimony to events in which God has acted for our salvation. That is to say, theological exegesis regards these texts as *Scripture*, not merely as a collection of ancient writings whose content is of historical interest. A bare description of the ideational content of biblical writings ("the theology of Luke" or the like) is therefore not yet theological in the sense meant here. Theological exegesis, as Meeks rightly but disapprovingly notes, seeks to read the Bible as normative for a community.

(2) Theological exegesis is *self-involving discourse.* Interpreters who read the Bible theologically approach the text with an awareness that we are addressed and claimed by the word of God that is spoken in the text, and we understand ourselves to be answerable to that word. For this reason, exegesis that is authentically theological will frequently contain sentences that employ pronouns in the first and second persons. A strictly third-person form of discourse lends itself to the mode of pure description, in which the author may stand apart, uninvolved in the text's world. Theological exegesis, however, draws us into the world of the text and demands response. As self-involving confessional acts, theological readings are closely interwoven with the practice of *worship.*

(3) At the same time, *historical study is internal to the practice of theological exegesis.* The reasons why this is so are themselves fundamentally theological: God has created the material world, and God has acted for the redemption of that world through the incarnation of the Son in the historical person Jesus of Nazareth. History therefore cannot be either inimical or irrelevant to theology's affirmations of truth. The more accurately we understand the historical setting of first-century Palestine, the more precise and faithful will be our understanding of what the incarnate Word taught, did, and suffered. The more we know about the Mediterranean world of Greco-Roman antiquity, the more nuanced will be our understanding of the ways in which the NT's epistles summoned their readers to a conversion of the imagination.[17]

---

of the ends and goods involved, are systematically extended" (*After Virtue: A Study in Moral Theory*, 2nd ed. [Notre Dame: University of Notre Dame Press, 1984 (1981)], 187).

17. See my *Conversion of the Imagination: Paul as Interpreter of Israel's Scripture* (Grand Rapids: Eerdmans, 2005).

(4) Theological exegesis attends to the *literary wholeness of the individual scriptural witnesses.* This, I would propose, is one of the signature contributions of biblical studies over the past fifty years to the task of theology. The Bible must be read neither as an anthology of disconnected theological sound bites nor, on the other hand, as a single undifferentiated story. Nor can its message be adequately grasped only through excerpts encountered in the church's liturgy. Rather, the Bible contains a chorus of different voices, and the distinctive integrity of each part in the chorus is essential to its polyphonic performance. This is especially true for texts such as the Gospels, which come to us in the form of cohesive narratives. It matters, as Irenaeus insisted, that we have not a single homogenized Gospel but, rather, a fourfold Gospel, in which the discrete voices of Matthew, Mark, Luke, and John can and must be heard. Theological exegesis attends lovingly to the distinctive testimony of each witness.

(5) My fifth point is the dialectical converse of the previous one: theological exegesis can never be content only to describe the theological perspectives of the individual biblical authors; instead, it always presses forward to *the synthetic question of canonical coherence.* This does not mean, of course, the assimilation of everything to a single doctrinal norm, as has happened sometimes when, for example, justification *sola fide* is made the single lens for interpreting all biblical texts. But it does mean that theological exegetes will seek the big picture, asking how any particular text fits into the larger biblical story of God's gracious action. (This is one of the points at which Luke Timothy Johnson and I have consistently differed. He believes we can simply listen to each canonical witness separately and then move directly to contemporary appropriation, whereas I insist that Christian theological exegesis has historically sought to allow the different biblical witnesses to "talk to each other" and to articulate some sort of complex unity.)[18]

(6) Theological exegesis does not focus chiefly on the hypothetical history behind the biblical texts, nor does it attend primarily to the meaning of texts as self-contained works of literature; rather, it focuses on these *texts as testimony.* This means we need to learn to stand where these witnesses stand and look where they point. Insofar as we do this, we will learn to see as they see; as Minear's *Eyes of Faith* promises, we will find our vision trained anew.

18. See, for example, Luke Timothy Johnson and William S. Kurz, *The Future of Catholic Biblical Scholarship: A Constructive Conversation* (Grand Rapids: Eerdmans, 2002), 129–30; compare my *Moral Vision of the New Testament* (San Francisco: HarperSanFrancisco, 1996), 187–205.

If we read the texts as testimony, we will find ourselves constantly reminded that the Bible is chiefly about God, not about human religious aspirations and power struggles.[19]

(7) *The language of theological exegesis is intratextual in character.*[20] In intratextual theological exegesis, our interpretations will remain close to the primary language of the witnesses rather than moving away from the particularity of the biblical testimony to a language of second-order abstraction that seeks to "translate" the biblical imagery into some other conceptual register. Of course, this sort of "translation" project was at the heart of Bultmann's hermeneutical program; however laudable its intention, it was theologically vacuous and unfruitful. As R. R. Reno complains, many contemporary failed attempts at theological exegesis commit precisely this same "translation" fallacy, without the same hermeneutical sophistication displayed in Bultmann's work.[21]

(8) Theological exegesis, insofar as it stays close to the language and conceptions of the NT witnesses, will find itself drawn into the Bible's complex web of *intertextuality*. The NT insistently cites and alludes to the OT, argues for a narrative continuity between the story of Israel and the story of Jesus, and interprets this continuity through discerning *figural* correspondences between the two. Consequently, theological exegesis will have to concern itself with tracing and interpreting these complex intertextual correspondences between the testaments.

(9) Theological exegesis thereby is committed to the discovery and exposition of *multiple senses* in biblical texts. Old Testament texts, when read in

19. See the first thesis of the Scripture Project, which declares that "God is the primary agent revealed in the biblical narrative" (Davis and Hays, *Art of Reading Scripture*, 1).

20. I use the term *intratextual* in the sense explained by George Lindbeck, *The Nature of Doctrine: Religion and Theology in a Postliberal Age* (Philadelphia: Westminster, 1984): "Intratextual theology describes reality within the Scriptural framework, rather than translating Scripture into extrascriptural categories. It is the text, so to speak, which absorbs the world, rather than the world the text" (118).

21. Reno, "Biblical Theology," passim. His essay gives dozens of examples, of which I cite only one for purposes of illustration. Whereas Paul in Rom 8:26–27 declares that the Spirit helps us in our weakness and intercedes with God, Luke Johnson's commentary on the passage transposes the categories into a discussion of "intimacy between the divine and human freedom" (Luke Timothy Johnson, *Reading Romans: A Literary and Theological Commentary*, Reading the New Testament [New York: Crossroad, 1997], 131; cited in Reno, "Biblical Theology," 391). This sort of move to the language of secondary reflectivity is not in itself inappropriate; indeed, it may be in some ways necessary. The difficulty appears when language of this sort overshadows or supplants the primary language of the text on which it is intended to comment.

conjunction with the story of Jesus, take on new and unexpected resonances as they prefigure events far beyond the historical horizon of their authors and original readers. The NT's stories of Jesus, when understood as mysterious fulfillments of long-ago promises, assume a depth beyond their literal sense as reports of events of the recent past. Texts have multiple layers of meaning that are disclosed by the Holy Spirit to faithful and patient readers.[22]

(10) Learning to read the text with eyes of faith is a skill for which we are trained by *the Christian tradition*. Consequently, theological exegesis knows itself to be part of an ancient and lively conversation. We can never approach the Bible as though we are the first ones to read it—or the first to read it appropriately. We know that we have much to learn from the wisdom of the people who have reflected deeply on these texts before us. Consequently, *theological exegesis will find hermeneutical aid, not hindrance, in the church's doctrinal traditions.*[23]

(11) Theological exegesis, however, goes beyond repeating traditional interpretations; rather, instructed by the example of traditional readings, theological interpreters will produce *fresh readings*, new performances of Scripture's sense that encounter the texts anew with eyes of faith and see the ways that the Holy Spirit continues to speak to the churches through the same ancient texts that the tradition has handed on to us. To put the same point in a slightly different way, the Spirit-led imagination, an imagination converted by the Word, is an essential faculty for the work of theological exegesis.

(12) Finally, when we speak of theological exegesis, particularly when we acknowledge the Spirit's role, we must always remember that we are speaking not chiefly of our own clever readings and constructions of the text but, rather, of the way that God, working through the text, is reshaping us. In his foreword to a recent collection of Minear's essays, J. Louis Martyn quotes the famous dictum of Johann Albrecht Bengel: "Apply yourself wholly to the text; apply the text wholly to yourself." Martyn, however, proposes that the maxim should be reworded to read, "Apply yourself wholly to the text, and the text will apply

22. See the fourth thesis of the Scripture Project: "Texts of Scripture do not have a single meaning limited to the intent of the original author. In accord with Jewish and Christian traditions, we affirm that Scripture has multiple complex senses given by God, the author of the whole drama" (Davis and Hays, *Art of Reading Scripture*, 2).

23. For a defense of this claim, see David S. Yeago, "The New Testament and the Nicene Dogma: A Contribution to the Recovery of Theological Exegesis," in *The Theological Interpretation of Scripture: Classic and Contemporary Readings*, ed. Stephen E. Fowl (Oxford: Blackwell, 1997). Fowl's edited collection is itself testimony to the point I am making here. For a recent and particularly illuminating case study, see Childs, *Isaiah as Christian Scripture*.

itself wholly to you!"[24] If it is true, as we confess with the author of the Letter to the Hebrews, that "the word of God is living and active, sharper than any two-edged sword" (Heb 4:12), then we may indeed expect to be transformed as we read. This means that theological exegesis must always be done from a posture of prayer and humility before the word. In the preface to the English edition of his Romans commentary, Karl Barth asks whom or what his book should serve. Here is how he answers the question: "No doubt it should be of service to those who read it. But, primarily and above all else, it must serve that other Book where Jesus Christ is present in His Church. Theology is *ministerium verbi divini*. It is nothing more nor less."[25] If this is true of theology in general, surely it is true a fortiori for theological exegesis.

"Go and Tell What You Have Seen and Heard": Theological Exegesis in Practice

In the final part of this article, I want to attempt an actual act of reading that will seek to illustrate theological exegesis in practice. I shall not at every point explain how this reading exemplifies the identifying marks of theological exegesis that I have just described, but I hope that some of the connections will be evident.

It has become a conventional view in modern NT criticism that the Gospel of Luke represents a "low" or "primitive" Christology.[26] According to this view, Luke portrays Jesus as a Spirit-anointed prophet, a teacher of divine wisdom, and a righteous martyr. Lacking, however, are any doctrines of preexistence and incarnation; lacking is any clear assertion of Jesus's identity with God. As we shall see, an attentive theological exegesis of Luke's Gospel gives us substantial reason to question this characterization of Lukan Christology.[27]

24. J. Louis Martyn, foreword to Paul S. Minear, *The Bible and the Historian: Breaking the Silence about God in Biblical Studies* (Nashville: Abingdon, 2002), 11.

25. Karl Barth, *The Epistle to the Romans*, trans. Edwyn C. Hoskins (London: Oxford University Press, 1933), x.

26. For a representative view, see, for example, John Drury, "Luke, Gospel of," in *A Dictionary of Biblical Interpretation*, ed. R. J. Coggins and J. L. Houlden (London: SCM, 1990), 410–13. Drury writes, "It has long been noticed that [Luke] has a 'lower' christology than the other evangelists, and a much lower one than John." Similarly, Christopher M. Tuckett observes, "Many have argued that, insofar as Luke's views can be discerned, the picture is fundamentally a 'subordinationist' one: Jesus is presented as above all a human being who is subordinate to God" ("The Christology of Luke-Acts," in *The Unity of Luke-Acts*, ed. Joseph Verheyden [Leuven: Leuven University Press, 1999], 148–49).

27. Many of the following exegetical observations are adapted from my essay "Die Be-

In Luke 7:18–23, the imprisoned John the Baptist sends messengers to question Jesus about his identity.[28] They ask, as John has instructed them, "Are you ὁ ἐρχόμενος ('the Coming One'), or shall we look for another?" The question is given particular emphasis by its repetition in verses 19 and 20 (in contrast to Matt 11:3); this is a good example of Luke's emulation of OT narrative style, but it also serves the important purpose of forcing the reader to linger over the question and to ponder its significance, particularly the significance of the term ὁ ἐρχόμενος. The carefully chosen language of the question evokes Ps 118:26//Ps 117:26 LXX, which is the culminating doxological passage of the cycle of Hallel Psalms (Pss 113–118): "Blessed is ὁ ἐρχόμενος in the name of the LORD." The Hallel Psalms were sung on the occasion of Israel's great national festivals of Tabernacles and Passover. Both of these festivals were associated with Israel's national liberation from bondage in Egypt and therefore also—in the first-century context—linked with the hope of a future liberation from Roman rule and the coming of a new king. Luke, more clearly than the other Synoptic Gospels, makes this royal hope fully explicit in his account of Jesus's triumphal entry to Jerusalem, as the crowd chants, using the words of Ps 118:26, "Blessed is ὁ ἐρχόμενος, *the king* who comes in the name of the Lord" (Luke 19:38).[29] Thus, reading retrospectively in the context of Luke's narrative, we see that John the Baptist's question in Luke 7:19–20 is a politically loaded query. He is asking whether Jesus intends to proclaim himself Israel's long-awaited ruler who will restore the kingdom of David. John is asking, "Are you the Coming One, the coming King?"

Jesus's answer speaks volumes without answering the question directly: "Go and tell John what you have seen and heard: the blind receive their sight, the lame walk, the lepers are cleansed, the deaf hear, the dead are raised, the poor have good news brought to them. And blessed is anyone who takes no offense at me" (Luke 7:22–23). The answer makes sense only when we recognize that it

freiung Israels im lukanischen Doppelwerk: Intertextuelle Erzählung als kulturkritische Praxis," in *Die Bibel im Dialog der Schriften: Konzepte Intertextueller Bibellektüre*, ed. Stefan Alkier and Richard B. Hays (Tübingen: Francke, 2005), 117–36.

28. A nearly identical account appears in Matt 11:2–6. This passage therefore belongs to material sometimes designated as coming from the hypothetical Q source. I am one of those who have serious doubts about the Q hypothesis, and in any case our chief concern here is not with source-critical issues. Unfortunately, space does not permit a comparison of the slightly different ways this story functions within Luke and Matthew; instead, our particular focus will be on theological exegesis of the passage in its *Lukan* setting.

29. Only Luke here has ὁ βασιλεύς as an explanatory gloss on "the Coming One" (cf. Matt 21:9; Mark 11:10).

echoes a number of motifs drawn from *Isaiah's* portrayal of the end of Israel's exile and God's eschatological restoration of the nation. The first and most important echo should remind John's emissaries of Isa 35:5–6a:

> Then the eyes of the blind shall be opened,
> and the ears of the deaf unstopped;
> then the lame shall leap like a deer,
> and the tongue of the speechless sing for joy.

These stirring images are part of Isaiah's vision of the exiled Israelites returning on a miraculous highway through the desert to Zion. Isaiah paints a picture of God's healing all that is broken, putting all things right in the eschatological time. The great Charles Wesley hymn "O for a Thousand Tongues" draws on precisely these images:

> Hear him ye deaf, his praise, ye dumb,
> your loosened tongues employ;
> Ye blind, behold your Savior come,
> and leap, ye lame, for joy.[30]

But Jesus's answer also sounds a second, slightly less prominent echo in the phrase "the poor have good news proclaimed to them." The Greek expression here, πτωχοὶ εὐαγγελίζονται, reminds us of the passage from Isa 61 that Jesus had earlier read in the synagogue in Nazareth to inaugurate his public ministry:

> The Spirit of the Lord is upon me,
> because he has anointed me to proclaim good news to the poor
> (εὐαγγελίσασθαι πτωχοῖς);
> he has sent me to proclaim release to the captives,
> and recovery of sight to the blind. (Luke 4:18–19)[31]

30. Charles Wesley, "O for a Thousand Tongues," *The United Methodist Hymnal* (Nashville: United Methodist Publishing House, 1989), 57.

31. The text of Isa 61 cited in Luke 4:18–19 follows the LXX much more closely than the MT, and it also includes a fragmentary echo of Isa 58:6 ("to let the oppressed go free"), as well as an allusion to the year of Jubilee (Lev 25:10). Each of these observations is of interest for the interpretation of Luke 4, but the scope of the present article precludes pursuing them in further detail.

On that occasion, Jesus had stunningly announced, "Today, this Scripture has been fulfilled in your hearing" (4:21). Thus, in Luke 7, Jesus's apparently cryptic response to John's disciples is actually a very clear, intertextually coded response.[32] By evoking Isa 35 and Isa 61, Jesus offers a scriptural interpretive framework for the miraculous deeds that John's disciples have seen him perform. The passages from Isaiah should signal to John—or to any hearer steeped in Israel's Scriptures—that Jesus's activity is indeed to be understood as the inauguration of the coming kingdom of God for which Israel had longed and for which John was waiting.

Yet these passages at the very same time gesture toward a dramatic reshaping of Israel's national hope. The motifs selected by Jesus in his answer to John's disciples pointedly avoid images of military conquest. They focus instead on actions of healing and restoration.[33] Precisely by doing so, they offer John and his followers a new, nonviolent image of "the Coming One" and teach them to read Israel's Scripture with new eyes. In effect, Jesus's act of teaching John's messengers how to "read" his own ministry in light of Isaiah's words is *in itself* part of his work of opening the eyes of the blind.

The concluding macarism, "blessed is he who takes no offense at me" (μὴ σκανδαλισθῇ ἐν ἐμοί, literally, "is not caused to stumble in me") should probably be understood as yet another echo—this time, pointing to Isaiah's image of the stone laid in Zion (Isa 28:16), which will also be a stone of stumbling for Israel (Isa 8:14; see the fusion of these same two texts in Rom 9:32–33). Isaiah's famous and enigmatic "stone" image draws a sharp contrast between the prophet's trust in God's promise and Israel's faithless reliance on military power as a source of security. The point is that John and his disciples should not "stumble" over Jesus's unexpected peaceful way of bringing in God's promised reign. (Luke later underscores his point narratively by telling the story of the two disciples on the road to Emmaus, who are leaving Jerusalem in disappointment *despite* having heard the report of the empty tomb. They say, "we had hoped that he was the one to redeem Israel" [Luke 24:21a]; that is, they had been expecting the conventional royal military redeemer.) The writer of the nineteenth-century hymn "Lead On, O King Eternal" gets the point just right:

32. For a full listing of the allusive parallels, see Dale C. Allison Jr., *The Intertextual Jesus: Scripture in Q* (Harrisburg, PA: Trinity Press International, 2000), 109–14.

33. The Dead Sea Scrolls have now yielded up evidence that other Jewish interpreters of this era drew upon precisely these same Isaianic texts as a description of the Lord's saving actions in the eschatological age. See particularly 4Q521.

> For not with swords loud clashing, nor roll of stirring drums;
> with deeds of love and mercy the heavenly kingdom comes.[34]

Luke sketches all this with economy of language and literary power though allusion and metalepsis.[35] The reader who knows the Psalter and Isaiah will get the point well enough. In light of the echoes from Ps 118 and Isaiah, the answer that we as readers are to supply to John's question is something like this: "Is Jesus the Coming One? Yes, he is the Coming King to which Ps 118 points, the eschatological deliverer anticipated every time the Hallel Psalms are sung. He is the one for whom we have hoped, but his coming kingdom must be interpreted not in terms of violent or coercive power, but in light of Isaiah's images of divine mercy and restoration."

There remains one more important thing to be said about this text. Jesus's answer to John hints at one more, still deeper truth at the heart of the good news Jesus is proclaiming. The texts from the prophet Isaiah that echo in Jesus's answer also adumbrate *the return of the Lord to Zion*. Israel is to be saved, according to Isaiah, not by a merely human leader who will bring them back from exile; rather, *God himself* will appear on the scene to lead the triumphant procession of returning exiles. As we have already seen, Jesus alludes forcefully to Isa 35:5 ("then the eyes of the blind shall be opened, and the ears of the deaf unstopped"). But *how* will these saving acts occur? Listen to the verse just before this, Isa 35:4: "Say to those who are of a fearful heart, 'Be strong, do not fear! *Here is your God. . . . He will come and save you*.'" Should we hear this echo as a metaleptic hint that the identity of this Coming One is something far greater than what John the Baptist envisioned?

The suggestion may seem farfetched until we consider more broadly the way in which the Evangelist Luke subtly narrates the identity of Jesus throughout his Gospel. Luke is the only one of the Gospel writers who regularly uses κύριος as a title for Jesus. Κύριος is, of course, the Greek word used by the Septuagint to translate the holy name of God, the Tetragrammaton (often dubiously rendered in modern English translations as "Yahweh"). There are at least fifteen instances in Luke where the evangelist refers to Jesus as the

34. Ernest W. Shurtleff, "Lead On, O King Eternal," in *The United Methodist Hymnal* (Nashville: United Methodist Publishing House, 1989), 580.

35. *Metalepsis* is a literary device in which an author quotes only a part of a precursor text, in such a way that the reader or hearer must recall the larger context from which the citation comes in order to grasp its full import. For further discussion, see my *Echoes of Scripture in the Letters of Paul* (New Haven: Yale University Press, 1989), 14–21; and also my *Conversion of the Imagination*, 2–3, and esp. n. 5.

κύριος.[36] Consider the following examples: "and why has this happened to me, that the mother of *my Lord* comes to me?" (Luke 1:43); "to you is born this day in the city of David a Savior, who is Christ *the Lord*" (2:11); "when *the Lord* saw her, he had compassion on her" (7:13); "Mary, who sat at *the Lord's* feet" (10:39); "*the Lord* turned and looked at Peter" (22:61); "*the Lord* has risen indeed" (24:34). Most appositely, within the very passage we are considering, we find this: "John summoned two of his disciples and sent them to *the Lord* to ask . . ." (7:18b-19a). In short, Luke quite remarkably applies the title κύριος both to the God of Israel[37] and to Jesus of Nazareth—occasionally in a way that suggests a mysterious fusion of divine and human identity in the figure of Jesus.[38]

The hermeneutical effect of Luke's repeated narrative usage of κύριος is not unlike the effect achieved at the end of Paul's Christ hymn in Phil 2, which astonishingly ascribes to Jesus the eschatological lordship that Isa 45:23 emphatically reserves for God alone: "so that at the name of Jesus every knee should bend . . . and every tongue should confess that Jesus Christ is κύριος, to the glory of God the Father" (Phil 2:10–11). In that same confession, Luke invites us to join. Consequently, when Jesus says to John's messengers, "Blessed is the one who takes no offense at me" (Luke 7:23), his blessing answers in call-and-response fashion the very text to which John's question alluded, Ps 118:26: "Blessed is the Coming One, the One who comes in the name of the Kyrios." It turns out, beyond all possible human power of anticipation, that Jesus is both ὁ ἐρχόμενος, the Coming One, *and*, in embodied form, ὁ κύριος, the LORD.

In view of these exegetical findings, I would hazard the following conclusion: the "low" Christology that modernist criticism has perceived in Luke's Gospel is an artificial construction achieved by excluding the hermeneutical relevance of the wider canonical witness, particularly the OT allusions in Luke's story. It is precisely by attending more fully to the OT allusions in Luke's Gospel that we gain a deeper and firmer grasp of the theological coherence between Luke's testimony and what the church's dogmatic tradition has affirmed about the identity of Jesus.

36. This tally does not count the vocative κύριε and other ambiguous instances.

37. Examples are numerous. Especially clear is Luke 1:16: "He will turn many of the people of Israel to *the Lord* their God."

38. For a thorough, theologically sophisticated analysis of this striking phenomenon in Lukan narrative Christology, see C. Kavin Rowe, *Early Narrative Christology: The Lord in the Gospel of Luke*, BZNW 139 (Berlin: de Gruyter, 2006). For an earlier, concise preview of his observations, see Rowe, "Luke and the Trinity: An Essay in Ecclesial Biblical Theology," *SJT* 56 (2003): 1–26.

And so, though we may be imprisoned and beset by doubt, though the time of the kingdom's coming seems slow, though the power of violence still seems to rule, we are taught by Luke—when his Gospel is read within the intertextual network to which it points—to recognize Jesus, the one who brings good news to the poor, as our LORD. Recognizing this, we find our eyes, like the eyes of the disciples on the road to Emmaus, opened to see in Moses and all the prophets the truth of the gospel's testimony: "Be strong, do not fear! *Here is your God. . . . He will come and save you.*"

3

Reading Scripture in Light of the Resurrection

The Offense of the Resurrection

On the issue of the resurrection, many preachers and NT scholars are unwitting partisans of the Sadducees. Because they deny the truth of Scripture's proclamation that God raised Jesus from the dead—or waffle about it—they leave the church in a state of uncertainty, lacking confidence in its mission, knowing neither the Scriptures nor the power of God.

As we stand on the cusp of postmodernity, many Christians are unsure about how to interpret the Bible and what role to give it within the church. At the same time, there is widespread confusion in the church about the NT's resurrection accounts. My proposal in this essay is that these two phenomena are linked: confusion about the resurrection has hindered the church's ability to interpret Scripture, and our ignorance of Scripture has obscured our understanding of the resurrection. Stated positively: *We interpret Scripture rightly only when we read it in light of the resurrection, and we begin to comprehend the resurrection only when we see it as the climax of the scriptural story of God's gracious deliverance of Israel.*

The NT's accounts of the resurrection of Jesus have proven particularly problematic for modern interpreters. Stories about the resurrection of a man crucified, dead, and buried contradict everything that orthodox post-Enlightenment historians take to be axiomatic about the nature of history

This essay was originally written as a contribution to the Scripture Project, at the Center of Theological Inquiry, Princeton, NJ. This was an ongoing collaboration of scholars from the years 1998 to 2002. My paper was presented there, discussed, and subsequently revised in light of the comments of colleagues who were participants in the project. I am indebted to them for much stimulating conversation, and also to Wallace Alston, the director of the Center, and to Robert Jenson, the senior scholar for research, both of whom graciously supported and hosted the research project.

and the reality in which we live. For that reason, the recent history of theology is replete with attempts to reinterpret the meaning of the NT's resurrection stories in ways that will not conflict with a modern scientific worldview. John Shelby Spong offers a blunt assessment: "If the resurrection of Jesus cannot be believed except by assenting to the fantastic descriptions included in the Gospels, then Christianity is doomed. For that view of resurrection is not believable, and if that is all there is, then Christianity, which depends on the truth and authenticity of Jesus' resurrection, also is not believable."[1] How, then, is "Christianity" to be salvaged without requiring acceptance of the New Testament's resurrection stories?

The most abidingly influential answer to this question in the twentieth century was given by Rudolf Bultmann, who offered the lapidary explanation that "Jesus rose in the kerygma." According to Bultmann, the NT's stories about a bodily resurrection and empty tomb are not in any sense factual descriptions of something that happened to Jesus of Nazareth, who had been put to death; rather, they are to be understood as expressions of the "Easter faith" of the first disciples. They are attempts to express in mythic imagery the early church's conviction that Jesus's life and death were in fact an expression of the unquenchable love and grace of God. In Bultmann's formulation, "The Easter-event as the resurrection of Christ is no historical event. . . . Resurrection faith is nothing other than faith in the cross as salvation-event."[2]

Bultmann's demythologized post-Kantian account of Easter faith continues to prevail in many circles of New Testament scholarship, including the work of Gerd Lüdemann[3] and of the scholars who have marketed themselves as the Jesus Seminar. Some interpreters who follow this line, like Bultmann himself, regard "Easter faith" as spiritually authentic and true, while others, such as Lüdemann, regard it as "only a pious wish" that ultimately has produced deceptive and destructive consequences.[4] Lüdemann and Spong have recently pro-

1. John Shelby Spong, *Resurrection: Myth or Reality? A Bishop's Search for the Origins of Christianity* (San Francisco: HarperSanFrancisco, 1994), 238.

2. Rudolf Bultmann, "Neues Testament und Mythologie," in *Kerygma und Mythos*, vol. 1, ed. Hans Werner Bartsch (Hamburg/Bergstedt: Herbert Reich-Evangelischer Verlag, 1948), 46–47, my translation. For a concise, sympathetic exposition of Bultmann's views on this issue, see John Painter, *Theology as Hermeneutics: Rudolf Bultmann's Interpretation of the History of Jesus* (Sheffield: Almond, 1987), 166–68.

3. Gerd Lüdemann, *The Resurrection of Jesus: History, Experience, Theology* (Minneapolis: Fortress, 1994).

4. For Lüdemann's public statement renouncing Christian faith, see his book *The Great Deception: And What Jesus Really Said and Did* (London: SCM, 1998), esp. "A Letter to Jesus,"

duced speculative accounts of the psychological states and experiences ("mass ecstasy," "grief work," etc.) that might have given rise to "Easter faith."[5]

On the other hand, not all interpreters have been ready to dispense with the notion, however vague, that something really did happen to Jesus, even if that "something" defies historical description. For example, Luke Timothy Johnson, a vehement critic of the methods of the Jesus Seminar, declares that "the Christian claim concerning the resurrection in the strong sense is simply not 'historical.' The problem in this case is, however, not with the reality of the resurrection. The problem lies in history's limited mode of knowing."[6] Johnson enters a plea for historical humility and a sober recognition of the limits of historical knowledge while holding open the claim that the resurrection of Jesus was nonetheless a real event.[7]

Johnson sometimes comes very close, however, to adopting the Bultmannian strategy of describing the resurrection exclusively through the filter of subjective faith experience. Consider the following passage from his book *The Real Jesus*:

> At the very heart of Christianity, therefore, is an experience and a claim. The experience is one of transforming, transcendent, personal power within communities that can be expressed in shorthand as "the gift of the Holy Spirit." The claim is that this power comes from Jesus, who was crucified but now lives by the life of God, and is expressed by the declaration "Jesus is Lord." . . . *Experience and conviction together form the primordial "resurrection experience" that founds the Christian movement and continues to ground it today.* . . . The resurrection experience that founded and grounds the Church is not based on the transitory encounters of a few people on Easter day or for forty days thereafter, but on the experience of power through Jesus by generations of people across the centuries and continuing still today.[8]

1–9. The phrase "only a pious wish" appears on p. 3, where Lüdemann asserts that the body of Jesus either rotted in the tomb or "was devoured by vultures and jackals."

5. For an extended imaginative reconstruction, see Spong, *Resurrection*, 242–60.

6. Luke Timothy Johnson, *The Real Jesus: The Misguided Quest for the Historical Jesus and the Truth of the Traditional Gospels* (San Francisco: HarperSanFrancisco), 136.

7. Spong can also make statements in this vein; see, e.g., *Resurrection*, 239, 256. It should always be acknowledged that his project is apologetic in character: he is seeking to affirm belief in "resurrection" (as he redefines it), not to debunk it.

8. Johnson, *Real Jesus*, 135, emphasis mine. Here Johnson sounds strikingly like Bultmann: "A merely 'reminiscent' historical account referring to what happened in the past cannot make the salvation-occurrence visible. . . . [T]he salvation-occurrence continues to take place in the proclamation of the word. The salvation-occurrence is eschatological

This account of resurrection is a textbook instance of a method of theological reflection—classically exemplified by Friedrich Schleiermacher—that George Lindbeck has characterized as "experiential-expressive": it begins with the religious experiences of believers as the primary data of theology and construes doctrinal claims as attempts to bring such inchoate experiences to expression.[9] There can be no doubt that the NT authors do describe the sort of transforming experiences to which Johnson points as an *effect* of the resurrection. It may be questioned, however, whether the narration of such experiences can stand as a fully adequate account of what they *mean* by resurrection. Particularly, it is doubtful that such an account provides an adequate hermeneutical framework for understanding the resurrection narratives we actually find in the Gospels, which speak of an empty tomb and a palpable, embodied risen Jesus who eats fish with his astonished disciples.[10]

Let us consider one final example of an attempt to reshape the understanding of "Christianity" to accommodate modernist epistemology. Robert W. Funk, the founder of the Jesus Seminar, has set forth on his website a programmatic manifesto titled "The Coming Radical Reformation: Twenty-One Theses." For purposes of illustration, I shall cite only four of the theses, culminating in Funk's declaration on the resurrection:

1) The God of the metaphysical age is dead. There is not a personal god out there external to human beings and the material world. We must reckon with a deep crisis in God talk and replace it with talk about whether the universe has meaning and whether human life has a purpose.

. . .

6) We should give Jesus a demotion. It is no longer credible to think of Jesus as divine. Jesus' divinity goes together with the old theistic way of thinking about God.

occurrence just in this fact, that it does not become fact of the past but constantly takes place anew in the present" (Rudolf Bultmann, *Theology of the New Testament*, trans. Kendrick Grobel, 2 vols. [New York: Scribner, 1951–1955 (1948–1953)], 1:302).

9. George Lindbeck, *The Nature of Doctrine: Religion and Theology in a Postliberal Age* (Philadelphia: Westminster, 1984), 16–17 et passim. To be fair to Johnson, we must recognize that he writes as a Roman Catholic for whom experience of the risen Lord is constantly mediated through liturgy and sacrament; therefore, the "experience" of which he speaks cannot be dissolved into purely individual subjectivity—the abiding danger of Protestant versions of experiential-expressive theology.

10. All the recent revisionist accounts of the NT's witness to the resurrection, of course, discount precisely these features of the NT witness as late legendary accretions to a more original and authentic testimony to visionary "experiences" of the resurrection.

7) The plot early Christians invented for a divine redeemer figure is as archaic as the mythology in which it is framed. A Jesus who drops down out of heaven, performs some magical act that frees human beings from the power of sin, rises from the dead, and returns to heaven is simply no longer credible. The notion that he will return at the end of time and sit in cosmic judgment is equally incredible. We must find a new plot for a more credible Jesus.

. . .

10) The resurrection of Jesus did not involve the resuscitation of a corpse. Jesus did not rise from the dead except perhaps in some metaphorical sense. The meaning of the resurrection is that a few of his followers—probably no more than two or three—finally came to understand what he was all about. When the significance of his words and deeds dawned on them, they knew of no other terms in which to express their amazement than to claim that they had seen him alive.[11]

Funk has spelled out aggressively and explicitly what seems to be implicit in the critical work of numerous other NT scholars who also do not believe that Jesus rose from the dead "except perhaps in some metaphorical sense." His declaration enables us to reflect clearly on what is at stake in our deliberations on this topic. The resurrection is the climactic element—indeed, the linchpin—of the biblical story of God's redemption of the world. Without it, the story falls apart, and there are, as Funk recognizes, wide-ranging systematic implications for theology. (Perhaps the most surprising feature of Funk's agenda is that he understands himself to be advocating a "reformation" rather than a refutation of Christianity.) The resurrectionless story that Funk envisions differs drastically from the story told by the Bible, and the canonical Scriptures of the Old

11. Robert W. Funk, "The Coming Radical Reformation: Twenty-One Theses," Westar/Jesus Seminar website, https://www.westarinstitute.org/resources/the-fourth-r/the-coming-radical-reformation/. For a fuller account of Funk's views, see his book *Honest to Jesus: Jesus for a New Millennium* (San Francisco: HarperSanFrancisco, 1996), 257–77. With regard to Funk's condescending suggestion that "they knew of no other terms in which to express their amazement," see the convincing argument of N. T. Wright that Jews in the Second Temple period had many terms and categories for describing visionary or revelatory experiences but that *resurrection* was not one of them. *Resurrection* referred unambiguously to the resurrection of the body, and it was symbolically associated with hopes for God's ultimate restoration and vindication of Israel. N. T. Wright, "Christian Origins and the Resurrection of Jesus: The Resurrection of Jesus as a Historical Problem," *Sewanee Theological Review* 41 (1998): 107–23. For a subsequent comprehensive study, see N. T. Wright, *The Resurrection of the Son of God* (Minneapolis: Fortress, 2003).

and New Testaments become for him an obstacle to be overcome ("we must find a new plot") rather than a source of good news and life.

But what if God really did raise Jesus from the dead? What if "resurrection" names not just the transformed self-understanding of Jesus's followers but rather God's mighty act of raising one particular man, who was crucified, dead, and buried, from the grave? Wouldn't that open up a totally different perspective for understanding the world and interpreting the Bible? In the brief scope of this essay, we shall explore this proposal by attending carefully to three Gospel passages that connect resurrection with the reading of Scripture.

Three Texts on Reading and Resurrection

John 2:13–22: Remembering Scripture and Jesus's Word

John's account of Jesus's protest action against trade and moneychanging in the temple appears near the beginning of his narrative. Rather than functioning, as it does in the Synoptic Gospels, as the culminating provocation that precipitates Jesus's arrest, it serves for John as a scene of dramatic foreshadowing. The story forges a symbolic identification between the temple and Jesus's own body in Jesus's enigmatic prophecy: "Destroy this temple, and in three days I will raise it up" (John 2:19). As the passage indicates, the meaning of this prophecy becomes intelligible—and its truth validated—only after the resurrection. Jesus's interlocutors misunderstand his saying because, in the dramatic irony typical of Johannine dialogues, they perceive only the surface literal sense and miss the hidden christological meaning. This meaning, of course, was inaccessible to them in the preresurrection situation.

The hermeneutical key to the passage is given explicitly in an authorial voiceover directed to the reader in John 2:21–22: "But he was speaking of the temple of his body. *When, therefore* (ὅτε οὖν), he was raised from the dead, his disciples remembered that he had said this; and they believed the scripture and the word that Jesus had spoken." The force of John's οὖν (not translated by the NRSV) is elusive, but it seems to imply something like this: "Jesus spoke *figuratively* about the resurrection of his own body; *therefore*, the meaning of his prophecy could be understood only after the resurrection, only after he had embodied its figural sense." It is not too much to suggest that John, early in his narrative, is teaching his readers how to read. Look beyond the literal sense, he whispers, and read for figuration. Read Scripture retrospectively, in light of the resurrection. If you do, you will see the temple as *prefiguring* the truth definitively embodied in Jesus.

But how does the reference to believing "*the scripture*" fit into this hermeneutical directive? There is no citation of Scripture in Jesus's saying. We could hypothesize that John is alluding to various uncited biblical passages about restoring the temple after the exile,[12] but there is a more immediate solution at hand in the passage itself. The key is to recognize the structural parallelism between verses 17a and 22a:

> 17a: His disciples remembered that it was written . . .
> 22a: [H]is disciples remembered that he had said this . . .

In both cases we find precisely the same wording in the Greek text: ἐμνήσθησαν οἱ μαθηταὶ αὐτοῦ ὅτι. In the first instance, the disciples are said to have remembered a scriptural text (Ps 69:9a: "Zeal for your house . . . has consumed me"); in the second, they are said to have remembered a word of Jesus ("Destroy this temple, and in three days I will raise it up"). Thus when John tells us that they "believed (a) *the scripture* and (b) *the word that Jesus had spoken*" (v. 22b), we should understand this as a summary comment about the whole narrative unit (vv. 13–22a), including the story of driving out the traders and moneychangers. If so—and here is the key point—"the scripture" that they believed was Ps 69.

What does a reading of Ps 69 after the resurrection disclose? In what sense can the disciples be said to have believed this scripture in a new way as a result of the resurrection?[13] The most important clue lies in the fact that the postresurrection reading sketched in John 2 requires us to understand Jesus as the *speaker*, the praying voice of the psalm: "Zeal for your house will consume *me*." This interpretation opens up the entire psalm, not just one half-verse of it, as a proleptic disclosure of the mystery of Jesus's identity.

Indeed, from a range of other evidence, we know that the early church did

12. Particularly interesting is Zech 14:21, the concluding verse of Zechariah's eschatological prophecy: "And there shall no longer be traders in the house of the Lord of hosts on that day."

13. Later in John's Gospel, we learn that the disciples' post-resurrection remembering is to be aided by the Paraclete, the Holy Spirit, who will recall and interpret Jesus's words for the community (John 14:25–26; 16:12–15). At one level, of course, we are to understand that Ps 69 foreshadowed Jesus's "zeal" for the house of God, as demonstrated in his angry rebuke of the merchants in the temple. At this level, to "believe the scripture" would be to accept the insight that this snippet (Ps 69:9a) was a hidden prophecy about something Jesus was later to do. This reading is facilitated by John's shifting of the verb tense: where Ps 69:9//Ps 68:10 LXX reads "Zeal for your house *has consumed* me" (κατέφαγεν, a second aorist form), John "remembers" the text to say ". . . *will consume* me" (καταφάγεται, a future form). The postresurrection perspective, however, contributes little to this interpretation.

read Ps 69 in precisely this way: as a passion psalm portraying Jesus as the righteous sufferer.[14] For example, Paul quotes the other half of the same verse that John cites in order to portray Jesus as one who suffers vicariously for the sake of others (Rom 15:3).[15] All four canonical Gospels say that on the cross Jesus was offered vinegar (ὄξος) to drink (Matt 27:48; Mark 15:36; Luke 23:36; John 19:29), a narrative detail whose correspondence with Ps 69:21//Ps 68:22 LXX can scarcely have escaped John's notice. Thus a reading of Ps 69 after the passion and resurrection of Jesus would disclose that the psalm is to be read as a poetic prefiguration of the suffering and vindication of Jesus the Messiah, whose voice "David" anticipated.

This interpretation was perhaps further encouraged by the fact that the Septuagint translated the obscure Hebrew phrase לַמְנַצֵּחַ ("to the leader"?) in the superscription of Ps 69 as εἰς τὸ τέλος ("for the end"), a phrase that early Christian interpreters could readily have understood as a directive to read the psalm as having eschatological reference.[16] From this perspective, to "believe the scripture" would mean to understand that Jesus is the speaker of the psalm taken as whole—or perhaps even of the Psalter as a whole—and that the sentence "Zeal for your house will consume me" should be read as a pointer to the destruction that came upon Jesus as a result of his zeal and faithfulness to God, a destruction prefigured in the psalm, foreshadowed prophetically by Jesus's own words, and narrated fully in the passion story.

Once one begins to read Ps 69 from a postresurrection perspective, the psalm's concluding turn to praise and thanksgiving (vv. 30–36) can also be read as a prefiguration of the resurrection. In that case, it is perhaps not sheerly coincidental that the psalm's final verses speak of God's saving Zion and *(re)building* the cities of Judah—an image that echoes suggestively in counterpoint with Jesus's prophecy that he will raise up the destroyed temple of his

14. C. H. Dodd observes a wide range of different citations of this psalm by various NT writers and concludes as follows: "The intention of the New Testament writers is clearly to apply the whole [of Psalm 69] to the sufferings and ultimate triumph of Christ" (C. H. Dodd, *According to the Scriptures: The Sub-structure of New Testament Theology* [London: Nisbet, 1952], 57–60, 96–97 [97]). See also Brian E. Daley, SJ, "Is Patristic Exegesis Still Usable? Some Reflections on Early Christian Interpretation of the Psalms," in *The Art of Reading Scripture*, ed. Ellen F. Davis and Richard B. Hays (Grand Rapids: Eerdmans, 2003), 69–88.

15. Elsewhere, he also cites vv. 22–23 of the psalm (following the wording of the LXX) as a depiction of the "hardened" Israel that rejects the gospel (Rom 11:9–10).

16. I have made this suggestion previously in Richard B. Hays, "Christ Prays the Psalms: Paul's Use of an Early Christian Exegetical Convention," in *The Future of Christology: Essays in Honor of Leander E. Keck*, ed. Abraham J. Malherbe and Wayne A. Meeks (Minneapolis: Fortress, 1993), 122–36. See particularly p. 127.

body.[17] One important implication of such a reading is that *the meaning of Jesus's resurrection is not to be understood apart from Israel's hope for deliverance and restoration; the resurrection is not an alternative to such hopes but rather a sign of their consummation.* To be sure, John does not cite these verses of the psalm, but if we follow his implied direction about reading the scripture and the saying of Jesus *together* in light of the resurrection, we belated disciples, long after the resurrection, may find ourselves recalling and understanding more than we could have imagined. If so, part of what we understand will be that Jesus's resurrection and the fate of Israel are inseparable.

Thus in John 2:13–22 the story of Jesus's death and resurrection is posited as the key that unlocks the interpretation of Scripture. Retrospective reading of the OT after the resurrection enables Jesus's disciples to "believe" in a new way both Scripture and Jesus's teaching and to see how each illuminates the other. Such retrospective reading neither denies nor invalidates the meaning that the OT text might have had in its original historical setting. Psalm 69 is fully comprehensible as an expression of Israelite piety: it is a prayer for deliverance in a time of trouble and suffering. When it is reread, however, in light of the NT's story of Jesus's passion and resurrection, it takes on additional resonances beyond those perceptible to its earlier readers. The figural correlation between the psalmist's prayer and the story of Jesus illuminates both in unexpected ways.[18]

Mark 12:18–27: Knowing the Scriptures and the Power of God

In this controversy story, Jesus is challenged by the Sadducees, who seek to discredit the idea of a resurrection of the dead.[19] (The story presupposes that Jesus was generally known to share the Jewish apocalyptic expectation of the resurrection of the dead; otherwise, the challenge from the Sadducees makes

17. This is an instance of the rhetorical device of metalepsis. For discussion of this figure, see Richard B. Hays, *Echoes of Scripture in the Letters of Paul* (New Haven: Yale University Press, 1989), 20 et passim.

18. This example illustrates what is meant by "figural reading." The retrospective interpretation of an OT text as a typological prefiguration of a subsequent person or event does not in any way negate the historical reality of the precursor. Both type and antitype are embraced together as concrete disclosures of God's activity in the world. Therefore, the hermeneutical current flows in both directions, and the "meaning" of each pole in the typological correlation is enhanced by its relation to the other. For a helpful discussion of figural reading and typology, see Hans W. Frei, *The Eclipse of Biblical Narrative* (New Haven: Yale University Press, 1974), 1–37.

19. For synoptic parallels, see Matt 22:23–33 and Luke 20:27–40.

no sense.) The Sadducees—about whom we know relatively little—were probably an aristocratic party that exercised influence in the political and religious establishment in Jerusalem during the era leading up to the war against Rome (66–70 CE). They rejected the doctrine of resurrection of the dead—apparently because it was not to be found in the law of Moses.[20] One suspects, additionally, that they may have found such apocalyptic ideas unsettling because they threatened the status quo of social power and privilege. Proclaiming resurrection turns the world upside down (cf. Acts 17:1–9) and holds out to the poor and lowly the hope of being vindicated while posing a worrisome prospect to those who have already received their consolation in the present life (cf. Luke 6:24).[21] Thus the Sadducees would have had a particular interest in debunking the belief in resurrection that was widely held among other Jews in the first century CE.[22]

In the story of Mark 12:18–27, the Sadducees conjure up an improbable tale about a woman who, under the provisions of levirate marriage law, is married in succession to seven brothers, all of whom die childless, with the woman being the last to go to the grave. In other circumstances this might provide the plot for a juicy murder mystery (with the woman as the chief suspect; cf. Tob 3:7–9), but the Sadducees have a different interest. They want to inquire how this scenario might inform theological reflection about resurrection: "In the resurrection, whose wife will she be?" The question is intended as a reductio ad absurdum.

Jesus's answer has three components: a put-down of his interlocutors (v. 24), a statement that the life of the resurrection will transcend sexual and marital relations as we know them (v. 25), and a cryptic attempt to demonstrate that the Pentateuch does, after all, provide warrant for the doctrine of resurrection (vv. 26–27). Each of these three components is of some importance for our reflections about reading Scripture in light of the resurrection.

First, the put-down. Jesus not only rejects the Sadducees' argument as silly but diagnoses the source of their error: "Is not this the reason you are wrong, that you know neither *the scriptures* nor *the power of God*?" (Mark 12:24). This

20. Josephus, *Ant.* 18.16–17; on the Sadducees' rejection of Pharisaic oral traditions, see *Ant.* 13.297.

21. See Richard Bauckham, "Life, Death, and the Afterlife in Second Temple Judaism," in *Life in the Face of Death: The Resurrection Message of the New Testament*, ed. Richard N. Longenecker (Grand Rapids: Eerdmans, 2002), 82.

22. As Bauckham convincingly argues, belief in resurrection of the dead was not a Pharisaic peculiarity: it was the Sadducees who held a distinctive minority opinion on this question.

opening rebuff frames the other elements of Jesus's response and directs our attention to what is theologically at stake in this controversy. To say that the Sadducees do not know the Scriptures is a direct affront to their competence as religious leaders. Presumably, in fact, their rejection of the resurrection rests precisely on appeals to the authority of Scripture: no such belief was taught by Moses, so it should not be accepted. By challenging them at this point, Jesus creates the expectation that he will produce scriptural evidence to discredit their skepticism—an expectation that he will fulfill, albeit in a surprising way, in verses 26–27. Just as importantly, he implies that knowledge of biblical content is not the same thing as "knowing the Scriptures" in the way that matters. The telling of this controversy story suggests that authentic knowledge of the Scriptures depends on a hermeneutic of resurrection, the ability to discern in Scripture a witness of God's life-giving power.

The reference to "the power of God" (τὴν δύναμιν τοῦ θεοῦ) has several possible meanings here. It could allude to the power of God to raise up children to the childless, the general power of God to raise the dead, or—most interestingly—the eschatological manifestation of God's glory at the time when the Son of Man is to be revealed seated at the right hand of *the Power* (τῆς δυνάμεως, Mark 14:62; Matt 26:64). Mark links this eschatological manifestation of God as Power with Daniel's vision of the Son of Man (Dan 7:13–14), which in turn is linked with the expectation of resurrection of the dead (Dan 12:2–3) and the vindication of the elect. Thus Jesus's accusation about the Sadducees' ignorance could be construed as a charge that they are ignorant of this eschatological vision: they are living only in the world of business as usual, heedless of the eschatological power of God that looms over the present. They know in advance what is and is not realistically possible, and so they foreclose the freedom of God to raise the dead.

Second, in verse 25 Jesus asserts that the life of resurrection will not conform to the patterns and categories that we know in the present life: "they neither marry nor are given in marriage, but are like angels in heaven." The Sadducees' derisive question actually reveals a plodding literalism that assumes the life of the world to come—in which they profess disbelief—could be nothing other than an extension of the existence we know now. The belief they reject, however, is a caricature of what Jesus and the NT writers mean by "resurrection." Jesus tries to get his adversaries to think outside the box, to conceive of the resurrection as a transformation, not just a continuation, of life as we know it. This is an extremely important point: to read and think in light of the resurrection is to open ourselves to "what no eye has seen, nor ear heard, nor the human heart conceived, what God has prepared for those who love him" (1 Cor 2:9). A hermeneutic of resurrection opens us up to eschatological surprises of grace, to blessings that confound our casuistic calculations.

Third, Jesus returns to the issue of what the Scriptures teach about resurrection and adduces a surprising text "in the book of Moses, in the story about the bush" (v. 26). Countering the Sadducean belief that the Law does not support the doctrine of resurrection, Jesus goes to the heart of God's self-revelation in the OT, God's appearance to Moses in the burning bush (Exod 3:1–6). How does this text support resurrection? Most NT commentators say that the argument turns on a grammatical technicality: because God says "I *am* the God of Abraham, the God of Isaac, and the God of Jacob," not "I *was* the God of Abraham . . . ," it must be inferred that these three patriarchs—who had long since departed earthly life—are to be found among the living, not the dead. It is often suggested, rather loosely, that this is a particularly "rabbinic" mode of argumentation.[23]

One difficulty, however, is that it is not at all clear how the argument, so construed, actually would support *resurrection*, as distinct from immortality of the soul. The Jewish apocalyptic doctrine of resurrection of the body envisioned the resurrection as part of God's comprehensive restoration of justice "on earth as it is in heaven." As long as injustice and suffering persist, as long as the world remains unredeemed, it would be a non sequitur to assert that the continued personal existence of the three great patriarchs in some other spiritual sphere could somehow prove the validity of belief in the resurrection. Generally, interpreters of Mark chalk this up as one of Jesus's weaker arguments and go on to the next passage—the more satisfying declaration of the double love commandment (Mark 12:28–34).

J. Gerald Janzen, however, has shown that the Exodus story reinforces resurrection in a much more theologically compelling way.[24] The God who speaks to Moses using the "three-ancestor formula" is a God who took the initiative to establish covenant relation with the patriarchs and to promise covenant blessings to their descendants. God consistently acted to protect and save them, even in the face of the most dire and impossible circumstances. God's faithfulness in securing the future of his chosen people is the sure basis on which the descendants of the patriarchs can continue to hope for the future. Therefore,

23. See, however, the rebuttal to this claim by D. M. Cohn-Sherbok, "Jesus' Defence of the Resurrection of the Dead," *JSNT* 11 (1981): 64–73.

24. J. Gerald Janzen, "Resurrection and Hermeneutics: On Exodus 3:6 in Mark 12:26," *JSNT* 23 (1985): 43–58. Janzen's argument builds on the earlier work of F. Dreyfus, "L'argument scriptuaire de Jésus en faveur de la résurrection des morts (Marc XII, vv. 26–27)," *RB* 66 (1959): 213–24.

God's use of the three-ancestor formula in Exod 3:6 implies that there must be an "analogy between the ancestral situations and the situation of the generation of Moses." Just as God delivered and saved the patriarchs, so he will do for his people in their plight in Egypt. Furthermore, if God acted to deliver his people from the "death" of slavery in Egypt, surely he will do so again in the future—not in precisely the same way, but in ways that are recognizably analogous. Consequently, Jesus's use of Exod 3:6 in support of the resurrection—the claim that God will finally save his beloved people from death—is nothing other than a metaphorical extension of the Exodus theophany's claim about God's identity. In other words, a "resurrectionist textual hermeneutics"[25] is already implicitly present in the book of Exodus, and Jesus's appeal to that book makes more explicit what is already there for those who have eyes to see.

Janzen offers yet one more turn in this provocative argument. The three-ancestor formula is a singularly appropriate rejoinder to the Sadducees' test story about the woman whose seven successive husbands fail to *raise up seed* (cf. Gen 38:8) for the first one (i.e., to perpetuate his line).[26] This failure corresponds symbolically to their denial that God will *raise up* the dead. The Sadducees' story is a story about historical existence ordered toward death, under death's reign. As Janzen notes, the stories of Abraham, Isaac, and Jacob are also stories of sterility despite divine promise and long-deferred hope; nonetheless, when read in full, they are stories of "ancestral sterility overcome by divine action." The story told by Genesis and Exodus is a story about God "who gives life to the dead and calls into existence the things that do not exist"—Paul's summary of the meaning of the Abraham story (Rom 4:17).[27] The story of God's life-giving power is evoked by Jesus's appeal to "the God of Abraham, the God of Isaac, and the God of Jacob." Once we know God as the God revealed in the patriarchal narratives, we perceive that giving life to the dead is not far-fetched but fundamentally in keeping with his character.[28] God's self-revelation from the burning bush, therefore, may indeed be understood as a witness to the resurrection.

Here—as in other passages where NT writers cite the OT—the allusive

25. Janzen, "Resurrection and Hermeneutics," 43.

26. The parallel in Matt 22:24 makes the link to the dispute about resurrection even more overt by using the verb ἀναστήσει ("raise up"), which is elsewhere used of resurrection. In Mark 12:19, the verb is ἐξαναστήσῃ (lit., "raise up out of").

27. Janzen, "Resurrection and Hermeneutics," 50–55. Janzen also notes Heb 11:11–12 as a significant reading of the story along similar lines.

28. Jon Levenson has recently argued in a similar fashion that the Torah supports the later rabbinic understanding of resurrection because its stories of God's miraculous intervention to ensure the continuance of the line of Abraham's seed are the "functional equiva-

ripples spread out widely from brief explicit citations to evoke larger narrative patterns. When these larger narrative patterns of the OT are brought into conjunction with the story of Jesus's death and resurrection, we are enabled to read Scripture with new eyes and to see Jesus as carrying forward the story of God's gracious life-giving power. To know the Scriptures and the power of God is to discern in Israel's story the working of the same God who raised Jesus from the dead.

Luke 24:13–35: Opening the Scriptures

The final passage we shall consider is Luke's account of the risen Jesus's encounter with two disciples on the road to Emmaus (Luke 24:13–35). In this episode Luke highlights Jesus's role as exegete of the biblical story: the risen Lord becomes the definitive interpreter of "the things about himself in all the scriptures" (v. 27).

Cleopas and his anonymous companion on the road to Emmaus are well acquainted with all the stories and traditions about Jesus's life, including the report of the empty tomb and the angelic proclamation of the resurrection (vv. 19–24). Nonetheless, they are departing Jerusalem in a state of gloomy disappointment: "But we had hoped that he was the one to redeem Israel" (v. 21a). This is a moment of wrenching irony: Jesus, the Redeemer of Israel, stands before them, yet they fail to recognize him.

Jesus scolds them for their failure to believe *the prophets*[29] (interestingly, not for their failure to believe Jesus's own predictions of his death and resurrection) and begins to instruct them all over again: "Then beginning with Moses and all the prophets, he interpreted to them the things about himself in all the scriptures." As Walter Moberly has observed, the risen Jesus offers no new visions from heaven or mysteries from beyond the grave but instead focuses on patient exposition of Israel's Scripture. The crucial truth lies there, not in some hidden heavenly revelation.[30] Furthermore, Luke's formulation suggests that testimony to Jesus is to be found "in all the scriptures" (ἐν πάσαις ταῖς γραφαῖς), not just in a few isolated proof texts. The

lent" of bringing life out of death (Jon D. Levenson, "Resurrection in the Torah? A Second Look" [2002 Palmer Lecture, Center of Theological Inquiry, Princeton, NJ, March 21, 2002]).

29. I am persuaded by C. F. Evans's suggestion that the rebuke should be translated, "Oh, how foolish you are, and how slow of heart to become believers on the basis of all that the prophets had said" (C. F. Evans, *Saint Luke*, TPINTC [London: SCM, 1990], 910).

30. R. W. L. Moberly, *The Bible, Theology, and Faith: A Study of Abraham and Jesus* (Cambridge: Cambridge University Press, 2000), 51.

whole story of Israel builds to its narrative climax in Jesus, the Messiah who had to suffer before entering into his glory. That is what Jesus tries to teach them on the road.

It is essential to teach them about Scripture because Scripture forms the hermeneutical matrix within which the recent events in Jerusalem become intelligible. Understanding can dawn only when these shattering events are brought into an interpretive dialectic with Israel's story: "As Jesus cannot be understood apart from Jewish scripture, Jewish scripture cannot be understood apart from Jesus; what is needed is an interpretation which relates the two—and it is this that Jesus provides (v. 27)."[31] The puzzled Emmaus disciples have all the facts but lack the pattern, the integrative interpretation, that makes them meaningful. Luke's tantalizingly brief summary of the meaning-pattern is offered in verse 26: "Was it not necessary that the Messiah should suffer these things and then enter into his glory?" (For Luke, entering "into his glory" refers to Jesus's resurrection and ascension.) Somehow, Jesus's exposition of Israel's Scripture will have to show the pervasive presence of this theme—which had never been perceived by anyone in Israel prior to the crucifixion and resurrection.[32]

Luke, as a skillful storyteller, does not yet give away all his secrets. He does not divulge the contents of this privileged exposition of the Bible by the risen Jesus. In order to see what Luke has in mind, we must await his second volume, where his accounts of the apostolic preaching draw heavily on scriptural texts.[33] The apostolic sermons exemplify the sort of readings that (we may suppose) Luke imagines Jesus to have offered on the Emmaus road. For example, Peter's Pentecost sermon finds in Ps 16:8–11 a prefiguration of Jesus's resurrection, and in Ps 110:1 a reference to Jesus's enthronement (Acts 2:22–36). Similarly, Peter's speech before the Jewish council reads Ps 118:22 as a prefiguration of Jesus's rejection, death, and vindication (Acts 4:8–12). To cite just one more example, Philip, in his encounter with the Ethiopian eunuch, finds "the good news about

31. Moberly, *Bible, Theology, and Faith*, 51.

32. As Professor Paul Meyer, in a written communication commenting on an earlier draft of this essay, observes, "what is not in doubt is the Messiah's glory. What needs explaining is that the path to this glory lies through the crucifixion."

33. Moberly points out that Luke's portrayal of Jesus's identity throughout his Gospel draws on OT texts, for example, the Spirit-anointed Servant of Isa 61 in Luke 4:16–21. Moberly, *Bible, Theology, and Faith*, 51–52. The point is well-taken, but most of the examples offered by Moberly do not clearly demonstrate the pattern of suffering and glorification of which Luke 24:26 speaks. The pattern appears more unambiguously in the Acts material.

Jesus" in the Isa 53 account of the suffering servant (Acts 8:26–40).[34] These passages provide clear models for the reading strategy that Luke 24:25–27 articulates in principle.

Yet strikingly, even Jesus's definitive peripatetic Bible study does not produce understanding and recognition in the Emmaus disciples, at least not immediately. The moment of recognition comes only as they sit at table and Jesus breaks bread with them (Luke 24:30–32)—an action that recalls Jesus's last supper with his disciples in Jerusalem (22:14–20). This point, too, is significant for understanding the hermeneutics of resurrection. We do not gain a grasp of Scripture's significance solely through lectures on the text; we come to understand the death and resurrection of Jesus as we participate in the shared life of the community, enacted in meals shared at table.[35]

For those who participate in the practices of sharing modeled by Jesus, an "opening" occurs. It is not by accident that Luke uses this word twice in quick succession. When Jesus broke the bread and gave it to them, their eyes *were opened* (διηνοίχθησαν, v. 31) to recognize him, and as they later recall his teaching, they say, "Weren't our hearts burning within us as he was speaking to us on the road, as he *opened* (διήνοιγεν) to us the Scriptures?" (v. 32). The disciples' faculties of perception are opened by God in such a way that they now recognize not only Jesus but also that the Scriptures have been opened by Jesus's interpretations. The same word appears once more in the following account of Jesus's teaching of the disciples in Jerusalem: "Then he opened (διήνοιξεν) their minds to understand the scriptures" (v. 45).[36] Reading in light

34. For an exposition of Acts 8:26–40 in light of Luke's resurrection themes, see Joel B. Green, "Witnesses of His Resurrection: Resurrection, Salvation, Discipleship, and Mission in Acts of the Apostles," in Longenecker, *Life in the Face of Death*, 227–46, esp. 233–35.

35. Moberly states the point concisely: "Christian understanding is inseparable from a certain kind of 'eucharistic' lifestyle and practice. It is to those who are willing to live and act as Jesus did that the way Jesus understood God and scripture is most likely to make sense" (Moberly, *Bible, Theology, and Faith*, 66). Moberly intends the term "eucharistic" to refer not just to liturgical ceremonies but to a broad range of practices that are "symbolically suggestive of the kind of action through which Jesus, the Christ, welcomed people and mediated God's kingdom to them" (65).

36. The second part of the story, Jesus's appearance to the gathered disciples (Luke 24:36–49), continues the motifs we have already seen in the Emmaus narrative while adding an antidocetic emphasis on the physically embodied form of the risen Jesus (vv. 38–43). The theme of Scripture fulfillment resurfaces in vv. 44–47. This time Jesus specifies more fully that there are things written about him in "the law of Moses, the prophets, and the psalms" that must be fulfilled (v. 44). The unusual threefold formula (in place of the more usual "the law and the prophets") may correspond loosely to the tripartite division of the Hebrew canon (Law, Prophets, and Writings), but it also highlights the particular importance of the

of the resurrection opens both text and reader to new, previously unimagined possibilities.

All three texts we have examined dramatize the hermeneutical nexus between Scripture and resurrection. Luke 24 proclaims overtly what was hinted by our first two passages, in John 2 and Mark 12: in the new situation created by the resurrection of Jesus, Israel's Scripture is to be comprehensively construed as a witness to the gospel. According to these Gospel texts, those who fail to read the OT this way have not yet understood it, at least not fully, for understanding is rendered possible only after the encounter with the risen Jesus. At the same time, the resurrection of Jesus will remain a mute, uninterpretable puzzle unless it is placed firmly within the OT's story of Israel. The disciples on the way to Emmaus had already heard it reported that Jesus was alive, but because they did not know how to locate this report within Israel's story, it seemed a curious and meaningless claim. Their incomprehension exemplifies the grimly ironic dictum with which Luke's parable of the rich man and Lazarus concludes: "If they do not listen to Moses and the prophets, neither will they be convinced even if someone rises from the dead" (Luke 16:31). The good news of Luke 24, however, is that the story does not end in incomprehension and hermeneutical failure, because the one who rose from the dead teaches us anew how to listen to Moses and the prophets.

Implications for Our Practices of Reading

What, then, does it mean to read Scripture in light of the resurrection? What are the *hermeneutical* consequences of standing on this side of the empty tomb? The following observations are preliminary reflections about how we might begin to answer this question.[37]

(1) God is the subject of the crucial verbs in the biblical story. When we

Psalms, read christologically, in early Christianity. In any case, Jesus declares that the Scriptures are full of foreshadowings of himself. A new element is added in v. 47—the claim that the mission to all nations is also adumbrated in Scripture. Thus the new resurrection-shaped reading of Scripture also finds in the OT a warrant for the preaching mission to the gentiles.

37. The following nine points are not intended to correspond precisely to the "Nine Theses on the Interpretation of Scripture." The *numerical* correspondence is coincidental. On the other hand, the *material* convergence of these points with the Nine Theses reflects the significant extent to which my own thinking has been influenced by the deliberations of the Scripture Project. The present essay seeks to demonstrate how the interpretive approach recommended in the Nine Theses might inform exegetical practice.

read Scripture in light of the resurrection, *we read it as a story about the power of the God who gives life to the dead* and calls into existence the things that do not exist. It is not a story about self-help, not a story about human wisdom, not a story about shaping our own identity. It is a story about God—a God who has revealed himself definitively through a mighty act beyond all human capacity, raising Jesus from the dead and transforming the cosmos. Therefore, anthropocentric readings are at best flattened and truncated accounts of the story.[38]

(2) When we read Scripture in light of the resurrection, *we understand Scripture as testimony to the life-giving power of God.* The resurrection of Jesus is not an isolated miracle but a disclosure of God's purpose finally to subdue death and to embrace us within the life of the resurrection. "As all die in Adam, so all will be made alive in Christ" (1 Cor 15:22). For that reason, a hermeneutic responsive to the resurrection can never be a hermeneutic of suspicion toward Scripture's word of promise. The God with whom we have to do is a God who wills life and wholeness for us. If we read the biblical story rightly as a story about this God, we will learn to read it in hopeful trust, open to joyous surprises. We will read with hearts open to the divine power disclosed in the resurrection—a power that overthrows all human systems of violence and oppression. (See Eph 1:17–23.)

(3) The NT's resurrection accounts teach us to *read the OT as Christian Scripture.* To read it in this way, as we have noted, does not mean to deny its original historical sense, nor does it preclude responsible historical criticism. Christians have a stake in seeking the most historically careful readings of the OT texts that we can attain. At the same time, however, in light of the NT's witness, we cannot confine the meaning of the OT to the literal sense understood by its original authors and readers, for these ancient texts have been taken up into a new story that amplifies and illumines their meaning in unexpected ways. The NT writers insist that we are to read Israel's story as a witness to the righteousness of God, climactically disclosed in Jesus Christ. They insist that Israel's Scriptures, understood in the fullest and deepest way, prefigure Jesus. This claim, of course, has important implications for Jewish-Christian dialogue. I would suggest that the goal of such dialogue should be not "tolerance" but respectful controversy between communities that make competing and partly incompatible claims about the meaning of Israel's story. In any case, the stories we have considered here show emphatically that a

38. This point accords with Brian Daley's observations about the emphasis on divine action in patristic biblical interpretation. See Daley, "Is Patristic Exegesis Still Usable?"

hermeneutic of resurrection will not treat the OT as superseded or obsolete. It has an indispensable role in bearing witness to the gospel.

(4) Reading in light of the resurrection is *figural reading*. Because the OT's pointers to the resurrection are indirect and of a symbolic character, the resurrection teaches us to read for figuration and latent sense. The Sadducees were literalists, but God seems to have delighted in veiled anticipations of the gospel. For that reason, resurrection is the enemy of textual literalism. Or, more precisely, resurrection reconfigures the literal sense of Scripture by catalyzing new readings that destabilize entrenched interpretations: the resurrection stories teach us always to remain alert to analogical possibilities and surprises. Resurrection-informed reading sees the life-giving power of God manifested and prefigured in unexpected ways throughout Scripture. It would therefore be a mistake to catalog, say, all the explicitly christological readings of OT texts in Luke-Acts and suppose that we had thereby exhausted the hermeneutical possibilities for understanding Scripture's witness to Jesus Christ. On the contrary, the Jesus who taught the disciples on the Emmaus road that all the Scriptures bore witness to him continues to teach us to discover figural senses of Scripture that are not developed in the NT.[39]

(5) To read Scripture in light of the resurrection is to *read with emphasis on eschatological hope*. The resurrection as a hermeneutical lens brings into focus the OT's propensity to lean forward with eager longing for God to make all things whole. I do not mean simply that texts such as Isa 25:6–8; Ezek 37; and Dan 12:2–3 take on new weight in light of the story of Jesus's resurrection—though of course they do. Rather, I mean that in light of the resurrection, the OT's narrative movement—from sterility to miraculous childbirth, from slavery in Egypt to freedom in the promised land, from exile to return—is to be interpreted as an adumbration of the eschatological hope signified in the NT by the resurrection of the dead. The logic of eschatological hope is structurally fundamental to the OT canon.

Reading in light of the resurrection in no way nullifies the cross. In some NT scholarship, there has been a tendency to disparage resurrection texts such as Luke 24 as "triumphalistic" in contrast to a Pauline *theologia crucis*. This tendency simply displays a misunderstanding of the way the NT's resurrection stories function: by vindicating the crucified Jesus, the resurrection marks the

39. For an excellent example of this open process of figuration, see the discussion of christological resonances of the Joseph story in Gary A. Anderson, "Joseph and the Passion of Our Lord," in Davis and Hays, *Art of Reading*, 198–215.

cross as "the decisive, apocalyptic event that makes sense of Israel's story."[40] Furthermore, the NT's resurrection stories, no less than the Old Testament's narratives, continue to celebrate God's acts of saving power as proleptic signs of the ultimate triumph of God's righteousness (as, e.g., 1 Cor 15:20–28 clearly indicates). In the time between Jesus's resurrection and parousia, therefore, the church lives under the sign of the cross while awaiting the consummation of God's promises. Thus the NT and the OT are closely analogous in their eschatological orientation and in their posture of awaiting God's deliverance in the midst of suffering.

(6) Reading Scripture in light of the resurrection produces an *epistemological transformation of the readers*. Having encountered the risen Jesus, we are forced—enabled—to revise our perceptual categories and our estimates of what is "real." The epistemological shift is nicely illustrated by Paul's rhetorical question in his speech before Agrippa: "Why is it thought incredible by any of you that God raises the dead?" (Acts 26:8). Paul, already trained as a Pharisee to expect the resurrection, now finds himself living in a world in which the truth of Jesus's resurrection shapes his commonsense view of daily reality. That someone might find resurrection incredible seems as odd to him as it would seem to us today that someone might still believe the earth to be flat. The resurrection produces a "conversion of the imagination" that causes us to understand everything else differently.[41]

Sarah Coakley has drawn attention to this phenomenon of transformed understanding in a fascinating essay, "The Resurrection and the 'Spiritual Senses': On Wittgenstein, Epistemology and the Risen Christ."[42] She explores the claim that the resurrection of Jesus might bring about "a transformation of the believer's actual epistemic *apparatus*."[43] She explains that Origen and Gregory of Nyssa, in their doctrine of the spiritual senses, suggest "how seeking and recognising the resurrected Christ require a *process* of change . . . ; it will involve an initial 'turning-around' morally,[44] then practice in seeing the world

40. Paul Meyer, written communication, April 26, 2002.

41. See Richard B. Hays, "The Conversion of the Imagination: Scripture and Eschatology in 1 Corinthians," *NTS* 45 (1999): 391–412; reprinted in Hays, *The Conversion of the Imagination: Paul as Interpreter of Israel's Scripture* (Grand Rapids: Eerdmans, 2005), 1–24.

42. Sarah Coakley, *Powers and Submissions: Spirituality, Philosophy, and Gender* (Oxford: Blackwell, 2002), 130–52.

43. Coakley, *Powers and Submissions*, 131.

44. By reminding us that the process of epistemic transformation also involves a moral "turning-around," Coakley draws attention to the process of character formation in community as an indispensable preparation for the faithful interpretation of Scripture. On this

differently, then only finally the full intimacy of 'spiritual/sensual' knowledge of Christ. What happens in this process is a transformation of one's actual epistemic capacities through their purgation."[45] The resurrection purges the deathbound illusions that previously held us captive and sets us free to perceive the real world of God's life-giving resurrection power.

The Gospel resurrection stories, then, expand our imagination and lead us to discern that God is at work within the sphere of physical time-space reality to transform and restore all things, negating death's power over the body. Our bodies become the vehicles and theaters of God's transforming power. That is why the gospel's epistemology privileges concreteness and anathematizes all docetism, Neoplatonism, and Kantian epistemological dualism. God the Creator raised Jesus from the dead; therefore, "flesh is precious."[46]

(7) The Gospel resurrection stories portray *the risen Jesus as both palpable and elusive.* A persistent motif of the appearance narratives, not just in Luke 24 but elsewhere as well, is that the disciples do not recognize the risen Lord at once. Furthermore, his presence seems to be oddly fleeting or intermittent. Luke Timothy Johnson, noting these elements of the story, speaks of a "dialectic of absence and presence at the heart of the resurrection faith."[47] This dialectic teaches us that, despite our new epistemological vantage point after the resurrection, we are not ourselves in control of the new knowledge we are given. The risen Christ is present where and when he chooses. Paradoxically, our new understanding depends on an event that we cannot possibly understand. Therefore, we are radically dependent on a God who insists on being known on his terms, not ours: "For my thoughts are not your thoughts, nor are your ways my ways" (Isa 55:8). A hermeneutic of resurrection, then, will teach us epistemic humility.

(8) In Luke 24, we have encountered the hint that *resurrection-empowered reading occurs primarily in the context of a shared life in community*, in the

---

theme, see esp. L. Gregory Jones, "Embodying Scripture in the Community of Faith," and R. W. L. Moberly, "Living Dangerously," in Davis and Hays, *Art of Reading*, 143–59 and 181–97.

45. Coakley, *Powers and Submissions*, 139–40. My remarks here have drawn attention primarily to the second stage of this process, the intellectual transformation through which we see the world differently. This need not necessarily be a long, drawn-out process. As Coakley notes, the NT's resurrection appearance stories "seem to involve 'epistemic transformations' much more instantaneous than those described in Origen's schema" (146).

46. Robert Morgan articulates this insight but curiously tries to integrate it into a Bultmannian hermeneutic that undercuts the point he is seeking to make (Robert Morgan, "Flesh Is Precious: The Significance of Luke 24.36–43," in *Resurrection: Essays in Honour of Leslie Houlden*, ed. Stephen Barton and Graham Stanton [London: SPCK, 1994], 8–20).

47. Luke Timothy Johnson, "Luke 24:1–11," *Int* 46 (1992): 58.

practice of breaking bread together. But here we must reckon with a hermeneutical circle. In Acts and the Epistles, it becomes abundantly clear that the resurrection is a generative event that creates a new community whose practices embody the message of resurrection. That embodiment, in turn, enables us to perceive the truth of the resurrection in Scripture. To take a single striking example, Luke narrates the sharing of possessions as an identity-defining practice of the early Jerusalem community and links this practice to the resurrection: "With great power the apostles gave their testimony to the resurrection of the Lord Jesus, and great grace was upon them all, *for* (γάρ) there was not a needy person among them, for (γάρ) as many as owned lands or houses sold them and brought the proceeds of what was sold. They laid it at the apostles' feet, and it was distributed to each as any had need" (Acts 4:33–35).[48] Thus the hermeneutics of resurrection is intimately linked with practices of discipleship and mission.[49]

(9) Finally, reading Scripture in light of the resurrection will provoke us to *rethink our methods for studying the Gospels*. New Testament scholars since the Enlightenment have, on the whole, been sympathizers of the Sadducees; that is to say, they have constructed historical accounts of the formation of the Gospel narratives that bracket out the resurrection as a real event in history. The theses of Robert Funk, quoted in the first section of this essay, offer a particularly egregious example, but Funk's proposals are in fact nothing more than extensions of modernist presuppositions that have influenced much mainstream NT exegesis for the past two centuries: God does not intervene in the processes of history; incarnation, resurrection, and judgment are mythological conceptions; Jesus could not have prophesied his own death and resurrection; the resurrection narratives are legendary; and so forth.[50] If, however, God did raise the crucified Jesus from his tomb, such critical commonplaces should be among the first elements of the status quo to be overturned. The problem was acutely described in 1909 in a penetrating essay by Adolf Schlatter:

48. The NRSV fails to translate the γάρ at the beginning of v. 34, thus obscuring the text's claim that the practice of sharing is the warrant that demonstrates the presence of God's grace and resurrection power in the community.

49. Green, "Witnesses of His Resurrection," 242; Stephen Barton, "The Hermeneutics of the Gospel Resurrection Narratives," in Barton and Stanton, *Resurrection*, 45–57, esp. 54–55. See also the discussion in Moberly, *Bible, Theology, and Faith*, 65–66.

50. Funk characterizes the views of his fellow participants in the Jesus Seminar as follows: "we all assume, they said, that Jesus' life ended with his crucifixion and death" (Funk, *Honest to Jesus*, 258).

> According to the sceptical position, it is true that the historian explains; he observes the New Testament neutrally. But in reality this is to begin at once with a determined struggle against it. The word with which the New Testament confronts us intends to be believed, and so rules out once and for all any sort of neutral treatment. As soon as the historian sets aside or brackets the question of faith, he is making his concern with the New Testament and his presentation of it into a radical and total polemic against it. If he claims to be an observer, concerned solely with his object, then he is concealing what is really happening. As a matter of fact, he is always in possession of certain convictions, and these determine him not simply in the sense that his judgments derive from them, but also in that his perception and observation is molded by them.[51]

What would critical study of the Bible look like if we heeded Schlatter's argument that dogmatics necessarily "permeates the whole course of historical work"[52] and that our location within the community of faith enhances rather than hinders our capacity to understand the past and the historical development of the tradition?[53] What would biblical criticism look like if we sought to develop a consistent critical approach from within the community that knows itself to be given life by the resurrection of Jesus of Nazareth? I do not mean to suggest that it is unheard of for NT scholars to be believers, but it is rare for them to ask how the resurrection—if it is true—ought to affect our methods for studying the history of the Synoptic tradition. To pursue this question consistently would be to create a disturbance as troubling to the NT guild as Jesus's protest action in the temple must have been to the moneychangers—or, perhaps, as troubling as the report of Jesus's resurrection must have been to the Sadducees.

51. Adolf Schlatter, "The Theology of the New Testament and Dogmatics," in *The Nature of New Testament Theology: The Contribution of William Wrede and Adolf Schlatter*, ed. and trans. Robert Morgan, SBT 2/25 (London: SCM, 1973), 122–24.

52. Schlatter, "Theology of the New Testament," 126.

53. By way of contrast, see the recent assertion of Gerd Lüdemann that "the pursuit of theology as an academic discipline should not be tied to the confession [of faith], and . . . if it is, it is not a true academic discipline" (quoted in Rob Simbeck, "Belief vs. Academic Freedom: Theology Professor Fights Ouster from Post Teaching Prospective Ministers," *Washington Post*, April 6, 2002, B9).

4

Figural Interpretation of Israel's Story

Does "Reading Backwards" Undermine the Inspiration of Scripture?

Someone has testified somewhere: "Long ago God spoke to our ancestors in many and various ways by the prophets, but in these last days he has spoken to us by a Son . . ." (Heb 1:1–2a). The "someone" who offered that testimony is, of course, the anonymous author of the Letter to the Hebrews. That testimony can serve as a stimulus to consider what is at stake in the distinction between the ways that God spoke long ago through the prophets and the way that God has spoken afresh in the Gospels.

My book *Echoes of Scripture in the Gospels* seeks to address precisely this distinction; it traces the many and various ways in which the writers of the four canonical Gospels received and reinterpreted Israel's Scripture in light of the astonishing new ways that God spoke in and through Jesus Christ.[1] One key emphasis in my book, however, has provoked a certain amount of murmuring in the academic guild: the practice of *figural exegesis* in the interpretation of the Gospels. This chapter will seek to clarify a few points and—as I shall suggest—to explore the possibilities of a renewed, Spirit-inspired freedom in biblical interpretation.

Reviewers of *Echoes of Scripture in the Gospels,* while generally appreciative of the book, have raised several concerns. Three questions have proven particularly persistent:

1. Richard B. Hays, *Echoes of Scripture in the Gospels* (Waco: Baylor University Press, 2016).

This chapter was originally delivered as the annual lecture for the Institute for Biblical Research meeting in Denver, Colorado, on November 16, 2018. I have edited the paper for publication, but I have retained some features of its oral presentation style. I am grateful for the invitation from the program chair, Mark Boda, and for the warm hospitality of the president, Tremper Longman, along with other members of the IBR board.

(1) *The question of method in identifying allusions and echoes.* When there is no quotation formula, how can we be sure an OT intertext is being echoed? Or how much of the original OT context is relevant for understanding the NT context in which an allusion appears? Some reviewers have judged that "the method lacks objectivity."[2]

(2) *The question of reader competence among first-century audiences.* Would the earliest gentile audiences, who did not have access to full copies of the Jewish Scriptures, have been able to recognize and interpret subtle intertextual references in the Gospels?

(3) *The question of comparative study of ancient Jewish exegetical traditions and practices.* To what extent are the Gospels following extant models of Jewish interpretation, or to what extent are they novel and innovative?

At present, in your hearing, I *won't* answer any of these questions. I have replied elsewhere to these concerns about original context and critical methodology.[3] And, at the end of the day, the most important matter is not the methodological prolegomena but the actual *readings* of the Gospel texts.[4]

I do, however, want to address a fourth concern that has surfaced in several reviews by authors writing from an avowedly evangelical perspective—and also in emails that sometimes pop up in my inbox from readers outside the academic guild. The concern is articulated differently by different critics. But it goes something like this: Are you saying that the OT prophets didn't make predictions about the coming of Jesus as Messiah? If you deny that, aren't you undermining the divine inspiration of Scripture? And aren't you diminishing the importance of authorial intention? If the Gospel writers were just "reading backwards," are you ascribing the figural correspondences between Old and New Testament to the narrative genius of the evangelists, rather than to the divine inspiration of the prophets? Or, as one critic put it, is figural exegesis just "a literary trick"?[5]

2. Thomas J. Savage, review of *Echoes of Scripture in the Gospels* by Richard B. Hays, *EuroJT* 26 (2017): 180.

3. Richard B. Hays, "Continuing to Read Scripture with the Evangelists: A Response," *JTI* 11 (2017): 85–99.

4. One reviewer who has recognized this point clearly is N. T. Wright, who observes that my book "contributes to [methodological] discussions only obliquely, by the simple method of 'Watch and you'll see.'" N. T. Wright, "Pictures, Stories, and the Cross: Where Do the Echoes Lead?," *JTI* 11 (2017): 50. In another place, he offers the judgment that "the many rich examples" offered in *Echoes of Scripture in the Gospels* "provide a better argument for the method than any amount of theoretical reasoning." N. T. Wright, private communication.

5. Tony Reinke, private communication, September 19, 2017.

What Is Figural Exegesis?

A classic definition of figural reading was articulated by Erich Auerbach, an eminent scholar of comparative literature:

> Figural interpretation establishes a connection between two events or persons in such a way that the first signifies not only itself but also the second, while the second involves or fulfills the first. The two poles of a figure are separated in time, but both, being real events or persons, are within temporality. They are both contained in the flowing stream which is historical life, and only the comprehension, the *intellectus spiritualis*, of their interdependence is a spiritual act.[6]

6. Erich Auerbach, *Mimesis: The Representation of Reality in Western Literature*, trans. Willard R. Trask (Princeton: Princeton University Press, 1953), 73; this is the translation of Erich Auerbach, *Mimesis: Dargestellte Wirklichkeit in der abendländische Literatur* (Bern: Franke, 1946). Auerbach's magisterial analysis of figural reading in the Western literary tradition was introduced into prominence in the world of theology by Hans W. Frei's influential study, *The Eclipse of Biblical Narrative* (New Haven: Yale University Press, 1974). Frei's account of the role of figural reading in "precritical interpretation" (particularly pp. 1–37) remains an illuminating point of entry to the discussion of the hermeneutical significance of figural interpretation. For detailed analysis of Auerbach and Frei, particularly in relation to Origen as a key figure in the history of figural interpretation, see John David Dawson, *Christian Figural Reading and the Fashioning of Identity* (Berkeley: University of California Press, 2002). Though figural reading fell into disfavor in modernity, there were significant voices in the twentieth century who began to argue for its recovery, particularly under the nomenclature "typology." Two of the most influential works were Leonhard Goppelt, *Die typologische Deutung des Alten Testaments im Neuen* (Gütersloh: Bertelsmann, 1939), translated into English by Donald H. Madvig as *Typos: The Typological Interpretation of the Old Testament in the New* (Grand Rapids: Eerdmans, 1982); and Jean Daniélou, SJ, *Sacramentum Futuri: Études sur les Origins des Typologie biblique* (Paris: Beauchesne, 1950), translated into English by Wulstan Hibberd as *From Shadows to Reality: Studies in the Biblical Typology of the Fathers* (London: Burns & Oates, 1960). The terms *typology* and *figural interpretation* are essentially synonymous, though the latter more clearly emphasizes the act of reception by the reader. In my own work, I have tended to prefer the terms *figural interpretation* or *figural reading* to *typology* for two principal reasons. First, within Roman Catholic circles, discussions of typology have chiefly emphasized the recovery of patristic traditions of interpretation rather than the ways in which the NT writers themselves freshly and distinctively read Israel's Scriptures. Second, within Protestant circles, particularly in some evangelical Protestant quarters, appeals to typology have sometimes been employed as an apologetic device to defend the historical factuality of the Bible and—to the point of the present essay—the predictive intention of the OT writers. Auerbach's emphasis on "figural interpretation," in my opinion, more helpfully focuses attention on the retrospective character of the hermeneutical processes that we find in the NT. For more recent studies that draw attention

Figural reading therefore is always a matter of "reading backwards," discovering previously unanticipated correspondences between a later event and an earlier text.

An example may clarify the point. The story of Jesus's raising the dead son of a widow at Nain (Luke 7:11–17) strikingly recalls the account of Elijah's raising the son of the widow at Zarephath (1 Kgs 17:17–24). But the narrative in 1 Kings is hardly a "prediction" of a future event. And the evangelist Luke offers no indication that he is intentionally alluding to the earlier story. Only a retrospective reading discloses the correspondence between Jesus's action and Elijah's. The correspondence or "rhyming" of the two stories suggests something about the mysterious continuity of God's action in history. From the perspective of Luke 7, we suddenly see Elijah as a prefiguration of Jesus, a prophet mighty in deed and word. And yet, at the same time, the interesting differences between the two accounts imply that in Jesus we encounter something far greater than Elijah.[7]

Did Luke want his readers to recognize the figural correspondence between the two stories? In light of many other clues in Luke's narrative, I am inclined to think so. In Luke 4:25–26, he has already mentioned Elijah's being sent to the widow at Zarephath in Sidon. And surely this figural correspondence is the sort of thing Luke means when he tells us that the mysterious risen Jesus explains to the befuddled travelers on the road to Emmaus "the things about himself in *all* the scriptures" (24:27). But if Luke wants us as readers to see the connection between Jesus's action and Elijah's, he does not say so explicitly.

Did the author of 1 Kings believe that he was writing a hidden prophecy about Jesus or about any future messiah? Surely not. He was simply narrating a marvelous story of how God had acted through the great prophet Elijah. In this case, the figural interpretation is necessarily performed by later interpreters of Luke's Gospel. I expect few readers of this essay will find this a surprising reading of Luke 7. The correlation between the two texts is well established in

to figural reading, see, e.g., Christopher R. Seitz, *Figured Out: Typology and Providence in Christian Scripture* (Louisville: Westminster John Knox, 2001) and *The Character of Christian Scripture: The Significance of a Two-Testament Bible* (Grand Rapids: Baker Academic, 2011); Stanley D. Walters, ed., *Go Figure! Figuration in Biblical Interpretation*, Princeton Theological Monograph Series (Eugene, OR: Pickwick, 2008); and Ephraim Radner, *Time and the Word: Figural Reading of the Christian Scriptures* (Grand Rapids: Eerdmans, 2016). For an approach to the question from a somewhat different angle, employing the category "mystery," see G. K. Beale and Benjamin L. Gladd, *Hidden but Now Revealed: A Biblical Theology of Mystery* (Downers Grove, IL: IVP Academic, 2014).

7. For discussion, see Hays, *Echoes of Scripture in the Gospels*, 237–39.

lectionaries, commentaries, and the church's homiletical traditions. It is even noted soberly in the margin of the Nestle-Aland text.

Here is my point: figural reading neither presupposes nor asserts that the author of the earlier text *predicted* or consciously anticipated its figural fulfillment in the later. In fact, the retrospective recognition of a pattern of correspondence usually comes as a surprise. The four Gospels of our NT are full of examples of unexpected, retrospectively recognized, figural linkages between Israel's story and the story of Jesus. Let us briefly consider just three such examples that illustrate the surprising "Aha!" experience that arises when those two stories are read in dialogue with one another.

Figural Readings in the NT: Three Illustrations

Jesus's Body as the Temple

We begin with an instance in which the Gospel writer explicitly instructs readers to read backwards. In John 2:17, after his account of Jesus's expulsion of merchants from the temple, John tells us that Jesus's disciples remembered a line from Ps 69: "Zeal for your house will consume me" (Ps 69:9). Read in isolation, this psalm is a prayer of lament, a plea for God's help in the midst of suffering. The psalmist's reference to "zeal for your house" is certainly not presented as a prophecy of a distant future event. It is, rather, a description of the hardship and rejection that the psalmist has already suffered.[8] Both the Hebrew original and the Greek translation (Ps 68:10 LXX) actually say, "Zeal for your house *has consumed me*" (MT: אֲכָלָתְנִי; LXX: κατέφαγέν με), making reference to something that has already happened. In order to highlight his interpretation of the psalm as a prefiguration of Jesus, John has changed the verb to a future tense: "Zeal for your house *will consume* me" (καταφάγεταί με). But Ps 69, taken by itself, offers no hint that it should be read as predicting a future messianic figure who would be consumed by zeal for the temple. This reading is possible only as a retrospective figural reading of the Davidic figure in Ps 69 as a mysterious prefiguration of the passion of Jesus.[9]

8. The final verses turn to an expression of hope and praise for God's impending deliverance (vv. 30–36); indeed, the final lines shift from individual lament to the expectation that God will save and rebuild Jerusalem and the cities of Judah (vv. 35–36). This literary feature of the psalm offers open possibilities for eschatological interpretation.

9. For further reflections on the retrospective christological interpretation of the Psalms, see Richard B. Hays, "Christ Prays the Psalms: Israel's Psalter as Matrix of Early Christology,"

In the narrative that follows in John 2, the evangelist reports Jesus's enigmatic saying about the destruction and raising up of the temple, and then explains, in an authorial aside to the reader, that Jesus's own body is in fact the temple. So, in John's interpretation, the temple itself, the physical place of God's presence to his people, becomes a figural precursor to the incarnation of God's presence in Jesus. The evangelist then tells us, "*After he was raised from the dead*, his disciples remembered that he had said this; and they believed the scripture and the word that Jesus had spoken" (John 2:19–22). No one in ancient Israel or in late Second Temple Judaism thought, prior to Jesus, that the temple was a prefiguration of a coming messiah who would himself be a new embodiment of God's presence. This figural interpretation of the temple is a retrospective reading—as John himself tells us: the disciples remembered and understood only later, after Jesus was raised from the dead.[10] As I have argued in *Echoes*, John is teaching his readers how to read. With the aid of the Spirit whom Jesus will send after his ascension, they are to read backwards to discover within Israel's Scripture a rich web of prefigurations of Jesus.[11]

Rachel Weeping and the End of Exile

Matthew, like John, seeks to offer his readers explicit pointers to the figural connections between Israel's Scripture and the events surrounding Jesus's life. Famously, after recounting Herod's slaughter of the innocent children, Matthew composes one of his numerous fulfillment quotations.

> Then was fulfilled what had been spoken through the prophet Jeremiah: "A voice was heard in Ramah, wailing and loud lamentation, Rachel weeping for her children; she refused to be consoled, because they are no more." (Matt 2:17–18)

This short passage creates a double rainbow of figuration. First, the slaughter of the infants in Bethlehem stands in obvious figural correspondence to Pharaoh's reign of terror in killing the Hebrew children in Egypt. Second, Matthew's

in *The Conversion of the Imagination: Paul as Interpreter of Israel's Scripture* (Grand Rapids: Eerdmans, 2005), 101–18.

10. For a concise account of this interpretation, see now also Christopher M. Blumhofer, *The Gospel of John and the Future of Israel*, SNTSMS 177 (Cambridge: Cambridge University Press, 2020), 81–86.

11. *Echoes of Scripture in the Gospels*, 281–345, esp. 311–14.

quotation of Jer 31:15 links the mourning over Herod's murders both to the matriarch Rachel and to the tragedy of Israel's exile in Jeremiah's time.

It is a debatable question whether Matthew's citation of Jeremiah is meant to evoke echoes of the larger context of Jer 31, with its promise of the end of exile and the establishment of a new covenant. In light of Matthew's interpretation of Jesus as the one who brings about the end of exile,[12] I am strongly inclined to settle the debate on the side of a deliberate Matthean metalepsis: that is, that readers are meant to recall the wider context of the quotation about Rachel's weeping.[13]

But here is the point that is not debatable: Jer 31:15 in its original context is not a prophecy about a future event in which a ruthless king will slaughter babies in order to assure the destruction of God's messiah. Instead, it is a poetic depiction of the mourning of the exiled people of Israel in Babylon in the sixth century BCE. When Matthew quotes this text and says that "what had been spoken through the prophet Jeremiah" was fulfilled, he surely does not mean that Jeremiah intended to predict a terrible event that was to happen six hundred years later. He means, I suggest, that by reading backwards through the lens of the story of Jesus, we can see that Jeremiah's words are newly filled with unexpected meaning. Jeremiah's prophecy is "filled up"[14] by the recognition of a triple figural correspondence: Israel in Egypt, Israel in the Babylonian exile, and Israel groaning under Herod's rule. For Matthew, this is not merely one more grim repetition of the cycle of violence in history ("Meet the new boss, same as the old boss"). Rather, Matthew is signaling that Jesus is the new king who has come to break the cycle of violence, to end the exile of God's people, and to institute the new covenant that Jeremiah saw through a glass darkly.

Jesus Laments and Offers Sheltering Wings

One last example, this time from Luke again. In the midst of his narrative of Jesus's traveling toward Jerusalem, Jesus pauses to intone a mournful lament over the city:

12. This theme is signaled already in Matthew's genealogy (Matt 1:11–17), as well as in Matthew's immediately preceding citation of Hosea's prophecy of the return of exiled Israel—"Out of Egypt I have called my son" (2:15).

13. See *Echoes of Scripture in the Gospels*, 113–17.

14. On this interpretation of πληρώθῃ in Matt 2:15 and other cognate usages in Matthew's fulfillment formulas, see Zack C. Phillips, "Filling Up the Word: The Fulfillment Citations in Matthew's Gospel" (PhD diss., Duke University, 2017).

> Jerusalem, Jerusalem, the city that kills the prophets and stones those who are sent to it! How often have I desired to gather your children together as a hen gathers her brood under her wings, and you were not willing! (Luke 13:34)

Unlike Matthew and John, Luke does not at this point quote any OT passage or offer any overt suggestion that Jesus's metaphor of himself as a bird offering sheltering wings should be linked figurally to any precursor texts. But if we listen for the echoes, they come loud and clear. In several vivid biblical passages, the LORD God is portrayed metaphorically as a bird that spreads its wings to protect Israel. In Deut 32—in the climactic Song of Moses—God is compared to an eagle that "stirs up its nest, and hovers over its young; as it spreads its wings, takes them up, and bears them aloft on its pinions," so also the LORD God alone guided, fed, and protected the chosen people (Deut 32:11–12). Or again, in Ps 91, the poet speaks reassuringly to those who "live in the shelter of the Most High" and proclaims this promise: "He will cover you with his pinions, and under his wings you will find refuge" (Ps 91:1–4).

What then are we to think when Jesus—who in Luke's narrative has never yet visited Jerusalem—laments that he has often desired to gather Jerusalem under his wings? And what are we to make of the fact that even though he knows he is on his way to be killed in Jerusalem, he does not cry out for refuge under God's wings? Instead, he portrays himself as the one whose wings long to shelter disobedient Israel. This image is one tiny but exquisite example of Luke's artful figural narration. The almost inescapable conclusion is that Jesus in Luke is somehow to be identified as the embodied presence of Israel's God.[15]

Luke does not draw attention to his hermeneutical method here. He does not instruct readers to track down Deut 32 and Ps 91 in order to grasp the full significance of Jesus's words. He does not claim that Moses and the psalmist predicted anything about Jesus's life and words. But he speaks the powerful image of sheltering wings and invites those who have ears to hear to listen.

As we read through the Gospels, we discover, on page after page, scores of such figural readings, texts where we find the evangelists looking backwards from the vantage point of the cross and resurrection and discovering images and stories from Israel's Scripture that light up like stained glass when the sun shines through it. They are reading retrospectively under the guidance of the Spirit and discerning new significances that no one could have predicted. And

15. See *Echoes of Scripture in the Gospels*, 260–61, and the surrounding exposition there.

this kind of reading is massively attested in the church's traditions of exegesis and artistic representation right up to the modern era.[16]

Evidence for the "Predictive Prophecy" Model in the New Testament?

In light of the great cloud of witnesses to figural reading that we find not only throughout Christian tradition but also in the Gospels themselves, why are some Christian critics uneasy about it? Their anxiety is provoked in part by a residual, perhaps unconscious, allegiance to a reductive modernist literalism. But it is also provoked, in part, by the fact that a few NT texts do in fact speak explicitly of predictive prophecy in the OT.[17]

The most important of these texts is Peter's Pentecost sermon in Acts 2, which names David as a prophet and interprets Ps 16 to mean that David explicitly foresaw the resurrection of the Messiah (Acts 2:25–32). The scope of this chapter does not permit a detailed exegesis of the passage, but at least three observations are pertinent.

First, it is impossible to quibble with the view that this Pentecost sermon does in fact exemplify an interpretation of the Psalms—both Ps 16 and Ps 110—as predictive prophecy. In this respect, it differs from the sort of figural exegesis found in many Gospel texts.

Second, it is noteworthy that in Acts 2 the quotation and interpretation of the psalm is based not on the Hebrew text of Ps 16 but on the Greek version, Ps 15 in the Greek Bible. It is an example of what Luke Timothy Johnson has rightly described as "Septuagintal midrash."[18] This fact strongly suggests that what we are reading here is not a transcript of what Peter may have said on that occasion but a Lukan composition. I am not at all worried about that, but it does suggest that we need to be clear about the literary character of the text we are dealing with.

Third—and this is the most important point—*Peter's speech is itself a strik-*

16. Frei's *Eclipse of Biblical Narrative* incisively analyzes and critiques the way in which academic biblical interpretation in modernity lost its grasp on the practice of figural reading.

17. The Gospel of Matthew, because of its prominent formula quotations, is frequently understood as the parade example of "proof from prophecy" that reads the OT as a grab-bag of messianic predictions. I once understood Matthew that way myself, but after detailed study, I came to see Matthew's Gospel as representing a far more complex and expansive approach to biblical hermeneutics. See *Echoes of Scripture in the Gospels*, 105–90.

18. Luke Timothy Johnson, *Septuagintal Midrash in the Speeches of Acts* (Milwaukee: Marquette University Press, 2002).

ing example of reading backwards. No Jewish interpreter prior to the day of Pentecost supposed that Ps 16 was a predictive prophecy about a future messiah. (And, by the way, David is never called a prophet in the OT.)[19] It is, rather, David's prayer for God's protection, and an expression of confidence in God's faithfulness. The concluding verses in the Hebrew text can indeed be understood as an expression of the psalmist's hope to be preserved from death, or even as a hope for some sort of resurrection to life in God's presence: "You do not give me up to Sheol, or let your faithful one see the Pit. . . . In your presence there is fullness of joy" (Ps 16:10–11). But to read this as a prophecy about the resurrection of a future messiah, as Peter does in this speech, is a revisionary retrospective hermeneutical move par excellence. So, perhaps paradoxically, the very description of Ps 16 as predictive prophecy is a retrospective *re-cognition* made possible only by rereading the text through the lens of the resurrection of Jesus.

Something similar may be said of another text that some worried reviewers have cited, a passage from 1 Pet 1:10–12. This text refers to prophets who "prophesied of the grace that was to be yours" and "testified in advance to the sufferings destined for Christ and the subsequent glory." Although no specific prophetic texts are cited here, the passage does seem to bear witness to an understanding of OT prophecy as predictive in character. Nonetheless, it also indicates that the prophets' knowledge was incomplete: they were seeking something, perhaps seeing through a glass darkly, but now what they devoutly sought has been fully revealed, "announced to you through those who brought you good news by the Holy Spirit sent from heaven." This way of understanding the relation between prophecy and gospel fits nicely together with the model articulated in Heb 1: God spoke through the prophets in various fragmentary and perhaps indistinct ways, but now in these last days, God has spoken definitively in the Son. And I add that, as 1 Peter suggests, the Holy Spirit sent from heaven brings the news that retrospectively integrates and clarifies what was spoken before. The prophetic word comes into focus in a new and surprising way.

The two passages we have considered so far as evidence for a nonfigural understanding of prophecy are taken from Acts and from an epistle. But something should also be said about the Gospel of John, which contains an explicit

19. As noted by Joseph Fitzmyer, *The Acts of the Apostles*, AB 31 (New York: Doubleday, 1998), 258. Fitzmyer does, however, adduce one citation from a Qumran text (1QPs[a] 27:2–11) and one passage in Josephus (*Ant.* 6.8.2 §166) that speak of David's activity of prophesying.

claim that Moses wrote about Jesus (John 5:46) and that Isaiah saw the glory of Jesus and "spoke about him" (12:41).

The reference to Moses in John 5 should probably be understood, in light of the hermeneutical direction given in John 2:17–22, as another indicator of retrospective interpretation. No one could have understood in advance that Moses was writing about Jesus, but in retrospect John interprets the manna in the wilderness, the bronze serpent on a pole, and other such elements of the pentateuchal narrative as figural anticipations of Jesus. The reference to Isaiah, however, points to something slightly different. When John writes that "Isaiah saw his glory," he is almost certainly referring to the throne vision in Isa 6, particularly since John has just in the preceding verses quoted a broadly paraphrased version of Isa 6:10, the command for the prophet to shut the eyes of the people. It appears that the Fourth Evangelist is asserting that the Lord whom Isaiah saw on the heavenly throne was actually Jesus.

To sum up: there are a few NT texts, including at least one in the Gospel of John, which proclaim that OT figures, such as David, Isaiah, and other prophets, had explicit visions that gave them foreknowledge of Jesus. These texts are few and far between but noteworthy.[20] As Simon Gathercole observes, there are certainly instances of intertextual "correspondences which might be seen as *prospective* rather than *retrospective*," particularly in relation to themes of promise and fulfillment.[21] What I want to suggest, however, is that the specific form of that fulfillment is consistently unexpected and astonishing, and, further, that the majority of the NT's "fulfillment" texts evoke figural correspondences with OT passages that were not previously understood as messianic prophecies. The few NT texts that do ascribe predictive intention to OT prophets should not be superimposed as prescriptive models for interpretation of the far greater number of texts in the Gospels that make no such assertions. We do not need to insist on one to the exclusion of the other.

Is predictive prophecy somehow inappropriate or impossible? As Paul would say, μὴ γένοιτο. Still, let it be observed that the great majority of examples of figural reading in the canonical Gospels presuppose and require the recognition that Jesus's fulfillment of scriptural prefigurations comes as a

20. In early Christian sources outside the NT, it would not be difficult to find other instances of literalistic interpretations of OT passages as predictive prophecy. Justin Martyr's *Dialogue with Trypho*, for example, provides numerous examples.

21. Simon Gathercole, "Reading Backwards," review of *Reading Backwards* by Richard B. Hays, *Reformation 21*, August 2015, http://www.reformation21.org/articles/reading-backwards.php.

poetic surprise, a surprise that *reconfigures* our understanding of the precursor texts and transforms any conscious intention of the OT authors.

What Is at Stake?

Why does all this matter? What is at stake in this discussion about the specific way in which the many and various writings of the prophets might prefigure God's speaking in these last days through his Son in the Gospels? The issues here are complex, and time would fail me to explore them fully. But let me at least sketch some of the key issues.

Original Sense and Authorial Intention?

The example of the four canonical evangelists should alert us to the possibility—indeed, the fact—that the meaning of Israel's scriptural texts cannot be narrowly restricted to the sense consciously intended by the original authors or understood by the original audiences of readers in ancient Israel. The Gospel writers were convinced that the events of Jesus's life, death, and resurrection were *revelatory*: they held the key to understanding all that had gone before. And the turning of this key opens the door to reassessment and transformation of the many and various ways that God had spoken in the past. The story of Jesus pulls back the veil.[22]

If we insist—as much modern criticism has done—that the legitimate interpretation of Israel's Scripture must be strictly constrained by the (historically reconstructed) intention of the original authors, we are declaring a priori that the Gospel writers were wrong and misguided and that their claims to revelatory retrospective reading are false. Oddly, both skeptical modern critics and staunch evangelical apologists have typically painted themselves into exactly this same hermeneutical corner, where they then battle over the same narrow turf—whether by debunking the Gospels' interpretations of the OT or by contending desperately that the authors of the OT's narratives and poems actually did intentionally (in some sense) forecast the details of Jesus's life. This misguided debate is generated—on both sides—by the rationalistic historicism of high modernity.

But the canonical evangelists, through their artful narration, offer us a

22. The following three paragraphs are adapted from *Echoes of Scripture in the Gospels*, 358–60.

different way to understand the NT's transformational reception of the OT as a paradigm-shattering but truthful disclosure of things "hidden from the foundation of the world" (Matt 13:35, freely quoting Ps 78:2). This hermeneutical sensibility locates the deep logic of the intertextual linkage between Israel's Scripture and the Gospels not in human intentionality but in the mysterious providence of God, who is ultimately the author of the correspondences woven into these texts and events, correspondences that could be perceived only in retrospect. In short, *figural interpretation discerns a divinely crafted pattern of coherence within the events and characters of the biblical narratives.*[23]

Rationalistic criticism either precludes such coherence from the outset or sees the Gospel stories as "prophecy historicized," a fictional mutation that disingenuously manufactures mythical tales by extrapolation from earlier biblical texts. The evangelists, by contrast, patiently insist that it was precisely the actual teachings and actions of Jesus that lived in the community's memory and subsequently catalyzed a retrospective recognition of unforeseen, divinely scripted, figural linkages with Israel's Scripture. After the resurrection, the community of Jesus's followers returned to reread Scripture under the guidance of the Spirit and experienced, again and again, an "Aha!" reaction.

Pictures versus Stories?

In his substantive and insightful review of *Echoes*, N. T. Wright suggests that there is an unresolved tension in my work between "pictures" and "stories."[24] By this distinction he means to indicate that figural exegesis focuses on isolated picture illustrations removed from their narrative and historical context, whereas stories point to a narrative and historical continuity. Wright rightly observes that I do not seem troubled by this dichotomy. This is because I think it is a false dichotomy. Auerbach's definition of figural interpretation, it should be recalled, stipulates that both poles of a figural correspondence are situated precisely within a temporal continuum, and that "they are both contained within the flowing stream which is historical life." This is one of the chief things that distinguishes figural reading from allegorical interpretation of the Philonic variety. And so, Wright is correct to presume that I do indeed

23. As Auerbach observes, in figural interpretation, "the connection between occurrences is not regarded primarily as a chronological or causal development but as *a oneness within the divine plan*, of which all occurrences are parts and reflections" (*Mimesis*, 555, emphasis mine).

24. Wright, "Pictures, Stories, and the Cross," 53–60.

intend the figural readings of the Gospels to be situated within the longer story of Israel—as the structure of each of my major chapters indicates.

Wright's basic concern is to insist on the primacy of a single continuous salvation-historical story. As he puts it aphoristically, "When we 'read backwards' in this way *we discover a forward-moving story coming to meet us.*"[25] And he is concerned that I do not affirm this point clearly enough.

If Wright is concerned about a linear historical continuity with Israel's past, Ben Witherington, on the other hand, poses a different possible criticism. He contends that the analysis in *Echoes* "goes in the opposite direction of the trajectory and flow and purpose of the Gospel narrative," for "the Gospel writers point us into the future not the past." The Gospel writers, Witherington says, do not want us "to scramble back to the OT and look at those words in their original contexts. To the contrary [they want] us to follow the story going forward to its eschatological conclusion . . . pointing forward to the conclusion of the salvation historical story."[26]

I confess that I find myself a little puzzled by the criticisms of these colleagues. Let me, therefore, go on record in reply to each of them. To Wright: Yes, the four evangelists see the story of Jesus in a relation of organic narrative continuity with Israel's story. (Though—perhaps in distinction from Wright?—I think that the four evangelists articulate and specify this continuity in strikingly different ways.) So it would be a mistake to understand figural exegesis as disconnected from narrative; indeed, the effect of figural reading is precisely to discern new and intricate threads of interconnection between the story of God's action in the days of our ancestors and the story of the ways God has now acted and spoken in Jesus. This is why each major chapter of my book contains a section on how figural exegesis illuminates *Israel's story* in the narrative of each evangelist.

And to Witherington: Yes, the four evangelists see the story of Jesus as pointing forward to a new eschatologically oriented story of what God is doing in the world. So it would be a mistake to understand figural reading as a backward-looking antiquarian obsession with the past; indeed, the effect of

25. Wright, "Pictures, Stories, and the Cross," 59.

26. B. Witherington, "Richard Hays' *Echoes of Scripture in the Gospels*: A Review," *Bible and Culture*, April 20, 2016, https://www.patheos.com/blogs/bibleandculture/2016/04/20/richard-hays-echoes-of-scripture-in-the-gospels-a-review/. In fairness, it should be noted that Witherington's review introduces this critique as a hypothetical critique that might be posed by "a literary critic of Richard's approach." But he then observes that this hypothetical critique, which he himself has actually written, "makes some valid points well worth considering."

figural reading in the Gospels is to show how in "these last days" we can newly discern how past, present, and future are interwoven by God's skillful and gracious hands. This is why each major chapter of my book contains a section on how figural exegesis illuminates *the mission and destiny of the church* in the narrative of each evangelist.

The Heart of the Matter

What is ultimately at stake in this whole discussion of the evangelists as readers of Israel's Scripture? Ultimately, this is not just a conversation about the best hermeneutical methodologies. It is not just a conversation about historical versus literary models for interpretation. And it is not just one more round of an ongoing acrimonious debate between "apocalyptic" and "salvation-historical" approaches in NT studies. Instead, this whole discussion is finally an attempt to wrestle with *fundamental theological issues.* I would like to conclude, then, by naming three such issues that I think are in fact at the heart of the matter.

First, a word about *God.* The testimony of the Gospel writers makes sense and has validity if and only if the God to whom the Gospels bear witness is *real*, and if he is the same God as the God of Abraham, Isaac, and Jacob. Further, their testimony makes sense only if that God has providentially scripted history. If I may put it this way, the Gospels presuppose that in some ultimate sense *God is the author* of the story of Israel. If that is not true, the NT's figural readings are merely clever imaginative fantasy. But if it *is* true, then these figural interpretations are deeply significant disclosures of God's identity. The figural unity of Scripture, OT and NT together, is nothing other than the astonishing literary outworking of God's self-revelation.

Second, a word about *Jesus.* The Gospels claim not only that God is the author of the story of Israel but also that Jesus is the climactic consummation of that story. But there is still more: through their pervasive evocations of Israel's Scripture, both subtle and overt, the evangelists portray Jesus as the embodiment of Israel's God. This finding flies in the face of two centuries of NT criticism that have argued, as Bart Ehrman asserts in one of his recent popularizations, that "the idea that Jesus was divine was a later Christian invention, one found, among our Gospels, only in John."[27] This is a conclusion

27. Bart D. Ehrman, *Jesus, Interrupted: Revealing the Hidden Contradictions in the Bible (and Why We Don't Know About Them)* (New York: HarperCollins, 2009), 249. See also his book *How Jesus Became God: The Exaltation of a Jewish Preacher from Galilee* (New York: HarperOne, 2014).

that can be reached and defended only by readers who are tone-deaf to the scriptural intertexts that form the theological foundation of the Gospels. To understand the Gospels within their own original Jewish historical milieu is to perceive that all four of them are narrating the astounding story of how the God of Israel was embodied in Jesus.

Third and last, a word about *the Holy Spirit*. As I have noted, one frequently expressed concern about *Echoes of Scripture in the Gospels* is that it places "an overemphasis upon the pole of the evangelists' narrative genius"[28] or, more strongly stated, that figural exegesis can be construed as just "a literary trick of the apostles to read Christ backwards into the previous Scripture."[29] The author of the Fourth Gospel would have found this a surprising, indeed, faithless, objection. In John 16, Jesus, as he prepares to leave his disciples, promises to send the Spirit to expand the imagination and understanding of those followers who will be charged to go on telling his story to the world:

> I still have many things to say to you, but you cannot bear them now. When the Spirit of truth comes, he will guide you into all the truth; for he will not speak on his own, but will speak whatever he hears, and he will declare to you the things that are to come. He will glorify me, because he will take what is mine and declare it to you. (John 16:12–14)

In light of the overall shape of John's narrative, we can see that the revelatory work of the Spirit would include, at a minimum, the role of the Holy Spirit in guiding the church's retrospective christological interpretation of Scripture. The Spirit will lead John the Evangelist to discover and proclaim previously unimaginable figural correspondences between Jesus and the temple, Jesus and the manna in the wilderness, Jesus and the Passover lamb. This does not show just that John was a clever writer. It shows that the Spirit of truth was at work to inspire John's retrospective poetic insight into the mysterious self-revelation of God in Jesus.

If I might dare to take this point one final step further, it would be to say only this: the Holy Spirit is still at work in the community of those who are called by Jesus "those who will believe in me through their word" (John 17:20). If John and the other evangelists are shaping a community through their word,

28. Alastair Roberts, review of *Echoes of Scripture in the Gospels* by Richard B. Hays, *Themelios* 41 (2016): 518. This phrase occurs as a qualification in the context of a generally positive review of the book.

29. Tony Reinke, private communication, September 19, 2017.

it would mean that we should learn from them a deep and careful attentiveness to story, metaphor, prefiguration, allusion, echo, irony, and paradox. We should be close readers immersed in the *language* of Scripture and alert to its complex figural interweavings. We do not need to be afraid of imaginative or metaphorical readings, and we do not need to insist that the meaning of OT texts must be rigidly restricted to what their original human authors intended. God indeed spoke to and through those authors. But in these last days, God has spoken—and continues to speak—through a Son, and through the Holy Spirit that he has sent to us. The Spirit removes the veil when Moses is read, and where the Spirit of the Lord is, there is freedom.

Part 2

HISTORICAL JESUS

5

Rebranding Jesus and the Pitfalls of Entrepreneurial Criticism

The message left on my answering machine by my brother-in-law, an attorney, sounded a tone of skeptical cross-examination: "I heard on my car radio today an interview with a New Testament scholar named Robert Funk. He's publishing a new version of the Gospels that claims to distinguish what Jesus really said from what the Gospel writers reported. Funk says it's based on the work of a group of leading Bible scholars. Are you involved in this? How can they claim to know what Jesus *really* said or didn't say? I have enough trouble proving in a court of law what somebody said six months ago! Should I take this book seriously?"

The Jesus Seminar Project

Indeed, a new book called *The Five Gospels*—the fruit of the labors of the much-publicized "Jesus Seminar"—claims to provide definitive new answers to the question, "What did Jesus really say?"[1] A panel of NT scholars, meeting over a period of several years, has given us a new red-letter edition of the four canonical Gospels, plus the Gospel of Thomas, with the words adjudged by a poll of these scholars actually to have been spoken by Jesus printed in red type. Other colors reflect their shadings of judgment about the historical reliability of the other sayings attributed to Jesus: pink for possibly authentic, gray for probably inauthentic, and black for certainly inauthentic. The introduction to the book suggests breezily that an "unofficial but helpful interpretation of the colors" would be as follows:

1. Robert W. Funk and Roy W. Hoover et al., *The Five Gospels: The Search for the Authentic Words of Jesus* (New York: Macmillan, 1993).

Red: That's Jesus!
Pink: Sure sounds like Jesus.
Gray: Well, maybe.
Black: There's been some mistake.

The results are offered up in a fresh translation—dubbed the "Scholars Version"—that seeks to "produce in the American reader an experience comparable to that of the first readers" by approximating "the common street language of the original."[2]

The grandiose dedication page of *The Five Gospels* invokes the names of three historic figures who hover as presiding genii over this ambitious work:

> *This report is dedicated to*
> GALILEO GALILEI
> *who altered our view of the heavens forever*
> THOMAS JEFFERSON
> *who took scissors and paste to the gospels*
> DAVID FRIEDRICH STRAUSS
> *who pioneered the quest of the historical Jesus*

Unnamed, however, is the one figure who might most appropriately symbolize the public face of this project: P. T. Barnum. The cochairmen of the Jesus Seminar, Robert Funk and John Dominic Crossan, have demonstrated an ingenuity for promotion that would surely have warmed the heart of that master American showman.

For the past seven years, the popular press has from time to time published eye-catching progress reports on the work of the Jesus Seminar under headlines such as "Most of Jesus' words ghostwritten," "Jesus probably didn't recite Lord's Prayer, scholars say," "Is the Bible the gospel truth?" and "Scholars compiling new Bible." And much humorous controversy has surrounded the Seminar's practice of voting on the authenticity of individual Jesus sayings by casting colored balls into a box. The publication of *The Five Gospels* was heralded by a feature story on National Public Radio (the broadcast heard by my brother-in-law), and the charismatic Crossan has broken through to a mass audience by appearing on *The Larry King Show*. Such publicity has been actively courted by members of the Seminar, who have from the beginning of their work explicitly aimed to disseminate their results as widely as possible in the public media.

2. Funk and Hoover et al., *The Five Gospels*, xii–xiv.

Of course, the knack for attracting popular attention is not necessarily to be despised. If indeed there were significant new findings, broadly accepted by leading NT scholars, concerning the historical facts about what Jesus taught, such findings would indeed be newsworthy. The basic questions to be asked about this project, therefore, concern not the Seminar's voting procedures or means of communicating its findings but rather the substance of its claims. What methods have been used to produce the results here proffered? What image of the historical Jesus emerges from these multicolored pages? (Actually, the pages are mostly black: more on this below.) To what extent are these methods and results genuinely representative of informed scholarly consensus? For reasons that I shall summarize briefly here, I must conclude that the operative methodology of the Seminar is seriously flawed, that it therefore inevitably produces a skewed portrait of Jesus's teachings, and that—contrary to the impression fostered by the book—the findings reported here represent the idiosyncratic opinions of one particular faction of critical scholars.

The aims of the Jesus Seminar are generally consonant with the work of historical scholarship since the Enlightenment: the participants seek to reconstruct the history of earliest Christianity. This project entails a critical interrogation of the Gospels as source documents, distinguishing, insofar as possible, the various streams of tradition and interpretation that underlie the canonical texts. The quest of "the historical Jesus"—as distinct from the church's subsequent representations of him—has engaged the efforts of NT scholars for the better part of two hundred years. Scholars have published hundreds of monographs on this subject, and every student who has taken a NT course in a college or seminary has been exposed to the complex problem of recovering a clear picture of the Jesus of history. Thus it is somewhat disingenuous for the editors of *The Five Gospels* to assert that the publication of this volume "represents a dramatic exit from windowless studies and the beginning of a new venture for Gospel scholarship."[3] The only new angle here is the decision to publish a complete edition of the Gospels that seeks to represent schematically a scholarly consensus about the authenticity of each individual sentence attributed to Jesus. In theory, the project could produce an interesting freeze-frame shot of the status of Gospel scholarship near the end of the twentieth century: not exactly the epoch-making scientific breakthrough of a Galileo, but a modestly worthwhile survey of opinion.

The difficulty arises, however, in the execution of the plan. The participants in this poll were those who chose to take part over a span of eight years in

3. Funk and Hoover et al., *The Five Gospels*, 1.

a seminar sponsored, not by one of the major scholarly societies such as the *Studiorum Novi Testamenti Societas* or the Society of Biblical Literature,[4] but by Funk's maverick entrepreneurial venture, the Westar Institute, located in Sonoma, California. This self-selected group, though it includes several fine scholars, does not represent a balanced cross section of scholarly opinion. Furthermore, the criteria for judgment that are employed in *The Five Gospels* are highly questionable.

Methodological Critique

For the sake of brevity, I shall note just four ways in which the methodology of the project is problematic.

First, there is the problem of the selection and dating of sources. The members of the Seminar determined—quite properly—that sayings attested in the earliest extant sources have the greatest claim to authenticity. But what are these earliest sources? The Jesus Seminar adopts the standard two-source theory as a solution to the synoptic problem: Mark is the earliest of the three Synoptic Gospels; in composing their Gospels, Matthew and Luke used Mark along with a hypothetical common source Q (short for the German *Quelle*, "source"), consisting primarily of sayings of Jesus. One would think, then, that this analysis ought to put the two synoptic sources, Mark and Q, on roughly equal footing as sources for authentic Jesus material. However, the Jesus Seminar dates the Q material earlier than the traditions found in Mark, during the period 50–70 CE. Mark, dated around 70 CE, in fact fares poorly in the Seminar's judgment as a source for Jesus sayings. Only one sentence in this entire Gospel receives the red-letter treatment: "Pay the emperor what belongs to the emperor, and God what belongs to God" (Mark 12:17).[5]

On the other hand, the extracanonical Gospel of Thomas is dated—for reasons never explained in the book—to the same early period as Q. This extraordinarily early dating of Thomas, along with the judgment that it is literarily independent of the synoptic tradition, becomes a crucial factor in the Jesus Seminar's weighting of evidence:

4. Indeed, more than ten years previously the Research and Publications Committee of the SBL rejected an overture from Funk to do a similar project under their auspices.

5. This translation, like all subsequent translations in this review, is taken from the "Scholars Version" of *The Five Gospels*.

> The first written gospels were Sayings Gospel Q and *possibly an early version* of the Gospel of Thomas. The Gospel of Mark was not composed until about 70 A. D. For these reasons alone, it is understandable that double attestation in the early independent sources Thomas and Q constitutes strong *documentary* evidence.[6]

This valuing of Thomas as an early and independent source is, however, a highly controversial claim. The traditional opinion among NT scholars has been that the Gospel of Thomas—a text known to us through a fourth-century Coptic text discovered at Nag Hammadi in Egypt—was composed in the second century, perhaps containing some independent tradition but heavily shaped by gnostic teachings.[7] Many scholars regard it as literarily dependent on the canonical Gospels, though this remains a debated issue.[8] No hint of these debates, however, is allowed to appear in the pages of *The Five Gospels*, which unhesitatingly treats the hypothetical Q and a hypothetical "early version of Thomas" as the crucial sources for locating authentic Jesus tradition.[9] Here some suspicion begins to arise concerning the candor of the editors of this book. They claim that they want to make the results of the best critical schol-

6. Funk and Hoover et al., *Five Gospels*, 26, emphasis added. Note, by the way, that double attestation in Mark and Q is by definition impossible, since Q material is defined as material shared by Matthew and Luke that does not come from Mark; on the other hand, the triple attestation of material shared by all three Synoptics is not given any evidential weight, since Matthew and Luke are simply following the Markan source.

7. For a helpful critique of the early dating of Thomas, see N. T. Wright, *The New Testament and the People of God*, Christian Origins and the Question of God 1 (London: SPCK; Minneapolis: Fortress, 1992), 435–43. For further updating of the arguments against the early dating and literary independence of the Gospel of Thomas, see now Mark Goodacre, *Thomas and the Gospels: The Case for Thomas' Familiarity with the Synoptics* (Grand Rapids: Eerdmans, 2012); and Simon Gathercole, *The Composition of the Gospel of Thomas: Original Language and Influences* (Cambridge: Cambridge University Press, 2012).

8. See, for example, Christopher M. Tuckett, "Thomas and the Synoptics," *NovT* 30 (1988): 132–57.

9. Some scholars have even sought to distinguish early and late redactional layers within the hypothetical document Q; this project can only be judged an exercise in fantasy. In fact, there are serious reasons to question whether "Q" ever existed. There is no such extant text, and there are no references in ancient Christian literature to such a collection of sayings. The parallels between Matthew and Luke can be explained in several ways, including the theory that Luke used both Matthew and Mark as sources. This view still leaves difficult problems, and it is decidedly a minority view, but it has been gaining some adherents in recent years. For extensive discussion, see E. P. Sanders and Margaret Davies, *Studying the Synoptic Gospels* (London: SCM; Philadelphia: Trinity Press International, 1989), 51–119.

arship available to the public, but their working method trades upon a controversial and implausible early dating of Thomas, without offering the reader any clue that this is a shaky element in their methodological foundation.[10]

The second major methodological issue is the Seminar's use of the criterion of dissimilarity for assessing the authenticity of Jesus tradition. This criterion posits that sayings material may be judged certainly authentic only when it is *dissimilar* both to antecedent Jewish tradition and to subsequent Christian tradition. Thus it is argued, for example, that Jesus probably did not say at his final meal with his disciples, "Have some, this is my body" (Mark 14:22, quoting from the Jesus Seminar's "Scholars [*sic*] Version"). Why? Because the church's liturgical tradition reports that he did; therefore, we cannot be sure that this saying was not read back into the story. On the other hand, Jesus almost certainly said, "Love your enemies" (Matt 5:44a). Why? Because it allegedly "cuts against the social grain" of Judaism[11]—and presumably it isn't anything the early church would have invented either.

The strict application of the criterion of dissimilarity has two immediately evident results. First, almost all the material in the Gospels is excluded as being either too Jewish or too Christian; this criterion is largely responsible for the fact that "82 percent of the words ascribed to Jesus in the gospels were not actually spoken by him, according to the Jesus Seminar."[12] (If one counts the possibly authentic sayings printed in pink type, the percentage of inauthentic material is significantly reduced.) Indeed, one is surprised that 18 percent remains untouched by this criterion, and one suspects that a more rigorous application could eliminate even more. For instance, the early church did teach love of enemies in a way that reflects direct dependence upon the OT rather than upon Jesus (cf. Rom 12:20–21, quoting Prov 25:21). Perhaps the Jesus Seminar was not sufficiently "critical" at this point. The second consequence is that the "Jesus" who emerges from this procedure is necessarily a free-floating iconoclast, artificially isolated from his people and their Scripture and from the movement that he founded.

As Nils Dahl rightly observed more than forty years ago, the criterion of dissimilarity must be applied in order to identify "a critically assured *minimum*," which must then be supplemented by other criteria and evidence.[13] Indeed, Jesus becomes comprehensible *precisely as a historical figure* only when

10. The one critical work on the Gospel of Thomas cited in the book's annotated bibliography is Stephen J. Patterson, *The Gospel of Thomas and Jesus* (Sonoma, CA: Polebridge Press, 1993). Polebridge Press, it should be noted, is Funk's own publishing operation.

11. Funk and Hoover et al., *Five Gospels*, 147.

12. Funk and Hoover et al., *Five Gospels*, 5.

13. Nils Alstrup Dahl, "The Problem of the Historical Jesus," in *Jesus the Christ: The*

he is placed in historical continuity with first-century Judaism and with emergent Christianity. As Dahl insisted,

> In no case can any distinct separation be achieved between the genuine words of Jesus and the constructions of the community. We do not escape the fact that we know Jesus only as the disciples remembered him. Whoever thinks that the disciples completely misunderstood their Master or even consciously falsified his picture may give fantasy free reign.[14]

The work of the Jesus Seminar exemplifies the fantasy that Dahl prophesied.

The third major methodological problem, closely related to the second, is the Jesus Seminar's tendentious insistence on finding a "non-eschatological Jesus."[15] The members assert repeatedly that Jesus did not proclaim a message of God's future intervention in history and final judgment. Instead,

> God was so real for him that he could not distinguish God's present activity from any future activity. He had a poetic sense of time in which the future and the present merged, simply melted together, in the intensity of his vision. But Jesus' uncommon views were obfuscated by the more pedestrian conceptions of John [the Baptist], on the one side, and by the equally pedestrian views of the early Christian community, on the other.[16]

Jesus's "poetic sense of time" was lost on the disciples, however: "Jesus' followers did not grasp the subtleties of his position and reverted, once Jesus was not there to remind them, to the view they had learned from John the Baptist." Consequently, according to the Seminar, nearly all the earliest Christian writings are infected by an eschatological perspective—including Q (thus the apocalyptic material in Q must be assigned to "late Q"!). But now, at last, the Jesus Seminar has come along to rescue "traces of that enigmatic sage from Nazareth—traces that cry out for recognition and liberation from the firm grip of those whose faith overpowered their memories."[17]

This must be deemed a "methodological problem" because the Jesus Seminar employs its conviction that Jesus was a noneschatological thinker as a

---

Historical Origins of Christian Doctrine, ed. Donald H. Juel (Minneapolis: Fortress, 1991), 97, emphasis his. This essay was originally published in Oslo in 1953.

14. Dahl, "Historical Jesus," 94.

15. Funk and Hoover et al., *Five Gospels*, 4.

16. Funk and Hoover et al., *Five Gospels*, 137.

17. Funk and Hoover et al., *Five Gospels*, 4.

stringent criterion for sorting the authenticity of the sayings material. Everything in the Gospels that smacks of Jewish apocalyptic eschatology is firmly consigned to black type. A "cameo essay" explains the reasons for this decision roughly as follows: the Gospels contain sayings proclaiming God's rule as both present and future; Jesus could not have said both things; the future eschatology appears "bombastic and threatening"; therefore, Jesus must have spoken of God's rule only as present reality. This is confirmed by the fact that the major parables of Jesus "do not reflect an apocalyptic view of history."[18] This bizarre claim can be supported only by screening the parables critically in such a way that their obviously apocalyptic elements are judged inauthentic. For example, one of the "major parables" said to illustrate Jesus's nonapocalyptic view of history is the parable of the corrupt judge (Luke 18:1–8). The Jesus Seminar deems verses 2–5 to be possibly authentic (pink) but verses 6–8 to be inauthentic (black). Why? Because the latter verses speak of God's eschatological vindication of his elect and of the future coming of the Son of Man; therefore, they must have been composed by Luke. The same sort of circular reasoning is applied to pericope after pericope in the Gospels to exclude future eschatology from Jesus's teaching.

In contrast to this arbitrary procedure, consider the following statement of the mainstream critical consensus by Elisabeth Schüssler Fiorenza, a scholar who can hardly be accused of traditionalist bias: "Exegetes agree that it is the mark of Jesus' preaching and ministry that he proclaimed the *basileia* of God as future and present, eschatological vision and experiential reality."[19] Characteristic of early Christian preaching is its *proleptic* eschatology, its conviction that God's coming kingdom has already begun to impinge upon the present in such a way that God's final justice is prefigured—but hardly fully realized—now. (For an elegant extended example, see Rom 8.) The Gospel tradition offers us strong reasons to believe, as Schüssler Fiorenza indicates, that a similar proleptic eschatology characterized Jesus's own proclamation. Only flat-footed rationalists could deem it impossible for both the present- and future-kingdom sayings to be held in Jesus's mind at the same time.

Finally, the attempt to assess the authenticity of Jesus's *sayings* in isolation from a more comprehensive reconstruction of the events of his life, ministry, and death is methodologically problematic. The Jesus constructed by the Jesus Seminar is a talking head, whose teachings bear no intelligible relation to his

18. Funk and Hoover et al., *Five Gospels*, 137.

19. Elisabeth Schüssler Fiorenza, *In Memory of Her: A Feminist Reconstruction of Christian Origins* (New York: Crossroad, 1983), 120.

death on a cross. If Jesus said only the sorts of things judged authentic by the Seminar, it is very difficult to see how he could have been mistaken by Jewish and Roman authorities as a messianic pretender who needed to be executed. Again, Dahl made the point dearly:

> One point in the life of Jesus is unconditionally established: his death. A historically tenable description of the life of Jesus would be possible only in the form of a description of his death, its historical presuppositions, and the events preceding and following it.[20]

More recently, E. P. Sanders's important book *Jesus and Judaism* takes a methodological path similar to that which Dahl had recommended, building its account of Jesus upon the events and actions of Jesus's career that can be most securely ascertained, rather than upon the tradition of his sayings, insisting that "a good hypothesis about Jesus' intention and his relationship with his contemporaries . . . should offer a connection between his activity and his death."[21] The result is a Jesus whose central concern was the hope of God's eschatological restoration of Israel—a theme that is emphatically consigned to black type in *The Five Gospels*. Indeed, though *Jesus and Judaism* was published in the year that the Seminar began its work (1985), the Seminar inexplicably ignores Sanders's methods and conclusions.

By contrast, rather than setting the sayings in a narrative context of historical events, the Jesus Seminar sees them as fragmentary materials mediated by oral tradition that—by its account—retains only short, memorable aphorisms and parables, floating free from association with any particular historical event. Allegedly, then, we can recover an approximation of "what Jesus really said" by applying general laws of oral transmission to strip away accretions and modifications.[22] One wonders whether the Seminar adopts too sanguine a view of its ability to work backwards from texts written down many years later to restore Jesus's pristine oral teachings.

In any case, the Seminar's concentration on Jesus's *words* as the primary evidence for historical knowledge about him is a late-blooming legacy of the otherwise defunct "New Quest of the Historical Jesus," a spinoff of Bultmannian existentialist theology that was briefly fashionable in the 1960s. The New Quest—some of whose original practitioners are among the members of the

20. Dahl, "Historical Jesus," 98.

21. E. P. Sanders, *Jesus and Judaism* (Philadelphia: Fortress, 1985), 22.

22. Funk and Hoover et al., *Five Gospels*, 25–29.

Jesus Seminar—sought to recover from Jesus's sayings and parables his "understanding of existence," detached from any particular claims about his life and actions. By drawing heavily upon the Gospel of Thomas and by packaging its results in a more user-friendly format than the abstruse hermeneutical musings of the "New Quest," the Seminar has updated this approach.

Whether it has thereby discovered anything that ought to be classified as historical knowledge is exceedingly doubtful. What the members of the Jesus Seminar have done, in effect, is merely to offer us an anthology of their favorite Jesus sayings. In this respect, as in several others, they do indeed follow the spiritual and intellectual example of Thomas Jefferson, who—though he declared himself a "Materialist" in contrast to the "Spiritualism" of Jesus—undertook the task of producing an expurgated edition of "The Life and Morals of Jesus of Nazareth Extracted Textually from the Gospels":

> Among the sayings and discourses imputed to Him by His biographers, I find many passages of fine imagination, correct morality, and of the most lovely benevolence; and others, again, of so much ignorance, so much absurdity, so much untruth, charlatanism, and imposture, as to pronounce it impossible that such contradictions should have proceeded from the same Being. I separate, therefore, the gold from the dross; restore to Him the former, and leave the latter to the stupidity of some, and roguery of others, of His disciples.

How did Jefferson distinguish between the sublime teachings of Jesus and the inventions of "the groveling authors" who wrote the Gospels? "The difference is obvious to the eye and to the understanding," for the authentic words of Jesus stand out from their setting in the Gospels like "diamonds in a dunghill."[23] For the Jesus Seminar, as for Jefferson, an a priori construal of Jesus and his message governs the critical judgment made about individual sayings. N. T. Wright accurately sizes up the Seminar's modus operandi:

> What is afoot . . . is not the detailed objective study of individual passages, leading up to a new view of Jesus and the early Church. *It is a particular view of Jesus and the early Church, working its way through into a detailed list of sayings that fit with this view.*[24]

23. Thomas Jefferson, as cited by F. F. Church in his introduction to *The Jefferson Bible: The Life and Morals of Jesus of Nazareth* (Boston: Beacon, 1989), 27–29, 17.

24. N. T. Wright, *Jesus and the Victory of God*, Christian Origins and the Question of God 2 (London: SPCK; Minneapolis: Fortress, 1996), 27, emphasis his.

As Wright observes, this is not necessarily a bad thing: any attempt at reconstructing the historical Jesus must operate with some general hypothesis that can be tested against the evidence: nothing is gained by "pseudo-atomistic work on apparently isolated fragments."[25] The difficulty with the work of the Jesus Seminar, however, even more than with Jefferson's scissors-and-paste job, is that so much of the evidence must be thrown away in order to save the hypothesis.

What portrait of Jesus emerges finally from the work of the Seminar? As we are repeatedly told, "He was a traveling sage who traded in wisdom."[26] The description pegs him—as some of the Seminar members have argued in other publications—as an itinerant Cynic philosopher, rather than as a prophet or the leader of a religious reform movement. He was a "laconic sage" who never initiated debates or controversies: "He is passive until a question is put to him, or until he or his disciples are criticized."[27] When he did speak, he spoke in parables and aphorisms, employing "exaggeration, humor, and paradox."[28] He shocked his contemporaries by calling for a reversal of roles and overturning people's ordinary expectations. He never spoke about himself, however, or claimed to play any distinctive role in the consummation of God's purposes. Certainly he never claimed to be the Messiah.

Some of the elements of this portrait are, of course, familiar from the canonical portrayals. The distortion lies more in what is denied than in what is affirmed. The depiction of Jesus as a Cynic philosopher with no concern about Israel's destiny, no connection with the concerns and hopes that animated his Jewish contemporaries, no interest in the interpretation of Scripture, and no message of God's coming eschatological judgment is—quite simply—an ahistorical fiction, achieved by the surgical removal of Jesus from his Jewish context. The fabrication of a non-Jewish Jesus is one particularly pernicious side effect of the Jesus Seminar's methodology. One would have thought that the tragic events of our century might have warned us to be wary of biblical scholars who deny the Jewishness of Jesus.

Evaluation of the Seminar's Aims and Claims

Who are the scholars that make up the membership of the Jesus Seminar? The group's publicity creates the impression that they represent a broad cross

25. Wright, *Jesus and the Victory of God*, 27.
26. Funk and Hoover et al., *Five Gospels*, 27.
27. Funk and Hoover et al., *Five Gospels*, 32–33.
28. Funk and Hoover et al., *Five Gospels*, 31.

section of this country's leading critical scholars. It is asserted that "the scholarship represented by the Fellows of the Jesus Seminar is the kind that has come to prevail in all the great universities of the world."[29] Though the Seminar expects to encounter hostile criticism, its work is said to be under attack principally "by conservative Christian groups" and by "those who lack academic credentials."[30] The casual reader of the introduction to *The Five Gospels* might suppose that no serious NT scholar would differ materially from the consensus represented by this book, were it not for the single telltale polemical reference to anonymous "elitist academic critics who deplored the public face of the seminar."[31] In fact—let it be said clearly—most professional biblical scholars are profoundly skeptical of the methods and conclusions of this academic splinter group. The membership of the Jesus Seminar does *not* include the overwhelming majority of the NT scholars who teach at the major graduate institutions in the United States. This may be verified by a check of the roster of seventy-four Fellows of the Seminar provided as an appendix.[32] Not one member of the NT faculty from Yale, Harvard, Princeton, Duke, University of Chicago, Union Theological Seminary, Vanderbilt, SMU, or Catholic University is involved in this project.[33] It probably goes without saying that the faculties of evangelical seminaries are not represented here. Nor are any major scholars from England or the Continent.

This is not to say that the Seminar participants are without credentials. They hold doctorates from reputable institutions, with Claremont and Harvard being the most heavily represented, in that order. The point is simply that this imaginative book has been produced by a self-selected body of scholars who hold a set of unconventional views about Jesus and the Gospels. They are of course free to publish these views; however, their attempt to present

29. In context, this sentence refers to critical scholarship that is controlled by "factual evidence," working from ancient texts in the original languages and submitting its findings to the judgment of peers. The rhetoric of the passage, however, is misleading, suggesting that all who disagree with the findings of the Jesus Seminar are not "critical scholars."

30. Funk and Hoover et al., *Five Gospels*, 35.

31. Funk and Hoover et al., *Five Gospels*, 34.

32. The introduction claims that "more than two hundred professionally trained specialists, called Fellows, joined the group" (34). The numerical discrepancy is nowhere explained.

33. Helmut Koester of Harvard, whose work on the Gospels significantly undergirds the methods of the Seminar, does not appear in the list of Fellows, but he is listed as a member of the translation panel that produced this book's "Scholars Version."

these views as "the assured results of critical scholarship"[34] is—one must say it—reprehensible deception.

The Seminar's disingenuous self-representation stands in service of a larger agenda: the deliberate creation of a new gospel. *The Five Gospels* is the realization of a vision clearly articulated by Funk in his keynote address at the opening meeting of the Jesus Seminar in 1985, subsequently published in *Forum*, the Westar Institute's journal. "The religious establishment has not allowed the intelligence of high scholarship to pass through pastors and priests to a hungry laity," and television preachers have "played on the ignorance of the uninformed." Thus, the Jesus Seminar rides to the rescue: "Our work . . . will spell liberty for . . . millions."[35] Funk opines that "we are having increasing difficulty these days in accepting the biblical account of the creation and of the apocalyptic conclusion in anything like a literal sense."[36] For him, the Bible's story of the world's history and destiny is a narrative fiction that has lost its credibility and usefulness in late modernity. It is not only the mythic beginning and ending of the Bible that have become problematic, however, but also the "hypothetical middle—Jesus of Nazareth." After all, as we are informed in *The Five Gospels*, "the Christ of creed and dogma, who had been firmly in place in the Middle Ages, can no longer command the assent of those who have seen the heavens through Galileo's telescope. . . . Copernicus, Kepler, and Galileo have dismantled the mythical abodes of the gods and bequeathed us secular heavens."[37]

> To put the matter bluntly, we are having as much trouble with the middle—the messiah—as we are with the terminal points. What we need is a new fiction that takes as its starting point the central event in the Judeo-Christian drama and reconciles that middle with a new story that reaches beyond old beginnings and endings. In sum, we need a new narrative of Jesus, a new gospel, if you will, that places Jesus differently in the grand scheme, the epic story.[38]

34. Funk and Hoover et al., *Five Gospels*, 34.

35. Robert W. Funk, "The Issue of Jesus," *Forum* 1.1 (1985): 8.

36. Funk, "Issue of Jesus," 11.

37. Funk and Hoover et al., *Five Gospels*, 2. The echoes of Bultmann become nearly deafening at this point. The astounding thing is that sentences so epistemologically naive can be written in 1993 by an author claiming to represent serious scholarship.

38. Funk, "Issue of Jesus," 12.

In the work of the Jesus Seminar, Funk's desideratum has been achieved: a new gospel that disposes of the embarrassments of apocalyptic ends. The pathos—or bathos—of the project resides in the incongruity between Funk's epic pretensions and the actual findings of the Seminar. Does the passive, politically correct, laconic sage who speaks in the red type of *The Five Gospels* have the capacity to remake our imaginative world and provide a new fiction within which millions might find meaning for their lives? Surely not.

But even if the grand design of liberating millions through a new gospel should fail to pan out, Funk also has a more modest and realistic aim: "If we are to survive as scholars of the humanities, as well as theologians, we must quit the academic closet. And we must begin to sell a product that has some utilitarian value to someone—or which at least appears to have utilitarian value to someone."[39] Presumably, in the commercial realm, *The Five Gospels* will fulfill this hope. This likelihood is immeasurably enhanced by the fact that one of the "Fellows" of the Jesus Seminar is moviemaker Paul Verhoeven (*Robocop, Basic Instinct*), who reportedly plans to turn the Seminar's findings into a Hollywood screenplay.

Funk's concern for the *appearance* of utilitarian value perhaps explains the peculiar way in which *The Five Gospels* deploys the rhetoric of empiricism ("empirical, factual evidence," "independent, neutral observers"), despite Funk's own earlier avowal that "our fictions, though deliberately fictive, are nevertheless not subject to proof or falsification."[40] If indeed, as Funk suggests, "we need a fiction that we recognize to be fictive,"[41] the present volume is an odd way of filling the prescription. *The Five Gospels* purports to offer precisely the opposite: a factual Jesus discovered by scientific methods and disentangled from the fictive Jesus rendered in the Gospel narratives. Truth in advertising would be served if Funk's 1985 essay were published in place of the book's present introduction.

So, when I return my brother-in-law's phone call, here is what I shall say: No, the case argued by this book would not stand up in any court. The critical study of the historical Jesus is an important task—perhaps important for reasons theological as well as historical—but *The Five Gospels* does not advance that task significantly, nor does it represent a fair picture of the current state of research on this problem. Some of its purported revelations are old news,

39. Funk, "Issue of Jesus," 10.
40. Funk, "Issue of Jesus," 11.
41. Funk, "Issue of Jesus," 12.

and many of its novel claims are at best dubious. No, I was not involved in the project, nor were any of my colleagues at Yale and Duke, all of whom share my view that the Jesus Seminar is methodologically misguided. Should you take it seriously? Only if you want to compare its findings to other scholarly reconstructions of Jesus of Nazareth. If you are interested in the problem, there are at least a dozen other books I would recommend in preference to this one. But their authors are less likely to be interviewed on the radio: no scandalous sound bites.

6

Story, History, and the Quest for Jesus

We are gathered here to celebrate the scholarly work of N. T. Wright. His prolific writings have reshaped the way many of us read the NT. His books have situated Jesus and Paul squarely on the map of Second Temple Judaism, while at the same time showing how a historically particular reading of Jesus and Paul as first-century Jews can enhance Christian theological interpretation. Tom has written extensively for both academy and church, and he has been one of our generation's most effective Christian apologists in a post-Christian culture. He is a devoted servant of the church, and he writes with grace, wit, and power. And so, this large crowd of friends and appreciative readers has come together to honor Tom Wright and his work.

Yet, at the same time, we have also come to reflect critically upon it. Those two aims (laudatory celebration and critical scrutiny) might seem to conflict, but in fact they do not. The greatest honor that can be shown to a scholar is for his or her work to be engaged deeply and tested rigorously by colleagues. Adulation is for rock stars—but patient, searching, truthful dialogue is for those we love. In the preface to *The New Testament and the People of God*, written eighteen years ago, Tom wrote:

> I frequently tell my students that quite a high proportion of what I say is probably wrong, or at least flawed or skewed in some way which I do not at the moment realize. The only problem is that I do not know which bits are wrong; if I did I might do something about it. . . . Serious debate and

This essay was originally presented as a paper at the Wheaton Theology Conference, at Wheaton College, on April 16, 2010, as part of a symposium intended to celebrate and critically engage the writings of N. T. Wright.

> confrontation is the stuff of academic life, and I look forward, not of course without some trepidation, to more of it as a result of this project.[1]

And so the essay that I offer today will seek to honor Tom as a true friend precisely by telling him which bits I think might be wrong. What you are about to hear, then, is the continuation of an unexpectedly challenging conversation between two friends.

For more than twenty-five years Tom Wright and I have been allies in various battles within the field of NT studies. The two of us have also been engaged in a long-running, mutually edifying conversation about the interpretation of Scripture; each of us has frequently drawn on the other's writings for inspiration and instruction. I regard Tom not only as an insightful interpreter of the NT and an eloquent preacher of the gospel but as one of my very closest friends.

It therefore came as a shock to me—and I think to him as well—when, at the Society of Biblical Literature (SBL) meeting in Boston in 2008, Tom delivered a withering attack on my most recent book project. The book was *Seeking the Identity of Jesus: A Pilgrimage*, coedited by Beverly Roberts Gaventa and me.[2] It was the subject of a review panel at SBL, and Tom had been asked to be one of the respondents. I knew he would find things in the book to criticize; it was, after all, a collection of essays by sixteen different scholars, and I myself disagreed with some of their arguments on various particular points. But I had expected that he would warmly welcome the book's fundamental approach and claims: that Jesus of Nazareth was a first-century Jew whose life and teachings could be understood only within the context of Israel's history and Israel's Scripture; that the identity of Jesus is reliably attested in the canonical Gospels (and not in extracanonical literature such as the various gnostic gospels); that the Jesus we find in the canonical NT is rightly understood in the church's subsequent confessional traditions—that is, the notion of Jesus as the incarnation of God is not a later fanciful aberration but a faithful construal of the figure we encounter in the Gospels; that after his crucifixion, Jesus was raised from the dead; consequently, he is not only a figure of past history, but he remains a living presence in the community of his people; and finally, that knowing Jesus rightly requires a lifelong process of discipleship, in which we

1. N. T. Wright, *The New Testament and the People of God*, Christian Origins and the Question of God 1 (London: SPCK; Minneapolis: Fortress, 1992), xvii–xviii.

2. Beverly Roberts Gaventa and Richard B. Hays, eds., *Seeking the Identity of Jesus: A Pilgrimage* (Grand Rapids: Eerdmans, 2008).

are conformed to the pattern of his life so that we seek to embody God's will in the world—or, to put this last point in a Wrightian idiom: true beliefs about Jesus cannot be separated from praxis that seeks to implement Jesus's kingdom agenda. All this, I expected, would be profoundly congenial to Tom's own scholarly commitments and conclusions.

But instead Tom greeted the book with sharp criticism, chiefly because he saw its approach to seeking Jesus as insufficiently historical. Our "pilgrimage," he said, was overdetermined by dogmatic concerns and theological traditions and inattentive to the realities of first-century history. Real pilgrims, Tom observed, would get their feet dirty on the dusty roads of ancient Palestine. But this book of essays was instead "a pilgrimage by helicopter," and its authors and editors were "pilgrims with suspiciously clean feet." The result was therefore, in his words, a "pseudotheological project of non-historical retrieval of Jesus." And much, much more in this vein.[3] A great deal of this critique was, I believe, wide of the mark. But it was delivered with the inimitable wit and dazzling rhetorical fireworks we have all come to admire in Tom's writing.

Now, my purpose in recounting this tale of a surprising showdown at SBL is not to set the stage for a rebuttal or to shift our attention today away from Tom's work to the book I coedited. Instead, my purpose is to set the stage for some reflections about the way in which we might most fruitfully understand the relation between story and history in our effort to grasp the truth about Jesus. Tom's visceral reaction to *Seeking the Identity of Jesus* exposed for both of us a large area of previously undiscovered, or at least unexamined, differences. In our subsequent conversations, I learned, for example, that he regards the theology of Karl Barth as the source of much mischief and error, and that he is deeply suspicious of the whole Barthian/postliberal project of "narrative theology" associated with the so-called Yale School of theologians such as Hans Frei and George Lindbeck. On his view, their "intratextual" hermeneutical approaches lead to an escapist denial of critical history and a detachment from the real world of historical events outside the text of the Bible. I, on the other hand, have been profoundly influenced by Barth and his heirs, and I believe Tom's negative evaluation of them is based on an unfortunate caricature of their theology. And so, the blowup in Boston exposed some important fault lines in the alliance between Tom and me. (Perhaps it was a little like the confrontation between Peter and Paul at Antioch: Tom believed I was not walking straight toward the truth of the gospel.) Consequently, this argument

3. These quotations are taken from N. T. Wright, "Pilgrims with Suspiciously Clean Feet" (paper presented at the annual meeting of the SBL, Boston, November 24, 2008).

has forced me to go back and reread Tom's work with new questions in mind to see what I missed before.

The questions concerning us in the present essay are these: How are we to understand the relation between story and history? What roles, if any, do the church's scriptural canon and tradition play in NT hermeneutics? Is there a legitimate discipline of historical inquiry that operates outside and apart from that tradition? If so, what claim does such a discipline have on determining the ways in which Christians know Jesus? In what ways might the historical study of Jesus play a role in apologetics or in conversation with non-Christians? And finally, what is the significance of the resurrection of Jesus for our epistemology?

Of course, to treat such huge questions is impossible in one short paper. All I can hope to do is offer a few summarizing observations and proposals. My remarks will proceed in three stages. First, I will sketch briefly my understanding of the ways in which Tom approaches these issues of story and history. Second, I will offer some reflections on the theological gains and losses entailed in Tom's working methodology. And finally, I shall venture some programmatic proposals about where we might go from here.

Approaching Jesus: The Wright Methods

The book in which Tom has most fully developed his account of the figure of Jesus is, of course, *Jesus and the Victory of God* (*JVG*). At the time of its publication in 1996, I wrote a blurb for the book jacket. That blurb still expresses accurately my view of the book's significance:

> Tom Wright's bold and brilliant book challenges us to rethink everything we thought we knew about the Jesus of history. Wright masterfully surveys the field of research on Jesus and proposes a fresh account of Jesus as a first-century Jewish apocalyptic prophet. . . . The result? A portrait of Jesus that situates him firmly "on the ground" in the politics of first-century Judaism while integrating the data of the Gospel traditions in fresh and surprising ways. Wright's sweeping hypothesis, presented in delightfully lucid prose, sets a benchmark for all subsequent investigations of the historical Jesus.[4]

4. Richard B. Hays, book jacket endorsement for N. T. Wright, *Jesus and the Victory of God*, Christian Origins and the Question of God 2 (London: SPCK; Minneapolis: Fortress, 1996).

But I now want to unpack a little more fully the judgments expressed in this blurb by analyzing the working methods Tom employs in the book. Exactly how does he challenge us to rethink our picture of Jesus, and how does he integrate the data in fresh ways?

One of the book's many virtues is that Tom is deeply reflective about methodological issues. He does not merely adopt the methods conventionally employed in historical study of the Jesus tradition; instead, he works out his own approach to the problem. The sophisticated methodological underpinnings of *JVG* are explained at length in his earlier book *The New Testament and the People of God*.[5] For the purposes of our present analysis, I want to highlight seven features of Tom's working method.

Descriptive Observations on Tom Wright's Historical Methods

(1) *Critical realism*. In *The New Testament and the People of God*, Tom devotes an opening chapter to the problem of epistemology. He rejects a naive historical positivism which supposes that "facts" about the world can be clearly and objectively discerned by the knower from a position of neutrality. But he also rejects a radical postmodernism that treats all knowledge as constructed by the knower and denies the possibility of true access to a reality external to the self. In place of these rival epistemologies, Tom opts for "critical realism," an epistemologically chastened position that recognizes both the role of the human agent's worldview in shaping perception—like the spectacles he or she wears—and, at the same time, the reality of the external world perceived by that agent. Through a process of trial and error, the testing of "fit" between worldview and evidence, the knower can gradually attain a reasonably accurate picture of the real world, including the real world of past history.

(2) *Hypothesis and verification*. This aspect of Tom's method is one of the ways in which his approach to Jesus differs radically from most other studies. In the twentieth century, studies of the historical Jesus usually sought to apply various criteria that enable the sifting of individual sayings and narrative units in the Gospels, separating the authentic from the inauthentic, assigning various levels of probability to their claim of historical factuality. The Jesus Seminar's color-coded edition of the Gospels is the most vivid visual representation of this methodology. The usual procedure is to extract the residue of "critically assured" units of tradition and build a picture of Jesus on that basis.

5. There is also a helpful brief summary of Wright's approach in Marcus J. Borg and N. T. Wright, *The Meaning of Jesus: Two Visions* (San Francisco: HarperSanFrancisco, 1999), 15–27.

But Tom rejects this whole approach out of hand. Instead, his method aims at "getting the evidence in." He takes the whole body of (canonical) traditions about Jesus and tries to develop a hypothesis about the identity of Jesus that will allow for maximum inclusion of the data. In fact, at no point in almost seven hundred pages of *JVG* does Tom say of any unit of Gospel material, "Jesus probably didn't say that," or "This is legendary embellishment." Instead, he tries to make all the pieces of the puzzle fit together as historically factual elements of his reconstruction. This is one of the reasons that many evangelicals love the book. Conversely, it is one of the things that causes many NT scholars in the academic guild to regard it with suspicion. The methodology requires initial immersion in the NT texts and other texts that provide insight into Jesus's cultural environment, followed by a highly intuitive, synthetic leap of induction that generates a master hypothesis. The master hypothesis is then—perhaps in circular fashion?—evaluated on the basis of its capacity to explain as much of the evidence as possible.

(3) *Skepticism about form and redaction criticism and about synoptic source criticism.* A corollary of the previous point is that Tom brackets out any use of the critical methods usually employed by Gospel scholars to distinguish stages of development within the tradition or relations of literary dependence among the three Synoptic Gospels. His reason for this radical methodological decision is simply stated: "If all this worked, and if most scholars agreed about it, it would be fine. But it doesn't, and they don't, and it isn't. Despite frequent claims, a century of research has failed to reach anything like consensus on a single one of the stages in question, let alone on the hypothetical developments in between."[6] Here I must register a slight qualm. On the question of synoptic literary relationships, something like the method of hypothesis and verification has been in play for a long time, and there is actually a very high degree of consensus among scholars on the priority of the Gospel of Mark, and the conclusion that both Matthew and Luke used Mark as a source. I myself would want to give this hypothesis considerably more weight in a historical reconstruction than Tom wants to allow. Tom's complete embargo on such considerations is another of the factors that has caused some NT critics to regard *JVG* as an apologetic tour de force.

(4) *Extensive use of Second Temple Jewish material.* Less distinctive to Tom's methodology, but deeply integral to it, is his broad engagement with Jewish sources from the Second Temple era. These texts and sources allow him to draw the map on which the Jesus of the Gospels is to be located. That map is

6. Borg and Wright, *Meaning of Jesus*, 20–21.

not the framework of the Christian credal tradition, or even of the canonical NT. Rather it is the "cultural encyclopedia"—the cultural framework of reference—of Jewish religion and culture in the ancient Mediterranean world. The important conversation partners for Tom's interpretation of Jesus are not Irenaeus or the Council of Chalcedon, not even the letter to the Hebrews or 1 Peter. Rather, the key conversation partners are Josephus, the Dead Sea Scrolls, 4 Ezra, and so on. (This attention to ancient Jewish sources is one of the characteristic features of what Tom has named "the Third Quest for the historical Jesus.") And here the polarities shift: at this point, Tom's method is much more in sync with the priorities of the academy and less in keeping with the perceptions of the church. This is certainly one of the points at which his critique of the book Beverly Gaventa and I edited is most acute: he simply thinks we have placed the Gospels in an anachronistic "encyclopedia of reception." (Not his term but Umberto Eco's.) It should be noted also that Tom is not merely mining ancient Jewish texts for parallels to this or that saying of Jesus. Rather, he is consistently reading them with an eye to discerning their worldview, asking about the story they tell about God, Israel, and the world. In this respect Tom's method is more sophisticated and holistic than the work one sometimes finds in the professional journals of the biblical academy.

(5) *Exclusive focus on the Synoptic Gospels.* By design, Tom's account of Jesus in *JVG* focuses on material found in the three Synoptic Gospels and excludes John from the picture almost entirely. Tom explains this methodological decision as a strategic move: since most Gospel scholars tend to regard the Fourth Gospel as later and full of highly theological, unhistorical material, he found it simpler to bracket out John in hopes of making his reconstruction of Jesus more accessible and credible to other scholars. Here I must register a small note of puzzlement. Given the radical ways in which Tom disregards scholarly consensus on other issues, why the sudden scruple here to conform to mainstream convention? And if his working method seeks to get all the evidence into the picture, surely the testimony provided by John is a necessary part of the puzzle, isn't it?[7]

(6) *Inattention to the literary and theological shape of individual Gospels. JVG* shows little or no interest in the distinctive literary contours of the individual canonical Gospels, or even in the distinctive theological witness of the

7. On the role of the Fourth Gospel in Wright's work, see Marianne Meye Thompson, "*Jesus and the Victory of God* Meets the Gospel of John," in *Jesus, Paul, and the People of God: A Theological Dialogue with N. T. Wright*, ed. Nicholas Perrin and Richard B. Hays (Downers Grove, IL: IVP Academic, 2011), 21–38.

individual evangelists. In my judgment this is a significant oversight, and I will have more to say about it in what follows.

(7) *Reconstruction of a Jesus behind the canonical Gospels.* Instead of attending to the distinctive portrayals of Jesus in the individual NT texts, Tom aims instead at something else: a reconstruction of the historical figure of Jesus behind the texts, including the construction of an account about Jesus's intentions and his self-understanding. Such an account necessarily involves a considerable amount of inference and speculation, because the Gospel writers—with the exception of John, who has been sent out of the classroom for the purpose of Tom's inquiry—actually give us rather little direct access to such information. But Tom regards this sort of "archaeological"[8] process of recovery as an essential part of the work of the historian. So the Gospels themselves become not the focus of attention but the windows through which Tom peers to find a Jesus outside and beyond the Gospels themselves.

Evaluative Reflections on Wright's Historical Methods

These last two points (inattention to the actual Gospels as literary texts and reconstruction of a Jesus behind the texts) seem a little odd given Tom's strong focus on story as a key to understanding Jesus. For example, he writes: "Since (a) stories are a key worldview indicator . . . and (b) a good part of the New Testament consists of stories, of narratives, it might be a good idea to consider how stories might carry, or be vehicles for, authority."[9] But in fact, upon closer examination, we see that the story in Tom's viewfinder is not exactly any of the specific stories actually told by the evangelists; rather, it is a critically abstracted construct, the master metanarrative of the Bible. It is Israel's grand story of creation, fall, covenant, exile, and return. More specifically, it is that metanarrative as told from within the perspective of late Second Temple Judaism's consciousness of "exile" and oppression, accompanied by a passionate hope for messianic deliverance.

Tom finds the locus classicus of this consciousness in the ardent prayer of Daniel (Dan 9:3–19), but a similar sketch of Israel's metanarrative can be found in the narrative frame of the Gospel of Matthew. Consider, for example, the evocative ending of Matthew's genealogy: "So all the generations from Abraham to David are fourteen generations; and from David to the deportation to Babylon, fourteen generations; and from the deportation to Babylon to the

8. On the use of *archaeological*, see Gaventa and Hays, *Seeking the Identity of Jesus*, 5.
9. Wright, *New Testament and the People of God*, 140.

Messiah, fourteen generations" (Matt 1:17). But again, I would note that Tom is not interested (at least not in *JVG*) in Matthew's theology; instead, his interest lies in tracing these ideas back into the mind of Jesus.

And so, in light of the methods he has employed, Tom arrives at the now well-known account of Jesus that he has offered with great passion and rigorous consistency over the past twenty years. Let us recall the key findings: the Jesus of Tom's historical reconstruction is a Jewish eschatological prophet who comes proclaiming the long-awaited coming of God's kingdom, the end of Israel's exile, and the return of YHWH to Zion. Indeed, Jesus is not just proclaiming the return of YHWH to Zion, he is embodying it, enacting it in such a way that his journey to Jerusalem actually is the long-awaited eschatological coming of Israel's God.

In all this I would suggest that there is at least some unresolved tension between theological and historical perspectives. In *The Meaning of Jesus: Two Visions*, published three years after *JVG*, Tom wants to say that history and theology are complementary; indeed, that both are necessary. And in *JVG* Tom can even assert that theological exegesis can be achieved through the historical study of Jesus.[10] It seems in principle that Tom's exposition of critical realism ought to allow faith an epistemological role, since we cannot avoid reading the evidence through the "spectacles" of our own worldviews. Yet in several weighty passages he seems to suggest that faith can obscure real history, or that hard-nosed history has a certain hermeneutical priority.[11]

One clear example is the passage near the end of *JVG* in which Tom speaks of Jesus's "awareness of vocation" to enact a "symbolic encoding" of the return of YHWH. Tom then distinguishes this claim sharply from Jesus's having a "'supernatural' awareness of himself" as being in some ontological relation to Israel's God. "Jesus did not," Tom writes, "'know that he was God' in the way that one knows one is male or female, hungry or thirsty, or that one ate an orange an hour ago." Rather, it was a sort of knowledge that can be discovered only by living into it, "like knowing one is loved." This is something very different from what Tom calls "pseudo-orthodox attempts to make Jesus of Nazareth

10. Wright, *Jesus and the Victory of God*, 662. Surely this formulation requires more careful exploration and explanation than Wright has so far given it in his work.

11. That is why Stephen Evans castigates Tom's work as philosophically slanted in the direction of "methodological naturalism" (C. Stephen Evans, "Methodological Naturalism in Historical Biblical Scholarship," in *Jesus and the Restoration of Israel: A Critical Assessment of N. T. Wright's* Jesus and the Victory of God, ed. Carey C. Newman [Downers Grove, IL: IVP Academic, 1999], 180–205). Evans's criticism is perhaps overdrawn, but I would suggest that he is in fact picking up some signals that really are there in Wright's work.

conscious of being the second person of the Trinity."[12] Christian theological tradition is by and large bracketed out—at least at the explicit level—in Tom's treatment of the evidence.

Or consider this passage on faith and history in *The Meaning of Jesus*: "The Jesus I know in prayer, in the sacraments, in the faces of those in need, is the Jesus I meet in the historical evidence—including the New Testament, of course, but the New Testament read not so much as the church has told me to read it but as I read it with my historical consciousness fully operative."[13] In that formulation, we hear, I think, a Tom Wright speaking who is still carrying the intellectual legacy of the liberal historicism of the First and Second Quests for the historical Jesus, the quests of the nineteenth and twentieth centuries. "The church" here seems to offer chiefly an oppressive and misleading hermeneutical framework that obscures the real Jesus. To discover that real Jesus we must bracket out the church's received traditions about him and reread the NT with a fresh (modernist?) historical consciousness. Only then will we truly know Jesus in two ways: through our own experience (prayer, etc.) and in our historical reconstruction. Experience and critical history rescue us from the misreading of Jesus bequeathed to us by the church. Tom does not always write about Jesus in these terms, but it is one important strand of his working methodology. And this is certainly the Tom Wright who was speaking on that difficult day in Boston.

The bracketing out of the church's theological tradition is also suggested by two other important features of *JVG*: the absence of the Gospel of John in the database used for reconstruction of the historical Jesus, and the deferral of the resurrection to a subsequent volume. Tom might well plead that these deferrals are either strategic or simply necessitated by the large scope of the topics. He did, after all, write an even longer subsequent volume on the resurrection! But I would still suggest that the omissions of John and the resurrection from *JVG* are hermeneutically significant. Clearly it makes a huge difference whether or not one reads the Synoptic Gospels in dialogue with John's proclamation that Jesus was the incarnation of the Logos or in light of the resurrection as the true climax of the story.[14]

Perhaps I could put my point here simply as a question to Tom: Now that you have worked through the evidence and written a comprehensive study of

12. Wright, *Jesus and the Victory of God*, 653.

13. Borg and Wright, *Meaning of Jesus*, 26.

14. See Richard B. Hays, "Reading Scripture in Light of the Resurrection," in *The Art of Reading Scripture*, ed. Ellen F. Davis and Richard B. Hays (Grand Rapids: Eerdmans, 2003), 216–38. (Chapter 3 in the present volume.)

the resurrection that concludes Jesus really was raised from the dead, should this finding retrospectively affect the content treated in *JVG*? If you were going to revise that volume for a second edition now, almost fifteen years later, would your assessment of the evidence have to be different in light of the findings of *The Resurrection of the Son of God*?

Theological Gains and Losses in Wright's Critical-Realist Historicism

It is time now to sum up what we have observed and reflect on what is gained and lost in Tom Wright's far-reaching and insightful account of the Jesus of history.

Gains

As *Jesus and the Victory of God* rolls on and the evidence accumulates, page after page, we find that Tom has achieved some impressive results. His construction of Jesus is wide-ranging, eloquent, and cohesive. From a theological point of view, here are the major gains that I see:

(1) *Reading in historical context and depth.* Tom narrates a Jesus who for the most part fits intelligibly into the history of Israel in the first century under Roman rule. His identity is thoroughly Jewish, and many of his actions and teachings come freshly into focus within the setting that Tom constructs. The Gospels themselves gain texture and precision when read alongside the extant corpus of ancient Jewish literature hoping for Israel's restoration and renewal.

(2) *Recovery of the political/pragmatic character of the gospel.* The Jesus who steps out of the pages of Tom's book is not an otherworldly, apolitical figure. He fits within a vivid political landscape of pragmatic collaborators, resistance fighters, would-be messiahs, and others struggling to sort out the national identity of a people trodden down by pagan powers but always dreaming that God would set them free and bring justice. Against this backdrop Jesus's prophetic proclamation of "the kingdom of God" recovers its properly explosive political meaning. So Tom's work goes a long way to overcome the misguided modernist divide between theology and politics.

(3) *Positive coherence of the synoptic storyline with OT/Israel.* One benefit of Tom's work that is not often enough recognized is that it goes a long way toward resolving the perennial problem of the relation between the Old and New Testaments. The Synoptic Gospels, on Tom's reading, narrate a linear

continuation of the story line of Israel's national struggles and hopes. The God who appears clearly in these pages is the God who made covenant with Israel, led them out of slavery in Egypt, gave them a promised land, banished them into exile because of their unfaithfulness, but nevertheless remains faithful to them. The NT then becomes, simply but profoundly, the story of God's restoration of his people Israel, and Jesus is "the one to redeem Israel" (Luke 24:21). I say this is a theological gain, though some of Tom's critics protest that his account overstates the salvation-historical continuity between Israel and church and underplays the radical newness of God's saving action in Christ's death and resurrection. I would like to go on record as saying that, theologically speaking, this is a misguided objection. Rather than diminishing the newness of God's saving action, Tom's account deepens our understanding of the way in which the death and resurrection of Jesus is not simply a matter of saving individuals from their personal guilt; instead, it is the culmination of God's astonishing large-scale plan to restore his covenant people and bring salvation to the whole world.

(4) *High Christology*. Perhaps the most surprising theological outcome of Tom's historical construction is the way in which, while working "from below" on the plane of historical events, it unexpectedly opens the door to the development of an exceedingly "high" Christology. Here is the now-famous concluding passage of Tom's account of Jesus's beliefs about himself and his mission:

> I propose, *as a matter of history*, that Jesus of Nazareth was conscious of a vocation: a vocation, given him by the one he knew as "father," to enact in himself what, in Israel's scriptures, God had promised to accomplish all by himself. He would be the pillar of cloud and fire for the people of the new exodus. He would embody in himself the returning and redeeming action of the covenant God.[15]

If that is what Jesus thought about his own identity, the subsequent development of the church's worship of him becomes more readily intelligible. From a historical point of view, if Jesus was a simple Galilean prophet and teacher, the church's later claims about his divinity have always appeared to be nothing other than a theological mistake, the superimposition of a mythological construct that Jesus himself would probably have found blasphemous. Not so on Tom's reading. But of course, while Tom's proposal that Jesus saw himself

15. Wright, *Jesus and the Victory of God*, 653, emphasis added.

as embodying the return of YHWH to Zion is the linchpin of his historical account, it is also the one feature of his reconstruction that has been seen as most unpersuasive to most of his colleagues who labor in the vineyard of "historical Jesus" studies.

(5) *Apologetic value.* Finally, from a theological point of view, one might hope—and I think Tom does hope—that his historical account of Jesus might have apologetic value and impact. He seeks to give us a historical narrative that takes in all the evidence and shows that the Gospels actually do give us a persuasive, coherent picture of what really happened in the life of Jesus—history *wie es eigentlich gewesen ist.* To the extent that Tom's construction works as "secular" history, it creates a bridge for dialogue with nonbelievers about Jesus. They can be invited to cross the bridge, to "come and see" who Jesus was[16] without first having to surrender their own historical consciousness and worldview. I fear, however, that this apologetic hope is illusory or at least exaggerated. But Tom's book may in fact serve a slightly different sort of apologetic function: it is not a sign for nonbelievers but for believers. It may allow uncertain believers to gain greater confidence about the historical credibility of the story that they already haltingly believe on other grounds.

Losses

The theological gains enumerated here are weighty. But I think a full assessment of *JVG* must also reckon with some factors that should be entered on the debit side of the theological ledger.[17]

(1) *Voices of the writers disappear.* First, as I have suggested already in my descriptive remarks, within Tom's project, the individual voices of the Synoptic Gospel writers disappear. The distinctiveness of the testimony of each individual Gospel witness is lost, or at least drowned out, by Tom's synthetic renarration of his account of Jesus. This is theologically regrettable, and it effectively turns back the clock and loses some of the very significant gains achieved by literary study of the Gospels over the past generation. As a reader of the NT I want to hear the complex polyphony of the choir of singers, not just a critically extracted unison melody.

(2) *Over-systematization.* The reference to a "critically extracted" melody

16. I choose the past tense of the verb "to be" deliberately. By contrast, see Leander E. Keck, *Who Is Jesus? History in Perfect Tense* (Columbia: University of South Carolina Press, 2000).

17. Perhaps some of the objections posed here may be counted as open questions, rather than losses.

points to my second concern: the danger of over-systematization. The question that haunts many readers of *JVG* is whether Tom's synthetic construct is too clever by half, whether it obsessively forces all the evidence into the single mold of the exile-and-return pattern. The parade example is Tom's interpretation of the parable of the prodigal son as a story about Israel's exile and restoration.[18] No matter how many times I read Tom's elegant treatment of the parable, I simply can't persuade myself that this is what Jesus meant when he told the story. There are two simple reasons for my incredulity.

First, Luke, the one Gospel writer who recounts this parable, does not seem to think it means what Tom thinks it means. He contextualizes it within a controversy between Jesus and the Pharisees and scribes about Jesus's practice of eating with sinners (Luke 15:1–2). In Luke 15 the parable is one of a string of three parables, following the lost sheep and the lost coin, about mercy and forgiveness. It requires a couple of tricky hermeneutical dance steps to get to Tom's reading about Israel's new exodus. I think finally he can get there only by assuming that the Jesus of history was really talking about national exile and return, but that Luke himself either failed to understand that theme or suppressed it deliberately. Tom never actually puts it that way, but I think that is the implicit logic of the argument. It seems to me that what Tom really has done to make a brilliant *homiletical* move, showing how the parable of the prodigal son *could* function metaphorically to illustrate his own major theme of Israel's exile and return. But merely to show the aptness of the metaphor is not to demonstrate historically that Jesus used the parable that way.

Second, Tom's reading of the parable is unprecedented in the history of interpretation. He points this out explicitly: "Years of scholarship have produced many commentaries on Luke, and many books on the parables. But none that I have been able to consult has noted the feature which seems to me most striking and obvious."[19] Indeed. Perhaps it is the case, then, that it is not really so "obvious." Perhaps we are dealing here not with a recovery of what Jesus really meant back in the first century but instead with a wonderful flash of poetic insight, the sort of artistic *poiēsis* that makes Tom such a fine preacher.

(3) *The church's confessional tradition.* All this raises the question of the relation of Tom's critical reconstruction of Jesus to the church's confessional tradition. He sometimes seems to insist that his account, as historical in character, is independent of that tradition. In the first place I must say that I doubt that. Tom Wright has never come to the NT as a neutral historian. His own

18. Wright, *Jesus and the Victory of God*, 125–31.
19. Wright, *Jesus and the Victory of God*, 126.

account of critical realism should serve amply to make the point. He comes to his reading of the Gospels as a believing Christian, formed intellectually and imaginatively by years of participation in the rich liturgical life of the Church of England; even as a Christian trying to think historically, he is engaged in the project of faith seeking understanding. But if that is the case, why not acknowledge that the church's tradition might provide aid rather than hindrance in seeking to understand the NT's witness about the identity of Jesus? Ben Meyer, one of the important influences on Tom's thinking, puts the point in the following way: it may be "*in the tradition generated by Jesus* that we discover what made him operate in the way he did."[20] Why then not acknowledge more forthrightly, Tom, that your reading of the historical evidence is actually stimulated by the church's orthodox confessional traditions, even if your reading fills in details and makes connections that the tradition has not often made before? Or, conversely, if your reading seems totally unprecedented in the church's whole tradition of reading—as in the case of the prodigal son parable—should that give you pause about whether your interpretation can persuasively claim historical validity? Should you think of it instead as a fresh constructive theological proposal, an exercise in typological reading, analogous (say) to Paul's reading of Christian baptism and the Lord's Supper as prefigured by Israel's exodus experience (1 Cor 10:1–22)?

(4) *The canon as authoritative for theology*. Another theological loss in Tom's project is a loss of clarity about the role of the canon of Scripture as authoritative for theology. (Or at least this is a potential danger in the project.) When we seek to know who Jesus is, how do we do that? Do we look to the narrative representations of Jesus in the canonical fourfold Gospel? Or must we instead read *JVG* to discover Tom Wright's reconstructed metanarrative as the distinctively authoritative construal of Jesus's identity? The problem here is the one long ago identified by Martin Kähler: the critical historian becomes in effect a Fifth Evangelist whose secondary reconstruction becomes the center of authority, perhaps even displacing the very texts it seeks to interpret.[21] One major difference between Tom and many other questers for the historical Jesus (such as Marcus Borg or John Dominic Crossan) is that he certainly does not intend to contradict or supplant the canonical accounts of Jesus. But at the end of the day the more strongly Tom emphasizes the distinctiveness of his account, the more acute the problem becomes.

20. Ben F. Meyer, *The Aims of Jesus* (London: SCM, 1979), 253, cited in Wright, *New Testament and the People of God*, 115, emphasis added.

21. Martin Kähler, *The So-Called Historical Jesus and the Historic Biblical Christ* (Philadelphia: Fortress, 1964 [1896]).

(5) *Narrative identity*. Finally, these problems may be restated in terms of the concept of narrative identity: how is identity rendered? Tom seems to locate the identity of Jesus in something like an abstracted pattern—the critically reconstructed story of Jesus as enacting the pattern of return from exile—rather than in the NT's specific narrative renderings. Paradoxically, at this point Tom's work bears a striking formal similarity to Hans Frei's classic study *The Identity of Jesus Christ*.[22] Frei of course said nothing about return from exile or restoration of Israel. But he saw Jesus's identity as enacted in a narrative pattern of self-emptying obedience to which the Gospels generally point. And, like Tom Wright, he made no effort to relate his proposed narrative pattern to the actual way the individual Gospels narrate the passion, death, and resurrection of Jesus. For Frei, the thing that mattered was a fundamental kerygmatic narrative pattern underlying all the canonical Gospel texts. It seems to me that Tom is actually doing something analogous, but he differs from Frei in insisting that the kerygmatic pattern he identifies was also present in the mind of the historical Jesus, consciously shaping his aims and actions. Against both Frei and Wright, I would like to propose that it is more theologically fruitful for interpretation of Jesus to adhere more closely to the actual specific narratives given us in the canonical Gospels: Matthew, Mark, Luke, and John.

Where Do We Go from Here? A Theological Assessment

First, I would like to arrange a conversation, in the near future, between my friends Tom Wright and Karl Barth. Maybe I could invite both of them to dinner. If they should accept the invitation, here is how I would introduce the dinner-table conversation: "Karl, I want you to listen to this passage from Tom's *Jesus and the Victory of God*":

> Those who have desired to explore and understand the incarnation itself have regularly missed what is arguably the most central, shocking and dramatic source material on that subject, which if taken seriously would ensure that the meaning of the word "god" be again and again rethought around the actual history of Jesus himself.[23]

22. Hans W. Frei, *The Identity of Jesus Christ: The Hermeneutical Bases of Dogmatic Theology* (Philadelphia: Fortress, 1975).

23. Wright, *Jesus and the Victory of God*, 661.

"And now, Tom, listen to this passage from Karl's *Church Dogmatics*": "The meaning of his deity—the only true deity in the New Testament sense—cannot be gathered from any notion of supreme, absolute, non-worldly being. It can be learned only from what took place in Christ."[24]

My point is that Tom and Karl ought to find they have more in common than Tom supposes. They are in full agreement, I think, that the incarnation forces us to rethink the very meaning of the word *god*, for in Jesus God is concretely present in a very surprising way. The particularity of incarnation requires a fundamental reconfiguration of our understanding of God. God is made known precisely in Jesus, not through general speculation or natural knowledge. Consider the opening of chapter fourteen of Barth's *Church Dogmatics*:

> The atonement is history. To know it, we must know it as such. To think of it, we must think of it as such. To speak of it, we must tell it as history. To try to grasp it as supra-historical or non-historical truth is not to grasp it at all. It is indeed truth, but truth actualised in a history and revealed in this history as such—revealed, therefore, as history.[25]

I would think Tom would applaud that! But I think my two friends Wright and Barth would still find plenty to argue about, because they still differ on the hermeneutical issue of how we come to know the truth about this historical figure of Jesus in whom God is embodied.

Second, we need to seek to overcome, with renewed determination, the pernicious dichotomy between story and history. Tom and I agree about that. Why, then, have we somehow come to think differently about the proper way of relating story and history? In pondering this question I stumbled across a particularly telling autobiographical insight offered by Tom in *The Meaning of Jesus*:

> I react against attempts to pull me back into the old split-level world . . . with the vigour of one who does not want to be imprisoned again in the attic (faith divorced from history) or the dungeon (history divorced from faith). This reaction will be understood, perhaps, by those who have experienced other liberations, for instance from heavy-handed traditional Protestantism or Catholicism.[26]

24. Karl Barth, *Church Dogmatics* 4/1, trans. G. W. Bromiley (Edinburgh: T & T Clark, 1956), 177.

25. Barth, *Church Dogmatics* 4/1:157.

26. Borg and Wright, *Meaning of Jesus*, 16.

This may go some way toward explaining Tom's vehement response to *Seeking the Identity of Jesus*: he perceived it as an attempt to imprison him again in the attic by banishing history and enforcing conformity to some sort of antihistorical disembodied faith.

But nothing could be further from the truth. In a significant essay in *Seeking the Identity of Jesus*, the theologian Robert Jenson confronts exactly this issue and asks a provocative question: "But what if the church's dogma were a necessary hermeneutical principle of historical reading, because it describes the true ontology of historical being?"[27] Let me paraphrase that: if it is true that Jesus was the incarnation of the Word, the fleshly embodiment of the one through whom all things were made—and if it is true that he was raised from the dead by the power of God and now reigns over the whole world (whether the world acknowledges it or not)—then it follows that the historical figure of Jesus cannot be rightly known or understood apart from the epistemological insight articulated precisely in the confession that Jesus is Lord—Jesus is the κύριος. This is where we ought to begin if we want to know the truth about Jesus.

This is the insight that Tom's whole historical Jesus project doesn't ever quite take on board. The "hypothesis" that Tom seeks to verify by pulling together the evidence of the Synoptics is not a naked inference from uninterpreted data. Rather, the hypothesis that Tom is testing is already encoded in the NT texts themselves as proclamatory stories, and already embedded in Tom's own worldview by virtue of his lifelong participation in a community that continues to retell the story. So the hypothesis-verification model can't escape the hermeneutical circle. Nor should it. Precisely because the church's dogma names a truth the world does not or cannot know, it rightly describes the truth about history in a way that secularist history is bound to miss.

Another way to put this point is to affirm that the resurrection of Jesus is the epistemological key to understanding the world and therefore the key to all history. If so, any history that does not begin from the vantage point of the resurrection of Jesus is perforce distorted because it denies or fails to grasp the true history of the world.

Conclusion

The fault line between Tom and me on story and history is broadly emblematic of a pervasive ambivalence in contemporary evangelical Christianity. The

27. Robert W. Jenson, "Identity, Jesus, and Exegesis," in Gaventa and Hays, *Seeking the Identity of Jesus*, 50.

desire for historical validation of Christian claims stands in some tension with a deeply felt desire for the postmodern recovery of canon and tradition as the necessary hermeneutical framework for understanding both Scripture and the world. Both Tom and I want both things, but we have different ways of seeking to integrate them. On the one hand, Tom insists that without historical investigation of the factuality of the Gospels, the story is vacuous, not least at the level of concrete action in the world. I insist, on the other hand, that without the canonical form of the story, we could never get the historical investigation right in the first place.

Throughout these critical reflections on Tom Wright's magisterial work, I have been seeking to extend a deep conversation between the two of us—that is to say, between the sort of colleagues whom Paul calls "fellow-workers belonging to God" (1 Cor 3:9). Ultimately, that conversation will end, I trust, not like the testy confrontation between Peter and Paul at Antioch, but more like the meeting in Jerusalem that led to the mutual recognition of the grace of God given to each, culminating in the giving of the right hand of κοινωνία. In that spirit, may faith and history unite; may story and history meet and embrace. May Richard and Tom embrace—and rejoice in the truth.

7

Catholic Tradition and the Quest for Jesus

Of the making of books about Jesus, there is no end; ordinarily, the appearance of one more might be merely an inducement to weariness of the flesh. But when the latest offering in this genre is a detailed study of the figure of Jesus by the Bishop of Rome, our curiosity may rightly be aroused. Joseph Ratzinger, now Pope Benedict XVI, brings to this task formidable credentials as a scholar and theologian. Consequently, his book—simply entitled *Jesus of Nazareth*—demands, and repays, careful attention.[1]

In the foreword, Ratzinger indicates that the book has had "a long gestation" (xi) and indicates that the first four chapters were completed in 2004, the year before his election to the papacy. He also gives a brief autobiographical sketch of his own encounter with the issues treated in his book. He lists "a series of inspiring books" about Jesus published in the 1930s and 1940s; their common denominator was that they "presented him as a man living on earth who, fully human though he was, at the same time brought God to men, the God with whom as Son he was one" (xi). That sentence could also stand as an excellent précis of Ratzinger's present work. Indeed, his book seems to be an attempt to recover and update the synthetic theological vision of these essentially precritical works while also incorporating the insights of the historical criticism that has gained official sanction in Roman Catholicism over the past sixty years.

One is surprised to find the statement on the first page of the foreword that it was only in the 1950s that "the gap between the 'historical Jesus' and the 'Christ of faith' grew wider and the two visibly fell apart." This can be understood only as another autobiographical statement of a thinker whose

1. Joseph Ratzinger, *Jesus of Nazareth: From the Baptism in the Jordan to the Transfiguration*, trans. Adrian J. Walker (London: Bloomsbury, 2007). References to the pagination will be in parentheses in the main text.

early experience was shaped chiefly by developments internal to Roman Catholicism. Elsewhere, in the Protestant world and in the universities of Europe, this gap had developed more than a century earlier and had reached crisis proportions well before World War I, as attested by Albert Schweitzer's landmark book of 1906, *The Quest of the Historical Jesus*. Schweitzer is never named in Ratzinger's study, though his interpretation of Jesus hovers in the background as a foil to some of Ratzinger's readings. In any case, Ratzinger regards the separation between the Christ of faith and the Jesus of history as a disaster for theology and for Christian faith more generally. His book attempts to remedy this situation.

Ratzinger's foreword also declares that "this book is in no way an exercise of the *magisterium*, but is solely an expression of my personal search 'for the face of the Lord' (cf. Ps. 27.8). Everyone is free, then, to contradict me" (xxiii–xxiv). Rather than seeking to contradict the author of this rich but puzzling book, however, this essay will attempt the sort of charitable, reasoned, critical conversation for which Ratzinger's own public pronouncements as pope have repeatedly called.

First Impressions

Jesus of Nazareth is not a complete account of Jesus's life. Rather, it is presented as the first part of a projected two-volume work,[2] treating only the first part of the public ministry of Jesus, as indicated in the book's subtitle, *From the Baptism in the Jordan to the Transfiguration*. This chronological framework is not, however, strictly observed in the book's actual content. For example, the chapter on "The Message of the Parables" focuses almost exclusively on Luke's parables of the Good Samaritan, the Prodigal Son, and the Rich Man and Lazarus, all of which occur in the Lukan narrative *after* the transfiguration. Similarly, Ratzinger's chapter on "The Principal Images of John's Gospel" draws heavily on material from the Farewell Discourses of John 13–16 (for example, the vine and the branches). John's Gospel does not include the transfiguration at all, but this material appears in John's account of Jesus's final evening with his disciples; presumably then, if John's story is superimposed on the synoptic narrative framework, this would also be post-transfiguration material.

2. The second volume was published as *Jesus of Nazareth: Part 2. Holy Week: From the Entrance into Jerusalem to the Resurrection*, trans. P. J. Whitmore (San Francisco: Ignatius, 2011). That volume, which appeared four years after the first, is not treated in this review.

In addition to the chapters already mentioned, the book includes chapters on the baptism of Jesus, the temptations of Jesus, the kingdom of God, the Sermon on the Mount, the Lord's Prayer, the disciples and "Two Milestones on the Way: Peter's Confession and the Transfiguration." The concluding chapter, "Jesus Declares His Identity," is a treatment of the titles "the Son of Man" and "the Son" along with a treatment of the "I am" sayings that feature prominently in John.

The genre of this book is puzzling. Is it a scholarly study of the historical figure of Jesus? An integrative theological account of the biblical foundations for the church's later articulation of trinitarian doctrine? A devotional meditation on the person of Jesus intended for prayerful appropriation by the faithful? An apologetic confrontation with secularism's barren and destructive view of humanity? The answer is that it is by turns all these things.

Likewise, one wonders who the intended readers of the book are. As readers we may on one page be caught up in a warmly moving devotional reflection on Jesus's unity with the Father and desire to bless humanity. Then we turn the page and find ourselves in the midst of a short critical survey of scholarly interpretations of the kingdom of God in the twentieth century, or a critical rebuttal to Bultmann's theories of pre-Christian gnostic sources for the Fourth Gospel's Christology. And perhaps on another page we find a couple of paragraphs on the difficulties with the way Western nations have offered aid to developing countries. The effect is to induce whiplash in the reader. One might say charitably that many different kinds of readers will find something engaging here. Or one might say less charitably that this is a book in need of a good editor who could help the author sort out the two or three different books that seem to have been struggling together in the womb during the book's long gestation period. As it stands, readers not interested in the history of historical Jesus scholarship are likely to find the intermittent surveys of critical opinion distracting, while readers like me who *are* interested in these matters are likely to find them sketchy and unsatisfying, even where we are inclined to be sympathetic to the positions that Ratzinger takes.

The Jesus of the Pope's Book

Given the range of topics treated in the book, a comprehensive engagement is impossible in the scope of this essay. Instead, I will simply identify some of the major themes that surface repeatedly in the book, note some methodological problems, and conclude with a few remarks about the book's virtues and contributions to the contemporary conversation about the identity of Jesus.

The single most dominant theme throughout the book is Jesus's "intimate unity with the Father" (6). The key to interpreting his identity and activity lies in his relation to God, which is ontologically grounded in his preexistent unity with the Father and expressed in his communion with the Father in prayer. Again and again Ratzinger quotes John 1:18: "No one has ever seen God; it is the only Son, who is nearest to the Father's heart, who has made him known."[3] The entire aim of Jesus's teaching and activity is to reveal his own union with God and to invite all humanity to share in an intimate, loving relation with God.

The second major theme of the book is the universal scope of Jesus's mission. While God's previous revealing and saving activity had been focused on the nation Israel, now in Jesus "God intends to come to all men." Ratzinger can even say, "This idea of universality will turn up again and again as the real core of Jesus' mission" (22). The contrast, therefore, between an ethnocentric Judaism and a universal Christianity is played out in many of the book's exegetical probes.

Third, Ratzinger downplays the apocalyptic content of Jesus's message. In fact, he argues, the idea that Jesus preached a message of "imminent expectation" for the coming of the kingdom of God "can actually be decisively ruled out" because it does not reckon adequately with the full range of statements in the Gospels about the kingdom, some of which clearly have a present dimension (58). Ratzinger declares that C. H. Dodd's emphasis on "realized eschatology" in the teaching of Jesus is "much more on the right track in terms of the real dynamics of the texts" (188) than the readings of exegetes who emphasize future apocalyptic themes in the Jesus tradition. Here, clearly, Ratzinger is jousting with the ghost of Schweitzer, who famously interpreted Jesus as a Jewish millenarian prophet whose apocalyptic hopes were mistaken and ultimately frustrated.

A less prominent but significant emphasis of *Jesus of Nazareth* is that Jesus, as the incarnate *Logos*, removes "the concrete political and social order" from "the directly sacred realm" (i.e., the specific requirements of the Torah) and transfers it to "the freedom of man" (118). This has the effect of "assigning reason its sphere of responsibility for acting within history" (126). For Ratzinger, this has two closely intertwined consequences: the exalting of human reason (though to be sure, not autonomous reason apart from God), and the refusal to identify Jesus with any particular political system or agenda. Ratzinger's Jesus stands apart from worldly politics. "Discipleship of Jesus offers no politically

3. The translation here follows Ratzinger's German text rather than standard English translations.

concrete program for structuring society" (114). Instead, the communion with God given by Jesus "frees men and nations . . . to work out their own juridical arrangements" (118). (Surprisingly, at this point Ratzinger finds himself in unlikely alliance with Garry Wills, a fierce critic of the papacy, whose recent book *What Jesus Meant* also insists that "Jesus had no political program."[4]) It is symptomatic that Ratzinger does not even comment on the fact that the Matthean version of the Lord's Prayer teaches the disciples to pray, "forgive us our *debts* as we forgive our *debtors*." Ratzinger treats this petition, without explanation, as a prayer about forgiveness of sins. There is a complex history of interpretation here, but the economic dimension of Jesus's teaching on prayer does not appear on Ratzinger's radar screen. Likewise, Luke's programmatic account of the beginning of Jesus's public proclamation in the synagogue at Nazareth (Luke 4:16–21)—in which he declares in Isaiah's words that the Spirit of the Lord has anointed him to proclaim good news to the poor and release to the captives—plays no structural role at all in this book. This is a striking omission.

In sum, Ratzinger's overall portrait of Jesus is strongly Johannine in character: grounded in high christological claims that Jesus was one with God, claiming a universalism that breaks the boundaries of Judaism, proclaiming a realized eschatology, and sketching a Jesus whose kingdom is not of this world (cf. John 18:36), whose teaching contains minimal social ethics. To Ratzinger's credit, he makes a serious case that these emphases are not confined to John's Gospel but can be found in the Synoptic Gospels as well. For example, on Ratzinger's reading, the Sermon on the Mount, with its strong implicit claim of Jesus's sovereignty over the Torah and its simultaneous summons to poverty and humility, contains "a hidden Christology" (99) that also comports with the Pauline message of Christ's *kenōsis* and descent to the cross. The arguments adduced are both interesting and complex, but the fact remains that it is the Gospel of John that imparts the fundamental shape to Ratzinger's portrayal of Jesus. The other New Testament texts are read selectively for corroborative testimony of this basically Johannine account.

Criticism

A book this ambitious inevitably makes controversial claims and invites critical discussion. I can only briefly enumerate some of the points where it seems

4. Garry Wills, *What Jesus Meant* (New York: Viking, 2006), 51.

to me that Ratzinger has either neglected important questions, left matters unclear, or chosen a path that seems methodologically problematical.

First, despite an emphatic endorsement of the historical-critical method (xv) and a robust insistence that the doctrine of incarnation requires faith to be based on historical truth, Ratzinger is appropriately aware of the limitations of historical knowledge. The resulting ambivalence about "history" runs like a fault line through the whole book. On the one hand, Ratzinger seems generally content to allow New Testament critics to operate within the field of history as usually conceived, and he readily acknowledges that the claim of Jesus's divinity "exceeds the scope of the historical method." On the other hand, he wants to "take this conviction of faith as our starting point for reading the texts with the help of historical methodology" (xxiii). But many historical critics would protest that such a starting point gravely compromises historical methodology. The total portrait of Jesus that Ratzinger draws stands in serious tension with the findings of historical criticism as conventionally practiced. I am sympathetic with many of his readings, but surely if "the aim unequivocally is not . . . to give up serious engagement with history," he owes us a more careful explanation of how he proposes to reconceive the practice of historical criticism to allow for the historical claims he wants to make.

This problem appears acutely in Ratzinger's very grudging and uneven acknowledgement of any historical distance between Jesus of Nazareth and the narrative representations of him in our canonical Gospels. To take a single example, Ratzinger cites Matt 5:17–18 as proof that "Jesus has no intention of abrogating the Ten Commandments" (71). That statement is certainly true of *Matthew*, the narrator of this account. But whether this passage in the Sermon on the Mount can be taken without further discussion as a reliable report of Jesus's views is a more complicated problem. Ratzinger tends to brush such complexities aside, even in the far more difficult case of the "I am" discourses in the Fourth Gospel.

Because of Ratzinger's pervasive tendency to treat the texts as transparent to the historical facts about Jesus, he also fails to be sufficiently attentive to the individual narrative shape and content of the four distinct witnesses of the canonical evangelists. Time and again he will dutifully note these differences but then brush them aside as inconsequential. To cite a single example, he quotes the differing versions of the "sign of Jonah" saying in Matthew and Luke, but then says blithely, without further explanation: "We do not need to analyze the differences between these two versions" (217). Why not? Surely it would make some difference to our historical picture of Jesus whether he used the Jonah story to predict his own resurrection after three days (Matthew) or whether he read the story as a typological precedent for his own prophetic mission of calling people to repentance (Luke). Each version of the saying resonates with theological concerns of the Gospel in which it appears. But reflection on such distinctions too rarely appears in Ratzinger's harmonizing readings of the texts.

Ratzinger's uneven attention to the theological and literary contours of the individual Gospels is perhaps just one manifestation of the fact that his critical dialogue partners in New Testament exegesis are, for the most part, the great scholars of earlier generations: Jeremias, Dodd, Bultmann, Schnackenburg, Barrett. There are exceptions: for example, Joachim Gnilka's commentary on Matthew and Pierre Grelot's *Les Paroles de Jésus Christ*, both published in the 1980s, are cited frequently.[5] But for the most part his definition of critical issues seems to be set by the problems of earlier generations. Bultmann's hypothesis of gnostic sources for John, already mentioned above, is a good example: this theory has more or less fallen into the dustbin of New Testament criticism, but Ratzinger still feels the need to refute it. At the same time, however, his work does not seem to be informed at all by the more recent and now much more influential work of great Catholic scholars such as Raymond Brown and John Meier. It is perhaps not surprising that an eighty-year-old scholar would continue to focus on the categories and questions that were current in the German academy during the era of his own training and more active scholarly career. But it is regrettable that he did not avail himself of a research assistant who could help him bring his discussion up to date. His dismissive discussion of Jesus as an apocalyptic teacher would profit greatly from engagement with the work of scholars such as E. P. Sanders and Dale Allison. And it would be fascinating to know what Ratzinger would think of the work of N. T. Wright, whose books on Jesus have become widely influential in the English-speaking world. But none of these figures appears even in Ratzinger's bibliography.

The deemphasis on apocalyptic elements in Jesus's thought is one particularly unfortunate feature of Ratzinger's account. A more resolutely historical approach would situate Jesus firmly in the apocalyptically oriented Judaism of his day. Such a finding hardly compels us to follow Schweitzer's conclusion that Jesus was deluded and disappointed, but it does require us to take seriously Jesus's identification with—and redefinition of—Israel's national hope, his formation of a countercultural Israel symbolized by the Twelve, and his

5. Joachim Gnilka, *Das Matthäusevangelium*, vol. 1: *Kommentar zu Kap 1,1–13,58*, 2nd ed., HThKNT 1/1 (Freiburg: Herder, 1986); Pierre Grelot, *Les Paroles de Jésus Christ* (Paris: Desclee, 1986).

orientation toward future eschatological judgment and vindication in the resurrection of the dead. Such motifs remain disappointingly peripheral in Ratzinger's treatment.

Equally disappointing is Ratzinger's skirting of the problem of the apparently anti-Jewish perspective in John's Gospel. Much recent scholarship has contextualized this Gospel's hostility toward "the Jews" in a historical setting later than the time of Jesus, after the "parting of the ways" between Judaism and emergent Christianity. Because Ratzinger insists, on the contrary, on reading the Johannine discourse material as historical reminiscence of what Jesus really said and taught, he is left with a Jesus who tells "the Jews" that their father is the devil (John 8:44). As far as I can see, Ratzinger never discusses this problem. But the issue cries out for attention in light of his privileging of the Johannine portrait of Jesus's identity.

Finally, one occasionally stumbles over glaring exegetical errors, such as the passing statement that Paul's Letter to the Galatians was written to *Jewish* Christians (100). (The letter was, on the contrary, written to *gentile* converts who were being pressured to adopt circumcision and Jewish customs.) One might have hoped that Ratzinger would be in a position to avail himself of better proofreaders to spare him such embarrassing mistakes.

Conclusion

This list of criticisms, however, should not be taken as a dismissal of the book's argument as a whole. I want to conclude by noting some of the impressive positive contributions of Ratzinger's devout and passionate rendering of the identity of Jesus.

First, apart from the vexing questions about the relation between history and faith, Ratzinger's synthetic theological reading of the canonical New Testament witnesses is both subtle and illuminating. It is indeed true that the Jesus of the Synoptics—the one who is Lord of the Sabbath and who teaches with an authority that transcends that of the scribes—is much more than a simple Galilean prophet. There are indeed intriguing links between the synoptic Christologies and the more overt high Christology of John. Ratzinger spots these links with a discerning eye and forces the reader to think seriously about them. He rightly shows that the messianic *Jubelruf* ("joyful shout") of Matt 11:25–27//Luke 10:21–22 is not, as often supposed, an incongruous intrusion into the Synoptic narratives; rather, it articulates an understanding of

Jesus's Sonship that is entirely consonant with other features of the narratives in which it appears.

Second, from beginning to end Ratzinger grounds his interpretation of Jesus in the Old Testament as well as the New. The significance of the Gospel stories is consistently explicated in relation to the Old Testament's typological prefiguration of Jesus, and Jesus is shown to be the flowering or consummation of all that God had promised Israel in many and various ways. The resulting intracanonical conversation offers many arresting insights into Jesus's identity and significance. Many of the connections that Ratzinger discerns are traditional in patristic exegesis, rather than original, but his explication of them is artful and effective. The church needs much more of this kind of reading.

Third, closely correlated with the constructive use of the Old Testament in Christology is Ratzinger's sympathetic appropriation of patristic exegesis more generally. Rather than ignoring the fathers or using them as foils for the allegedly more reliable interpretations of modernity, Ratzinger draws them into the conversation as wise and illuminating commentators on the figure of Jesus in the Gospels. Thus, he provides a fine model for the integrative appropriation of the church's tradition in the reading of Scripture.

Finally, the book is full of luminous passages that offer a fruitful basis for meditation on the mysterious and gracious figure of Jesus. If one focuses on these sections of the book, it must be judged a great success. This book is the distillation of the wisdom of one who has lived long in prayer and reflected deeply on Jesus's unity with the Father. From this, there is much spiritual benefit to be gained and much to be learned.

But if Ratzinger intends his work to be taken seriously as *history*, his second volume will need to set forth more clearly how the practice of history-writing should be done in the new world revealed by incarnation, cross, and resurrection. If he does that, it will become more evident that his account of the historical Jesus poses a frontal challenge, not a modest amendment, to the assumptions and methods of post-Enlightenment historiography.

8

A Modest Sketch of Jesus of Nazareth

Why Not Begin with Jesus?

Books on NT ethics often begin with an extensive treatment of the ethical teachings of Jesus. Wolfgang Schrage's *The Ethics of the New Testament*, for example, devotes more than one hundred pages to a discussion of "Jesus' Eschatological Ethics," before turning to a brief sketch (twenty-five pages) of "Ethical Accents in the Synoptic Gospels."[1] In such a presentation, the focus of interest lies on Schrage's historical reconstruction of the figure of Jesus, while the Gospel writers are treated as editors who make slight adjustments to a received body of historical tradition. In the present book, I have placed much less emphasis on the historical Jesus and much more on the ethical perspectives of the individual evangelists. A word of explanation for this methodological decision is perhaps in order. Why not begin with a reconstruction of the ethics of the historical figure Jesus of Nazareth?

First of all, I reiterate that the purpose of this book is not to trace the history of early Christian ethics. A study intending to present the historical background and development of Christian ethics would, to be sure, have to begin with some account—however sketchy—of the ethics of Jesus. But that is a different matter from the aim of this book: to reflect on how the church's life should be shaped by the NT witnesses.

Second, despite the apparent objectivity of beginning with an appeal to the

1. Wolfgang Schrage, *The Ethics of the New Testament*, trans. David E. Green (Philadelphia: Fortress, 1988 [1982]). See also Allen Verhey, *The Great Reversal: Ethics and the New Testament* (Grand Rapids: Eerdmans, 1984).

This essay, originally entitled "Excursus: The Role of 'the Historical Jesus' in New Testament Ethics," is excerpted from my book *The Moral Vision of the New Testament: Community, Cross, New Creation* (San Francisco: HarperSanFrancisco, 1996), 158–66.

"historical," the history of NT research demonstrates that efforts to reconstruct the historical Jesus have been beset by subjectivity and cultural bias. Albert Schweitzer's classic study *The Quest of the Historical Jesus* amply documented this difficulty in nineteenth-century "life of Jesus" research,[2] and the problem continues unabated in the present renewed outpouring of studies of the historical Jesus.[3] The temptation to project upon the figure of Jesus our own notions of the ideal religious personality is nearly irresistible.[4] As Martin Kähler sagely observed almost one hundred years ago, the critic who reconstructs a "historical Jesus" inevitably becomes a "fifth evangelist," cutting and pasting the tradition so as to articulate a new vision of Jesus for his or her own time.[5] Sometimes this outcome of historical inquiry is explicitly embraced, as in the programmatic comments of Robert Funk, the founder of the "Jesus Seminar":

> We are having increasing difficulty these days in accepting the biblical account of the creation and of the apocalyptic conclusion in anything like a literal sense. . . . But our crisis goes beyond these terminal points: it affects the middle as well. . . . To put the matter bluntly, we are having as much trouble with the middle—the messiah—as we are with the terminal points. What we need is a new fiction that takes as its starting point the central event in the Judeo-Christian drama. . . . In sum, we need a new narrative of Jesus, a new gospel, if you will, that places Jesus differently in the grand scheme, the epic story.[6]

Funk's remarks clearly acknowledge a point not always stated with such candor: the act of historical reconstruction is necessarily a hermeneutical en-

2. Albert Schweitzer, *The Quest of the Historical Jesus*, trans. W. Montgomery (New York: Macmillan, 1968 [1906]).

3. See, for example, Luke Timothy Johnson's evaluation of John Dominic Crossan's exhaustive study, *The Historical Jesus: The Life of a Mediterranean Jewish Peasant* (San Francisco: HarperSanFrancisco, 1991): "Perhaps after all these authors [Crossan and John P. Meier] have not escaped the tendencies so acutely described by Schweitzer. Does not Crossan's picture of a peasant cynic preaching inclusiveness and equality fit perfectly the idealized ethos of the late twentieth-century academic?" ("A Marginal Mediterranean Jewish Peasant," *Commonweal* 119 [1992]: 26).

4. For a broad account of different images of Jesus as mirrors of general cultural history from the first century to the present, see Jaroslav Pelikan, *Jesus through the Centuries: His Place in the History of Culture* (New Haven: Yale University Press, 1985).

5. Martin Kähler, *The So-Called Historical Jesus and the Historic Biblical Christ*, trans. Carl E. Braaten (Philadelphia: Fortress, 1964 [1896]).

6. Robert W. Funk, "The Issue of Jesus," *Forum* 1.1 (1985): 5–6.

deavor. Insofar as the historian rejects the interpretive frameworks of the Gospel writers, some other framework must be provided. This is not necessarily a bad thing, but the recognition of this point does undercut one of the principal arguments for beginning the study of NT ethics with the historical Jesus: to do so is not to attain some greater degree of objectivity or factual security. It would be a curious act of intellectual hubris to suppose that our speculative reconstruction could give us a picture of Jesus immune to the vicissitudes of subjectivity.

In fact, we have a better chance of holding our own predispositions in abeyance—and thus allowing our communities to be shaped by Scripture—if we follow the procedure adopted in this book of treating each Gospel individually and attending to its narrative logic, its representation of the figure of Jesus, and its consequent moral world. Because each Gospel has a determinate structure and content, the interpretive imagination is given a set of constraints that guide and limit the range of viable readings. This range is narrower than the range of possible critical reconstructions of Jesus. Thus, we are more likely to reach consensus about literary and theological readings of the individual Gospel texts than about the historical figure who stands behind them all. The evidence for this claim may be found in the scholarly secondary literature; there is a far higher degree of agreement about, say, the theology of Matthew than about the content of the teaching of the Jesus of history. Of course, this is not to say that the Gospels are "foolproof" compositions[7] or that each Gospel has a univocal meaning. Debates still rage about various points, such as Luke's attitude toward Judaism. Mark is a more ambiguous text than the other three Gospels, offering less narrative closure and therefore inviting a greater diversity of interpretations. Nonetheless, it makes sense to claim modestly that NT ethics will find a more stable starting place if we begin with the moral visions of the individual texts than if we try to begin by reconstructing Jesus.

That is one of the reasons that Rudolf Bultmann opined that the preaching of Jesus belongs not to the theology of the NT but to its presuppositions.[8] Jesus is, after all, not one of the NT writers. His life and death constitute the subject matter for the NT's narration and reflection, but if the aim of our inquiry is the ethics of the NT, the ethical teaching of the historical Jesus will enter the picture only indirectly, as it is filtered through the compositional purposes

7. As Meir Sternberg (*The Poetics of Biblical Narrative: Ideological Literature and the Drama of Reading* [Bloomington: University of Indiana Press, 1985], 48–56, 230–35) claims for the Hebrew Bible.

8. Rudolf Bultmann, *Theology of the New Testament*, vol. 1, trans. Kendrick Grobel (New York: Scribner, 1951 [1948]), 3.

of the evangelists. The theological function of the NT canon is to designate precisely these interpretations of Jesus as authoritative for the continuing life and practice of the community. Therefore, the historian's reimagining of Jesus, however informative and interesting, can never claim the same normative theological status as the four diverse canonical accounts. Consequently, in a work (such as the present one) that aims to read the NT as normative for the church's ethical reflection, it makes more sense to stay with the texts and to interpret the moral visions that confront us there, in the Jesus rendered by the four individual evangelists.

Having said all that, however, it must be acknowledged that the question about the Jesus of history will not go away, because the question of truth looms. If the canonical accounts of Jesus were in fundamental conflict with what actually happened, if they were sheer fabrications of religious fanaticism or wishful thinking,[9] then Christians would be, in Paul's words, of all people most to be pitied. If the NT writers based their moral visions on a distorted or fundamentally mistaken view of what Jesus of Nazareth actually did and taught, then the church's subsequent reliance on these texts would be misplaced. Historical inquiry can never prove the truth of the kerygma, but historical inquiry might *disconfirm* it; consequently, intellectual integrity demands some investigation of what can be known historically about Jesus, even if our historical knowledge is subject to serious limitations. As Ernst Käsemann formulated the problem, the Jesus of history must ultimately serve as a criterion against which the NT's diverse formulations of the kerygma must be measured; otherwise, we are in danger of "falling into docetism and depriving ourselves of the possibility of drawing a line between the Easter faith of the community and myth."[10] By pressing the question about the Jesus of history, we seek to avoid falling into an enthusiastic religious subjectivity that ignores the question of what God has done *extra nos* in the world.

It is far beyond the scope of the present book to undertake a full treatment of the problem of the historical Jesus. Nonetheless, it is perhaps not a gratuitous gesture for me to give a brief account of the general outlines of

9. As claimed, for example, by Burton Mack (*A Myth of Innocence: Mark and Christian Origins* [Philadelphia: Fortress, 1988]).

10. Ernst Käsemann, *Essays on New Testament Themes*, trans. W. J. Montague, SBT 41 (London: SCM, 1964 [1960]), 34; see also Käsemann, *New Testament Questions of Today*, trans. W. J. Montague and W. F. Bunge (Philadelphia: Fortress, 1969 [1965]), 23–65. For an exposition of Käsemann's views on this topic, see Bernhard Ehler, *Die Herrschaft des Gekreuzigten: Ernst Käsemann Frage nach die Mitte der Schrift*, BZNW 46 (Berlin and New York: de Gruyter, 1986), 161–273.

my understanding of Jesus, especially since much attention has been given in the popular press to revisionist representations of Jesus as an itinerant Cynic philosopher specializing in aphoristic wisdom sayings. The Jesus portrayed in the findings of the Jesus Seminar is indeed far removed from the Jesus depicted by Matthew, Mark, Luke, and John.[11] The following sketch will display my own assessment of the evidence, pointing to a historical figure who might reasonably stand behind the canonical traditions.

Methods for the Quest

What methods should be followed in assessing the historical value of the traditions about Jesus that are available to us? The following list of methodological guidelines indicates the procedures that I think appropriate in seeking to reconstruct the Jesus of history. Although I cannot defend in detail here my reasons for adopting these guidelines, they offer the reader some basis for understanding and evaluating the conclusions that follow.[12]

- Jesus must be located organically within first-century Palestinian Judaism. He neither rejected nor sought to supersede the faith of his people Israel.
- Jesus's life and teaching stand in some relation of continuity with the movement that he initiated—that is, the church.[13] (The effect of these first two guidelines is to counteract the "criterion of dissimilarity," which decrees that we can be most confident of the authenticity of the tradition when it represents Jesus as standing out of sync with first-century Judaism and with emergent Christianity.)
- A reconstructed narrative account of Jesus's life must yield some plau-

11. For my critique of the Jesus Seminar, see Richard B. Hays, "The Corrected Jesus," *First Things* 43 (1994): 43–48 (chapter 5 in the present volume). See also Ben Witherington III, *The Jesus Quest: The Third Search for the Jew of Nazareth* (Downers Grove, IL: IVP Academic, 1995), 42–57; and Luke Timothy Johnson, *The Real Jesus: The Misguided Quest for the Historical Jesus and the Truth of the Traditional Gospels* (San Francisco: HarperSanFrancisco, 1996).

12. Readers conversant with the literature in the field will recognize that my approach to method has been significantly shaped by Nils Alstrup Dahl, *Jesus in the Memory of the Early Church* (Minneapolis: Augsburg, 1976); see also *Jesus the Christ: The Historical Origins of Christological Doctrine* (Minneapolis: Fortress, 1991); E. P. Sanders, *Jesus and Judaism* (Philadelphia: Fortress, 1985); and Sanders, *The Historical Figure of Jesus* (London: Allen Lane, 1993).

13. Dahl, *Jesus the Christ*, 81–111.

sibly continuous picture of how Jesus's activity and fate led, within the social and religious world of ancient Judaism, to the formation of the church. How did events move from *a* to *b*? What is necessary to account for the development?[14]

- The reconstruction must pose some plausible explanation for the relation between Jesus's life and teaching, on the one hand, and his death, on the other.[15] Why did Jesus die on a cross? And how could his death have been interpreted at such an early date as having redemptive efficacy?
- The sayings traditions must not be weighed more heavily than the historical narrative materials. Both are essential to a coherent picture of Jesus.[16]
- The Gospel of John should not be dismissed in principle as a historical source, despite its heavily theological agenda. All four Gospels, after all, are theological. The Fourth Gospel claims to be based on eyewitness testimony. Even though John is more difficult to use with confidence as a historical source, its claims should not be dismissed out of hand.
- The Gospel of Thomas is a second-century gnostic text. Though it may contain some independently transmitted traditions of Jesus's sayings, it is demonstrably dependent upon the synoptic tradition,[17] and it is therefore of secondary value as a historical source. Similarly, the Gospel of Peter, alleged by some to contain tradition older than the synoptic passion narratives,[18] is a second-century text derived loosely from the synoptic accounts; it has little or no independent historical value.[19]

14. See John K. Riches, *Jesus and the Transformation of Judaism* (New York: Seabury, 1982); and A. E. Harvey, *Jesus and the Constraints of History* (Philadelphia: Westminster, 1982).

15. Dahl, *Jesus the Christ*, 98–99; Sanders, *Jesus and Judaism*, 22.

16. E. P. Sanders (*Jesus and Judaism*) gives priority to narrative materials about events in Jesus's career. This is a helpful corrective to the prevailing tendencies of previous research. I would insist, however, that the significance of the events can hardly be understood apart from the sayings traditions.

17. Christopher M. Tuckett, "Thomas and the Synoptics," *NovT* 30 (1988): 132–57; N. T. Wright, *The New Testament and the People of God*, Christian Origins and the Question of God 1 (London: SPCK; Minneapolis: Fortress, 1992), 440–43; Mark Goodacre, *Thomas and the Gospels: The Case for Thomas' Familiarity with the Synoptics* (Grand Rapids: Eerdmans, 2012); Simon Gathercole, *The Composition of the Gospel of Thomas: Original Language and Influences* (Cambridge: Cambridge University Press, 2012).

18. See, e.g., John Dominic Crossan, *The Cross That Spoke: The Origins of the Passion Narrative* (San Francisco: Harper & Row, 1988).

19. Raymond E. Brown, "The Gospel of Peter and Canonical Gospel Priority," *NTS* 33 (1987): 321–43; see also, *The Death of the Messiah: From Gethsemane to the Grave*, 2 vols. (New York: Doubleday, 1994), 1317–49.

- The burden of proof lies upon claims concerning the inauthenticity of material in the Gospel tradition, not upon claims for authenticity. The criteria of multiple attestation and coherence are far more important than the criterion of dissimilarity, which is useful primarily for targeting points of maximum historical probability.
- Wisdom lies in humility. Claims to historical knowledge should not transgress the constraints of modesty. We know less than we are fond of supposing.[20]

The Life and Teachings of Jesus: A Proposed Reconstruction

(1) *The center.* Jesus was a Jew from Nazareth in Galilee who was put to death in approximately 30 CE by the Roman governor Pontius Pilate on a charge of insurrection.

That is the center, the fixed datum and reference point from which our reconstruction must proceed. Beyond this, all our other remarks will possess decreasing certainty. I do not believe that we can reconstruct the sequence of events in Jesus's public career. We know the beginning (his baptism by John) and the end (his crucifixion), and we have a drawerful of snapshots that go somewhere in the middle, but we cannot confidently reconstruct a dramatic development. The one event that can be placed with some confidence is his demonstration in the temple against the moneychangers and sellers of animals. Presumably, this temple incident was the precipitating factor in his arrest and execution.[21]

(2) *Jesus's background.* Jesus came from Galilee. This is in itself a significant fact, for it indicates that his roots were in a region that was marginal in relation to the established religious and political centers of power in Judaism.[22] About

20. Thus, I am less confident than Ben Witherington (*The Christology of Jesus* [Minneapolis: Fortress, 1990]) that we can gain access, as historians, to Jesus's self-understanding. See Luke Timothy Johnson, *The Real Jesus: The Misguided Quest for the Historical Jesus and the Truth of the Traditional Gospels* (San Francisco: HarperSanFrancisco, 1996), 81–104.

21. Sanders, *Jesus and Judaism*, 61–76.

22. John P. Meier (*A Marginal Jew: Rethinking the Historical Jesus*, vol. 1: *The Roots of the Problem and the Person*, ABRL [New York: Doubleday, 1991]), who emphasizes the marginality of Jesus, writes, "Jesus, the poor layman turned prophet and teacher, the religious figure from rural Galilee without credentials, met his death in Jerusalem at least in part because of his clash with the rich aristocratic urban priesthood. To the latter, a poor layman from the Galilean countryside with disturbing doctrines and claims was marginal both in the sense of being dangerously antiestablishment and in the sense of lacking a power base in the capital. He could be easily brushed aside into the dust bin of death" (9).

his early life we know almost nothing. Tradition says that he was an artisan or the son of an artisan (Mark 6:3; Matt 13:55). He seems to have studied the Scriptures deeply, but this does not necessarily imply formal training as a rabbi. We can trace his public career from his baptism by John the Baptist, an event that the Gospels retain in memory despite a certain embarrassment about it (e.g., Matt 3:13–15). It is possible, but not certain, that Jesus may have been, prior to his baptism, a disciple of John. This would mean that he would have held an apocalyptic expectation of the coming of God's messiah to establish the rule of God's righteousness (i.e., the kingdom of God).

(3) *Jesus's movement*. Jesus soon struck out on his own and became a controversial public figure, a man who was widely perceived as a prophet mighty in word and deed. He assembled a group of disciples around himself and taught them. He singled out twelve of them as symbolic heads of the new eschatological Israel, which he proclaimed and hoped to bring into being. This symbolic act is a clear sign that he understood his movement in terms of "restorationist eschatology"; in other words, he was anticipating that God would act to restore Israel to its lost glory.[23]

Jesus also attracted a large following among the fringe and outcast groups in Palestinian society.[24] Sinners and tax collectors, cripples, lepers, prostitutes—all the folks who were disdained by educated citizens with taste and theological education: this was the constituency of the Jesus movement. (One thinks of the characters in Flannery O'Connor's short stories.) Part of his appeal for these groups derived from his reputation as a healer and miracle worker. I think that we should credit the historical truth of this picture.[25] Even where the Gospels show some discomfort with this portrayal of Jesus, it is never denied, only qualified so that he is seen as a reluctant miracle worker who intends his healings to point to a truth that continues to elude the popular perception.

(4) *Jesus's message*. Jesus spoke characteristically in parables and stories that declared the imminent bursting in of God's kingdom, bringing grace and mercy in unexpected ways in unexpected places. (Interestingly, Jesus's mode of parabolic discourse was generally not emulated in the early Christian tradition.) The parables of the coming kingdom must be taken closely together with his warnings of apocalyptic judgment: he preached that the kingdom of God would bring the radical restoration of God's justice, setting things right but bringing judgment and destruction on those who resist God's will. The

23. Sanders, *Jesus and Judaism*, 98–106.

24. Crossan, *Historical Jesus*.

25. Here again I find myself in agreement with Crossan, *Historical Jesus*, 303–53.

tendency in some recent NT scholarship to sever the message of grace from the message of judgment and to regard the latter as inauthentic is the natural—and misleading—consequence of isolating Jesus from the Jewish prophetic tradition within which all his words and actions must be understood.

Jesus's message was controversial and threatening to the established institutions of religious and political power in his society: the message carried with it a fundamental transvaluation of values, an exalting of the humble and a critique of the mighty. The theme of *reversal* seems to have been pervasive in his thought. To "the chief priests and the elders of the people," for example, he declared: "the tax collectors and the prostitutes are going into the kingdom of God ahead of you" (that is, becoming adherents of the Jesus movement; Matt 21:31). This reversal motif is built into the deep structure of Jesus's message, present in all layers of the tradition; thus, the criterion of multiple attestation validates this theme as a foundational element of Jesus's teaching. We find it in *sayings*—for example, "Whoever would save his life will lose it, and whoever loses his life for my sake and the gospel's will save it" (Mark 8:35 RSV)—and in the Beatitudes, especially in the Lukan version (Luke 6:20–26), which is likely to be more original than Matthew's spiritualized account. We find it in *parables*: the prodigal son (Luke 15:11–32), the unjust steward (Luke 16:1–8). We find it in *controversy pronouncements*: for example, Matt 21:31, cited above. And, perhaps most tellingly, we find it in Jesus's *actions*, his association with the unclean and outcasts.

It is unlikely that Jesus proclaimed an abrogation or even a critique of the Law. His critique seems to have been directed instead at those who *professed* allegiance to the Law while ignoring its weightier demands, its fundamental thrust toward justice and mercy. In this respect, he stood squarely in the prophetic tradition. This is first and foremost the way in which the historical Jesus should be understood: he was a prophet in the tradition of the prophets of Israel, warning of God's judgment on Israel, calling Israel to repentance and acknowledgment of God's justice in human affairs.

It is likely that Jesus explicitly interpreted his own mission in terms of paradigms provided by Israel's prophetic texts. If he understood himself to be gathering eschatological Israel, surely he thought of this action in terms suggested by Isaiah (cf. Luke 7:18–23). If he pronounced a word of judgment on the temple when Israel refused his summons, he did so in terms that evoked echoes of Jeremiah's temple sermon (Mark 11:15–17; cf. Jer 7:1–15).

Jesus spurned violence as the appropriate instrument of God's righteousness (see Mark 10:42–45). He taught love of enemies and rejected any suggestion of armed resistance to authority, even Roman authority. This combination of nonresistance with his inflammatory critique of those in power inevitably finds its consequence in the cross. Thus, it is not improbable that Jesus came to understand his own vocation in terms of necessary suffering and death.

(5) *The response: violent rejection.* Jesus's activity and proclamation brought him squarely into conflict with the guardians of order in Jewish society. Whether it was Jesus's intention or not, his proclamation of the kingdom of God was inevitably heard as a revolutionary manifesto; the whole Gospel tradition is full of this. People wanted to make him king (John 6:15), and Peter's confession (Mark 8:29) means nothing other than this. It was this popular perception that finally proved his undoing: the inscription on the cross proves that he was executed as one who claimed to be "king of the Jews." And indeed, it would appear that he refused to get himself off the hook by denying the charge. Thus, we have a situation pregnant with ambiguity. The whole shape of the tradition indicates that Jesus—in contrast to other figures in Jewish history of the era, such as Bar Kochba—persistently refused to claim that he was the messiah (cf. John 10:24). His whole message entailed a rejection of the violence and nationalism implied in the popular understanding of that title. Yet his words and deeds incited in the people a vivid expectation that he might, after all, be the one who would deliver Israel. There is a deep irony here. One might almost see Jesus as a victim crushed between the jaws of opposing historical forces. He rejected the way of violent revolution and so disappointed the hopes of many of his own followers; but because he excited—perhaps contrary to his own intention—popular messianic hopes, he was executed by the authorities as a potential danger to the stability of the social order. The reasons for his demise may have been similar to those adduced by Josephus for the execution of John the Baptist:

> When others too joined the crowds about him, because they were aroused to the highest degree by his sermons, Herod became alarmed. Eloquence that had so great an effect on mankind might lead to some form of sedition, for it looked as if they would be guided by John in everything that they did. Herod decided therefore that it would be much better to strike first and be rid of him before his work led to an uprising, than to wait for an upheaval, get involved in a difficult situation and see his mistake.[26]

So Jesus also was executed as a revolutionary, or at least as a potential security threat—as indeed he was, though not in quite the sense the authorities feared.

(6) *God's answer: resurrection.* Shortly after Jesus's death, the same followers

26. Josephus, *Ant.* 18.118.

who had fled in terror when he was arrested began proclaiming that he had been raised from the dead and had appeared to them. They understood this as a vindication of his whole life and message, particularly of his status as God's anointed one, the Messiah. They also saw his resurrection as the proleptic realization of the final triumph of God's kingdom in history, the foreshadowing of the general resurrection of the dead: as lightning is to thunder, so Jesus's resurrection is to the consummation of all things. There were no independent witnesses to the disciples' claim outside the community, however—no "independent sightings." Jesus did not appear in the temple and chastise his opponents; he did not appear to Pilate or in Rome to Caesar.

Nonetheless, the resurrection, just as much as the other events of the story, must be assessed as a historical event. It is told as such in the narratives. Certainly, it is a mysterious event, but it is *not* presented as a vision, a dream, a theological inference, or an ineffable event in the hearts of those who loved him. It is told as another remarkable event within the narrative, as the bodily resurrection of the man Jesus, leaving the tomb empty, conversing with his disciples, showing them his hands and his feet, eating fish with them. This is the historical event that alone renders the development of the church historically explicable. This is the historical event in the light of which all our history must be interpreted anew.

With this conclusion, I part company with many NT scholars and theologians who think it inappropriate to describe the resurrection as a historical event.[27] One may readily concede that the historical factuality of the resurrection cannot be affirmed with the same level of confidence as the historical factuality of the crucifixion. All historical judgments can be made only with relative certainty, and the judgment that Jesus rose from the dead can be offered—from the historian's point of view—only with great caution. The character of the event itself hardly falls within ordinary categories of experience.[28]

27. For example, Günther Bornkamm, *Jesus of Nazareth*, trans. Irene McLuskey and Fraser McLuskey (New York: Harper & Row, 1960 [1956]), 180: "The event of Christ's resurrection from the dead, his life and his eternal reign, are things removed from historical scholarship. History cannot ascertain and establish conclusively the facts about them as it can with other events of the past. The last historical fact available to them is the Easter faith of the first disciples." For different assessments, more open (in varying degrees) to considering the resurrection as a historical event, see Wolfhart Pannenberg, *Jesus: God and Man*, trans. Lewis L. Wilkins and Duane A. Priebe (Philadelphia: Westminster, 1977 [1964]), 80–106; Luke Timothy Johnson, *The Writings of the New Testament: An Interpretation* (Minneapolis: Augsburg, 1986), 98–113; Sanders, *Jesus and Judaism*, 320; and Sanders, *Historical Figure of Jesus*, 276–81.

28. See the helpful discussion by Johnson, *Writings of the New Testament*, 98–113.

Still, something extraordinary happened shortly after Jesus's death that rallied the dispirited disciples and sent them out proclaiming to the world that Jesus had risen and had appeared to them. Reductive psychological explanations fail to do justice to the widespread testimony to this event within the original community and to the moral seriousness of the movement that resulted from it. The best explanation is to say that God did something beyond all power of human imagining by raising Jesus from the dead.

To make such a claim is to make an assertion that redefines reality.[29] If such an event has happened in history, then history is not a closed system of immanent causes and effects. God is powerfully at work in the world in ways that defy common sense, redeeming the creation from its bondage to necessity and decay. That is precisely what the early Christians believed and proclaimed:

> I pray that the God of our Lord Jesus Christ, the Father of glory, may give you a spirit of wisdom and revelation as you come to know him, so that, with the eyes of your heart enlightened, you may know what is the hope to which he has called you, what are the riches of his glorious inheritance among the saints, and what is the immeasurable greatness of his power for us who believe, according to the working of his great power. *God put this power to work in Christ when he raised him from the dead* and seated him at his right hand in the heavenly places, far above all rule and authority and power and dominion, and above every name that is named, not only in this age but also in the age to come. (Eph 1:17–21)

Implications for Christian Ethics

All of this has far-reaching implications for Christian ethics. If God really did raise Jesus from the dead, everything that Jesus taught and exemplified is vindicated by a God more powerful than death. He must therefore be seen as the bearer of the truth and the definitive paradigm for obedience to God. The NT writers seek in their own ways to develop the moral implications of this confession for the life of the community.

29. The epistemological—and therefore ethical—consequences of faith in the resurrection are far reaching. The topic is too massive to be examined here. One theologian who has seen the dimensions of the issue is Oliver O'Donovan (*Resurrection and Moral Order: An Outline for Evangelical Ethics*, rev. ed. [Grand Rapids: Eerdmans, 1994]).

The foregoing historical sketch of the figure of Jesus of Nazareth is fundamentally congruent with the witness of the evangelists, though each of them highlights different aspects and introduces other themes not included in this minimal historical reconstruction. We may summarize some of the motifs within the NT that would be highlighted if my historical account were read in counterpoint with the canonical witnesses:

- The continuity of the gospel with Israel's heritage would be highlighted. Jesus's activity pointed toward the creation of a restored Israel, proleptically figured in the community of his disciples. Insofar as the church seeks to maintain continuity of its life and witness with the historical Jesus, it must consciously ground its identity in the tradition of Israel and wrestle with the issues posed both by Israel's election and by Israel's unfaithfulness. The struggle with this tension was central to Jesus's career.
- The apocalyptic character of Jesus's preaching would remain determinative for the symbolic world of the Christian community. The historical reality of the resurrection validates both apocalyptic hope and apocalyptic critique of the status quo in a world alienated from its creator.
- The reversal of "normal" conceptions of status and power was central to the message of Jesus and would remain central for a community that carries on his legacy. The kingdom of God belongs to the poor, the outcasts, the weak, the children. Wherever the church becomes acclimated and deferential to conventional human authority that rests upon pride and coercion, it has lost continuity with the Jesus of history.
- Jesus's emphatic reaffirmation of the prophetic call for justice and mercy as the hallmarks of God's covenant people suggests that a community bearing his name ought to return again and again to the prophets to find its ethical bearings.
- Jesus's rejection of violence and his call to love the enemy would be given prominence in any ethic that looked to the historical Jesus for direction.
- Jesus of Nazareth died on a cross. Those who follow him can hardly expect better treatment from the world. Insofar as the community of faith follows the path of the Jesus of history, it should expect suffering as its lot.

As we have seen, each of these points is dramatized in one way or another by the canonical evangelists. Thus, in one sense, the reconstruction of the historical Jesus adds nothing new to NT ethics. If it adds anything at all, it is merely what Luke calls ἀσφάλεια, a confidence in the truth of the things about which we have been instructed by the storytellers who wrote the Gospels. They did not invent their portrayals of Jesus out of whole cloth; rather, they were assembling pieces already cut according to his pattern. For the church, it is perhaps important to know that the obedience of faith was lived out in history by the flesh-and-blood man Jesus, for his example teaches us that to trust in the power of God over history is not to trust in vain.

Part 3

PAUL

9

Christology

Paul's Story of God's Son

In the midst of a battle against the "superapostles" who were corrupting the faith of the fledgling church he had planted in Corinth, Paul blurts out this fearful complaint:

> But I am afraid that as the serpent deceived Eve by its cunning, your thoughts will be led astray from a sincere and pure devotion to Christ. For if someone comes and proclaims *another Jesus than the one we proclaimed*, or if you receive a different spirit from the one you received, or a different gospel from the one you accepted, you submit to it readily enough. (2 Cor 11:3–4)

Another Jesus?[1] Of course, Paul does not mean some other person altogether—say, Jesus Barabbas rather than Jesus of Nazareth. If the preaching of the superapostles involved a case of mistaken identity, their mistake lay not in identifying the wrong individual but in mischaracterizing Jesus. These other preachers were presenting an *account of Jesus* that Paul regarded as distorted. This in turn suggests that *Paul's own preaching must have included his own very*

1. It is a point of more than passing interest that Paul describes the battle in these terms, rather than saying, for example, "If someone comes and proclaims another doctrine of justification than the one we proclaimed . . ."

This essay was originally composed as a contribution to the Identity of Jesus Project, at the Center of Theological Inquiry, Princeton, NJ. This was an ongoing collaboration of scholars from the years 2003 to 2006. My paper was presented there, discussed, and subsequently revised in light of the helpful engagements offered by colleagues from various theological subdisciplines, to whom I am grateful. Once again, thanks are due to Wallace Alston and Robert Jenson, the leaders of CTI, for their enthusiastic support and hospitality for this project.

specific account of the identity of Jesus, his own particular way of telling the Jesus story. What, then, was the character of Paul's Jesus?

From one point of view, Paul offers remarkably little information about Jesus.[2] If we had only Paul's letters as a source for knowledge about the man Jesus, here is what we would know:

> Jesus was born of a woman, "under the Law," that is, as a Jew (Gal 4:4). He was a descendant of Israel's great king, David (Rom 1:3). He had brothers, one of whom was named Jakobos ("James," Gal 1:19; 1 Cor 9:5). He forbade divorce (1 Cor 7:10–11), and he commanded that preachers of his message should receive financial support for their preaching (1 Cor 9:14). He instructed his followers to celebrate a communal meal in his memory (1 Cor 11:23–25). The wording of this tradition ("This cup is the new covenant in my blood") suggests that Jesus understood his impending death as a decisive event that would inaugurate a new chapter in the story of Israel's relation to God. Further, it suggests that he expected to meet a violent end, and he was right: he was crucified (1 Cor 2:2; Gal 3:1; Phil 2:8). Although crucifixion was a Roman punishment, some of Jesus's own Jewish countrymen opposed him and played a role in his violent death (1 Thess 2:14–15). He was buried; then, on the third day, he arose from the dead and appeared to many of his followers (1 Cor 15:3–8).[3]

In short, although the points of contact between Paul and the Gospels are significant, we get limited information from Paul about "the Jesus of history." He does not tell us that Jesus proclaimed the kingdom of God or that he taught in parables or that he performed healings and miracles or that he clashed with the Pharisees over interpretation of the Law. (The last of these points is a remarkable silence in light of Paul's own troubled deliberations about the Torah.) Still less do we gain from Paul any sense of Jesus's individual personal characteristics: was he solemn or fun loving, reclusive or extroverted? And what did he look like? Paul's silence on such matters is not surprising, since he was not a follower of Jesus during Jesus's earthly life; indeed, there is no

2. For surveys of the critical investigation of this problem, see Victor P. Furnish, *Jesus according to Paul* (Cambridge: Cambridge University Press, 1993); and David Wenham, *Paul: Follower of Jesus or Founder of Christianity?* (Grand Rapids: Eerdmans, 1995).

3. Occasionally, it is suggested that in a few other passages Paul may allude to specific sayings of Jesus (e.g., Rom 8:15–16; 12:17; 13:8; Gal 4:6; 5:14; 1 Thess 4:15–17), but Paul himself gives no indication that these passages are based on the authority of Jesus's teaching. The "word of the Lord" in 1 Thess 4:15 probably refers to a word of Christian prophecy.

reason to think that Paul ever met Jesus.[4] We might conclude from this brief survey of the matter that the Pauline Epistles have little to contribute to an exploration of the identity of Jesus.

Such a conclusion, however, would clash with one other salient fact: on virtually every page of his letters, Paul talks about Jesus. This fact has sometimes been obscured by the way that modernist biblical scholarship has organized information, separating out bits of "historical" data that correlate with the Gospels (as in the above sketch) from Paul's "Christology" with only the former regarded as significant for the Jesus quest. To be sure, the fragments of biographical information summarized above show that Paul's Jesus was a human historical figure of the first century CE, but the identity of Jesus, as Paul describes it, is a much wider reality. Jesus Christ, according to Paul, is the preexistent Son of God through whom all things exist; he freely took human form and surrendered himself to suffering and death for the sake of reconciling the world to God; by virtue of his resurrection he is exalted as Lord over the world, which he transforms and sustains with his life-giving power; and he will come again to judge the world and to bring about the final redemption of all things. To speak rightly of the identity of Jesus in Paul's letters, we must take this wider, cosmic frame of reference into account.

Thus, the distinction between "the Jesus of history" and "the Christ of faith" is misleading when applied to Paul's writings. For Paul, Jesus Christ is a single person whose identity is disclosed in a seamless narrative running from creation to the cross to the resurrection to the eschaton. The historical details of his earthly life, such as his death by crucifixion, are no more and no less a part of his identity than are his role in creation and his present lordship in the community of those who call upon his name.

The aim of the present essay, then, is to trace this narrative identity through the letters of Paul,[5] following its plotline as limned in the "Christ hymn" of

4. A statement in 2 Cor 5:16 has sometimes been understood to mean that Paul was personally acquainted with Jesus of Nazareth: "Even though we once knew Christ from a human point of view (κατὰ σάρκα; lit., "according to the flesh"), we know him no longer in that way." Paul's contrast, however, is not between knowledge of the human Jesus and of the divine Christ; rather, it is between the old, fleshly *way* of knowing and the new epistemological perspective given through God's apocalyptic act of new creation. See J. Louis Martyn, "Epistemology at the Turn of the Ages," in *Theological Issues in the Letters of Paul* (Nashville: Abingdon, 1997), 89–110.

5. For the purposes of this inquiry, I have surveyed not only the seven letters whose authorship is generally uncontested but also Colossians and 2 Thessalonians. The arguments against Pauline authorship of these letters are not in my judgment persuasive. I have not

Phil 2:5–11: preexistent glory, cruciform abasement, transformative exaltation, eschatological consummation. Wholly apart from the question of correspondence to the historical data given in the Gospels, what is the story of Jesus Christ told in the letters of Paul?[6]

Preexistent Glory

Jesus the Agent of Creation

Several passages in Paul's letters refer to Jesus's role in the creation of the world. The anchor point for this element of Jesus's identity is 1 Cor 8:6, perhaps a very early confessional formula: "For us there is one God, the Father, from whom are all things and for whom we exist, and one Lord, Jesus Christ, through whom are all things and through whom we exist." This formula is an adaptation of Israel's Shema (Deut 6:4–5), which proclaims the oneness of God as the heart of Israel's faith. By applying this language to Jesus Christ, Paul is describing him not as a second character alongside God but as (mysteriously) one with God, who brought the world into existence.[7]

As the active agent in creation, Jesus is also the bearer of divine glory, as, for example, in 2 Cor 4:6: "For it is the God who said, 'Let light shine out of darkness' (Gen 1:1–3), who has shone in our hearts to give the light of the knowledge of the glory of God in the face of Jesus Christ." Jesus manifests the divine glory because, in his preexistent state, "he was in the form of God" (Phil 2:6). These elements of preexistent glory and creative power are given their fullest development in Col 1:15–17, again perhaps part of an early confession or hymn:

> He is the image of the invisible God, the firstborn of all creation; for in him all things in heaven and on earth were created, things visible and invisible,

included Ephesians and the Pastoral Epistles, whose authorship seems to me to be more seriously in doubt.

6. Similar approaches have been taken by Leander E. Keck, "'Jesus' in Romans," *JBL* 108 (1989): 443–60; Stephen E. Fowl, *The Story of Christ in the Ethics of Paul: An Analysis of the Function of the Hymnic Material in the Pauline Corpus*, JSNTSup 36 (Sheffield: JSOT Press, 1990); and Douglas A. Campbell, "The Story of Jesus in Romans and Galatians," in *Narrative Dynamics in Paul: A Critical Assessment*, ed. Bruce W. Longenecker (Louisville: Westminster John Knox, 2002), 97–124.

7. N. T. Wright, *The Climax of the Covenant: Christ and the Law in Pauline Theology* (Edinburgh: T & T Clark, 1991), 120–36.

> whether thrones or dominions or rulers or powers—all things have been created through him and for him. He himself is before all things, and in him all things hold together.

These passages are strongly reminiscent of several earlier texts that speak of the role of divine Wisdom in creation (e.g., Prov 8:22–31; Wis 9:1–2, 9–10); this linkage suggests that Paul is ascribing to Jesus Christ attributes that earlier Jewish texts had associated with God's eternal creative wisdom.[8]

Closely linked to this aspect of Jesus's identity are Paul's startling declarations that Christ was the rock from which Israel drank in the wilderness (1 Cor 10:4; cf. Wis 11:4) and that the unfaithfulness of Israel's wilderness generation put Christ to the test (1 Cor 10:9).[9] Jesus Christ, who was before all things, was present in sustaining the people of Israel during the exodus, and their rebellion was therefore also in some sense against him.[10] For Paul, then, Jesus's identity is not limited to the lifespan of his activity as a Galilean prophet in Paul's own generation.

Jesus the Son of God

Paul often refers to Jesus as God's Son. The title has royal connotations, as in Ps 2:7, and this nuance is emphasized by Rom 1:3–4 (". . . his Son, who was descended from David according to the flesh and was declared to be Son of God with power according to the spirit of holiness by resurrection from the dead, Jesus Christ our Lord"). Jesus is David's heir, who is to reign not only over Israel but also over the gentiles (1:5), as Paul proclaims in the climactic peroration of Romans: "The root of Jesse shall come, the one who rises to rule the Gentiles; in him the Gentiles shall hope" (Rom 15:12). Indeed, the title Χριστός ("Christ"), often thought to have become for Paul merely a proper name, has by no means lost its messianic connotations, as hinted by several passages where he uses it with the definite article: "Welcome one another, therefore, just as ὁ Χριστός (lit., the Christ) has welcomed you" (Rom 15:7;

8. Note also the connection between Rom 10:6–7 and Bar 3:29–30.

9. The text-critical problem in 1 Cor 10:9 is difficult, but on balance Χριστόν ("Christ") seems to be the better reading than κύριον ("the Lord"). In view of Paul's characteristic use of κύριος to refer to Jesus Christ, the textual difference may not in any case be theologically significant.

10. Nowhere else does Paul so explicitly connect God's saving and revealing activity in Israel's past to the figure of Jesus, but this one passage may be the tip of a substantial christological iceberg.

cf. Rom 9:5; 15:3; 2 Cor 1:5; 2:14; Phil 1:15, 17; 3:7; Col 2:6; 3:1, 4).[11] Wherever in Paul's letters we read the name "Christ," the suggestion that he is the royal Son, Israel's expected King, is not far in the background.

More often, however, Paul's designation of Jesus as God's Son has another set of associations more prominently in view. The "sending" formulas in Gal 4:4–5 and Rom 8:3–4 portray Jesus as preexistent Son dispatched by the Father on an errand of rescue for a world held in bondage: "But when the fullness of time had come, God sent his Son, born of a woman, born under the law, in order to redeem those who were under the law, so that we might receive adoption as children" (Gal 4:4–5).[12] These formulas envision an apocalyptic scripting of human history and speak of God's Son as a preexistent agent commissioned to enter human existence for a redemptive mission.[13]

Further, that mission requires the Son's death: "He who did not spare his own Son, but gave him up for us all, will he not also give us all things with him?" (Rom 8:32 RSV). Here the Father-Son language suggests both the *love and intimacy* within the mysterious divine reality and, at the same time, the truth that the identity of the Son is distinctively expressed in the costly *sacrificial act of his death*. (We should hear in this an echo of Abraham's offering up of Isaac: "[you] have not withheld your son, your only son" [Gen 22:16]. The Akedah prefigures Jesus's death, as well as the blessing that his death offers to Abraham's seed.) Thus, the sacrifice of the Son is, from one point of view, the costly act of God the Father. Paul can also speak of it, however, as the Son's own act of loving self-offering: "the Son of God, who loved me and gave himself for me" (Gal 2:20). Consequently, the sending and death of the Son enact a mysterious fusion of agency between Father and Son. This is expressed most tellingly in the extraordinary claims of Rom 5: "But *God* proves his love for us in that while we still were sinners *Christ* died for us. . . . [W]hile we were enemies, we were reconciled to *God* through the death of *his Son*" (Rom 5:8, 10).

In such passages, the identity of Jesus is bound up inextricably with the

11. As a glance at the concordance will show, there are dozens of instances in which Paul uses some form of the definite article with Χριστός, but it is difficult to know how many should be taken as indicators of its titular force. The ones I have cited here are among those that would merit careful study.

12. James D. G. Dunn has questioned whether Paul thought of Christ as preexistent, but his treatment of these texts in his *Theology of Paul the Apostle* (Grand Rapids: Eerdmans, 1998), 277–79, is more measured than in his earlier *Christology in the Making: A New Testament Inquiry into the Origins of the Doctrine of the Incarnation*, 2nd ed. (London: SCM, 1989 [1980]).

13. Cf. John 3:16–17; 1 John 4:9–10, 14.

loving, sacrificial, saving activity of God. That is why Paul can assert that "in [Christ] the whole fullness of deity dwells bodily" (Col 2:9), with the result that "in Christ God was reconciling the world to himself" (2 Cor 5:19). The reference to Jesus as "Son of God" affirms his divine origin and identity, precisely as expressed in his sacrificial death.

Jesus Prefigured in Scripture

Although Paul, in contrast to Matthew, offers few explicit proofs showing that Jesus is the fulfillment of prophecy, he does at many points suggest that Scripture prefigures the identity of Jesus. Curiously, Paul's most explicit statement of this claim has been obscured by most modern English translations. Paul begins his letter to Rome with the following words: "Paul, a slave of Jesus Christ, called to be an apostle set apart for the gospel of God, which was pre-promised through the prophets *in holy writings concerning his Son*, who came from the seed of David according to the flesh . . ." (Rom 1:1–3, my translation).[14] Here is an explicit claim that the writings of the OT prophets spoke of God's Son, a claim reinforced at several places later in the letter, such as the statement that Israel was entrusted with "the oracles of God" (3:2);[15] the assertion that "the righteousness of God" is "attested by the law and the prophets" (3:21); and Paul's christological interpretations of Isaiah's stone of stumbling (9:33), Deuteronomy's word that is "near" the people (10:6–11), and Isaiah's Deliverer who "will banish ungodliness from Jacob" (11:26). Indeed, these passages illuminate the meaning of Paul's declaration in Rom 10:4 that Christ is τέλος νόμου: he is the goal toward which the Law points.[16] Most of all, Paul's belief that the OT prefigures Jesus is shown in the climactic chapter 15 of Romans, in Paul's christological reading of the Psalms (15:3, 9) and the prophecy of Isaiah about "the root of Jesse" (15:12).

Thus, for Paul, the identity of Jesus Christ is grounded in the ancient story of God's elect people Israel. His death and resurrection took place "in accor-

14. The NRSV reads the phrase περὶ τοῦ υἱοῦ αὐτοῦ as a modifier of εὐαγγέλιον θεοῦ, producing the translation "the gospel of God, which he promised beforehand through his prophets in the holy scriptures, *the gospel* concerning his Son . . ." This is a possible interpretation, but it is hardly the most natural reading of the Greek word order.

15. On "the oracles of God" as Paul's way of referring to Israel's Scripture in its role of mysteriously prefiguring Christ and the gospel, see Richard B. Hays, *The Conversion of the Imagination* (Grand Rapids: Eerdmans, 2005), 98–99.

16. See Richard B. Hays, *Echoes of Scripture in the Letters of Paul* (New Haven: Yale University Press, 1989), 75–77.

dance with the scriptures," as the confessional formula of 1 Cor 15:3–5 insists. This hermeneutical conviction has enormous implications for opening up new insights into the identity of Jesus: Paul believes that the reader for whom the veil is removed in Christ will see in Israel's Scripture "the glory of the Lord" and will be transformed into the image of Christ that appears there (2 Cor 3:12–18).[17]

Cruciform Abasement

Jesus the Self-Giving Servant

Paul appeals repeatedly to the *pattern* of Jesus's self-giving or self-emptying for the sake of others. This theme of Jesus's exemplary self-sacrifice plays a central role in Paul's pastoral admonitions (e.g., Rom 15:1–3, 7–9; 1 Cor 11:1 [cf. 8:11]; 2 Cor 8:9; 12:9–10; Gal 2:20; 6:2; Phil 2:5–11; 3:7–17; 1 Thess 1:6).[18] The most extended of these passages is Phil 2:5–11, where Christ is said to have emptied himself and become a slave, culminating in his death on the cross. For Paul, Christ's pattern of self-sacrificial emptying, or *kenōsis*, is a model that his followers are called to emulate: "Let each of you look not to your own interests, but to the interests of others. Let the same mind be in you that [*is*] in Christ Jesus" (Phil 2:4–5).[19] The humility (ταπεινοφροσύνη, 2:3) that is to characterize the community of the church reflects the character of Christ's own action: he humbled himself (ἐταπείνωσεν ἑαυτὸν, 2:8). This call to humility must have surprised Paul's first readers, for ancient popular philosophy was no more fond of lowliness and abasement than is political rhetoric in our own day. But Paul insists that the character of Jesus was shown forth in the cross and that his cruciform identity therefore provides a distinctive model to which the community must be conformed. Precisely in this way, "in the midst of a crooked and perverse generation," they will "shine like stars in the world" (Phil 2:15).

It is against this background that we should interpret a series of charac-

17. Hays, *Echoes of Scripture in the Letters of Paul*, 122–53.

18. On the expression ὁ νόμος τοῦ Χριστοῦ ("the law of Christ," Gal 6:2) as a designation for the pattern of Christ's burden bearing for others, see Richard B. Hays, "Christology and Ethics in Galatians: The Law of Christ," *CBQ* 49 (1987): 268–90; and David G. Horrell, *Solidarity and Difference: A Contemporary Reading of Paul's Ethics* (London: T & T Clark, 2005), 222–31.

19. On the "ethical" interpretation of the passage, and on supplying the present tense of the verb "to be" in v. 5, see Markus Bockmuehl, *The Epistle to the Philippians*, BNTC (London: A & C Black, 1997), 121–25.

ter qualities attributed to Christ that also set the moral tone for the Pauline churches: "the compassion of Christ Jesus" (Phil 1:8), "the love of Christ" (2 Cor 5:14; cf. Rom 8:35), "the meekness and gentleness of Christ" (2 Cor 10:1), "the steadfastness (ὑπομονή) of Christ" (2 Thess 3:5). Insofar as the community embodies these attributes, it faithfully *mirrors* the identity of Jesus to an otherwise uncomprehending world. It must always be remembered that for Paul it is Jesus's *death* in which these attributes are definitively disclosed (i.e., not in his attitude toward little children or his interpersonal sensitivity in discussion with his critics).[20]

Jesus the Paradigm of Faithfulness

In speaking of Jesus's death, we must also give careful attention to πίστις Ἰησοῦ Χριστοῦ: "the faith [or faithfulness] of Jesus Christ." Some variant of this formula appears seven times in Paul's letters (Rom 3:22, 26; Gal 2:16 [2x], 20; 3:22; Phil 3:9; see also Eph 3:12). While often translated as "faith *in* Jesus Christ," this Pauline expression refers not in the first instance to our act of "believing in" Christ but rather to Jesus Christ's gracious, self-sacrificial death on a cross. This death is simultaneously an act of human faithfulness, obedience to God "all the way to death" (Phil 2:8, my translation)—the obedience that Adam had failed to offer—and an act of divine faithfulness to the promises made to Israel. Christ's people participate in this "faith of Jesus Christ" in much the same way that they participate in the compassion or meekness of Christ: by being drawn into participation in him, they are conformed to the shape of his life. The faithfulness of Jesus is closely connected to his obedience (Rom 5:19). Yet because πίστις Χριστοῦ functions in a special way as a synecdoche for the saving event of the cross,[21] it points with particular emphasis to the climactic event in the life of "the Son of God, who loved me and gave himself for me" (Gal 2:20). The faithfulness of Jesus Christ in his death on the cross is the central *defining* act for his identity; it marks him as the singular, irreplaceable individual in whom God's will for the salvation of a faithless world is made effectual.[22]

20. We have already noted a very few passages in which Paul refers to Jesus as an authoritative teacher (1 Cor 7:10–11; 9:14), or as the initiator of traditions that are to be kept by his followers (1 Cor 11:23–26). Though these passages may seem to us exceedingly sparse, they are present in Paul and should be noted as part of his total account of Jesus's identity.

21. Campbell, "Story of Jesus in Romans and Galatians," 121.

22. See Richard B. Hays, *The Faith of Jesus Christ: The Narrative Substructure of Galatians 3:1–4:11*, 2nd ed., The Biblical Resource Series (Grand Rapids: Eerdmans, 2002 [1983]), xxi–lii.

Thus, for Paul, there is no right knowledge of the identity of Jesus apart from the cross. That is why he tells the Corinthians he "decided to know nothing among them except Jesus Christ, and him crucified" (1 Cor 2:2). Paul's struggles with rival preachers often turned precisely on this issue: the super-apostles in Corinth were preaching a powerful, glorious, rhetorically polished Jesus rather than a crucified Lord; the rival missionaries in Galatia sought to avoid persecution and to remove "the offense of the cross" by preaching circumcision (Gal 5:11; 6:12); and in Philippians, Paul derides his adversaries as "enemies of the cross of Christ" (Phil 3:18). Whether by precept or by example, these other early Christians were proclaiming "another Jesus" because they were not allowing the crucifixion to stand at the heart of their account of his identity. Paul, on the other hand, returns again and again to the cross as the touchstone of his interpretation of Jesus's identity (see, e.g., 1 Cor 1:23–24, 30; 2 Cor 13:4; Gal 3:1; 6:14; Phil 2:8; Col 1:20).[23]

Jesus the Agent of Redemption

Jesus's death not only exemplifies radical obedience but also brings about the redemption of the world. Paul declares that Jesus died "for our sake," but how are we to understand the logic of this claim? Paul's letters employ a kaleidoscopic diversity of metaphors to hint at the meaning of Jesus's death for the "weak," the "ungodly," and the "sinners" (Rom 5:6–8)—that is, for "all" (2 Cor 5:14–15).

One cluster of metaphors focuses on sacrificial and substitutionary images: God put Jesus forward as a propitiation (ἱλαστήριον, Rom 3:25), or as a sin offering (περὶ ἁμαρτίας, Rom 8:3). Closely connected to this field of images are Paul's assertions that Jesus became a curse for us (Gal 3:13), or that for our sake God "made him to be sin who knew no sin" (2 Cor 5:21). All these passages pose notorious exegetical challenges, but the common thread seems to be that Jesus's death is the death of a sacrificial victim who absorbs into himself the consequences of human sin so that his blood has an atoning effect. Wherever we find Paul writing that God "handed him over" (Rom 4:25; 8:32; 1 Cor 11:23)[24]

23. In this respect, Paul's message presents a stark alternative to accounts that offer us a Jesus conjured out of Q and the Gospel of Thomas, a Jesus who is a wisdom teacher and spinner of aphorisms, a Jesus without a cross.

24. In 1 Cor 11:23, the phrase sometimes translated "on the night when he was betrayed" reads literally "on the night when he was handed over (παρεδίδετο)." In light of the clear parallels in Rom 4:25 and 8:32, where the same verb appears, we should understand the traditional formula in 1 Cor 11:23 to refer not to Judas's act of betrayal but to God's "handing over" of Jesus to death. Beverly Roberts Gaventa has argued persuasively that this "handing over" language, beyond its sacrificial connotations, refers to God's surrender of his own Son

or that he died "for our sins" (e.g., Rom 4:25; 1 Cor 15:3; Gal 1:4; cf. Col 2:13–14; 1 Thess 5:10), we are within this metaphorical field.

The metaphor of Jesus as the paschal lamb, which appears only in 1 Cor 5:7, is not to be conflated with the notion of Jesus's death as atonement for sin. It adds another dimension of meaning by interpreting Jesus's death through "new exodus" imagery: it suggests both that God's work of liberating us from bondage has begun in Christ's death and that God's people must therefore, as in the Passover, "clean out the old leaven," which symbolizes the old life of impurity.

In other passages, Paul uses the metaphor of reconciliation. This language is drawn not from the imagery of the sacrificial cult but from the discourse of political negotiation.[25] Somehow, through Jesus's death, the alienation that previously separated warring parties has been overcome, and barriers have been broken down, not only between God and humanity (Rom 5:10–11; 2 Cor 5:18–20) but also between human beings who were previously at odds with one another (Rom 15:7–9).[26] Wherever we find Paul referring to "peace with God through our Lord Jesus Christ" (Rom 5:1) or the peacemaking function of the cross (Col 1:20), we see another facet of Jesus's identity, as the one who reconciles enemies through surrendering his own life.

Thus, through a variety of different metaphors, Paul portrays Jesus's death as the pivotal event in the salvation of the world. Jesus is the one who was given up (or gave himself up, as in Gal 1:4; 2:20) to bring about this mysterious redemptive outcome.

Transformative Exaltation

Jesus the Agent—and Firstfruits—of New Creation

Paul's proclamation of Christ crucified, however, is not the end of the story. As 1 Cor 15 declares, after his death and burial "he was raised on the third day

to "anti-god powers" in order paradoxically to defeat those powers and redeem humanity (see Gaventa, "God Handed Them Over: Reading Romans 1:18–32 Apocalyptically," *ABR* 53 [2005]: 42–53, esp. 52–53). On this reading, Rom 4:25 and 8:32, along with 1 Cor 11:23, should be understood in the context of God's cosmic apocalyptic triumph over the powers. (See also my comments on "Jesus the Triumphant Rescuer," below.)

25. Cilliers Breytenbach, *Versöhnung: Eine Studie zur paulinischen Soteriologie*, WMANT 60 (Neukirchen: Neukirchener Verlag, 1989).

26. This theme is given an especially rich ecclesiological development by the author of Ephesians (Eph 2:11–22).

in accordance with the scriptures," and he appeared to a chain of witnesses, culminating in Paul himself. This astounding turn in the story vindicates Jesus as "Son of God with power" (Rom 1:4). In this way, it discloses a new dimension of his identity: "For he was crucified in weakness, but lives by the power of God" (2 Cor 13:4). The resurrection, effected by God the Father (Gal 1:1; 1 Thess 1:10), reconfirms Jesus's relation to the Father, for he is now exalted to the right hand of God, where he intercedes for us (Rom 8:34).

The resurrection of Jesus also spills over into saving effects for the world. He was "raised for our justification" (Rom 4:25), and his resurrection is both the source and attestation of his life-giving power: "If the Spirit of him who raised Jesus from the dead dwells in you, he who raised Christ from the dead will give life to your mortal bodies also through his Spirit that dwells in you" (Rom 8:11; cf. 6:4–11). This effusion of life is not merely a secondary effect of the resurrection of Jesus; it is integral to his identity, for while "'the first man, Adam, became a living being' (Gen 2:7); the last Adam became a life-giving spirit" (1 Cor 15:45). Consequently, his identity cannot be understood apart from the company of those who are destined to share his resurrection (1 Thess 4:13–18): he is the "first fruits of those who have fallen asleep" (1 Cor 15:20–23), the "firstborn from the dead" (Col 1:18). To know who he is is to know him as the "firstborn within a large family," who will ultimately share in his glory (Rom 8:29–30).

For Paul, Jesus is the antitype of Adam: "For as all die in Adam, so all will be made alive in Christ" (1 Cor 15:22). He is (to borrow a term from Hebrews) the ἀρχηγός of a new humanity, the initiator and representative figure of a whole new creation brought into being through his obedient death and resurrection from the grave.

Jesus the Triumphant Rescuer

By virtue of his resurrection, Jesus is frequently portrayed by Paul as *Christus Victor*, as one who has come to "snatch us out of the grasp of the present evil age."[27] The metaphor of liberation sounds again and again through Paul's letters. Christ has set us free (Gal 5:1); we are no longer captive under the law (Gal 4:3–5; Col 2:14), no longer enslaved to the powers of sin and death (Rom 6:18; 7:25; 8:2), no longer separated from God by the principalities and powers (Rom 8:31–39). Even though the completion of this rescue operation

27. This is J. Louis Martyn's colorful translation of Gal 1:4 (Martyn, *Galatians*, AB 33A [New York: Doubleday, 1997], 81).

remains in the eschatological future (1 Thess 1:10; Rom 8:18–25; 11:25–27), the resurrection has assured Jesus's ultimate triumph so that Paul can already exclaim, "Thanks be to God, who gives us the victory through our Lord Jesus Christ" (1 Cor 15:57).

Jesus the Benefactor

With extraordinary frequency, Paul represents Jesus as the source of peace and blessing. This theme appears not only in Paul's characteristic salutations and benedictions, where we find various versions of the χάρις ("grace") formula (Rom 1:7; 16:20; 1 Cor 1:3; 16:23; 2 Cor 1:2; 13:13; Phlm 25; etc.), but also scattered profusely throughout the letters, in endless variation but always identifying Jesus as the giver of wonderful gifts and consolations. He is the source of the "free gift of righteousness" (Rom 5:17; 6:23) or "harvest of righteousness" (Phil 1:11), of "eternal life" (Rom 5:21), of "the blessing of Christ" (Rom 15:29), of "the peace of Christ" (Col 3:15; 2 Thess 3:16; cf. Rom 5:1), of the "yes" to all God's promises (2 Cor 1:19–20), of "redemption" (Rom 3:24–26), of "the grace of God" (1 Cor 1:4), of "encouragement" (Phil 2:1), of "eternal comfort and good hope" (2 Thess 2:16), and on and on. In short, Jesus is represented as the *benefactor and sustainer* of the community of faith, an inexhaustible fountain of grace.

Jesus the Kyrios

Jesus can be such a benefactor only because he is exalted to the right hand of God and now reigns "until he has put all his enemies under his feet" (1 Cor 15:25). As the Risen One, Jesus is now *Lord*; accordingly, κύριος ("Lord") is one of Paul's favorite titles for Jesus. The title signifies his sovereign authority. To confess him as "Lord" is at the heart of Christian practice (Rom 10:9; 1 Cor 12:3), and to make such a confession is a performative, self-involving act of submission to him. Consistent with this image of submission, Paul describes himself as the slave of Christ (Rom 1:1; Gal 1:10); he can also apply the metaphor (if it *is* a metaphor) to his fellow apostolic workers (Phil 1:1; Col 4:12) and to all who are called into Christ's service (1 Cor 7:22). That is why, Paul argues, Christians should not pass judgment on one another: they are all slaves of Christ and therefore accountable to no one other than their one true Master (Rom 14:4; cf.14:7–12; Col 3:22–4:1). As the Master, Jesus sends his slave Paul on whatever errands he chooses and works through him to spread the gospel (Rom 1:5; 15:18–19; 1 Cor 3:5; 4:1; Gal 1:16; 1 Thess 3:11). Yet it is precisely as

Christ's slave that Paul also receives the authorization that empowers his apostolic work (e.g., 1 Cor 4:1–5; 2 Cor 10:7–8; Gal 1:10–12).[28] Only for that reason can he make the extraordinarily bold claim that his mission is to "take every thought captive to obey Christ" (2 Cor 10:5).

The portrayal of Jesus as κύριος carries with it one further set of sweeping implications about Jesus's identity, for κύριος is the word characteristically used by the Septuagint to render the Tetragrammaton, the unutterable name of God. Paul can thus quote Old Testament passages that in their original context refer to the God of Israel and interpret them as references to the Lord Jesus Christ. The most striking instance of this is Phil 2:9–11, which declares that God highly exalted the crucified Jesus so that

> at the name of Jesus
> every knee should bend . . .
> and every tongue should confess
>   that Jesus Christ is κύριος,
>   to the glory of God the Father. (2:10–11)

The text echoes Isa 45:22–23, a relentlessly monotheistic text:

> Turn to me and be saved,
>   all the ends of the earth!
>   For I am God, and there is no other.
> By myself I have sworn,
>   from my mouth has gone forth in righteousness
>   a word that shall not return:
> "To me every knee shall bow,
>   every tongue shall swear."

Thus, according to Phil 2:9–11, the obedient submission that was to be rendered to God alone is now to be directed to Jesus Christ. Similarly, Paul appropriates Joel 2:32 ("Then everyone who calls on the name of the Lord shall be saved") as a word that pertains to those who call on *Jesus* as Lord (Rom 10:9, 12–13).[29] Paul's identification of Jesus as Lord thus converges with

28. On this theme, see Dale B. Martin, *Slavery as Salvation: The Metaphor of Slavery in Pauline Christianity* (New Haven: Yale University Press, 1990).

29. See C. Kavin Rowe, "Romans 10:13: What Is the Name of the Lord?," *HBT* 22 (2000): 135–73.

his "Son of God" language to underscore the mysterious oneness of Jesus with God. Only for that reason can he be the one in whom faith/trust is rightly to be placed (Gal 2:16; Phil 1:29; Col 2:5; Phlm 5).

Jesus Embodied in the Church

We come now to what may be the most startling aspect of Paul's portrayal of the identity of Jesus: Paul and his communities know Jesus Christ not only as Lord—not only as the Master who holds sovereign authority over the church—but also as personally united with his people in such a way that they become his "body." He is actually present in and through them. After the resurrection, Jesus's identity is not confined to a single localized physical body; he embraces and receives into himself all those whom he calls. Consequently, he manifests his identity to the world through this complex corporate reality.[30]

The well-known "body of Christ" text in 1 Cor 12 makes this point forcefully: "For just as the body is one and has many members, and all the members of the body, though many, are one body, so it is with Christ" (12:12). As Paul develops the analogy, he does not say that the church has many members, like a physical human body.[31] Rather, he says that Christ has many members, which, like the members of the human body, have diverse functions. Thus, the term "Christ" in 1 Cor 12:12–27 refers to this multimembered corporate entity. The seriousness with which Paul takes this claim is illustrated by his use of the same image earlier in the letter, in his vehement argument against the Corinthians' practice of going to prostitutes: "Do you not know that your bodies are members of Christ? Should I therefore take the members of Christ and make them members of a prostitute? Never!" (6:15).

The more closely we study Paul's letters, the more we are forced to recognize that this is for him not merely a figure of speech. The church really is the body of Christ, because Christ lives in us: "I have been crucified with Christ; and it is no longer I who live, but it is Christ who lives in me" (Gal 2:19b-20a).[32] The

30. Later Christian theology referred to this corporate aspect of Christ's identity as the *totus Christus*, the "whole Christ" (Augustine, *On Christian Doctrine* 3.31.44).

31. Many students are surprised to discover that the term ἐκκλησία ("church") appears in the passage only at 12:28.

32. Paul's "I" here is not merely autobiographical but also exemplary; he presents his experience of dying to his old life and living in union with Christ as a model or pattern that he expects all Christians to share. See Beverly Roberts Gaventa, "Galatians 1 and 2: Autobiography as Paradigm," *NovT* 28 (1986): 309–26.

line of distinction between Christ and his people has become blurred if not erased altogether. "My" personal identity has been taken up into Christ.

Here, if anywhere (someone might protest), surely we must make a distinction between the historical man Jesus and the risen "supernatural" Christ. After all, Paul never calls the church "the body of Jesus." A careful examination of the evidence, however, shows that such a distinction does not consistently stand. The key text is 2 Cor 4:10–11: "[We are] always carrying in the body the death of Jesus, so that the life of Jesus may also be made visible in our bodies. For while we live, we are always being given up to death for Jesus' sake, so that the life of Jesus may be made visible in our mortal flesh." What Paul says of himself applies more generally to the identity and vocation of the church: our lives and our bodies become the locus of the manifestation of *Jesus's* life. Here, as elsewhere, "Jesus" and "Christ" are names that Paul can use interchangeably to refer to the same person.

If that is so, then our investigation of the identity of Jesus must take into account the numerous passages in which Paul describes the participation of the church in Christ's sufferings, in the power of his resurrection, and in the resultant transformation of human social experience within the body of Christ.[33] Our understanding of the identity of Jesus Christ will somehow have to include his present embodiment in the community of those called by his name, a community that lives in suffering and weakness but also displays, in a distinctive way, the hope of freedom from sin and abolition of divisive distinctions of nationality, social rank, and gender.

We must hasten to say that claims about the church as the theater of the identity of Jesus always remain subject to the eschatological reservation: we see through a glass darkly. Paul describes himself as being in the agony of childbirth "until Christ is formed in you," that is, in the Galatian churches (Gal 4:19). This suggests that we do not yet see Christ's identity rightly displayed in the church. On the one hand, Paul can write that "all of us, with unveiled faces, seeing the glory of the Lord [Jesus] as though reflected in a mirror, are being transformed into the same image from one degree of glory into another" (2 Cor 3:18). Here is the eschatological vision, already shining forth in the community (see also Col 1:27). On the other hand, Paul never forgets that "we hope for what we do not see" (Rom 8:25), and that the identity of Jesus Christ

33. See esp. Rom 6:3–11; 8:17, 29–30; 2 Cor 12:7b–10; Gal 3:27–29; 6:14; Phil 3:7–11; and Col 1:24—the last of these is the extraordinary text in which Paul declares that through his own sufferings he is "completing what is lacking in Christ's afflictions for the sake of his body, that is, the church" (Col 1:24).

will be fully manifest in the church only when he comes as the Savior from heaven, who "will transform the body of our lowliness (ταπεινώσεως; cf. Phil 2:8) that it may be conformed to the body of his glory, by the power that also enables him to make all things subject to himself" (Phil 3:20–21).

Eschatological Consummation

Jesus the Agent of Final Judgment and Salvation

Paul's account of Jesus contains a prominent eschatological element. The same Jesus Christ who was the preexistent creator, who was crucified and rose from the dead, will also come at the end of the age to judge the world and to complete his saving work. The image of Jesus as judge, though it is highlighted in the creeds and in the church's iconographic traditions, strikes late modern sensibilities as offensive, and it has fallen into neglect in our time. In Paul, however, we find repeated references to Jesus as the agent of eschatological judgment: "For all of us must appear before the judgment seat of Christ, so that each may receive recompense for what has been done in the body, whether good or evil" (2 Cor 5:10; see also Rom 2:16; 14:4; 1 Cor 4:5; Phil 1:10; 2:16; 1 Thess 5:23).

Alongside such images, however, we find Paul more often proclaiming that the purpose of Christ's future coming is to bring to completion the salvation of his people. Paul portrays Jesus not only as judge but also as advocate who intercedes for us in the final judgment (Rom 8:33–34). His intercession will succeed against all cosmic accusers and adversaries, for nothing can separate us from "the love of God in Christ Jesus our Lord" (8:35–39). He will come as the eschatological "Deliverer" (11:26), and he will *rescue* us from "the wrath that is coming" (1 Thess 1:10). He will gather his people to be with him forever (1 Thess 4:16–17; 2 Thess 2:1) and complete the good work that he has begun among them (Phil 1:6) by banishing ungodliness, taking away their sins, and sanctifying them entirely (Rom 11:26–27; 1 Cor 1:7–8; 1 Thess 5:23). At Christ's future coming his people will be fully conformed to him and share his glory (Rom 8:29–30; Phil 3:20–21; Col 3:4).

"That God May Be All in All"

Paul's story about the identity of Jesus contains one last surprising twist. At that eschatological day, when every knee bows and every tongue confesses that

Jesus Christ is Lord, when his triumph over all things, including the power of death, is complete and all things are put under his feet in subjection—then, at that moment, he will hand over the kingdom to God the Father. "The Son himself will also be subjected to the one who put all things in subjection under him, so that God may be all in all" (1 Cor 15:24–28). Thus, the grand conclusion of the plot shows that the identity of Jesus Christ is still consistent. In the day of eschatological consummation, he is still the same obedient, self-emptying Son on whose act of radical self-giving the salvation of the world depends. If the story had any other ending, he would indeed be "another Jesus."

Jesus's Identity and Ours

Paul's Jesus Christ is the protagonist of an epic story that moves from creation to the climactic events of cross and resurrection to the final judgment and salvation of the world. Thus, Paul's account of Jesus has the unity of a personal identity unfolded across time. Jesus the weak, suffering servant is not a contradiction or a paradox alongside Jesus the triumphant, conquering Lord. The identity of Paul's Jesus is encapsulated precisely in the narrative line and cannot be abstracted from it.

Someone might ask what value there is in seeking a synthetic account of Jesus as a character in Paul's letters. Is it purely a literary parlor game? Will this project merely retrace a mythological plot that corresponds neither to the historical reality of the life of Jesus nor to the theological needs of our own time? My answer to this is twofold.

First, if critical history is our interest, there is great value in asking how Jesus looked through Paul's eyes, since Paul is our earliest extant witness. The usual procedure of taking the Gospels (written twenty to forty years later) as the primary frame of reference and asking how Paul matches up is historically anachronistic. The first step is to clarify what *Paul* tells us about the identity of Jesus; only then, as a second step, can we compare Paul's Jesus to information from other sources. One striking result of this procedure is to show that the account of Jesus as Lord and Redeemer of the world is not—as is sometimes asserted—a late doctrinal invention of the church in the second or third century; rather, it belongs to the very earliest layers of tradition to which we have access.

Second, reckoning with Paul's account of the identity of Jesus requires us to expand the frame within which we decide what is "real." If "reality" is rightly described by Paul's declaration that "one has died for all, therefore all have died," then his next moves follow compellingly: we no longer know κατὰ σάρκα, according to the flesh; the old has passed away. We are living in the realm of new creation (2 Cor 5:14–17). Our very concept of personal identity undergoes a mind-stretching transformation, including our own personal identities: we are transformed by the story of Jesus Christ, and we find ourselves living *within* that story rather than at a critical distance from it. If Paul's story of Jesus Christ is true, then we too have been crucified with Christ and will be raised with him. In the story of Jesus Christ we find our own.

10

Soteriology

Christ Died for the Ungodly

Soteriology and Story

When Paul seeks to articulate how human beings are saved, does he answer the question by telling a story? Or, perhaps to put the matter more cautiously, do Paul's soteriological affirmations rest upon a narrative substructure? If so, what implications does this have for our understanding of Paul's theology?

It is no longer surprising to find "Paul" and "narrative" in the same sentence. Over the past twenty years, a number of significant studies have highlighted various narrative elements in Paul's thought. In addition to my own efforts in this regard, I would mention particularly the contributions of Norman Petersen, Stephen Fowl, N. T. Wright, Ben Witherington, Luke Timothy Johnson, Sylvia Keesmaat, Michael Gorman, and A. Katherine Grieb.[1] A recent collaborative volume of essays by leading British NT scholars, under the editorship of Bruce

1. My own early reflections on this matter are now further developed in a new introduction to the second edition of *The Faith of Jesus Christ: The Narrative Substructure of Paul's Theology in Galatians 3:1–4:11*, 2nd ed., The Biblical Resource Series (Grand Rapids: Eerdmans, 2002 [1983]), xxi–lii. See also Norman R. Petersen, *Rediscovering Paul: Philemon and the Sociology of Paul's Narrative World* (Philadelphia: Fortress, 1985); Stephen Fowl, *The Story of Christ in the Ethics of Paul: An Analysis of the Function of the Hymnic Material in the Pauline Corpus*, JSNTSup 36 (Sheffield: Sheffield Academic Press, 1990); N. T. Wright, *The New Testament and the People of God*, Christian Origins and the Question of God 1 (London: SPCK; Minneapolis: Fortress, 1992); Ben Witherington III, *Paul's Narrative Thought World: The Tapestry of Tragedy and Triumph* (Louisville: Westminster John Knox, 1994); Luke Timothy Johnson, *The Real Jesus* (San Francisco: HarperSanFrancisco, 1997), 117–22; Sylvia Keesmaat, *Paul and His Story: (Re)interpreting the Exodus Tradition*, JSNTSup 181 (Sheffield: Sheffield Academic Press, 1999); Michael Gorman, *Cruciformity: Paul's Narrative*

This paper was originally presented in the Pauline Soteriology Group at the Annual Meeting of the Society of Biblical Literature, Atlanta, November 24, 2003.

Longenecker, has produced a stimulating discussion of *Narrative Dynamics in Paul*.[2] This way of thinking about Paul's letters has entered the mainstream of discourse in the field. A single citation will illustrate my point: In his magisterial study of *The Origins of Christian Morality*, Wayne Meeks writes as follows:

> We have not thought of Paul as a storyteller, for the Jesus stories of the Gospels are absent from his letters. Yet his use of narrative is very important . . . because Paul's central concern was to use the narrative [of Jesus] to form a moral community. The pivotal story for Paul was simple and astounding: God's son and anointed one was the very Jesus who was most shamefully crucified, dead, and buried, but whom God then raised from the dead, exalted to share his own throne and very name in heaven, to sit at God's right hand as Lord until all things would be subjected to him and God alone would reign in righteousness over all his people and creation. The drama of Paul's career turns on his recognition that that story shattered and recreated his own conception of a life lived in obedience to God's will.[3]

Meeks's summary of Paul's story is of course drawn from 1 Cor 15, a text to which we shall return below. His description focuses on the importance of narrative for understanding Paul's moral teaching and community-forming practices. My assignment in the present paper, by contrast, is to reflect upon the ways in which attention to narrative may be fruitful for interpreting Paul's *soteriology*. (As we shall see, though, a narrative approach to Paul's theology will suggest that the relationship between "soteriology" and "community formation" is closer than we might have thought.)

There are good reasons for suggesting that any soteriology—not just Paul's distinctive one—inescapably bears a narrative character. The theologian Michael Root explains the reason for this inescapable linkage:

> Narrative is not merely ornamental in soteriology, but constitutive. . . . Soteriology is the moment within theological reflection at which the narrative

Spirituality of the Cross (Grand Rapids: Eerdmans, 2001); and A. Katherine Grieb, *The Story of Romans* (Louisville: Westminster John Knox, 2003).

2. Bruce W. Longenecker, ed., *Narrative Dynamics in Paul: A Critical Assessment* (Louisville and London: Westminster John Knox, 2002). For an extended review of this important book, and for a fuller discussion of the question of narrative in Paul's letters, see Richard B. Hays, "Is Paul's Gospel Narratable?," *JSNT* 27 (2004): 217–39.

3. Wayne A. Meeks, *The Origins of Christian Morality: The First Two Centuries* (New Haven: Yale University Press, 1993), 196.

> form of the Christian message cannot be avoided. Soteriology presumes two states of human existence, a state of deprivation (sin, corruption) and a state of release from that deprivation (salvation, liberation), and an event that produces a change from the first state to the second. It presumes then the sufficient conditions of a narrative: two states and an event that transforms the first into the second.[4]

Accordingly, an analysis of Paul's soteriology would necessarily seek to describe how Paul's letters narrate the passage from one state to the other. And yet, soteriology is not simply a matter of repeating the story, for it is always necessary to elucidate "how the reader is included in the story and how the story then is or can be the story of that reader's redemption."[5] The interpreter must connect the stories of later readers, as a later sequence in the narrative, to the story of Jesus. This interpretive process necessarily involves what Root calls "narrative redescriptions of the story of Jesus . . . that make it clear *how* it is the story of redemption." Consequently, "*it is by the construction of such augmented forms of the story of Jesus that the soteriological task is carried out.*"[6]

When we examine Pauline soteriology we are considering two levels of discourse that are distinguishable in principle, if difficult to keep separate in practice: (1) Paul's soteriological redescriptions of the story of Jesus and (2) our own augmented narrative constructions that seek to explain Paul's narrative redescriptions. The focus of this essay will be primarily on the first level, but Paul's language is sufficiently condensed and allusive to provoke us into continuing attempts to fill gaps by recourse to our own acts of narration. (For example, most accounts of "the faith of Jesus Christ" as soteriologically efficacious fall into the latter category.)

As these opening remarks suggest, I regard the narrative character of Paul's soteriology as clearly evident. Indeed, I would contend that Paul's statements about salvation are unintelligible apart from a narrative framework. How then are we to respond to Francis Watson's skepticism, expressed in his essay, "Is There a Story in These Texts?"[7] Watson argues that Paul proclaims a sheer vertical incursion of God's grace into the world; this divine action cannot be confined to the horizontal temporal plane within which human stories are

4. Michael Root, "The Narrative Structure of Soteriology," in *Why Narrative? Readings in Narrative Theology*, ed. Stanley Hauerwas and L. Gregory Jones (Grand Rapids: Eerdmans, 1989), 263–64.

5. Root, "Narrative Structure of Soteriology," 266.

6. Root, "Narrative Structure of Soteriology," 267, emphasis original.

7. Francis Watson, "Is There a Story in These Texts?," in Longenecker, *Narrative Dynamics*, 231–39.

told. Consequently, Paul's message is "an essentially nonnarratable gospel."[8] This surprising opinion, proffered by a scholar of Watson's ability and buttressed by citations from the redoubtable authority of Karl Barth, requires a serious response.

The structure of the present essay, then, will be as follows. We shall first examine two key Pauline texts (1 Cor 15 and Rom 5) in which he makes explicit soteriological claims; our purpose will be to explore whether there are signs here of a narrative structure—whether these passages offer what Root calls a narrative redescription of the story of Jesus as the story of redemption. In light of our reading of these two passages, we shall then propose a few general observations about the narrative pattern of Paul's soteriology and its significance for theological reflection. Finally, by way of conclusion, we shall reply to Watson's thesis that Paul's gospel is nonnarratable.

Narrative Soteriology in Two Pauline Texts

1 Corinthians 15:1–28

A full exegesis of this dense passage is out of the question here; we must content ourselves with a few observations pertinent to our topic.

Paul begins this climactic chapter of his letter by recalling for his Corinthian readers the content of the gospel that he had originally preached to them. This passage is of particular importance for our present purposes because it is one of the relatively infrequent places where Paul uses the verb σῴζω: the εὐαγγέλιον that Paul proclaimed is a word in which the Corinthians now stand and through which they are being saved (σῴζεσθε; note the present tense) if they hold it fast. Salvation depends upon a message that can be formulated in words, a message that can be received and passed on (15:3). Further, this message takes precisely the form of a story. The content of the salvation-bringing good news is articulated in the confessional formula of verses 3b–5: "that Christ died for our sins in accordance with the Scriptures, and that he was buried, and that he was raised on the third day in accordance with the Scriptures, and that he appeared to Cephas, then to the twelve." Despite Watson's misgivings, it is difficult to see this kerygmatic tradition as anything other than the plot synopsis of a story—indeed, precisely the sort of story that appears in more developed form in the passion/resurrection narratives of the later canonical Gospels.

8. Watson, "Is There a Story in These Texts?," 239.

In 1 Cor 15:3b–5 the soteriological claim is stated but not explained: "for our sins" is given no immediate elucidation, and the twofold reference to the accordance of Christ's death and resurrection with the Scriptures remains somewhat enigmatic. At the very least, however, the emphasis on the Scriptures requires us to interpret the saving significance of Jesus's death and resurrection in relation to the ancient story of God's dealings with Israel. The story of Jesus's death and resurrection is placed within the matrix of the story of Israel. This hint cries out for further explication, which Paul of course provides elsewhere, but not here.

In verses 6–11, we find Paul's own augmentation of the story that is encapsulated in the confessional tradition of verses 3b–5. The risen Christ appeared, he declares, to many other witnesses and ultimately to Paul himself. This event is narrated as an event in our world of time and space, one of a sequence of similar appearances to various witnesses, "most of whom are still alive, though some have died" (v. 6). Paul's own experience of transformation from persecutor to apostle is in itself a sign of the power of God's saving grace at work (vv. 8–10). In these verses we see the "two states" of existence to which Root refers. Paul's transformation from one to the other—from "unfit" to graced—is said to have been effected by the appearance of the risen Christ directly to him. This begins to suggest how the story might be a saving story: in Paul's case, it produced personal transformation from a life of violence to a life of grace-empowered service.

In verses 12–19, a few further nuances appear. It is at last said explicitly rather than indirectly that *God* raised Christ (v. 15). Further, Paul now implies that deliverance from sin, connected by the confessional formula to Christ's death (v. 3), is dependent also on the reality of Christ's resurrection (v. 17). Likewise, in verses 18–19 we find the first indication that the resurrection of Jesus is the ground of our hope for deliverance from death—a point that Paul will develop more fully in the following paragraph. In any case, the effect of these verses is to assert strongly that the soteriological power of Paul's message depends upon the integrity of the story summarized in the confessional formula. Unless the story is true that "he was raised on the third day," there is no εὐαγγέλιον.

Up to this point, Paul has offered a selective redescription of the story of Jesus, focusing particularly on cross and resurrection, but he has not yet explained "how the reader is included in the story" (as Root says). Though he has asserted that the story is a saving story (vv. 1–2), its soteriological logic remains unclear. In verses 20–28, however, we get a more complete account, which also extends the narrative line into the eschatological future. Christ is "the first fruits of those who have died," and all who are "in" him will share ultimately in the resurrection that has come through him. Here, Christ is the ἀρχηγός of the new humanity in typological contrast to Adam; he is the great symbolic protagonist, who will lead his people out of bondage to death. "But each in his order: Christ the first fruits, then at his coming those who belong to Christ" (v. 23). Paul then unfolds the plot line in further detail: the risen Christ reigns from heaven but continues to battle against every power hostile to God. Ultimately he will subdue them all, including the last enemy, death. When that happens, he ("the Son") will hand over the kingdom to God the Father.

Once again, it should be beyond dispute that we are reading a précis of a narrative. The story of Jesus, rooted somehow in Israel's story and coming to its decisive turning point in the cross and resurrection, extends through the present time in which cosmic warfare is underway to an eschatological consummation in which the dead will be made alive and Christ, the triumphant ruler, will offer one final act of self-emptying submission to the Father.

Further, this narrative is a saving story because Christ's people will share in his resurrection and his triumphant destiny. All of this is fleshed out (as it were) in verses 35–58. "The trumpet will sound, and the dead will be raised imperishable, and we will be changed" (v. 52). The key point for our purposes is this: the soteriological logic of the story is *participatory*: the story of Jesus's death and resurrection is a saving story because Paul and his readers somehow mysteriously *participate* in the destiny of Jesus, the story's protagonist.[9] His story prefigures and embodies the destiny that "those who belong to Christ" will share at the end (τὸ τέλος, vv. 23–24).

Thus, the soteriology of Paul's gospel story operates within an eschatological dialectic framed by temporal markers *in the unfolding narrative*. On the one hand, Paul has already been transformed from persecutor to bearer of grace; the Corinthians, formerly gentile idolaters, have been brought into a new eschatological community of God's people, in which they can be "steadfast, immovable, always excelling in the work of the Lord, because [they] know that in the Lord [their] labor is not in vain" (v. 58).

On the other hand, the παρουσία of Christ is *not yet* (v. 23); consequently, patience and faithfulness are necessary in this interval where the cosmic war against God's enemies remains incomplete. The Corinthians can neither de-

9. For further reflection on this aspect of Paul's soteriology, along with further bibliographical references, see Richard B. Hays, "What Is 'Real Participation in Christ'? A Dialogue with E. P. Sanders on Pauline Soteriology," in *Redefining First-Century Jewish and Christian Identities*, ed. Fabian E. Udoh et al. (Notre Dame: University of Notre Dame Press, 2008), 336–51.

clare themselves to have arrived fully in the new age nor dismiss the urgency of hope for that age to come. Such a temporally conditioned dialectical consciousness makes sense only within the framework of the story: "But each in his own order . . ."

Romans 5:6–11

We focus here on a narrower slice of text, once again fraught with more exegetical problems than we can possibly address within the scope of this essay. Our heuristic question remains whether there is a soteriological narrative in or behind the passage.

Romans 5 begins with a summary passage (vv. 1–2) that recapitulates the argument of the letter's first four chapters and begins the transition to the next phase of the argument.[10] Because Jesus "was handed over to death for our trespasses and was raised for our justification" (4:25—note that this plot summary corresponds closely to 1 Cor 15:3b–5), we may now have peace with God and hope to share the glory of God. In verses 3–5, Paul begins for the first time in the letter to speak of the sufferings of the present time and of the importance of hope (cf. 8:18–25; again, these sentences frame the believer's present experience within an eschatological narrative). Verse 5 expresses assurance that such hope is not in vain "because God's love has been poured into our hearts through the Holy Spirit that has been given to us."

The paragraph to which we now turn our attention, verses 6–11, provides an explanatory expansion (γάρ, v. 6) of what is meant by the reference in verse 5 to "God's love." These verses are actually parenthetical in relation to the main line of argument, but they reveal some of the deep presuppositional structure of Paul's soteriology. They answer the implicit question, "What do you mean by 'God's love' and on what basis do you claim to have received it?" It is therefore telling that Paul once again responds by narrating, in capsule form, a story: "For while we were still weak, at the right time (κατὰ καιρὸν; note the temporal reference and compare Rom 9:9 [!] and Gal 4:4) Christ died for the ungodly." This self-sacrificial act of Christ, extraordinary by human standards (Rom 5:7), is in some mysterious way not merely the act of a noble human being but also an act of God: "But *God proves his love for us* in that while we still were sinners Christ died for us" (v. 8). There is a mysterious logic at work

10. A very good text-critical argument can be made that the main verb in v. 1 should be read as ἔχωμεν, a hortatory subjunctive. The implications of this reading cannot be developed here, but it would highlight the shift into a new mode of argument.

here: Paul claims that the death of Jesus is his own act of self-sacrificial love (v. 6; cf. Gal 2:20b) and faithful obedience (Rom 5:19), and yet simultaneously the act of God, "who did not withhold his own Son, but gave him up for all of us" (Rom 8:32—a text that echoes the Akedah, Gen 22:16). Paul's pithy plot summary in Rom 5:6–8 highlights the gracious and costly divine initiative in rescuing human beings from a state of weakness, sin, and alienation. (These verses amplify Paul's description of God in 4:5 as the one "who justifies the ungodly.") The rest of the paragraph (vv. 9–11) then emphasizes our resultant transformation from one state into another: we were sinners, but now we have been justified by his blood (v. 9); we were enemies, but now we have been reconciled to God through the death of his Son (v. 10).

In light of this brief summary, Watson's claim that the gospel is "nonnarratable" seems extremely odd. In Rom 5:6–11 Paul concisely narrates God's already accomplished action to deliver us from sin and estrangement through the death of Jesus. This pivotal event has effected a change from a state of deprivation and bondage to a state of reconciliation and hope. Further, Paul places this redemptive action in a temporal frame that still looks to the future for its completion: having been justified and reconciled, we will be saved (σωθησόμεθα, vv. 9, 10; note the future tense) in the eschatological judgment. When Paul writes in v. 10 "much more . . . will we be saved by his life," he is almost surely referring to the resurrection of the body (cf. 8:11, 23). Thus, the soteriological narrative of Rom 5 encompasses past, present, and future.

It requires no ingenuity or artifice to recognize in Paul's statements here another "narrative redescription" of the same story we encountered in 1 Cor 15. Romans 5 focuses more on the death of Jesus as a reconciling act of divine love, while 1 Cor 15 focuses more on the resurrection of Jesus as a sign of the eschatological triumph in which we shall participate by virtue of union with him. In that sense, the two narrative redescriptions have different soteriological emphases, but they are profoundly unified as interpretations of the same story—the story of Jesus's death, resurrection, and eschatological victory.[11] If we fail to recognize that the two passages are offering explications of the same story, we might see Rom 5 and 1 Cor 15 as two fragmentary and competing soteriologies. I hope that my brief interpretive remarks here have been sufficient to indicate how mistaken such a reading would be.

If there were world enough and time, we could similarly analyze Rom 5:12–21, which is full of references to the soteriological transformation effected through participation in Christ. The Adam/Christ typology suggested in 1 Cor

11. Cf. Meeks, *Origins of Christian Morality*, 196.

15:22 (and 15:45–49) is much more fully developed here, in a way that highlights Christ's *act* of righteousness and obedience as the initiation of a new humanity, the means through which God's grace triumphs in the world and leads us to "eternal life through Jesus Christ our Lord" (Rom 5:21). Watson's insistence that the deeds of Adam and Christ are incommensurable misses the point.[12] The question is not whether Adam and Christ are precisely comparable figures within a single historical continuum, but whether the action of Jesus is *narrated* as an event that delivers humanity from a state of bondage to a state of righteousness and life. I do not see how it is possible to give anything other than an affirmative answer to this question.

The Grammar of Paul's Narrative Soteriology

We should be cautious about generalizing from these two texts to comprehensive claims about Pauline soteriology. Nonetheless, on the basis of what we have observed, I am willing to float a few hypotheses about the "grammar" of Paul's soteriological narrative.

(1) *God's saving act is not a bolt from the blue that bears no relation to the story of Israel.* Rather, God's act in Christ is said to happen κατὰ τὰς γραφάς; its intelligibility depends upon its relation to Israel's Scripture. For example, the eschatological triumph of the Christ is expressed and interpreted through an allusion to the royal (messianic) exaltation promised in Ps 110:1 (1 Cor 15:25), and his triumph over death is to be understood in counterpoint to the story of Adam. The passages we have examined do not develop the narrative connections very fully, but they gesture in the direction of placing the story of salvation within the matrix of Israel's Scripture. The question of how to specify and explicate the narrative continuities then becomes a major project for theology. One might put it this way: the hermeneutical rule that the saving event occurred κατὰ τὰς γραφάς serves as a stimulus to the narrative imagination, for one requirement of Christian soteriology is to generate "augmented forms of the story of Jesus" (Root's phrase again) that discern patterns of narrative unity between Israel's story and the gospel. We can see Paul working this out in many and various ways throughout his correspondence.

(2) The saving story is *apocalyptic in character*, and it therefore posits a tension between the present time and the hoped-for future consummation. In 1 Cor 11:23–26, Paul, after retelling the story of the Lord's Supper, comments:

12. Watson, "Is There a Story in These Texts?," 235–39.

"For as often as you eat this bread and drink the cup, you proclaim the Lord's death until he comes." The Lord's Supper becomes a repeated act of narration, such that to be in Christ is to find oneself located within this still-unfinished story. Similarly, in Rom 5 we find a poignant contrast between a present state of reconciliation to God and a hoped-for future salvation. Paul's narrative soteriology accounts for this already/not yet tension in his thought. This tension is not, strictly speaking, a "dialectic," as it is often described. It is, rather, a consequence of finding ourselves within an unfinished plot line. Still, for those who live within the symbolic world of this story, the future consummation is guaranteed by Christ's resurrection, and all thought and action are strongly shaped by apocalyptic hope.

(3) The soteriological narrative hinges on the *death and resurrection of Jesus*. Jesus's death is both an expression of God's love and Jesus's own act of fidelity. The latter emphasis comes strongly to the fore in Rom 5, where Paul refers to this self-sacrificial death as efficacious through "one man's act of righteousness" (δι' ἑνὸς δικαιώματος) and "one man's obedience" (vv. 18–19). As Luke Johnson has contended, this narrative pattern explicates the meaning of πίστις Ἰησοῦ Χριστοῦ.[13] A further implication of this narrative grammar is that, because the many are made righteous by this one act of Jesus (v. 19), we can never suppose that we are saved by our own actions and choices. Such actions are always derivative, always responsive to the prior gracious initiative of God in Christ.

(4) The logic of Paul's soteriological narrative is *participatory*. We receive salvation insofar as we are united with Christ and belong to him. This has far-reaching implications. I mention only a couple of them here. For one thing, a participatory soteriology ensures that salvation always has an *ecclesial* character: we are not saved as solitary individuals, but we become incorporate in Christ so that our fate is bound together not only with him but also with our brothers and sisters in him. Second, participation in Christ entails conformity to the pattern of self-sacrificial love that he embodied and enacted on our behalf (as Gal 2:19b–20 elegantly suggests). Therefore, a narrative soteriology will always highlight the ethical implications of participation in Christ: our lives become shaped in accordance with his pattern of action.[14] These two points,

13. Luke Timothy Johnson, "Romans 3:21–26 and the Faith of Jesus," *CBQ* 44 (1982): 77–90.

14. This point is nicely developed in John Barclay, "Paul's Story: Theology as Testimony," in Longenecker, *Narrative Dynamics in Paul*, 133–56. See also Gorman, *Cruciformity*.

taken together, indicate why I remarked in the opening section of this essay that soteriology and community formation are closely linked.

A Nonnarratable Gospel? A Reply to Francis Watson

I promised to reply to Francis Watson's judgment that Paul's gospel proclaims a nonnarratable vertical incursion of God's grace. My comments on 1 Cor 15 and Rom 5 have already shown that I think the evidence is strongly stacked against this interpretation. It remains only to offer a few methodological comments to clarify, if possible, where my real disagreements with Watson do and do not lie, and to seek to understand why he advances his provocative but, in my judgment, mistaken antinarrative reading of Paul.[15] Given the limitation of time, I offer three points for discussion.

First, Watson asserts, as though the point were decisive, that Paul, in contrast to the evangelists, "is simply not a storyteller."[16] Yet this point has never really been in dispute. In the sense that Watson means this statement, I agree with it. The question is not whether Paul is a "storyteller" but whether his theology is to be understood as direct commentary upon a soteriological narrative. In *The Faith of Jesus Christ*, for example, I described Paul's discursive argumentation as belonging to the mode of "primary reflectivity" rather than foundational narrative language. My interpretive approach is set forth in the opening chapter:

> Paul does not, of course, simply retell the story in his letters, although he alludes to it constantly. He assumes that his readers know the gospel story, and his pervasive concern is to draw out the implications of this story for shaping the belief and practice of his infant churches. . . . It is possible, however, to identify Paul's allusions to his story of Jesus Christ, to discern some features of its narrative "shape," and to examine the way in which this story operates as a constraint governing the logic of Paul's argumentation.[17]

15. If I had more time to develop this section into a full essay response, I might entitle it "Francis Watson: Ein Versuch, ihn zu Verstehen."

16. Watson, "Is There a Story in These Texts?," 232. (Hereafter, page references are given in parentheses in the text.) As Watson acknowledges, the *narratio* of Galatians provides an exception to this rule.

17. Hays, *The Faith of Jesus Christ*, 6.

What I and others have attempted to demonstrate is that Paul's theological language is grounded in story and that his letters must be interpreted as theological reflection on the first-order kerygmatic narrative about Jesus. (See for a very helpful development of this approach the richly detailed essay of Douglas Campbell, "The Story of Jesus in Romans and Galatians."[18]) All this applies to the present discussion of soteriology as well. The narrative statements we have discussed in this essay are condensed summarizations of a plotline, upon which Paul comments in order to demonstrate its saving significance.

Second, Watson and I are in agreement that Paul does in fact place his soteriology in conversation with scriptural stories (234). Further, we agree that he does not merely repeat the story of Israel: he is a revisionary reader who transforms Israel's story in the retelling—but I would add, as Watson would not, that the transformation is performed precisely by reading it through the lens of the story of Jesus. (See for example the revisionary renarration of the story of Sarah and Hagar in Gal 4:21–5:1, noting particularly the climactic comment in 5:1.) To say that Paul's soteriology is grounded in narrative is to affirm the constant *intertextual* character of Paul's discourse: Paul's letters are always in hermeneutical engagement with other "texts," both Israel's story and the early church's narrative of the εὐαγγέλιον of Jesus Christ.

Third, Watson and I agree that the gospel "announces a definitive, unsurpassable divine incursion into the world" (232). But we differ over whether it is possible to tell the story of this incursion and whether Paul in fact does so. Since the evidence that Paul does indeed do so is so straightforward, one must attempt to understand what Watson is actually resisting when he balks at describing the gospel in narrative terms. If I understand him correctly, he is worried that to describe the gospel as "narrative" is to compromise its transcendent character by absorbing it into the temporal process of human affairs. For example, Watson writes:

> The Christ event is sui generis and does not exist on the same horizontal plane as the scriptural narrative(s) that nevertheless bear witness to it. The grace of the one man Jesus Christ is the gift of God, and the divine act of giving occurs within the vertical plane rather than the horizontal one. Paul's gospel, then, is not itself a "story," since its vertical construal of God's act as a movement of descent and ascent inhibits the linear, temporal extension that a "story of Jesus" would require. (239)

18. Douglas Campbell, "The Story of Jesus in Romans and Galatians," in Longenecker, *Narrative Dynamics in Paul*, 97–124.

For Watson, this divine act "lies beyond the scope of human storytelling." Surely this is so, however, only if we define "narrative" a priori as limited to the ordinary plane of human agency, of finite cause and effect—i.e., only if we decide before the fact that "narrative" can describe only human actions, never God's action. That is why Watson repeatedly posits peculiar dichotomies such as the following: "The death of Jesus is not an event within a temporal flow; it is an absolute and unsurpassable event that determines who Jesus is, who God is, and indeed who we are" (234).

To cut to the bottom line, it seems to me that such dichotomies are the legacy of idealist Kantian philosophy and would have appeared exceedingly puzzling to Paul. Paul has no doubt that the act of God can be narrated or that the death of Jesus was a specific event within human history. To say that is not to deny its transcendent significance or that it is also the act of God. Rather, it is to affirm the paradigm-shattering incarnational claim that God really has acted in history, indeed that we know God only there. Paul writes: "God proves his love for us in that while we still were sinners Christ died for us." This sentence demonstrates not only that the gospel can be narrated but also that it must be; the demonstration of God's love is precisely an event that occurred within our temporal flow, an event which nonetheless redefines everything else within the temporal plane in which it occurred. The dichotomy between "horizontal" and "vertical" imposes upon us a false choice. Any talk about "the act of God" which denies its temporal/narrative concreteness necessarily denies that it is a real *act* in time and therefore threatens to undo its soteriological reality *pro nobis*, its actual engagement in the life of creation.

On first reading Watson's essay, I was surprised to find him appealing to Karl Barth in defense of his antinarrative reading. After all, it is Barth above all others who has given decisive impetus to the recent theological interest in narrative.[19] But upon reflection, I realized that Watson is invoking the Barth of the *Römerbrief* and the first volume of the *Church Dogmatics*. Watson's reading of Paul would be corrected and enriched if he would attend more closely to the mature Barth, who opens the great fourteenth chapter of his dogmatics by writing "Die Versöhnung ist Geschichte . . . Wer von ihr reden will muss sie als Geschichte *erzählen*."[20]

19. I am thinking here, of course, of the influence of Barth on the work of Hans Frei and his students. See also David Ford, *Barth and God's Story: Biblical Narrative and the Theological Method of Karl Barth in the Church Dogmatics* (Frankfurt am Main: Lang, 1981).

20. "The atonement is history . . . Whoever would speak of it must narrate it as history" (*Kirkliche Dogmatik*, vol. 4, *Die Lehre von der Versöhnung*, part 1 [Zollikon-Zurich: Evangelischer Verlag, 1953], 171, translation and emphasis mine). The German *Geschichte*

The paradigmatic text for Barth's narration of the atonement is Phil 2:5–11, which he reads as the story of "The Obedience of the Son of God." Someone might fear that such a narration of the humiliation and obedience of the Son of God would absorb the gospel into the temporal flow of finitude. But Barth, on the contrary, insists that only in such narration is the gospel rightly to be grasped:

> We may believe that God can and must only be absolute in contrast to all that is relative, exalted in contrast to all that is lowly, active in contrast to all suffering, inviolable in contrast to all temptation, transcendent in contrast to all immanence, and therefore divine in contrast to everything human, in short that He can and must be only the "Wholly Other." But such beliefs are shown to be quite untenable, and corrupt and pagan, by the fact that God does in fact be and do this in Jesus Christ.[21]

It is precisely because God has done this in Jesus Christ that the gospel is narratable, and for this reason Pauline soteriology is always bound up with the narrative of grace.

is of course slightly ambiguous. My particular interest here is in Barth's choice of the verb *erzählen* ("narrate").

21. Karl Barth, *Church Dogmatics*, vol. 4, *The Doctrine of Reconciliation*, part 1, trans. G. W. Bromiley (Edinburgh: T & T Clark, 1956 [1953]), 186.

11

Apocalyptic

New Creation Poetics in Galatians

The Theological Keynote of Galatians: The "Grace and Peace" Salutation (Gal 1:3–5)

> Grace to you and peace from God our Father and from the Lord Jesus Christ, who gave himself for our sins, so that he might rescue us from the present evil age, in accordance with the will of our God and Father, to whom be the glory forever. (Gal 1:3–5)

Thus runs the opening salutation of Paul's Letter to the Galatians. It is generally recognized that the openings of Paul's Epistles are not inconsequential; they are artfully composed to signal the chief themes and concerns of the letters that they introduce. Yet until rather recently, the apocalyptic opening lines of the Letter to the Galatians have rarely been given their full weight as a thematic key to the letter's message.

There are several possible reasons for the overlooking of verses 3–5. Sometimes interpreters have zoomed in on Paul's forceful assertion in 1:1 of a divine authorization for his own apostleship—clearly a major topic in the first two chapters of the letter. Other times interpreters have found their attention arrested by Paul's abrupt θαυμάζω in verse 6. In the absence of a preliminary thanksgiving paragraph, this expression of dismay plunges many interpreters immediately into an attempt to reconstruct the historical problem in Galatia that evoked Paul's impassioned missive. Or again, Protestant theological exegesis has often thumbed its way quickly past the letter's opening to reach the juicy central section of the letter (Gal 3–4), with its convoluted and challenging

This essay was originally presented as a paper at the St. Andrews Galatians and Theology Conference, University of St. Andrews, Scotland, July 2012.

argument about Law, faith, and justification—themes not mentioned in the first chapter. Or alternatively, some readers are drawn particularly to the hortatory and ethical "payoff" of the argument in chapters 5 and 6. Finally, partly because of the absence of "justification" language in the letter opening, and partly because of Paul's uncharacteristic use of the plural "sins" in the announcement that Christ "gave himself for our sins" (1:4), critics have often suggested that in 1:3–5 Paul is simply quoting a traditional formula that fails to express the distinctive substance of his own thought—or even stands in some tension with it.[1]

I suggest, however, that in Galatians, as in every other Pauline epistle, the opening lines highlight precisely the themes that lie at the theological heart of the letter. The salutation of Galatians allusively encapsulates the story of Jesus Christ, sent forth by God the Father into the world to rescue human beings from bondage to sin and death—that is, bondage to "the present evil age"—through his own self-giving death (and resurrection! [1:1]). It is *this* story that provides the narrative framework within which Paul proclaims his urgent message about the justification of gentiles and constructs his arguments against the requirement of circumcision for the Galatian believers.

During the past generation, a number of important developments in the study of Pauline theology have created the hermeneutical conditions necessary for a fresh reading of the letter that brings these themes into proper focus. First among these developments is a new attention to the *narrative* character of Paul's thought, as opposed to construals that approach the letters through a strictly conceptual/propositional filter.[2] But just as important for our present concerns is the paradigm-challenging work of J. Louis Martyn, whose magisterial commentary on Galatians offers a comprehensive reading of Galatians as an *apocalyptic* proclamation of the gospel. Here is Martyn's vivid translation of Gal 1:4: Jesus Christ "'gave up his very life for our sins,' so

1. J. Louis Martyn goes so far as to suggest that Paul cites the formula in order to "correct it by means of an additional clause" (*Galatians*, AB 33A [New York: Doubleday, 1997], 90). Cf. James D. G. Dunn, *The Theology of Paul's Letter to the Galatians* (Cambridge: Cambridge University Press, 1993), 42–44.

2. My own work has played some role in this shift toward narrative. I also draw attention, however, to the contributions of N. T. Wright, James D. G. Dunn, Ben Witherington III, Michael Gorman, and Douglas Campbell. For one significant survey and assessment of the narrative turn in Pauline interpretation, see Bruce W. Longenecker, ed., *Narrative Dynamics in Paul: A Critical Assessment* (Louisville: Westminster John Knox, 2002). Interestingly, this collection of essays on narrative in Paul contains only a few slight passing references to Gal 1:3–4.

that he might snatch us out of the grasp of the present evil age."[3] From start to finish in his commentary, Martyn describes God's saving action through the imagery of invasion and battle, and he presses the case for reading Paul as an apocalyptic theologian.

Martyn's work has become so widely influential for the current generation of Pauline scholarship that it now seems almost incredible to recall that just over thirty years ago, J. Christiaan Beker could describe Galatians as an anomalous contingent *exception* to Paul's otherwise coherent proclamation of a gospel centered on the eschatological cosmic triumph of God. Indeed, Beker saw Galatians as such a nonapocalyptic outlier that it threatened to undo his own advocacy of Paul as a thoroughgoing apocalyptic theologian.[4] Martyn's provocative work has stimulated much debate, and Douglas Campbell's recent massive work *The Deliverance of God* has likewise pressed the case for reading Paul as a radical apocalyptic thinker.[5]

In this essay, I shall not attempt to give a detailed review of the current vigorous debates about "apocalyptic" in Paul.[6] But I do want to offer a few broad observations about the contours of some key issues that have surfaced through Martyn's work and the various responses to it.

Marks of Apocalyptic Theology in Galatians

The major advocates of "apocalyptic" are using the term not chiefly to identify the historical sources of specific motifs in Galatians—and still less to identify

3. Martyn, *Galatians*, 81.

4. J. Christiaan Beker, *Paul the Apostle: The Triumph of God in Life and Thought* (Philadelphia: Fortress, 1980), 58.

5. Douglas Campbell, *The Deliverance of God: An Apocalyptic Rereading of Justification in Paul* (Grand Rapids: Eerdmans, 2009).

6. For a critical perspective on the use of the category of "apocalyptic" to characterize Paul's thought, see, e.g., R. Barry Matlock, *Unveiling the Apocalyptic Paul: Paul's Interpreters and the Rhetoric of Criticism*, JSNTSup 127 (Sheffield: Sheffield Academic Press, 1996); also N. T. Wright, "Paul in Current Anglophone Scholarship," *ExpTim* 123 (2012): 367–81, esp. 372–74. For a more thoroughly developed account of Wright's critique of the apocalyptic school of interpreters, see his book *Paul and His Recent Interpreters: Some Contemporary Debates* (Minneapolis: Fortress, 2015), 135–218. For interpretations that embrace the category of "apocalyptic," see, e.g., Martinus C. de Boer, "Paul, Theologian of God's Apocalypse," *Int* 56 (2002): 21–33; Douglas K. Harink, "Paul and Israel: An Apocalyptic Reading," *ProEccl* 16 (2007): 359–80; and Beverly Roberts Gaventa, *Our Mother Saint Paul* (Louisville: Westminster John Knox, 2007).

the genre of the letter.[7] Instead, they are using "apocalyptic" as a descriptor for a certain profile of *theological* claims and commitments. These theological tendencies in Paul are presumptively characterized as *analogous* to the underlying theological claims and commitments of Jewish apocalyptic thought. According to this reading, there is a family resemblance, a sort of theological DNA, that Galatians shares with Jewish apocalyptic texts, despite many evident surface differences. We may identify three salient characteristics of this apocalyptic DNA, as it is described by the scholars who champion the apocalyptic reading of Galatians.

(1) The most fundamental of these underlying theological commitments is the insistence on *divine initiative and action* as the ground of salvation and hope, as opposed to any human religious practice or subjective disposition. This theological stance is elegantly expressed in Paul's rhetorically skillful self-correction in Gal 4:9: "But now that you know God—or rather, now that *you have been known by God.*" The grammatical correction signals the deep theological grammar of Paul's gospel. *God* is the primary agent, and human beings are the receivers of God's gracious action—just as in the letter opening, it is by God's gracious will that Jesus Christ gave himself to rescue us from the present evil age.

(2) The reference to "the present evil age" highlights the second key apocalyptic perspective found in Galatians: a scheme of *two ages*. In the old age, humans were in bondage to sin and death. With the inbreaking of the new age, however, there is a "new creation" (6:15), a new era of freedom, righteousness, and life. As the expression "new creation" suggests, this new age comes about entirely through God's initiative, not from any human design or action. Everything is made new in Christ. To unpack what Paul means by speaking of "new creation" in Gal 6, we may refer to his fuller exposition of this same image in 2 Cor 5:17: "If anyone is in Christ—new creation! The old things have passed away. Look! The new has come into being." Further, according to Martyn's reading, there is a radical *discontinuity* between the old age and the new. The death and resurrection of Jesus create a caesura in time and history; consequently, there can be no direct connection between the past and the present.

(3) To some advocates of apocalyptic in Paul, this radical discontinuity between the ages suggests a third feature of Pauline apocalyptic thought: *a sharp break with Judaism, with "salvation history," and with Israel*—at least with

7. As noted by Leander E. Keck, "Paul and Apocalyptic Theology," *Int* 38 (1984): 229–41.

Israel as defined in the past. Paul speaks of his "former life in Judaism" (1:13)[8] and can say that he has "died to the law" (2:19). He refers to life under Torah as "slavery" (4:9, 25; 5:1) and warns the Galatians that if they undergo circumcision, they will be "cut off from Christ" (5:2–4). These radical disjunctions and apparent disavowals of Israel's sacred law allegedly make sense only in light of Paul's apocalyptic conviction that a new age has dawned, in which the Torah belongs to the past. During the old age, its function was to be a παιδαγωγός until Christ came, but now that in the fullness of time πίστις has arrived on the scene, the Torah is superseded and no longer valid (3:23–25).

It is this third aspect of the "apocalyptic" interpretation of Galatians that is most problematic—and at the same time most convergent with the Reformation's traditional law/gospel antithesis and its concomitant anti-Jewish readings of Paul. Even where contemporary "apocalyptic" interpreters are sensitive—as indeed J. Louis Martyn is[9]—to the theological dangers of such a position, they nonetheless tend to portray Paul as having broken decisively with Israel's history.

A Proposal: Reshaping the Hermeneutical Imagination

In the present essay, I argue that the first two features of the apocalyptic interpretation that I have described are on target as readings of Galatians: Paul does insist on the priority of divine initiative, and he does read present existence through the lens of a two-age schema, in which Jesus Christ has inaugurated a new creation. But I also suggest that the third tendency of many contemporary apocalyptic interpretations—the claim of radical discontinuity between present and past, between church and Israel—fails to describe with sufficient nuance either the way in which two-age thinking actually works in Jewish apocalyptic thought or the complex way in which Paul engages Israel's Scripture and tradition. I contend that Paul's understanding of the new age in Christ leads him not to a *rejection* of Israel's sacred history but to a *retrospective hermeneutical transformation* of Israel's story in light of the story of God's startling redemptive actions: God has sent his Son to rescue us and redeem the

8. On the interpretation of Paul's term Ἰουδαϊσμός, see now the valuable essay by Matthew Novenson, "Paul's Former Occupation in *Ioudaismos*," in *Galatians and Christian Theology: Justification, the Gospel, and Ethics in Paul's Letter*, ed. Mark W. Elliott et al. (Grand Rapids: Baker Academic, 2014), 24–39.

9. See, e.g., J. Louis Martyn, "Galatians, an Anti-Judaic Document?," in *Theological Issues in the Letters of Paul* (Nashville: Abingdon, 1997), 77–84.

whole world, and God has sent forth the Spirit to confirm and continue God's transforming work in the community of God's people in Christ—a community that now embraces Jews and gentiles together without distinction. All this requires a dramatic rereading of Israel's story, but what is required is precisely a *rereading*, not a repudiation.[10]

After all, as Paul strikingly claims in Gal 3:8, Scripture *foresaw* that God, out of his own faithfulness to his promises, would justify the gentiles, and Scripture *pre-proclaimed the gospel to Abraham*. From this it follows that Paul's passionate engagement with scriptural interpretation in his Letter to the Galatians is not simply a reluctant concession to his opponents; rather, it is a necessary component of his own apostolic mission. Paul seeks to teach his gentile readers how to discover and interpret the complex hermeneutical relationship between Israel's story and the new creation in Christ.

Another way to put this point is to say that the dichotomy between apocalyptic and salvation history is false. Israel's sacred history is indeed a preparation for the gospel, but Paul does not understand that history as a simple linear progression toward triumphant fulfillment; rather, the story has to be reread retrospectively under the guidance of the Spirit in light of its fulfillment in Christ. However, God's "apocalyptic" act in Christ does not simply shatter and sweep away creation and covenant; rather, it hermeneutically reconfigures creation and covenant, under the guidance of the Spirit, in light of cross and resurrection.

All of this means that to understand "apocalyptic" in Paul, we must attend to *the gospel's imaginative remaking of the world*. To interpret the apocalyptic rhetoric and theology of Galatians, we must reflect on the *poetics* of the letter, the way in which Paul deploys language and imagery to reshape the symbolic world in which his readers live and move.

If we pick up Galatians and read through the Greek text from start to finish, we find ourselves immersed in a sea of images and sensibilities that may indeed be called apocalyptic, in the sense that they are revelatory of a world charged with spiritual conflict and spiritual power. There is no clearly defined dispensationalist scheme here, except for Paul's urgent conviction that when the time had fully come, God sent forth his Son, and everything changed. Reading this letter plunges us into a drama in which Paul, the zealous devotee of Jewish law who was persecuting the church and trying to destroy it, suddenly receives what he calls "the apocalypse of Jesus Christ" and finds himself seized by the commission to proclaim good news about Jesus Christ to the gentiles (1:11–16).

10. On these themes, see Richard B. Hays, *The Conversion of the Imagination: Paul as Interpreter of Israel's Scripture* (Grand Rapids: Eerdmans, 2005).

Reading this letter plunges us into a drama in which God's Spirit is afoot in the world so palpably that Paul can impatiently ask his readers to recall just how they first received this Spirit that is now performing mighty works (δυνάμεις) in their midst (3:1–5). Reading this letter plunges us into a drama in which the powers of Spirit and Flesh are at war with each other (5:16–17), and the community now given life by the Spirit is called to stand fast and not submit to oppressive powers seeking to subjugate them again to slavery (4:8–11; 5:1).

This is not the world of the university classroom. It is more like the world of Martin Luther's hymn "Ein' feste Burg," particularly its third stanza:

> And though this world, with devils filled,
> should threaten to undo us,
> We will not fear, for God has willed
> his truth to triumph through us.[11]

Paul writes as a charismatic preacher; he writes as a strong poet. His arguments depend on rich narrative allusions, on metaphorical linkages, and even on fanciful allegorical interpretation. His logic is more associative than linear. And his rhetoric is aggressive and hyperbolic. Paul can say that his readers at one point would have torn out their own eyes for him (4:15); he can breathe the wish that the rival troublemaking preachers would castrate themselves (5:12); and he can declare metaphorically that he has been crucified along with Christ (2:19).

Apocalyptic Themes and Imagery: A Catalog

It may be useful to consider a short catalog of some elements in Galatians in which we see Paul's *poiēsis* at work, shaping the apocalyptic imaginative matrix within which he wants his readers to see the world. Here is a selective list of some of the images and motifs that appear in the letter:[12]

11. Martin Luther, "A Mighty Fortress Is Our God" ("Ein' feste Burg ist unser Gott"), hymn 110 in *The United Methodist Hymnal: Book of United Methodist Worship*, trans. Frederick H. Hedge (Nashville: United Methodist Publishing House, 1989 [1853]). Original German text:

> Und wenn die Welt voll Teufel wär'
> Und wollt' uns gar verschlingen,
> So fürchten wir uns nicht so sehr,
> Es soll uns doch gelingen.

12. For a similar list of "apocalyptic expressions" in Galatians—a shorter list, but with fuller interpretative comments—see Martyn, *Galatians*, 97–104.

1 God raised Jesus Christ from the dead (Gal 1:1).

2 Christ died "to rescue us from the present evil age" (1:4; cf. 2:20).

3 Human beings may receive messages from angels, who may be either authentic messengers of God (3:19; 4:14) or deceptive and malevolent (1:8).

4 Paul received his gospel as a divine revelation (ἀποκάλυψις, 1:1, 11–12, 16), and God chose to reveal (ἀποκαλύψαι) his Son in and through Paul (1:16). Further, Paul's decision to go to Jerusalem was directed κατὰ ἀποκάλυψιν (2:2).

5 The opponents of Paul's message are "false brothers" (2:4), who presumably stand under a curse (1:9). Those who are led astray from Paul's gospel are "bewitched" (3:1).

6 Paul has died to the Law through being "crucified with Christ," and now Christ lives in him (2:19–20). Indeed, through Christ's death the whole world has been crucified, and Paul has been crucified to the world (6:14). He bears the στίγματα of Christ on his body (6:17).

7 The Spirit is a power palpably active in the community and working miracles (3:5).

8 Scripture (ἡ γραφή) speaks in oracular fashion to prophesy future events (3:8–9; cf. 4:21–31).[13]

9 Israel, because of disobedience, stands under the curses of Deut 27–28 (Gal 3:10).

10 Christ has redeemed "us" (Israel?) from the curse pronounced by the Law through absorbing the curse in his death on a cross (3:13).

11 Paul's use of Χριστός to describe the agent of redemption and salvation strongly suggests that the term should be understood to refer to a Messiah figure (3:16).[14]

12 The phrase "sons of God" in 3:26 refers to the eschatological people of God, disclosed only at the end time (cf. Rom 8:19).[15] Those who are

13. These events are in the future from the perspective of the scriptural text, but not from the perspective of Paul and his readers; one thing that sets Galatians apart from most apocalyptic literature is that it does not prophesy or speculate about events in future time.

14. On this, see N. T. Wright's essay for the St. Andrews conference, "Messiahship in Galatians?," in Elliott, *Galatians and Christian Theology*, 3–23. Note also the use of σπέρμα as recipient of the promises (3:16, 19), and its messianic sense in 2 Sam 7:12–14a LXX. For a significant study reexamining the use of Χριστός as a messianic title in Paul, see Matthew V. Novenson, *Christ among the Messiahs: Christ Language in Paul and Messiah Language in Ancient Judaism* (Oxford: Oxford University Press, 2012).

15. See James M. Scott, *Adoption as Sons of God: An Exegetical Investigation into the Background of υἱοθεσία in the Pauline Corpus*, WUNT 2/48 (Tübingen: Mohr Siebeck, 1992);

sons and daughters of God have "put on Christ" and entered, at least proleptically, into an existence where the antinomies of the old age—the distinctions of race, class, and gender—are rendered insignificant (Gal 3:26–28).

13 Paul says that both he and his readers were once enslaved under τὰ στοιχεῖα τοῦ κόσμου (4:3; cf. 4:8–9). But God has sent forth his Son to liberate his people and to send the Spirit upon them and make them "heirs" (4:4–7). As Rodrigo Morales has shown, this image of the giving of the Spirit was traditionally understood in Second Temple Judaism as a sign of the eschatological restoration of Israel.[16]

14 Paul depicts himself as being "in labor" with his converts until Christ is eschatologically formed in them (4:19).[17]

15 Paul's allegorical reading of the Sarah/Hagar story contrasts "the present Jerusalem" in slavery with the eschatological "Jerusalem above, which is free" (4:25–26).

16 The community now awaits "the hope of righteousness" (5:5). This should be understood as the community's earnest hope for eschatological fulfillment, as in Rom 8:18–25. But those who live by the flesh will not "inherit the kingdom of God"—another clear reference to future eschatological hope (Gal 5:21). By contrast, those who "sow to the Spirit" will "reap eternal life" (6:8).

17 Several phrases point to Paul's expectation of an eschatological day of reckoning: those who trouble the Galatians will incur God's final judgment (5:7–10). The sowing/reaping imagery of 6:7–9 employs a traditional set of metaphors for eschatological judgment.

18 The formerly salient distinction between circumcision and uncircumcision has been rendered meaningless by God's "new creation" (6:15). Those who live into this reality can be described as "the Israel of God," God's eschatological people (v. 16).

More detailed exegesis would no doubt identify still more eschatological/apocalyptic ideas and images in the letter. But this list of some of the more obvious examples suffices to show how thoroughly Paul is seeking to reshape the imagination of his readers, seeking to narrate them into a symbolic world where

and Susan G. Eastman, "Whose Apocalypse? The Identity of the Sons of God in Romans 8:19," *JBL* 121 (2002): 263–77.

16. Rodrigo J. Morales, *The Spirit and the Restoration of Israel*, WUNT 2/282 (Tübingen: Mohr Siebeck, 2010), esp. 41–77.

17. On the eschatological overtones of this labor/birthing imagery, see Gaventa, *Our Mother Saint Paul*, 29–39.

God the Father, Jesus Christ the Son of God, and the Spirit are powerfully at work to bring a new world into being.

Shall we use the term "apocalyptic" to describe the imaginative *poiēsis* enacted in Paul's language? The question is really just a semantic quibble. This much is clear: the symbolic world created by Paul's imagery is one in which all the initiative in the rescue of God's people belongs to God. It is a world in which the death and resurrection of Jesus have decisively transformed the conditions of all human existence, so that the times before and after these events are qualitatively different from each other. Looking back at Israel's Scripture from the perspective of the new age, we can see that God had always scripted the story to prefigure God's action in Christ to justify the nations of the world and bring them into unity with Israel, but only in retrospect does this interpretation of Scripture become evident. The news of God's redemptive transformation of the world has been conveyed by divine revelation to Paul. The world disclosed in this revelation is a world alive with superhuman powers, who are engaged in conflict and seeking to enslave or liberate human beings. Although God has decisively achieved the rescue of his people through the cross, the consummation of God's transforming righteousness remains a future hope. In this situation "the Israel of God" is summoned to walk under the guidance of the Spirit and resist the seduction of the powers of the old age, who seek to suck them back into slavery.

This is the story told—perhaps better, the picture drawn—by Paul's language in Galatians. It is a remarkable poetic performance, giving expression to the gospel with epic narrative sweep and linguistic power. Within the storied world that Paul portrays, I now want to focus on three motifs that can illuminate ongoing theological reflection today. The three motifs are God as Father (*paternity*), Jesus's death as the pivotal liberating event (*passion*), and union with Christ (*participation*).

Major Motifs and Images in the Narrative World of Galatians

Paternity and Sonship: The Adoption of Gentiles into the Covenant People

In Galatians, Paul uses the word "Father" (πατήρ) only a few times to name God,[18] but the passages in which it does appear are fraught with theological significance. There are two key passages: 1:1–5 and 4:3–7.

18. The designation of God as Father appears in all thirteen letters of the extended Pauline corpus.

First, in the letter's opening salutation, Paul names God as Father three times. He amplifies his usual greeting formula ("Grace to you and peace from God our Father") in two striking ways. He opens the letter by asserting first that his commission as an apostle comes "through Jesus Christ and God the Father," not from any human source (1:1). And then he expands the "grace and peace" formula by adding a phrase that describes Jesus's action of self-giving to rescue us from the present evil age as an action performed "in accordance with the will of our God and Father" (1:4). Thus, God the Father is portrayed here as the initiating source behind Jesus's saving action, as well as the one who commissions the dissemination of the gospel to the world through Paul's apostolic activity.

Second, the dramatic narrative passage in Gal 4:3–7 even more clearly portrays God as the Sender,[19] the sovereign initiator of the saving event: in the fullness of time *God sent forth his Son* to redeem (i.e., emancipate) his people under the Law, so that they might receive the status of sonship. Further, to those who do receive this status, God sent the Spirit into their hearts, a Spirit who in turn enables them to cry out "Abba! Father!" Whether their cry is one of grateful praise or anguished petition is not clear in the context.[20]

In either case, this passage demonstrates that our interpretation of God's paternity must embrace not only the texts in which Paul refers directly to God as πατήρ but also the texts in which he refers to Jesus as "Son of God" and/or to God's people as "sons [and daughters] of God." Paternity and sonship are complementary images that require each other. Thus, alongside the two passages already noted, we should take particular note of 2:20, where "the Son of God" is described as the one "who loved me and gave himself for me." As a result of this self-donation of the Son, Paul has lost his independent existence and now lives "by the faithfulness of the Son of God."[21] In all three of these passages where Christ is designated as "Son of God," Paul is drawing attention to his self-sacrificial death and highlighting the redemptive effect of that death.[22] Furthermore, in a mysterious way, the Son's redemptive death effects υἱοθεσία,

19. On this designation for God in Paul's master narrative structure, see Richard B. Hays, *The Faith of Jesus Christ: The Narrative Substructure of Galatians 3:1–4:11*, 2nd ed., The Biblical Resource Series (Grand Rapids: Eerdmans, 2002 [1983]), 90–117.

20. The parallel in Rom 8:14–17 suggests the former.

21. On this interpretation, see Hays, *Faith of Jesus Christ*, 153–55.

22. The verb ἐξαγοράσῃ in 4:5 echoes ἐξηγόρασεν in 3:13, thus linking the Son's redemptive act to his cursed death on a cross.

bringing his people into union with himself in such a way that they too become υἱοί (3:26; 4:6–7) and thereby become "[heirs] through God" (4:7).[23]

The theme of "inheritance" for the "sons of God" is of particular importance because it shows that Paul now thinks of his Galatian gentile readers as "heirs according to promise" (3:29), de facto participants in the covenant people Israel. It is the people Israel to whom the promise of an inheritance (κληρονομία) had long been given, starting with Abraham. This is precisely the focus of Paul's concern in the lengthy argument of 3:6–4:7.

Furthermore, it is the people Israel concerning whom God instructed Moses to say to Pharaoh, "Israel is my firstborn son" (Exod 4:22). And Israel's filial tie to God is also invoked by the prophet Isaiah, who cries out, "You, O LORD, are our father; our Redeemer from of old is your name" (Isa 63:16). Or again, in Isa 64, the prophet pleads with God:

> Yet, O LORD, you are our Father;
> we are the clay, and you are our potter;
> we are all the work of your hand.
> Do not be exceedingly angry, O LORD,
> and do not remember iniquity forever.
> Now consider, we are all your people. (64:8–9)

And again, in the prophecy of Jeremiah, God answers Israel's prayers by reaffirming his paternal relation to the people who will ultimately return from exile:

> With weeping they shall come,
> and with consolations I shall lead them back,
> I will let them walk by brooks of water,
> in a straight path in which they shall not stumble;
> for I have become a Father to Israel,
> and Ephraim is my firstborn. (31:9)

In later Second Temple Judaism, these prophetic traditions about fatherhood and sonship are tied closely to the hope that God will restore Israel and that they will obediently keep the commandments of the Torah. For a clear example, see *Jubilees* 1:23–25:

23. On this theme, see Scott, *Adoption as Sons of God.*

> And I shall create for them a holy spirit, and I shall purify them so that they will not turn away from following me from that day and forever. And their souls will cleave to me and to all my commandments. And they will do my commandments. And I shall be a father to them, and they will be sons to me. And they will all be called "sons of the living God." And every angel and spirit will know and acknowledge that they are my sons and I am their father in uprightness and righteousness. And I shall love them.[24]

Thus, when Paul assures the Galatians that "you are all sons of God through the faithfulness of Jesus Christ" (3:26) and reminds them that the Spirit enables them to cry "Abba! Father!" and to claim the status of "heirs," he is saying in metaphorical language that they are now participants in "the Israel of God" (6:16), partakers in the covenant of promise, members of God's family whom he is bringing out of metaphorical exile. But their status of sonship is now granted and assured, not because of their obedience to Torah, but because of Jesus Christ's faithful death for their sake and their union with him through baptism. So God's covenant with Israel is not renounced but reconfigured.

These background intertexts show that the language of God's paternity and the sonship of those who belong to Christ is *not* meant to refer primarily to some sort of affective piety or individual experience of spiritual intimacy with God; rather, when Paul tells the Galatians that they are "sons of God," this is *covenant* language that assures the Galatians of their participation in the covenant community of God's people.[25] Thus, any Christian theology that takes its bearings from Galatians needs to grapple with its apocalyptic emphasis on the fatherhood of God—made manifest through his redemptive action of creating a new eschatological covenant community, in which Jew and Greek, slave and free, male and female are all equally "sons of God."[26]

24. Translation from O. S. Wintermute, "Jubilees," in *The Old Testament Pseudepigrapha*, vol. 2, ed. James H. Charlesworth (New Haven: Yale University Press, 1983), 54. For discussion of this passage, see Scott, *Adoption as Sons*, 107–9, 114, 178–80. For further relevant examples, both in the OT and in Second Temple Jewish texts, see the discussion in Marianne Meye Thompson, *The Promise of the Father: Jesus and God in the New Testament* (Louisville: Westminster John Knox, 2000), 35–55. See also Morales, *Spirit and Restoration*, 43–48, 127–31.

25. After surveying the use of "Father" language for God in the OT and in Second Temple Judaism, Thompson observes, "It is this very notion of God as Father who gives his children an inheritance that is crucial to Paul's argument in Romans and Galatians. God the Father has, through the Spirit, made Jews and Gentiles together 'heirs of God and joint heirs with Christ' (Rom. 8:16–17; cf. Gal. 4:6)" (*Promise of the Father*, 116–17).

26. On this theme, see Brendan Byrne, *"Sons of God"—"Seed of Abraham": A Study of*

Passion: The Death of Jesus as Saving Event

As we have already noted, the keynote salutation in Galatians emphasizes that "the Lord Jesus Christ gave himself for our sins." This opening declaration alludes to the passion story of Jesus's death and places the cross at the heart of Paul's proclamation. The allusion is sounded again in 2:19b–20, this time with an explicit mention of Paul's co-crucifixion with "the Son of God who loved me and gave himself for me." This reference to the Son's loving death—the letter's only mention of "love" prior to the hortatory material in chapter 5—ensures that Paul's directives to the community to serve one another in love and to "fulfill the law of Christ" by bearing one another's burdens (5:13–14; 6:2) will be understood as admonitions to conform their lives to the self-giving pattern of Jesus Christ's death.[27] And the image of the cross is at last brought front and center at the beginning of chapter 3, as Paul, after the extended *narratio* of chapters 1 and 2, directly confronts the Galatians about their own faithless folly: "O foolish Galatians, who has bewitched you, before whose eyes Jesus Christ was portrayed (προεγράφη) as crucified (ἐσταυρωμένος)?" Paul here refers to the vivid *poiēsis* of his own preaching: in his initial proclamation to the Galatians, he vividly narrated the story of the passion of Jesus, his death on the cross, as an act of self-giving for the sake of all.[28]

The apostle continues to hammer home this theme insistently through the rest of the letter. For example, just a few sentences later, Paul explains that Christ accomplished his act of redemption by becoming a curse for us through being hanged on a tree (3:13). Because these texts so firmly bind the themes of redemption and rescue to the cross, at least two more subsequent passages also serve to remind the readers of Jesus's death:

---

the Idea of Sonship of God of All Christians in Paul against the Jewish Background, AnBib 83 (Rome: Biblical Institute Press, 1979), esp. 189–90.

27. On this interpretation of "the law of Christ" in 6:2, see Richard B. Hays, "Christology and Ethics in Galatians: The Law of Christ," *CBQ* 49 (1987): 268–90.

28. It is also possible that Paul's προεγράφη (3:1) alludes to his own physical scars, which in 6:17 he calls τὰ στίγματα τοῦ Ἰησοῦ, as a graphic visible portrayal of Christ's crucifixion. This is a possible secondary sense, but the meaning of προεγράφη as referring to vivid public narration is well established and should be taken as the primary sense of Paul's expression here. See the evidence cited by Hans Dieter Betz, *Galatians: A Commentary on Paul's Letter to the Churches in Galatia*, Hermeneia (Philadelphia: Fortress, 1979), 131n39. See also B. S. Davis, "The Meaning of *Proegraphē* in the Context of Galatians 3.1," *NTS* 45 (1999): 194–212.

> God sent forth his Son . . . in order that he might *redeem* those under the Law. (4:4–5, my translation)

> For freedom Christ has set us free. (5:1)

In addition to these references, I would also continue to commend strongly the interpretation of Paul's several references to the faithfulness of Jesus Christ (πίστις Ἰησοῦ Χριστοῦ, 2:16, 20; 3:22; 3:26) as metonymic allusions to the story of Jesus's faithful self-giving death on the cross.[29] If this reading is adopted, it adds even more weight to Paul's emphasis on the cross as the crux of his gospel.

In the final hortatory section of the epistle, Paul several more times refers to the cross as the heart of his proclamation. He alleges that to preach circumcision would be to avoid persecution for "the offense of the cross" (5:11; 6:12), and he declares his intention to boast in nothing other than "the cross of our Lord Jesus Christ" (6:14). These texts bear obvious links with Paul's more extended treatment of the foolishness of the κήρυγμα of the cross in 1 Cor 1:18–2:5. But Gal 6:14–15 extends the imagery of the cross into a remarkable apocalyptic dimension: through the cross of Christ, the *world* has been crucified, and Paul has been crucified to the world. It is this cataclysmic death of the old κόσμος, through the cross, that has cleared the way for "new creation" (v. 15)—presumably brought into being through the resurrection of Jesus (1:1) and the work of the Spirit. The cross thus becomes the crucial pivotal event at the heart of the cosmic apocalyptic drama in which Paul sees himself and his churches living and acting. Thus any Christian theology that takes its bearings from Galatians will need to grapple with what we might call its apocalyptic *staurocentricity*.

Participation in Christ

Underlying both the paternity/sonship imagery and the imagery of the cross is a third closely related but distinguishable image: the motif of the believing community's union with Christ. Why and how is the cross a saving event rather than a terrible cosmic tragedy? Why and how do former pagans become God's sons and receive the inheritance promised to Abraham? Paul's answer to both questions is the same: a mysterious union, a fusion of identities, has occurred, in such a way that Jesus has enacted our destiny in his death and resurrection, and we find ourselves caught up into him, incorporated into his life. Paul uses a variety of metaphors to characterize this union with Christ. Consider the following examples:

29. Hays, *Faith of Jesus Christ*. See esp. the "Introduction to the Second Edition," xxi–lii.

1 Paul has been crucified with Christ so that he no longer lives, but Christ lives in him. Or to put it a little differently, the life that he lives, he lives by the faithfulness of the Son of God (2:19–20).
2 Christ is the one messianic "seed" (σπέρμα) envisioned in God's promise to Abraham. Because he has received the promise (through his death and resurrection), we too receive it because we are "in" him and belong to him (3:16, 29).
3 In baptism we have been plunged into Christ, and we are now "clothed with Christ," so that we are all one in him (3:27–28).
4 Paul is a mother who is suffering the pangs of childbirth until Christ is fully formed in the Galatians (4:19).

The shorthand version of these metaphorical depictions is the simple formula "in Christ," which Paul uses repeatedly to characterize his own existence and the existence of his churches (Gal 1:22; 2:4, 17; 3:14, 26, 28; 5:6). The second-order theological term that best describes the soteriological logic of all these passages—a term not used by Paul himself, but an apt summary of the force of these texts—is "participation in Christ." Gregory of Nyssa, in his reading of Paul, focuses clearly on this theme. His word for "participation" is μετουσία—a term that could usefully be adopted by Pauline scholarship today.[30]

This participatory soteriology is the dominant paradigm in Galatians for understanding the way in which Christ rescues his people.[31] In this respect, at least with regard to Galatians, E. P. Sanders was right to contend that "the main

30. There is a particularly illuminating discussion of "participation" in Gregory of Nyssa's treatise *On Perfection*. For a brief discussion of the light shed on Paul by the comparison to Eastern patristic sources, see Richard B. Hays, "What Is 'Real Participation in Christ'?," in *Redefining First-Century Jewish and Christian Identities: Essays in Honor of Ed Parish Sanders*, ed. Fabian E. Udoh et al. (Notre Dame: University of Notre Dame Press, 2008), 336–51, esp. 347–49. For a study of participatory soteriology in Paul, see Daniel G. Powers, *Salvation through Participation: An Examination of the Notion of the Believers' Corporate Unity with Christ in Early Christian Soteriology*, CBET 29 (Louvain: Peeters, 2001). Yet Powers makes only slight use of patristic sources and does not cite Gregory of Nyssa at all.

31. The themes of participation in Christ and conformity to Christ have been particularly illuminated by Michael J. Gorman in two important studies: *Cruciformity: Paul's Narrative Spirituality of the Cross* (Grand Rapids: Eerdmans, 2001) and *Inhabiting the Cruciform God: Kenosis, Justification, and Theosis in Paul's Narrative Soteriology* (Grand Rapids: Eerdmans, 2009). Gorman's use of the term "theosis" in his more recent book has stirred controversy among some Protestant interpreters, but readers who attend carefully to his exposition of the term will see that he is using it in a sense that corresponds closely to the participatory and transformative soteriology found in Galatians and in Paul's other letters.

theme of Paul's theology is found in his participationist language rather than in the theme of righteousness by faith."[32] Participation in Christ is certainly more foundational to the argument of Galatians than is any forensic conception of justification. Thus, any Christian theology that takes its bearings from Galatians must grapple with its apocalyptic vision of μετουσία: union with Christ as the means and meaning of salvation.

Paul's Apocalyptic *Poiēsis* as Theological Source and Stimulus

Reflections on the Theological Implications of Paternity, Passion, and Participation

What are the theological consequences and implications of the reading of Galatians offered in this essay? I have proposed that we should read the whole letter through the lens of 1:3–5. Paul's own introduction of his epistle frames his sharply critical pastoral response to the Galatian churches within a cosmic narrative about God's Son, Jesus Christ, who was sent forth by God the Father and gave himself up on the cross in order to rescue us from the present evil age. Consequently, if we are to take our theological bearings from Galatians, the church must work out all its teaching and all its moral and ecclesial practices within the world created through this decisive event and through the telling and retelling of this story.

The story is apocalyptic in the sense that it focuses resolutely on God's inbreaking action to end an age of slavery and bring into being a new age, indeed a new creation. But it is also very different from many other Jewish apocalyptic narratives—including Paul's own narratives in some of his other letters[33]—in that it lacks any specific speculations about future events,[34] and it seems unconcerned with contemporary political events and powers. If we place Galatians and Daniel on the table alongside each other—or Galatians and Revela-

32. E. P. Sanders, *Paul and Palestinian Judaism: A Comparison of Patterns of Religion* (Philadelphia: Fortress, 1977), 552.

33. I am thinking here particularly of 1 Cor 15:21–28, 50–57; 1 Thess 4:13–18; and even Rom 8:18–39.

34. The letter does gesture rather vaguely toward a future "hope of righteousness" (5:5) and God's ultimate judgment of human beings (5:7–10; 6:7–9), but these eschatological expectations are not presented as imminent, and they are given little specificity. Even the future hope of resurrection is not explicitly mentioned in Galatians.

tion—these differences stand out immediately in sharp relief. Thus, if Galatians is "apocalyptic," it is apocalyptic in its own particular transformative mode.

The hermeneutically transformative effect of this remarkable epistle is the product of Paul's *poiēsis*—his imaginative renarration of a symbolic world in which the gospel story reshapes everything. In this essay I have singled out three major motifs within that imaginative renarration. In conclusion I turn to a few brief suggestions about how each of these motifs might come into play in our theological reflection today.

(1) *God the Father acts freely and graciously to rescue his people, in a totally unexpected way, to create a new covenant community of the "sons of God."* This new community is continuous with the covenant community of Israel reaching all the way back to Abraham yet at the same time is discontinuous in its surprising inclusion of gentiles as God's sons and daughters. The relation between continuity and discontinuity is worked out through scriptural exegesis that demonstrates how God's unexpected action was prefigured and promised in Israel's Scripture, whose true original sense is now at last disclosed through the apocalypse of Jesus Christ. This complex retrospective hermeneutical reconfiguration of "the Israel of God" complicates any attempt at simple judgment about whether Paul is or is not a supersessionist. A corollary of this point is that Pauline interpreters ought to quit lobbing the accusation of "supersessionism" at one another.[35]

(2) *The cross is the decisive event that is the pivot point of the ages, ending the curse, ending humanity's slavery to the στοιχεῖα τοῦ κόσμου, and opening the way to the new creation.* It is remarkable that in Galatians, in contrast to his other letters, Paul pays relatively little attention to the resurrection of Jesus.[36] As we have seen, the resurrection of Jesus is foregrounded in the opening salutation; consequently, we know that Paul regards it as a key part of the gospel story. But in this particular letter, he makes it do remarkably little specific critical work. To be sure, when he declares, "It is no longer I who live, but Christ lives in me"

35. For a particularly unfortunate example, see Douglas Harink's treatment of N. T. Wright in *Paul among the Postliberals: Pauline Theology beyond Christendom and Modernity* (Grand Rapids: Brazos, 2003), 151–207.

36. By contrast, see Daniel Kirk's helpful discussion of resurrection as a central theme in Romans: J. R. Daniel Kirk, *Unlocking Romans: Resurrection and the Justification of God* (Grand Rapids: Eerdmans, 2008). For an argument that the future resurrection of the dead plays an important *implicit* role in Galatians, see N. T. Wright, *The Resurrection of the Son of God*, Christian Origins and the Question of God 3 (London: SPCK; Minneapolis: Fortress, 2003), 219–25: "Though Galatians does not mention the resurrection explicitly, there are many points at which it is so close to the surface that we can see it just below the waterline" (224).

(2:20), it is the *risen* Christ who is portrayed as the active agent in Paul's new life. But in Galatians it is the death of Jesus on a cross that occupies most of Paul's attention and seems to fire his pastoral imagination.

The effect of this *staurocentric* narrative strategy is to highlight the radically transformative character of the gospel drama. To give one example, consider Gal 2:21: "I do not nullify the grace of God. For if righteousness comes through the law, then Christ died for nothing." The very fact that such a drastic measure as the death of Jesus Christ was necessary demonstrates both the depth of the human predicament of bondage to death—which the Law was powerless to rectify (3:21)—and at the same time the astonishing grace and love of God that conceived and executed such a costly rescue operation.

It is highly significant that God's means of carrying out this rescue is through the incarnation and self-giving death of Jesus, rather than through the violent conquest of enemies.[37] Paul formulates the logic of this position in his later Letter to Romans: "God proves his love for us in that while we were still sinners Christ died for us. . . . For if while we were enemies, we were reconciled to God through the death of his Son, much more surely, having been reconciled, will we be saved by his life" (5:8, 10). Thus, as Michael Gorman rightly observes, for Paul the cross is the definitive sign of "God's nonviolent reconciliation."[38] This has wide-ranging implications that Christian theology and theological ethics must seek to address ever anew.

(3) *In Galatians, human beings receive the benefits of God's saving action through incorporation in Christ.* The logic of salvation is *participatory*. For Christian theology, the ripple effects of this insight are extensive. It means, first of all, that the distinction between justification and sanctification is at best artificially heuristic and at worst positively misleading. One little phrase in Galatians indicates how closely these aspects of soteriology are bound together: in Gal 2:17, Paul can speak of "seeking to be justified in Christ." Justification in fact means inclusion in the covenant community of God's people, and as we have seen, that inclusion takes place in and through union with Christ. So justification and sanctification should never be pried apart.

Of equal importance, Paul's emphasis on participation in Christ necessarily leads to a strong ecclesiology that is integral to Paul's soteriology. To

37. That is one reason why Martyn's metaphor of Christ's action as an "invasion" is potentially misleading. See now the helpful essay of Susan G. Eastman, "Apocalypse and Incarnation: The Participatory Logic of Paul's Gospel," in *Apocalyptic and the Future of Theology: With and Beyond J. Louis Martyn*, ed. Joshua B. Davis and Douglas Harink (Eugene, OR: Wipf & Stock, 2012), 165–82.

38. Gorman, *Inhabiting the Cruciform God*, 129–60.

be "in Christ" entails participation in the church, because "you are all one in Christ Jesus" (3:28). That is why the radical vision of Gal 3:28 (neither Jew nor Greek, neither slave nor free, no "male and female") is not just a utopian social program. Instead, it is a normative vision of the new community that Jesus Christ has actually brought into being in the church. That is why Paul can complain that Cephas and his segregationist friends at Antioch were "not walking straight toward the truth of the gospel" (2:14). The truth of the gospel is that there is one table where all the members of God's family, who all equally participate in Christ, share in the meal that embodies that communion. Any social arrangement that divides the one table into two is a denial of the new creation and a betrayal of our μετουσία in Christ.[39]

Reflections on the Style of Paul's Pastoral Theology

Of course, there are many significant theological themes in Galatians that I have not attempted to address here. For example, I have said too little about faith and about the role of the Spirit in the new creation.[40] But the three motifs I have identified offer at least a starting place for conversations about Paul's apocalyptic *poiēsis*. Yet I want to offer three concluding remarks not about the thematic substance of Paul's theology in Galatians but about its *style*—the manner in which Paul writes as a pastoral theologian in this letter. I hazard the suggestion that each of these points might offer some useful instruction for theology in our time.

(1) *Paul writes as a hermeneutical theologian.* Confronted with a fundamental challenge to his understanding of the gospel, his response is to return to a close and passionate reading of Israel's Scripture. Contrary to the once-influential view of Adolf von Harnack that Paul engaged in OT interpretation only when forced to counter the views of judaizing opponents,[41] we should instead follow the much older and wiser opinion of Origen: Paul as "teacher

39. For a prescient treatment of this theme, see Nils Alstrup Dahl, "The Doctrine of Justification: Its Social Function and Implications," in *Studies in Paul* (Minneapolis: Augsburg, 1977), 95–120.

40. If I were determined to keep my alliterative pattern going, I could add to my discussion of paternity, passion, and participation two additional sections on *pistis* and *pneuma*. But I forbear.

41. Adolf von Harnack, "Das Alte Testament in den Paulinischen Briefen und in den Paulinischen Gemeinden," *Sitzungsberichte der Preussischen Akademie der Wissenschaften: Philosophischhistorische Klasse* 12 (1928): 124–41; also appeared as an offprint booklet (Berlin: de Gruyter, 1928).

of the Gentiles" was deeply concerned about teaching his converts how to read Scripture.[42] In order to do this, he brought Israel's Scripture into a new generative conversation with the story of the death and resurrection of Jesus Christ. In the case of Galatians, we see that this hermeneutical strategy produced reconfigured readings of the stories of Abraham, Sarah, and Hagar as well as surprising engagements with Deuteronomy and Habakkuk. We would do well to emulate this pastoral strategy; when facing challenges, we should constantly return to the study of Scripture.

(2) *Paul is not afraid to think big.* Faced with a vexing controversy in his churches, he frames the problem in relation to a cosmic narrative of the gospel, a narrative of how, in the fullness of time, God the Father sent forth his Son. He does not appeal to custom or convention or to opinion polls. Instead, he retells the gospel story and thinks about the problem in radical terms. Surely that is one of the reasons why Galatians has perennially exercised such influence in the theological imagination of the church. Our kneejerk tendency, by contrast, is to fiddle with adjustments and compromises, with procedural rules and refinements of recent political arrangements in the church. Paul might dare us to think bigger about fundamental questions.

(3) *Paul is not afraid of polemic.* I offer this observation with some trepidation, because in some sectors of the church there is already all too great a readiness to adopt a polemical tone similar to Paul's brutally undiplomatic "O brainless Galatians, who has bewitched you?" (3:1). But I equally suspect that in other theological circles—and certainly in many approaches to pastoral care and preaching—the default tone has instead become one of unconditional, nonjudgmental inclusivity, a tone that greets any and all opinions and practices with tepid, suffocating tolerance. To the extent that this is an accurate diagnosis of a certain malaise in "mainstream" Protestantism, Galatians may come as a bracing blast of fresh air, with its uncompromising call: "Stand firm, . . . and do not submit again to a yoke of slavery" (5:1). Galatians reminds us that there are times when the truth of the gospel really is at stake, when we must not yield submission even for a moment to forces that would compromise or undermine the liberating message of Jesus Christ. The difficult task, of course, is to discern when those times are at hand, when we are confronting a *status confessionis.* We may receive help on such discernment if we return to Galatians again and

42. Origen, in *Hom. Exod.* 5.1, writes that the apostle Paul, "'teacher of the Gentiles,' taught the church which he had gathered from among the Gentiles, how to understand the books of the Law" (Origen, *Origen: Homilies on Genesis and Exodus*, trans. Ronald E. Heine, FC 71 [Washington, DC: Catholic University of America Press, 1982], 275, translation amended).

again and reflect analogically on the powerful story it tells, a story of paternity, passion, and participation. And if we succeed in faithfully reading Galatians analogically as a word to the church in our time (as Luther did in his time), we too will be participating in the practice of apocalyptic *poiēsis*.

12

PNEUMATOLOGY

The Spirit in Romans 8

An Intertextual Approach to Paul's Language about the Spirit

New Testament scholarship has found it difficult to work out appropriate categories for grasping the apostle Paul's language about the Holy Spirit. For almost ten years in the 1980s and 1990s, I participated in a working group of scholars in the Society of Biblical Literature that focused on the topic of Pauline Theology. We debated endlessly about the meaning of terms such as justification, faith, and law. We grappled with Paul's views of Israel and the relation between Jews and gentiles. We pondered the ways in which Paul's theological arguments are tailored to address particular historical circumstances in Paul's churches. We argued about whether Paul was an apocalyptic thinker. But a retrospective look at the volumes of essays produced by that group shows that we paid remarkably little attention to the topic of the *Spirit* in Paul.[1] Indeed, if Paul himself had dropped in on one of our SBL meetings and asked this distinguished group of scholars whether we had considered the role of the Holy Spirit in his thought, I suspect that many would have answered, like the

1. The SBL Pauline Theology Group published four volumes of essays: Jouette M. Bassler, ed., *Pauline Theology*, vol. 1 (Minneapolis: Fortress, 1991); David M. Hay, ed., *Pauline Theology*, vol. 2 (Minneapolis: Fortress, 1993); David M. Hay and E. Elizabeth Johnson, eds., *Pauline Theology*, vol. 3 (Minneapolis: Fortress, 1995); and E. Elizabeth Johnson and David M. Hay, eds., *Pauline Theology*, vol. 4, SBL Symposium Series 4 (Atlanta: Scholars, 1997). The first three volumes in the series have subsequently been reprinted as volumes 21–23 in the SBL Symposium Series (Atlanta: Scholars, 2002).

This essay was presented at a conference on the theme "Geist," at the Johann Wolfgang Goethe-Universität, Frankfurt, Germany, on June 19, 2009. It was first published in German as "Intertextuelle Pneumatologie: Die paulinische Rede vom Heiligen Geist," *ZNT* 25 (2010): 30–37.

bewildered disciples in Ephesus, "No, we have not even heard that there is a Holy Spirit" (Acts 19:2).

This slight exaggeration serves to make a point. We find it hard to give a clear account of Paul's teaching about the Spirit—or perhaps it would be more accurate to say not "Paul's teaching" but rather Paul's *language* about the Holy Spirit, for Paul rarely if ever thematizes the Holy Spirit as a topic for instruction in his churches. Perhaps he comes closest to it when he scolds the Corinthians for their abuse of the gifts of the Spirit, but even here he hardly treats the Spirit as a dogmatic topic for systematic exposition. Instead, he seems to assume that his readers already possess some substantial knowledge about the Spirit. And so he refers to it allusively, employing affirmations about the Holy Spirit to support his arguments about other matters.

For example, Paul demands of the "foolish Galatians" that they answer only one decisive question: "Did you receive the Spirit from works of the Law, or from the message of faith?" (Gal 3:2, my translation). The very form of the question assumes that receiving the Spirit is such a clear and powerful experience that it can provide a firm fulcrum giving Paul leverage for the teachings that follow. The meaning of any experience, however, is notoriously slippery; we always must find language and concepts to interpret it. In what sense can the blessing promised to Abraham be identified with the Spirit experience of a congregation of gentiles in a much later time? What *is* this Spirit (πνεῦμα) that Paul believes his readers have received? Is it an impersonal supernatural power or substance? How is it related to God's own presence, or to the person and work of Jesus?

These are precisely the sorts of questions that theological interpretation seeks to address. Yet Paul's statements about the Spirit are so diverse and apparently unsystematic that dogmatic reflection upon them is notoriously difficult. In some places, Paul can use language that appears proto-Trinitarian (e.g., Rom 8:9–11), linking the Spirit almost indistinguishably with the presence and activity of God and Christ. Sometimes the Spirit seems to be a "person" possessing will and agency (1 Cor 12:11). Other times, however, the Spirit seems to be merely an impersonal instrument of the divine will, or a kind of potent celestial fluid poured out to produce effects in the world (Gal 3:5). Alternatively, sometimes Paul seems to talk about the Spirit as a sphere of power or influence, like an electromagnetic field into which God's people are drawn (Rom 8:9a: "you are not in the flesh; you are in the Spirit"); yet other times Paul can use the phrases "in spirit" or "spiritual" in a way that seems to signify some inner mystical intuition (Rom 2:29; 1 Cor 5:3a) or even the figurative sense of a text, as opposed to its literal surface meaning (2 Cor 3:6). Finally, when Paul uses πνεῦμα with no modifying adjective, it is sometimes nearly impossible (as in Rom 12:11 or 1 Cor 14:15) to determine whether he is using the term theologically to refer to the divine Holy Spirit or anthropologically to refer to the human spirit (as in 1 Cor 2:11). What are we to make of all this?

To be sure, there have been attempts to address such questions in a thoroughgoing way and to classify Paul's various usages of πνεῦμα in some comprehensive manner. One thinks particularly of the lengthy article in Kittel's *Wörterbuch*, or more recently, substantial monographs by Friedrich W. Horn and Gordon Fee.[2] Such studies suffer, however, from two basic difficulties. First, because the Holy Spirit is elusive of human understanding (cf. 1 Cor 2:6–16), our attempts at dogmatic definition may prove reductive and inadequate to the mysterious realities of which Paul speaks. Second, although these critical studies have explored the historical antecedents and conceptual structure of Paul's thought about the Spirit, they have given relatively little attention to the *intertextual* character of Paul's discourse about the Spirit. In particular, the significance of the OT as the linguistic matrix for Paul's Spirit language has played a relatively minor role in most critical investigations. For example, Fee treats "The Spirit in the Old Testament" and "The Intertestamental Developments" only in a ten-page appendix at the very end of a nine-hundred-page book. Horn's *Stellenregister* lists only seventeen OT references, and the great majority of these appear in his preliminary chapter on "Voraussetzungen Paulinischer Pneumatologie," rather than in his actual exposition of the key Pauline texts.

The task of the present essay, then, is to explore the implications of thinking about Pauline pneumatology from an intertextual perspective. Careful definition is necessary here. An intertextual reading of Paul's language about the Spirit is not simply concerned with identifying the "sources" of Paul's statements. Nor will it be limited to those passages in which Paul explicitly quotes a scriptural text. Rather, an intertextual approach will offer readings that place Paul's letters in a dialogical relationship with other texts that share the cultural framework (or "encyclopedia") of Paul himself and the early readers of his letters.[3] For example, an intertextual reading might place Paul's letters in

2. Friedrich W. Horn, *Das Angeld des Geistes: Studien zur paulinischen Pneumatologie*, FRLANT 154 (Göttingen: Vandenhoeck & Ruprecht, 1992); Gordon D. Fee, *God's Empowering Presence: The Holy Spirit in the Letters of Paul* (Peabody, MA: Hendrickson, 1994).

3. The term *encyclopedia* as a way of referring to the text's cultural framework was coined by Umberto Eco. See Stefan Alkier, "Die Bibel im Dialog der Schriften und das Problem der Verstockung in Mk 4," in *Die Bibel im Dialog der Schriften: Konzepte intertextueller Bibellektüre*, ed. Stefan Alkier and Richard B. Hays (Tübingen: Francke, 2005), 8: "Die *En-*

counterpoint with Isaiah—particularly with passages such as Isa 44:2–3—and explore whether such a reading seems to shed light on Paul's language about the Spirit. Even if we cannot prove definitively that Paul derived his ideas about the Spirit from a text such as Isa 44:2–3, we do know that Paul was well acquainted with Isaiah and cited it frequently, expecting his readers to understand his citations and allusions.[4] Thus, it can be a fruitful exercise to read Paul in intertextual juxtaposition with Isaiah and to see whether such a reading seems to shed light on Paul's language about the Spirit.

Further, an intertextual reading asks about the *semantic effects* produced when the two texts are read in dialogue with each other. Stefan Alkier provides a helpful guideline: "Von Intertextualität sollte man nur sprechen, wenn das Interesse an der Erforschung von Sinneffekten besteht, die durch die Beziehung mindestens zweier Texte entstehen und zwar von Sinneffekten, die keiner der beiden Texte für sich allein gesehen eröffnet."[5] Thus, to investigate intertextual pneumatology in Paul is to open up imaginative space to consider the metaphorical impact of the poetic fusion of two different worlds of discourse (Isaiah's in the eighth century BCE. and Paul's in the first century CE), or perhaps three (counting our own world).

Of course, intertextual reading is in principle hardly limited to studying the ways in which NT authors read Israel's Scripture. For example, one could also pursue an intertextual reading of Paul's language about the Spirit alongside Stoic texts that speak of πνεῦμα.[6] Within the limited space of the present essay, however, we cannot hope to offer a comprehensive treatment of all the possible

zyklopädie is dabei der kulturelle Rahmen, in den der Text eingestellt wird und von dem aus sich Leerstellen des Textes füllen lassen."

4. On this topic, see Florian Wilk, *Die Bedeutung des Jesajabuches für Paulus*, FRLANT 179 (Göttingen: Vandenhoeck & Ruprecht, 1998) and "Paulus als Nutzer, Interpret und Leser des Jesajabuches," in Alkier and Hays, *Die Bibel im Dialog der Schriften*, 93–116; J. Ross Wagner, *Heralds of the Good News: Isaiah and Paul "In Concert" in the Letter to the Romans*, NovTSup 101 (Leiden: Brill, 2002); and Richard B. Hays, "'Who Has Believed Our Message?' Paul's Reading of Isaiah," in *The Conversion of the Imagination: Paul as Interpreter of Israel's Scripture* (Grand Rapids: Eerdmans, 2005), 25–49.

5. Alkier, "Bibel im Dialog der Schriften," 8. (Translation: "One should speak of intertextuality only when the interest remains firmly on the investigation of meaning effects that arise through the relationship of at least two texts, and specifically on the meaning effects that neither of the two texts, considered individually, opens up.")

6. For a treatment of this theme in the Stoics, see Eduard Schweizer's article on πνεῦμα in *TWNT* 6:394–449. Interestingly, the major comparative study by Troels Engberg-Pedersen (*Paul and the Stoics* [Edinburgh: T & T Clark, 2000]), gives little attention to Stoic conceptions of πνεῦμα. See the important critique of J. Louis Martyn, "De-apocalyticizing Paul: An Essay Focused on *Paul and the Stoics* by Troels Engberg-Pedersen," *JSNT* 86 (2002): 61–102.

intersections between Paul's writings and various ancient cultural repertoires. Instead, I want to offer a limited exploratory probe that will demonstrate some of the possibilities for a fresh intertextual reading of Paul's pneumatology. For this purpose, I will focus on a single Pauline passage that contains a dense concentration of references to the Spirit: Rom 8. The intertextual reading offered here will concentrate on the intertextual dialogue between this text and a few key OT texts, with some attention to the way in which those texts were heard and appropriated also in other Jewish writings of the Second Temple era.[7]

The Spirit's Activity in Romans 8

The word πνεῦμα ("spirit") appears no fewer than twenty times in Rom 8. Although the expression "Holy Spirit" appears nowhere in the chapter, the great majority of these instances clearly seem to refer to "the Spirit of God" (8:9—also in the same verse called "the Spirit of Christ"). In many of these references, the Spirit is imaged as an active power. There have been earlier hints of the Spirit's active role in Rom 1:4 and 5:5, but it is only in this climactic eighth chapter that the Spirit emerges fully on stage as an agent who *does* things. Paul's closely interwoven statements about the Spirit's activity can be grouped into three categories: the Spirit gives life; the Spirit leads God's children; and the Spirit groans and intercedes for us. In each case, Paul's language evokes rich resonances of Israel's Scripture.

The Spirit Gives Life

The Spirit's life-giving role is the keynote of Rom 8, for the Spirit is first introduced here as "the Spirit of life" (8:2). It is the "law" (νόμος) of "the Spirit of life in Christ Jesus" that "has set you free from the law of sin and of death"—the oppressive condition that Paul has described insightfully in chapter 7. Romans 8:2 has sometimes been interpreted to mean that it is some noetic "principle"

7. My thinking on this topic has been stimulated by the work of two scholars writing in English whose contributions are perhaps not (or not yet) very well known in Germany: Sylvia C. Keesmaat, *Paul and His Story: (Re)Interpreting the Exodus Tradition*, JSNTSup 181 (Sheffield: Sheffield Academic Press, 1999); and Rodrigo J. Morales, *The Spirit and the Restoration of Israel: New Exodus and New Creation Motifs in Galatians*, WUNT 2/282 (Tübingen: Mohr Siebeck, 2010). Keesmaat's study was originally a doctoral thesis written at Oxford University under the direction of N. T. Wright, and I had the pleasure of directing Morales's doctoral dissertation at Duke University.

of life in Christ that sets captives free. But the subsequent references to the Spirit's life-giving *action* make it clear that this exegesis of 8:2 cannot be correct. Rather, the Spirit who gives the mindset (φρόνημα) that produces life and peace (v. 6) is a *power* that actually dwells in the believer (v. 9). Further, even though the human body is dead because of sin, Paul says not, as we might expect, that the human spirit is alive, but rather that the Spirit itself *is* "life because of [God's] righteousness" (v. 10). This shows that Rom 8:10 should not be understood to express an anthropological dualism: Paul is not saying that our human spirits will live even when our bodies die. Rather, he is saying that the Spirit of God is the power of life that overcomes our enslavement to death. This is made unmistakably clear in the following sentence: the Spirit is "the Spirit of [the One] who raised Jesus from the dead," and for that reason we can trust that this same Spirit "will also give life to [our] mortal bodies" (v. 11). This is an anticipatory reference to the resurrection of the body—a hope firmly reiterated in verse 23 ("the redemption of our bodies" from bondage to decay).[8] The Spirit's life-giving role is ultimately confirmed by the eschatological resurrection of the body, but the same life-giving power of the Spirit is also already at work in the present to shape and transform God's people; consequently, they are no longer in the grip of sin but are freed to fulfill the righteous command of God by walking in the power of the Spirit (v. 4).

Nowhere in Rom 8:1–11 does Paul quote a scriptural text or allude overtly to Israel's Scripture. Nonetheless, his account of the Spirit's activity in this passage comes more sharply into focus when we place it alongside several OT passages, especially Ezek 36:26–28:

> A new heart I will give you, and *a new spirit I will put within you*; and I will remove from your body the heart of stone and give you a heart of flesh. *I will put my spirit within you*, and make you follow my statutes and be careful to observe my ordinances. Then you shall live in the land that I gave to your ancestors; and you shall be my people, and I will be your God.

In its original context, this is a word of divine promise about the restoration of Israel from exile. According to Ezekiel's prophecy, Israel's disobedience defiled the land, and so God judged them "in accordance with their conduct and

8. On the central role of resurrection in Romans, see N. T. Wright, *The Resurrection of the Son of God*, Christian Origins and the Question of God 3 (London: SPCK; Minneapolis: Fortress, 2003), 241–66; and J. R. Daniel Kirk, *Unlocking Romans: Resurrection and the Justification of God* (Grand Rapids: Eerdmans, 2008).

their deeds" and scattered them among the nations (36:16–19). But God now declares his intention to gather Israel from diaspora, bring them back to the land, and purify them (vv. 22–25). The promise of "a new spirit" is then meant to ensure that the people will follow God's commandments faithfully and live in a restored covenant relation to God. Interestingly, the "new spirit" of verse 26 is further specified in verse 27 as "*my* spirit"—i.e., the Spirit of God, which God promises to put "within you."

Exactly the same promise is reiterated in the next chapter of Ezekiel, following the great vision of the valley of dry bones. The prophet follows God's command to prophesy over the bones, "and the breath/spirit (MT: רוּחַ, LXX: πνεῦμα) came into them, and they lived (LXX: ἔζησαν), and stood on their feet, a vast multitude" (Ezek 37:10). In the concluding words of the unit, God offers the prophet an explicit interpretation of the vision: the bones are the house of Israel, and God intends to open their graves, raise them up, and bring them back to the land (vv. 11–12). And, most significantly for our reading of Romans, God instructs Ezekiel to say to the people, "*I will put my spirit within you, and you shall live* (LXX: ζήσεσθε)" (v. 14).

Thus, in Ezek 36 and 37, God promises to restore Israel by placing his Spirit within his people to raise them from the dead, give them new life, and empower a new obedience from the heart (cf. also Jer 31:31–34). The congruence of these motifs with Rom 8:1–11 is compelling: just as God's Spirit will give life to the dry bones, so the Spirit of the one who raised Jesus from the dead will indwell God's people and "give life to your mortal bodies" (Rom 8:11). This explains God's answer to Paul's cry, "Who will rescue me from this body of death?" (7:24). And, furthermore, this life-giving Spirit will also produce a new radical obedience in those who walk according to the Spirit, an obedience that the Law was powerless to produce (8:3–4).

What, then, is the effect of reading Rom 8 in intertextual counterpoint with Ezek 36–37? It suggests that Paul is concerned to proclaim much more than the salvation of individuals from the power of sin; his field of vision is also corporate and cosmic. The deliverance achieved in Jesus Christ is somehow linked with the restoration of a *people* who will bring honor to God's name by walking in the power of the Spirit; hence, Paul's emphasis on the transformed *conduct* that characterizes the new life in the Spirit (esp. Rom 8:3–13). And when Paul speaks of "no condemnation for those who are in Christ Jesus" (v. 1), their reprieve from judgment parallels the fate of Israel according to Ezekiel: they were judged according to their deeds and scattered, but they will be brought back to life simply because of God's free and merciful life-giving action. Ezekiel describes that life-giving restoration by using the metaphor of resurrection. For Paul, however, the image is more than metaphorical: because God has raised Jesus from the dead, he now envisions an eschatological future in which "the redemption of our bodies" will actually take place in a restored and liberated new creation (vv. 18–25). Thus Paul both draws upon Ezekiel's imagery and transforms it hermeneutically through his gospel of the death and resurrection of Jesus.

Most of all, in Rom 8 Paul is echoing Ezekiel's image of the Spirit as being placed *within* God's people as the source of new life: "I will put my spirit within you, and you shall live" (Ezek 37:14). Paul does not quote this text, but everything he says in Rom 8 about the life-giving power of the Spirit resonates powerfully with this promise.[9] Life is the result of the divinely given indwelling presence of God's own Spirit.

In light of these impressive parallels, why does Paul not quote the Ezekiel passage at this point? We can be reasonably sure that he knows the text, because he alludes to it pointedly in 2 Cor 3:3, where he speaks of Christ's writing "with the Spirit of the living God, not on stone tablets, but on fleshy tablets of the heart." This complex allusion draws both on Jeremiah's image of a new covenant written on the heart (Jer 31:33) and Ezekiel's promise that God will replace Israel's heart of stone with a new heart of flesh (36:26; cf. 11:19).[10] This second independent allusion to Ezek 36 strengthens the probability that Paul knew the text well. Why, then, does he not refer to it more explicitly? Such questions about what Paul did *not* choose to write are impossible to answer. Perhaps in Rom 8 Paul was not consciously alluding to Ezekiel at all; perhaps that text's depiction of the Spirit as the giver of resurrection life was simply part of his encyclopedia of production, at a subconscious level. It seems more likely, however, there was some conscious poetic artistry at work in Paul's discourse. Romans 8 is, after all, a highly skillful and elevated rhetorical composition. Poets and preachers have long known that sometimes the most powerful intertextual allusions are subliminal: to explain every poetic allusion is to deaden metaphorical discourse. In his victory speech on the night of his election as

9. It is also noteworthy that Ezekiel directly links the promise of the Spirit with the promise of renewed possession of the land (e.g., Ezek 36:24–30; 37:14a). This might provide, at some deep level, a partial explanation for Paul's puzzling equation in Galatians of the reception of the Spirit with the fulfillment of the promise to Abraham (offspring and land). If in Ezekiel land is linked to Spirit, perhaps by metonymy the latter comes not only to represent but finally to occlude and supplant the former. But if so, Paul does not explain his process of reasoning.

10. For a discussion of OT echoes in the passage, see Richard B. Hays, *Echoes of Scripture in the Letters of Paul* (New Haven: Yale University Press, 1989), 122–53.

President of the United States, Barack Obama did not quote Martin Luther King Jr. explicitly, but his speech contained several elegant allusive transformations of phrases from King's most famous speeches. Obama did not draw attention to his allusions, but those with ears to hear were able to hear. Perhaps Paul was doing something similar in Rom 8. There is no way to be sure of Paul's intention. But what we can say is this: an intertextual reading of Ezek 36–37 and Rom 8 is both literarily and theologically illuminating.

Of course, Paul's portrayal of the Spirit as a life-giving power does not draw exclusively on this single intertextual echo. A much subtler one may be found in Rom 5:5: "the love of God is poured out in our hearts through the Holy Spirit that is given to us." This image may again be reminiscent of Ezekiel's promise of a new spirit within God's people, but the specific language of Rom 5:5 corresponds more closely to an important image from Isa 44:3: "I will *pour my spirit* upon your descendants, and my blessing on your offspring." Like the passage from Ezekiel, this oracle in Isaiah belongs to a larger prophecy of the end of exile and the restoration of Israel. It is, interestingly, the only passage in the OT that directly associates the terms "spirit" and "blessing" (here in synonymous parallelism). When Paul uses the image of the *outpouring* of the Spirit, therefore, we may well hear an echo of this word of promise in Isaiah.

The case for such a reading has been strengthened by an important study by Rodrigo Morales, demonstrating that Isa 44:3 was appropriated also by a liturgical fragment from Qumran, known as the Words of the Luminaries. In this text we find a prayer thanking God for remembering his covenant promises, regathering the people, and putting into their hearts the desire to obey the commandments. All of this is of course closely parallel to Ezek 36. But then we find this explanation of the way in which God has changed Israel's previously disobedient heart: "you have poured out your Holy Spirit upon us, [to be]stow your blessings to us" (4Q504 5.15–16). Morales observes that this passage offers clear evidence that other Jewish interpreters in Paul's time focused on Isa 44:3 as a promise of Israel's eschatological redemption through the reception of the Holy Spirit.[11] This finding confirms that Isa 44 also belongs appropriately

11. Rodrigo J. Morales, "The Words of the Luminaries, the Curse of the Law, and the Outpouring of the Spirit in Gal 3,10–14," *ZNW* 100 (2009): 268–78. See also the similar passage *Testament of Judah* 24.2–3: "And the heavens will be opened upon him to pour out the spirit as a blessing of the Holy Father. And he will pour out the spirit of grace upon you. And you shall be sons in truth, and you will walk in his first and final decrees" (translation from H. C. Kee, "Testament of the Twelve Patriarchs," in *The Old Testament Pseudepigrapha*, ed. James H. Charlesworth [New Haven: Yale University Press, 1983], 801). Morales rightly observes that the *Testament of Judah* cannot with confidence be treated as a pre-Christian Jewish source,

to the intertextual field within which we should read Paul's discourse about the Spirit as a life-giving power poured into the heart. In Rom 5, Paul's most significant hermeneutical transformation of this tradition is to identify the outpouring of the Spirit with the *love* of God, a motif not found explicitly either in Isa 44 or in the Words of the Luminaries.

The Spirit Leads God's Children

Returning to Rom 8, we find in Rom 8:14–15 a new and different portrayal of the activity of the Spirit. Here the Spirit is said to *lead* the "sons of God." This language is strongly reminiscent of the terms in which Israel recalled the exodus from Egypt, when the Lord went in front of the people "in a pillar of cloud by day, *to lead them* along the way, and in a pillar of fire by night" (Exod 13:21). Particularly significant is the retrospective account of the exodus found in Deut 32, for here the people of Israel are described as God's children (v. 5), his sons and daughters (vv. 19–20). God is pictured as their father (LXX: πατήρ, v. 6; cf. v. 18), who alone *led* (LXX: ἦγεν, v. 12) them in the wilderness. Thus, as Sylvia Keesmaat has observed, when Paul writes, "all those who are led by the Spirit of God, these are sons of God" (Rom 8:14), "the echoes of Deuteronomy 32 which can be perceived in Romans 8 are abundant."[12] The case for hearing such echoes is strengthened both by the prominence of Deut 32 (the Song of Moses) in Jewish tradition and by Paul's own frequent citations of and allusions to this text.[13] The intertextual linkage is reemphasized when Paul continues in his next sentence to say, "For you did not receive a spirit of *slavery* leading back again into *fear*, but you received a spirit of adoption (or *sonship*), in which we cry 'Abba, *Father* (πατήρ)'" (Rom 8:15). Here again, it seems that Paul is describing the situation of his Christian readers in Rome by using exodus metaphors. They should not be afraid and desire to return to "the house of slavery," as did the Israelites in the desert. (E.g., Exod 14:10–12: "In great *fear* the Israelites cried out to the Lord. They said to Moses, . . . 'What have you done to us, bringing us out of Egypt? . . . For it would have been better for us to *be slaves* to [NRSV: "serve"] the Egyptians than to die in the wilderness.'") Instead, they should continue to recognize the leading of the

for it may reflect Christian influence or even authorship. Nonetheless, if our interest is in intertextual reading rather than sources, this text may still provide significant insight into the encyclopedia of production within which Paul's letters were read at an early date.

12. Keesmaat, *Paul and His Story*, 61.

13. For further discussion of Paul's use of Deut 32, see Hays, *Echoes of Scripture in the Letters of Paul*, 93–94, 163–64.

Spirit of God, which confirms their status as "sons," causes them to cry to God as Father, and shows the way to freedom.

Similar images appear once again in another retrospective retelling of the exodus story in Isa 63:7–14, a passage that laments Israel's unfaithfulness and calls upon God to remember and save them. The prophet declares that Israel, though they were God's children, "rebelled and grieved [God's] holy spirit" (v. 10), and he asks, "Where is the one who *put within them his holy spirit* (!) . . . ?" (v. 11). He then recalls the dividing of the sea, and wonders where God is, "who *led them* through the depths" (v. 13). The prophecy poignantly continues with a cry to God as Father, seeking his saving intervention in the present time:

> For you are our *father,*
>   though Abraham does not know us
>   and Israel does not acknowledge us;
> you, O LORD, are our father;
>   our Redeemer from of old is your name. (v. 16; cf. also 64:8)

Thus in Isa 63 we see a clustering of imagery related to the exodus that resonates strongly with Rom 8:14–15. The Spirit is depicted as the presence of God that led God's children/sons in the exodus, and Isaiah longs for the return of God's presence (e.g., Isa 64:1) to bring about a new exodus that will restore Israel's freedom and reaffirm God's compassionate fatherhood of his people. These are precisely the events that Paul proclaims, in Rom 8:14–15, as having taken place through Jesus Christ and the presence of the Holy Spirit in the community of God's people.

The motif of a new exodus appears likewise in Isa 43:1–7, a passage that emphatically declares, "Do not fear, for I am with you" (Isa 43:5; cf. 43:1). It is particularly striking to read this text in the LXX, which affirms not only that God will "lead" his "sons and daughters" (v. 5) whom he has "redeemed" and "called" (vv. 1, 7) but also that they are "glorified" because God "loves" them (v. 5). All of this seems to foreshadow the unfolding emphases of Paul's argument in Rom 8, for he not only argues that the sons of God are led by the Spirit and moved to call to him as "Father" (vv. 14–15); he also goes on to say that they need not fear the sufferings of the present time, for God has called, justified, and glorified them, and nothing can separate them from the love of God (see especially vv. 30, 39).

Was Paul consciously alluding to these texts from Exodus, Deuteronomy, and Isaiah, in the expectation that his readers would perceive the allusions? We cannot say for sure. We do know, however, that the exodus tradition stood at the very center of Israel's national identity and memory, and indeed at the center of their understanding of God. These are hardly obscure texts. It is precisely the centrality of these texts in Israel's historical imagination that enables Paul to renarrate the condition of his readers *metaphorically*—just as the authors of Deuteronomy and Isaiah had done before him—within the symbolic world of the exodus story. Michael Fishbane, observing the various metaphorical transformations of the exodus tradition within the Hebrew Bible, writes of "the capacity of the exodus paradigm to elicit memory and expectation." Further, he observes,

> the very capacity of a historical event to generate future expectation is dependent on the transfiguration of that event by the theological intuition that in it and through it the once and future power of the Lord of history is revealed. Without such symbolic transformation, the exodus would never have given birth to hope.[14]

Paul is the heir of Israel's conviction that the power of God was disclosed in the exodus, and Rom 8 is a powerful example of the "symbolic transformation" of which Fishbane speaks. Therefore, only an intertextual reading of Paul's language about the Spirit in Rom 8 can disclose the full range and depth of his vision for the church as a people eschatologically redeemed by the same living God who led Israel out of Egypt.

The Spirit Groans and Intercedes for Us

Finally, in light of the above intertextual readings of Paul's language about the Spirit, we may venture a slightly more speculative proposal that seeks to clarify one puzzling feature of Rom 8: Paul's account of the Spirit's interceding for the people of God with "inarticulate groans" (v. 26). This is a notoriously difficult passage for exegesis. How are we to translate and interpret Paul's expression στεναγμοῖς ἀλαλήτοις? Does it refer, as some English translations have rendered it, as "sighs too deep for words"? (Perhaps following Luther's "mit unaussprechlichem Seufzen.") Is Paul talking about some silent inner form of prayer? Or does he refer, as some interpreters suggest, to the Spirit-inspired phenomenon of speaking aloud in unintelligible cries and tongues?[15]

14. Michael Fishbane, *Text and Texture: Close Readings of Selected Biblical Texts* (New York: Schocken, 1979), 140.

15. See, e.g., Ernst Käsemann, "Der gottesdienstliche Schrei nach der Freiheit," in *Paulinische Perspektiven* (Tübingen: Mohr, 1969), 211–36.

Either way, what motivates him to use this extraordinary image to describe the Spirit's work of intercession?

First, we must note that Paul has already introduced the sound of groaning into the text in verses 19–23, where he speaks of the whole creation yearning to be set free from "*slavery* [NRSV: "bondage"] to decay" in hope of obtaining "the freedom of the glory of the children of God." If our foregoing analysis of echoes of exodus in Rom 8:14–15 is correct, it would seem that Paul has now transposed the exodus paradigm to another imaginative level, describing creation's bondage to death as analogous to Israel's slavery in Egypt, and envisioning the eschatological redemption of all creation as a new and final exodus, in which the whole created world will share in Israel's experience of redemption and freedom. If so, Paul's statement that creation "is groaning together" (συστενάζει, v. 22) can hardly fail to remind the reader who has ears to hear of Israel's groaning in slavery in Egypt:

> The Israelites *groaned* (LXX: κατεστέναξαν) under their *slavery*, and cried out. Out of the *slavery* their cry for help rose up to God. God heard their *groaning* (στεναγμόν), and God remembered his covenant with Abraham, Isaac, and Jacob. (Exod 2:23–24)

Or again:

> I have also heard the *groaning* (στεναγμόν) of the Israelites whom the Egyptians are holding as *slaves*, and I have remembered my covenant. (Exod 6:5; see also Acts 7:34)

It is the more remarkable, then, that Paul, who has just spoken of the indwelling Spirit of God as leading and assuring God's children, now asserts that it is not only the enslaved creation that groans but also "we ourselves, who have the first fruits of the Spirit." Even those who have received the Spirit "groan (στενάζομεν) inwardly while we wait for adoption, the redemption of our bodies" (Rom 8:23). That is, the children of God share fully in creation's suffering and agonized groaning—and in this respect, they still stand analogously in the situation of Israel in bondage in Egypt, awaiting God's deliverance.

Further, this groaning of creation is described in terms of "labor pains" (Rom 8:22). The suffering of the present time is not merely meaningless, random suffering, but it is part of a painful, hope-filled process leading to the birth of the new age. Here, Paul has appropriated a common apocalyptic symbol (see, e.g., Mark 13:8; Rev 12:2; 1QH^{a} 11.6–8).[16] In Rom 8, the exodus imagery and the apocalyptic imagery of cosmic suffering as leading to new birth are superimposed upon one another. This fusion of images makes the text difficult to interpret if we are looking for a single simple decoding of its multilayered metaphorical language. But an intertextual perspective will acknowledge the overlay of these different symbolisms and reflect on the complex semantic effect produced by their simultaneous presence—like the sounding of dissonant notes in a single chord.

But Paul has saved his most dramatic intertextual effect for his depiction of the activity of the Spirit. God does not stand apart from the creation's suffering. God does not just *hear* the groaning of creation and of the children of God who groan along with it (as in the Exodus story). Rather, God's Spirit *joins in the groaning*: "Likewise, the Spirit helps us in our weakness; for we do not know how to pray as we ought, but that very Spirit intercedes *with inarticulate groans* (στεναγμοῖς ἀλαλήτοις) [NRSV: "sighs too deep for words"]. . . . [T]he Spirit intercedes for the saints according to the will of God" (Rom 8:26–27). Reading this remarkable description, the reader who has noted Paul's repeated allusions to Isaiah's prophecies of God's redemption of Israel might recall this one as well:

> For a long time I have held my peace,
>   I have kept still and restrained myself;
> now I will cry out like a woman in labor,
>   I will gasp and pant. (Isa 42:14)

God declares through Isaiah that his activity of judgment and redemption will cause him to cry out like a woman in labor. And now, in Rom 8, Paul declares that the Spirit of this same redeeming God will join together with creation's groaning in labor pains to intercede (paradoxically) for the ultimate deliverance of the saints and the world.[17]

16. The antecedents of the apocalyptic use of the "birth-pangs" image are to be found in Israel's prophetic literature (e.g., Isa 13:6–8; 26:16–18; Jer 6:24; Mic 4:9–10). In these passages the image chiefly describes the suffering of Israel under God's judgment, but in Mic 4:10 the suffering is preparatory to redemption, and in Isa 26 the description of futile labor pains is immediately followed by a promise of resurrection: "the earth will give birth to those long dead" (Isa 26:19). For discussion of Paul's use of this imagery, see Beverly Roberts Gaventa, *Our Mother Saint Paul* (Louisville: Westminster John Knox, 2007), 32–34, 56–59.

17. For the reference to Isa 42:14 and further discussion of this motif, see Keesmaat, *Paul and His Story*, 122.

It would go beyond the available evidence to assert that Paul had thought through all this, and that he calculatingly drew upon these scriptural texts to argue for a doctrine of the Spirit's redemptive participation in suffering. But by using language that echoes and evokes these traditions from Israel's Scripture, Paul certainly has created a text laden with intertextual resonances. We can affirm unhesitatingly that these scriptural texts belonged to Paul's encyclopedia of production; further, we can suggest that readers who share these same canonical texts as part of their encyclopedia of reception will be moved to creative theological reflection within the metaphorical field created by these intertextually resonant images. Such readings are likely to yield a nuanced pneumatology, for readers will come to realize that the Holy Spirit about which Paul writes is *simultaneously* to be understood as the breath that animates dry bones and gives life to the dead; as the pillar of cloud and fire that led the children of God out of slavery and through the sea; and as the intimate presence of God's own self participating with us in labor and groaning while we await the final disclosure of creation's freedom.

13

Gospel

For Gentiles Only?

Paradigm shifts in Christian theology have often turned upon revolutionary readings of Paul's Letter to the Romans: Augustine, Luther, and Barth found in Romans the catalyst for their epoch-making insights, and each in turn offered a fresh overall construal of the letter. Stanley K. Stowers, professor of religious studies at Brown University, now seeks to produce a "rereading" of Romans whose effects would be of comparable scope: *A Rereading of Romans: Justice, Jews, and Gentiles.*[1] Indeed, he explicitly sets out to undo the interpretations of his great predecessors, who have (erroneously, he believes) read into Romans "systems of sin and salvation" that would have been unintelligible to readers in Paul's time. Through his revisionary reading, he hopes to recover "a kind of Christianity that existed before Christianity became a religion of an intrinsically sick human nature and its cure" (329).

Stowers's ambitious effort fails in the end to account for everything in Romans; indeed, there is much material in the letter that resists his novel construction. Still, we learn a great deal from him along the way, for he is a learned and acute interpreter. In the following discussion of *A Rereading of Romans,* I shall first summarize his argument, then identify some of its important contributions, and finally offer a critique of his proposals. I shall conclude with an epilogue offering some reflections about the relation between Stowers's project and the tasks of Christian theology.

1. Stanley K. Stowers, *A Rereading of Romans: Justice, Jews, and Gentiles* (New Haven: Yale University Press, 1994). References to *A Rereading of Romans* are given in parenthetical citations.

Stowers's Proposed Reading of Romans

According to Stowers, interpreters of Romans, at least from Augustine onward, have persistently misread the letter by superimposing upon it anachronistic schemes of Christian doctrine and failing to understand its original purpose and audience. Paul had no conception, Stowers asserts, of "Christianity" as a new religion or of Christians as a "third race" distinct from Jews and gentiles. If that is so, Romans must be read very differently. One tragic consequence of the traditional misreading has been to produce anti-Jewish interpretations of many passages in the letter. Stowers insists, however, that such interpretations can be overcome by a more historical reading. His programmatic question is this: "How can one read Romans afresh as a letter from the Greco-Roman world of the first century C. E.?" (6). Such a reading will seek to identify the cultural codes that were available to Paul's first-century gentile readers and to show how the letter might be intelligible in the context of these codes.

The following summary highlights six major theses, both methodological and substantive, of Stowers's work. Nowhere does Stowers himself itemize precisely this set of affirmations. This summary represents my own distillation of the points that I take to be distinctive and of central importance in his argument.

(1) *Romans is addressed to an exclusively gentile audience.* Stowers is careful to indicate that he is speaking not of the original empirical readers at Rome but of the readers encoded in the text: "The encoded audience is a feature of the text itself. I can know with certainty that the audience in the text is Gentiles at Rome who know something about Jewish scripture and Jesus Christ, but I can only speculate about who actually read the letter. . . . Separating the encoded reader from the empirical reader helps one to see that the encoded audience is always a rhetorical strategy of the text" (22). Stowers's insistence that this encoded audience is entirely non-Jewish, which can be maintained only with some difficulty, is crucial to his reading.

(2) *Romans must be read against the backdrop of Greco-Roman literature and moral philosophy.* Stowers draws on his extensive knowledge of ancient Greco-Roman texts to sketch an intellectual and literary context for Paul's letter, ranging from "the moral politics of the Augustan revolution" as the rhetorical presupposition of Rom 1:18–32 (52–65) to Euripides's *Medea* as the background for Rom 7 (260–64) to the Homeric story of the footrace at the funeral games of Patroclus (in book 23 of the *Iliad*) as the "allusive background metaphor" for Romans 11 (312–16). The book simultaneously highlights such Greco-Roman cultural factors and polemicizes against "the fantasy that Paul had some biblical doorway into the culture of ancient Israel and a super culture-blocker that prevented him from inhabiting even his own [Greek] language" (316). Stowers

by no means denies the presence or importance of biblical themes and allusions in Paul's thought; however, he contends that the Greco-Roman cultural setting "controls" his use of the scriptural texts by providing the "framework of meaning" within which biblical texts are read (316).

(3) *For the encoded gentile audience, a major theme of Romans is "self-mastery."* In a world where Hellenistic philosophy focused persistently on gaining control of the passions and desires, Paul's letter can be read as offering gentiles a new and more powerful means of self-mastery. Indeed, Paul tells "the story of God's righteous action through Jesus Christ" in such a way that "Christ becomes an enabler of the disciplined and restored self" (42). In Stowers's view, this understanding of the gospel was so prevalent in antiquity that he can describe Galen, a cultured second-century outsider, as watching intently for "the latest achievements in this *self-potential movement* that endlessly elaborated the theme of control" (81, emphasis mine). To be sure, Paul's gospel provides a new spin on this theme by stressing the initiative and power of God as the indispensable means of gaining control over the passions, but (per Stowers) the theme of mastering desire remains central to the argument of Romans.

(4) *Major portions of Romans should be read not as Paul's own voice but as "speech in character."* Stowers (widely known for his earlier important study *The Diatribe and Paul's Letter to the Romans*[2]) stresses the dialogical character of the letter. To "follow" Paul's argument, he contends, we must at numerous points posit a change of speaker, similar to what we find in Arrian's *Discourses of Epictetus*. Even though there are no explicit markers in the text to indicate change of speakers, ancient readers trained in the conventions of *prosōpopoiia* ("speech in character," the dramatic representation of various contrasting views for the purpose of instruction) would have had little trouble picking up the clues in the text and assigning the different lines to the right characters (esp. 16–21).

Thus, for example, Stowers reads Rom 2:17–4:23 as an extended dialogue between Paul and an imaginary interlocutor, a pretentious Jewish teacher who presumes the ability to instruct gentiles in keeping the Law (144–250). At several turns, Stowers's exegesis of the text depends on assigning statements in the text not to Paul but to this imagined opponent. To cite another example, Rom 7:7–25 should be read, according to Stowers, not as Paul's own voice but as an expression of the struggles of a gentile "god fearer" who has attempted without success to gain control over his passions by keeping the commandments of the Law (264–84).

(5) *Paul assumes that God's covenant with the Jewish people remains intact*

2. Stanley K. Stowers, *The Diatribe and Paul's Letter to the Romans*, SBLDS 57 (Chico, CA: Scholars Press, 1981).

and that they are rightly related to God through it. Here Stowers stands within a recent interpretative trajectory pioneered by Krister Stendahl, John Gager, and Lloyd Gaston.[3] Stowers suggests that for Paul the worship and sacrifices at the temple in Jerusalem had continuing validity and efficacy: indeed, Paul "assumed that the temple system would continue in the age to come" (96). Even though Paul nowhere states these views explicitly, they are the necessary corollary of the idea that the Mosaic covenant is unbroken and sufficient for the Jewish people, which Stowers is convinced was the viewpoint of Paul: "The minute one begins to imagine the books of Moses concretely and to think about how these writings functioned among Jews in Paul's time, the idea of Paul saying that the law, with its divinely ordained institutions, cannot make Jews acceptable to God becomes absurd" (190).

In order to uphold this position, Stowers must counter the traditional interpretation of Rom 9–11 as Paul's anguished meditation over Israel's rejection of the offer of salvation through Christ. Thus, he proposes a revisionary reading contending that Paul is concerned not about Israel's failure to find salvation but about their failure to recognize the legitimacy of the gospel of Jesus Christ as God's means of reconciling the gentiles to God (285–316). Accordingly, Stowers argues (though not, it seems, with perfect consistency throughout the book) that the gospel of Christ's death and resurrection is exclusively—or at least primarily—for gentiles.[4] Thus, Rom 3:21–26, for example, which has traditionally been read as a proclamation of God's provision of universal atonement through the death of Christ, speaks, according to Stowers's reading, only of "God's justice toward the gentile peoples" (202–6).

(6) *The faithfulness of Jesus Christ (πίστις Ἰησοῦ Χριστοῦ, 3:22) refers to Jesus's renunciation of his messianic powers and prerogatives, allowing himself to be killed rather than using his divine power to execute judgment on the unrighteous (213–14)*. Thus, Jesus's death is to be interpreted not in terms of sacrificial blood atonement but as an act of gracious forbearance, a model of "adaptability to

3. Krister Stendahl, *Paul among Jews and Gentiles* (Philadelphia: Fortress, 1976); John Gager, *The Origins of Anti-Semitism* (Oxford: Oxford University Press, 1983); Lloyd Gaston, *Paul and the Torah* (Vancouver: University of British Columbia Press, 1987).

4. After the original appearance of this review (*CRBR* 9 [1996]: 27–44), Professor Stowers, in private correspondence, protested strongly that I had misconstrued his position on this crucial point. I have not attempted to revise the review for inclusion in the present volume, but I would urge readers to consult Stowers's book for themselves to judge whether I have misread him. I certainly did not mean to caricature his interpretation. If I have inadvertently misrepresented his position on this point, some of my critique is wide of the mark, though it would still apply to other interpreters who hold the view that Paul embraced a two-covenant schema in which Jews could be saved apart from Christ.

the needs of others" (219). The effect of the death of Jesus was to postpone the judgment of the world in order to give gentiles the opportunity to repent and live righteously. This aspect of Stowers's reading is only sketchily developed, but it plays an important role in his overall construction for two reasons: (a) it allows him to interpret most of the letter's language about "faith" as a reference to Jesus's action rather than the subjective response of the believer; and (b) it allows him to integrate Paul's Christology with his ethics, thereby linking the hortatory part of the letter (chs. 12–15) closely with the argument of the first eleven chapters.

This brief sketch of these six theses conveys some sense of the wide-ranging scope of Stowers's argument, but it hardly suggests the weight and density of his discourse. Stowers works hard to account for the overall coherence of Romans, and he demands that the reader work hard along with him. After an introductory chapter explaining the need for a new interpretation and a second chapter highlighting the importance of "self-mastery" in Greco-Roman culture, Stowers's approach is to work painstakingly through a close reading of each particular passage under consideration, demonstrating how it is to be read in light of his hypotheses. The argument becomes repetitious at points, no doubt because Stowers finds repetition necessary to counteract the subliminal power of traditional readings, but it constantly pushes the reader to rethink the letter comprehensively in relation to the proposed hypotheses and in relation to a rich compendium of Greco-Roman sources.

Stowers's interpretative work, however, is exegetically uneven. Some points of particular interest to him are buttressed by massive argumentation, while other key claims rest almost entirely on bald assertion, with remarkably little exegetical support (see below). Similarly, the weight of Stowers's attention is unevenly distributed through the letter, falling disproportionately on Rom 1–4. Only after two hundred and fifty densely packed pages does he reach Rom 5, but the final twelve chapters of the letter are treated in less than eighty pages. This is perhaps a mercy to the reader. Had Stowers continued his exposition in comparable detail, the book would have run close to a thousand pages (i.e., it would be comparable in length to the recent two-volume commentary of James D. G. Dunn, of whom Stowers is sharply critical [22–29]).[5] Apparently, having established the foundation for his rereading of Romans in his detailed treatment of the first four chapters, Stowers feels able to treat the rest of the epistle more economically; after all, he is not attempting to write a commentary. It would, however, be fascinating to see him attempt such a project in the future, because the commentary genre would compel him to deal more thoroughly with some details of the text that fit awkwardly into his construction.

5. James D. G. Dunn, *Romans*, 2 vols., WBC (Dallas: Word, 1988).

Significant Contributions of Stowers's Reading

Even though several of Stowers's basic theses remain unpersuasive (as I shall try to show later), his fresh approach to Romans yields a number of valuable contributions. It is not possible to mention all of them in this essay, but the following points are representative.

Stowers offers a plausible account of how some themes in Romans might have been heard by first-century gentiles. He ably executes the imaginative exercise of rereading the text through the perspective of an ancient gentile reader. This reading opens up a number of insights that have remained mostly hidden in the Augustinian tradition of theological interpretation. For example, it is indisputable that self-mastery was indeed a pervasive concern of popular philosophical traditions in this period and that Hellenistic Jewish writers frequently played upon this theme by representing Judaism as a superior "school for self-mastery" (58–65). There are indeed passages in Romans that seem to evoke similar concerns, and Stowers compels us to read such passages with new eyes.

To cite one case, even if Paul has more than gentiles in mind in Rom 7:7–25, it is difficult to deny that Stowers provides an illuminating account of how this notoriously difficult passage might sound to a gentile godfearer who continues to struggle with mastering the desires of the flesh. Furthermore, Stowers's suggestion that such a reader might hear this passage in counterpoint with *Medea* is compelling. The imagination of ancient moral philosophers was captured by the passage in which Medea, preparing to execute her terrible revenge, declares, "I am being overcome by evils. I know that what I am about to do is evil but passion is stronger than my reasoned reflection and this is cause of the worst evils for humans."[6] Stowers adduces impressive quotations from Epictetus, Plutarch, Galen, and Ovid, showing that this statement became a *locus classicus* for subsequent debates about the will and moral psychology in the Greco-Roman world. Of course (as Stowers acknowledges) Paul's solution to the problem of ἀκρασία (lack of self-mastery) differs dramatically from the solutions offered by the moral philosophers, but Stowers's discussion demonstrates that Rom 7 should be heard in counterpoint with this ongoing tradition.

Another way of putting this point is to say that Stowers enriches our understanding of the complex intertextuality of Paul's discourse. Though my own work has focused on Israel's Scriptures (rather than Greek literature and philosophy) as the primary intertextual matrix for Paul's thought,[7] I welcome

6. Euripides, *Medea* 1077–1080, quoted in Stowers, *Rereading of Romans*, 260.

7. Richard B. Hays, *Echoes of Scripture in the Letters of Paul* (New Haven: Yale University Press, 1989).

Stowers's contribution also insofar as it further allows us to hear the resonances of Paul's language more precisely and subtly.

Another example of this kind is Stowers's observation about the meaning of "weakness" (ἀσθένεια) in the Hellenistic philosophical tradition. He quotes Cicero's statement that weakness is "an unwholesome aversion and loathing for certain things . . . an intense belief, persistent and deeply rooted, which regards a thing that need not be shunned as though it ought to be shunned."[8] Romans 14–15 should be read, Stowers suggests, against the backdrop of the psychagogic tradition, in which the "weak" person was given "therapy" by the philosopher in order to overcome such weakness: "Thus the weak and the strong [in Romans 14–15] . . . are not groups or parties or theological positions, as New Testament scholars have thought, but dispositions of character" (321). This example shows how Stowers's reframing of the letter within Greco-Roman cultural codes might lead to far-reaching reassessments of conventional theories about the audience and purpose of the letter. It has become conventional to take Paul's discussion of the weak and the strong in Romans as an appeal for unity in a church divided by factions; Stowers's observations call at the very least for careful reevaluation of such hypotheses.

On another matter, Stowers's interpretation of πίστις Ἰησοῦ Χριστοῦ supports a growing movement in Pauline studies toward understanding "the faithfulness of Jesus" as the decisive soteriological event in Paul's gospel. One particular contribution of *A Rereading of Romans* is to suggest how this interpretation integrates the various parts of the letter and links the hortatory section of chapters 12–15 more firmly to chapters 1–4. Here Stowers builds on the prior work of others,[9] but, by treating this problem in the context of a comprehensive rereading of Romans, he formulates the issue in appropriately radical terms. Once "righteousness" in Romans has been reinterpreted,

8. *Tusculanae disputationes* 4.23, 26, cited in Stowers, *Rereading of Romans*, 46.

9. E.g., George Howard, "On the 'Faith of Christ,'" *HTR* 60 (1967): 459–65; Howard, *Paul: Crisis in Galatia*, 2nd ed., SNTSMS 35 (Cambridge: Cambridge University Press, 1990); Luke Timothy Johnson, "Romans 3:21–26 and the Faith of Jesus," *CBQ* 44 (1982): 77–90; Richard B. Hays, *The Faith of Jesus Christ: An Investigation of the Narrative Substructure of Galatians 3:1–4:11*, 2nd ed., The Biblical Resource Series (Grand Rapid: Eerdmans, 2002) [original publication: SBLDS 56 (Chico, CA: Scholars Press, 1983)]; Hays, "ΠΙΣΤΙΣ and Pauline Christology: What Is at Stake?," in *Society of Biblical Literature 1991 Seminar Papers*, ed. Eugene H. Lovering (Atlanta: Scholars Press, 1991), 714–29; Sam K. Williams, "Again *Pistis Christou*," *CBQ* 49 (1987): 431–47. For a defense of the objective genitive interpretation see James D. G. Dunn, "Once More Pistis Christou," in *Society of Biblical Literature 1991 Seminar Papers*, ed. Eugene H. Lovering (Atlanta: Scholars Press, 1991), 730–44 [reprinted as an appendix to Hays, *Faith of Jesus Christ*, 2nd ed., 249–71].

as it was by Käsemann,[10] in terms of God's own apocalyptic saving power, the meaning of πίστις must change accordingly ("faith" to "faithfulness"). By pressing his challenge against the older Augustinian-Lutheran construal of the letter as a whole, Stowers clears the way for a fresh reading in which Jesus's own faithfulness becomes the central saving event.

Unfortunately, Stowers's constructive explanation of πίστις Ἰησοῦ Χριστοῦ (213–26) remains blurry and speculative, in part because Paul himself never fully narrates the events to which the compressed formula alludes. Thus, Stowers concedes, he cannot finally prove his thesis that "the saving act for Paul was Jesus' decision not to exercise his messianic mandate" (222). Still, Stowers's work moves the debate on this problem forward; above all, he rightly insists that its solution must be found in a reading that intelligibly coordinates Paul's Christology, soteriology, and ethics. The traditional Augustinian reading has always found such coordination difficult.

As the foregoing examples show, on numerous particular exegetical points, Stowers cuts through the confusion and sets forth helpful readings. Here is a list of some further instances, briefly described.

1 Stowers repeatedly calls attention to the ways in which English translations of Romans have been shaped—or even twisted—by the presuppositions of traditional Christian soteriology. See, for example, his remarks on Rom 9:27 (302).[11] One comes away from this book with a deepened appreciation of the truth that all translation is interpretation.

2 In Rom 2:14–15, Stowers takes φύσει as a modifier of ἔχοντα, rather than ποιῶσιν, thus yielding the translation, "For when gentiles, not having the law by nature, do the things of the law."[12] This interpretation rightly does away with the anomaly of Paul's apparent endorsement of the theoretical possibility that "natural law" might somehow enable gentiles to attain righteousness apart from Torah and apart from Christ. Regrettably, Stowers does not give credence to Cranfield's further suggestion that the gentiles who "do the things of the law" might be gentile Christians (cf. Rom 2:25–29 alongside 7:6, and 2 Cor 3:1–6).[13]

10. Ernst Käsemann, "The Righteousness of God in Paul," in *New Testament Questions of Today*, trans. W. J. Montague and W. F. Bunge (London: SCM; Philadelphia: Fortress, 1969 [1965]), 168–82; and Käsemann, *Commentary on Romans*, trans. G. W. Bromiley (Grand Rapids: Eerdmans, 1980 [1973]).

11. Cf. Hays, *Echoes of Scripture in the Letters of Paul*, 68.

12. Here Stowers follows C. E. B. Cranfield, *The Epistle to the Romans*, 2 vols., ICC (Edinburgh: T & T Clark, 1975), 1:156–57, though without acknowledgment.

13. For the most recent defense of the latter interpretation, see N. T. Wright, "The Law

3 In several places, Stowers's hypotheses help to make sense of the textual tradition of the letter. In light of his construal of the argument, he takes the hortatory subjunctive ἔχωμεν ("let us have") as the original reading in 5:1. This reading is strongly attested in the manuscript evidence, but most translations, under the power of the Augustinian-Lutheran interpretative tradition, opt for the poorly attested indicative ἔχομεν ("we have"). (In a minor lapse, Stowers explains the problem as though it were a question of whether to interpret the ambiguous form ἔχω as subjunctive or indicative [248–49], but anyone who has studied the exegesis of this verse will understand what he means to say.) Or again, in 8:2 Stowers accepts the better-attested second-person pronoun, σε, as the original reading, rather than the first-person, με. The second-person pronoun fits well into the dialogical structure proposed by Stowers; in his view, later scribes who did not know how to read the *prosōpopoiia* changed the reading to the first-person pronoun to accord with Romans 7.

Every careful reader of this book will discover many such minor epiphanies lurking within Stowers's learned exposition of the letter. The major contribution of the book, however, is not merely to shed light on this or that minor exegetical problem in Romans but rather to press for a fresh coherent reading of the argument as a whole. In his preface, Stowers acknowledges that he has consciously adopted a "rhetorical stance" in this book, by which he seems to mean that he has sharpened his differences with traditional theological readings and even polemically attacked such interpretations. Revealingly, he then remarks that "the book contains a series of arguments against ways that I have read Paul's great letter, *an argument with myself*" (vii, emphasis mine). Any readers who find the rhetorical tone of the book disturbing would do well to bear this prefatory acknowledgment in mind.

Clearly, the argument has been going on in Stowers's mind for a long time. The preface thanks friends who read an earlier draft of the book as long ago as 1983 and indicates that the book was essentially complete before the appearance of the NRSV in 1989, which helps to explain the book's relative lack of engagement with critical literature on Paul and Romans that has appeared since the late 1980s. For example, Stowers quite remarkably makes no reference to Watson, Wedderburn, Westerholm, Segal, Donfried, or the essays on

in Romans 2," in *Paul and the Mosaic Law*, ed. James D. G. Dunn (Tübingen: Mohr Siebeck, 1996), 131–50.

Romans in Hay and Johnson, many of which were originally presented at the SBL Pauline Theology Group in 1992.[14]

In any case, by pushing his admittedly idiosyncratic case as far as it will go, Stowers forces us to reexamine the global construals that govern our own readings of Romans and to ask about the cultural codes or theological assumptions that may be driving our readings.

Critique of Stowers's Proposals

Of the six major theses summarized earlier, I believe that two are fundamentally mistaken: that the "encoded audience" of Romans is entirely non-Jewish, and that Paul assumes the continuing sufficiency of the Mosaic Law as the basis for Israel's relation to God. These two theses are very closely interwoven in Stowers's argumentation, and in the following remarks I shall try to distinguish them and show why they cannot be maintained in light of the text of Romans. Two other issues highlighted in the theses enumerated above also require further comment: the theme of "self-mastery," and Paul's use of "speech in character." Stowers's claims about these matters clearly do have a sound basis in the text, but certain questions must be raised about the emphasis that he places upon the former and the method that he employs for analyzing the latter.

First, who is the audience of Romans? Stowers flatly asserts that "the text explicitly addresses itself only to gentiles and nowhere explicitly encodes a Jewish audience" (30). The primary evidence that the implied readers of Romans are gentiles is to be found in the following passages.

In Rom 1:5–6 Paul writes, "We have received grace and apostleship to bring about the obedience of faith among all the Gentiles . . . among whom you also are called to belong to Jesus Christ" (my translation). Stowers takes this as a clear statement that Paul envisions exclusively gentile readers. This is an understandable inference, but the ἐν οἷς ("among whom") of 1:6 is ambiguous. The relative clause should not necessarily be translated "including yourselves

14. Francis Watson, *Paul, Judaism, and the Gentiles*, SNTSMS 56 (Cambridge: Cambridge University Press, 1986); A. J. M. Wedderburn, *The Reasons for Romans* (Edinburgh: T & T Clark, 1988); Stephen Westerholm, *Israel's Law and the Church's Faith: Paul and His Recent Interpreters* (Grand Rapids: Eerdmans, 1988); Alan F. Segal, *Paul the Convert: The Apostolate and Apostasy of Saul the Pharisee* (New Haven: Yale University Press, 1990); Karl P. Donfried, ed., *The Romans Debate*, rev. ed. (Peabody, MA: Hendrickson, 1991); David M. Hay and E. Elizabeth Johnson, eds., *Pauline Theology*, vol. 3, *Romans* (Minneapolis: Fortress, 1995).

who are called" as in the NRSV. It could also be interpreted to mean "among whom you are, you who find yourselves called." In other words, the clause would affirm that the Roman readers of the letter are *located geographically* among the gentiles.[15]

In Rom 1:13, Paul declares that he hopes to "reap some harvest among you as I have among the rest of the Gentiles." The formulation clearly does presuppose a primarily gentile readership. Similarly, 15:15–16 indicates that Paul thinks of his act of writing the letter as an expression of his calling to be an apostle to the gentiles in order to bring "the offering of the Gentiles" to God.

In Rom 11:13, Paul says, "Now I am speaking to you Gentiles." This direct address is consistent with the rhetoric of Rom 9–11, in which he continually speaks about the Jewish people in the third person plural, rather than addressing them. Stowers offers a detailed exegetical argument (287–89) that 11:13 should not be understood to indicate that Paul turns only in this limited section of the letter to address gentile readers.

That constitutes the entire body of evidence upon which Stowers's thesis of an exclusively gentile audience is based. It is one thing to say that Paul is writing to a predominantly gentile audience, an observation with which nearly all commentators would agree, but it is quite another thing to maintain the thesis that nowhere in the letter are Jewish readers in view. There are, in fact, several passages that raise serious questions about Stowers's thesis.

When Paul sounds the keynote of his letter in Rom 1:16, he proclaims that the gospel is "the power of God for salvation to everyone who believes, to the Jew first and also to the Greek." Here both Jews and gentiles are mentioned in the third person, and the presumption is created that Paul's ensuing exposition of the gospel will address both equally. This presumption is fully borne out by the evidence of the first four chapters.

Romans 2:17 explicitly encodes a *Jewish* addressee: "But if you call yourself a Jew and rely on the law and boast of your relation to God." This text is potentially fatal to Stowers's reading. Consequently, he insists repeatedly that the "Jew" here is not really among the encoded readers of the letter, but that this figure is a fictitious construct of Paul's diatribal style, introduced in order to instruct the gentile readers: "One should not confuse depicting a Jew with encoding a Jewish audience" (44). We should not, however, allow this evidence to be dismissed quite so easily.

We must recall that Stowers has adamantly distinguished between the empirical readers of the letter and the readers encoded in the text; thus, it makes

15. Cranfield, *Epistle to the Romans*, 1:68.

no sense for him to claim that 2:17 is not really addressed to Jews. The fact is that, at the explicit level of the textual surface, a Jew is addressed (not "depicted," as Stowers misleadingly puts it). In 2:17 the "encoded explicit reader" is a Jew, even though Stowers might be able to claim that the "encoded implicit reader" is still the gentile audience. (For these terms, see Stowers's discussion on p. 21.) Moreover, even if we grant Stowers's point that the Jew of 2:17–29 is a character constructed for Paul's rhetorical purposes, we must ask what those purposes might be. Stowers's own explanation of how such rhetoric works is worth quoting in full:

> The teacher giving the diatribe speaks to an imaginary person who represents a certain vice. The apostrophe characterizes this type of person, *and the sharp censure of the teacher against this fictitious person is actually a censure for students in the audience who fit the type*. The teacher, who has been speaking abstractly of this type of behavior, uses the apostrophe to drive the message home in a sharp but indirect way that *criticizes any hearers to whom the indictment is applicable*. (11–12, emphasis mine)

If Rom 2:17–29 is "a censure for students in the audience who fit the type," what else can we infer but that the encoded audience of Romans includes Jews, perhaps Jewish Christians, who boast in their possession of the Law?

In Rom 4:1, Paul refers to Abraham as "our ancestor according to the flesh." Such a reference makes sense only if the question of 4:1 is addressed to a fellow Jew, a fellow descendant from Abraham "according to the flesh." Stowers argues that this passage is still part of Paul's dialogue with the imaginary Jewish teacher and therefore says nothing about the implied audience of the letter. Even if 4:1 is still part of a diatribal dialogue, however (as I believe it is), the same points made concerning 2:17 apply here also.

In Rom 7:1, Paul says, "I am speaking to those who know the Law." Stowers rightly observes that this does not, strictly speaking, indicate a Jewish audience. He suggests that Paul is thinking of and speaking to gentile Godfearers. More likely, in view of the other evidence I have adduced here, Paul's phrasing includes both Jews and Godfearers.

Romans 15:7–13, the grand summation of the letter's argument, poses severe difficulties for Stowers's hypothesis, for there Paul exhorts his readers to "welcome one another . . . for the glory of God," following the example of Christ, who welcomed Jews and gentiles in order that they might join together in praising God. Most commentators see here a clear appeal for Jewish and gentile Christians to receive one another. Stowers, however, suggests—with virtually no supporting exegetical argument—that the passage means simply that "gentiles are to accept one another" (133).

Finally, the greetings in chapter 16 of Romans are addressed to a variety of persons, including several who are almost certainly of Jewish descent. Stowers acknowledges this fact: "Five of those greeted in chapter 16, including Prisca and Aquila, may be Jews and probably are" (75). Surely those to whom the greetings are addressed are among the encoded audience of the letter? In fact, Stowers's reading of the letter concludes with chapter 15 and omits chapter 16 from consideration. This is surely not coincidental, for some of the strongest evidence for the mixed Jewish/gentile composition of the Christian community at Rome comes from that chapter.

In short, Stowers can maintain his claim of a non-Jewish audience only by selective use of the evidence: the passages addressed to gentile readers are taken to be determinative, and the passages addressed to Jewish readers are dismissed by various arguments that are far from compelling. The evidence presented here suggests that we will do better to continue reading the letter as addressed both to Jewish and to gentile readers. If that is correct, of course, the relevant cultural codes for reading the letter must include not only Greco-Roman literature and philosophy but also specifically Jewish traditions, of the sort cataloged thoroughly by Dunn in his commentary.[16]

"Why," asks Stowers rhetorically, "does the traditional reading of Romans erase the gentile audience and replace it with 'Christians, both Jews and gentiles'?" His answer is, "The erasure is a hermeneutical move that facilitates reading the letter as canonical scripture of the orthodox catholic church" (33). We might ask in turn why Stowers's reading erases the Jewish audience and replaces it with "gentiles only." My answer is that the erasure is a hermeneutical move that facilitates reading the letter as innocuous for Jewish-Christian relations in a pluralistic culture. That observation leads directly to the second thesis of Stowers's book that demands careful critique.

Is the gospel that Paul proclaims for the Jews? Although Stowers (unlike Stendahl and Gaston) does not place Jewish-Christian relations explicitly at the center of his deliberations, he argues repeatedly that the traditional Christian misreading of Romans has produced slanderous misrepresentations of Judaism. According to Stowers's reading, Paul saw his missionary obligation as focused exclusively on the gentiles, who, *unlike Jews*, needed the gospel to bring them into right relation with God and into mastery of their desires. The Jews were already God's covenant people. The inference lies constantly at hand

16. Dunn, *Romans*.

that for the Jewish people the death and resurrection of Jesus were not necessary. Or, to put it more cautiously, the death and resurrection of Jesus were not intended by God as saving events for Israel. According to Stowers, Paul

> never argues or implies the end of God's covenant with the Jews. . . . [I]n Paul's day the temple system was still working and Christianity was not a distinct religion. Nowhere does Paul mount an argument about the inadequacy of the covenant and the temple system. To prove that Jews are under sin in the way the gentiles are, Paul would have had to argue that the Law's system of repentance and holiness was not working. (129)

Stowers sets his view of Paul's thought in direct contrast to E. P. Sanders,[17] who maintains that in Paul's view "faith in Christ" is an "entrance requirement" for Jews and gentiles alike, and that Paul finds Judaism wanting because "it is not Christianity."[18] For Stowers, it is precisely the concept "Christianity" that is problematical: Paul had no clear-cut notion of Christianity as a religion of salvation with new entrance requirements. The only important question was how gentiles could be redeemed from their moral confusion and weakness. Jews, however, did not need salvation through Christ.

Stowers's construction founders badly on the evidence of Romans. We have already noted that Paul begins his argument by declaring that the gospel is "the power of God *for salvation* to everyone who believes, *to the Jew first* and also to the Greek" (1:16). Stowers never, as far as I am able to see, gives any serious discussion to this statement or considers how deeply it challenges his thesis. Similarly, Stowers's detailed reading of the opening chapters of the letter fails to come to terms with the way in which Paul's argument drives inexorably toward the affirmation of 3:22 that "there is no distinction" between human beings before God's justice. Jews and Greeks together stand condemned, and Jews and Greeks together are delivered by God's righteousness through the faithfulness of Jesus Christ. Stowers attempts to exempt Jews by arguing that Rom 3:20 applies "only to gentiles or perhaps to extremely wicked and unrepentant Jews" (190). This simply will not wash.

The unit of thought in Rom 3:9–20 begins by denying that Jews are any better off than gentiles and affirming that "all, both Jews and Greeks, are under

17. E. P. Sanders, *Paul and Palestinian Judaism: A Comparison of Patterns of Religion* (Philadelphia: Fortress, 1977); and Sanders, *Paul, the Law, and the Jewish People* (Philadelphia: Fortress, 1983).

18. Sanders, *Paul and Palestinian Judaism*, 552; see the discussion in Stowers, *Rereading of Romans*, 24–25.

the power of sin" (3:9). This radical charge is then warranted by a collection of scriptural citations (3:10–18), most of which in their original setting referred to gentiles. Paul, however, radicalizes and universalizes them. His hermeneutical warrant for this move is stated explicitly in 3:19: "We know that whatever the Law says, it speaks to those who are under the Law (i.e., Israel), so that every mouth may be silenced (i.e., no boasting; cf. 2:17; 3:27), and *the whole world may be held accountable to God*." When Paul goes on to say in this context that "there is no distinction, since all have sinned and fallen short of the glory of God" (3:22–23), it is unmistakably clear that he means "no distinction between Jew and gentile." Both are saved by God's gracious initiative through Jesus Christ. It is certainly true that Paul does not know the term "Christian"; but it is equally unmistakable that in Romans, as in his other letters, he thinks of the church as a new people bound together "in Christ" in such a way that the distinction between Jew and gentile loses its relevance (cf. Gal 3:27–29).

How, then, does Stowers deal with the "no distinction" of Rom 3:22? For the most part, he simply lets it slide by without comment. At one point, however, he offers his own translation to show how he understands the passage. The relevant portion is as follows:

> For there is no difference [which makes Jews alone worthy of God's mercy] since all have sinned and are in need of God's glory. They [the ungodly/gentiles] are made right freely by his grace through the redemption in Jesus Christ. (223)

Here, without argument or justification, Stowers introduces a full stop at the end of 3:23 and provides a new grammatical subject ("the ungodly/gentiles") for the sentence beginning in verse 24. This is exegetically indefensible, for the participle δικαιούμενοι in verse 24 modifies the πάντες of verse 23. Those who are "made right freely" are precisely the "all" who have sinned without distinction.

Throughout the book, Stowers is forced to produce labored interpretations to preserve the thesis that Jews are fully in right relation with God through the Law. For example, he suggests, without basis in the Greek text, that Rom 4:14 should be read, "If *only* those whose status springs from the law are heirs, Abraham's faithfulness has been made useless and God's promise is unkept" (246). (Notice, by way of contrast, his sharp criticism [302] of translators who introduce the word "only" into 9:27.) Or again, he makes the remarkable claim that 5:1–11 "announces the reconciliation of *the gentiles*" (248), not Jews, to God. Why then does Paul write this section using first-person plural pronouns? "God proves his love for us in that while we were still sinners Christ died for us" (5:8). Is not Paul here, as a Jew, including his own fate along with that of his gentile readers? Later, Stowers ascribes this formulation to Paul's "doctrine of adaptability," meaning that for the sake of his mission he "identifies himself with the religious experience of the gentile audience" (292).

After working through explanations of this kind page after page, one starts to suspect a tendentious special pleading. On the one hand, Stowers wants to read the text without introducing dogmatic constructs to filter the interpretation. On the other hand, the manifold statements in the letter that present the death and resurrection of Jesus as the singular apocalyptic event through which God has wrought the salvation of the world—Jew and gentile alike—are repeatedly explained away by convoluted arguments or, alternatively, by unsupported assertions. In short, it seems that Stowers's thesis about the independent validity and sufficiency of Judaism as a religion takes on the status of a dogmatic constraint that controls his exegesis in a way at least as heavy-handed and artificial as the traditional Christian theology that he rejects. Many thinkers at the end of the twentieth century may wish that Paul and other first-century Christians had adopted a different attitude toward Judaism, but wishing will not make it so. The text of Romans resists Stowers's reading on this point. As John Barclay notes, Paul, despite his claims of loyalty to Jewish tradition, "was generally distrusted by his Jewish contemporaries and condemned in many synagogue trials (2 Cor 11:24)."[19] These things remain inexplicable in Stowers's construction.

Paul in fact takes a complex, dialectical stance toward Israel, affirming God's faithfulness to the covenant promises, agonizing over the Jewish people's rejection of the proclaimed gospel (9:1–5; 9:30–10:4; 10:14–21), and expecting God's eschatological salvation of all Israel (11:25–32).[20]

My reservations about Stowers's other two theses can be explained more briefly.

First, is self-mastery an adequate category for capturing Paul's message? While Stowers convincingly demonstrates the importance of self-mastery among Paul's contemporaries, the weight of emphasis given to this motif in his reading of Romans threatens to create the impression that Paul was a

19. John Barclay, review of Stowers, *A Rereading of Romans*, *JTS* 46 (1995): 651.

20. For more extensive discussion of the question of Paul and Israel, see Richard B. Hays, *The Moral Vision of the New Testament* (San Francisco: HarperSanFrancisco, 1996), 409–17, and the literature cited there. For important Jewish studies of Paul that disagree with Stowers on this key issue, see Segal, *Paul the Convert*; Daniel Boyarin, *A Radical Jew: Paul and the Politics of Identity* (Berkeley: University of California Press, 1994).

moral philosopher offering one more scheme for self-improvement. In light of Stowers's debunking of "salvation" as a category for understanding Paul's gospel and his rejection of the concept of "an intrinsically sick human nature," the reader of Stowers's book sometimes may wonder whether his analysis of the human predicament is considerably less radical than Paul's. According to Stowers, the death of Jesus merely buys time for people to straighten out their lives and offers a good example to be imitated. One misses here a sense of humanity's profound alienation from a holy God and of the persistent costly love of that God, "who did not withhold his own Son, but gave him up for all of us" (8:32). Such matters recede curiously into the background in Stowers's treatment of Romans. Perhaps if he had engaged more fully in sympathetic dialogue with Augustine, Luther, Calvin, Wesley, and Barth (the representatives of the theological tradition that he seeks to supplant), or even with more recent interpreters such as Cranfield, Käsemann, Dunn, and the SBL Pauline Theology Group,[21] he would have been able to give a more satisfying account of these great themes of the letter.

Secondly, how do we know who is talking in this or that Romans passage? Stowers is undoubtedly justified in pointing to the conventions of *prosōpopoiia* and diatribal dialogue as formal elements in the rhetoric of Romans. The stylistic traces of these devices are clearly present, as Stowers showed in his dissertation.[22] The difficulty, however, is to know what methodological controls govern the assignment of various lines in the text to different speakers. How do we know where such "speech in character" begins and ends, and (perhaps even more difficult to determine), within these dialogical sections, how do we know whether it is Paul or the fictitious interlocutor speaking at any given moment? Stowers freely offers proposed reconstructions of these dialogues, but he offers few explanations for his proposals. For example, in Rom 4:1–2, how do we know that it is the interlocutor who asks the question in verse 1, and supplies the additional consideration in verse 2a, and how do we know that Paul's own voice interjects, "but not before God" in 4:2b (234)? Perhaps more challenging still is the identification of the speaker in Rom 7:7–25. Stowers's suggestion that the character speaking here is a gentile Godfearer is interesting, but what would count as evidence for or against such a claim? How could the original audience of the letter have inferred such an identification of the

21. Cranfield, *Epistle to the Romans*; Käsemann, *Commentary on Romans*; Dunn, *Romans*; Hay and Johnson, *Pauline Theology*.

22. Stowers, *Diatribe and Paul's Letter to the Romans*.

character? Stowers's study, for all its detail, is surprisingly uninformative about such methodological issues.

Epilogue: Historical Explanation and the Tasks of Christian Theology

I have contended that Stowers's provocative book falls considerably short of his goal of providing a new historical reading of Romans that will overturn the readings of a dominant Western theological paradigm, even though many of his criticisms of that paradigm are just and accurate. The reasons given so far for my judgment have been primarily exegetical. That is, even given the task that Stowers has set for himself, I do not believe that his reading executes the project successfully. But questions may also be raised at another, more fundamental, level about the character and purpose of Stowers's undertaking.

We may put the question this way: What, finally, is this book seeking to accomplish? What response would Stowers desire from a reader persuaded by his arguments? Stowers describes himself, not as a theologian, but as "a historian of early Christian literature" (4). As a historian, does he seek simple intellectual assent from his readers? The self-acknowledged rhetorical tone of the book (vii) and the passion of his arguments suggest that something more is at stake here. Presumably, he would at least want Christian readers to relinquish certain anti-Jewish stereotypes and prejudices. To that extent at least, he would presumably commend his reconstruction of Paul's thought as a valid normative model. But would he also want his readers to enter Paul's first-century Greco-Roman thought world and endorse its "decline of civilization narratives" (85–100)? Presumably not. Would he want them to learn to exercise the sort of self-mastery through the Holy Spirit promised by Paul's letter? Would he want them to believe Paul's myth of "the Messiah who delayed" (213–26) and to emulate his flexible self-abnegation? What criteria might be employed to make such decisions?

We can give no answers to these questions because the book itself neither asks nor answers them. The book has no hermeneutical dimension, or at least its hermeneutical agenda (if there is one) is not made explicit. Consequently, there is a strange flatness to the work. For some reason, Stowers thinks it urgent for us to take up the imaginative task of reading Romans in light of first-century Greco-Roman cultural codes. But why?

Furthermore, he seems to think we might be better readers of the letter if we were unencumbered by two thousand years of tradition, if we had found this text somewhere in a ruin as a papyrus scroll "filled from side to side with unbroken and unpunctuated lines of Greek letters" (4). Why would such a reading be better than the readings influenced by generations of interpreters who have labored lovingly over the text and sought to shape their lives in accordance with its teaching? Could the church's tradition be an aid to interpretation, rather than solely a hindrance?

I raise these questions, not because Stowers's work is idiosyncratic, but because it typifies a certain sort of historical work that does not make its hermeneutical aims explicit. Taken at face value, Stowers's study would have the effect of isolating Romans in a historical past relatively inaccessible to us, like a museum piece displayed in a sealed, temperature-controlled, glass case. Yet, at the same time, the pathos of Stowers's presentation beckons the reader to care somehow more deeply about reading this text rightly, not just as an ancient cultural construction but as a text that exerts some claim upon us. Regrettably, Stowers gives his readers no guidance about such matters. This is by no means to say that historical work is of no value. I am insisting only that historical work must finally be in service of something or someone.[23]

In short, I am suggesting that Stowers's project falls short of its own implicit goals because it is insufficiently theological. The roll of great misreaders invoked at the beginning of this essay—Augustine, Luther, and Barth—read Romans passionately under the conviction that it was the vehicle of the word of God. Their readings were powerful and influential precisely because they were interpreting the text in and for a community, the church, that understood its identity to be formed by the text they were interpreting. If Stowers really hopes efficaciously to challenge the traditional theological paradigm for reading Romans, he will have to write a sequel to *A Rereading of Romans* in which he takes a stand and shows us what the implications of his reading might be for forming communities that practice the obedience of faith.

23. For a powerful example of what a hermeneutically engaged historical rereading of Paul might look like when offered by a reader *outside* the Christian theological tradition, see Boyarin, *Radical Jew*.

14

ISRAEL

Hope for What We Do Not Yet See

> Whenever a long delay casts us into despair, let us remember this word *mystery*. By this Paul clearly instructs us that the manner of [Israel's] conversion will be unique and unprecedented, and that therefore those who attempt to measure it by their own judgment will be in error.
>
> John Calvin[1]

Why Does Paul Tweak Isaiah's Text?

In his commentary on Romans, John Calvin observes, with his usual careful attention to detail, that Paul's quotation of Isaiah in Rom 11:26b–27 diverges from the actual text of Isa 59:20–21. Having made this observation, however, Calvin dismisses the exegetical difficulty of the citation with a fascinatingly casual assessment:

> Paul, however, does not quote the passage in Isaiah word for word. . . . We need not worry ourselves unduly on this matter; for the point which we are to consider is how appropriately the apostles adapt to their purpose the proofs which they adduce from the Old Testament. They desire only to point to the passages, in order to direct their readers to the fountain itself.[2]

In other words, Calvin takes Paul to be gesturing loosely toward the passage in Isaiah rather than attending closely to its wording. Consequently, Calvin

1. John Calvin, *The Epistles of Paul the Apostle to the Romans and to the Thessalonians*, trans. R. Mackenzie, Calvin's Commentaries (Grand Rapids: Eerdmans, 1960), 254. All subsequent quotations are taken from this edition.

2. Calvin, *Romans*, 255–56.

proceeds to comment not on what *Paul* actually wrote but on "the fountain itself," the text of Isa 59, observing that the prophet "says expressly, that a Redeemer shall come to Sion; and he adds, that he will redeem those in Jacob who shall return from their transgression." Of course, this proclamation differs significantly from what Paul says in Romans: Paul writes that the Redeemer shall come *from* Zion, not *to* it, and that *he* will take away the sins of Jacob, with no explicit proviso that they must first repent from their transgression.

Calvin is not unaware of the discrepancies, but he waves them off as a matter of small concern:

> Although the expression used by the prophet, "shall come to Zion" (Isa 59.20), suited his purpose better, Paul felt no scruple in following the commonly accepted translation which reads, "A redeemer shall come out of Zion."[3]

Calvin attributes no particular significance to the form of the translation that Paul actually chose to cite. Likewise, mindful that the last part of Paul's citation also does not come from Isa 59, Calvin opines that the words found in Rom 11:27 must be derived from Jeremiah (i.e., the promise of a new covenant), even though Paul's actual wording only very indirectly recalls the words of Jer 31:34.[4]

In contrast to the great Reformer's assurance that we "need not worry ourselves" about the anomalies in Paul's citation of Isaiah, recent NT scholarship has worried a great deal about the peculiarities of Paul's reception and interpretation of Israel's Scripture. Romans 11:25–27 has become an intensely

3. Calvin, *Romans*, 256. It is not clear why Calvin assumed that Paul's citation was following "the commonly received translation," for the Greek manuscript tradition of Isaiah overwhelmingly supports the reading ἕνεκεν Σιων. Was Calvin aware of later Greek manuscripts that, under the influence of Rom 11:26, read ἐκ Σιὼν? (For details, see J. Ross Wagner, *Heralds of the Good News: Isaiah and Paul 'in Concert' in the Letter to the Romans*, NovTSup 101 [Leiden: Brill, 2002], 284.) Or was he simply assuming that Paul must have used a source with such a reading?

4. Calvin writes, "Although Paul had briefly touched in the last prophecy quoted from Isaiah on the office of the Messiah, in order to advise the Jews of what they were chiefly to hope for from Him, he deliberately added these few words from Jeremiah for the same purpose. The words which he adds do not appear in the former passage." In Calvin's view, Paul has to supply a reference from Jeremiah to the divine initiative in the removal of sins because otherwise the expectation of conversion of an obstinate people would seem incredible (Calvin, *Romans*, 256). He does not seem to be aware of Isa 27:9 as the source of the words cited in Rom 11:27b.

contested locus for exegesis—not least because it presents a crucial text for theological reflection about God's faithfulness to Israel and the relationship between the church and the Jewish people.[5]

Among exegetes who have wrestled with these matters, N. T. Wright holds a place of preeminence for the depth and clarity of his engagement with Rom 9–11.[6] From his earliest work in *The Climax of the Covenant* (1991), through his commentary on Romans in the *New Interpreters Bible* (2002), all the way up to his magisterial *Paul and the Faithfulness of God* (2013), Wright has consistently highlighted distinctive features of Paul's citation of Isaiah in Rom 11:25–27. His attention to those features has led him to champion an interpretation of Rom 11:25–27 that challenges much modern critical opinion.[7]

It should be noted, however, that in one key respect Wright's reading of the passage aligns closely with the judgment of Calvin about the meaning of Paul's declaration that "all Israel shall be saved" (11:26a). Thus Calvin:

> Many understand this of the Jewish people, as if Paul were saying that religion was to be restored to them again as before. But I extend the word *Israel* to include all the people of God, in this sense, "When the Gentiles have come in, the Jews will at the same time return from their defection to the obedience of faith. The salvation of the whole Israel of God, which

5. Michael Wolter devoted his Presidential Address at the 2017 General Meeting of the Studiorum Novi Testamenti Societas to the interpretation of this difficult passage (Michael Wolter, "Ein exegetischer und theologischer Blick auf Rom 11.25–32," *NTS* 64 [2018]: 123–42). Regrettably, Wolter's article appeared in print well after the present essay had been completed and sent to press; therefore, I was not able to engage his arguments in this discussion of the passage. Readers of Wolter's piece will recognize that his interpretation differs significantly from N. T. Wright's and from my own—particularly on the meaning of "all Israel." I would, however, note that Wolter's emphasis on the LXX Psalms as the source of Paul's anomalous use of ἐκ Σιὼν in his citation of Isa 59:20 is independently convergent with one of my major arguments in the pages that follow here.

6. The present essay was written as a contribution to a Festschrift in his honor: "Hope for What We Do Not See: The Salvation of All Israel in Romans 11.25–27," in *One God, One People, One Future*, ed. John Anthony Dunne and Eric Lewellen (London: SPCK, 2018), 545–72.

7. N. T. Wright, *The Climax of the Covenant: Christ and the Law in Pauline Theology* (Edinburgh: T & T Clark, 1991; Minneapolis: Fortress, 1992), 231–57; Wright, "Romans," in *Acts, Introduction to Epistolary Literature, Romans, 1 Corinthians*, ed. Leander E. Keck, *NIB* 10 (Nashville: Abingdon, 2002), 393–770, esp. 687–93; Wright, *Paul and the Faithfulness of God*, Christian Origins and the Question of God 4 (London: SPCK; Minneapolis: Fortress, 2013), 1231–52 (hereafter cited as *Faithfulness*). For Wright's concise summary of the points at which his interpretation of Rom 11:25–27 challenges received scholarly opinion, see *Faithfulness*, 1231–32.

> must be drawn from both, will thus be completed, and yet in such a way that the Jews, as the first-born in the family of God, may obtain the first place." . . . In the same way, in Gal 6.16, he calls the Church, which was composed equally of Jews and Gentiles, the Israel of God.[8]

Though Wright makes only glancing reference to Calvin in a footnote,[9] he has arrived at the same destination by a different route. It is a lengthy route, carefully mapped out. Indeed, as far as I am able to judge, in the whole history of Pauline exegesis no one else has developed a more extensive defense of the interpretation of πᾶς Ἰσραήλ in Rom 11:26 as the one people of God composed of Jews and gentiles together.[10]

In my opinion, as I shall explain below, Wright's reading of "all Israel" is convincing, and his arguments are both sound and powerful. I believe, however, that several other details of his interpretation of Rom 11:25–27 could be both qualified and amplified. The aim, then, of the present essay will be to carry forward the conversation about Paul's interpretation of Israel's Scripture in the specific locus of Rom 11:25–27. I shall query a few aspects of Wright's interpretation and offer some complementary suggestions about this difficult passage.[11] My remarks will fall into three parts: first, a summary of some of the strongest points in Wright's reading; second, an examination of several questions that require additional critical exploration; and finally, a few constructive exegetical suggestions, particularly about the role of the Psalms in the intertextual network of interpretation that underlies Rom 11:25–27.

Wright's Reading of Romans 11:25–27: Ground Gained

Wright's comprehensive exegesis of the passage has, in my opinion, established firm ground on a number of crucial points. Whatever else may be said about these verses—and indeed about Rom 9–11 more broadly—we must acknowl-

8. Calvin, *Romans*, 255.

9. Wright, *Faithfulness*, 1239n672.

10. I refer here specifically to his treatment of 11:26a, but his interpretation of this verse must be understood in the broader context of his reading of Rom 9–11 as a whole (*Faithfulness*, 1156–1258).

11. I am profoundly grateful to Tom for dedicating his magisterial work on Paul to me. I trust that my engagement with his reading of Rom 11:25–27, while critical at certain points, will be understood as an appreciative conversation between friends who care deeply about getting the exegesis right.

edge the force of his reading on at least the following six points. In my judgment the strength of his exegesis has effectively placed the burden of proof on any interpreter who would dispute any of these six findings.[12]

(1) *The contingency of the argument.* Paul is not writing a treatise on election or predestination; he is writing an apostolic pastoral letter. Its particular target audience in Rom 9–11 is a community of gentile Christians in Rome who may be tempted to claim superior status or to regard themselves as having supplanted the Jewish people within God's special favor (11:13, 17–24, 25, 28–32). Again and again Paul asserts that God is mysteriously at work to bring Jews and gentiles alike into the sphere of his unfathomable mercy. Gentile followers of Christ are therefore admonished not to be proud or condescending toward Jews who have, at least in the present time, not believed the gospel.

(2) *The continuity of the argument.* Romans 11:25–27 is not a sudden revelation of a new mystery that contradicts what Paul has said in the preceding chapters of the letter. This is one of the most compelling aspects of Wright's exposition. He demonstrates the carefully crafted continuity of Paul's argument through the entirety of Romans, particularly the way in which 11:25–27 concisely summarizes exactly what Paul had asserted in 11:11–24: branches have been broken off the olive tree (Israel), but they can be grafted back in "if they do not remain in unbelief" (ἐὰν μὴ ἐπιμένωσιν τῇ ἀπιστίᾳ, v. 23). The "mystery" (μυστήριον, 11:25), then, is not a sudden bolt from the blue; rather, it is precisely a disclosure of the insight that Paul has reached through meditation on the course of his apostolic mission in conjunction with his christologically inflected rereading of Israel's Scripture.[13] (Cf. Rom 16:25–26, where Paul's gospel proclamation of Jesus Christ is said to be "according to the revelation of the mystery [μυστήριον] that was kept silent for long ages but now made known *through prophetic scriptures* to all the Gentiles" [my translation].) The μυστήριον is mysterious precisely because it entails a reversal of the narrative order in which Paul, along with his Jewish kinsmen, had expected salvation to come to Israel and to the nations.[14]

12. The summary that follows refers to Wright's exposition in *Faithfulness*, 1231–52.

13. See Nils Dahl's characteristically incisive formulation: "Paul introduces this statement as the disclosure of a revealed mystery. Yet the solution draws the conclusion of the preceding arguments. We should probably not think of a sudden, unmediated revelation granted to Paul but rather of a mystery hidden in Scripture until its explanation was unveiled" (Nils Alstrup Dahl, *Studies in Paul* [Minneapolis: Augsburg, 1977], 152). Wright aptly notes Dahl's judgment (*Faithfulness*, 1232).

14. Speaking of this reversal and the unexpected way in which the gentile mission leads to Israel's salvation, Francis Watson, noting the motif of Israel's "jealousy" in Deut 32:21,

(3) *Gentile believers "come in" to Israel.* When Paul writes of the fullness of the gentiles "coming in" prior to the salvation of all Israel, *into what* does he expect them to come? Wright answers that they are to come in to *Israel*, precisely as the olive-tree metaphor in 11:17–24 has indicated.[15] As wild olive branches they are grafted onto the tree, which is undoubtedly a symbol for Israel.[16] This image is fully consistent with Paul's well-attested theological conviction that his gentile converts have been taken up into the story of Israel. Paul insists that Abraham is the father of circumcised and uncircumcised alike (Rom 4). In his view, the non-Jewish Christians at Corinth "used to be Gentiles" (1 Cor 12:2), but now they are to regard Moses and the people of Israel in the wilderness as "our forefathers" (1 Cor 10:1–4).[17] As Wright compellingly observes, gentile believers in Jesus have, in Paul's view, received circumcision of the heart and can now rightly be described as "Jews" (Rom 2:25–29); accordingly, Paul can encourage his Philippian converts who "worship in the Spirit of God" and confess Jesus as Messiah to join him in declaring "we . . . are the circumcision" (Phil 3:3). In light of such texts, it also seems highly likely that when Paul invokes a blessing on "the Israel of God" (Gal 6:16), he is referring to all those, gentile and Jew alike, who share a common identity in Christ (Gal 3:26–29).[18]

---

writes: "If Paul has learned all this through a 'mystery' or special revelation (11:25), the revelation has come to him in and through his meditation on the Song of Moses" (Francis Watson, *Paul and the Hermeneutics of Faith* [London: T & T Clark, 2004], 449). In light of Rom 11:26–27, we may add that Isa 59 and 27 also played a significant role in Paul's scriptural meditation, along with other texts to be discussed below.

15. In support of this interpretation, see also Ulrich Wilckens, *Der Brief an die Römer*, vol. 2, EKKNT 6/2 (Zurich: Benziger Verlag; Neukirchen-Vluyn: Neukirchener Verlag, 1980), 254–56; Leander E. Keck, *Romans*, ANTC (Nashville: Abingdon, 2005), 276, 286; and Robert Jewett, *Romans: A Commentary*, Hermeneia (Minneapolis: Fortress, 2007), 700–701.

16. Against, e.g. James D. G. Dunn (*Romans*, vol. 2, *9–16*, WBC 38B [Dallas: Word, 1988], 680) who joins a line of exegetes including Ernst Käsemann in suggesting that Paul is here dependent on "pre-Pauline tradition that stems from Jesus." Dunn therefore suggests an allusion to the synoptic language of "entering the kingdom," although Paul does not use that expression anywhere in the present context.

17. On this point, see Richard B. Hays, *Echoes of Scripture in the Letters of Paul* (New Haven: Yale University Press, 1989), 91–104; and Hays, *The Conversion of the Imagination: Paul as Interpreter of Israel's Scripture* (Grand Rapids: Eerdmans, 2005), 8–12.

18. This reading of Gal 6:16 and Rom 11:26 is challenged by Susan Eastman, "Israel and Divine Mercy in Galatians and Romans," in *Between Gospel and Election: Explorations in the Interpretation of Romans 9–11*, ed. Florian Wilk and J. Ross Wagner, WUNT 257 (Tübingen: Mohr Siebeck, 2010) 147–70; and Eastman, "Israel and the Mercy of God: A Re-reading of Galatians 6.16 and Romans 9–11," *NTS* 56 (2010): 367–95. These two careful essays argue that "the Israel of God" can only refer to ethnic Israel rather than to a redefined Israel inclusive

(4) *Paul's kinspeople, the Jewish people, can find salvation only through confessing Jesus Messiah as Lord.* There is no separate dispensation for Jews apart from Christ. Paul has insistently argued throughout Romans that "there is no distinction" between Jew and gentile with respect to God's saving action. This is the whole burden of Rom 1–4. The righteousness of God is revealed through the faithfulness of Jesus Christ for all who trust in him (Rom 3:21–24). And, in case his readers may have forgotten the point, he hammers it home again in Rom 10:9–13: everyone who confesses that Jesus is Lord and believes that God has raised him from the dead will be saved (v. 9). Precisely with respect to this point "there is no distinction between Jew and Greek; the same Lord [Jesus] is Lord of all" (v. 12). Thus, whatever Rom 11:26–27 means, it cannot mean there is a *Sonderweg*, a separate path of salvation for Israel—or for some part of Israel—apart from trusting in the one whom Paul proclaims to be Israel's Messiah.[19] That is why Paul anguishes over many of his own kinspeople who have not accepted the gospel (9:1–5), and that is why he continues to pray earnestly "that they may be saved" (10:1)—surely meaning that they may not "remain in unbelief" (11:23).

(5) *The meaning of καὶ οὕτως (11:26a) is "and thus"—not "and then."* It refers to *manner*, not temporal sequence. In other words, it points back to the events summarized in verse 25 (the hardening of a part of Israel and the incoming of a plenitude of gentiles to stir Israel to jealousy) as the surprising *manner in which* the salvation of "all Israel" will occur.[20] As Wright puts it, "and *that*, the entire sequence of 11.11–24, summed up in 11.25, is *how* 'all Israel' will be saved."[21]

(6) *"All Israel" means the one people of God, composed of Jews and gentiles who have come to place their trust in Jesus Messiah.* The cumulative force of the previous five points leads almost inescapably to Wright's conclusion that "all

of both gentiles and Jews who confess faith in Jesus. For the reasons briefly sketched above, I am not finally convinced by her arguments, but her work must be weighed carefully by anyone seeking to understand the issues.

19. For statements opposing the *Sonderweg* reading, see, for example, Dahl, *Studies in Paul*, 152–55; E. P. Sanders, *Paul, the Law, and the Jewish People* (Philadelphia: Fortress, 1983), 192–96; Dunn, *Romans*, 2:691; Scott Hafemann, "The Salvation of Israel in Romans 11:25–32: A Response to Krister Stendahl," *ExAud* 4 (1988): 38–58; Reidar Hvalvik, "A 'Sonderweg' for Israel: A Critical Examination of Current Interpretation of Romans 11.25–27," *JSNT* 38 (1990): 87–107; Wagner, *Heralds of the Good News*, 297–98; Keck, *Romans*, 285–86; Jewett, *Romans*, 702; J. R. Daniel Kirk, "Why Does the Deliverer Come ἐκ Σιών (Romans 11.26)?," *JSNT* 33 (2010): 81–99.

20. The lexical arguments for a temporal interpretation are very slight, and the temporal sense is not elsewhere attested in Paul.

21. Wright, *Faithfulness*, 1241.

Israel" in Rom 11:26a is Paul's way of describing the whole people of God, the whole body of those who confess Jesus as Messiah and Lord, and thereby find salvation within the christologically reconfigured covenant with Israel's God. Wright's detailed exegesis thus leads him to substantial agreement with Calvin (cited above) and with the classic formulation of Karl Barth:

> "All Israel" is the community of those elected by God in and with Jesus Christ both from the Jews and also from the Gentiles, the whole Church . . . in the totality constituted by the remnant continuing in and with the original stem Jesus Christ, by the wild shoots added later from the Gentiles, and by the branches which were and are finally grafted in again.[22]

Wright notes that Paul had, significantly, launched this whole train of argument in 9:6 with the declaration that "not all who are from Israel are Israel (οὐ γὰρ πάντες οἱ ἐξ Ἰσραήλ, οὗτοι Ἰσραήλ)." And Paul further insists that it is "the children of promise" who are truly reckoned as the "seed" of Abraham (9:8). We should not forget that *in Galatians he had argued vehemently that the uncircumcised gentile believers in Galatia were precisely among the "children of the promise" (Gal 4:28), Abraham's heirs*. Thus, for Paul to include Jewish and gentile Christians together under the designation "Israel" is fully consistent with deep currents in his theology. Wright characterizes this locution as a "polemical redefinition,"[23] but I am not sure that is quite the right description. Instead, I would suggest that Paul's designation of Jewish and gentile believers together as "all Israel" is simply the *constructive exegetical outworking* of Paul's hermeneutical project, his sustained effort to interpret his mission to the nations through a retrospective reading of Israel's Scripture in light of the

22. Karl Barth, *Church Dogmatics*, vol. 2, *The Doctrine of God*, part 2, trans. G. W. Bromiley (Edinburgh: T & T Clark, 1957 [1955]), 300. I cannot resist observing with some satisfaction that Wright has been led via his exegesis to concur with Barth—at least on this point. Joseph A. Fitzmyer (*Romans*, AB 33 [New York: Doubleday, 1993], 623–24) compiles a formidable list of patristic commentators who advocated this interpretation, including Irenaeus, Clement of Alexandria, Theodore of Mopsuestia, Theodoret of Cyrrhus, and (in some but not all of their writings) Origen and Augustine. Fitzmyer himself judges that such a reading of "all Israel" cannot be correct. I would suggest, however, that the early prevalence of this interpretation should at least give pause to modern commentators who reject it out of hand. The unpopularity of such a reading in the late twentieth century is surely in part influenced by the laudable desire of exegetes in a post-Holocaust era to interpret Paul in a way they imagine to be more helpful for Jewish-Christian dialogue.

23. E.g., Wright, *Faithfulness*, 1242.

ἀποκάλυψις of Jesus as Messiah. The redefinition is not so much "polemical" as it is exegetical and kerygmatic.

Ground Still to Be Explored: Open Questions

Despite the substantial ground gained by Wright's wide-ranging interpretation, there is still some rough territory remaining to be explored. On several points, there is need for greater clarity. Some of these questions may not be susceptible to definite resolution this side of the eschaton. Nonetheless, it is important to identify them, because they appear to me to represent points of continuing uncertainty (or possible vulnerability) in Wright's position. Once again I offer a list of particular points, coincidentally also six in number, this time in interrogative form.

(1) *What is the sense of ἀπὸ μέρους?* The meaning of ἀπὸ μέρους in Rom 11:25 is often left murky by commentaries on Romans. Wright leaves no such ambiguity; he clearly states his preference for a partitive interpretation ("a hardening has come upon *a part of* Israel") as opposed to a temporal one ("a hardening has come *for a while* upon Israel"). He concedes the possibility of a temporal meaning, pointing to Rom 15:24 as an instance, but then writes, "But it is in my judgment far more likely that Paul is here referring to the 'hardening' coming upon *one part* of Israel, as in 11.1–7, especially verse 7."[24] Insofar as Wright gives reasons for this judgment, they appear to rest on his larger construal of the logic of the discourse, rather than on lexical investigation of the meaning of the prepositional phrase. Perhaps we can advance the discussion, at least a little, by tracking down how ἀπὸ μέρους functions in other relevant contexts.

Beyond the present passage, Paul uses this expression only four times in his letters. In Rom 15:15 he tells his readers, "on some points (ἀπὸ μέρους) I have written to you rather boldly by way of reminder." That is a periphrastic rendering, but the sense here is apparently partitive and not temporal. The phrase occurs twice more in the opening chapters of 2 Corinthians. In 2 Cor 1:14 he tells the Corinthians, "you have known us *in part*." And in 2 Cor 2:5 he writes, "But if anyone has caused pain, he has caused it not to me, but to some extent (ἀπὸ μέρους)—not to exaggerate it—to all of you." Again, these uses of the expression are clearly *not* temporal. In light of these parallels, I am inclined to doubt that ἀπὸ μέρους in Rom 15:24 should be taken in a temporal sense—a

24. Wright, *Faithfulness*, 1239.

sense otherwise unattested in either the NT or the LXX. Romans 15:24 could instead be translated literally as follows: "For I do hope to see you on my journey and to be sent on by you (i.e., given provisions and resources), once I have been *in part* filled up (i.e., supplied) by you."[25] It should be observed that in all of these other Pauline usages, the phrase ἀπὸ μέρους functions adverbially. It does not occur elsewhere in the NT.

In the extant Greek versions of Israel's Scriptures, the prepositional phrase ἀπὸ μέρους occurs only seven times. In three of the instances (Num 34:3; Josh 18:15, 20), it is a geographical term referring to an area of land (one thinks of the colloquial English expression "in those parts" to designate a geographical region). In one other case the term is used to describe a part (the extremity) of a cherub's wings (1 Kgs 6:24). But the last three instances offer potentially closer parallels to the sense of this terminology in Rom 11:25. The phrase ἀπὸ μέρους appears in the rendering of Judges 18:2 in Codex Alexandrinus: καὶ ἐξαπέστειλαν οἱ υἱοὶ Δαν ἐκ τῶν συγγενειῶν αὐτῶν πέντε ἄνδρας ἀπὸ μέρους αὐτῶν ("And the Danites sent from their clan five men from their part").[26] A similar partitive use of the phrase to designate a portion of a larger group of people appears in Neh 7:70 LXX: καὶ ἀπὸ μέρους ἀρχηγῶν τῶν πατριῶν ἔδωκαν εἰς τὸ ἔργον ("And *some of the heads* of ancestral houses contributed to the work"). Finally, in Theodotion's text of Dan 1:2, we read this: "And the Lord gave into his hand Joakim king of Judah, *and part of the vessels of the house of God* (ἀπὸ μέρους τῶν σκευῶν οἴκου τοῦ θεοῦ)." All three of these examples illustrate the use of ἀπὸ μέρους to designate one part of a greater whole. Of course, in Romans Paul is not alluding to any of these passages, but they do demonstrate an idiomatic use of the expression ἀπὸ μέρους in biblical Greek that closely approximates the partitive interpretation given to ἀπὸ μέρους in Wright's reading of Rom 11:25.

To summarize: a survey of the uses of ἀπὸ μέρους in Paul and in the Greek versions of Israel's Scriptures gives little or no support to a temporal interpretation. The only possible example of such a sense is Rom 15:24, and even that instance is questionable. In all the other relevant comparative passages, a partitive sense is clear. As we have noted, in all of the Pauline passages apart from Rom 11:25 ἀπὸ μέρους is used adverbially, not adjectivally. Following

25. Interestingly, the KJV renders the relevant clause as "if first I be somewhat filled with your company." Most modern translations opt for a temporal rendering, as suggested by BDAG, 633: "for a while." It is noteworthy that BDAG offers no other examples of this alleged temporal sense of the phrase.

26. This could, of course, be interpreted as another instance of the geographical sense: "from their territory."

this pattern in Rom 11:25 would yield a translation such as "a hardening has partially come upon Israel." In view of the entire foregoing discourse (branches cut off, etc.) this could hardly mean that individual Israelites were left with only some sort of partial faith.[27] In all likelihood, therefore, even granting the technical adverbial sense, the sentence probably means nothing different from what Wright has suggested: "a hardening has come upon part of Israel." The examples cited above from Greek versions of Judges, Nehemiah, and Daniel confirm that such a usage of ἀπὸ μέρους would be idiomatic in biblical Greek in a historical period not far removed from Paul. On balance, I would judge that the evidence favors Wright's interpretation. It should be emphasized, further, that if Wright is correct about the sense of ἀπὸ μέρους, it follows that *"Israel" in verse 25 might well have the same meaning as "Israel" in verse 26: the whole body of the people of God made up of Jewish and gentile believers together.*[28] Part of the totality of *that* Israel is presently hardened, but ultimately, Paul believes, they will come to embrace the saving confession of Jesus as Lord.

(2) *What is the significance of ἄχρι οὗ?* A very different judgment applies to the adverbial clause introduced by ἄχρι οὗ in 11:25. There is no doubt of its temporal meaning: ἄχρι οὗ means "until," and the translation of the clause is uncontroversial: "until the fullness (πλήρωμα) of the Gentiles has come in." Paul's articulation of the "mystery" appears to anticipate a definite future endpoint[29] at which the full divinely ordained number of gentiles will have "come in" to Israel. And Paul's sentence implies that precisely after that definite endpoint the "hardening" that has come upon "a part of Israel" will be removed.[30] To most interpreters, the language here strongly suggests an eschatological scenario, analogous to the apocalyptic visions of Revelation. (For an

27. Wright is probably correct to say that this would, strictly speaking, be nonsensical. From Paul's perspective, either individual Israelites have been hardened, or they have not; either they have believed in Jesus, or they have not. Wright remarks, "in view of 11.1–10, being 'partly hardened' would make as much sense as being 'partly pregnant'" (*Faithfulness*, 1239n668). As Leander Keck observes (*Romans*, 279), the qualifier ἀπὸ μέρους "distinguishes nonbelieving Israel from the Christian Jews, who by definition are not among the hardened."

28. For slightly different reasons, Wright makes a similar observation about the sense of "Israel" in v. 25 (*Faithfulness*, 1244).

29. BDAG (160) describes ἄχρι as a "marker of continuous extent of time *up to a point*" (emphasis mine). Florian Wilk observes that ἄχρι οὗ "bezeichnet in den Briefen des Paulus stets ein konkretes Ereignis der Zukunft als Endpunkt eines Tuns oder Zustands; und zwar entweder das Kommen Christi selbst—sei es 'ins Fleisch' (Gal 3:19) oder zur Parusie (1 Kor 11:26)—oder ein Geschehen, das mit ihm eng verbunden ist (1 Kor 15:25)" (*Die Bedeutung des Jesajabuches für Paulus*, FRLANT 179 [Göttingen: Vandenhoeck & Ruprecht, 1998]), 68.

30. It is probably the temporal force of ἄχρι οὗ that has (perhaps subconsciously)

especially interesting parallel, see Rev 2:25: "Only hold fast to what you have *until I come* [ἄχρι οὗ ἂν ἥξω].") Wright, however, has consistently resisted this interpretation of the passage. He believes that Paul, rather than foreseeing a fixed eschatological endpoint, envisions an indefinite period during which the number of believing Jews will gradually increase in "a steady flow of Jews into the church, by grace through faith."[31] As he puts it in his most recent extended interpretation of the passage, "not only will gentiles continue to 'come in,' but the remnant itself will become very much larger, moving toward an eventual 'fullness' (verse 12)."[32]

It appears to me that Wright is (understandably) reacting against an opinion that was briefly popular among some late twentieth-century exegetes but now largely rejected by most recent commentators—namely, the opinion that Paul envisioned no evangelistic mission to the Jewish people prior to the parousia, and that God would at the time of the eschaton suddenly save all Jews through some mysterious means unrelated to their placing trust in Jesus as the Messiah. For reasons explained above, I also regard this view as unsustainable as an exegesis of Paul's argument. It is not clear, however, that the only alternative to such a view is Wright's picture of a gradual influx of Jews into the community that confesses Jesus as Lord. Paul clearly does hope that in the present time some of his own people will be moved to jealousy by the gentile mission and brought to faith. The existing "remnant" (11:5), including Paul himself, already bears witness to such a possibility, and Paul has emphatically agreed that other apostles, such as James and Cephas and John, should continue their mission of proclaiming the gospel message to the circumcised (Gal 2:9). But such an understanding of a present-time mission to the Jewish people hardly precludes the possibility of a future dramatic event, after "the fullness of the Gentiles has come in," that will bring many more (τὸ πλήρωμα αὐτῶν, Rom 11:12) to be "grafted in again" through coming to acknowledge Jesus as Lord (11:23–24).

Paul's hope for a radical eschatological transformation in the future is amply attested in other passages in his letters (e.g., 1 Thess 1:9–10; 4:13–18; Phil 3:20–21; 1 Cor 15:20–28), including other portions of Romans (13:11–14). Especially pertinent is Rom 8:18–25, which speaks of a hope that the whole creation "will be set free from its bondage to decay and will obtain the freedom of the

---

led some interpreters to inappropriately impose a temporal sense on καὶ οὕτως in the following clause.

31. Wright, *Climax of the Covenant*, 249.

32. Wright, *Faithfulness*, 1239.

glory of the children of God"—while acknowledging that in the present time believers continue to groan and wait in hope for that which they do not see. Part of what Paul does *not* see in this "not yet" time is a large-scale turning of the Jewish people to confess Jesus as Messiah and Lord; hence, his sorrow, anguish, and earnest prayers for them (9:1–5; 10:1–4). Yet that large-scale turning is precisely what Paul envisions in 11:25–27 as an event that will not occur "*until* the fullness of the Gentiles has come in."

(3) *How does Paul interpret ὁ ῥυόμενος?* This line of thought leads on to the citation that Paul adduces in 11:26b–27 as the scriptural confirmation of his foregoing argument. How will the large-scale eschatological turning of unbelieving Israel occur? The answer is given in a blended citation drawn from Isa 59:20–21 and 27:9, perhaps with wording influenced by echoes of other texts. Here is the quotation as Paul presents it (with words that are not found in Isa 59:20–21 in italics):

> And in this way all Israel will be saved, as it is written:
> *Out of* Zion (ἐκ Σιὼν) will come the Deliverer (ὁ ῥυόμενος);
> he will banish ungodliness from Jacob.
> And this is my covenant with them,
> *when I take away their sins.*

The distinctive form of this composite citation poses several crucial issues. Who is "the Deliverer" and how are we to interpret his "coming"? In the original context of Isa 59, the Deliverer is Israel's God, who sees that there is no justice and "no one to intervene" (Isa 59:15–16); he therefore dons his armor and comes powerfully *to* Zion as Israel's champion and Redeemer (59:16b-20). Paul, reading retrospectively, sees here a figural anticipation of the coming of *Jesus* as Israel's Messiah and Deliverer. (This is a vivid example of the way in which Paul's figural christological exegesis identifies Jesus as the embodiment of Israel's God.)[33] The identification of Jesus as the Deliverer is confirmed

33. Exactly on point is the frequently cited judgment of E. P. Sanders (*Paul, the Law, and the Jewish People*, 194): "'The Deliverer,' as most scholars agree, is almost certainly Christ in Paul's understanding. . . . But for the present question, whether or not Paul thought of the salvation of Israel apart from Christ, it matters little whether he understands 'the Deliverer' to be God or Christ; for it is incredible that he thought of 'God apart from Christ,' just as it is that he thought of 'Christ apart from God.' . . . To suppose that the 'the Deliverer' could be for Paul 'God apart from Christ' seems to expect of him an unthinkable abstraction." David Capes (*Old Testament Yahweh Texts in Paul's Christology*, WUNT 2/47 [Tübingen: Mohr

by the strong parallel in 1 Thess 1:9–10, where Paul commends the formerly pagan Thessalonian believers who have "turned to God from idols, to serve a living and true God, and to wait for his Son from heaven, whom he raised from the dead—*Jesus who delivers us from the wrath that is coming* (Ἰησοῦν τὸν ῥυόμενον ἡμᾶς ἐκ τῆς ὀργῆς τῆς ἐρχομένης)." In light of this Pauline intertext, interpreters of Romans have judged almost unanimously that in Rom 11:26–27 Paul has construed Isa 59:20 to prefigure a future coming (παρουσία) of Christ in power to raise the dead, gather all the people of God (including the presently unbelieving remnant) to himself, and to establish his rightful lordship over all creation (as in 1 Thess 4:13–18; Phil 3:20–21; 1 Cor 15:20–28; Rom 8:18–23).[34]

Despite the widespread evidence for this narrative pattern in Paul's thought, Wright has resisted *the communis opinio* that Rom 11:26–27 refers to an eschatological future event of Christ's parousia. Instead, Wright maintains, the "coming" of the Deliverer refers to the proclamation of the gospel to the nations, preeminently by Paul himself, whose preaching is "the fulfillment of the Isaianic promise of the herald announcing God's kingdom (10.15, citing Isaiah 52.7)."[35] In the next section, we will consider the question of whether the apostolic proclamation could itself be identified as the coming of the Deliverer. For the moment, I simply want to register the opinion that Wright underestimates the weight of the evidence in favor of the parousia interpretation. He does note the parallel in 1 Thessalonians but brushes it aside a little too casually:

> True, Paul can use the verbal equivalent of the noun *ho ruomenos*, "the Deliverer," when referring to Jesus' return and his delivering of his people from the wrath to come. But that does not mean that whenever he uses a cognate word he must always be referring to the "second coming."[36]

Siebeck, 1992], 102) notes in passing that Paul interprets "the Deliverer" christologically in Rom 11:26. Surprisingly, however, Capes does not develop an interpretation of the passage as a significant instance in which Paul considers Jesus "a manifestation of Yahweh."

34. Also relevant is Rom 7:24b–25a: "Who will deliver (ῥύσεται) me from this body of death? Thanks be to God through Jesus Christ our Lord!" While the timing of the hoped-for deliverance is not specified in this compact outcry, Rom 8 exposits the temporal framing dialectically. Deliverance is *both* a present reality (vv. 1–11) and an urgent future hope (vv. 18–25).

35. Wright, *Faithfulness*, 1250–51.

36. Wright, *Faithfulness*, 1251.

I offer two rejoinders. First, a technical quibble: ὁ ῥυόμενος is in fact not a noun but a participle used substantively. And in 1 Thess 1:10 what we find is once again precisely the participial form, this time in the accusative case: τὸν ῥυόμενον. A good case could be made here for interpreting Paul's construction as a substantive use of the participle in apposition to the proper name "Jesus," expressing a titular sense identical to that in Isa 59:20/Rom 11:26. This would yield a translation such as "Jesus, our Deliverer from the wrath that is coming." My point is that in 1 Thess 1:10 Paul uses not "a cognate word" but exactly the same word in a slightly different grammatical construction, both times in contexts that refer to eschatological salvation.

Second, and perhaps more significantly, this seems to be an unusual instance where Wright has selectively excluded the relevance of a larger dominant narrative structure for the interpretation of a particular local exegetical context. Elsewhere throughout Tom's massive oeuvre he emphatically advocates reading individual texts within the context of a larger story, a foundational narrative that unifies and illuminates the individual writings of the Bible as a whole, and of Paul's situationally specific statements in particular. Surely, however, Paul's overall unifying narrative structure points to the consummation of God's saving action in an eschatological future event when the dead are to be raised and Christ's lordship is at last to be made fully manifest. It is not clear to me why that larger narrative pattern should suddenly be ruled out of play in our interpretation of an eschatologically freighted text such as Rom 11:25–27. The connection between Rom 11:26 and 1 Thess 1:10 is not simply a random verbal parallel; both texts appropriate ὁ ῥυόμενος, Isaiah's descriptor of Israel's God, as a title for Jesus in his role as bringer of eschatological salvation.[37] For that reason, the eschatological narrative pattern presupposed by 1 Thess 1:9–10 is directly pertinent to the interpretation of the passage in Romans.

(4) *Why does Paul say the Deliverer will come ἐκ Σιών*? Here we return to the exegetical problem that Calvin sought to sweep under the rug. The textual issues have been exhaustively studied and can be briefly summarized. The Hebrew text of Isa 59:20 says that the Redeemer will come *to* Zion (לְצִיּוֹן). The LXX renders this, a little broadly, as ἕνεκεν Σιων ("for the sake of Zion"). Paul has altered the quotation to read ἐκ Σιών ("from Zion"). Scholars have espoused various opinions on the question of whether Paul's tweaking of the text was deliberate (to further his argument) or unintentional and inconsequential (i.e., he was following a *Vorlage* with a variant rendering).[38] Indeed,

37. In addition to Isa 59:20, see also Isa 49:7.

38. Dietrich A. Koch (*Die Schrift als Zeuge des Evangeliums*, BHT 69 [Tübingen: Mohr

those who think Paul is not responsible for the alteration usually contend—as Calvin did—that the wording of the MT or the LXX would actually have served his argument better than the form he does cite. Wright, however, comes down firmly in favor of the view that the change "cannot be accidental" and that Paul has himself "adjusted" the text to fit his understanding of what God is surprisingly doing in the events of his own time. This adjustment is part of Paul's "redefinition of Jewish eschatology around Jesus and the spirit." Here is Wright's explanation of the textual change:

> Salvation is coming *from* Zion to the nations. Paul is not reinscribing the older centripetal tradition [i.e., the pilgrimage of the nations to Zion], but nor is he abandoning the old belief that when Israel's God finally acted to fulfill his promises to his people the gentile nations would come under his rule, whether for rescue or for ruin. Rather, he is transforming the tradition into a centrifugal movement: the Redeemer now comes, with the gospel, *from* Zion to the world, and as a reflex (exactly as in 11.11–15) will "banish ungodliness from Jacob."[39]

This account of the textual alteration fits neatly into place alongside Wright's insistence that the coming of the Deliverer is not a future event. Instead, the "coming" of the Deliverer is collapsed—I find it hard to choose another word—into the dissemination of Christian preaching throughout the pagan world (as perhaps in accord with Rom 10:6–9, 17–18). Wright does not elaborate on this point, but its implications are clearly spelled out by J. R. Daniel Kirk in a lucid essay that converges with many aspects of Wright's interpretation. Kirk recognizes the possible difficulty of identifying ὁ ῥυόμενος unqualifiedly with the phenomenon of the preached message. Nonetheless, appealing to Rom

Siebeck, 1986], 177) opines that the unaltered LXX text would have been more suitable to Paul's argument and that the alteration to ἐκ Σιών is for Paul "funktionslos." For that reason he concludes that the text form in Rom 11:26 is taken over from pre-Pauline tradition. For similar positions on the question, see Christopher D. Stanley, "'The Redeemer Will Come ἐκ Σιων': Romans 11:26–27 Revisited," in *Paul and the Scriptures of Israel*, ed. Craig A. Evans and James A. Sanders, JSNTSup 83/SSEJC 1 (Sheffield: JSOT, 1993), 118–42; and Wilk, *Die Bedeutung des Jesajabuches*, 40. For the contrary view that Paul himself is responsible for the textual alteration, see Shiu-Lun Shum, *Paul's Use of Isaiah in Romans*, WUNT 2/156 (Tübingen: Mohr Siebeck, 2002), 236–39; Wagner, *Heralds of the Good News*, 280–81n196 (an especially strong refutation of Stanley on this point) and 285–86n208; Jewett, *Romans*, 703; and Kirk, "Why Does the Deliverer Come ἐκ Σιών (Romans 11.26)?," 83–86.

39. Wright, *Faithfulness*, 1250.

10:20 ("I became manifest [ἐμφανὴς ἐγενόμην] to those who did not ask for me"), he confronts the question squarely:

> Thus, as Paul reads Isaiah, "the deliverer," be it God or Christ, is *a suitable metonymy for the message that brings salvation.* In interpreting ὁ ῥυόμενος in Rom 11:26, then, it is highly plausible that the figure indicates Christian proclamation.[40]

On this reading, the apocalyptic future dimension of the gospel is (at least for Rom 11) dissolved, and the hoped-for saving action of Christ is deemed to occur in Paul's immediate present time through the proclaimed word.

What are we to make of this? It must be conceded that Wright's position (likewise Kirk's) has the virtue of consistency. My worry is that the consistency is perhaps purchased at the rather high price of absorbing Jesus into the kerygma[41] and excluding the future apocalyptic elements of Paul's eschatology and soteriology, elements that may contribute to a more complex, mysterious, and untidy picture of Rom 11:25–27 than the one Wright paints.[42]

Wright is no doubt correct to reject the suggestion that "Zion" in Rom 11:26 refers to the heavenly Jerusalem, as in Paul's allegorical exposition of the story of Sarah and Hagar in Gal 4:26. Even where Paul elsewhere refers to Christ's

40. Kirk, "Why Does the Deliverer Come ἐκ Σιών (Romans 11.26)?," 92, emphasis mine. I take the interpretation that I have cited here from Kirk to be essentially identical to Wright's understanding of the way in which Paul understood the declaration that "The Deliverer will come from Zion." Kirk challenges Wright's understanding of πᾶς Ἰσραὴλ as the church of Jews and gentiles together, but concurs with his rejection of the parousia interpretation and with his argument that the gentile mission is the instrument through which the salvation of "all Israel" will be accomplished.

41. Rudolf Bultmann would no doubt applaud from beyond the grave. (Of course, he would be able to do that only if he was after all mistaken about the mythological character of belief in some sort of postmortem existence.)

42. I am mindful that Wright is sharply critical of the use of the word "apocalyptic" as a meaningful descriptive term in characterizing Paul's theology. This problem would require another essay to address. Here I use the term simply to gesture toward Paul's expectation of a dramatic future event that would include Christ's coming in power and glory, the resurrection of the dead, and the creation of a new world in which the powers of Sin and Death are decisively abolished, a world in which God's justice reigns visibly forever. Despite Wright's disapproval of the term "apocalyptic" as a descriptor for Paul's theology, he elsewhere affirms all these elements of the story that Paul's theology tells and interprets. This leads to an important point: Wright's resistance to the future-parousia interpretation of Rom 11:25–27 should not be understood as a denial that Paul specifically hoped for the future coming of Christ; instead, it is a more specific and limited position on the meaning of Rom 11:25–27 in its context.

coming from heaven (e.g., 1 Thess 1:9–10; Phil 3:20–21), he makes no reference to Jerusalem, or to any "heavenly city." Much more apposite is Robert Jewett's observation: "Paul's formulation 'from Zion' is consistent with the composite creed that opens his letter concerning Jesus 'descended from David' (1.3) and with the reminder that Christ came from the Israelites (9.5) and that it was in 'Zion' that the stone of stumbling was laid."[43] In view of these considerations, Kirk concludes that in Rom 11:26 "Zion functions as a metonymy for Jerusalem or the people of Israel"—i.e., that Paul's formulation emphasizes Jesus's historical, earthly roots in the people of Israel.[44]

(5) *Does "covenant" in Rom 11:27 refer to Jeremiah's "new covenant"?* In some of his earlier work, Wright seems to suggest that Rom 11:27 contains a quotation from Jer 31:34. In *Paul and the Faithfulness of God*, however, he offers a more qualified formulation: "Rom 11.27, affirming that God's covenant will consist of his forgiving his people's sins, while at one level obviously quoting Isa 59.21 and 27.9, at another level resonates powerfully with Jer 31.33–34."[45] Wright is not alone in hearing such a resonance. We have already noted that Calvin connected the "covenant" of Rom 11:27 to Jeremiah's promise of a new covenant (Jer 31:31–34 [38:31–34 LXX]). Nor was this reading original with Calvin; it is attested in Thomas Aquinas's commentary on Romans, and no doubt has deeper roots in patristic exegesis. It is also supported, to one degree or another, by several modern commentators.[46]

Despite the antiquity and pervasiveness of this intertextual reading, the actual wording of Paul's citation is drawn almost entirely from the two Isaiah passages, with minor modifications. The words quoted in Rom 11:27a simply continue Paul's quotation of Isa 59:20–21; they are taken verbatim from Isa 59:21a (καὶ αὕτη αὐτοῖς ἡ παρ' ἐμοῦ διαθήκη). And the words quoted in the last bit of Paul's composite citation (ὅταν ἀφέλωμαι τὰς ἁμαρτίας αὐτῶν, Rom 11:27b) are a slight modification of words drawn from Isa 27:9 LXX: ὅταν ἀφέλωμαι αὐτοῦ τὴν ἁμαρτίαν. For contextual reasons, Paul's quotation changes the singular τὴν ἁμαρτίαν to the plural τὰς ἁμαρτίας and also shifts the possessive pronoun to the plural, in keeping with his focus on the soteriological fate of a

43. Jewett, *Romans*, 703–4. See also Fitzmyer, *Romans*, 624.

44. Kirk, "Why Does the Deliverer Come ἐκ Σιών (Romans 11.26)?," 91. This interpretation was already suggested by Thomas Aquinas; see "Selections from Thomas Aquinas' *Commentary on Romans*," trans. Eugene F. Rogers, Jr., in *The Theological Interpretation of Scripture: Classic and Contemporary Readings*, ed. Stephen E. Fowl (Oxford: Blackwell, 1997), 331. Aquinas notes a parallel in John 4:22: "Salvation is from the Jews."

45. Wright, *Faithfulness*, 1247n697, acknowledging a corrective offered by Wagner, *Heralds of the Good News*, 290.

46. For example, Barrett, Cranfield, Dahl, Dunn, and Fitzmyer.

large group of people. Apart from the single key term διαθήκη—which might provide a catchword link between Isa 59 and Jer 38 LXX—the only possible traces of allusion to Jeremiah would be the reference to "sins" in the plural,[47] along with the plural pronoun. That is a slender basis indeed for tracing an intertextual allusion. By contrast, Isa 59:20–21 is obviously linked to Isa 27:9 by references to God's action of turning away ungodliness (59:20) or removing lawlessness (27:9) *from Jacob*.

Given Paul's concern to affirm the *continuity* of God's covenant relationship with Israel, he might well have chosen for rhetorical reasons to avoid explicitly invoking Jeremiah's image of a "*new* covenant." Whether that be so or not, my main point here is that, *in defending the proclamation that "all Israel will be saved," Paul sticks closely to language drawn from Isaiah*. This has two implications worth noting. First, we should be cautious about building our interpretation of Rom 11:25–27 on Jeremiah's picture of a "new covenant." Second, when Paul writes that the Deliverer will come ἐκ Σιών, his departure from the wording of Isa 59:20 becomes all the more surprising and noteworthy.

(6) *What is the temporal reference of ὅταν ἀφέλωμαι?* Here the issue can be sharply stated: Does Paul's citation of Isaiah point to an indefinitely repeatable future possibility ("whenever I take away their sins") or to a specific future occurrence at some unspecified point in time ("at the point when I take away their sins")? Once again Wright stakes out a definite position.

> What is particularly telling is the exact form of the quotation from Isaiah 27 at the end of 11.27, *hotan ophelōmai*, "*whenever* I take away" their sins. The natural reading of this is not to refer to one single action, a unique, one-off saving event at the end of all things, but to an indefinite future possibility. It could of course mean 'whenever it may be that I perform that single action', but it could equally mean "at whatever time, however frequently repeated, people 'turn to the lord and have the veil removed,' as in 2 Corinthians 3.15."[48]

47. Even here, Jer 38:34 has the genitive τῶν ἁμαρτιῶν, in contrast to the accusative τὰς ἁμαρτίας in Rom 11:27. (The accusative case is of course dictated by the fact that the noun is the direct object of the verb ἀφέλωμαι from Isa 27:9.) The verbal echo of Jer 38 LXX is indistinct at best. Perhaps more pertinent is the echo of Isa 59:2: διὰ <u>τὰς ἁμαρτίας</u> ὑμῶν ἀπέστρεψεν τὸ πρόσωπον αὐτοῦ ἀφ' ὑμῶν τοῦ μὴ ἐλεῆσαι. This comes from the Lord's indictment of Israel that introduces the chapter from which Paul has just quoted in Rom 11:26–27a; the verbs ἀπέστρεψεν and ἐλεῆσαι resonate with the immediate context in Rom 11:25–32. See also Isa 59:12.

48. Wright, *Faithfulness*, 1251. Wright's reference to 2 Cor 3:15 appears to be a typographical error; 2 Cor 3:16 is intended.

A good deal is at stake here for Wright. His scenario of a gradual influx of Jewish people drawn over time to confessing Jesus as Lord requires that ὅταν + aorist subjunctive must indicate an indefinitely repeatable future possibility. This grammatical point is, however, like so many other things in this passage, contested. The strongest counterstatement appears in Robert Jewett's Hermeneia commentary. Jewett declares firmly that, on grammatical grounds, God's action of taking away "Jacob's" sins must be understood as a single action at a future point in time: "The citation refers to a condition that must be fulfilled before the covenant can be restored: 'when I shall have taken away their sins.'"[49]

Some of the examples cited in BDAG, to which Jewett appeals, would support his interpretation. It appears to me, however, that passages such as Matt 5:11 would instead support Wright's case: "Blessed are you when people revile you and persecute you and utter all kinds of evil against you" (μακάριοί ἐστε ὅταν ὀνειδίσωσιν ὑμᾶς καὶ διώξωσιν καὶ εἴπωσιν πᾶν πονηρὸν καθ' ὑμῶν). Here it would seem artificial to insist on translating as "Blessed are you when people shall have (on one definite future occasion) reviled you and persecuted and uttered all kinds of evil against you." Surely what is envisioned here in Matthew's ὅταν + aorist subjunctive construction is precisely the kind of repeated future action that Wright sees in Rom 11:27b.

I would judge that on this point the strictly grammatical evidence is inconclusive. Wright's position is a possible exegetical option: the construction in Rom 11:27b allows for indefinitely repeated future action. But this interpretation can be argued (either pro or con) only on contextual grounds, as Wright has attempted to do in *Paul and the Faithfulness of God.*

Let us pause for an overview of the uncertain terrain we have sought to map. Our exploratory expedition has arrived at these findings:

1 In Rom 11:25, Wright is almost certainly correct to translate "a hardening has come upon *part of* Israel."
2 However, his interpretation underestimates the way in which ἄχρι οὗ points to a definite future endpoint at which the "fullness of the Gentiles" will have been grafted into Israel.
3 When Paul cites Isaiah's prophecy of the coming of "the Deliverer," he is thinking of Jesus, who fulfills and embodies the hope that God would come to rescue his people. Wright recognizes the christological force of the quotation in Rom 11:26 but underestimates the significance of

49. Jewett, *Romans*, 706, citing in support BDAG, 731. (Jewett also cites BDF § 318, 333, 379, 382. But none of these paragraphs in BDF appears directly relevant to the case at hand.)

the parallel in 1 Thess 1:9–10. His resultant reading wrongly excludes possible reference to a future triumphant coming of Christ.

4 Wright is surely correct to insist that Paul's alteration of the quotation of Isa 59:20 to read ἐκ Σιών must be taken as significant. His suggestion that the coming of the Deliverer "from Zion" should be interpreted as a reference to the spread of the gospel to the gentile world is a possible and coherent reading. But this interpretation has the effect of minimizing the unfulfilled future eschatological dimension of Paul's thought and collapsing the person Jesus Christ into the preached word.

5 Despite venerable interpretative precedent, we should be cautious about assuming an intertextual allusion to Jeremiah's "new covenant" in Rom 11:25–27.

6 The last clause of Rom 11:27 blends Isa 27:9 into Paul's citation. The grammatical construction here (ὅταν + aorist subjunctive) refers to something that is to happen in an indefinite future time. On the basis of grammar alone, however, it is not possible to determine whether Paul understands this to indicate a single future event or an indefinitely repeatable possibility.

A Path Forward: Echoes of the Psalms?

Paul's anomalous reading of ἐκ Σιών in his citation of Isaiah confronts us with a crux for the exegesis of Rom 11:25–27. Our sifting of the evidence so far suggests that much turns on the interpretation of this phrase. What does Paul mean by saying that the Deliverer will come *from* Zion?

Occasionally attempts have been made to identify a single intertextual source for this unexpected wording. One proposed candidate is Isa 2:3, with its depiction of the pilgrimage of the nations to Jerusalem to receive instruction: "For out of Zion [ἐκ γὰρ Σιων] shall go forth instruction [νόμος], and the word of the LORD from Jerusalem."[50] But skeptics have understandably balked

50. Wright made this suggestion in *Climax of the Covenant*, 250–51, and reaffirms it as a possible echo in *Faithfulness*, 1249–50. For a more extended exposition of this position, see Christopher R. Bruno, "The Deliverer from Zion: The Source(s) and Function of Paul's Citation in Romans 11:26–27," *TynBul* 59 (2008): 119–34. The same proclamation that the νόμος would go forth from Zion appears almost verbatim in Micah 4:2 LXX, lacking the γάρ found in Isa 2:3.

at finding such a highly specific allusion on the basis of a single preposition (ἐκ), especially since Paul never elsewhere refers to a pilgrimage of the nations to Jerusalem and never invokes Isa 2 as justification for his gentile mission.[51] Wright, who has himself pointed to Isa 2:3 as a possible background to Rom 11:26, has qualified this view in his more recent work by observing that in view of "Paul's redefinition of Jewish eschatology around Jesus and the spirit . . . it would make no sense to undo this powerful theology by reinstating the earthly Jerusalem as the place to which the nations should go to find salvation."[52] Therefore, as Wright notes, if there is any possible allusion to Isa 2:3 in Rom 11:26, it would require a reversal, or transformation, of Isaiah's scenario.

Commentators on Romans often make passing reference to a few other scriptural passages in which the phrase "from Zion" appears, chiefly in the Psalms, but rarely do they attribute much significance to these as intertexts.[53] More typically, the commentary tradition takes Paul's alteration of Isaiah as odd but insignificant.

I would propose a different way of proceeding. The phrase ἐκ Σιων appears eight times in the Greek Psalter: Ps 13:7; 19:3; 49:2; 52:7; 109:2; 127:5; 133:3; and 134:21.[54] Reading these psalms cumulatively, one sees that all of them (except the very brief Ps 133) speak of God's sending help to Israel or coming to save Israel. I think it unlikely that Paul "intended" in Rom 11 to allude to any one of these psalms in particular. But I think it highly likely that the language of these psalms was imbedded in Paul's bones, and that when he was writing passionately to the Romans about the mystery of Israel's salvation the wording of these texts rose spontaneously to his mind. Rather than discussing all eight instances, the following discussion will offer a brief survey of the occurrences of ἐκ Σιων in five psalms that offer particularly rich examples of the "encyclopedia of production" that informed Paul's tweaking of Isaiah.

51. Terence L. Donaldson, *Paul and the Gentiles: Remapping the Apostle's Convictional World* (Minneapolis: Fortress, 1997), 187–97. For Donaldson's dismissal of an allusion to Isa 2:3 in Rom 11:26, see 329n66.

52. Wright, *Paul and the Faithfulness*, 1250.

53. Wright mentions Ps 14:7 but does not explicate its significance for Rom 11:25–27 (*Faithfulness*, 1249–50). Perhaps he regards it as self-evident? He also cites Deut 33:2, which is of doubtful relevance, since it speaks of the Lord coming from Sinai, not Zion.

54. In the following pages, references to chapter and verse in the Psalms will follow the LXX numeration.

Ps 13:7 LXX/ Ps 52:7 LXX

> Who will bring the salvation of Israel (τὸ σωτήριον τοῦ Ισραηλ)
> out of Sion (ἐκ Σιων)?
> When the Lord brings back (ἐπιστρέψαι) the captivity of
> his people,
> let Jacob exult, and Israel be glad.

Psalm 13 is particularly significant for our present investigation[55] because *earlier in Romans Paul had quoted it at some length* in a catena of texts that present a withering indictment of human sinfulness (Rom 3:10–18; see esp. vv. 10–12, which draw directly from Ps 13:1–3). Thus the yearning of the psalm's final verse (v. 7), a wish for Israel's salvation, prefigures the movement of Paul's whole letter from indictment to the proclamation of God's action for the salvation of his people.[56] The fact that Paul has previously cited a part of Ps 13 greatly enhances the likelihood that he knows its concluding expectation that Jacob/ Israel will be brought back by the Lord. This is an example of the way in which the criterion of *recurrence* can lend confidence to proposed intertextual readings.[57] It is also highly significant that Rom 3:15–17 includes, within the same catena, material directly quoted from Isa 59:7–8—the same chapter that Paul cites in Rom 11:26–27. Thus, there is a three-way linkage between Ps 13, Isa 59, and Romans (3:10–18 + 11:26–27). One suspects that we are seeing here only a glimpse of a more complex intertextual web.[58] Further, the reference in Ps 13:7 to *Jacob* as the object of God's saving action provides an additional link to Isa

55. I focus my remarks here on Ps 13 LXX. Almost everything said here is also applicable to the nearly identical Ps 52 LXX.

56. A fascinating note: the word for "salvation" here in the Hebrew text (Ps 14:7) is יְשׁוּעַת (*yeshuath*). Would Paul possibly have been aware of the serendipitous subtextual connection between the Hebrew name of Jesus (*Yeshua*) and the Greek σωτήριον? If so, he never draws attention to it. But cf. Matt 1:21.

57. Hays, *Echoes of Scripture in the Letters of Paul,* 30; Hays, *Conversion of the Imagination,* 37–38.

58. It should also be noted that allusions to Isa 59:17 show up in 1 Thess 5:8 and Eph 6:14, 17. Florian Wilk (*Die Bedeutung des Jesajabuches,* 239–42) sketches out a whole network of connections between Rom 11:26–27 and intertexts in Isa 59:9–60:3, as well as Isa 27:6–13. To follow his intriguing pointers would take us too far afield from the present purposes of this essay, but his exegesis merits deeper deliberation. Wagner (*Heralds of the Good News,* 287–89) also helpfully observes the many connections between Isa 59, Rom 3, and Rom 11.

59:20/Rom 11:26, which declares that God "will turn away (ἀποστρέψει) ungodliness *from Jacob*." Interestingly, one of the minor ways in which Ps 52 LXX differs from Ps 13 LXX is that its concluding affirmation of God's restoration of Jacob/Israel shifts from exhortation ("let Jacob exult, and Israel be glad") to future promise: "Jacob will rejoice and Israel will be glad" (Ps 52:7 LXX).

Ps 19:2 LXX

This psalm opens with a prayer that God will come to the rescue of Israel's king:

> May the Lord answer you in the day of trouble.
> May the name of the God of Jacob protect you.
> May he send you help from the sanctuary
> and come to your aid from Zion (ἐκ Σιων). (Ps 19:1–3)

Because this is a prayer offered for the king, rather than for the sinful people, it has less direct resonance with Rom 11:26. It is noteworthy, however, that the God whose support is invoked is named as "the God of Jacob." This is the God who will send help *from Zion*; the synonymous parallelism here suggests that Zion is regarded as the sanctuary, the place of God's dwelling.

Ps 49:2 LXX

Here the LXX differs from the Hebrew text in a way that suggests an interesting resonance with Isa 59:20/Rom 11:26.

> Out of Sion (ἐκ Σιων), the excellence of his beauty, God will come visibly (ἐμφανῶς ἥξει).

This "coming" of God from Zion in a visible manifestation is, we learn as the psalm continues, for the purpose of summoning his people ("who made a covenant with me") to judgment (vv. 4–6). But as the speech of the judge unfolds, it turns from rebuke to invitation and promise: "Call on me in the day of trouble; I will deliver you, and you shall glorify me" (v. 15). Once again, as in Ps 13, the movement of the psalm—from judgment to the promise of salvation offered by the God who will come *from Zion*—anticipates the narrative shape of Paul's argument in Rom 11.

Ps 109:2 LXX

The final instance we shall consider offers another example of the importance of noting the recurrence of allusion to a highly significant precursor. Psalm 109 LXX//110 MT is of course cited repeatedly as a prefiguration of Christ's exaltation at the right hand of God in the Synoptic Gospels, in Acts, and in the Letter to the Hebrews. Though Paul never quotes this psalm overtly, he clearly alludes to Ps 109:1 in his depiction in 1 Cor 15:20–28 of Christ's eschatological triumph over the power of death: "For he must reign until [God] *has put all things in subjection under his feet*" (15:25). In view of this distinct allusion, Paul's declaration in Rom 8:34 that the risen Christ is now "at the right hand of God" should likewise be understood to presuppose Ps 109 (see also Eph 1:20; Col 3:1). If Paul's language seems to assume deep familiarity with this christologically freighted psalm, then perhaps we should also follow the Nestle-Aland apparatus in discerning allusions to Ps 109:5 in Rom 2:5 ("the day of his wrath") and—intriguingly, but more distantly and doubtfully—to Ps 109:4 ("the Lord has sworn and will not change his mind [οὐ μεταμεληθήσεται]") in Rom 11:29 ("the gifts and the calling of God are irrevocable [ἀμεταμέλητα]"). In light of this scattering of allusions, both certain and less certain, in Paul's letters, it is perhaps not farfetched to hear also in Rom 11:26 an echo of Ps 109:2 LXX:

> The Lord will send out from Zion (ἐκ Σιων) your rod of power.

In the context of the psalm, the power that goes forth ἐκ Σιων is said to subdue and destroy enemies rather than to rescue Israel, though the two things may be closely related. In any case, Ps 109 LXX is another text that appears to be stored deeply in Paul's memory bank, and his allusions to it in other contexts indicate that he understood it as a prefiguration of Christ's eschatologically triumphant lordship. If this psalm was one of the subliminal intertexts that caused Paul to modify Isa 59:20 by writing ἐκ Σιών rather than ἕνεκεν Σιων, then the case is strengthened for interpreting Rom 11:26, alongside 1 Thess 1:10, as a reference to a *future* coming of the Deliverer to turn away the ungodliness of Jacob and accomplish the salvation of all Israel.

To sum up: the Psalms presented Paul with a range of texts in which the expectation of God's help coming ἐκ Σιων was associated with the rescue or salvation of Israel. In some of these psalms, the coming of help from Zion was interpreted as God's power issuing forth from the sanctuary—i.e., the temple in Jerusalem, the dwelling place of God (*not* from some otherworldly venue). Further, some of these psalms depict God as a righteous judge who enacts a narrative movement from condemnation of the guilty to a final rescue/salvation of Israel. Exactly that same pattern is present in Isa 59, which begins by announcing to Israel that "your iniquities have been barriers between you and your God, and your sins have hidden his face from you," but concludes by narrating God's decision nonetheless to intervene by coming as Deliverer of Israel. Romans 3:10–18 is a key text showing that Isa 59 (the key text quoted in Rom 11:25–27) is interwoven in Paul's mind with Ps 13/Ps 52. Further, Paul elsewhere alludes to Ps 109 in contexts that associate it with the resurrection of the dead and Christ's final triumph. If Ps 109:2 is part of the intertextual reservoir from which Paul drew (whether consciously or unconsciously) the words ἐκ Σιών and imported them into his citation of Isa 59:20, it is more rather than less likely that he interpreted Isaiah's prophecy as a picture of a dramatic future "coming" of Christ, as in 1 Thess 1:9–10; 4:13–18—not simply as a portrayal of the church's preaching of the gospel to the gentiles.

Conclusion

In the modern era, some NT scholars, seeking to escape the shadow of an ugly history of Christian anti-Jewish bias, have sought to find in Rom 11 a basis for affirming gentile Christianity and Judaism as separate but equal paths to relationship with God, perhaps through two separate but equal covenants. This interpretative project is, however, doomed to exegetical failure. Tom Wright, while acutely aware of the vital hermeneutical and ethical issues surrounding Jewish-Christian relations in our time, has charted another course. He has insisted on interpreting Paul within his own historical context as a Jew who believed Jesus to be Israel's Messiah and Lord. Whatever we might wish Paul to have said, or whatever we might think is theologically necessary to say in a post-Holocaust world, we must reckon first of all with what Paul actually said and meant. It is a salutary discipline to distinguish descriptive exegesis from constructive theological reflection.[59] (And, I hasten to add, to keep the two in close, urgent conversation.) Wright's exegesis of Rom 11:25–27 has gone a long way toward clarifying the passage; I am deeply grateful for what I have

59. E. P. Sanders models such a distinction in the closing pages of *Paul, the Law, and the Jewish People* (192–99). He argues on exegetical grounds that Paul believed Jews could be saved only through faith in Christ. He indicates, however, that he himself would "vote against" such a theological proposition today, and he speculates that perhaps Paul himself might now do the same, in view of the fact that his expectation that the Redeemer would come soon turned out to be mistaken.

learned from him. The present essay has sought to engage his exegesis appreciatively, while also suggesting some ways in which it could be sharpened and, in some instances, corrected. It remains for me then to state positively what the text means.

The "mystery" to which Paul refers (11:25) is the unexpected narrative sequence in which God's saving plan for the world has unfolded and will one day be completed: a hardening has come upon a part of ethnic Israel, with the result that they have rejected the message that Jesus is Lord and Messiah. This hardening has allowed many gentiles to "come in," i.e., to be grafted into Israel. There will come a day when the "fullness of the gentiles" (its number and extent known only to God) will have embraced the faith and been incorporated, through Christ, into the "olive tree," the people of God. In the meantime, while a "remnant" of ethnic Israel has believed (and more individuals may continue over time to confess Jesus as Lord), ethnic Israel as a whole remains in the status of being branches "cut off" by unbelief. But their current status is not their final destiny. There will come a day in the future when Christ will come as the Deliverer and (in some way that we cannot now know) turn "Jacob" away from its present "ungodliness" and unbelief. At that time, they will acknowledge him as Lord (as in Rom 10:9; Phil 2:10–11). When that happens, the fullness of the whole people of God made up of Jews and gentiles together in Christ (Rom 11:12 + 11:25)—that is, "all Israel"—will be saved. (Paul's καὶ οὕτως in Rom 11:26 points to the surprising reversal of the eschatological script expected by many Jews in his day: the nations will "come in" first, with the majority of ethnic Israel later, following a period of "hardening.") This unfathomable future event is linked with Christ's coming in power, the resurrection of the dead, and the final establishment of God's justice. The Deliverer, then, will be seen to have come "from Zion" in at least two senses: his saving power will come forth from God's own dwelling place (that is perhaps, as Wright proposes, through Jesus himself as the locus of God's presence), and from Jesus's specific historical identity as a human being rooted in the people of Israel. (In other words, salvation will not come from an alien god but from Israel's own Messiah, whom Paul can describe paradoxically as "the Messiah κατὰ σάρκα, God over all," Rom 9:5). But for the present, our appropriate role is one of humility: both soteriological humility about being incorporated by God's mercy into his people Israel and epistemological humility about our capacity to know exactly how the faithfulness of God will finally be consummated.

As Tom writes concerning Paul's olive tree metaphor, "part of the point of using picture-language is after all to be evocative and not mathematically precise."[60] My worry about his painstakingly thorough exegesis of the picture language in Rom 11:25–27 is that he has not sufficiently heeded his own admonition, that he has sought to delimit the force of Paul's open-ended, poetic, intertextual language too strictly: to insist that the coming of the Deliverer from Zion can mean *only* the mission of the church, not the eschatological parousia of the Lord. I would suggest, to the contrary, that we should keep both possibilities open. That would do more justice to Paul's agonized wrestling in Rom 9–11, which seems designed to gesture toward hope for something that we do not yet see.

60. Wright, *Faithfulness*, 1211.

15

Paul, Acts, and Early Christian Proclamation

Comparing the Theologies of Paul and Acts

Philipp Vielhauer's influential essay "On the 'Paulinism' of Acts" forcefully articulated the case for seeing the theology of Acts as far removed from the thought of the apostle Paul. Vielhauer's working method was to examine the *speeches* that Luke places in Paul's mouth and to compare their theology to the theology found in Paul's letters. The comparison was carried out in regard to four theological loci: natural theology, Law, Christology, and eschatology. In these four areas, Vielhauer found little common ground between Luke and Paul; indeed, he repeatedly concluded that Luke did not know, or did not understand, the distinctive emphases of Pauline theology. "To summarize: the author of Acts is in his Christology pre-Pauline, in his natural theology, concept of the law, and eschatology, post-Pauline. He presents no specifically Pauline idea. . . . [H]e no longer stands within earliest Christianity, but in the nascent early catholic church."[1]

In this essay I will propose that, in light of significant advances in NT studies over the past half century, additional evidence ought to be taken into

1. Philipp Vielhauer, "On the 'Paulinism' of Acts," in *Studies in Luke-Acts*, ed. Leander E. Keck and J. Louis Martyn (Nashville: Abingdon, 1966), 48–49; originally published as "Zum 'Paulinismus' der Apostelgeschichte," *EvT* 10 (1950–1951): 1–15. The Keck and Martyn volume was reprinted in a new edition in 1980 (Philadelphia: Fortress, 1980). Vielhauer's essay was also reprinted in David P. Moessner et al., eds., *Paul and the Heritage of Israel*, LNTS 452 (London: T & T Clark, 2012), 3–17. All page references in these notes refer to the original 1966 edition of *Studies in Luke-Acts*. Vielhauer's essay oddly fails to consider how an author who "no longer stands within earliest Christianity" could have a "pre-Pauline" Christology.

A version of this essay was first presented at the Reception of Paul Seminar, the SNTS meeting in Aberdeen, Scotland, 2006. I am appreciative of the helpful comments from that session.

account in forming a fuller picture of the theological relationship between Paul and the author of Acts.[2] Since the original publication of Vielhauer's work in 1950, our understanding of "Pauline theology" has undergone certain chastenings and adjustments. More recent scholarship has offered us a more complex picture of Paul, particularly with regard to his relationship to Judaism. If indeed Paul's thought remained deeply rooted in a Jewish apocalyptic worldview, and if much of his theological reflection was generated and sustained by Israel's Scripture—and I would argue that both of these statements are accurate readings of Paul—then Vielhauer's comparison would require fundamental reconsideration.

Furthermore, Vielhauer's method of looking almost exclusively at the content of the *speeches* ascribed in Acts to Paul has the effect of restricting the evidence too narrowly. If our aim is to compare Paul's theology to the theology of *Acts*, it will hardly do to examine only the content of a few speeches; we must consider the whole shape of the Lukan narrative and the theology that comes to expression in and through that narrative. It is perhaps not surprising that an essay written in Germany in 1950 would overlook the significance of *narrative* as a vehicle of theological reflection,[3] and it would be foolish and ungracious of us to chide Vielhauer for failing to employ narrative criticism—as foolish as it would be to chide Luke for failing to apply historical-critical methods in his exegesis of the Psalms. Nonetheless, in our own reading of Acts, we can surely do better.

For example, we cannot simply assume—as Vielhauer does—that Paul's Areopagus speech in Acts 17 gives an adequate summary of Luke's own theology (Vielhauer inexplicably asserts that this speech appears at "the high point of [Luke's] book";[4] regrettably, this judgment illustrates the severe limitations of Vielhauer's method for interpreting narrative texts). As Beverly Gaventa and other narratively oriented critics have shown convincingly, the rhetoric of the speeches in Acts is always carefully tailored to the apologetic situation within the unfolding plot of Acts, always keeping in view the symbolic world

2. For critical reassessments of Vielhauer, see, e.g., H. Douglas Buckwalter, *The Character and Purpose of Luke's Christology*, SNTSMS 89 (Cambridge: Cambridge University Press, 1996), 231–72; and François Bovon, "The Law in Luke-Acts," in *Studies in Early Christianity*, WUNT 161 (Tübingen: Mohr Siebeck, 2003), 59–73.

3. On the lengthy history of the neglect of narrative in German theology and biblical scholarship, see Hans Frei, *The Eclipse of Biblical Narrative: A Study in Eighteenth and Nineteenth Century Hermeneutics* (New Haven: Yale University Press, 1974).

4. Vielhauer, "On the 'Paulinism' of Acts," 34.

of the characters being addressed within the narrative setting.[5] Luke's theology, therefore, cannot necessarily be directly extrapolated from any single speech in the story, not even the speeches of "reliable" characters such as Peter and Paul. One must read the narrative as a whole to see how Luke gradually builds up his picture of the significance of Jesus and the redemptive action of God. Consequently, our ultimate judgment about the "Paulinism" of the theology of Acts should not depend exclusively on whether Luke's narrative has placed an adequate summary of "Pauline theology" in the mouth of the character of Paul. We may find influences of and parallels to Pauline thought elsewhere in the narrative.

Indeed, some of the most "Pauline" theological elements in the story of Acts are actually to be found in the speeches and stories of *Peter*. It has sometimes been argued that the Acts of the Apostles seeks to domesticate Paul by absorbing him into the Petrine theological discourse of early catholic Christianity.[6] I would like to suggest, on the contrary, that *Luke is narrating Peter into the Pauline worldview as he understands it*, recruiting Peter as a supporter of the Pauline mission to the gentiles. But to state that claim is to run ahead of our investigation.

I would like to propose an investigative method different from Vielhauer's. Rather than looking only at the Pauline speeches, I suggest that we begin by looking at passages in Acts that quote or clearly allude to the OT. As we do so, our heuristic questions will be as follows: Which OT texts are being cited? Do we find overlap between the passages Luke cites and the texts that Paul refers to in his letters? If so, do Luke and Paul read the texts similarly or divergently? In short, we will be asking about the *intertextuality* of Acts with respect both to the OT and to Paul. Are Luke's intertextual engagements of Israel's story on the same trajectory as Paul's, or not?

A word of explanation about "intertextuality" is necessary before I begin.[7] I am not asking whether it can be shown that Luke uses Paul's letters as a "source," or whether we can identify verbatim agreements of Luke's text with Pauline material. It can be shown rather easily that there is very little, if any,

5. See Beverly Roberts Gaventa, "The Overthrown Enemy: Luke's Portrait of Paul," in *SBL Seminar Papers, 1985*, ed. K. H. Richards (Atlanta: Scholars, 1985), 439–49.

6. For a brief survey of this scholarly trend, see Alan J. Thompson, *One Lord, One People: The Unity of the Church in Acts in Its Literary Setting*, LNTS 359 (London: T & T Clark, 2008), 3–10; see also, e.g., Ernst Käsemann, "Paul and Nascent Catholicism," *JTC* 3 (1967), 14–27, esp. 17–18.

7. On this topic more generally, see Richard B. Hays, Stefan Alkier, and Leroy A. Huizenga, eds., *Reading the Bible Intertextually* (Waco: Baylor University Press, 2009).

such material in Luke-Acts. The question, rather, is whether Luke's readings of the OT live and move and have their being within the same intertextual field as Paul's readings.[8] Are they talking about the same texts, and are they thinking about these texts in similar ways? To put the same question in slightly different terms, do Paul and Luke belong to an interpretive community that shares a recognizably common "encyclopedia of reception" (to use Umberto Eco's term) for interpreting Israel's Scripture?[9] Or do they seem to belong to two different interpretive communities that are receiving these scriptures in notably different ways?

Acts has far too many OT citations to be treated thoroughly in this short essay, and it would in any case be tedious to work through the full list. I propose instead to select a few examples of OT reading in Acts and to demonstrate that they manifest significant points of contact with the Pauline tradition. One final disclaimer: I am not attempting to show that the author of Luke-Acts was in fact Luke the physician, a companion of Paul on his journeys (in fact, I do not have a settled opinion about this issue). Rather, like Vielhauer, I am interested simply in a theological comparison of the two writers—or, to be more precise, I am interested in a *hermeneutical* comparison of the two writers: How does each one operate as a reader of Scripture, and are there any signs of Luke's engagement with Pauline traditions of scriptural exegesis?

OT Readings in Acts: Some Examples

Overlap between Luke and Paul in Explicit Citations of the OT

We begin with a few cases in which Luke explicitly quotes a text that was previously referenced by Paul in his letters (I use the term "referenced" to include both explicit citations and direct allusions, for reasons that will appear in the discussion of the examples below).

(1) *Acts 2:17–21/Joel 2:28–32.* Peter's Pentecost sermon takes its point of departure from an extensive quotation of the prophet Joel, climaxing in the declaration that "*everyone who calls on the name of the Lord shall be saved*" (Acts

8. This way of posing the issue presumes that Luke is not simply compiling traditional sources haphazardly; rather, he is to be understood as a literary artist and theologian who is shaping his material with particular theological and literary aims.

9. As Stefan Alkier explains, "The *encyclopedia* is the cultural framework in which the text is situated and from which the gaps of the text are filled" ("Intertextuality and the Semiotics of Biblical Texts," in Hays, Alkier, and Huizenga, *Reading the Bible Intertexually*, 8).

2:21, citing Joel 3:5 LXX).[10] We are probably meant to remember this passage at the conclusion of the sermon when Peter calls his hearers to repent and be baptized in the name of Jesus in order to receive forgiveness of sins and the Holy Spirit, "for the promise is for you, for your children, and for all who are far away, *everyone* whom the *Lord* our God *calls* to him" (Acts 2:38–39). Certainly, the "promise" refers to the affirmation in the preceding clause that "you will receive the gift of the Holy Spirit" (see also Luke 24:49). But—in view of the emphasis here on the universal scope of the promise, and the way that προσκαλέσηται (Acts 2:39) sounds an answering echo to ἐπικαλέσηται (v. 21)—it seems likely that, at the same time, we should also interpret "the promise" as a reference to the word of assurance given in Joel's prophecy: "Everyone who calls on the name of the Lord shall be saved."[11] If so, this would provide an artful *inclusio* for Peter's sermon. Whether that be so or not, it is indisputable that Joel's prophecy of salvation for those who call upon the name of the Lord stands as the keynote for Luke's account of the first Christian preaching, and that this prophecy, read within the wider narrative of Acts, already prefigures the message of salvation that will go forth to the gentile world.

It is of more than passing interest, then, that Paul employs precisely the same text in Rom 10 in support of his argument that the gospel is a word of salvation for Jew and Greek alike. "For there is no distinction between Jew and Greek; the same Lord is Lord of all and is generous to all who call on him. For, '*Everyone who calls on the name of the Lord shall be saved*'" (Rom 10:12–13). In both Acts 2 and Rom 10, Joel 3:5 LXX becomes a major text prefiguring the proclamation of the gospel. Not incidentally, both texts almost certainly understand "the Lord" to be the Lord Jesus. In Romans the link of 10:9 to verses 12–13 makes this identification unambiguous,[12] and in Acts, the connection between 2:21 and 36 leads to the same conclusion.[13] Thus, both of our authors are reading Joel's reference to "the Lord" christologically.

10. On the whole matter of scriptural interpretation in the Pentecost sermon, see David P. Moessner, "Luke's 'Plan of God' from the Greek Psalter: The Rhetorical Thrust of 'The Prophets and the Psalms' in Peter's Speech at Pentecost," in *Scripture and Traditions: Essays on Early Judaism and Christianity in Honor of Carl R. Holladay*, ed. Patrick Gray and Gail R. O'Day, NovTSup 129 (Leiden: Brill, 2008), 223–38.

11. It is also to be noted that Joel 3:5 LXX ends with these words: καὶ εὐαγγελιζόμενοι, οὓς κύριος προσκέκληται. Undoubtedly, Luke's use of the verb προσκαλέσηται (Acts 2:39) re-sounds the echo of Joel's prophecy.

12. C. Kavin Rowe, "Romans 10:13: What Is the Name of the Lord?," *HBT* 22, no. 2 (2000): 135–73.

13. For an analysis of Luke's use of κύριος, see C. Kavin Rowe, *Early Narrative Christology: The Lord in the Gospel of Luke*, BZNW 139 (Berlin: de Gruyter, 2006).

(2) *Acts 2:34–35/Ps 110:1.* Another key text in Peter's web of OT witnesses in the Pentecost sermon is Ps 110:1, "The Lord said to my Lord, 'Sit at my right hand, until I make your enemies your footstool'" (Acts 2:34–35).[14] In its context in the sermon, the citation asserts the appropriateness of calling Jesus κύριος (v. 36), in view of his resurrection and exaltation to the right hand of God. Paul alludes to the same passage in 1 Cor 15:25 to affirm the ultimate eschatological triumph of Christ in overcoming even death so that those who are "in Christ" will ultimately share in his resurrection. The argumentative purposes of the two citations differ, but in both cases, Ps 110 is read christologically as an affirmation of Christ's eschatological victory over death. Interestingly, Paul's reference to this psalm in 1 Cor 15 appears with no citation formula, indicating that it is already understood by his readers as part of their symbolic world.[15] Or, to rephrase the point, the christological interpretation of Ps 110 already belongs to the "encyclopedia of reception" for Paul's gentile readers in Corinth. (At least, Paul's rhetoric treats it as belonging to that encyclopedia.) [16] Luke's use of the same text in the Pentecost sermon belongs to the same circle of interpretive convention. The fact that this circle includes also the synoptic tradition (Mark 12:35–37 par.), 1 Peter (1 Pet 3:22), and the Letter to the Hebrews (Heb 1:13) is an interesting fact, whose significance we shall consider in the conclusion of the present essay.

(3) *Acts 13:47/Isa 49:6.* In Acts 13, Paul's initial "word of exhortation" in the synagogue at Pisidian Antioch contains a concise summary of Israel's history and a cluster of OT quotations highly reminiscent of Peter's Pentecost sermon (13:32–37, quoting Ps 2:7; Isa 55:3 LXX; and Ps 16:10), as well as a quotation of Hab 1:5. All of this has the effect of situating Paul's message within the long story of God's elective grace toward Israel, and the accompanying threat of God's judgment ("Beware, therefore, that what the prophets said does not happen to you," Acts 13:40).

Our immediate concern, however, is with the words spoken by Paul and Barnabas on the following Sabbath, when they encounter opposition to their

14. On this passage, see David P. Moessner, "*Two* Lords 'at the Right Hand'? The Psalms and an Intertextual Reading of Peter's Pentecost Speech (Acts 2.14–36)," in *Literary Studies in Luke-Acts: Essays in Honor of Joseph B. Tyson*, ed. Richard P. Thompson and Thomas E. Phillips (Macon, GA: Mercer University Press, 1998), 15–32.

15. For the pervasive influence of Ps 110 in early Christianity, see David M. Hay, *Glory at the Right Hand: Psalm 110 in Early Christianity*, SBLMS 18 (Nashville: Abingdon, 1973), esp. 35, 39, 50–51.

16. Similarly, Paul's reference to Christ's place "at the right hand of God" in Rom 8:34 also suggests an allusion to Ps 110:1.

message. They declare that they will leave the synagogue and turn to the gentiles, and they find a scriptural warrant—indeed, a command—for this decision in Isa 49:6: "I have set you to be a light for the Gentiles, so that you may bring salvation to the ends of the earth" (Acts 13:47). Readers of Acts have known since the first account of Paul's conversion that he is God's chosen instrument "to bring my name before Gentiles and kings and before the people of Israel" (9:15). The explicit citation of Isa 49:6 in Acts 13 gives a prophetic scriptural grounding for this vocation.[17] Here in Acts 13, Isa 49 is interpreted not in a christological sense but as a commission for the early Christian mission to the gentiles. It is Paul and Barnabas who find themselves addressed by God's word in Isa 49: they are the ones sent forth as a light to the nations. Precisely this same passage informs Paul's self-description of his apostolic vocation in Gal 1:15–16: like the servant figure of Isa 49:1–6, he was set apart from his mother's womb for the task of proclaiming good news to the nations. The centrality of this text for defining Paul's understanding of his own vocation is shown once again in 2 Cor 6:2, where—at the climax of a passage declaring his role as an ambassador for Christ—he cites Isa 49:8: "At an acceptable time I have listened to you, and on a day of salvation I have helped you." Clearly this is one point where the portrayal of Paul in Acts corresponds closely to the Paul we encounter in the letters: he is sent by God on a mission to the gentiles, and *Isa 49 is the key text, in both cases, for defining and sustaining the mission.* In all the passages just mentioned (Acts 13; Gal 1; 2 Cor 6), Paul draws upon this OT text in the course of defending and justifying the legitimacy of his ministry. It may occasion some surprise that in none of these passages is the servant who brings light to the nations identified as Jesus by either of our authors; rather the interpretation of Isaiah's prophecy is focused on Paul and his missionary associates.[18]

(4) *Acts 28:25–28/Isa 6:9–10.* The final Scripture quotation in Acts appears in Paul's parting admonitory word to the Jewish leaders in Rome who have assembled to hear his message. Luke tells us that some were convinced, but others disbelieved. On their way out the door, they are reminded by Paul of the gloomy prophecy of Isaiah about the people's incapacity to hear the prophetic word and to turn in response to it (Acts 28:25–28, quoting Isa 6:9–10 in almost verbatim agreement with the LXX). The effect of this citation is once more to link Paul's own prophetic ministry of proclamation to Isaiah's.

17. Isaiah 49 also underlies a number of other passages in Luke-Acts that refer to the task of bringing light to the gentiles (e.g., Luke 2:32; Acts 26:17–18).

18. The christological interpretation of the "light to the gentiles" motif does appear, however, in Acts 26:23 as well as in Luke 2:32.

In my view, the citation should *not* be interpreted to mean that Luke finally gives up on the Jewish people and embraces a supersessionist theology, any more than such a view should be attributed to the prophet Isaiah himself. This is the third time in the narrative of Acts that Paul declares his intention to go to the gentiles (earlier in 13:46–48 and 18:5–6); yet, as many commentators have observed, after each of the first two pronouncements he continues to reach out to the synagogues and the Jewish people, though with results that are at best mixed. Reading the Isaiah citation within its original literary context would lead us rather to suppose that it is a prophetic judgment oracle meant to provoke repentance and faith; and perhaps Paul's citation of it functions in a similar way. If so, Paul's announced intention to take the message of "the salvation of God" to the gentiles (28:28) should be understood as part of his missionary strategy to make his own people jealous and thus save some of them (Rom 11:13–14).

In any case, as this link to Rom 11 suggests, we find Paul's passionate treatment of the problem of Israel's unbelief in Rom 9–11 drawing upon precisely this same tradition of Isaiah's proclamation to a people who have "eyes that would not see and ears that would not hear" (Rom 11:8). The scriptural citation in Rom 11:8 is a complicated conflation of three different texts: the phrase πνεῦμα κατανύξεως echoes Isa 29:10; the idea that God has *given* them this disability "down to this very day" echoes Deut 29:3 LXX; and the reference to unseeing eyes and unhearing ears seems to blend Deut 29 with Isa 6:9. We cannot here delve into the complexities of this blended citation.[19] The salient point for our present purpose is that Paul addresses the pressing issue of Israel's stubborn rejection of the gospel by evoking the tradition of Isaiah's vocation to preach to a people seemingly incapable of seeing and hearing—precisely the same image with which Luke leaves his readers in Acts 28. Once again here, we find a significant convergence between Luke's portrayal of Paul and Paul's own deployment of Scripture to reflect on Jewish response and nonresponse to the gospel.

Additionally, in Rom 11:9–10, immediately following his reference to Isa 6, Paul amplifies his judgment on Israel by citing Ps 68:23–24 LXX, the same psalm cited by Luke to describe God's judgement on Judas (Acts 1:20a). Both of these quotations presuppose the common early Christian tradition of reading this psalm as a foreshadowing of Jesus's passion and death—a reading that shows up in Rom 15:3; John 2:17; and in the tradition attested in all four Gospels

19. For a full discussion, see J. Ross Wagner, *Heralds of the Good News: Isaiah and Paul 'In Concert' in the Letter to the Romans*, NovTSup 101 (Leiden: Brill, 2002).

that Jesus on the cross was offered vinegar to drink. It is precisely because Jesus is understood to be the speaker of the psalm that the psalm's condemnations of enemies can be applied to those who reject him as Lord. Thus, in Acts 1:20 Luke's loose citation of Ps 69:26 (68:26 LXX) is an excellent example of the way in which his reading of Scripture presupposes the same hermeneutical frame of reference that we find in Paul's use of the same psalm. It is not merely a random prooftext: it can be applied to Judas because of the prior conviction that the psalm is to be interpreted christologically.

Allusions and Echoes in Acts 10:34–43

We turn now to look all too briefly at the way in which Luke alludes to scriptural texts that he does not quote directly. Even though these passages do not entail explicit citation, they are no less important for reassessing the Paulinism of Acts from an intertextual point of view. Precisely where no explicit quotation is necessary, the shared hermeneutical assumptions may be most powerfully present. The scope of the present essay allows us to consider only one significant example.

As suggested by the copious marginal references in Nestle-Aland[27], Peter's compact sermon to the household of the gentile centurion Cornelius is dense with scriptural allusions. We cannot now attend to all of these, but I want to call attention to a few of them that suggest points of contact with Paul's readings of scripture. In 10:36, Peter declares that God "*sent* (ἀπέστειλεν) the word to the sons of Israel, preaching peace through Jesus Christ (εὐαγγελιζόμενος εἰρήνην διὰ Ἰησοῦ Χριστοῦ)—this one is Lord of all." The reference to "preaching peace" almost surely echoes Isa 52:7, which Paul quotes explicitly in Rom 10:15 to describe the role of Christian preachers, who are "*sent* (ἀποσταλῶσιν) . . . preaching (εὐαγγελιζομένων) good news." It should also be remembered that in Rom 10 Paul has just driven home the point that the central content of Christian preaching is that Jesus Christ is Lord (Rom 10:9–12). Thus, Peter's exclamation in Acts 10:36 that Jesus Christ is "Lord of all" seems to presuppose precisely the same complex of ideas that appear in Rom 10, and both of these texts are in turn dependent on Isaiah's language about the messengers who bring the good news of Israel's redemption from exile.[20] At the

20. The Nestle-Aland[27] text of Acts 10:36 includes a completely conjectural emendation that would omit the phrase οὗτός ἐστιν πάντων κύριος as a gloss. Such speculations in the absence of any textual evidence are of doubtful value in a critical edition of the Greek text. However, by calling attention to the slightly intrusive character of the phrase, this text-critical suggestion might cause us to consider even more strongly the possibility that

same time, I would suggest that the phrase "preaching peace through Jesus Christ" is even a clearer echo of Rom 5:1: "we have peace with God through our Lord Jesus Christ." In short, Peter's opening words to Cornelius sound very much as though they could have been lifted out of the pages of Paul's Letter to the Romans.

The second allusion in Acts 10 to which I would like to draw attention is found in Peter's announcement that "God raised him on the third day (ἐν τῇ τρίτῃ ἡμέρᾳ)" (10:40), a phrase that appears to echo Hos 6:2. Of course, in Acts 10, there is no sign of a citation formula, and we might miss the allusion were it not for Paul's earlier adamant confession that "he was raised on the third day (τῇ ἡμέρᾳ τῇ τρίτῃ) *in accordance with the scriptures*" (1 Cor 15:4). Of course, there is no reason to think this allusion to Hosea is distinctively Pauline; it appears also in the Matthean and Lukan passion predictions. But it is Paul who draws attention to the conformity of this detail to *Scripture*. Interestingly, while Matthew's version of the passion predictions passes over this point in silence, only Luke highlights that the killing and resurrection of Jesus on the third day belongs to that which is "written about the Son of Man by the prophets" (Luke 18:31; cf. 24:46). One wonders whether this is another point—perhaps comparable to the formulation of the Lord's Supper tradition—where Luke shares a common tradition with Paul, a tradition that connects the promise of Jesus's resurrection to Hos 6:2.

The last scriptural echo in Peter's sermon to Cornelius that is of special interest for our present purposes is considerably less distinct but nonetheless of some importance. Peter begins his speech by saying, "I truly understand that God is not one who shows partiality (προσωπολήμπτης), but in every nation the one who fears him and does righteousness is acceptable to him" (10:34–35). The unusual word προσωπολήμπτης seems to echo the language of the scriptural maxim that God "is not partial and takes no bribe" (Deut 10:17, repeated in 2 Chr 19:7 and slightly elaborated in Sir 35:12–13). But the strongest echo of all, the closest verbal parallel, is to Paul's declaration in Rom 2:11: οὐ γάρ ἐστιν προσωπολημψία παρὰ τῷ θεῷ. This parallel is of special interest, because in Romans Paul articulates this characterization of God's impartiality precisely in the midst of an argument that God treats *Jews and gentiles alike*. They are equally under judgment for doing evil (2:9) and equally granted "glory and honor and peace" for doing right (v. 10). Indeed, this argument is developed throughout Rom 2:1–16, and it stands as part of the foundation for Paul's over-

its presence here is a sign of the intertextual influence of Rom 10, where Jesus's lordship is so prominently featured.

arching argument that the gospel is "the power of God for salvation to everyone who believes, *to the Jew first and also to the Greek*" (1:16 and throughout the first four chapters of Romans). In short, the maxim of divine impartiality, which had traditionally been used to underwrite the claim that God does not favor the rich over the poor,[21] that God gives justice to the orphan and the widow, becomes in Paul's hands a theological argument for the acceptance of gentile believers into the people of God through Jesus Christ. And of course, this is precisely the use to which Luke puts the same maxim in the pivotal story of Acts 10. I would submit that once again we might well suppose some intertextual relationship between Acts 10 and Rom 2, even though there is no direct quotation. At the very least, this fundamental element of Luke's theological program stands within the trajectory launched by Paul's theological justification for the mission to the gentiles.

The Pauline and Lukan use of "divine impartiality" as a support for acceptance of gentiles is not entirely without foundation in the Torah text from which the maxim originally comes. In Deut 10, Moses proclaims that though all heaven and earth belong to God, he has "set his heart in love" on Israel and chosen them out of all the peoples of the earth; nonetheless, God's impartiality means that he also "loves the stranger" (וְאֹהֵב גֵּר, 10:18). This creates a presumptive obligation for Israel also to "love the stranger, for you were strangers in the land of Egypt" (v. 19). In the LXX, however, Deuteronomy's גֵּר is rendered by προσήλυτος. This translation creates a linguistic bridge that easily permits a crossing to the Pauline use of "divine impartiality" as a warrant for the extension of God's grace to gentile *converts* to the faith. Neither Paul nor Luke makes such a connection to Deut 10:17–19 explicit, but it seems likely that this interpretation belongs to the intertextual field of hermeneutical assumptions underlying both Rom 2 and Acts 10.

One could continue to multiply examples. Again and again, when we scratch the surface of Luke's scriptural citations and allusions, we find a hermeneutical substratum that is shared with Paul. It seems to me that the best explanation for the evidence we have considered is not that Luke is using Paul's letters directly as a source but rather that both of them participate in a common intertextual field, a community of interpretation in which numerous texts from Israel's Scriptures have been highlighted, read through the lens of the message of Jesus's death and resurrection, and thereby reinterpreted as witnesses to the gospel and warrants for the emergent mission to the gentile world. The list of interpretive conventions that Paul and Luke share could

21. As reflected in Jas 2:1 and 2:9.

be extended. For example, both participate in the hermeneutical convention of reading some of Israel's psalms as the speech of Jesus the Messiah (e.g., Acts 2:25–28; Rom 15:3, 9). Both of them presuppose, perhaps following Deut 33:2 LXX, that angels were involved in giving the Law at Sinai (Acts 7:38; Gal. 3:19). Both use ὁ δίκαιος—probably on the basis of Hab 2:3–4—as an epithet for Jesus the Messiah (as in Acts 3:14; 7:52; 22:14), or so I would contend.[22] And so forth. Rather than continuing to pile up such evidence, however, it may be more fruitful—since this paper constitutes only a preliminary probe of these matters—to take a step back and outline the broad contours of a "theology" that Acts and Paul share in common, as disclosed by the methodology we have been pursuing here.

The Lukanism of Paul? Intertextual Common Ground: Shared Theological Themes and Convictions

To be sure, there are many facets of Paul's theology, as reflected in his letters, that appear nowhere in the pages of Acts. If the history of interpretation of the Pauline letters proves nothing else, it shows that Paul was a profound and subtle thinker. His second-order theological reflection is richly detailed and not easily represented through Luke's medium of storytelling. Nonetheless, the intertextual approach that we have begun to explore in this paper does in fact suggest that we may be able to describe the profile of a certain set of theological themes and convictions shared by Paul's letters and the author of Acts. I would summarize this profile in the following list of affirmations.[23]

(1) *At the heart of the gospel message stand the crucifixion and resurrection of Jesus.* These events happened "according to the Scriptures." Vielhauer, by contrast, asserts that in Acts "nothing is said of the saving significance of the cross of Christ."[24] This statement is true, in the sense that Luke gives no explication comparable to Paul's reflections on the death of Jesus as "judgment upon all mankind and at the same time reconciliation."[25] And at the same time, Luke emphasizes repentance and forgiveness of sins in a way that finds little parallel in Paul. Yet

22. For a full statement of this argument, see Richard B. Hays, *The Conversion of the Imagination: Paul as Interpreter of Israel's Scripture* (Grand Rapids: Eerdmans, 2005), 119–42.

23. Not everything in the list that follows is directly based on the exegetical observations of the preceding pages of this essay. Where I am filling out the outline with new textual material, I will provide references, without being able to explicate them fully.

24. Vielhauer, "On the 'Paulinism' of Acts," 45.

25. Vielhauer, "On the 'Paulinism' of Acts," 44.

the two are agreed that the *story* of Jesus's death and resurrection constitutes the heart of the message (in contrast, let us say, to various known or hypothetical "early Christianities" that concentrate on Jesus as wisdom teacher or on gnosis as a means of escape from materiality). And they agree that the cross and resurrection mysteriously constituted God's will, as attested by Scripture.

(2) *Jesus was raised "on the third day" and he is now exalted,* in accordance with Ps 110:1, to the right hand of God, where his status as Lord is now manifest through the gifts he pours out on his people.

(3) *Paul was divinely called to a special prophetic role as the proclaimer of God's good news to the gentile world.* This role was prefigured in Isaiah's vision of a servant sent as a "light to the gentiles."

(4) According to Acts, *Paul's preaching of the gospel was accompanied by "signs and wonders"* (Acts 14:3; 15:12; 19:11–12), a claim consistent with Paul's own testimony (Rom 15:18–19; 2 Cor 12:12). Luke sets these miraculous events in direct parallelism to the works performed by Jesus (Acts 2:22) and through the name of Jesus by the Jerusalem apostles (Acts 4:30; 5:12). These mighty works, as well as the proclamation of the message, were empowered by the Holy Spirit. For both authors, the work of the Holy Spirit is manifest through speaking in tongues, prophecy, healings, and other such signs.

(5) *Paul's missionary preaching to gentiles, in the narrative of Acts, summoned them to turn from idols "to the living God"* (Acts 14:15; 26:17–20), in accordance with Paul's own summary of his original preaching to the Thessalonians (1 Thess 1:9–10).

(6) *Conversion in response to the preaching of the message about Jesus is described, in language derived from Joel 3:5 LXX, as "calling on the name of Lord,"* and it is an integral part of the message of Paul, as well as of Acts, that *all* who call on the name of the Lord will be saved. The promise of God's mercy is universally inclusive of all who will receive it.

(7) For both authors, *the scriptural term κύριος applies to Jesus,* thus mysteriously fusing his identity with the God of Israel.

(8) A corollary of point number 6 is that *gentiles are to be received fully among the followers of Jesus without having to obey all the commandments of Israel's Law.* Paul and Luke are both insistent advocates of a Law-free mission to the gentiles and both place the theological justification for this mission at the heart of their writings. Indeed, Luke's narrative enlists *Peter,* particularly in Acts 10–11 and 15, as a star witness in support of this Pauline gospel. The prophecies of Isaiah play an important role in justifying this mission, as does the maxim of God's impartiality, rooted in Deut 29, homiletically explicated in Rom 2, and narratively enacted in Acts 10–11.

(9) For both of our authors, *the unbelief of many in Israel when offered the good news of the gospel constitutes a significant theological challenge.* In both cases, this challenge is met through appeal to the prophecies of Isaiah concerning Israel's blindness and deafness. Thus, this anomalous state of affairs is also attributed to the mysterious will and working of God. Paul, more clearly than Luke, envisions an eschatological redemption in which all Israel will be saved; nonetheless, Luke holds open the possibility of a future time when God will restore the kingdom to Israel (Acts 1:6–7, perhaps also 3:21), and he continues to refer to the gospel message as "the hope of Israel" (28:20; cf. Luke 24:21a).[26]

(10) *Christ will come again* (Acts 1:11; 1 Thess 4:13–18) in power to bring about the resurrection of the dead (Acts 26:6–8; 1 Cor 15:20–28), and to act as "judge of the living and the dead" (Acts 10:42; 17:31; 2 Cor 5:10; Rom 14:10b–12).

Much more could be said, but this sketch identifies some of the most important points. (I have said nothing at all about matters of biographical detail: Paul as a Pharisee, as persecutor of the church, as one who has always lived with "a clear conscience before God" [Acts 23:1; Phil. 3:6].)

Concluding Reflections

The sketch above does not constitute anything like a full summary of the theology of Paul, or of Luke-Acts. Nor is it my intention to deny that major differences of emphasis and sensibility remain between Paul and Luke. Harmonization of these two major NT witnesses is not the purpose of the present essay. Rather, my ultimate intention is to achieve a more nuanced and rounded picture of each of these figures than Vielhauer's sharply dichotomous essay suggested. Surely a judicious reading of Acts and the Pauline letters will have to acknowledge that there are substantial areas of commonality between them as well as real differences.

In this initial thought experiment, I have suggested that a study of the ways that Acts and Paul employ Scripture might provide a vantage point for observing some of these areas of commonality. In general terms, the consequences of this approach are at least twofold.

(1) On the one hand, Vielhauer's judgment that "Acts is not intended as kerygma or as 'witness'"[27] can be regarded only as a historical curiosity, a ten-

26. See Klaus Haacker, "Das Bekenntnis des Paulus zur Hoffnung Israels nach der Apostelgeschichte des Lukas," *NTS* 31 (1985): 437–51.

27. Vielhauer, "On the 'Paulinism' of Acts," 44.

dentious offshoot of a certain twentieth-century theological program hindered by a blind spot for narrative interpretation and overdetermined by existentialist philosophical commitments. Luke is much more deeply immersed in the ongoing story of Israel and in the interpretation of Israel's Scriptures than Vielhauer believed. In light of the evidence presented even in this brief essay, Vielhauer's bizarre judgement that in Acts the "claim of the Jews to be the people of God was replaced by the idea of natural man's immediacy to God, and the significance of Judaism was relativized to that of a venerable *antiqua religio*" is simply untenable.[28] In a word, then, Luke's theology is more Jewish, more scriptural, and more kerygmatic than Vielhauer recognized—and in all these respects, Luke's thought seems to represent an intelligible trajectory from within a Pauline symbolic world. The theology of Acts can be seen as an organic outgrowth of the Pauline tradition that maintains its roots in at least some of Paul's characteristic themes and concerns.

(2) On the other hand, Paul emerges as a more "Lukan" figure than one would ever guess from reading Vielhauer. Vielhauer has indeed identified certain points where there are real divergences between Luke and Paul. (To take the most striking example, I have a great deal of trouble imagining the author of Galatians acquiescing in the conciliatory gestures narrated in Acts 21:17–26.) Nonetheless, rereading Paul through the intertextual lens of Acts does enable us to see *precisely in his letters* a charismatic Jewish Paul, a figure grounded in apocalyptic hope, exercising a powerful wonder-working ministry (even while also undergoing suffering and rejection for his message), and focused above all on his God-given calling to proclaim the good news of Israel's God to the gentile world. He is at once more deeply Jewish and more theologically consonant with emergent proto-catholic Christianity than Vielhauer's account would suggest. This appears with particular clarity when we attend to his strategies of scriptural interpretation.

(3) These comments lead to one final remark. The search for a distinctive "Paulinism"—along with the tacit presupposition that "Paulinism" ought to be strongly privileged over other perspectives in the NT—may lead to a significant perspectival distortion in our reading of the material. A careful rereading of Vielhauer will show that he was indeed aware of some of the points of contact that I have described in this essay (for example, the similarities between the Pauline and Petrine sermons in Acts), but that he found them

28. Vielhauer, "On the 'Paulinism' of Acts," 48–49. Vielhauer's position is also significantly problematized by the recent work of C. Kavin Rowe on Acts 17; see "The Grammar of Life: The Areopagus Speech and Pagan Tradition," *NTS* 57 (2011): 31–50.

uninteresting because the points of agreement between Paul and Luke were to be found not where Paul speaks with a distinctive voice but at the points where both of these authors are simply reflecting the common views of "the earliest congregation." This was assumed to prove that Luke did not adequately represent "Paulinism."

But why think about the question in these terms? Why privilege the solitary religious genius? For example, there is nothing distinctively "Pauline" about the use of Ps 110:1 to describe Jesus's exaltation to the right hand of God. This appears to belong to the common stock of hermeneutical property within early Christianity; as we have already noted, a similar reading of the text shows up in the Synoptics, 1 Peter, and in Hebrews. But does this make the convergence between Paul and Luke on their use of this motif less significant and interesting? Would it not be equally valuable to seek, as I have sought to do in this paper, to discern the ways in which both Paul and Luke participate in a wider community of intertextual discourse, share certain hermeneutical assumptions, and converge on quite a number of highly significant theological affirmations? To be sure, Luke writes a generation later than Paul's heyday. His concerns differ, and his literary strategy for presenting the gospel through a complex story, narrated καθεξῆς, differs dramatically from the genre of Paul's urgent and highly particular pastoral letters, with their dense theological discourse. But precisely as we observe these differences, we might do well to echo one of Paul's own metaphors for describing the distinct but complementary contributions of different interpreters of the word: Paul planted, Luke watered, but God gave the growth.

Part 4

NEW TESTAMENT THEOLOGY

16

Christology

Jesus in the Apocalypse of John

A Profusion of Images

Who is Jesus in the Apocalypse of John? This visionary book deploys a kaleidoscopic profusion of imagery to depict its chief protagonist. Jesus is portrayed as exalted revealer of prophetic mysteries, faithful witness and martyr, first-born from the dead, Son of God, the Coming One, the Son of Man, the future judge of the world and giver of life, the Lion of the tribe of Judah, the root of David, the Lamb who was slaughtered, the shepherd who guides his people to springs of the water of life, the child given birth by the woman clothed with the sun, the conquering rider on a white horse, the bright morning star, the Lord of lords and King of kings, the one who is Alpha and Omega, and much more.[1]

Faced with such a diverse array of images—which could, on an unsympathetic reading, be regarded as chaotic and self-contradictory—studies of the Christology of the book of Revelation have tended to pursue one of two interpretative strategies: (1) seek to identify different *sources, traditions, or social settings* from which the book's depictions of Jesus are derived;[2] or (2) focus

1. For a more comprehensive list of christological titles in Revelation, see Loren L. Johns, *The Lamb Christology of the Apocalypse of John: An Investigation into Its Origin and Rhetorical Force*, WUNT 2/167 (Tübingen: Mohr Siebeck, 2003), 217–21.

2. See, e.g., Loren T. Stuckenbruck, *Angel Veneration and Christology: A Study in Early Judaism and in the Christology of the Apocalypse of John*, WUNT 2/70 (Tübingen: Mohr Siebeck, 1995); and Thomas B. Slater, *Christ and Community: A Socio-Historical Study of the Christology of Revelation*, JSNTSup 178 (Sheffield: Sheffield University Press, 1999).

This essay was presented at a conference on "The Book of Revelation: Theology, Politics, and Intertextuality," at Duke Divinity School on October 7–10, 2010, under the joint sponsorship of Duke and the McDonald Agape Foundation.

on specific titles or images as the *key* to the book's Christology.[3] The present essay will take a different approach. I do not deny that John the Seer draws upon sources and traditions. I do not deny that some images in the book (e.g., the Lamb) are weightier than others. Nor do I deny that some of the images stand in a certain tension with others. I would suggest, however, that it is most *theologically* fruitful to read the Apocalypse's christological imagery as manifesting a complex unity. Its christological unity is best grasped through a reading that treats the book as a literary whole, acknowledges diversity and intertextual interplay, and lets the tensions stand—just as wise readers do when encountering any complex work of literature.[4] Jesus in the book of Revelation is a multifaceted character whose identity unfolds gradually within the work as a whole; to understand his identity, we are required to absorb the full range of representations that we encounter throughout the book; to interpret those representations, insofar as we are able, within the imaginative frame of reference ("encyclopedia of reception")[5] of the Christian communities of Asia Minor at the end of the first century CE; and to ask how the complex person we encounter in this complex text might engage or challenge the symbolic world in which we live and move.

It is this last part of the interpretative task from which biblical interpreters often shrink. But the Apocalypse does not want to permit its readers a position of wise neutrality: it pronounces blessing on those who keep the words of the prophecy (Rev 22:7) and dire warnings to those who fail to hear what the Spirit is saying. The Apocalypse summons readers to enter sympathetically into the intertextually rich symbolic world of the story it tells, in all its grandeur and confusing complexity. Only by doing so will we come to understand its depiction of the identity of Jesus.

Within a single short essay we cannot explore all the facets of Jesus's identity that such a reading might discover. I want to propose, therefore, that we

3. For example, Traugott Holtz, *Die Christologie der Apokalypse des Johannes*, TU 85 (Berlin: Akademie-Verlag, 1962); Johns, *Lamb Christology of the Apocalypse of John*; and Konrad Huber, *Einer gleich einem Menschensohn: Die Christusvisionen in Offb 1,9–20 und Offb 14,14–20 und die Christologie der Johannesoffenbarung*, NTAbh, new series, 51 (Münster: Aschendorff, 2007).

4. This approach has much in common with Richard Bauckham, *The Theology of the Book of Revelation* (Cambridge: Cambridge University Press, 1993); and Joseph L. Mangina, *Revelation*, Brazos Theological Commentary on the Bible (Grand Rapids: Brazos, 2010).

5. See Stefan Alkier, "Intertextuality and the Semiotics of Biblical Texts," in *Reading the Bible Intertextually*, ed. Richard B. Hays, Stefan Alkier, and Leroy A. Huizenga (Waco: Baylor University Press, 2009), 3–21: "I call the external relationships of the text, in dependence upon Umberto Eco, its encyclopedic relationships. The *encyclopedia* is the cultural framework in which the text is situated and from which the gaps of the text are filled" (8).

attend to two major strands of the book's narrative representation of Jesus: *Jesus as sharer in the identity of God* and *Jesus as faithful witness.* After examining these two strands, we will offer some concluding reflections about how these very different motifs play in counterpoint to illumine the identity of Jesus.

Jesus as Sharer in the Divine Identity

We begin in an unusual and slightly daunting place. In the prophetic word to the church in Thyatira, Jesus (the glorious "one like a Son of Man," 1:13) chastises the community for tolerating the false prophetess Jezebel and issues this dire warning:

> Beware, I am throwing her on a bed, and those who commit adultery with her I am throwing into great distress, unless they repent of her doings; and I will strike her children dead. And all the churches will know that I am the one who searches minds and hearts, and I will give to each of you as your works deserve. (Rev 2:22–23)

Here we encounter the threatening, judgmental Jesus that many contemporary readers of Revelation find so problematic. Before grappling with this aspect of Jesus's identity, however, I want to draw attention to an easily overlooked feature of Jesus's self-description in this prophetic word. Jesus's stern judgment against the "children" of Jezebel is meant to teach the churches to recognize two aspects of Jesus's identity and action: "I am the one who searches minds and hearts" (ἐγώ εἰμι ὁ ἐραυνῶν νεφροὺς καὶ καρδίας) and "I will give to each of you according to your works" (δώσω ὑμῖν ἑκάστῳ κατὰ τὰ ἔργα ὑμῶν). Each of these actions is elsewhere in Jewish tradition and in early Christianity ascribed exclusively to God. The parallels to two passages in Paul's Letter to the Romans are particularly striking. In Rom 8:27, Paul declares that the "the One (i.e., God) who searches hearts (ὁ δὲ ἐραυνῶν τὰς καρδίας) knows what is the mind of the Spirit, because the Spirit intercedes for the saints according to the will of God." And earlier in the same letter, Paul declares that God's wrath is being stored up against those who refuse to repent (cf. Rev 2:22: ἐὰν μὴ μετανοήσωσιν), because God is the one "who will repay to each one according to his works" (ὅς ἀποδώσει ἑκάστῳ κατὰ τὰ ἔργα αὐτοῦ, Rom 2:6).

I am by no means suggesting that Revelation is literarily dependent on Romans. Instead, Revelation's close parallels to Paul's statements about God simply demonstrate that these affirmations of God's supernatural perspicacity and just repayment according to works were commonplace maxims in the ancient Jewish and Christian cultural encyclopedia. Indeed, the maxim about

God's repayment of human works is a near citation of Prov 24:12, where the wider context, particularly in the LXX rendering, bears especially close relation to Revelation's affirmation about Jesus:

> the Lord knows the hearts of all (κύριος καρδίας πάντων
> γινώσκει),
> and he who formed breath in everyone,
> he himself knows all things,
> who renders to each one according to his works (ὃς ἀποδίδωσιν
> ἑκάστῳ κατὰ τὰ ἔργα αὐτοῦ).

My point here is a simple one: the prophetic warning in Rev 2:23 ascribes to *Jesus* a power (knowing hearts and rewarding or punishing deeds) that Israel's Scripture ascribed to God *alone*.[6] Similar transferred ascriptions appear pervasively in Revelation, and they hint that Jesus is the possessor of divine power and prerogative. Precisely because this example appears unobtrusively in Rev 2:22–23, without fanfare or authorial comment, it all the more powerfully discloses the symbolic world from which John's prophecy issues. In that world, Jesus knows and does what only God can know and do.[7]

Other similar transferrals of divine attributes to the person of Jesus, both in descriptions of actions and in visual imagery, are more explicit.

One of the major christological motifs in the Apocalypse is the identification of Jesus as the "one like a Son of Man," the figure who appears in the eschatological prophecy of Dan 7:13–14, "coming with the clouds of heaven" to receive universal dominion.[8] From the opening lines of the book, Revelation identifies Jesus as the embodiment of this figure, beginning with a solemn declaration that echoes and fuses Dan 7:13 and Zech 12:10:

> Look! He is coming with the clouds;
> every eye will see him,
> even those who pierced him;
> and on his account all the tribes of the earth will wail. (Rev 1:7)

6. See also Ps 62:12b.

7. Cf. Bauckham, *Theology of the Book of Revelation*, 63: in Revelation, "Since Christ shares the one eternal being of God, what Christ is said to do, in salvation and judgment, is no less truly and directly divine than what is said to be done by 'the One who sits on the throne.'"

8. On the complexities of the Son of Man motif in Revelation, see Huber, *Einer Gleich einem Menschensohn*.

In Dan 7, the Son of Man figure is a representative of an eschatologically triumphant Israel; the "one like a Son of Man" is the visionary symbolization of Israel's final vindication and triumph over enemies and oppressive empires.[9] But when Jesus first appears in John's vision as the glorious Son of Man (Rev 1:9–20), the iconography of his appearance includes an important additional detail that suggests divine identity:

> Then I turned to see whose voice it was that spoke to me, and on turning I saw seven golden lampstands, and in the midst of the lampstands I saw one *like the Son of Man*, clothed with a long robe and with a golden sash across his chest. *His head and his hair were white as white wool, white as snow*; his eyes were like a flame of fire, his feet were like burnished bronze, refined as in a furnace, and his voice was like the sound of many waters. In his right hand he held seven stars, and from his mouth came a sharp, two-edged sword, and his face was like the sun shining with full force. (Rev 1:12–16)

The imagery of the head and hair white as wool is drawn *not* from Daniel's description of the "one like a Son of Man" but rather from his portrayal of "the Ancient of Days" seated on the throne in the heavenly throne room (Dan 7:9), and John's depiction of the Son of Man as a fiery presence (eyes "like a flame of fire" and a face "like the sun") is also reminiscent of the God of Israel in Daniel's vision: "His throne was fiery flames, and its wheels were burning fire. A stream of fire issued and flowed out from his presence" (Dan 7:9–10). Thus, from Jesus's first appearance on the stage of the drama of Revelation, he is *intertextually* marked as bearing the visible signs of divine identity. Or, to put the point another way, the figures of the Ancient of Days and the Son of Man—two distinct figures in Dan 7—are iconographically blended in Revelation's portrayal of Jesus.[10]

John's depiction of Jesus's fiery countenance is repeated in the prophetic address to the church in Thyatira: "And to the angel of the church in Thyatira

9. See N. T. Wright, *The New Testament and the People of God*, Christian Origins and the Question of God 1 (London: SPCK; Minneapolis: Fortress, 1992), 291–97. For further discussion of the various interpretations of the Son of Man's identity in Dan 7, see John J. Collins, *Daniel: A Commentary*, Hermeneia (Minneapolis: Fortress, 1993), 304–10.

10. Interestingly, the OG text of Dan 7:13 reads, ἐπὶ τῶν νεφελῶν τοῦ οὐρανοῦ ὡς υἱὸς ἀνθρώπου ἤρχετο, καὶ ὡς παλαιὸς ἡμερῶν παρῆν, as compared to Theodotion's μετὰ τῶν νεφελῶν τοῦ οὐρανοῦ ὡς υἱὸς ἀνθρώπου ἐρχόμενος ἦν καὶ ἕως τοῦ παλαιοῦ τῶν ἡμερῶν ἔφθασεν. One wonders if such a reading influenced the Seer's conflation of the figures in Rev 1:12–16.

write: These are the words of the Son of God, who has eyes like a flame of fire, and whose feet are like burnished bronze" (Rev 2:18). This is the only place in the entire book where the title "Son of God" appears, and, as we have seen, it is precisely to this church that Jesus asserts his divine power to search hearts and mete out judgment according to each person's works (vv. 22–23).

The role of the Son of Man as judge of the world is signaled again in the vision of Rev 14:14–20, where "one like a Son of Man" seated on a cloud wields a sickle to reap the harvest of the earth—another well-known symbol for final judgment. This passage is sometimes taken as evidence of an angelomorphic Son of Man Christology—that is, a conceptuality in which the Son of Man is an angelic figure of intermediate status between God and humanity—because here the Son of Man figure acts in response to the bidding of "another angel" who comes out of the heavenly temple (v. 15) and because the Son of Man's reaping action is paralleled by an apparently different angel who swings a sickle to "gather the clusters of the vine of the earth" and to throw them "into the great wine press of the wrath of God" (vv. 17–20).[11] As Loren Stuckenbruck comments, it is "logically problematic to modern readers why the author has not attempted to introduce terms which would keep his christological and angelological categories more separate."[12] This vision may be compared to the Matthean interpretation of the parable of the wheat and the weeds, where the Son of Man sends angelic reapers to perform the eschatological harvest and to throw the weeds "into the furnace of fire" (Matt 13:36–43). In Matthew, the distinction between the Son of Man and the angels is clearer than in the vision of Rev 14:14–20. Nonetheless, readers of Revelation who have followed the prophecy from its beginning in chapter 1 will clearly identify the Son of Man figure on a cloud (Rev 14:14) as Jesus, and for such readers there can be little doubt of his dominion over the angels, as well as the whole earth.

The problem that Stuckenbruck identifies arises chiefly when Rev 14:14–20 is treated as a separate form-critical unit of material rather than as part of a total composition. It is certainly possible that the passage may derive from an earlier source in which the Son of Man is an angelic figure, but within the literary context of the book of Revelation, he can be none other than Jesus, who has already been disclosed as bearing the divine identity. Within this reading, the function of Rev 14:14–20 is to assert once more the role of Jesus as the exalted Son of Man who will execute just judgment on the earth.

11. On this passage, see Huber, *Einer Gleich einem Menschensohn*, 218–69; Stuckenbruck, *Angel Veneration and Christology*, 240–45.

12. Stuckenbruck, *Angel Veneration and Christology*, 241.

This divine role has been repeatedly assigned to Jesus throughout the text. It appears especially in the letters to the seven churches (e.g., Rev 2:5, 16, 22–28; 3:2–5, 16, 21) as well as at other points in the visionary sequences (e.g., 6:16–17; 11:15–18), and it culminates in the christological vision of the rider on a white horse who "judges in righteousness" (19:11). For that reason, even though there is no explicit mention of Jesus in the brief description of final judgment of the dead in 20:11–15, the reader of the whole book will surely surmise that the book of life (20:12, 15) is none other than *the Lamb's* book of life (13:8), and that when Death and Hades are thrown into the lake of fire (20:14), the agent of their overthrow must be none other than Jesus, the Living One who now holds "the keys of Death and of Hades" (1:18).[13]

It should be emphasized that final judgment in the book of Revelation means not only punishment of the wicked but also the granting of life, consolation, and rewards to the faithful. This is emphasized throughout the letters to the seven churches (Rev 2:7, 11, 17, 26–28; 3:4–5, 10–12, 21), and it is given particularly powerful emphasis in 7:9–17, where the *Lamb* (Jesus) is portrayed—in a paradoxical formulation—as the *shepherd* who will protect and guide his people to "springs of the water of life" (echoing Ps 23), where God will "wipe away every tear from their eyes" (echoing Isa 25:8). This vision anticipates the book's climactic image of the new Jerusalem, where God himself will dwell with mortals, wipe away all tears, and abolish death and pain forever (Rev 21:1–4). Readers who have fully grasped the christological depth of the Apocalypse will almost certainly understand that if "the dwelling (σκηνή) of God is among human beings," then God's embodied presence in their midst cannot be understood apart from the embodiment of the divine presence in Jesus.

The mysterious coinherence of the identity of God and the identity of Jesus (*Verbindungsidentität*, to use the term proposed by C. Kavin Rowe),[14] is nowhere expressed more remarkably than in Revelation's deployment of the divine title "the Alpha and the Omega." This terminology appears only in the opening and closing sections of the book. Its first occurrence is the sonorous declaration of Rev 1:8, where the speaker is none other than the one God of Israel, the cosmic creator and ruler: "'I am the Alpha and the Omega (τὸ ἄλφα καὶ τὸ ὦ),' says the Lord God, who is and who was and who is to come, the Almighty (ὁ παντοκράτωρ)." Similarly, when the title reappears in 21:6, the speaker again is a voice from the divine throne who self-identifies as "God"

13. The passive verb ἐβλήθησαν in Rev 20:14 almost surely signifies divine action.

14. C. Kavin Rowe, *Early Narrative Christology: The Lord in the Gospel of Luke*, BZNW 139 (Berlin: de Gruyter, 2006), 201.

(v. 7). In this second instance, the "Alpha and Omega" title is supplemented and interpreted by the appositional expression, "the Beginning and the End" (ἡ ἀρχὴ καὶ τὸ τέλος). But in the third and final appearance of this divine title (22:13), we encounter a highly significant variation. Here the speaker is one who is "coming soon . . . to repay according to everyone's work" (v. 12)—precisely the office already claimed for Jesus in 2:23. And in this final reiteration, the title "the Alpha and the Omega" has now acquired a third synonymous epithet, "the First and the Last" (ὁ πρῶτος καὶ ὁ ἔσχατος). So the final cadence sounds like this: "I am the Alpha and the Omega, the First and the Last, the Beginning and the End" (22:13). But ὁ πρῶτος καὶ ὁ ἔσχατος has already appeared as a title specifically for Jesus, "[the one] who was dead and came to life," in 1:17 and 2:8. Thus, however remarkable it may seem, the reader should not be surprised when the same revelatory voice that speaks as Alpha and Omega finally announces, "*It is I, Jesus*, who sent my angel to you with this testimony for the churches" (22:16). In the end of the book of Revelation, it is *Jesus* who can say, "I am the Alpha and the Omega, the First and the Last, the Beginning and the End."

Readers who have already heard Jesus assert himself to be "the First and the Last" (1:17, 2:8)—if their ears are attuned to echoes of Isaiah's prophecies—will already have heard a theme preparatory to the climactic christological cadence of Rev 22:13. The title "the First and the Last" (ὁ πρῶτος καὶ ὁ ἔσχατος) is strongly reminiscent of the divine declaration in Isaiah 44:6:

> Thus says the Lord, the King of Israel,
> and his Redeemer [!], the Lord of Hosts:
> I am the First and I am the Last (MT: אֲנִי רִאשׁוֹן וַאֲנִי אַחֲרוֹן);
> besides me there is no god.

Or again, readers might recall Isa 48:12:

> Listen to me, O Jacob, and Israel, whom I called:
> I am He; I am the First, and I am the Last (MT: אֲנִי רִאשׁוֹן אַף אֲנִי אַחֲרוֹן).

Thus, even in the early part of the Apocalypse, in the letters to the churches, Jesus has already spoken the self-description that belongs only to the One who can say "besides me there is no other God."[15] By fusing "First and Last" with

15. See Bauckham, *Theology of the Book of Revelation*, 25–28; Bauckham, *God Crucified:*

"Alpha and Omega," Rev 22:13 clearly brings Jesus into a shared identity with the God of Israel, who has said, "My glory I will not give to another" (Isa 48:11). The only possible implication, within the symbolic world of Revelation, is that Jesus and God are one; their identity is a *Verbindungsidentität*. Otherwise, the claims made here by and for Jesus are simply blasphemous profanations of the name of God.[16]

A similar phenomenon appears in John the Seer's depiction of worship around the heavenly throne in Rev 4 and 5.[17] In chapter 4, the four living creatures around the throne and the twenty-four elders offer praise to "our Lord and God" who is "worthy . . . to receive glory and honor and power" (ἄξιος εἶ, ὁ κύριος καὶ ὁ θεὸς ἡμῶν, λαβεῖν τὴν δόξαν καὶ τὴν τιμὴν καὶ τὴν δύναμιν, 4:11). But when the new figure of the slaughtered Lamb appears in the throne room in chapter 5, the elders are joined by a great chorus of angels singing, "Worthy (ἄξιον) is the Lamb that was slaughtered to receive power (τὴν δύναμιν) and wealth and wisdom and might and honor and glory (τιμὴν καὶ δόξαν) and blessing" (5:12). The Lamb that was slaughtered—clearly a symbol of Jesus Christ—is now deemed worthy of receiving precisely the same praise addressed to God in the first part of the throne room vision. And this point is finally driven home explicitly by the sung acclamation of "every creature in heaven and on earth and under the earth and in the sea." They all sing together:

Monotheism and Christology in the New Testament (Grand Rapids: Eerdmans, 1998), 53–54. Interestingly, while the divine title appears in the Apocalypse as ὁ πρῶτος καὶ ὁ ἔσχατος, this Greek rendering does not precisely follow the LXX, where we find ἐγὼ πρῶτος καὶ ἐγὼ μετὰ ταῦτα (Isa 44:6) and ἐγώ εἰμι πρῶτος, καὶ ἐγώ εἰμι εἰς τὸν αἰῶνα (48:12). There can be no doubt that the Apocalypse is echoing the divine self-disclosure as respresented in Isaiah; therefore, it would appear that in Revelation, we are encountering either a tradition of Greek translation independent of the LXX or a direct translation from Hebrew by the author himself.

16. In this context, it is interesting to note that when Christ appears in eschatological triumph as the rider on a white horse (Rev 19:11–16), his name is said to be a mystery: "he has a name inscribed that no one knows but himself" (v. 12). In our conference at Duke, Tobias Nicklas suggested to me that the Rider's name must remain unknown because it is the ineffable divine name (cf. Exod 3:13–15). I am grateful for this interesting suggestion, which supports my line of argument in this essay.

17. For an illuminating theological analysis of the christological implications of these chapters, see C. Kavin Rowe, "For Future Generations: Worshipping Jesus and the Integration of the Theological Disciplines," *ProEccl* 17 (2008): 186–209, esp. 190–96. The following sketch of the passage recapitulates and builds upon Rowe's reading.

> To the One seated on the throne and to the Lamb
> be blessing and honor (τιμή) and glory (δόξα) and might forever
> and ever! (Rev 5:13)

And lest this acclamation be thought an aberration, it receives the "Amen" endorsement of the four living creatures and the elders in the final verse of the chapter (5:14). So the Lamb is included within the praise addressed to God.

The startling character of this inclusion is highlighted all the more forcefully by Revelation's incorporation, later in the book, of what Stuckenbruck has called "the refusal tradition," in which an angelic figure rejects the attempt of the human visionary to offer veneration or worship and redirects worship to God alone (Rev 19:10, 22:8–9; cf. Tob 12:16–22; *Apoc. Zeph.* 6:11–15; *Mart. Ascen. Isa.* 7:18–23, 8:1–10, 15; 2 *Enoch* 1:4–8; 3 *Enoch* 1:7, 16:1–5).[18] The stark contrast between all creation's worship of the Lamb and the angel's emphatic refusal of worship ("You must not do that! . . . Worship God!" Rev 19:10; 22:9) shows that the worship of Jesus, the Lamb, cannot be thought to violate the prohibition of idolatrous worship.[19]

The Lamb's sharing in the divine identity is reinforced at the end of the book in John's vision of the new Jerusalem, where "the river of the water of life" flows "from the throne of God and of the Lamb" (22:1). Most strikingly, "the throne of God and of the Lamb will be in it [the city], and his servants will worship *him* (αὐτῷ)" (v. 3). Here, in view of the compound antecedent (God and the Lamb) we would expect the plural pronoun αὐτοῖς. But the seemingly ungrammatical singular αὐτῷ makes a deeper point of theological/christological grammar: God and the Lamb are one.[20] That is why this Lamb can be named "Lord of lords and King of kings" (17:14; cf. 1:5). But what is the significance of the fact that this Lamb who mysteriously shares the exalted identity of God is at the same time "the Lamb that was slaughtered"? The an-

18. Stuckenbruck, *Angel Veneration and Christology*, 75–103, 245–61.

19. Rightly Bauckham, *Theology of the Book of Revelation*, 58–63: "the worship of Jesus must be understood as indicating the inclusion of Jesus in the being of the one God defined by monotheistic worship" (60).

20. I am not necessarily suggesting that the author of the Apocalypse is consciously making this point. Rather, his odd grammatical construction attests, perhaps unreflectively, to a fundamental theological intuition that the church centuries later would seek to articulate in a more systematic fashion. Again, Bauckham observes the grammatical issue here: John is "even prepared to defy grammar for the sake of theology" (*Theology of the Book of Revelation*, 60).

swer to that question is closely bound together with Jesus's identity as the one who faithfully testified to God's truth through his death.

Jesus as Faithful Witness

The opening salutation formula of the book offers "grace to you and peace . . . from Jesus Christ, the faithful witness, the firstborn from the dead, and the ruler of the kings of the earth" (Rev 1:4–5). The programmatic prominence of the epithet "the faithful witness" (ὁ μάρτυς ὁ πιστός) leads us to expect that the Christology of the Apocalypse will place heavy emphasis on Jesus's role as one who testifies to the truth. The actual expression "faithful witness" appears as a christological title, however, in only one other place in the book: the letter to the church in Laodicea is introduced as "the words of the Amen, the faithful and true witness (ὁ μάρτυς ὁ πιστός καὶ ἀληθινός)" (3:14). And the same qualities are ascribed—probably in titular form—to the rider on a white horse who comes to execute the final triumph of God: "Then I saw heaven opened, and there was a white horse! Its rider is called Faithful and True (πιστὸς . . . καὶ ἀληθινός)" (19:11). We should not make the mistake of supposing, however, that Jesus's role as faithful witness is confined to those few passages in which he is given this specific designation.

The concept of witness bearing (μαρτυρία) is central to the message of Revelation and to its hortatory purposes. John the Seer describes himself as one "who testified to the word of God and to the testimony of Jesus Christ, everything that he saw" (ὅς ἐμαρτύρησεν τὸν λόγον τοῦ θεοῦ καὶ τὴν μαρτυρίαν Ἰησοῦ Χριστοῦ ὅσα εἶδεν, Rev 1:2). So John himself is a witness, and that to which he bears witness is said to be "the μαρτυρία of Jesus Christ." Commentators debate whether the genitive construction here is objective ("the testimony about Jesus Christ") or subjective ("the testimony given by Jesus Christ"). Both meanings are possible, and I would suggest that a careful reading of the book as a whole will require us to hear both senses simultaneously.[21]

On the one hand, John tells us that his exile on the island of Patmos is "because of the word of God and the testimony of Jesus" (Rev 1:9), that is, presumably because of his own prophetic activity of proclaiming Jesus, not Caesar, as the true Lord and King. Similarly, we are told later that the dragon

21. For discussion of this problem see Sigve K. Tonstad, *Saving God's Reputation: The Theological Function of* Pistis Iesou *in the Cosmic Narratives of Revelation*, LNTS 337 (London: Continuum, 2006), 170–71, 179–82.

is making war on "those who keep the commandments of God and hold the testimony of Jesus" (12:17). Perhaps the clearest example of this objective genitive sense is found in Rev 20:4, where the Seer witnesses "the souls of those who had been beheaded for their testimony of Jesus (διὰ τὴν μαρτυρίαν Ἰησοῦ) and for the word of God." In this class of references, we should include also John's depiction of the souls under the altar in the heavenly throne room, those "who had been slaughtered for the word of God and for the testimony which they held" (6:9). In all of these instances, "the testimony of Jesus" constitutes an act of countercultural resistance through public prophetic proclamation of Jesus as Lord, an act of resistance that leads to persecution and (ultimately) martyrdom.[22]

On the other hand, there are also several suggestions in the text that Jesus himself is one who bears testimony, as the opening declaration of his role as "Faithful Witness" certainly indicates. In part, this refers to his role as the revealer of the visions given to the Seer: "I, Jesus, have sent my angel to testify (μαρτυρῆσαι) to you concerning these things for the churches" (22:16). This sense of Jesus as the revealer of testimony is confirmed in his final words in the book: "The one who testifies to these things (ὁ μαρτυρῶν ταῦτα) says, 'Surely I am coming soon.' Amen. Come, Lord Jesus!" (22:20). Here it appears that the entire book of Revelation constitutes Jesus's own testimony. Thus, there is a strong case to be made that "the testimony of Jesus" encompasses both the proclamation about him and the revelation that he supplies.

Beyond these grammatical observations about the multivalence of the construction διὰ τὴν μαρτυρίαν Ἰησοῦ, however, I would propose that "the testimony of Jesus" must include the memory or message of Jesus's own faithful suffering and death. This is suggested first of all by the interesting fact that the martyr Antipas in Pergamum is described as ὁ μάρτυς μου ὁ πιστός μου (2:13)—precisely echoing Revelation's programmatic description of Jesus himself as ὁ μάρτυς, ὁ πιστός (1:5). It is likewise noteworthy that the martyred souls in 6:9 are said to have been slaughtered (ἐσφαγμένων) on account of

22. We see the same pattern in the fate of the "two witnesses" in Rev 11:3–10, who give testimony (μαρτυρία) and are therefore attacked and killed by "the beast that comes up from the bottomless pit." Although there is no specific reference here to "the testimony of Jesus," readers are surely to understand that these witnesses are carrying the same gospel message for which other witnesses in the text are said to undergo martyrdom. See also 19:10, where the angelic messenger describes himself to John as "a fellow slave with you and your brothers who hold the testimony of Jesus." Here, though presumably the angel is not subject to persecution by the empire, he is declaring solidarity with those witnesses who do hold fast to the message and suffer as a result of their testimony.

their testimony—precisely the same verb used to describe the identity of the slaughtered Lamb in 5:6, 9, 11. Again, we should observe carefully how John describes the triumph of God's faithful over the adversarial dragon in chapter 12: "they have conquered him *by the blood of the Lamb* and *by the word of their testimony* (διὰ τὸν λόγον τῆς μαρτυρίας αὐτῶν), for they did not cling to life even in the face of death" (12:11). Here is an unmistakable statement that the "testimony" that conquers evil is not merely a verbal message; instead, it is an embodied testimony, enacted through a confession that refuses the way of violence and undergoes death, just as Jesus did, at the hands of earthly powers.[23] That is why witnesses of this kind can be said to have the Lamb's name written on their foreheads (14:1); they are the ones who "follow the Lamb wherever he goes" (v. 4)—which surely means following his example of testimony through the way of the cross.

Consequently, when John declares that he has "testified to the word of God and to the testimony of Jesus Christ, *everything that he saw*" (1:2), we must surmise that the ματυρία he *saw* includes the vision of Jesus as the slaughtered but triumphant Lamb—that is to say, Jesus as the crucified Lord. And precisely in his identity as slaughtered Lamb, Jesus provides the pattern, the example, and the prototype for those who follow him wherever he goes. Their identity as suffering witnesses is patterned on Jesus's identity as Faithful Witness, which finds its definitive embodiment in his own death on a cross.

Only in that sense can we rightly understand his prophetic promise to the church at Laodicea: "To the one who conquers I will give a place with me on my throne, just as I myself conquered and sat down with my Father on his throne" (3:21). To "conquer," as in 12:11, is to follow Jesus's own example of conquering through a faithful submission to death.[24] This paradoxical symbolic inversion

23. There is an important and interesting parallel here to the account found in the Pastoral Epistles of Jesus's faithful confession before earthly power: "In the presence of God, who gives life to all things, and of Christ Jesus, who in his testimony before Pontius Pilate made the good confession (Χριστοῦ Ἰησοῦ τοῦ μαρτυρήσαντος ἐπὶ Ποντίου Πιλάτου τὴν καλὴν ὁμολογίαν), I charge you to keep the commandment without spot or blame until the manifestation of our Lord Jesus Christ, which he will bring about at the right time—he who is the blessed and only Sovereign, the King of kings and Lord of lords" (1 Tim 6:13–15). The concluding christological title in 1 Tim 6:15 closely parallels the acclamations of Jesus in Rev 17:14 and 19:16. Thus, 1 Timothy concurs with Revelation in paradoxically describing Jesus as faithful martyr/witness who suffers at the hands of earthly powers and simultaneously as the One who rules over all such powers.

24. For that reason, the NRSV's inclusive-language translation of Rev 21:7 results in an unfortunate reduction of the christological symbolism of the text: "*Those who conquer* will inherit these things, and I will be *their* God and *they* will be my *children*." But in fact the

lies at the heart of the entire book of Revelation. To put the point aphoristically, I would suggest that the conquering power of the Lamb in Revelation can be best understood when it is interpreted through the intertextual lens of the Gospel of John, in which Jesus conquers the world (John 16:33) by being lifted up on the cross in such a way that his death will draw all humanity to himself (12:32–33). Thus, the passion narrative is the christological subtext that undergirds all of the Apocalypse's references to Jesus as Faithful Witness/Martyr.

The Lamb on the Throne: God Crucified and Triumphant

These preliminary explorations in the Christology of the Apocalypse have demonstrated something of the depth and complexity of this visionary work. I would like to draw out some of the implications of my reading by making four points—two methodological observations and two substantive claims.

(1) *The necessity of intertextual interpretation.* The Christology I have described is not entirely to be found in the explicit surface statements and affirmations of the text. It arises from reflective intertextual interpretation of the Apocalypse as a document embedded in a particular encyclopedia of production, a discursive space shaped by dialogue with precursor texts. For example, the full import of describing Jesus as "the First and the Last" can be discerned only in relation to the precursor texts in Isaiah that emphatically declare the God of Israel to be "the First and the Last." Readers unfamiliar with Israel's Scripture are likely to underinterpret the radical and shattering christological implications of Revelation's imagery. Consequently, interpretation of the message of Revelation requires the recovery and amplification of numerous intertextual echoes that will be inaudible to many readers today. One effect of recovering these echoes will be to highlight the astonishing claim that Jesus is a sharer in the divine identity.

(2) *The implications of canonical reading.* A related but distinguishable point is that the Christology of Revelation is brought rightly into focus by a reading

---

substantive participle and following pronouns in the Greek text are all singular: ὁ νικῶν κληρονομήσει ταῦτα καὶ ἔσομαι αὐτῷ θεὸς καὶ αὐτὸς ἔσται μοι υἱός ("*The One who conquers* will inherit these things, and I will be God to *him*, and *he* will be a *Son* to me"). I would propose that reading Rev 21:7 alongside 3:21 suggests a complex but deliberate ambiguity: the primary referent of ὁ νικῶν in 21:7 is Jesus himself, God's Son, who shares the promised inheritance with those who follow his pattern of conquering through faithful endurance of death—and so ὁ νικῶν can be referred secondarily to those who follow his way and thereby show themselves to be God's sons/children (as in the NRSV).

that places it firmly within the canon of the NT—or at least within the narrative world of the four canonical Gospels. The image of the triumphant "Lamb that was slaughtered" is unintelligible apart from the Gospel narratives of Jesus's crucifixion and resurrection. And it should be noted that the interpretation of Jesus's crucifixion as the "slaughter" of a "lamb" almost certainly presupposes a canonical/intertextual reading of the passion story in light of Isa 53:7:

> He was oppressed, and he was afflicted, yet he did not open his mouth;
> like a lamb that is led to the slaughter (LXX: ὡς πρόβατον ἐπὶ σφαγὴν ἤχθη),
> and like a sheep that before its shearers is silent,
> so he did not open his mouth.

Most Christian readers effortlessly and unreflectively perform this sort of intertextual reading so that the otherwise puzzling figure of the slaughtered Lamb on the throne occasions no particular difficulty. But it should be noted that apart from the narrative context provided by the Gospels, as well as by Isa 53, this aspect of the christological imagery of the Apocalypse would be at best opaque.

Further, I would suggest that a similar point can be made about the image of Jesus as "Faithful Witness." Such an interpretation of Jesus presupposes not only the explicit description of Jesus as a revealer in the Apocalypse but also the influence of at least two other streams of NT Christology. First, the image of Jesus as "Witness" appears prominently in the Gospel of John, climactically in the trial scene before Pontius Pilate: "For this I was born, and for this I came into the world, *to testify to the truth* (ἵνα μαρτυρήσω τῇ ἀληθείᾳ)" (John 18:37; cf. also 3:31–33; 8:18). And second, Paul's references to the faithfulness of Jesus Christ (πίστις Ἰησοῦ Χριστοῦ) in his obedient self-giving death may undergird Revelation's portrayal of Jesus as the faithful one.[25] Further, as I have already noted,[26] the image of Jesus as faithful oppositional witness in the face of Roman power is brought fully to expression in the Pauline tradition in 1 Tim 6:13.

One of the major hermeneutical implications of reading Revelation within the canonical framework of the NT is to serve as a check and corrective on

25. For an incisive analysis of πίστις Ἰησοῦ in Revelation, see Tonstad, *Saving God's Reputation*, 157–94. On the Pauline material, see Richard B. Hays, *The Faith of Jesus Christ: The Narrative Substructure of Galatians 3:1–4:11*, 2nd ed. (Grand Rapids: Eerdmans, 2002 [1983]), and the literature cited there.

26. See note 23 above.

interpretations that seek to read the violent militaristic imagery of the Apocalypse literalistically. If Jesus wins his victory over the world through his faithful death on a cross (as all the rest of the NT documents insist), and if Revelation's figurative depictions are to be read in intertextual concert with these other texts, then the triumphant rider who is "clothed in a robe dipped in blood" (Rev 19:13) must be wearing a garment drenched with his *own* blood, and the "sharp sword" that comes "from his mouth . . . to strike down the nations" (v. 15) must be the proclaimed word of the gospel (as in Eph 6:17), not a literal sword of iron that kills enemies.[27]

The larger point, however, is not only that placing Revelation within the NT canon leads to a nonviolent reading of the text but that the book's vivid depictions of God, Christ, and the church must all be construed as part of a larger narrative whole. Such a reading will cause hermeneutical implications to run both ways. On the one hand, the wider NT narrative creates hermeneutical constraints on the interpretation of Revelation's symbolism; on the other hand, Revelation's apocalyptic worldview broadens and deepens the radical implications of the NT's other stories and letters—it discloses vividly that our lives are placed in a cosmic frame of reference.

(3) *The narrative embodiment of proto-Chalcedonian Christology.* I turn now to two substantive findings of this brief study of the Christology of the Apocalypse. One of the most striking features of the analysis we have pursued here is that it seems to show that the presentation of Jesus in this book is what we might call "proto-Chalcedonian." Jesus in Revelation is a figure who shares fully in the divine identity, yet at the same time, he is a human figure who suffered a martyr's death at the hands of an earthly empire. Only so can he rightly say of himself, "I was dead, and see, I am alive forever and ever; and I have the keys of Death and of Hades" (1:18). Thus he is simultaneously the example par excellence of human faithfulness (the prototypical martyr) *and* the Alpha and the Omega, the one who is worthy to receive worship and honor that belongs to God alone. This is not merely a retrospective projection of a later doctrinal standard onto a primitive Christian text; rather, this paradoxical duality of the

27. "Thus the only weapon the Rider needs, if he is to break the opposition of his enemies, and establish God's reign of justice and peace, is the proclamation of the gospel" (G. B. Caird, *The Revelation of St. John the Divine*, HNTC [New York: Harper & Row, 1966], 245). For a reading of Revelation that more fully develops this line of interpretation, see Richard B. Hays, *The Moral Vision of the New Testament: Community, Cross, New Creation* (San Francisco: HarperSanFrancisco, 1996), 169–85. A similar approach to reading Revelation is also now comprehensively supported by Sigve K. Tonstad, *Revelation*, Paideia Commentaries on the New Testament (Grand Rapids: Baker Academic, 2019).

identity of Jesus is embedded deeply in the symbolic logic of the text itself.[28] The book of Revelation does not attempt to explain its paradoxical Christology through any sort of ontological analysis or second-order conceptual reasoning; rather, its presentation of Jesus's identity operates in the realm of narrative and poetic figuration. It is not hard to see how the book's symbolic representations—along with similar material in the other NT documents—subsequently stimulated (indeed, we might say, *demanded*) second-order reflection. But the Apocalypse itself offers vision and proclamation, not "theology" as a mode of discourse. At best, we could say that theology and Christology are implicit in the text's *poiēsis*.

(4) *The politics of eschatological justice*. Finally, Revelation's portrayal of the identity of Jesus impacts our understanding of *politics*. The theme of the conference that gave rise to this essay was "The Book of Revelation: Theology, Politics, and Intertextuality." I have sketched here the manifold ways in which careful *intertextual* reading can inform our grasp of the *theology* implicit in the book. In these concluding remarks, I also want to highlight the way in which the Christology of the Apocalypse points toward certain *political* implications.[29] In the interpretation of the Apocalypse, it becomes evident that literary, theological, and political readings are inextricably interwoven.

The two components of the christological paradox we have examined converge to encourage the formation of a confessing community of followers of the Lamb, a community that poses a fundamental challenge to the powers of the present world. On the one hand, Jesus as Faithful Witness/Martyr stands in opposition to the false and blasphemous claims of the dragon, the empire that exercises "authority over every tribe and people and language and nation" so that "all the inhabitants of the earth will worship it, everyone whose name has not been written from the foundation of the world in the book of life of the Lamb that was slaughtered" (13:7–8). Jesus the Lamb dies as a victim of this false power, but precisely by so doing exposes its evil and its illegitimacy. On the other hand, because this same Jesus is in fact "the ruler of the kings of the earth" (1:5), the "Lord of lords and King of kings," his victory over the oppressing earthly powers is both assured and final (17:14). Thus, both in his

28. See David S. Yeago, "The New Testament and the Nicene Dogma: A Contribution to the Recovery of Theological Exegesis," in *The Theological Interpretation of Scripture: Classic and Contemporary Readings*, ed. Stephen E. Fowl (Oxford: Blackwell, 1997), 87–100.

29. On this question, see especially N. T. Wright, "Revelation and Christian Hope: Political Implications of the Revelation to John," in *Revelation and the Politics of Apocalyptic Interpretation*, ed. Richard B. Hays and Stefan Alkier (Waco: Baylor University Press, 2012), 105–24.

humanity (Faithful Witness) and his divinity (Alpha and Omega), Jesus stands triumphant: "the kingdom of this world has become the kingdom of our Lord and of his Messiah, and he will reign forever and ever" (11:15).[30] The derisive lament over the fall of Babylon the great—with its military power, its mercantile wealth, its immorality, and its violence (18:1–24)—is the apocalyptic disclosure of God's final judgment on the present political order. This politics of wealth and violence, the politics of "Babylon, the mighty city" (18:10), is judged and supplanted by God's new polis, the new Jerusalem, in which God dwells with his people and wipes away all tears (21:1–4). This eschatological vision of justice looms over present political reality and subjects it to judgment.[31]

The consequent effect of Revelation's political vision is summed up eloquently by Oliver O'Donovan: "It conveys to us a hope that in the life which we are summoned to live with Christ we may experience, as a social reality, that authority of truth and righteousness which our experience of political society on earth has consistently denied us." Consequently, those who proclaim the message of the Apocalypse to challenge the injustice of the prevailing political powers are "confronting a false political order with the foundation of a true one."[32] Those who "follow the Lamb wherever he goes" (14:4) will find that the Christology of this mysterious visionary Apocalypse leads us ultimately to justice and life. The slaughtered Lamb, the Faithful Witness, is also the One who stands, as Alpha and Omega, at the beginning and end of history. For that reason—and only for that reason—we can join John the Seer in patient endurance while we live, act, and bear witness in light of his apocalyptic vision of the healing of the nations.

30. Once again, we see a construction in which an (implied) plural subject (the Lord and his Messiah) anomalously becomes the grammatical subject for a third-person singular verb (βασιλεύσει: "he will reign"). The grammatical irregularity may once again implicitly testify to the *Verbindungsidentität* of God and Christ.

31. See Elisabeth Schüssler Fiorenza, *The Book of Revelation: Justice and Judgment* (Philadelphia: Fortress, 1985).

32. Oliver O'Donovan, "The Political Thought of the Book of Revelation," *TynBul* 37, no. 1 (1986): 90.

17

Covenant

New Covenantalism in Hebrews

A Proposal: The Proclamation of "New Covenantalism" in Hebrews

Does the Letter to the Hebrews articulate a supersessionist theology? For a long time, there has been a clear consensus among interpreters that it is so, that Hebrews emphatically represents Judaism as a religion now rejected and replaced by Christianity. In the course of my research for this essay, I came across the following representative assessment: "The Letter to the Hebrews is the paradigmatic illustration in the New Testament" of "supersessionist hermeneutics." Indeed, because the entire letter is built on "the rhetorical ground structure of inference from the lesser to the greater," it repeatedly "annuls" the texts it cites from Israel's Scripture, and its typological reading strategy is therefore "relentlessly supersessionist."

I fear, however, that such assessments are too often grounded in a superficial reading of the evidence. In the example I have just cited, the author is merely using Hebrews as a rhetorical foil to make contrasting positive judgments about Pauline hermeneutics; this author's generalizing claims about the supersessionist hermeneutics of Hebrews are not based on any serious exegesis of the text itself. I make this accusation with some confidence because these quotations are taken from a book called *Echoes of Scripture in the Letters of Paul.*[1] In that book, published in 1989, it appears that Richard Hays was merely reflecting what he took to be the *communis opinio* at that time, for he offers no actual argumentation, merely a summary characterization of Hebrews. In light

1. Richard B. Hays, *Echoes of Scripture in the Letters of Paul* (New Haven: Yale University Press, 1989), 177, 99, 98.

This essay was originally presented as a paper at the St. Andrews Conference on Scripture and Theology, University of St. Andrews, Scotland, in 2006.

of the current state of discussion, however, I believe it is necessary to revisit the question and to subject Hays's judgment to critical scrutiny. In particular it may be useful to look more closely at the way in which appeals to the OT actually function in the argumentation of the letter.

At least since the time of John Chrysostom, Hebrews has been read as a stern warning to Jewish converts to the Christian faith not to fall back into Jewish practices. In the course of the argument, the author of Hebrews asserts that God's "first covenant" (Heb 8:7) with the people of Israel—that is, the covenant established at Sinai—is now "obsolete" (so most translations of 8:13 read) and has been replaced by "a better covenant, which has been enacted through better promises" (v. 6). The mediator of this new covenant is Jesus, who is explicitly said to be of superior status to Moses (8:6; 3:1–6). That certainly sounds like a textbook illustration of Christian supersessionism.

Despite this clear first impression—and indeed, after centuries of Christian interpretation, one can hardly describe it as a hasty first impression—several scholars have recently begun to question the supersessionist paradigm for reading Hebrews and to propose new models for understanding the text more sympathetically within a complex reconstruction of first-century Judaism. So, for example, Charles P. Anderson argues that Hebrews is to be read within the context of Jewish apocalyptic thought, and that the heirs of the new age are assumed in Hebrews to be of Jewish descent; the gentile mission is nowhere in view in the text.[2] Several of the essays in the recent volume edited by Gabriella Gelardini seek to reopen the question of the relation between Judaism and the Letter to the Hebrews. Gelardini herself suggests that Hebrews is a homily composed specifically for *Tisha be-Av*, a crucial day of fasting in the Jewish liturgical calendar that "commemorates and mourns over the sins of Israel and the covenant curse that followed upon them."[3] Pamela Eisenbaum, in a paper delivered at the 2005 SBL meeting, proposes a social and literary setting for Hebrews after the destruction of the Jerusalem temple, in a time when Jews and Christians alike were experiencing social and religious dislocation; consequently, the author is not attacking Judaism but "attempting to

2. Charles P. Anderson, "Who Are the Heirs of the New Age in the Epistle to the Hebrews?," in *Apocalyptic and the New Testament: Essays in Honor of J. Louis Martyn*, ed. Joel Marcus and Marion L. Soards, JSNTSup 24 (Sheffield: JSOT Press, 1989), 255–77.

3. Gabriella Gelardini, "Hebrews, an Ancient Synagogue Homily for *Tisha Be-Av*: Its Function, Its Basis, Its Theological Interpretation," in *Hebrews: Contemporary Methods—New Insights*, ed. Gabriella Gelardini (Leiden: Brill, 2005), 121. See also, in the same volume, Elke Tönges, "The Epistle to the Hebrews as a 'Jesus-Midrash,'" 89–105.

fill a desperate theological and social void."[4] Her essay in the Gelardini volume argues that Hebrews should be clearly distinguished from the work of later Christian writers such as Barnabas, Melito of Sardis, and Justin Martyr, who undertake an explicit polemic against Judaism. Instead, she writes, what we find in Hebrews is "in some ways neither Judaism nor Christianity." The letter represents "a unique form of Judeo-Christian religiosity that perhaps existed briefly when Rome was the common enemy of Jews and believers in Jesus and before the rhetoric of Christian and Jewish leaders could construct firm boundaries between Judaism and Christianity."[5]

The examples I have just cited—regardless of whether their particular proposals ultimately prove persuasive—are not idiosyncratic. They are part of a broader scholarly landscape, in which we are increasingly recognizing that the process of identity formation of distinct "Christian" and "Jewish" communities in the first century was a complex and gradual matter, and that the "border lines"—to use Daniel Boyarin's term—were sometimes indistinct.[6] If we return to a fresh reading of Hebrews in light of this insight, we may notice a number of interesting things that might have eluded us before. One of my students recently proposed the following thought experiment: "Forget that there ever was such a thing as Christianity, let alone Christianity as a predominantly Gentile movement. Now reread Hebrews with this renewed absence of knowledge. Is there anything that would lead one to conclude that the author of this homily is anything other than a Jew (albeit a messianic one) weighing in on a controversy within his own religion?"[7] Carrying out this experiment, we notice that

4. Pamela Eisenbaum, "Hebrews, Supersessionism and Jewish-Christian Relations" (unpublished paper presented at Hebrews Consultation, SBL Annual Meeting, Philadelphia, 2005), 1.

5. Pamela Eisenbaum, "Locating Hebrews within the Literary Landscape of Christian Origins," in Gelardini, *Hebrews: Contemporary Methods*, 236–37.

6. Daniel Boyarin, *Border Lines: The Partition of Judea-Christianity* (Philadelphia: University of Pennsylvania Press, 2004). See also Judith Lieu, "'I Am a Christian': Martyrdom and the Beginning of 'Christian' Identity," in *Neither Jew nor Greek? Constructing Christian Identity* (Edinburgh: T & T Clark, 2003).

7. T. J. Rogers, seminar discussion paper, February 27, 2006. Compare the judgment of Andrew T. Lincoln: "The notion of this document's relation to Judaism could be held to be an anachronistic one, if it suggests that author and readers saw themselves as standing outside their religious heritage and having an attitude toward its basic set of convictions from which they had now distanced themselves by converting to Christianity. Rather, from their own perspective, it was not so much that Judaism was defunct but more that their religion and its central symbols had now been decisively fulfilled in Christ" ("Hebrews and Biblical Theology," in *Out of Egypt: Biblical Theology and Biblical Interpretation*, ed. Craig

the Letter to the Hebrews nowhere speaks of Jews and gentiles, nowhere gives evidence of controversies over circumcision or food laws,[8] criticizes nothing in the Mosaic Torah except for the Levitical sacrificial cult,[9] and contains no polemic against Jews or Jewish leaders—thereby differing dramatically from texts such as Matthew, John, and Revelation. Nowhere does Hebrews suggest that the Jewish people have been replaced by a new and different people of God. Indeed, it appears that the addressees of the letter are considered part of God's "house," the same house over which Moses was faithful—that is, "the house of Israel" (3:1–6; 8:10).

To pose the question whether Hebrews is "supersessionist," then, runs the risk of imposing anachronistic categories on the text.[10] Read from a later gentile Christian perspective—say in Chrysostom's fourth-century Constantinople, or the liberal Protestant culture of nineteenth-century Germany—Hebrews seems obviously to be rejecting "Judaism."[11] If, however, we stay

---

Bartholomew, Mary Healy, Karl Möller, and Robin Parry, Scripture and Hermeneutics Series 5 [Grand Rapids: Zondervan, 2004], 334).

8. The possible exception to this statement is Heb 13:9, "It is well for the heart to be confirmed by grace, not by foods which have not benefited those who walk in them" (my translation). NRSV's broadly periphrastic translation ("It is well for the heart to be strengthened by grace, not by *regulations about food*, which have not benefited those who observe them") clearly does presuppose that there is a polemic here against Jewish food law. I would suggest, on the contrary, the possibility that the term "foods" (βρώμασιν) in this verse serves as a metaphor for the "strange teachings" just referred to in v. 9a. This would be consistent with the author's earlier use of "food" as a metaphor for the teaching that sustains growth to maturity (5:11–14, where the term is στερεᾶς τροφῆς). The metaphor of teaching as a form of sustenance goes back at least to Deut 8:3. In any case, the NRSV's introduction of the idea of "regulations" that must be "observed" supplies a set of categories that are far from explicit in the text of Heb 13:9.

9. Shaye J. D. Cohen ("The Significance of Yavneh: Pharisees, Rabbis, and the End of Jewish Sectarianism," *HUCA* 55 [1984]: 27–53]) observes that Jewish sectarian movements characteristically defined themselves in opposition to the priests and temple cult: "Hence a common feature of Jewish sectarianism is the polemic against the Temple of Jerusalem: its precincts are impure, its cult profane, and its priests illegitimate" (43). For this reference, I am indebted to Anderson, "Who Are the Heirs?," 277n44.

10. On the difficulties surrounding the attempt to define "supersessionism," see, e.g., Bruce Longenecker, "On Israel's God and God's Israel: Assessing Supersessionism in Paul," *JTS* 58 (2007): 26–44. Note especially his comment on p. 40: "If we were to imagine that supersessionism *per se* is anti-Jewish, then perhaps whole swaths of Early Jewish literature would need to be similarly characterized—a bizarre result, itself indicating that something is wrong in the house of supersessionist studies."

11. Again, see Lincoln ("Hebrews and Biblical Theology," 334): "Once the separation had clearly set in after 135 AD and Hebrews became a text whose later readers were pri-

within the text's own narrative world, such a claim may appear unwarranted, even puzzling. For that reason, it may be unhelpful to describe the teaching of Hebrews as a form of "Christianity" over against "Judaism"; rather, it is better described as a form of Jewish sectarian "New Covenantalism."

In the remainder of this essay, then, I shall not focus directly on the question whether the theology of Hebrews is supersessionist. Instead, I propose to ask this slightly different question: *How does the letter's New Covenantalism engage and carry forward the heritage of Israel?* What happens to Israel's story in the hands of our rhetorically artful author? To anticipate the outcome of such an inquiry, we will find both continuity and discontinuity. On the one hand, Israel's story is continued, reaching a climax in the figure of Jesus—just as the author's portrayal of him as the ἀρχηγὸν καὶ τελειωτὴν of faith stands at the climax of a chronologically ordered retelling of Israel's long heritage of radical trust in God (11:1–12:2). Yet, on the other hand, Jesus, as the climactic figure of the story, also introduces a major plot twist: he becomes the mediator of a new covenant that not only sustains but also *transforms* Israel's identity.

It is precisely the revisionary transformation of Jewish tradition, however, that produces the further difficulty so acutely posed by A. J. M. Wedderburn in a recent essay: Does the argumentation of Hebrews inadvertently saw off the branch on which the author sits? That is, does the logic of the letter's Christology and soteriology depend upon Jewish cultic categories that are ultimately undermined and invalidated in the course of the author's own argument? If so, is the letter, as Wedderburn suggests, finally incoherent?[12] The question can hardly be ducked by any serious theological reading of the text, and we shall return to it in the final part of this paper.

Exegetical Grounds for Claiming Newness

Every reader of Hebrews will immediately recognize that this letter is massively concerned with interpretation of Israel's Scripture, and there have been a number of important technical studies of the biblical exegesis found in the text.[13] Time would fail me to recount and evaluate these works. The particular

marily Gentile Christians who had little contact with the Judaism of their own time, then its denigration of the earlier stage of Judaism would easily have been thought to apply to Judaism as such."

12. A. J. M. Wedderburn, "Sawing Off the Branches: Theologizing Dangerously *Ad Hebraeos*," *JTS* 56 (2005): 393–414.

13. See, for example, Jean van der Ploeg, "L'exégèse de l'Ancien Testament dans l'Epitre

question that will engage our attention here is how Hebrews finds warrants for its revisionary "New Covenantalism" precisely within the texts acknowledged by Jewish interpreters as authoritative Scripture.[14] What are the exegetical grounds on which Hebrews can base its transformational assertion that the Sinai covenant has been replaced by a new and better one? I would suggest that the author of Hebrews sets forth at least eight major exegetical arguments to this effect.

Eight Exegetical Arguments

(1) *The revelatory new message is spoken through a Son who is ontologically superior to the prophets and intermediaries through whom the word previously came.* This claim is stated forcefully in the very first sentence of the text (1:1–2)—a sentence that also establishes a strong temporal distinction between the *past*

aux Hébreux," *RB* 54 (1947): 187–228; G. B. Caird, "The Exegetical Method of the Epistle to the Hebrews," *CJT* 5 (1959): 44–51; Simon J. Kistemaker, *The Psalm Citations in the Epistle to the Hebrews* (Amsterdam: Soest, 1961); Markus Barth, "The Old Testament in Hebrews: An Essay in Biblical Hermeneutics," in *Current Issues in New Testament Interpretation*, ed. William Klassen and Graydon F. Snyder (New York: Harper, 1962), 53–78, 263–73; Kenneth J. Thomas, "The Old Testament Citations in Hebrews," *NTS* 11 (1964–65): 303–25; George Howard, "Hebrews and the Old Testament Quotations," *NovT* 10 (1968): 208–16; Friedrich Schröger, *Der Verfasser des Hebräerbriefes als Schriftausleger*, Biblische Untersuchungen 4 (Regensburg: Pustet, 1968); Rowan A. Greer, *The Captain of Our Salvation: A Study in the Patristic Exegesis of Hebrews*, BGBE 15 (Tübingen: Mohr Siebeck, 1973); Graham Hughes, *Hebrews and Hermeneutics: The Epistle to the Hebrews as a New Testament Example of Biblical Interpretation*, SNTSMS 36 (Cambridge: Cambridge University Press, 1979); R. T. France, "The Writer of Hebrews as a Biblical Expositor," *TynBul* 47 (1996): 245–76; Herbert W. Bateman, *Early Jewish Hermeneutics and Hebrews 1.5–13: The Impact of Early Jewish Exegesis on the Interpretation of a Significant New Testament Passage*, American University Studies 193 (New York: Peter Lang, 1997); Pamela M. Eisenbaum, *The Jewish Heroes of Christian History: Hebrews 11 in Literary Context*, SBLDS 156 (Atlanta: Scholars, 1997); Peter Enns, "The Interpretation of Psalm 95 in Hebrews 3.1–4.13," in *Early Christian Interpretation of the Scriptures of Israel: Investigations and Proposals*, ed. Craig A. Evans and James A. Sanders, JSNTSup 148 (Sheffield: Sheffield Academic Press, 1997), 352–63; Stephen Motyer, "The Psalm Quotations of Hebrews 1: A Hermeneutic Free Zone?," *TynBul* 50 (1999): 3–22; and George H. Guthrie, "Hebrews' Use of the Old Testament: Recent Trends in Research," *CBR* 1 (2003): 271–94.

14. A similar question was posed half a century ago by Caird; his essay ("Exegetical Method of the Epistle to the Hebrews"), originally presented as his presidential address to the Canadian Society of Biblical Literature and Exegesis in 1958, still repays careful reading and reflection.

in which the prophets spoke (πάλαι) and the present in which the Son has spoken (ἐπ' ἐσχάτου τῶν ἡμερῶν τούτων). This eschatological disjunction between two times establishes a frame of reference that is fundamental to the letter's hermeneutics. The *exegetical* basis for the Son's ontological superiority—even to the angels through whom the word of God came in the past (2:2)—is found in a remarkable florilegium of OT texts (1:5–13, quoting Pss 2:7; 45:6–7; 102:25–27; and climactically 110:1; cf. also 2 Sam 7:14) that are read as direct divine speech from God the Father addressing the Son. (Particularly striking is the author's interpretation of Ps 45, in which God, as speaker of the psalm, addresses the Son as ὁ θεός.) Because Jesus is the Son, he also stands above Moses, who was "faithful in all God's house as a servant, *to testify to the things that would be spoken later*" (3:5). Thus, the word of God spoken through Moses has a provisional, forward-pointing quality, and when we read later of a new covenant of which Jesus is the mediator (8:6), we may be sure it is superior because of the superior ontological status of Jesus the Son (3:1–6).

(2) According to the argument of Heb 3:7–4:13, *Israel's entry to the promised land cannot be understood as the final "rest" promised to God's people.* The argument hinges on an exegetical observation: Ps 95 is spoken to Israel by David[15] much later than the time of Joshua and the wilderness generation. This is spelled out very carefully in 4:7–9:

> Again he sets a certain day—"today"—saying through David *much later*, in the words already quoted,
>
> "Today, if you hear his voice,
> do not harden your hearts."
>
> For if Joshua had given them rest, God would not speak *later* about another day. So then, a sabbath rest still remains for the people of God.

Consequently, whatever blessing Israel may have received in the past remains provisional, looking to an eschatological future. We find here also evidence of the author's pervasive hermeneutical conviction that Scripture is "living and active" (4:12), addressing the readers immediately in their own time, "today."

(3) Psalm 110, already cited in Heb 1 as a proof for the glory and sovereignty of the Son, returns in Heb 5–7 as the source of the extraordinary claim that *Jesus is "a priest forever according to the order of Melchizedek"* (Ps 110:4). Once

15. Note that this exegetical claim rests on the Septuagintal superscription of Ps 94.

the identification of Jesus as the "priest" addressed in Ps 110 has been made, numerous implications are traced out carefully in chapter 7. Because Scripture gives no genealogy of Melchizedek and does not narrate his death, he is said to "remain a priest forever" (Heb 7:3), thereby symbolizing the risen Jesus, who lives forever (v. 8). This interpretation highlights the wording of Ps 110:4 ("You are a priest *forever*"), while also presupposing the message of Jesus's resurrection.[16] This is crucial for the New Covenantalist argument, because Jesus, who has become a priest "through the power of an indestructible life" (Heb 7:16), thereby holds his priesthood permanently, in contrast to the mortal levitical priests, whose priesthood was ephemeral because of their mortality (vv. 23–25). In the midst of this argument, in verses 11–19, we encounter once again, as in chapters 3–4, the argument that the Psalms come later chronologically than the Pentateuch: the Law of Moses speaks of a priesthood "according to the order of Aaron," but then Scripture later, through David, speaks of "another priest arising." The fact that God finds it necessary to declare later, in Ps 110, a new eternal priesthood according to the order of Melchizedek implies the "setting aside of an earlier commandment" (ἀθέτησις . . . προαγούσης ἐντολῆς, Heb 7:18; see the wider context in vv. 11–19). One more exegetical observation supports this astonishing construction: this appointment of a new priesthood was confirmed not just by a commandment but by an *oath* sworn by God in Ps 110:4: "The Lord has sworn and will not change his mind: 'You are a priest forever . . .'" (quoted in Heb 7:20–22). For Hebrews, this demonstrates explicitly that Jesus is "the guarantee *of a better covenant*" (v. 22; the term "covenant" seems to be applied here rather narrowly to the establishment of a particular type of *priestly* service.) Finally, the argument from chronological sequence is driven home one more time in 7:28: because the oath of Ps 110 came *later than the Law* (μετὰ τὸν νόμον), it follows that the eternal Son appointed as priest by this oath takes the place of the "high priests" appointed by the Law.

(4) Closely tied to the argument about Jesus's priesthood is the letter's portrayal of *the earthly sanctuary as a "sketch and shadow" (ὑποδείγματι καὶ σκιᾷ) of the heavenly sanctuary in which Jesus has offered his perfect sacrifice*. Here, too, an exegetical argument supports this claim. Hebrews 8:5 points to Exod

16. On the central role of resurrection in the argument of Hebrews, see David M. Moffitt, *Atonement and the Logic of Resurrection in the Epistle to the Hebrews*, NovTSup 141 (Leiden: Brill, 2011). See also William L. Lane, "Living a Life in the Face of Death: The Witness of Hebrews," in *Life in the Face of Death: The Resurrection Message of the New Testament*, ed. Richard N. Longenecker (Grand Rapids: Eerdmans, 1998), 247–69; N. T. Wright, *The Resurrection of the Son of God*, Christian Origins and the Question of God 3 (London: SPCK; Minneapolis: Fortress, 2003), 457–61.

25:40 as evidence for the secondary and inferior character of the wilderness tabernacle constructed by Moses. The logic of the argument is somewhat obscured, however, by the NRSV's periphrastic translation. Here is a more literal rendering: the priests who offer gifts according to the Law in the earthly sanctuary "serve a sketch and shadow of the heavenly one, *just as it was made known in a divine oracle* to Moses, when he was going to complete the tent; for 'See,' it says, 'you will make everything *according to the typos* that was shown to you on the mountain.'" The point of the sentence in Greek is not, as the NRSV suggests, that Moses was sternly warned to follow directions closely.[17] Rather, the point that interests the author of Hebrews is that Exod 25:40 describes what Moses saw on the mountain as the τύπος, the ideal heavenly pattern; the divine voice thereby reveals that the earthly sanctuary is only a "sketch and shadow" of that reality. (As commentators regularly note, we find a very similar reading of Exod 25:40 in Philo's *On the Life of Moses*.)[18] This interpretation of Heb 8:5 is confirmed in the next chapter, when our author insists that Christ's priestly work was not performed in a humanly made ἀντίτυπος but in the real thing, in heaven (9:23–24). All of this serves the New Covenantal argument by emphasizing once again that the role of the sanctuary prescribed in the Torah was provisional in character, never intended to be other than a foreshadowing of the reality of Christ's priestly offering. The same point is underscored by the repeated character of the Levitical sacrifices, set in contrast to the definitive sacrifice offered once for all (ἐφάπαξ) by Jesus (9:12). My chief point here is that, once again, the argument of Hebrews turns on the exegesis of an OT text: the Exodus narrative itself is used to prove the secondary and derivative character of the earthly sanctuary.

(5) The clearest expression of "New Covenantalism" in Hebrews appears, of course, in chapter 8, where the author quotes in extenso Jeremiah's prophecy of "a new covenant with the house of Israel" (8:8–13, citing Jer. 31:31–34 [38:31–34 LXX]) and argues—once again employing a version of the argument from sequence—that *the promise of a new covenant implies that the old one was in some way deficient.* God's very speech-act of referring to a new covenant effectually consigns the first covenant to the past (see especially 8:13). Because

17. Notice that the NRSV reshapes the logic of the sentence, leaving καθώς untranslated and relocating the γάρ. In the Greek sentence, it is much clearer that the quotation of Exod 25:40 provides the warrant for the primary assertion made in the first clause of Heb 8:5a.

18. See, among many other references in Philo, *Moses* 2.74. For discussion, see Harold W. Attridge, *The Epistle to the Hebrews*, Hermeneia (Philadelphia: Fortress, 1989), 222–24. The independently attested presence of this interpretation in Philo demonstrates that the interpretative strategy of Hebrews can hardly be labeled anti-Jewish at this point.

this passage is central to the topic considered in this paper, we must devote a little more time to consideration of it.

(a) First, we should note that the comments with which Hebrews frames the Jeremiah quotation are more ambiguous than English translations ordinarily suggest. In 8:8a, there is a difficult text-critical problem: should we read αὐτούς (with ℵ*, A, D*, et al.) or αὐτοῖς (with p[46], ℵ[2], B, D[2], m, et al.)? In the one case, we would translate, "For, finding fault with them, he says . . ." In the other case, we would translate, "For, finding fault [with the first covenant], he says to them . . ."[19] The former interpretation has the advantage of agreeing with the actual content of the quotation, which indicates that the demise of the first covenant was a result of the people's failure to keep it: "they did not continue in my covenant, and so I had no concern for them, says the Lord" (v. 9). But, on the other hand, the latter interpretation agrees better with the framing argument in Heb 8, which seems to locate the fault not in the people's unfaithfulness but in the covenant itself: "If that first covenant had been *faultless* (ἄμεμπτος), no place would have been sought for a second" (8:7; cf. Rom. 8:3). Because the immediately following first word of Heb 8:8, μεμφόμενος, picks up the language of *fault*, it is more natural to suppose that the blame falls on the earlier covenant—an inference reinforced in verse 13 by the author's concluding comment, which addresses the passing away of the covenant itself. Thus, it is not hard to see how the divergent textual traditions in verse 8a might have arisen: one reading correlates better with the framing argument of Hebrews, the other with what the Jeremiah quotation appears to say. Theologically speaking, it is not too difficult to put these ideas together. The inadequacy of the first covenant may be thought to consist precisely in its inability to create an obedient people, as suggested also in 10:1: the sacrifices offered under the Law can never "make perfect those who approach." Consequently, the people's failure to continue in the covenant is itself a symptom of the covenant's shortcoming, and God's solution to this problem is the creation of a new covenant in which the Law will be effectually written on the hearts and minds of the people (8:10–11).

(b) Our author's concluding comment in verse 13 is perhaps slightly less negative than suggested by the NRSV, which uses the word "obsolete" to describe the first covenant. What Hebrews actually says is that God has "made old" the first covenant (πεπαλαίκεν). Once again, this must be understood as an *exegetical* remark: it is precisely by the speech-act of declaring a new cove-

19. For a defense of the latter interpretation, see Johannes L. P. Wolmarans, "The Text and Translation of Hebrews 8.8," *ZNW* 75 (1984): 139–44.

nant, in Jer 31:31, that God has made the previous one old. A literal translation of Heb 8:13a would read, "In saying 'new' he has made the first old." The point is significant not only because it once again offers a strong textual/exegetical warrant for understanding Hebrews as an expression of New Covenantalism but also because it indicates that the change of covenant hinges upon an act of God, an eschatological declaration that brings a new situation into being.

(c) As we have observed briefly before, our author gives no indication in his comments that this new covenant is meant for anyone other than "the house of Israel and . . . the house of Judah" (8:8). The gentile church appears nowhere in the picture. Harold Attridge asserts that Heb 8 ignores Jeremiah's message of hope for Israel and remarks—wrongly, in my judgment—that "our author is not particularly interested in the context of what he cites."[20] On the contrary, in light of the pervasive "new exodus" imagery throughout Hebrews, it seems more probable that Hebrews represents a form of Jewish "restoration eschatology";[21] indeed, the burden of proof would lie strongly on any other way of reading the text. The Qumran texts, of course, provide a clear precedent for the use of "new covenant" language by a Jewish sectarian community to describe their own system of teachings and practices over against other Jewish interpretative options.[22]

(d) As we have already noted, the author of Hebrews is not interested in a blanket abolition of the Mosaic Torah. Rather, his concern focuses narrowly on the cultic practice of offering sacrifices for sins under the first covenant, particularly on the Day of Atonement, as Heb 9 will show. The new covenant instituted by Jesus provides an alternative way for purification and atonement through Jesus's once-for-all offering of his own blood. But to generalize the new covenant language of Heb 8 into a comprehensive negation of Torah is to go far beyond anything found in the text.

The cumulative force of these observations is to suggest that the classic "new covenant" chapter in Hebrews has often been overinterpreted through a supersessionist hermeneutical framework. *The possibility should at least be considered that the author's use of the new covenant image in Hebrews envisions not*

20. Attridge, *Hebrews*, 227.

21. On this topic, see E. P. Sanders, *Jesus and Judaism* (Philadelphia: Fortress, 1985), 77–119. I am also indebted to my student Alicia Myers for her unpublished paper "Exodus Typology in Hebrews 8:3–13" (Duke University, 2006), which argues for reading the new covenant imagery of Hebrews in light of Israel's "new exodus" tradition.

22. See 1QpHab 2.1–10; 1QS (Community Rule) 6.18–19; 8.20–21; 19.34; 20.11–13. For discussion of these passages, see Susanne Lehne, *The New Covenant in Hebrews*, JSNTSup 44 (Sheffield: JSOT Press, 1990), 43–54.

the rejection but the restoration of Israel; if so, Heb 8 is less discontinuous with the original sense of Jer 31 than Christian historical critics have often supposed.

(6) Yet another scriptural argument for newness appears in the tenth chapter of Hebrews, this time quoting Ps 40—or, more precisely, Ps 39 LXX. The author is arguing in defense of the boldly stated thesis that "it is impossible for the blood of bulls and goats to take away sins" (Heb 10:4). How can this be so, if these sacrifices are in fact explicitly commanded in the Torah? And how then are sins to be dealt with? The answers to these questions are found in the Septuagintal psalm text: *God takes no pleasure in (the former) sacrifices, but God has prepared a body for Jesus so that Jesus will be able to offer himself as the one truly pleasing sacrifice (Heb 10:5–10).* We learn here, perhaps with some surprise, that the speaker of this psalm is in fact Jesus, and that he uttered these lines "when he came into the world."[23] As Hebrews reads the psalm, it explicitly declares that the ancient animal sacrifices are now replaced by the once-for-all offering of Jesus (ἐφάπαξ again), and that his death was an act of radical obedience to God's will, in accordance with what is written in Scripture ("the scroll of the book"). While a modern historical-critical interpreter can pose numerous objections to this interpretation—starting with the fact that the LXX's phrase "a body you have prepared for me" departs drastically from the Hebrew text—the argument has a certain undeniable force if one grants the hermeneutical assumption that Jesus is the speaker in the psalm. Once again here we encounter an exegetical argument based on the sequence of statements in the text: the text *first* states that God has not taken pleasure in sacrifices and offerings according to the Law and *then* provides an alternative in the psalmist's declaration of willing obedience. This sequence allows the author of Hebrews to conclude that "he abolishes the first in order to establish the second" (10:9).

(7) *The great roll call of heroes of faith in chapter 11 offers rich resources for answering our question about how Hebrews engages and carries forward the story of Israel.* Strikingly, what we find here is not so much a "salvation history" as a catalog of examples that illustrate the open-ended future orientation of faith. The chief emphasis of the whole chapter is not just that the biblical characters mentioned here are virtuous examples but that their faith remained fixed on promises that were substantially unfulfilled. As the author's summary puts it near the conclusion of the litany, "Yet all these, though they were

23. On the hermeneutical convention of treating the Psalms as prayers of Jesus Christ, see Richard B. Hays, "Christ Prays the Psalms: Israel's Psalter as Matrix of Early Christology," in *The Conversion of the Imagination* (Grand Rapids: Eerdmans, 2005), 101–18.

attested through faith, did not receive the promise, *since God had provided* (προβλεψαμένου: lit., "foreseen") *something better* so that they would not, apart from us, be made perfect" (11:39–40). The "something better" foreseen by God is of course the new covenant instituted through the work and example of Jesus, who is the ἀρχηγὸν καὶ τελειωτήν of faith. The story of Israel, then, looks forward in eager expectation to Jesus, who brings it to its proper climax (12:1–2). The central message of this retelling of the OT narrative is powerfully articulated in a summary excursus that our author inserts in the middle of his discussion of Abraham (11:13–16). Precisely because these verses digress from the listing of specific examples, they flag the theme that is the hermeneutical key to the whole chapter: "All of these died in faith without having received the promises, but from a distance they saw and greeted them." Even Scripture's greatest heroes continually lived in a state of eschatological expectation, and Israel's story remains incomplete. The figure of Isaac invoking "blessings concerning things to come" (περὶ μελλόντων εὐλόγησεν, v. 20) stands nicely as a synecdoche for the chapter as a whole. In this sense, the exegetical strategy of Heb 11 is typological; we are meant to read Israel's whole story in a figural way as pointing forward to the reality embodied in Jesus. This is shown most clearly by the author's account of Abraham's offering of Isaac, which is presented here as a prefiguration of the death and resurrection of Jesus. Abraham is said to have "considered the fact that God is able even to raise someone from the dead—and ἐν παραβολῇ, he did receive him back" (v. 19).[24] In a parable! This weighty comment gives us the necessary hermeneutical clue to read the whole story of Israel. It is all a vast figural narrative whose true meaning is finally disclosed in Jesus. (I do not mean that Hebrews doubts the historical factuality of the OT narratives; far from it. The point is that the events narrated in Scripture actually happened and that they nonetheless point forward to a christological meaning beyond themselves.)[25]

(8) Finally, even the hortatory material in chapter 12 carries forward this typological reading of the story of Israel by subtly suggesting that *the readers of the letter should identify with Israel in the wilderness*. Perhaps the clearest indication of this connection is found in 12:15, which warns the readers to take care that no "root of bitterness" spring up. This is a clear allusion to Deut 29:18, where the expression "root of bitterness" refers to apostates whose hearts turn

24. For an argument, from a Jewish point of view, that the hope of resurrection is indeed to be found in the Torah, see Jon D. Levenson, *Resurrection and the Restoration of Israel: The Ultimate Victory of the God of Life* (New Haven: Yale University Press, 2006).

25. The most illuminating discussion of figural interpretation known to me remains that of Hans Frei, *The Eclipse of Biblical Narrative* (New Haven: Yale University Press, 1974), 17–37.

away into idolatry and thus bring the Deuteronomic covenant curses down upon the heads of the people. Almost surely, when they hear the warning "See to it that no one fails to obtain the grace of God" (Heb 12:15a), readers are meant to recall the earlier lengthy discussion in chapters 3 and 4 that warned them against having "an evil, unbelieving heart that turns away from the living God" (3:12) and fails, like Israel in the wilderness, to enter God's rest. Similarly, the admonition in Heb 12:5–11 to accept suffering as a sign of belonging to God's family, though it is expressed through a quotation of Prov 3:11–12, undoubtedly echoes the topos addressed to Israel corporately in Deut 8:5: "Know in your heart that as a parent disciplines a child so the LORD your God disciplines you."[26] The immediately following word of encouragement in Heb 12:12–13 draws its imagery directly from the second-exodus traditions of Isaiah: the call to lift drooping hands and strengthen weak knees alludes directly to Isa 35:3, and the call to make "straight paths" probably evokes the promise of end of exile found in Isa 40. Whether or not readers of the letter would have heard these OT allusions, there can be no mistaking the reference to the exodus in the chapter's rhetorical climax (Heb 12:18–29). The images of God's terrifying presence at Mount Sinai create the backdrop for a stunning dissimile, in which the readers are to see that though they have *not* come to the blazing fire and darkness associated with the giving of the first covenant, they are in a situation even more terrifying as they stand before "the heavenly Jerusalem" (v. 22) if they refuse the covenant now offered them by "the one who warns from heaven" (v. 25).[27]

Summary Reflections on the Hermeneutical Strategy of Hebrews

It is time to take stock of what we have observed in this survey of our author's persistent arguments in Hebrews that Scripture itself bears witness both to the newness and to the superiority of the new covenant offered through Jesus Christ. Our conclusions can be summarized fairly briefly.

(1) *First, there is not a trace of anti-Judaism in these texts,* or any sense that God has rejected Israel in favor of gentile believers in Jesus. All of the warnings about Israel's faithlessness and failure are expressed in the language and imag-

26. This insight was impressed upon me by the research of another Duke doctoral student, Matthew Thiessen, who noted that exactly the same disciplinary imagery found in Heb 12 appears also in Wis 11:19–20 and in Philo (*Moses* 1.199 and *On the Preliminary Studies* 163–177) to describe Israel's period of testing in the wilderness: Matthew Thiessen, "Hebrews and the End of the Exodus," *NovT* 49 (2007): 353–69.

27. On the figure of dissimile, see Hays, *Echoes of Scripture in the Letters of Paul,* 140–43.

ery of Deuteronomy, the Psalms, and the Prophets. In this respect, Hebrews is no more supersessionist than Jeremiah. The identity of the implied reader of Hebrews appears to be thoroughly Jewish, as suggested by the traditional title, ΠΡΟΣ ΕΒΡΑΙΟΥΣ.

(2) *Israel's Scripture is read as a living and active word* in and through which God continues to speak directly to his people. Nowhere do we find anything analogous to Paul's denigration of the "letter" or the merely written form of Israel's sacred text.[28] In Hebrews, Scripture is repeatedly cited as authoritative and regarded with great reverence.

(3) When the old covenant is contrasted unfavorably to the new, *the specific deficiency of the old is described exclusively in terms of the ancient sacrificial cult as a means of atonement for sins*. At no point does Hebrews suggest that the OT is legalistic, that it leads to self-righteousness, that its moral laws are in any way inadequate, or that its conception of God stands in need of correction.

(4) What I have called *the argument from sequence* is repeatedly invoked by the author of Hebrews. This suggests both an alertness to the *narrative* order of Israel's Scripture and a conviction that God's purpose has a sequential, linear logic to it; the most recent revelation "in these last days" is fuller and more comprehensive than what was revealed in former times. This is surely a relatively unusual way of thinking in Mediterranean antiquity, which normally thought of ancient truth as superior to new ideas. The persistent emphasis in Hebrews on the *new* results not from an evolutionary idea of progress, but from the conviction that God has acted through the death and resurrection of Jesus to do something unprecedented—that is, to inaugurate a new covenant for Israel, precisely as Israel's ancient Scripture had anticipated.

(5) *Exodus typology* repeatedly surfaces throughout the letter's argument. The story of the exodus becomes the narrative template for the author's interpretation of the situation of the community in the present time. Readers of the letter are not encouraged to gloat over their superiority to unfaithful Israel; rather, they are encouraged to understand themselves as standing in a situation precisely analogous to the situation of Israel in the wilderness.[29] Matthew Thiessen aptly summarizes the effect created by this theological and

28. In my view, Paul's antithesis between the letter and the spirit (2 Cor 3:6) should not in fact be interpreted as a denigration of Scripture—far from it—but his bold figurative language in this difficult passage has left open the possibility of a misreading along these lines. On the interpretation of 2 Cor 3, see Hays, *Echoes of Scripture in the Letters of Paul*, 122–53.

29. In this respect, the exhortations of Hebrews closely parallel the hermeneutical strategy of Paul in 1 Cor 10:1–22. For analysis of this text, see Hays, *Echoes of Scripture in the Letters of Paul*, 91–104; Hays, *Conversion of the Imagination*, 8–12.

rhetorical device: "The Letter to the Hebrews thus envisions its audience at the very same spot that the book of Deuteronomy envisions the people of Israel: at the doorstep of God's promised land of rest."[30]

(6) A corollary of the last point is that *Hebrews—despite its conviction that Jesus has in fact completed his atoning work in the heavenly sanctuary—retains a remarkably open-ended eschatology* that continues to look to the future for the consummation of salvation. This future-oriented hope appears repeatedly throughout the letter; to take a single example, consider 9:28: "so also Christ, having been offered once to bear the sins of many, will appear a second time, apart from sin, to those who are eagerly awaiting him for salvation." Both author and readers are conscious of being engaged in a struggle in the present time. This is powerfully articulated in the hortatory word of the final chapter: "For here we have no lasting city, but we are looking for the city that is to come" (13:14). People who speak in this way make it clear that they stand within Israel's ongoing and unfinished story. Hebrews, like Deuteronomy, teaches its readers to understand themselves as "the wandering people of God."[31] A strong dialectical eschatology tends to temper triumphalist supersessionism, for those who know that they have no lasting city are likely to recognize that they themselves stand under impending judgment. Perhaps they are also more likely to recognize the provisional character of their own understanding and to acknowledge that God's ultimate redemptive grace may yet hold surprises.

(7) Implicit in all we have been saying is that *Hebrews reads Israel's story figurally*. Just as the earthly sanctuary is a figurative representation that points truly to the heavenly typos, so also the events of Israel's past took place ἐν παραβολῇ. Understood rightly, they point beyond themselves to foreshadow the reality embodied in Jesus. This is precisely the point at which the charge of supersessionism often arises, but wrongly so. The typological strategy of Hebrews does not—contrary to the earlier opinion of Hays (!)—"annul" Scripture, nor does it disinherit Israel. On the contrary, it embraces and confirms Israel's story as truly revelatory, even though incomplete. Those throughout Israel's past who looked to God in faith saw and welcomed the promises "from a distance" but nonetheless truly. Abel, Enoch, Noah, Abraham, Sarah, Isaac, Jacob,

30. Thiessen, "End of the Exodus," 369.

31. In that sense, Ernst Käsemann correctly identified a central theological motif of the letter, even though his speculations about the letter's history-of-religions background have proven unsustainable (Ernst Käsemann, *Das wandernde Gottesvolk: Eine Untersuchung zum Hebräerbrief*, 2nd ed., FRLANT 55 [Göttingen: Vandenhoeck & Ruprecht, 1957 (1939)]).

Joseph, Moses, Rahab, Gideon, Barak, Samson, Jephthah, David, Samuel, and the prophets all truly belong to the great cloud of witnesses.[32]

But what of their genetic descendants among the Jewish people at the time of the writing of the Letter to the Hebrews? What of those within the house of Israel and the house of Judah who do not recognize Jesus as the mediator of a new covenant? In all honesty, we must acknowledge that the question never comes up in this letter. There is no passage analogous to Rom 9–11 in which the fate of unbelieving Israel is directly contemplated. The usual Christian response has been to assume that they are excluded from salvation. But I would like to offer another theological possibility. Would not the logic of Hebrews' own symbolic world allow us to propose that they, too, insofar as they continue to trust in the God of Abraham, Isaac, and Jacob, greet the promises from afar? If so, perhaps Christian interpreters could and should transitively reverse the affirmation with which Heb 11 ends: the "something better" that God has prepared for us surely must include the hope that we will not be made perfect apart from them.[33]

Hebrews as Self-Consuming Artifact

Granting all that we have observed here, the question of the final theological coherence of the Letter to the Hebrews remains unanswered. I promised in my opening remarks to address Wedderburn's contention that Hebrews saws off the branch on which it sits. Both with regard to its quasi-Platonist cosmology and with regard to its appropriation of the imagery of the OT sacri-

32. The position taken here stands in some contrast to that of Eisenbaum, *Jewish Heroes of Christian History*. In this work, her dissertation, Eisenbaum argues that "the heroes of Hebrews are alienated individuals with no national affiliation" (219). This interpretative strategy allows them to be reappropriated as a part of Christian history: "The author of Hebrews no longer sees scripture as the history of Israel; it is now the pre-Christ history of Christians. Abraham and Moses are not Israelites or Jews, they are *Christians*" (220, emphasis in original). Just as the present essay represents a rethinking of my earlier understanding of Hebrews, so Eisenbaum's more recent work (see notes 4 and 5, above) suggests that a reconsideration of her earlier judgments on this matter is necessary.

33. A word of clarification: by venturing this proposal, I do not mean to suggest that the author of Hebrews would have envisioned a two-covenant scheme in which the Jewish people can be saved apart from Christ. Rather, I mean to suggest a possibility closely analogous to Paul's hope in Rom 11:25–36 that in some now unforeseeable way God's eschatological salvation *through Christ* will include not only the great cloud of Israel's witnesses who lived before the time of Jesus but also "all Israel" in later times as well.

ficial cult, Wedderburn writes, "the author's argument leads him to positions which seemingly call in question the presuppositions on which his previous argument had been based and on which it depended for its force and validity."[34] The pervasive use of the imagery of sacrifice in Hebrews illustrates the problem: if the blood of animals actually had no power to take away sins and if God desires only radical human obedience, not blood sacrifices (10:4–10), then why is it necessary for the heavenly sanctuary to be purified with the blood of Christ (9:23–26), and why does our author insist that the blood of Christ is necessary to purify our conscience (9:14)? As Wedderburn observes, "Hebrews seems to persist resolutely with cultic terminology even after it has, to all intents and purposes, dealt the cultic way of thought a coup de grace." According, then, to Wedderburn's reading, "the imagery cannot be taken at face value, but rather comes apart at the seams as soon as one examines it closely enough."[35] This is not necessarily a bad thing in Wedderburn's view, because it exposes the paradoxes and contradictions inherent in any human attempt to speak about God. The problem is, however, that, in contrast to an intentionally "self-subverting" apophatic theologian like Pseudo-Dionysius, our author stumbles into these problems naively. "The fault of the *auctor ad Hebraeos* is not so much his incoherence as his failure to perceive that he has been incoherent and that he indeed must be incoherent, given the nature of that which he sets out to describe."[36]

Wedderburn's sharp questions raise issues close to the heart of the mystery of the hermeneutics of Hebrews—and, I would suggest, issues of crucial importance for grasping how this letter's New Covenantalism carries forward Israel's tradition—or fails to. Nonetheless, I would propose that Wedderburn stops just short of grasping how the self-subverting arguments of Hebrews actually function rhetorically and theologically.

In order to approach this question, I must take you on an unexpected detour by explaining briefly the central thesis of a book by Stanley Fish, entitled *Self-Consuming Artifacts*.[37] This is an early work by Fish (1972), written back in the days when he still believed there was a text in this class and that the text exercised powerful and specifiable effects upon the reader. Fish distinguishes between two types of literature, which he calls "self-satisfying" and

34. Wedderburn, "Sawing Off the Branches," 393.

35. Wedderburn, "Sawing Off the Branches," 409.

36. Wedderburn, "Sawing Off the Branches," 413.

37. Stanley E. Fish, *Self-Consuming Artifacts: The Experience of Seventeenth-Century Literature* (Berkeley: University of California Press, 1972). Subsequent citations of this work will be given by parenthetical page numbers in the text.

"self-consuming." The self-satisfying type reinforces the opinions its readers already hold and validates their categories for interpreting the world. The self-consuming type, on the other hand, unsettles and challenges its readers and destabilizes their interpretative categories; it seeks to produce "nothing less than a conversion" (2). The characteristic argumentative strategy of such works is dialectical, and the author takes the role of the "good physician" who prescribes medicine that may be painful but ultimately produces "a kind of saving by undoing" (2, citing John Milton). These pieces of literature are "self-consuming" in two senses: first, "the reader's self (or at least his inferior self) is consumed as he responds to the medicinal purging of the dialectician's art," and second, "that art, like other medicines," is itself consumed—the text negates or deconstructs itself as it leads the reader to the desired end (3). Fish's point is nicely articulated by a citation from Wittgenstein's *Tractatus Logico-Philosophicus* that he places as an epigraph to his study:

> My propositions serve as elucidations in the following way: anyone who understands me eventually recognizes them as nonsensical, when he has used them—as steps—to climb up beyond them. (He must, so to speak, throw away the ladder after he has climbed up it.) He must transcend these propositions, and then he will see the world aright. (vi)

Now one might suppose that this sort of paradoxical self-negation in literature would be a characteristic of modern and postmodern texts, but Fish compellingly traces it back to antiquity. His textbook examples are Plato's *Phaedrus* and Augustine's *On Christian Doctrine*. The bulk of the study treats seventeenth-century authors such as Donne, Herbert, Bunyan, and Milton. What all of these authors have in common, according to Fish, is a deep perception of the ultimate inadequacy of rational discursive categories to grasp transcendent truth. They therefore use language not "to construct internally coherent artifacts whose strength lies in their conformability to the limitations of the human mind," but rather "to push [their] auditors beyond their confining horizons" (21).

Listen to Fish's description of the characteristic strategy of this sort of dialectical art: "the reader is first invited to consider a problem in terms with which he is likely to be familiar (and therefore comfortable) and then forced by some unexpected turn in the argument to reconsider not the problem, but the terms" (32). Through the repeated application of this argumentative strategy, at ever higher levels, the reader's understanding of the concepts employed in the argument is "refined to the point where the concepts more or less disappear"

(32). That is, the signs in the text finally point away from the text itself until the reader is able to see beyond it. And what is beyond it will, in the case of Fish's example of Augustine, always be "another instance of the only lesson the Bible ever teaches: love of God and love of one's neighbor for the sake of God. Anything else is an illusion, created by the distorted glass of a limited and darkened perspective" (22).

In light of all this, I offer you a simple proposition: the self-subverting tendencies that Wedderburn finds in Hebrews should serve as clues that this λόγος τῆς παρακλήσεως is precisely the sort of self-consuming artifact that Fish describes, meant to lead the reader beyond its own rhetoric to an encounter with the living God. Wedderburn seems certain, for reasons he does not explain, that the unknown and unknowable author of Hebrews was oblivious to the paradoxical character of his homily. I see no reason to make this uncharitable assumption about an author of such remarkable rhetorical skill—but in any case all we have is the text itself. The author died, but through his text he still speaks. And it seems to me that his text functions in very much the same way that Fish so discerningly delineates. Let me illustrate with three examples.[38]

(1) Readers of Hebrews are invited to consider the problem, in terms universally familiar in Hellenistic antiquity, of *how they might ascend from the finite realm of sense impression to the heavenly world*. They are offered a way to do this through Jesus, the Son of God, "the reflection of God's glory" who is exalted above the angels. But unexpectedly, they discover that this preexistent heir of all things shared in blood and flesh, that the new means of access to the nonmaterial heavenly realm is through the curtain of Jesus's flesh, and that he has cleansed their consciences through the embarrassingly palpable act of sprinkling his own human blood around in the heavenly sanctuary, in the very presence of God. *This stunning paradox short-circuits the categories of the Platonic worldview* and invites the readers to reconsider the terms—to rethink what they thought they knew about reality, particularly about the relation between God and creation. Perhaps the heavenly world is not so nonmaterial as we thought.

(2) Readers of Hebrews are invited to consider *the problem of how they might receive atonement for sins*—a problem particularly pressing for Jewish readers if Eisenbaum is right in placing Hebrews after the destruction of the Jerusalem temple. They are reassured that they do have a faithful and compas-

38. The first two examples that follow are the issues raised by Wedderburn's essay, here narrated in a way that demonstrates the usefulness of Fish's categories for interpreting the textual tensions in Hebrews that Wedderburn finds so unsatisfactory. One clarification is perhaps necessary: Fish does not discuss Hebrews in his book; the application of his categories to Hebrews is my own.

sionate new high priest in Jesus, who can sympathize with their weaknesses and who will represent them before God. But unexpectedly, they discover that this high priest is also the sacrificial victim whose death and offering of his own blood was the once-for-all act that brought an end to the sacrificial system and instituted a new covenant in which "there is no longer any offering for sin" (10:18). *This stunning paradox short-circuits the categories of the Mosaic covenant* and invites the readers to reconsider the terms—to rethink what they thought they knew about reality, particularly the connection between sacrifice and forgiveness.

(3) One final example—and with this example, we leave behind the issues raised by Wedderburn and return to the problem of supersessionism with which this essay began. Readers of Hebrews are invited to consider *the problem of how they might carry forward the story of Israel*—perhaps in a time when Israel's very existence as a people was fundamentally threatened by the loss of Jerusalem, their historic political and spiritual center. They are encouraged to identify themselves as Israel in the wilderness, exhorted directly by the word of God not to grumble and rebel, not to harden their hearts, and to seek to enter the land of promised rest. They are inspired by the stories of Israel's patriarchs and heroes who trusted in God in times of terrible adversity. They are assured that though they may be suffering now they are being disciplined as God's own children, just as Deuteronomy had explained, and they are exhorted to show endurance and trust in God. All these categories would be deeply familiar to faithful Jews of the Second Temple era. They are even assured, as the argument reaches its climax in chapter 12, that in their wilderness journey they have moved beyond the terrifying mountain where God spoke to Moses, and that in this new exodus experience they have come to the very verge of entering "the city of the living God, the heavenly Jerusalem" where they will receive an unshakeable kingdom. But unexpectedly, in the final chapter of the homily, they are not invited to enter the city. Instead, they are called to go "outside the camp," to the place where Jesus suffered "outside the city gate in order to sanctify the people by his own blood." They are called to bear the same abuse he suffered, "for here we have no lasting city" (13:12–14). In short, while awaiting "the city that is to come," they are summoned to look to Jesus, the pioneer and perfecter of faith who endured the cross, and to allow their lives to be conformed to the example of his faithfulness. *This paradoxical vocation short-circuits the categories of triumphalist politics and religion*, and it invites the readers to reconsider the terms—to rethink what they thought they knew about reality, particularly about the relation between Israel's God and self-satisfying religion.

Hebrews, then, however elegant its rhetorical surface, is finally a self-consuming artifact. Readers drawn into this dialectical discourse of the new covenant will find themselves challenged, destabilized, and ultimately transformed. The New Covenantalism of Hebrews is certainly not supersessionist in the classic sense that it replaces one religious system with a new stable religious system that allows readers to stand in a position of secure superiority. Instead, they find themselves "naked and laid bare" (4:13); they are summoned on a pilgrimage in which they identify with Israel in the wilderness and are constantly compelled to confess, "Here we have no lasting city." To use Fish's descriptions one last time, Hebrews is not "a presentation that leaves the mind complacent and self-satisfied"; rather, it is a self-consuming "presentation that unsettles the mind and demands, literally, that it change" (76–77).[39] The Letter to the Hebrews therefore does precisely what Augustine, on Fish's reading, claims a sermon should do: "a sermon that is true to Augustine's *ars praedicandi* will in the end give itself over to God, just as it will give over to God the selves of its charges. It will thus be self-consuming" (42–43). This is so for one fundamental theological reason: the author of Hebrews has deeply grasped the theological truth that stands at the climax[40] of the letter's argument: "indeed our God is *a consuming fire*" (12:29).

39. Like Augustine's teaching, Hebrews demands "a total reorientation (conversion) of being, which involves an inversion of earthly values and a rejection of conventional ways of knowing, a turning of the world, as our natural faculties receive it, upside down" (Fish, *Self-Consuming Artifacts*, 23).

40. If Craig Koester's rhetorical analysis is correct, this powerful depiction of God is located right at the beginning of the homily's peroration (*Hebrews*, AB 36 [New York: Doubleday, 2001], 83–86, 554–57).

18

Humanity

Bultmann's Misreading of Pauline Anthropology

"Man Prior to the Revelation of Faith," the title of the first major section of Rudolf Bultmann's treatment of "The Theology of Paul," already hints at the contours of his interpretation of Paul's thought. Bultmann proposes a reading that focuses on "Man"—that is, on theological *anthropology*. And the "plot" of this reading is scripted by an *ordo salutis* in which everything hinges on the existential decision of the individual person to respond in faith to God's grace. As I shall explain, this approach to interpreting the theology of Paul—an approach meant to address the apologetic concerns of the mid-twentieth-century German academy—now seems deeply problematical.

The task of composing a critical evaluation of this section of Bultmann's hugely influential *Theology of the New Testament* has been, for me, a trip back in the time machine to a very different era in NT studies—an era that formed the ethos of my own early theological education but that now seems remote and rather strange. It is a bit like the disconcerting experience of going back to one's high school reunion after more than forty years: there are familiar and welcome memories, but one also quickly becomes aware of how much has changed, how one's own view of the world has been altered across time, and how impossible it is to go home again.

I first read Bultmann in 1967, as an undergraduate. My now dog-eared and taped-together paperback copy of Kendrick Grobel's English translation subsequently accompanied me through the years of seminary, served as a frequent reference and sparring partner during my doctoral studies, and came off the shelf often when I later taught seminars on NT theology. Yet to read through the whole thing freshly now is to be confronted anew by the strangeness and instability of Bultmann's ambitious project. Is it really possible to "translate" Paul's Christ-centered Jewish apocalyptic discourse into the idiom of a demythologized twentieth-century existentialism? When the question is posed that way, a negative answer seems inevitable.

Yet anyone seeking to pursue the theological interpretation of Scripture is faced with a formidable task analogous to Bultmann's project: to give a faithful descriptive explication of the historically situated content of the biblical texts while at the same time seeking to be guided, as Bultmann put it, by "the presupposition that they have something to say to the present."[1] The critique that I shall offer in the following pages may therefore, precisely in and through its severity, serve as a chastening and cautionary word to all of us who try to meet the challenges of theological hermeneutics in our own day and to grapple with what these texts have to say to us.

In the compass of this brief essay, I cannot possibly engage all the exegetical issues raised in Bultmann's extended treatment of "Man Prior to the Revelation of Faith."[2] I propose, therefore, to focus attention on four of Bultmann's major methodological decisions, key structural choice points that shape his presentation of Paul's thought. They are as follows: (1) Bultmann's decision to explicate Paul's theology chiefly as anthropology, (2) the decision to read Paul against the history-of-religions backdrop of a hypothetical Hellenistic Christianity influenced more by mystery religions and Gnosticism than by Israel's Scripture and Jewish tradition, (3) the decision to focus on individual words and concepts as the primary vehicle for interpreting Paul's theology, and (4) the explicit decision to employ a demythologizing hermeneutic to unfold the "real intention" underlying Paul's explicit statements. Our discussion of these interrelated methodological moves will identify several substantive theological issues that demand scrutiny. But at every point, it should be recognized, Bultmann's treatment of the issues in Pauline theology is heavily conditioned by the *methodological* commitments that frame his analysis.

1. Rudolf Bultmann, *Theology of the New Testament*, trans. Kendrick Grobel, 2 vols. (New York: Scribner, 1951–1955 [1948–1953]), 2:251. Subsequent citations of this work appear in the text and provide the volume and page numbers in parentheses.

2. Parenthetically, I wonder just a little about Grobel's English rendering of Bultmann's chapter title. The German is "Der Mensch vor der Offenbarung der πίστις." Bultmann's "vor" might be understood as having a sense that is not only temporal but also figuratively spatial: man (standing) before the revelation of faith. The ambiguity of the German would be better preserved if the English translation of the unit were given as "Man before the Revelation of Faith."

Theology as Anthropology

In the opening pages of "Man Prior to the Revelation of Faith," Bultmann describes his reasons for focusing his discussion on Paul's *anthropology*. Observing that Pauline theology is "not a speculative system," he affirms that Paul is concerned not with some notion of God *in se*, but "only with God as he is significant for man, for man's responsibility and man's salvation." Thus, "every assertion about God is simultaneously an assertion about man and vice versa. For this reason, and in this sense, Paul's theology is at the same time anthropology." Likewise, "every assertion about Christ is also an assertion about man and vice versa; and Paul's christology is simultaneously soteriology" (1:190–91). These statements—reminiscent of the famous methodological meditation at the beginning of Calvin's *Institutes*[3]—are certainly accurate observations about Paul's thought. Paul's discourse about God and Christ is always concerned to explicate God's action *pro nobis*, and therefore his theological and christological affirmations do necessarily entail anthropological and theological corollaries.

Having begun, however, with these unimpeachable observations, Bultmann suddenly leaps to an assertion that seems unwarranted and one-sided: "Therefore, Paul's theology can best be treated as his doctrine of man: first, of man prior to the revelation of faith, and second, of man under faith, for in this way the anthropological and soteriological orientation of Paul's theology is brought out" (1:191). Why is this approach "best"? Why not the other way around? Why are the anthropological and soteriological dimensions of Paul's theology not best explicated as entailments of his proclamation about God's action in and through Jesus Christ (as Bultmann's contemporary Karl Barth insisted they should be)? This is a fateful decision because it determines the vantage point for all that follows. Everything in Paul's complex theological reflections is seen, as it were, from the side of the human experience, rather than from the side of the narrative proclamation of the gospel. Here Bultmann is following a well-established trajectory in German Protestant theology that dates back at least to Friedrich Schleiermacher. But I would venture the suggestion that this

3. "Nearly all the wisdom we possess, that is to say, true and sound wisdom, consists of two parts: the knowledge of God and of ourselves" (John Calvin, *Institutes of the Christian Religion*, ed. John T. McNeill, trans. Ford L. Battles, LCC 20 [Philadelphia: Westminster, 1960], 1.1.1, p. 35). It is telling, however, to note how Calvin finally decides to proceed: "Yet, however the knowledge of God and of ourselves may be mutually connected, the order of right teaching requires that we discuss the former first, then proceed afterward to treat the latter" (*Institutes* 1.1.3, p. 37). Bultmann makes the opposite methodological choice.

methodological decision causes him to place the accents of Paul's thought in the wrong places. Indeed, I would suggest that—contrary to Bultmann's own intention—he risks reducing Paul's message to an anthropocentric meditation on human religious psychology, its limits, and its possibilities. (I am mindful of the small irony that here I am applying a bit of Bultmannian *Sachkritik* to the master of the method.)

To take a particularly striking example, after citing 1 Cor 15:24–26, a dramatic passage that declares that Christ will hand all things over to God the Father after triumphing over all powers, including death as the final enemy, Bultmann remarkably comments, "In reality, he is thereby only [!] expressing a certain understanding of existence:[4] The spirit powers represent the reality into which man is placed as one full of conflicts and struggle, a reality which threatens and tempts" (1:259). Here Paul's proclamation of God's eschatological triumph over evil and death is converted through Bultmann's anthropocentric emphasis into a message about our human *Daseinsverständnis*; consequently, it becomes a rather banal affirmation that we live in a world where we are surrounded by conflicts and difficulties.

One can find similar examples strewn throughout the pages of "Man Prior to the Revelation of Faith," not always so dramatically reductive as this one, but consistently focusing on *human experience* as the chief subject matter of Paul's thought. We shall return to a further consideration of this *Tendenz* in Bultmann's interpretation when we consider his methodological commitment to demythologizing the texts. Here, however, I am calling attention to the way in which he systematically focuses on the *anthropological* content of Paul's writings as their real and primary sense. This primary focus on anthropology is, it seems to me, a significant reversal of the polarity of Paul's proclamation. Paul emphasizes again and again that his message is a word of revelation—ἀποκάλυψις—from and about God as disclosed in Jesus Christ. To cite just two examples, consider the following emphatic passages:

> For I want you to know, brothers and sisters, that the gospel that was proclaimed by me is not of human origin (κατὰ ἄνθρωπον); for I did not receive it from a human source (παρὰ ἀνθρώπου), nor was I taught it, but I received it through a revelation of Jesus Christ (δι᾿ ἀποκαλύψεως Ἰησοῦ Χριστοῦ). (Gal 1:11–12)

4. German original: "In Wahrheit kommt darin nur ein bestimmtes Daseinsverständnis zum Ausdruck" (*Theologie des Neuen Testaments*, 4th ed. [Tübingen: Mohr, 1961 (1948–1953)], 1:259). All subsequent citations of Bultmann's German text are taken from this edition.

> And we also thank God continually because, when you received the word of God, which you heard from us, you accepted it not as a human word (lit., "a word of human beings," λόγον ἀνθρώπων) but as it actually is, the word of God, which is indeed at work in you who believe. (1 Thess 2:13)

Bultmann would no doubt say, with justification, that each of these passages is concerned with "God as he is significant for man, for man's responsibility and man's salvation." But this statement runs the risk of misconstruing the *directionality* of Paul's soteriological grammar: the gospel for Paul is a proclamation of good news about *God* and *God's* action for the salvation of the world. This is of course the precise point of controversy in Ernst Käsemann's well-known critique of his teacher: Bultmann's anthropological focus fails to grasp the gospel as the *power* of God for salvation and domesticates it into a word about the possibility of a new self-understanding.[5] It may be a telling fact that neither of the above passages (Gal 1:11–12 and 1 Thess 2:13) appears in the index of scriptural passages cited in Bultmann's *Theology of the New Testament*—an omission all the more startling in a presentation that purports to take "the *Revelation* of Faith" as a hinge point for understanding Paul's thought.

The Hellenistic Thought World and the Erasure of Israel

At the very outset, Bultmann situates Paul "within the frame of Hellenistic Christianity," influenced by its thought forms but also at the same time calling attention to "the problems latent in the Hellenistic proclamation" (1:187). To

5. In his watershed essay "The Righteousness of God in Paul," Käsemann sharply takes issue with Bultmann's translation of Rom 1:16 as "the possibility of salvation (*Die Möglichkeit zum Heil*) is the Gospel." Käsemann writes, "Characteristically, Bultmann chooses the translation which substitutes for the motif of the God who acts and creates and who prevails in the Gospel the quite different motif of an alleged anthropological 'given'" (Käsemann, *New Testament Questions of Today*, trans. W. J. Montague and W. F. Bunge [London: SCM; Philadelphia: Fortress, 1969 (1965)], 173n4). This essay originally appeared as "Gottesgerechtigkeit bei Paulus," *ZTK* 58 (1961): 367–78, and was included, with additional notes, in *Exegetische Versuche und Besinnungen*, vol. 2 (Göttingen: Vandenhoeck & Ruprecht, 1964), 181–93. Again, in a later vigorous polemic against Hans Conzelmann (another of Bultmann's students), Käsemann complains that "misunderstandings . . . arise when one starts from the alternative between theology and anthropology, reduces faith to self-understanding and ends up in a liberal-Protestant variant of Christ as the cultic deity who brings the true gnosis to his people" (Ernst Käsemann, *Perspectives on Paul*, trans. Margaret Kohl [Philadelphia: Fortress, 1971], 77n27; originally *Paulinische Perspektiven* [Tübingen: Mohr Siebeck, 1969], 138n27). It is not hard to see that this barb is really aimed at the master, Bultmann himself.

be sure, Bultmann duly notes Paul's own roots in Hellenistic Judaism. But he questions the tradition that Paul was a pupil of Gamaliel in Jerusalem (Acts 22:3) and finds the most significant fact about Paul's upbringing to be the fact that he was a native of Tarsus in Cilicia, for "in his home city he came into contact with Hellenistic culture and became acquainted with popular philosophy and the phenomena of religious syncretism." Bultmann is not certain whether it was "in his pre-Christian period" that Paul absorbed "theological ideas of this syncretism (those of the mystery-religions and of Gnosticism)," but he opines that such ideas do surely "come out in his Christian theology" (1:187). As this preliminary summary would suggest, Bultmann's account of Paul's history-of-religions background exercises a major influence on his analysis of Paul's thought. Repeatedly in the pages of "Man Prior to the Revelation of Faith," Bultmann explicates various elements in Paul's conceptual world as arising from Hellenistic influences of one sort or another, even when he sees Paul critically qualifying these elements.

Particularly striking is the number of instances in which he identifies hypothetical "Gnostic" sources or backgrounds for Paul's ideas and images. In 2 Cor 5:1–8, Paul "comes very close to Hellenistic-Gnostic dualism" in his deprecation of present embodied existence but avoids this problem by his wish to be "further clothed" in a heavenly body rather than "unclothed" (1:201–2). Again, in 1 Cor 15:44–45, Paul is "influenced . . . by Gnostic usage, with the result that he uses *psyche* in a deprecatory sense. . . . *Psyche* is now (as in Gnosticism) the merely natural, earthly vitality in contrast to the divinely given capacity for eternal life" (1:204).

Indeed, Bultmann (remarkably) finds gnostic motifs throughout Paul's emphatic discussion of the resurrection of the body in 1 Cor 15. For example, "the drama described in 1 Cor 15:20–28 does not come from the tradition of the creation-story, but from Gnostic cosmology and eschatology" (1:228). On the contrary, most NT scholarship today would see this text as one of the passages in Paul that most robustly gives expression to *Jewish apocalyptic* tradition, but Bultmann affirms repeatedly that the notion of God's cosmic triumph derives from a Hellenistic gnostic milieu. Not only in 1 Cor 15 but also in Rom 8:18–39, "Paul is able to appropriate the cosmological mythology of Gnosticism because it enables him to express the fact that the perishable 'creation' becomes a destructive power whenever man decides in favor of it instead of for God" (1:230). Or again, in Paul's account of Adam's transgression as the universal cause of human bondage to sin (Rom 5:12–19), "Paul is unquestionably under the influence of the Gnostic myth" (1:251). (Interestingly, neither here nor in any of the other passages cited in this paragraph does Bultmann specify *what* gnostic myth he has in mind or cite any actual textual evidence for it.) To cite one last example, Bultmann explains the notoriously difficult Gal 3:19 as follows: "Paul can take up the Gnostic myth of the giving of the Law by angels in order to prove that the Law of Moses is not attributable to God himself" (1:268).

All of this is deeply problematical for at least two reasons. First, the older hypothesis of a well-developed pre-Christian Gnosticism, a hypothesis beloved by the *Religionsgeschichtliche Schule* of the early twentieth century, has foundered on the rocks of subsequent scholarly investigation, chiefly because of the absence of textual evidence for such a phenomenon. All the texts that attest a developed system of gnostic mythology date from a historical period demonstrably later than Paul's letters.[6] Many of the narrative or dramatic elements that Bultmann ascribed to a hypothetical Gnosticism are much more easily explained as developments within Paul's own native Jewish tradition, particularly in its apocalyptic forms.

More deeply troubling than Bultmann's speculative hypotheses about Paul's Hellenistic intellectual horizons, however, are the *absences* and gaps in the picture he draws of Paul's thought world. One can read through page after page of "Man Prior to the Revelation of Faith" and find only the most cursory nods to the importance of Israel's Scripture for Paul's theology. Bultmann's Paul has turned his face primarily toward the worlds of Hellenistic philosophy, mystery religions, and gnostic speculation; he seeks in various ways to counter or transform the mythological elements in those worlds, but their symbolic universe nonetheless provides the conceptual furniture for Paul's imagination. By contrast, the story of Israel's election, the fate of God's elect people, the reliability of God's covenant promises to Israel, the Jewish hope for resurrection of the dead, and the actual language of Israel's scriptural story appear only on the periphery of Bultmann's portrait of Paul.[7]

Indeed, while Bultmann does take note of Paul's wrestling with the significance of the Law, the role of that Law has become almost entirely a negative one for the person who has come to faith. Bultmann offers a lengthy and convoluted discussion of the role of Law for "Man Prior to the Revelation of Faith" (1:259–69), but the bottom line of that discussion is this: "*the ultimate purpose*

6. As Bentley Layton notes, "the earliest surviving reference" to an actual group called γνωστικοί appears in the writings of Irenaeus of Lyon, around 180 CE. And none of the writings identified with "Gnosticism" (a notoriously difficult term to define) appeared before the second century CE (*The Gnostic Scriptures* [Garden City, NY: Doubleday, 1987], 5–8).

7. On this point, see also Richard B. Hays, *Echoes of Scripture in the Letters of Paul* (New Haven: Yale University Press, 1989), 7–8.

of the Law is to lead man to death and thereby to let God appear as God" (1:267, emphasis original, both in German and in the English translation).

In order to arrive at this conclusion, Bultmann offers a whole series of highly debatable exegetical judgments about particular passages. He interprets Rom 10:4 to mean that Christ is the *termination* of the Law rather than its goal (τέλος, 1:263). As I have argued elsewhere, this is almost surely a misreading of the text; within the argument of Rom 10, Paul is asserting that Christ is the true end to which Israel's Law points.[8] Again, referring to Gal 5:4 ("You are severed from Christ, you who would be justified by the Law; you have fallen away from grace," RSV), Bultmann asserts that the very effort to keep the Law is already in itself sinful in principle, because it presumes that one can thereby achieve salvation through "self-powered striving" (1:264). But, as much recent commentary has shown, this reading superimposes the Reformation's concern about "self-powered striving" upon an argument that actually is chiefly concerned with whether gentiles must adopt the practices and markers of Jewish ethnic identity.

To give one more example, Bultmann argues that Paul's image of the Law as a παιδαγωγὸς . . . εἰς Χριστόν (Gal 3:24) means that "the 'educating' done by the Law leads . . . into sin" and that this leading into sin is precisely "the purpose of the Law in the history of salvation" (1:266–67). All this is based on the doubtful assertion that Gal 3:19 ("Why then the Law? It was added because of transgressions [τῶν παραβάσεων χάριν]") means that the Law was given "to evoke transgressions"—a reading clearly at odds not only with the internal logic of the metaphor of the παιδαγωγός but also with Gal 3:23, which affirms that "before faith came, we were imprisoned *and guarded* . . . until faith would be revealed."[9] Paul is arguing that the Law had a protective and propaedeutic function, not that it tempted the Jewish people into sinful self-powered striving that led to pride and alienation from God.[10]

8. Hays, *Echoes of Scripture in the Letters of Paul*, 75–77.

9. In this context Bultmann also imports into Rom 4:13–16 the idea that the Law's purpose was to lead humanity into sin. He achieves this interpretation by offering a "translation" into which he has interpolated his own parenthetical gloss asserting that the purpose of the Law was "to yield wrath" and "to cause transgression"—statements not to be found in Paul's text at Rom 4:13–16 (1:265–66).

10. Interestingly, while in my judgment Bultmann's presentation misconstrues the role of the Law in Paul's thought, it does have the virtue of recognizing that Paul's "conversion was not the result of an inner moral collapse. . . . It was not rescue from the despair into which the cleavage between willing and doing had allegedly driven him. His was not a conversion of repentance" (1:188). At this point, Bultmann's interpretation anticipates a

What is almost entirely missing here is adequate attention to Paul's insistence that "the Law is holy, and the commandment is holy and just and good" (Rom 7:12). And more fundamentally, what is missing on Bultmann's radar is any recognition that Paul's argument in Romans is passionately concerned to show that "God has not rejected his people whom he foreknew" (Rom 11:2a). The ongoing significance of Israel as a people is simply elided (or erased) throughout Bultmann's ingenious reading of Paul, and the notion that Paul is concerned to uphold the integrity of God's promises to Israel seemingly plays no role in his interpretation. At every point, instead, the discussion focuses on "Man" (*der Mensch* or *die Menschen*) as a naked generic subject, not significantly conditioned by a specific history (unless it is "the history of mankind," 1:266), and certainly not by God's election of a specific people. I would suggest that Bultmann's neglect of the story of Israel is but one aspect of his larger inattention to the significance of narrative in Paul's thought.[11] But that observation leads directly into our third set of methodological observations.

Theology as Word Study

In retrospect, one of the most curious and unfortunate features of Bultmann's presentation is his methodological decision to approach the exposition of Paul's theology of "Man Prior to the Revelation of Faith" through stringing together a series of word studies on individual terms and concepts: σῶμα, ψυχή, σάρξ, and so forth—in other words, his decision to approach the topic through a study of "anthropological concepts" (*die anthropologischen Begriffe*). Of course, this approach was influenced by the methodology then current in the field of biblical studies, as reflected in Kittel's *Theologisches Wörterbuch zum Neuen Testament*—a methodology that has subsequently come under severe criticism and fallen decidedly out of favor.[12] What I have to say on this matter, therefore, will hardly come as a surprise to most readers today.

The word-study approach has two closely related drawbacks. First, words

theme later highlighted by Krister Stendahl in his landmark essay "The Apostle Paul and the Introspective Conscience of the West," *HTR* 56 (1963): 62–77.

11. On this criticism of Bultmann, see Richard B. Hays, *The Faith of Jesus Christ: The Narrative Substructure of Paul's Theology in Gal 3:1–4:11*, 2nd ed. (Grand Rapids: Eerdmans, 2002 [1983]), 47–52.

12. For the classic broadside against the Kittel methodology, see James Barr, *The Semantics of Biblical Language* (Oxford: Oxford University Press, 1961); see esp. "Some Principles of Kittel's Theological Dictionary," 206–62. Bultmann was, of course, a major contributor

do not carry semantic freight apart from contexts in which they are used. The Kittel approach tends to treat words as concepts whose sense is to be determined through a diachronic investigation of their history, rather than through careful synchronic observation of their usage in particular arguments or contexts. It would be unfair to say that Bultmann completely ignores the contexts in which Paul's anthropological terms occur, but it would be fair to say that he is more interested in developing an understanding of the terms themselves than in explicating the arguments in which they actually appear. So, for example, Bultmann can quite remarkably declare in the very beginning of his explanation of σῶμα ("body") that it would be a "methodological error" to allow our understanding of the term to be influenced by Paul's use of it in 1 Cor 15:35–50, because in this passage "Paul lets himself be misled into adopting his opponents' method of argumentation," and so in this text "he uses the *soma*-concept in a way not characteristic of him elsewhere." Paul's usage of the term here, Bultmann contends, is in fact "un-Pauline" (1:192). The underlying assumption here is that Paul must have an ideal or normative *concept* of σῶμα that transcends his actual use of the term in any particular context—even, in this case, a context where he is making repeated and emphatic use of it in an effort to correct what he regards as the misunderstanding of his readers.

Bultmann's assertion that Paul has been "misled" by his opponents would suggest he recognizes that in 1 Cor 15 the apostle is addressing a particular pastoral situation, a situation that has created certain rhetorical exigencies. But Bultmann neither outlines his understanding of that situation nor attempts to show clearly how Paul's argument confronts it. Instead, he immediately starts surveying other passages more congenial with his own proposal that σῶμα in Paul most fundamentally indicates that "*Man is called sōma in respect to his being able to make himself the object of his own action or to experience himself as the subject to whom something happens*" (1:195, emphasis original). If Paul's passionate discussion of the resurrection body in 1 Corinthians fails to fit this definition, it can simply be set aside as uncharacteristic of Paul's genuine theology. In sum, Bultmann's methodology undervalues both the historically contingent character of Paul's letters[13] and the rhetorical function of the anthropological terms as he actually uses them in his arguments.

to *TWNT*; over the course of his career, he composed twenty-six articles for that widely used reference work.

13. By way of contrast, see the methodology employed by the SBL Pauline Theology Group, which sought to explore Paul's theology through studying the contingent development of his "theologizing" in individual letters. The essays produced by this collaborative group were published in four volumes: Jouette M. Bassler, ed., *Pauline Theology*, vol. 1,

The second major drawback of Bultmann's word-study approach may be illuminated by asking a simple question: why should an exposition of Paul's theology take its starting point from an exposition of the concept of σῶμα? This choice of starting point seems both arbitrary and fragmenting in its effect. If we look to Paul's own discourse, we do not find him launching into disquisitions on the meaning of isolated anthropological terms. Instead, when he identifies the fundamental themes of his own message, he offers concise summaries of a kerygmatic narrative focused on God's saving action in Christ. Consider the following examples:

> You turned to God from idols, to serve a living and true God, and to wait for his Son from heaven, whom he raised from the dead—Jesus, who rescues us from the wrath that is coming. (1 Thess 1:9–10)

> But when the fullness of time had come, God sent his Son, born of a woman, born under the law, in order to redeem those who were under the law, so that we might receive adoption as children. (Gal 4:4–5)

> For I tell you that Christ has become a servant of the circumcised on behalf of the truth of God in order that he might confirm the promises given to the patriarchs, and in order that the Gentiles might glorify God for his mercy. (Rom 15:8–9a)

> For I handed on to you as of first importance what I in turn had received: that Christ died for our sins in accordance with the scriptures, and that he was buried, and that he was raised on the third day in accordance with the scriptures, and that he appeared to Cephas, then to the twelve. (1 Cor 15:3–5)

After citing these examples of Paul's encapsulations of his gospel, I decided to look them up in the index of Bultmann's *Theology*. Here is what I found: according to the index, none of them is discussed anywhere in Bultmann's exposition of "The Theology of Paul." In the preliminary opening pages ("Presuppositions and Motifs of New Testament Theology"), there are just a few glancing references to 1 Thess 1:9–10 and 1 Cor 15:3–5 as part of the kerygma of

Thessalonians, Philippians, Galatians, Philemon (Minneapolis: Fortress, 1991); David M. Hay, ed., *Pauline Theology*, vol. 2, *1 and 2 Corinthians* (Minneapolis: Fortress, 1993); David M. Hay and E. Elizabeth Johnson, eds., *Pauline Theology*, vol. 3, *Romans* (Minneapolis: Fortress, 1995); and E. Elizabeth Johnson, ed., *Pauline Theology*, vol. 4, *Looking Back, Pressing On*, SBL Symposium Series 4 (Atlanta: Scholars, 1997).

the earliest church and/or the Hellenistic church prior to Paul. But Bultmann does not treat them as part of his exposition of Paul's own theology. And, again according to the index, there are no references at all anywhere in Bultmann's book to Gal 4:4–5 or to Rom 15:8–9. These are astonishing omissions.[14]

My point is this: by focusing his exposition of "Man Prior to the Revelation of Faith" on isolated anthropological terms, Bultmann submerges the *story* that constitutes the heart of Paul's gospel. He offers a number of luminous insights into the meaning of this or that term that Paul uses. (See, to cite a single example, his incisive paraphrase of Rom 8:13: "He who derives life out of the transitory must, himself, perish with the perishing of the transitory" [1:247].) But the overall shape of Paul's proclamation is simply lost, replaced by Bultmann's own preoccupation with how human beings can find authentic existence. The stripping away of the kerygmatic narrative allows Paul's anthropological terms to be factored out of his narrative world, paraphrased in modern terminology, assigned a new prominence as proto-philosophical concepts, and eclectically reconstructed into a twentieth-century existentialist theological program whose contours would have been perplexing to the first-century apostle. This reconfiguration of Paul's theology is facilitated by the word-study method, which is particularly well suited to extract concepts (*Begriffe*) while discarding the narrative—or "mythic"—framework in which the concepts originally are found. But this observation leads to the final methodological decision that we must consider in assessing Bultmann's treatment of Paul: his demythologizing hermeneutic.

Demythologizing the Gospel

Bultmann's hermeneutical program of demythologizing the NT has been exhaustively debated by NT scholars and theologians—or at least it was a generation ago. Even if the intensity of the debate has waned in recent years, the importance of the issues raised by Bultmann is perennial. The fundamental

14. I note parenthetically that the index is not comprehensive; instead, it offers a list of "New Testament Passages Discussed (a selection of the more important)." (In the German original, *Stellenverzeichnis [in Auswahl]*.) In fact, in Bultmann's later discussion of "Christ's Death and Resurrection as Salvation-Occurrence," there are passing references to 1 Cor 15:1–4 (1:293) and Gal 4:4–5 (1:297). Still, the fact that these references can be excluded from the "more important" passages discussed speaks volumes about the lines of emphasis in Bultmann's treatment. Similarly, it is worth noticing that the index includes passages from the NT and the Apostolic Fathers but not from the OT.

problem, as Bultmann saw it, is that the NT writers lived and wrote within an ancient worldview characterized by a primitive cosmology that is no longer believable for modern persons living in a scientific age. Consequently, theological interpretation of the NT requires that its "mythological" stories and concepts be translated into different philosophical and linguistic categories that nonetheless preserve and reveal the "real intention" that is implicit in the mythological language employed by the NT authors.

Bultmann's *Theology of the New Testament* is neither an explanation nor a defense of the program of demythologizing; rather, it presupposes the necessity of such a program. The book therefore functions as a *performance*, an embodiment, of the sort of interpretation that Bultmann had advocated in his earlier essays on hermeneutics.[15] The task of such an interpretation is chiefly, as Bultmann pictures it, "the explication of believing self-understanding" (2:251). This conception of the task of NT theology explains, in part, Bultmann's pervasive anthropological focus and his palpable discomfort with the Jewish apocalyptic elements in Paul's proclamation. But it also leads to theological difficulties.

All of this is well-worked ground. My chief task in the last section of this chapter, therefore, is simply to illustrate the way in which Bultmann's demythologizing program manifests itself in his account of "Man Prior to the Revelation of Faith" and to assess the consequences of this approach.

Near the beginning of his treatment of Paul's anthropological concepts, in the discussion of the concept of σῶμα, Bultmann explicitly flies the flag for his hermeneutical agenda. He is grappling with Paul's discussion of the resurrection of the body—an idea that Bultmann finds distinctly problematical. He writes as follows:

> If man were no longer *soma*—if he no longer had a relationship to himself—he would no longer be man. Since Paul's capacity for abstract thinking is not a developed one, and he therefore does not distinguish terminologically between *soma* in the basic sense of that which characterizes human existence and *soma* as the phenomenon of the material body, he connects the idea of somatic existence in the eschatological consummation with a mythological teaching on the resurrection (I Cor. 15). . . . In distinction from this mythology, the real intention of Paul must be made clear. It is that he asserts specific human existence, both before and beyond death, to

15. See particularly "New Testament and Mythology," in *Kerygma and Myth: A Theological Debate*, vol. 1, ed. Hans Werner Bartsch, trans. R. H. Fuller (London: SPCK, 1953 [1941]), 1–44.

> be a somatic existence in the basic sense defined above [i.e., an existence in which man has a relationship to himself]. (1:198)

One must credit Bultmann with putting his hermeneutical cards on the table. Paul, says Bultmann, not having had the benefit of education in a German university, had not developed the "capacity for abstract thinking" necessary to conceive of an existence beyond death in which human beings, having no material body of any kind, will still be capable of having a relationship to themselves. (Whatever that might mean.) Therefore, the "unfortunate consequence" (1:198) is that Paul has recourse to a "mythological teaching on the resurrection" in which he imagines the existence of a "spiritual body." But Bultmann somehow knows that Paul's "real intention" lies not in what he actually wrote but in the abstract idea of a nonmaterial self "determined by the power of God which reconciles the cleft between self and self within a man and hence does presuppose a relationship of man to himself" (1:199).

I can only register the impression that Bultmann's interpretation of Paul at this point is both condescending and reductionistic. In addition, it is unclear whether Bultmann is still envisioning an existence "beyond death" in any temporally future sense, or whether Paul's apocalyptic eschatological vision of the resurrection hope has been subtly replaced by the concept of an integrated personal selfhood that might be attained, or anticipated, within life as we know it in the present age. I say intentionally that this is "unclear," because in the passage cited above we find, as often in Bultmann, a certain slippage between Paul's mythological/apocalyptic language and Bultmann's existentialist reappropriation of it. Whether the ambiguity is intentional or not, there remains a gray area in which Bultmann distances himself from the literal-referential sense of Paul's theological affirmations while still inhabiting them confessionally in some transferred metaphorical sense. At the same time, Bultmann asserts that this transferred sense is Paul's "real intention," even though the conceptualities he employs would have been unavailable to Paul or anyone else in the first century. Perhaps Bultmann's argument would be better served if he had avoided the language of "intention" and argued instead that Paul's formulations are groping dimly toward a reality that can now be more adequately named in a different (modern) linguistic register.

We find something similar in the later discussion of "flesh" and "sin" as "powers to which man falls slave." Bultmann writes,

> Paul can speak of both as personal beings as if they were demonic rulers—but in such a way that we do not have the right actually to ascribe to him

> a mythological concept of "flesh" or "sin." . . . Little as all this constitutes realistic mythology—it is not that but figurative, rhetorical language—it is, nevertheless, clear that this language stamps *flesh and sin as powers to which man has fallen victim* and against which he is powerless. The personification of these powers expresses the fact that man has lost to them the capacity to be the subject of his own actions (*sein Subjekt-sein*). . . . [T]he subject-self, the true self of a man, is inwardly split. . . . Therefore, "I" and "I," self and self, are at war with each other. (1:244–45, emphasis original)

In this instance, Bultmann judges that Paul is already speaking figuratively, rather than in the language of "realistic mythology." Thus, strictly speaking, no demythologizing hermeneutic is necessary at this point. When Paul speaks of flesh and sin as "powers," he is in fact deliberately talking about an inward division in the human subject. But if that is the case, does it really make sense to say that the individual has "fallen victim" to these powers, and that he or she "has lost *to them* (*an sie*) the capacity" to be the subject of personal action? What, in this case, is the antecedent of the pronoun "them"? Does Paul really mean nothing more than that the rational will is overridden by other elements within the human psyche? Or should we instead consider the possibility that Paul really does believe in the existence of suprapersonal forces that oppress and enslave human beings?[16]

In light of this analysis, it is not hard to see why Bultmann can conceive of salvation chiefly as "a new understanding of one's self" that takes place through a process of individual decision. The individual sinner "is confronted by the gospel [the German here is actually *Botschaft*—not *Evangelium*] when it reaches him with the decision whether or not he is willing to understand himself anew and to receive his life from the hand of God" (1:269). It is important to get the balance right here: Bultmann is not saying that individuals can simply decide, as a project of self-improvement, to overcome their own dividedness or master their own baser impulses. Rather, the "decision" (*Entscheidung*) for a new self-understanding is always a "decision in regard to the grace which encounters man in the proclaimed word" (1:269). So the decision for a new self-understanding is always responsive in character, always answering God's offer of grace. But Bultmann is very clear that "through Christ . . . there was

16. See Beverly Roberts Gaventa, "The Cosmic Power of Sin in Paul's Letter to the Romans," in *Our Mother Saint Paul* (Louisville: Westminster John Knox, 2007), 125–36. See now also Robert Ewusie Moses, *Practices of Power: Revisiting the Principalities and Powers in the Pauline Letters* (Minneapolis: Fortress, 2014).

brought about no more than the *possibility* of life," a possibility that must be embraced and actualized by the individual decision of faith (1:252).

It remains notoriously unclear exactly *how*, for Bultmann, the proclaimed word of Christ's death and resurrection enables or facilitates this new self-understanding, since this message is for Bultmann neither an account of Christ's death as a blood atonement that enables forgiveness of sins nor a true story about a cosmic event in which Christ has liberated humanity from the grip of hostile powers. But since the task of this essay is only to focus on Bultmann's treatment of "Man Prior to the Revelation of Faith," we need not attempt here to resolve this puzzle. The central point for now is that the human predicament is for Bultmann one of inward division and self-misunderstanding; accordingly, salvation is to be conceptualized in noetic terms as a transition into a new integrative interpretation of one's own self before God.

The besetting theological danger here is that of the reduction of theology to anthropology *simpliciter*. Both Barth and Käsemann leveled precisely this charge at Bultmann. On the basis of his account of Pauline theology, I would judge the charge to be justified. As we have already seen in the opening section of the present essay, Bultmann can astonishingly interpret Paul's account of Christ's eschatological triumph over the powers of sin and death (1 Cor 15:20–28) to express "only . . . a certain understanding of existence" that portrays our human reality "as one full of conflicts and struggle" (1:259). Or to take another example, he can write, "knowledge of God as Creator contains primarily (*vor allem*) knowledge of man—man, that is in his creatureliness and in his situation of being one to whom God has laid claim" (1:228–29). Does Bultmann really mean *vor allem*, or is this a case of rhetorical exaggeration to make the more modest point that the doctrine of creation should never be isolated from human recognition of our finitude and dependence upon God? Whatever judgment one makes about questions of this kind, it is at least clear that Bultmann repeatedly leaves himself open to being understood in reductionist terms.

Conclusion

In sum, we have seen that the opening section of Bultmann's treatment of Pauline theology makes a series of consequential methodological decisions that project an image of Paul filtered through the hermeneutical lenses of a philosophically sophisticated blend of twentieth-century existentialism and dialectical theology. Bultmann's Paul is a man of the Hellenistic world, immersed in critical dialogue with Gnosticism and mystery religions and only tangentially linked to his own Jewish heritage—except insofar as that heritage is the source of a lethal boasting that must be renounced in order to arrive at the new self-understanding made possible by the gospel. The narrative kerygmatic confessions of the early Hellenistic church belong to the presuppositional background of Paul's thought, but his real theological contribution lies in his nuanced development of a series of anthropological concepts that insightfully depict the human condition. For this reason, Paul's theology is first of all to be understood as anthropology—or, more precisely, as the exposition of "believing self-understanding." This line of interpretation is made possible through a demythologizing hermeneutic that reads beneath the surface of Paul's mythologically laden language to expose the "real intention" of his message. That real intention focuses on the possibility that individuals may attain a new self-understanding by making a decision in response to the proclaimed word, a new self-understanding that overcomes divided personal identity and receives life as a gift from the hand of God (1:269).

In this demythologized account of Paul's thought, certain crucial elements are dramatically downplayed or missing altogether: the election of Israel, the constitutive role of Israel's Scripture, the cosmic centrality of the *narrative* of the death and resurrection of Jesus (except as a stimulus to new self-understanding), the corporate character of redemption in Christ (and consequently the role of the church in God's eschatological purposes), the breaking down of the barrier between Jew and gentile, and the radical hope for resurrection of the body and God's apocalyptic triumph over death and evil in the world. Some of these themes will resurface at least briefly in Bultmann's exposition of "Man under Faith" (1:270–352). But because the soteriological *solution* offered by the gospel must correlate with the diagnosis of the *problem* confronted by "Man Prior to the Revelation of Faith," the positive depiction of the condition of the believer in the latter part of Bultmann's account will remain individualistic and focused on a revised self-understanding.

It will be evident to the reader that in my judgment there would be "a more excellent way" to describe Paul's theology. That way would start by telling the story of God's action in Christ to fulfill the scriptural promises to Israel and redeem the creation that is in bondage to sin and death; the corollary analysis of the human condition would follow from that fundamental narrative. Christological narrative would assume primacy over anthropological concepts, and Paul's "real intention" would not be disjoined from the stories and images that are the primary content of his kerygmatic summaries. Whatever we might say about the human condition prior to the revelation of faith would be situated within the story of God's self-disclosure to Israel, as hermeneutically reconfigured by the cross and resurrection.[17]

Of course, to work out such a presentation of Paul's theology would be a huge undertaking. In any case, such a presentation would be significantly sharpened and refined by respectful critical attention to Bultmann's wide-ranging and theologically searching depiction of Paul's thought. Any serious fresh engagement with the theology of Paul will perforce emulate Bultmann's conviction that Paul still has much to say to the present—even if what we hear him saying is rather different from what Bultmann heard.

17. For one illustration of the alternative approach toward which I am gesturing, see chapter 9 in the present volume: "Christology: Paul's Story of God's Son."

19

Law

Whose World Is It, Anyway?

Worlds in Collision

It is an honor to be invited to present this lecture in the McDonald Distinguished Scholar Lecture Series here at the Center for the Study of Law and Religion. At the same time, it is a daunting task to be invited to address the question, "What does Christian theology offer the world of law?" My first response, perhaps just a little facetious, is to echo Alasdair MacIntyre's well-known questions by asking, "Whose world? Which law?" (Perhaps while I am at it, I should ask "Whose theology?" But presumably you have invited me to speak because you want to know what *my* theology might offer. And if you ask a NT scholar to speak, you are going to get a heavy dose of NT theology.)

Whose world? Which law? When we start to ask such questions, several texts from the Acts of the Apostles come to mind, for Luke the evangelist offers a fascinating account of the way in which the earliest Christian preachers fanned out through the Mediterranean world and began to encounter various local and imperial legal authorities. For example, consider the story in Acts 18 of the apostle Paul's arrest in Corinth and his hearing before the Roman proconsul Gallio:

> But when Gallio was proconsul of Achaia, the Jews made a united attack on Paul and brought him before the tribunal. They said, "This man is persuading people to worship God in ways that are *contrary to the law*." Just as Paul was about to open his mouth, Gallio said to the Jews, "If it were a matter of crime or serious villainy, I would be justified in accepting the complaint

This essay was presented as the 2015 McDonald Distinguished Scholar Lecture at the Center for the Study of Law and Religion, Emory University.

> of you Jews; but since it is a matter of questions about words and names and *your own law*, see to it yourselves; I do not wish to be a judge of these matters." And he dismissed them from the tribunal. (Acts 18:12–16)

Here we see the collision of two worlds—or, rather, three. The Jews in Corinth perceive Paul's evangelistic, apocalyptic, messianic world as a threat to their orderly, traditional religious world; consequently, they drag Paul to the civil legal authority and accuse him of persuading people to worship God in a way that is "contrary to the law" (παρὰ τὸν νόμον). Their artful accusation exploits a semantic ambiguity in the word νόμος. Their real concern is that they consider Paul's teaching to be contrary to Torah, that is, contrary to the Law of Moses. But they carefully frame their accusation to Gallio so as to insinuate that Paul's teaching is subversive of the world of Roman order, the Roman law. No doubt we readers of Acts are meant to recall the uproar in Thessalonica just one chapter earlier, an uproar caused by the Jewish accusation that the Christian preachers, including Paul, have "turned the world upside down" by "acting contrary to the decrees of the emperor, saying that there is another king named Jesus" (Acts 17:6–7).

But before Paul can even begin to defend himself, Gallio curtly dismisses the case by characterizing the complaint as a dispute about "your own law" (that is, Jewish religious law) and therefore not pertinent to the world of Roman law. In short, he says to them, "It's your problem, not mine, and your law is irrelevant to the concerns of my law." The attempt by Paul's adversaries to conflate two senses of "law" fails. (Paradoxically, if Gallio had allowed Paul to speak, he might have discerned at least dimly that the new world proclaimed by Paul did in fact contain the potential to turn the Roman order upside down; hence the delicate narrative irony of this episode.)[1]

Our discussions of a theological perspective on law, however, are often susceptible to the semantic slippage that Gallio cannily avoided. We are constantly tempted to read the NT's words about νόμος as general statements about civil law or human positive law. We will do well to remember, on the contrary, that when the NT writers speak about νόμος they are usually speaking very specifically about Israel's scripturally disclosed Law, the divinely given Torah.

1. For a nuanced discussion of the issues raised by this passage, see C. Kavin Rowe, *World Upside Down: Reading Acts in the Graeco-Roman Age* (Oxford: Oxford University Press, 2009), 57–62.

The Narrative Framing of Law

The juxtaposition between the νόμος of the Jewish plaintiffs in Corinth and the νόμος of Gallio the Roman proconsul draws our attention to something crucial that Christian theology offers to our understanding of law: there is no such thing as a law that has normative force and validity outside of a particular cultural system, or—to put the point in a more biblical fashion—outside of a particular *story*. The biblical account of the origin of Torah makes this point very clear. The Law is derived neither by some sort of democratic process nor by reason's unaided contemplation of the night sky; rather, the Law is given by God to a people he has graciously chosen, rescued from slavery in Egypt, and led to the foot of Mount Sinai, where he summons his servant Moses to receive a revelatory disclosure of God's order and God's will. The giving of Israel's Law is embedded in a much longer story of election, covenant, and gracious deliverance. That is why the Ten Commandments are prefaced with an encapsulated recollection of that story: "I am the LORD your God, who brought you out of the land of Egypt, out of the house of slavery; you shall have no other gods before me" (Exod 20:2–3). The laws given to Moses have binding force because they are the decrees of a Lawgiver who is first of all creator and savior of the people to whom they are given.

Apart from such a story, the rules of any particular system of law will be merely arbitrary assertions of power by those who hold positions of privilege, or at best socially constructed compromises, a social contract to limit the power of human beings to inflict harm on one another. Why, for example, should we assert the truthfulness of the laws of Western liberal democracy over the claims of Islamic law as rigorously interpreted by the Islamic State?[2] If we are honest with ourselves, we will see that our preference for one over the other is a consequence of our embeddedness in a cultural community shaped by the long traditions of Judaism and Christianity, now inflected (and to some degree diluted) by modernity's secularized story of human freedom.

But to the extent that law is losing its authority in a postmodern society subliminally infected by a Nietzschean worldview, that is a direct result of our culture's drift away from the biblical story. The theologian Robert Jenson has diagnosed this situation of postmodern malaise in an incisive essay, "How the World Lost Its Story." Jenson writes,

2. On the role of Islamic law in shaping the agenda of the Islamic State, see the fascinating account given in Graeme Wood, "What ISIS Really Wants," *The Atlantic*, March 2015.

> The entire project of the Enlightenment was to maintain realist faith [in a narratable world] while declaring disallegiance from the God who was that faith's object. The story the Bible tells is asserted to be the story of God with His creatures; that is . . . there is a true story about the universe because there is a universal novelist/historian. Modernity was defined by the attempt to live in a universal story without a universal storyteller.[3]

With respect to law specifically, we might well add to Jenson's insight the observation that the universal storyteller is also the universal judge. In the world narrated by the Bible, the moral order defined by the Law receives its grounding and normativity in God's character, God's will, and—it must be emphasized—God's grace. The Law of the Lord is a gift to be received joyfully, the psalmist declares, because it revives the soul, makes wise the simple, rejoices the heart, and enlightens the eyes (Ps 19:7–8).

At any rate, my main point here is that any particular body of law finds its place and meaning within *some* story. What Christian theology offers to the world of law is a story that offers assurance of truth, promises human wholeness, and holds out the confident eschatological hope that justice will finally prevail so that the earth will be full of the knowledge of the Lord as the waters cover the sea (Isa 11:9). Of course the question posed not only to Gallio but also to our contemporary jurisprudence is whether the world of law wants to acknowledge and receive the gift that Christian theology offers.

Roles of Law within the Christian Story

In the theological traditions that flow from the Reformation, there is a well-known topos about three "uses" of the Law—here referring to the Law of Moses. The three uses are (roughly sketched) to restrain sin before the coming of Christ, to convict the conscience so as to make sinners aware of their need for grace, and to provide a positive guide for the moral life for those who have come to know themselves justified by faith. I would suggest that this schema, while identifying some key motifs in the relevant NT texts, focuses too narrowly on an individualized conception of an *ordo salutis* and omits some significant aspects of NT's portrayal of the roles of Israel's Law. In the short time we have here today, I would like to give a descriptive sketch of

3. Robert W. Jenson, "How the World Lost Its Story," *First Things*, October 1993, 19–24, 21.

four roles of the Law in the biblical story[4] as read through the lenses of the NT, and then, in a subsequent set of second-order hermeneutical reflections, suggest some implications for our question about what Christian theology might offer to our own understanding of law, in the "lowercase" sense of law in a democratic society. So, first, a brief description of the four roles of Law in the biblical story.

First Role: The Law Defines the Identity of the People of God

In the NT's vision of the world, the Law is not merely a negative restraining force to curb human sinfulness, though it can sometimes be so described (for example, 1 Tim 1:8–9). It also creates a positive form of life for the embodied identity of a distinct people in the world. That is why Paul can refer to the Jewish people with shorthand expressions such as [οἱ] ἐν τῷ νόμῳ ("those who are in the Law," Rom 3:19) or οἱ ἐκ νόμου ("those [who live] on the basis of the Law," Rom 4:14). Those who have been chosen by God as members of the covenant people are called to obey the Law fully and unconditionally (for example, Deut 30:11–14). This obligation is, however, not a burden but a blessing: it holds the promise of life (Deut 30:15–20; cf. Ps 19, cited above). That is why Paul can assert that the "advantage of the Jew" is "much, in every way" (Rom 3:1–2). Israel is given a privileged knowledge of God's will and a commission, therefore, to be a "light to those who are in darkness" (Rom 2:19, echoing Isa 49:6, though not without a certain ironic critical edge).

Precisely because the Law is an identity-creating power, scholars such as James D. G. Dunn and N. T. Wright have argued that Paul's phrase "works of the Law" should be understood to refer not to merit-acquiring deeds but chiefly to the distinctive identity-marking practices such as circumcision, dietary observances, and Sabbath keeping that set the Jewish people apart from their gentile contemporaries. As Michael Winger has summarized this interpretation, "*Nomos* is what Jews do."[5] And because the Law does have this function of marking out a distinct social group with a privileged knowledge of God's ways, it can unfortunately become the ground for "boasting," a tendency that Paul devastatingly lampoons in Rom 2:17–24. It can be distorted to become a "badge" of ethnic pride. But the entire NT—Gospels, Paul, Hebrews,

4. My exegetical observations here are partly adumbrated in an earlier essay. Richard B. Hays, "Three Dramatic Roles: The Law in Romans 3–4," in *The Conversion of the Imagination: Paul as Interpreter of Israel's Scripture* (Grand Rapids: Eerdmans, 2005), 85–100.

5. Michael Winger, *By What Law? The Meaning of Νόμος in the Letters of Paul*, SBLDS 128 (Atlanta: Scholars, 1992), 109.

James, and all the rest—bears witness that using the Law as a basis for self-righteous pride and exclusion of others is a *misinterpretation*, an abuse of the Law. This observation points to the second role of the Law in the NT, a role distinctively identified by Paul.

Second Role: The Law Pronounces Condemnation

The Reformation's "second use of the Law" rightly identifies a theme that is especially prominent in Paul's Letter to the Romans: the Law pronounces categorical judgment on the unrighteousness of all human beings, Jews and Greeks alike: "There is no one who is righteous, not even one" (Rom 3:10, paraphrasing Eccl 7:20), and all are under the power of Sin (Rom 3:9). It is important to note that Paul here envisions Sin as a cosmic power that holds humanity in bondage, with the result that all have turned away from God into disobedience and violence, as chillingly depicted in Paul's catena of OT citations in Rom 3:10–18. The Law therefore speaks, especially to those who are "in the Law," "so that every mouth may be silenced, and the whole world may be held accountable to God" (Rom 3:19). It is important to see that Paul is not here articulating a comprehensive doctrine about the Law—as some varieties of Protestant theology have sometimes assumed. Rather, within the rhetorical design of this particular letter, he is "seeking to destabilize an entrenched position that associates the Law with the privileged status of the elect Jewish people."[6] Nonetheless, the comprehensive force of the indictment remains: the Law strips away human pretense and exposes the depth of human folly and evil before the face of a righteous God who is our ultimate judge: "All have sinned and fall short of the glory of God" (Rom 3:23).

Third Role: The Law Prefigures the Righteousness of God in Jesus Christ

Fortunately for humanity, the Law is not only an accuser and a source of condemnation, for the Law also prefigures the saving righteousness of God, as disclosed in Jesus Christ. Paul insists not only that the Law is "holy and just and good" (Rom 7:12) but also that the gospel message of God's righteousness/justice (δικαιοσύνη θεοῦ) in Jesus Christ is "attested (μαρτυρουμένη) by the Law and the prophets" (Rom 3:21). This is almost certainly what Paul means, I believe, when he declares in Rom 10:4 that "Christ is the end of the Law."

6. Hays, "Three Dramatic Roles," 93.

The Greek here is τέλος γὰρ νόμου Χριστὸς. Paul is not saying that Christ terminates the Law; rather, he is proclaiming that the Law has all along pointed to Christ, who is its τέλος in the sense that he is its *goal*, the disclosure of its true meaning and purpose. This reading is corroborated by the consistent testimony of all four Gospels and Acts that Israel's Scriptures bear witness to Jesus. In the Gospel of John, Jesus tells his interlocutors, "If you believed Moses, you would believe me, for he wrote about me" (John 5:46). And in the climactic conclusion of the Gospel of Luke, the risen Jesus tells his astounded disciples that "everything written about me in the Law of Moses, the prophets, and the psalms must be fulfilled" (Luke 24:44).

In the time permitted here, I can hardly scratch the surface of this topic, but suffice it to say that this claim about the prefigurative function of the Law opens up wide-ranging implications for how Christian theology reads the Law *retrospectively* as a figural narrative disclosure of something beyond its original literal sense.[7] That is why Paul can insist that his gospel does not negate the Law but rather upholds it (Rom 3:31). For example, he rereads the story of Abraham (notice here that he treats this biblical narrative as part of "the Law") as a prefiguration of the story of Jesus Christ and sees God's reckoning of righteousness to Abraham as a promise that will also be reckoned to those "who believe in him who raised Jesus our Lord from the dead, who was handed over to death for our trespasses and was raised for our justification" (Rom 4:24–25). Clearly here, the meaning and implications of the term νόμος have expanded far beyond the minimal sense of a code of behavioral rules or legal constraints.

Fourth Role: The Law Informs the Moral World of the Community of Faith

And yet, the Law does nonetheless also inform the moral vision of the community of faith. The moral stances of the NT authors on many issues of conduct (for example, care for the poor, sexual ethics, and abhorrence of idolatry) are deeply and specifically shaped by the provisions of Israel's Law. And Jesus's double love commandment that mandates love of God and love of neighbor, often taken as the epitome of NT ethics, is nothing other than a direct citation of two legal texts from Torah (Matt 22:37–40, citing Deut 6:5 and Lev 19:18).

7. For a broader discussion of the NT's retrospective figural hermeneutic, see Richard B. Hays, *Reading Backwards: Figural Christology and the Fourfold Gospel Witness* (Waco: Baylor University Press, 2014).

It is important to recognize, however, that Israel's Law is also hermeneutically filtered and even reconfigured in the NT texts. For example, Matthew foregrounds Hos 6:6 ("I desire *mercy*, not sacrifice") as a hermeneutical key to understanding the Law (Matt 9:9–13; 12:1–8), and Jesus, in this same Gospel, admonishes the scribes and Pharisees for neglecting "the weightier matters of the Law: justice and mercy and faith" (23:23). To take another example, Paul proclaims that "the one who loves another has fulfilled the Law" (Rom 13:8), perhaps echoing Jesus's teaching—but if so, without attribution to Jesus. In some cases the hermeneutical reconfiguration may involve an intensification of the Law's commandments, as in the series of six antitheses in the Sermon on the Mount ("You have heard that it was said . . . but I say to you"), or in the case of Jesus's teaching on divorce, which radicalizes the Law's modest regulation of divorce (Deut 24:1) by precluding divorce altogether on the basis of the Law's narrative of God's creation of man and woman for each other (Mark 10:2–9), or at least severely restricting the permission of divorce to cases of sexual infidelity (Matt 19:3–9).

Perhaps the most striking hermeneutical reconfiguration of Torah, however, is related to the point I have already made about the New Testament's reading of the Law as prefiguration of Christ. The conviction that Jesus is the *embodiment of Torah*—certainly pervasive in the Christology of John's Gospel—perhaps also underlies Paul's repeated appeals to his communities to imitate Christ by humble service to others. For example, Gal 6:2: "Bear one another's burdens, and in this way you will fulfill the law of Christ (τὸν νόμον τοῦ Χριστοῦ)."

Christian Perspectives on the Role of Law in a Democratic Society

How might the NT's teaching on the Law of Israel be received hermeneutically in a way that could inform our reflections on the role of law in a pluralistic democratic culture? The question is complicated for many reasons, not least because the semantic gap between "Law" as God's divinely ordained will for humankind and "law" as a democratically devised system for channeling the will of the people constructively makes it impossible to map "applications" of the biblical discourse on Law directly onto legal problems of our time. The only possible way to relate the two senses of law is through a process of metaphorical or analogical comparison that will propose imaginative links between the two. Because of our time constraints, I can only offer a few brief suggestions to serve as provocations for our conversation together.

(1) *The NT's teaching on the Law illuminates our understanding of human identity and the human condition.* The recipients of biblical Law are addressed as people made in the image of God, capable of hearing and responding to the Law, and indeed destined for covenant partnership with God. As God's creatures, therefore, they have a certain a priori dignity and value. At the same time, the perfect Law of God exposes their brokenness and sinfulness—indeed, it exposes their captivity to patterns of behavior that are destructive to themselves and to others. As Paul insists, they are "under the power of Sin." The dialectic between human freedom and human fallenness, between human possibility and human perversity, illumines both the necessity of law and the challenge faced by every attempt to legislate human flourishing.

(2) *The NT highlights the limitation of the power of law to make us whole or to make us good.* This limitation is expressed vividly by Paul in Rom 8:

> For the law of the Spirit of life in Christ Jesus has set you free from the law of sin and of death. For God has done what the Law, weakened by the flesh, could not do: by sending his own Son in the likeness of sinful flesh, and to deal with sin, he condemned sin in the flesh, *so that the just requirement* (δικαίωμα) *of the Law might be fulfilled in us,* who walk not according to the flesh but according to the Spirit. (Rom 8:2–4; cf. Acts 13:39)

This same text suggests, however, not only the limits of what law can do but also something more hopeful, for it suggests that the deepest remedy for the broken human condition is not restraint and punishment but forgiveness and reconciliation. This might by analogy lead us to conclude that our best hopes for amelioration of our troubled social order would lie not in the proliferation of punitive laws but in the various movements that aim at "restorative justice."[8]

(3) *The Law, despite lacking the ultimate power to transform human character, nonetheless implicitly points beyond itself to a goal of the transformation of human hearts and communities.* This emphasis shows up in many NT texts. In Matthew, Jesus announces that he has come not to abolish the Law or the Prophets but to fulfill them (Matt 5:17). That fulfillment is not simply a matter of bringing predictions to completion; rather, it is a matter of transforming the hearts and minds of disciples so that they hunger and thirst for righteousness

8. See Christopher D. Marshall, *Compassionate Justice: An Interdisciplinary Dialogue with Two Gospel Parables on Law, Crime, and Restorative Justice*, Theopolitical Visions 15 (Eugene, OR: Cascade Books, 2012).

and seek to create an embodied community that is "the light of the world" as Isaiah had prophesied (Matt 5:6, 14–16; Isa 49:6). Whatever the Law's limitations, it offers "a shadow of the good things to come," as the Letter to the Hebrews has it (Heb 10:1). Several NT texts evoke Jeremiah's prophetic hope for a new covenant in which God's Law will be written on human hearts, so that they will know and fulfill the will of God (see Heb 8:4; Rom 2:25–28; 2 Cor 3:2–3, all alluding to Jer 31:33). The analogies here to our secular civil law are perhaps distant, but one thinks for example of civil rights laws that mandate fair and equal legal treatment of all persons regardless of race. At one level, of course, such laws regulate only outward conduct and policy, but surely we hope that over time these laws will in fact inculcate new and more generous attitudes even in social environments where hostility and condescension might once have been the norm. Only time will tell.

(4) Precisely because the biblical story distinguishes between the Law of the Lord and the laws of worldly empires, as we saw in the story of Paul's arraignment before Gallio, *the biblical text opens up a space that provides critical leverage on the contingent laws produced by secular governments*. Because there is "another king named Jesus," the positive laws of secular rulers can never be ultimate, and the possibility of principled civil disobedience is real. Daniel speaks boldly to King Nebuchadnezzar: "If our God whom we serve is able to deliver us from the furnace of blazing fire and out of your hand, O king, let him deliver us. But if not, be it known to you, O king, that we will not serve your gods and we will not worship the golden statue that you have set up" (Dan 3:16–18). And in Acts, we hear Peter and the apostles defying the orders of the chief priest and the council in Jerusalem: "We must obey God rather than any human authority" (Acts 5:29). The horrifying failure of German Christianity in the Nazi era was its inability to make such a distinction and to resist an evil regime; by contrast, the power of the testimony of the Confessing Church lay in its clear-minded recognition that baptism was a more fundamental identity marker than nationality, and that at times resistance is necessary in the name of a God who rules over the nations. This is so because God is ultimately the judge of all, as compellingly articulated in Israel's tradition:

> Listen therefore, O kings, and understand;
> learn, O judges of the ends of the earth.
> Give ear, you that rule over multitudes and boast of many nations.
> For your dominion was given you from the Lord,
> and your sovereignty from the Most High;
> he will search out your works and inquire into your plans.

Because as servants of his kingdom you did not rule rightly,
or keep the law,
or walk according to the purpose of God,
he will come upon you terribly and swiftly,
because severe judgment falls on those in high places.
For the lowliest may be pardoned in mercy,
but the mighty will be mightily tested. (Wis 6:1–6)

The secular analogue of this teaching would be at least this: governments are always subject to be held accountable to standards of justice, and individuals may rightly oppose and resist unjust laws or governments that fail to follow just laws that do exist. Of course, once again such a dictum leads back to the question, "Whose justice?" Christian theology offers an answer to all who have ears to hear.

Conclusion: What Does Christian Theology Offer to the World of Law?

A dose of humility. A sign of hope. And ground to stand on, even in the face of suffering.

A dose of humility. Christian theology can help the world of law know itself and recognize the contingent character of even its own best institutions; theology provides a critical capacity for the world to assess its social practices and particular laws in light of divine justice.

A sign of hope. Christian theology can offer the world of law a vision of a transformed community that seeks not just its own good but the good of others. The paradigm for such a community is the self-emptying, merciful figure of Jesus. Even those who doubt or reject the truth of Christian claims about this man invariably recognize the compelling power of communities that seek to embody his vision and follow his example. The world of law should honor such communities and seek to encourage institutions that emulate them in whatever ways are possible.

A ground to stand on in the face of suffering. Finally, Christian theology holds out the hope that the injustice that persists in the world will not have the last word. The Christian story is neither naive nor sanguine about the actual conditions of human suffering under unjust rulers in the world. I did not read you the ending of the story of Gallio's dismissal of the complaint against Paul. Here it is, just two sentences: "Then [the crowd] seized Sosthenes, the official of the synagogue, and beat him in front of the tribunal. But Gallio paid no attention to any of these things" (Acts 18:17). Here is a ruler derelict in doing justice, indifferent to violence right in front of his nose. And of course the NT could hardly be unaware of the miscarriages of justice under the *pax Romana*, for the central event of the NT story is the unjust crucifixion of an innocent man who was the very embodiment of God's justice. Nonetheless, the resurrection declares that injustice and death will not finally prevail. As Desmond Tutu repeatedly told his compatriots who were resisting apartheid in South Africa, "Don't give up hope. I've read the end of the book: we win!"

In short, Christian theology *asks* the world of law what story does frame its own self-understanding. And Christian theology *offers* the world of law a story that makes sense of our experience of human dignity, human evil, and our hope for justice.

20

CONFESSION

Romans and the Nicene Creed

The Confessional Tradition as "Divine Pedagogy"

As some interpreters have recently sought to recover an authentically theological approach to interpreting Scripture, it has slowly begun to dawn on some of us that we might actually find guidance, rather than hindrance, in the church's doctrinal traditions. A suggestion such as this could seem surprising only to interpreters trained in resolutely modernist exegetical methods—that is to say, interpreters like me. Even though we may have assumed vaguely that our own ecclesial communities stood in continuity with the message of the Bible, and even though we believed that our exegetical work was meant to serve and inform the teaching and preaching of these communities, it would never have occurred to most of us to take the inherited confessional standards of these communities as *hermeneutical* guidelines for our professional exegetical work. Indeed, this would have seemed to skew the task of interpretation in an unfortunate—indeed, "uncritical"—way.

Consider, for example, the labors of the Pauline Theology Group that thrived in the Society of Biblical Literature during the 1980s and '90s, a lively group for which I was privileged to serve on the steering committee. For ten years, we passionately pondered the theologies of the individual Pauline letters and debated (inconclusively) whether it was possible to articulate some sort of synthetic theology found in the letters as a whole. But never did it occur to us to consult a *theologian* about our problems. We were, after all, critical exegetes, confident that our linguistic and historical skills gave us the necessary privileged insight into interpreting these documents. And still less did it occur

This essay was originally presented as a paper in the Theological Hermeneutics of Christian Scripture Group at the 2009 Annual Meeting of the Society of Biblical Literature in New Orleans.

to any of us to ask whether the ecumenical creeds of the church might offer some useful perspective on the coherence of Paul's thought. Those creeds were, after all, later developments; surely, then, it would have been anachronistic to project their doctrinal formulations back onto the first-century texts.

In the years since then, however, some of us have been moved to consider these matters in a different way. For example, the Scripture Project, an interdisciplinary group of biblical scholars, theologians, and historians, sponsored by the Center of Theological Inquiry in Princeton, struggled for several years with the question of how we might best read Scripture together. Among the theses we finally agreed on were these:

- Scripture is rightly understood in light of the church's rule of faith as a coherent dramatic narrative.
- Faithful interpretation of Scripture invites and presupposes participation in the community brought into being by God's redemptive action—the church.
- The saints of the church provide guidance in how to interpret and perform Scripture.[1]

At the same time, many other voices from various corners of the academy have begun to explore similar claims. David Yeago's justly famous programmatic essay, "The New Testament and the Nicene Dogma," contends that the church's later dogmatic formulations were not alien superimpositions on the NT but rather well-considered interpretive performances that explicitly articulated the implicit christological "judgments" present in the NT writings themselves.[2] Or, as Kavin Rowe has put it, the development of the doctrine of the Trinity was "the unpacking of the internal theological logic behind the particular form of scripture's grammar."[3]

Rusty Reno's series preface to the Brazos Theological Commentary states the case with provocative clarity:

1. Ellen F. Davis and Richard B. Hays, eds., *The Art of Reading Scripture* (Grand Rapids: Eerdmans, 2003), 1, 3, 4.

2. David S. Yeago, "The New Testament and the Nicene Dogma: A Contribution to the Recovery of Theological Exegesis," in *The Theological Interpretation of Scripture: Classic and Contemporary Readings*, ed. Stephen E. Fowl (Oxford: Blackwell, 2001), 87–100.

3. C. Kavin Rowe, "The Trinity and the New Testament" (paper presented in the Development of Early Trinitarian Theology Group at the 2009 Annual Meeting of the Society of Biblical Literature in New Orleans).

> This series of biblical commentaries was born out of the conviction that dogma clarifies rather than obscures. . . . [T]he Nicene tradition, in all its diversity and controversy, provides the proper basis for the interpretation of the Bible as Christian Scripture. . . . Doctrine, then, is not a moldering scrim of antique prejudice obscuring the Bible. It is a crucial aspect of the divine pedagogy, a clarifying agent for our minds.[4]

These are bold words. But even some of us who are sympathetic to such claims are still trying to figure out exactly how a proposal such as this works out in practice. *How*, exactly, does the credal tradition clarify our actual *exegesis* of the biblical texts? (Some of the early volumes in the Brazos series were not altogether helpful or reassuring in this respect!)[5]

And so, when the organizers of the Society of Biblical Literature Group on Theological Hermeneutics of Christian Scripture asked me to offer a paper on theological interpretation of Paul's Letter to the Romans, I found myself pondering questions such as these: What would it mean to read Romans through the lens of the Nicene credal tradition? How would Romans look different if I approached the text in light of the hermeneutical framework articulated in the creeds? Would I notice things I had missed before? Or, to turn the question around the other way, would reading Romans alongside the classical creeds allow Paul to instruct us in the proper exegesis of the *creeds*? Would Romans expand and enrich the compressed confessional language of these dogmatic statements? Or might we discover certain points of critical tension between the two? If so, what implications would follow for our own constructive theological work? And so this essay is a reflective experiment, an exercise in retraining myself to see differently and inviting others to join me in musing about questions such as these; it is what Reno calls an "experiment in postcritical doctrinal interpretation."[6]

When I posed these questions, one realization struck me immediately. Since the Reformation, the interpretation of Romans has focused relentlessly on debates about Paul's view of the Law and the meaning of justification by faith. But these are topics not addressed at all in the church's ecumenical creeds. Might it be, then, that our Protestant preoccupation with the question

4. R. R. Reno, series preface in *Matthew*, by Stanley Hauerwas, Brazos Theological Commentary on the Bible (Grand Rapids: Brazos, 2006), 12.

5. See, for example, C. Kavin Rowe and Richard B. Hays, "What Is a Theological Commentary?," *ProEccl* 16 (2007): 26–32, a response to Jaroslav Pelikan, *Acts*, Brazos Theological Commentary on the Bible (Grand Rapids: Brazos, 2005).

6. Reno, series preface, 14.

of justification has created a certain hermeneutical distortion and occluded other significant theological themes in Romans?

I hasten to add that I do not think we can or should do away with "justification" as an important motif in Pauline theology: Romans has an ample share of forensic language—and I believe it is Paul's own language, not merely the language of an imagined interlocutor.[7] I am simply asking whether the creed offers us a different lens through which to view the letter, a lens that brings other very different motifs more clearly into focus.

In this brief essay, then, I propose to focus attention on the third article of the creed—the portion of the confession that speaks of the Holy Spirit, the church, baptism, and the resurrection of the body. Here is the pertinent passage from the Nicene-Constantinopolitan Creed:

> And [we believe] in the Holy Spirit, the Lord and Giver of life, who proceeds from the Father, who together with the Father and Son is worshiped and glorified, who spoke through the prophets; and in one holy, catholic, and apostolic church. We confess one baptism for the forgiveness of sins. We look forward to the resurrection of the dead and the life of the world to come. Amen.[8]

So, what happens if we reread Romans through the lens of this confession of faith?[9]

7. For a sharp critique of the treatment of "justification" in the Protestant theological and exegetical tradition, see Douglas A. Campbell, *The Deliverance of God: An Apocalyptic Rereading of Justification in Paul* (Grand Rapids: Eerdmans, 2009). Campbell offers a rhetorical analysis of the Letter to the Romans that assigns some of the forensic statements in Rom 1–4 to a fictive interlocutor who serves as a foil for Paul's own presentation of an apocalyptic gospel of God's unconditional grace. My statement above is meant to indicate respectful skepticism about Campbell's reading of Rom 1–4.

8. On the history and development of the creed, see J. N. D. Kelly, *Early Christian Creeds*, 3rd ed. (London: Longman, 1972 [1950]). For helpful theological commentary and reflection on the specific credal affirmations, see Luke Timothy Johnson, *The Creed: What Christians Believe and Why It Matters* (New York: Doubleday, 2003), from which the translation cited above is, taken (37–38). For a theological treatment of the interdependence of the credal tradition and the formation of the Christian canon, see Robert W. Jenson, *Canon and Creed*, IBC Interpretation Resources (Louisville: Westminster John Knox, 2010). For theological commentary on the slightly different formulations found in the Apostles' Creed, see Roger E. Van Harn, ed., *Exploring and Proclaiming the Apostles' Creed* (Grand Rapids: Eerdmans, 2004).

9. This "rereading" is diametrically opposed to the method of rereading proposed by Stanley K. Stowers in *A Rereading of Romans: Justice, Jews, and Gentiles* (New Haven: Yale

The Holy Spirit in Romans

First of all, reading Romans through the lens of the third article shifts our attention away from the metaphorical courtroom drama of the letter's first four chapters and refocuses our gaze on other portions of the letter that highlight the role of the Holy Spirit in God's work of transforming a weak and broken humanity. In particular, Rom 8, with its emphasis on the Spirit as "Giver of life," comes into focus as the climactic passage that most clearly narrates God's solution to the death-bound human condition. It is surprising to find how relatively little has been written on the Spirit as a major theme of Romans. (Gordon Fee's massive study *God's Empowering Presence* is of course the major exception in English to this generalization.)[10] The most important German monograph on the Spirit in Paul, Friedrich Wilhelm Horn's 1992 work *Das Angeld des Geistes: Studien zur paulinischen Pneumatologie*, has major chapters on 1 Thessalonians and 1 Corinthians and a third chapter with briefer treatments of 2 Corinthians, Galatians, and Philippians. But there is no individual chapter on Romans—a remarkable omission.[11] The third article of the creed,

University Press, 1994). Stowers contends we can best understand Romans by removing it completely from any sort of doctrinal or confessional context. See my review of Stowers in *CRBR* 9 (1996): 27–44, now included as chapter 13 in the present volume.

10. Gordon D. Fee, *God's Empowering Presence: The Holy Spirit in the Letters of Paul* (Peabody, MA: Hendrickson, 1994). In the world of recent Pauline scholarship on this topic, special note should be taken of the work of James D. G. Dunn and Douglas Campbell, both of whom have recognized the distinctive and determinative significance of the Spirit in Paul's thought. See, for example, Dunn's treatment of Rom 8 in *Romans*, vol. 1, *1–8*, WBC 38A (Waco: Word, 1988), esp. 412–13, 433–46, 457–64, and 486–95. Similarly, Dunn's *The Theology of Paul the Apostle* (Grand Rapids: Eerdmans, 1998) includes significant comments about the Spirit in Romans; see especially 422–24, 430, 435–38, and 642–49. Douglas Campbell (*The Quest for Paul's Gospel* [London: T & T Clark, 2005]) argues that "pneumatology is the key to the soteriological mechanism that lies at the heart" of Paul's thought (60; see also his comments on 38–42 and 74–80, the latter focusing especially on Rom 8). In light of this important observation, one is surprised to find relatively little sustained discussion of the Spirit in *The Deliverance of God* (see note 7 above); see, however, 62–73 and 707–11. For a significant new contribution to the topic of the Spirit in Paul, see now Volker Rabens, *The Holy Spirit and Ethics in Paul: Transformation and Empowering for Religious-Ethical Life*, WUNT 2/283 (Tübingen: Mohr Siebeck, 2010). On the whole, however, where the topic of the Spirit is treated explicitly, as in Ernst Käsemann's classic essay, "The Cry for Liberty in the Worship of the Church," in *Perspectives on Paul*, trans. Margaret Kohl (Philadelphia: Fortress, 1971 [1969]), 122–37, there has been a tendency for exegesis in the Reformation traditions to treat the experience of the Spirit as a problem that Paul has to assess critically in light of the experience of suffering.

11. Friedrich Wilhelm Horn, *Das Angeld des Geistes: Studien zur paulinischen Pneuma-*

however, summons us to consider the liberating, life-giving Spirit of Rom 8 as a central theme of Paul's gospel message.

But it is not only Rom 8 that assumes larger significance in light of the creed's promptings. We might also take note of the way in which the argument of Romans is framed *pneumatologically*, beginning and end, by two key references to the Spirit.

First, in Rom 1:4, Paul informs his readers that Jesus "was publicly identified as God's Son in power *according to the Spirit of holiness* (κατὰ πνεῦμα ἁγιωσύνης), *through his resurrection from the dead.*" The exact manner in which the Spirit was at work in effecting and/or proclaiming the resurrection of Jesus is not explained in this compact formulation. But on any reading of the text, *Holy Spirit* and *resurrection*, key components of the third article, are foregrounded by Paul in his opening summary of the gospel. Further, this gospel is said to have been "promised ahead of time through [God's] prophets" (v. 2)—another function of the Spirit, who, according to the creed, "spoke through the prophets."

Then, in Rom 15:13, at the climax of the letter's *peroratio*, Paul breathes this prayer for his Roman readers: "May the God of hope fill you with all joy and peace in trusting, so that you overflow with hope *by the power of the Holy Spirit.*" This eschatologically oriented prayer, with its emphasis on the Spirit's work of infusing hope, should remind readers of an earlier rhetorically climactic passage in the middle of the letter, where Paul declares that "hope does not put us to shame, because the love of God has been poured out in our hearts *through the Holy Spirit that has been given to us*" (5:5). (And this text in turn anticipates many aspects of Paul's description of the Spirit's work in ch. 8.) Similarly, the prayer in 15:13 for the Spirit to fill the readers with "joy and peace" recalls the major summary dictum of 14:17: "For the kingdom of God is not food and drink but righteousness and peace and joy *in the Holy Spirit.*" Thus, these passages, which are both structurally crucial and rhetorically prominent in Paul's presentation, alert the reader to the role of the Spirit in promising the gospel in advance, making the promise effectual through the resurrection of Jesus, disclosing the good news to the world, pouring out the love of God in the hearts of those who hear the message, and sustaining them with joyful hope for the future—a future hope focused on the eschatological resurrection of the dead.

tologie, FRLANT 154 (Göttingen: Vandenhoeck & Ruprecht, 1992). See also the critique of Horn in Volker Rabens, "The Development of Pauline Pneumatology: A Response to F. W. Horn," *BZ* 43 (1999): 161–79.

Other Credal Themes: Church, Baptism, Resurrection

Given the Trinitarian structure of the creed, the credal themes of church, baptism, and resurrection are to be understood as subheadings that explicate further aspects of the work of the Spirit.[12] Consequently, these themes, too, will surface in a role of greater prominence in our thought experiment of reading Romans through the lens of the creed. I shall comment briefly on each in turn.

"One Holy, Catholic, and Apostolic Church"

It is commonly observed that the word ἐκκλησία appears in Romans only in chapter 16, and then only with reference to other Christian communities in the Mediterranean world, never in reference to the communities of believers in Rome. One consequence of this observation is that we rarely hear much about ecclesiology in Romans,[13] and it is sometimes suggested that Paul does not regard the Roman gatherings as properly established "churches" under apostolic authority.[14] But this seems to me to be a speculative construal of the evidence that places too much weight on an *argumentum e silentio*, the absence of a single lexical item in the letter. Regardless of what Paul may have thought about the establishment and polity of the Roman communities of believers, he regards them as fellow participants in the "one body in Christ" (12:5), and he repeatedly addresses them as ἀδελφοί (1:13; 7:1, 4; 8:12; 10:1; 11:25; 12:1; 15:14, 30; 16:17), his favored term for fellow believers. Further, his pastoral counsel to them in chapters 14 and 15 insistently presupposes that they should treat one another as

12. While of course I cannot explore here the historical complexities surrounding the emergence and development of the creed, I will presuppose that its outline originated in the context of baptismal catechesis and that its structure is fundamentally Trinitarian (see Kelly, *Early Christian Creeds*, 30–61). If so, the creed's affirmations concerning church, baptism, and resurrection are to be understood as subheadings under the rubric "We believe . . . in the Holy Spirit" and therefore as implications or aspects of the Spirit's saving activity.

13. Among the rare explicit discussions of ecclesiological themes in Romans, see Pablo T. Gadenz, *Called from the Jews and from the Gentiles: Pauline Ecclesiology in Romans 9–11*, WUNT 2/267 (Tübingen: Mohr Siebeck, 2009); and Peter Oakes, "Made Holy by the Holy Spirit: Holiness and Ecclesiology in Romans," in *Holiness and Ecclesiology in the New Testament*, ed. Kent Brower and Andy Johnson (Grand Rapids: Eerdmans, 2007), 167–83.

14. See, for example, Günter Klein, "Paul's Purpose in Writing the Epistle to the Romans," in *The Romans Debate*, ed. Karl P. Donfried, rev. ed. (Peabody, MA: Hendrickson, 1991), 29–43, esp. 39: "Paul can consider an apostolic effort in Rome because he does not regard the local Christian community there as having an apostolic foundation." Among other things, Klein notes here the absence of the word "church" in the prescript (41–43).

brothers and sisters in Christ; the strong parallels to 1 Cor 8–10 are universally acknowledged. In short, all the evidence suggests that Paul regards his Roman readers as part of the one community of the people of God, even if they have factional divisions and struggles similar to his churches in other cities.

Indeed, scanning Romans through the credal lens casts light on numerous passages that emphasize a strong functional ecclesiology in the letter. The scope of the present essay does not permit detailed study of these passages, but we may briefly survey several of the more important ones. The Romans are beloved by God and κλητοὶ ἅγιοι (1:7)—certainly a designation reserved for members of the one elect people of God. The whole discussion of Abraham in chapter 4 as "our father in the sight of God" (vv. 16–17) is meant to show that Jewish and gentile believers alike are part of the one people united in trusting the one God (as Paul has insisted in 3:27–31); thus, whether circumcised or uncircumcised, surely it follows that they partake equally of God's grace in the one ἐκκλησία. Further, they are all to participate together in presenting their bodies as one corporate living sacrifice (12:1) and therefore, as already noted, to function cooperatively as interdependent members of one body in Christ (vv. 3–8). Indeed, the lengthy hortatory section that runs from 12:1 to 15:13 paints a wide-ranging picture of the church. It is a diverse community, made of up Jews and gentiles, embracing a range of different practices. Consequently, though they may be conflicted in the present, they are called to pursue "[the things that] make for peace and for mutual upbuilding" (14:19; cf. 15:2), and their life together is eschatologically ordered toward a vision of unity so that in the present they may "live in harmony with one another" and "together . . . with one voice glorify the God and Father of our Lord Jesus Christ" (15:5–6). If that does not qualify as an account of the one holy, catholic church, it is hard to imagine what would so qualify. I suggest, therefore, that Romans is in fact an exceedingly rich source for the development of ecclesiology. The creed names and sharply focuses the ecclesiocentric character of Paul's apostolic message and ministry.[15]

Of course, in recent NT studies, these ecclesial features of Romans are commonly studied from a *sociological* point of view, so that the accent falls on the social history of the early church in Rome.[16] This is, to be sure, an

15. See further Richard B. Hays, *Echoes of Scripture in the Letters of Paul* (New Haven: Yale University Press, 1989).

16. Among the landmarks here are Wayne A. Meeks, *The First Urban Christians: The Social World of the Apostle Paul*, 2nd ed. (New Haven: Yale University Press, 2003 [1983]); Peter Lampe, "The Roman Christians of Romans 16," in *The Romans Debate*, ed. Karl P. Donfried, rev. ed. (Peabody, MA: Hendrickson, 1991 [1977]), 216–30; Robert Jewett, *Romans: A Com-*

important topic for exploration, and scholarship on these topics has yielded important insights. But a reading of Romans through the lens of the creed will also discover a strong confessional affirmation of the church as a central reality in God's redemptive action of reclaiming sovereignty over an alienated creation and putting things right in a newly constituted humanity in Christ. Even the prosaic list of greetings in chapter 16, read through the lens of the creed, starts to look like an instantiation of practical ecclesiology. All these people who have labored in the apostolic mission of the gospel are bound together in a circle of grace by Paul's words of greeting. And they, along with the recipients of the letter, are encouraged to "greet one another with a holy kiss" (16:16a). Why? Because they belong to the fellowship of "all the churches of Christ" (v. 16b)—and therefore to the one holy, catholic, apostolic church.

"We Confess One Baptism for the Forgiveness of Sins"

To read Romans through the lens of the creed will also focus our attention sharply on the baptismal language that appears in the letter, preeminently in Rom 6. But here we encounter an interesting point of tension. Whereas the creed, in the English translations known to most of us, speaks of "one baptism for the forgiveness of sins" or "remission of sins," Paul in Rom 6 says nothing about "forgiveness." Instead, he portrays baptism as union with Christ's death and rising to new life, with the result that those who have undergone baptism have been *set free from the power of Sin*. Baptism, according to Paul, is not simply a transaction in which we receive "forgiveness" for our offenses. Rather, its effect is to abolish Sin's grip on our bodies (6:6). And we find once again that this new freedom from Sin's power is bound in the closest possible way to *resurrection*, both the already accomplished resurrection of Jesus and the anticipated resurrection in which "we will also live with him" (v. 8).

How are we to deal with the apparent tension at this point between the creed and the text of Romans? If I might offer a tentative suggestion, I would call attention to the fact that the Greek text of the creed reads ἓν βάπτισμα εἰς ἄφεσιν ἁμαρτιῶν. I would suggest that, in this case, Rom 6 might encourage us to understand that the noun ἄφεσις should retain its connotation of "release" from captivity, just as in the passage from Isa 61 read by Jesus in Luke 4:18, declaring that the *Spirit* has anointed him to proclaim ἄφεσις to the captives—here, certainly not "forgiveness" but "liberation." If so, a credally informed reading of Romans would

mentary, Hermeneia (Minneapolis: Fortress, 2007); and Francis Watson, *Paul, Judaism, and the Gentiles: Beyond the New Perspective*, rev. ed. (Grand Rapids: Eerdmans, 2007 [1986]).

produce two reciprocal effects. On the one hand, the creed focuses attention on the Spirit-powered, ecclesially centered practice of baptism as a key locus of God's saving work: that is, Rom 6 is to be read not simply as an ad hoc apologetic reply to a hypothetical charge of antinomianism but as integral to the liberative logic of the gospel. And at the same time, on the other hand, Rom 6 enables—indeed, requires—us to read the creed with new eyes. On this reading, the creed would not chiefly emphasize baptism as a way to find forgiveness; instead, it would proclaim baptism's liberating power that sets us free to "walk in newness of life" (6:4). So we should translate: "We confess one baptism for release from sins."[17] This is a helpful illustration of the way in which a "postcritical doctrinal interpretation" might prove fruitful on multiple fronts at once.

"We Look Forward to the Resurrection of the Dead and the Life of the World to Come"

Time would fail me to review the many passages in Romans where the resurrection of the body stands at the heart of Paul's argument—a theme strangely neglected in many readings of the letter. Fortunately, however, a careful study of these passages has recently been published by J. R. Daniel Kirk, in his book *Unlocking Romans: Resurrection and the Justification of God*.[18] So, gesturing in the direction of Kirk's analysis, I will simply say that reading Romans in light of the third article of the creed illuminates many passages in which resurrection is either proclaimed or presupposed, beginning with the reference to Jesus's resurrection in the letter's opening salutation (1:4) and climaxing at 11:15: "For if [Israel's] rejection brings the reconciliation of the world, can their acceptance mean anything less than life from the dead?" But the remainder of this essay will concentrate particularly on Rom 8 and offer a few brief exegetical observations about the way in which the creed brings Paul's teaching on the resurrection into focus—and vice versa.

While Paul elsewhere writes more extensively about the future resurrection, particularly in 1 Cor 15,[19] nowhere in Paul's extant letters does he more strongly

17. One should, of course, note the plural, ἁμαρτιῶν, here; the creed's formulation, unlike Paul, does not seem to envision sin as a personified power.

18. J. R. Daniel Kirk, *Unlocking Romans: Resurrection and the Justification of God* (Grand Rapids: Eerdmans, 2008). On the central role of resurrection in Romans, see also N. T. Wright, *The Resurrection of the Son of God*, Christian Origins and the Question of God 3 (London: SPCK; Minneapolis: Fortress, 2003), 241–66.

19. See my discussion of this passage in *1 Corinthians*, IBC (Louisville: Westminster John Knox, 1997), 252–82.

relate "the resurrection of the dead and the life of the coming age" to the work of the Holy Spirit than in this passage in Rom 8. The word πνεῦμα appears no fewer than twenty times in Rom 8. Although the precise expression "Holy Spirit" appears nowhere in the chapter, the great majority of these instances clearly refer to "the Spirit of God" (8:9—also in the same verse called "the Spirit of Christ").[20] Paul's closely interwoven statements in this chapter about the Spirit's activity may be divided into three categories: (1) the Spirit gives life, (2) the Spirit leads God's children, and (3) the Spirit groans and intercedes for us.[21] Interestingly, only the first of these actions of the Spirit is mentioned in the creed. Here is an example of a way in which Romans expands and enriches the credal formula. But in each case, Paul's language evokes rich resonances of Israel's Scripture—hardly a surprise because he is writing about the Spirit who "spoke through the prophets."

(1) *The Spirit's life-giving role* is the keynote of Rom 8, for the Spirit is first introduced here as "the Spirit of life" (v. 2). Again, recall that the creed identifies the Spirit as "the Lord, the Giver of life." The Spirit that gives life is not an attribute or aspect of the ἄνθρωπος; rather, the Spirit that produces life and peace (v. 6) is a divine *power* that actually dwells in believers (v. 9) and overcomes our enslavement to death. This is made unmistakably clear in verse 11: this indwelling Spirit is "the Spirit of [the One] who raised Jesus from the dead," and for that reason we can trust that this same Spirit "will give life to [our] mortal bodies also." This is certainly an anticipatory reference to the resurrection of the body—a hope firmly reiterated in verse 23 ("the redemption of our bodies" from bondage to decay). The Spirit's life-giving role will ultimately be confirmed by the eschatological resurrection of the body, but the same life-giving power of the Spirit is also *already* at work in the present to shape and transform God's people; consequently, they are no longer in the grip of sin but are freed to fulfill the righteous command of God by walking in the power of the Spirit (v. 4).

Thus, Rom 8 explicates an ambiguity in the creed: to confess the Holy Spirit as "Giver of life" is to refer *both* to the life-giving power that promises future resurrection of the body *and* to the transforming effects of that power in the believing community's present existence. In other words, the Spirit's life-giving role includes empowerment for obedience. This point is far clearer in Paul than in the credal tradition.

20. One might ask whether this parallelism between "Spirit of God" and "Spirit of Christ" sheds any light on the question at issue in the *filioque* controversy.

21. The observations that follow here are adapted and abbreviated from a fuller treatment in my "Intertextuelle Pneumatologie: Die paulinische Rede vom Heiligen Geist," *ZNT* 25 (2010): 30–37, to be found now in English translation in chapter 12 of the present volume.

(2) A second, closely related action of the Spirit is its role in *leading the children of God out of slavery and into freedom* (8:14–15, echoing the language of Exod 13 and Deut 32).[22] This same Spirit bears witness with our spirit that we too, like Israel, are "children of God" (Rom 8:15b–16). Here, Paul offers a much fuller account of the Spirit's action than we find in the creed: the Spirit acts to provide guidance, secure adoption, and offer assurance of belonging to God's family. And just at this point we may suspect that the truncation of these themes in the creed is related to its lack of a robust affirmation of the election of Israel. As often noted, the omission of Israel from the creed is a grievous oversight that has had tragic consequences in the church's doctrinal tradition. The effect of reading the Nicene-Constantinopolitan Creed alongside Rom 8 is to remind us that the work of the Spirit cannot be understood properly apart from the story of Israel. To put it aphoristically, there is no pneumatology without Israelology.[23]

(3) Finally, and most remarkably, Paul depicts the Spirit as *groaning along with the suffering of a creation that groans in bondage to decay while it awaits the life of the world to come*. This groaning Spirit intercedes for us, according to the will of God, even in our complete inability to pray properly (8:22–27). This extraordinary account imparts a deep poignancy to the verb that introduces the final clause of the creed: προσδοκῶμεν—we *wait*. We look forward with eager longing for the resurrection and the life of the world to come.[24] Paul helps us read this concise credal phrase from a position of historically situated weakness, as an expression of urgent, pained hope rather than as a smug, complacent claim to know the ending in advance. And in turn, so understood, the creed informs the many different future eschatological images in Romans, all of which are imbued with a yearning for the coming age.[25]

But why does Paul describe the Spirit as interceding for us "with inartic-

22. See Sylvia C. Keesmaat, *Paul and His Story: (Re)Interpreting the Exodus Tradition*, JSNTSup 181 (Sheffield: Sheffield Academic Press, 1999), 61. See also N. T. Wright, "Romans," in *Acts, Introduction to Epistolary Literature, Romans, 1 Corinthians*, ed. Leander E. Keck, *NIB* 10 (Nashville: Abingdon, 2002), 590–94.

23. And the same dictum applies a fortiori to ecclesiology. (*Sine Israel nulla ecclesia.*) The connection between "ecclesiology" and "Israelology" is drawn from the work of George A. Lindbeck. See, for example, "Confession and Community: An Israel-like View of the Church," *The Christian Century* 107 (1990): 492–96; reprinted in the collection of his essays entitled *The Church in a Postliberal Age*, ed. James J. Buckley (Grand Rapids: Eerdmans, 2002), 1–9.

24. In a word, I am suggesting that the creed's προσδοκῶμεν should be heard in harmony with the ἀποκαραδοκία of Rom 8:19.

25. For example, Rom 5:1–5, 9–10; 7:24–25; 8:18–39; 9:1–3; 11:11–12, 25–32; 13:11–14.

ulate groans" (8:26)? If we have decided to read Romans through the lens of a Trinitarian credal statement, can it really be said that *God* the Holy Spirit enters so fully into the pain of the unredeemed creation that the creation's groans are not merely *heard* by God—as God heard the groaning of the children of Israel in slavery in Egypt (Exod 2:23–24)—but actually echoed and amplified by the divine Spirit's own groans? Have we reached a place where Paul's radical statements about the Spirit simply cannot be squared with the Trinitarian credal tradition? Μὴ γένοιτο.

The key to grasping this paradox is to be found in yet another biblical text, if we recall the creed's affirmation that the Spirit "spoke through the prophets." The text I have in mind is Isa 42. As Sylvia Keesmaat has observed, this prophetic text, which declares God's intention to redeem Israel through a new exodus, carries language that resonates powerfully with Rom 8.[26] In Isa 42, God is announcing "new things" (v. 9) and promising to act at last to save and restore his people Israel. And here is what God says:

> For a long time I have held my peace,
> I have kept still and restrained myself;
> now I will cry out like a woman in labor,
> I will gasp and pant. (Isa 42:14)

God declares through Isaiah that his activity of judgment and redemption will cause him to cry out like a woman in labor. And now, in Rom 8, Paul declares that it is the *Spirit* of this same redeeming God who will join together with creation's groaning in labor pains to intercede for the ultimate deliverance of the saints and the world.

And so, if we hold Scripture and creed together, we will come to recognize that when we say, "We believe in the Holy Spirit," we are confessing faith in a God who participates with us in labor and groaning while we await (προσδοκῶμεν) the final disclosure of creation's freedom in the life of the world to come.

26. Keesmaat, *Paul and His Story*, 122.

21

Eschatology

"Why Do You Stand Looking Up into Heaven?"

> Besides this, you know what time it is, how it is now the moment for you to wake from sleep. For salvation is nearer to us now than when we became believers; the night is far gone, the day is near.
>
> Rom 13:11–12a

Millennial Fever and Backlash

As the twentieth century staggers to its close, the symptoms of millennial fever are on display all around us.

- *This American Life*, a radio show on National Public Radio, features an interview with a devout Christian woman who has calculated on the basis of biblical prophecies that Jesus will descend from heaven and bring the world to an end on October 19, 1999.
- A syndicated newspaper story tells of a man who, regarding himself as the messiah and believing the end to be at hand, would lie on the floor in his workplace and "pretend he was nailed to the cross, frightening coworkers and customers." (The story helpfully goes on to explain that this worker's behavior may be protected by state and federal laws prohibiting religious discrimination in the workplace.)[1]
- An anxious Seventh Day Adventist, having heard a report that the pope

1. Raleigh *News and Observer*, May 16, 1999.

This essay was originally invited as a contribution to a symposium of papers appearing in the year 2000 in the journal *Modern Theology*. The editors sought to bring together various historical and theological perspectives on eschatology in light of the turn of the millennium.

has issued a statement encouraging Christians to observe Sunday as a day of rest, phones my office to ask whether I, as a NT scholar, think this might be a harbinger of a new oppressive legal order that will mandate Sunday worship and forbid Adventists from observing the Sabbath, thus ushering in the reign of the Antichrist in the year 2000.

- On the internet, rumors fly that the dreaded Y2K bug will bring down civilization as we know it and perhaps inaugurate the reign of the Antichrist.

These tidbits of news, which could be multiplied many times over, illustrate a widespread popular tendency to believe that human history has reached a desperate state of corruption and that God's final judgment is surely at hand. The current wave of speculation about the year 2000 may be artificially fueled by news media looking for livid curiosities in order to sell news "product"; nonetheless, there is a deep strain of belief in American popular Christianity that the Bible points to an apocalyptic end of all things that is to occur within the current generation. Such beliefs are held not merely by fringe sectarian groups such as the ill-fated Branch Davidians but also by millions of ordinary American Christians who continue to line the pockets of TV evangelists and authors of speculative books on the endtime.[2]

On the other hand, such millennium fever receives its due portion of derision from many sides—not only from comics and pundits who count themselves among the cultured despisers of religion but also from Christian scholars, pastors, and laity who consider themselves too "modern" to countenance such foolishness and who regard apocalyptic ideas as an embarrassing throwback to naive fundamentalism. Thus, in the backlash against millennialist literalism, many Christians have categorically dismissed the NT's apocalyptic imagery. With greater or lesser theological reflection, they have come to think that all ideas about the second coming of Christ are quaint speculations that should be shed by mature, educated believers. The rising millennial fever, with its periodic outbreaks of bizarre or even violent behavior, confirms their worst suspicions and leads to widespread scoffing at the eschatological visions of the NT writers. Where this reaction occurs, the already tenuous authority of the NT in the church is further undermined.

2. In 1991, Elisabeth Schüssler Fiorenza reported that Hal Lindsey's sensationalistic book, *The Late, Great Planet Earth* had sold *seven million* copies since its original publication in 1970 (*Revelation: Vision of a Just World* [Minneapolis: Fortress, 1991], 8). It is a curious fact that sales figures for such books, sold primarily through chains of "Christian bookstores," are not included in the bestseller lists of the *New York Times* and other "mainstream" media.

Yet such a reaction is both hasty and self-defeating, for apocalyptic categories are neither peripheral nor dispensable; they stand at the heart of the gospel of Jesus Christ, as proclaimed and interpreted by the NT writers. The resurrection itself is an apocalyptic event, and it can be understood as a saving event for the world only within the framework of the NT's dialectical already/not yet eschatology. Thus, Christians who scoff at apocalyptic are sawing off the branch on which they sit—or, to give the metaphor a more biblical turn, tearing out the roots of a tree of which they themselves are the branches. Apocalyptic narrative and apocalyptic expectation are integral to the logic of the gospel.

In order to develop this claim, we must first distinguish between specific millennial speculation and apocalyptic eschatology. The NT writers actually discourage the former, while insisting on the latter. The distinction appears clearly in a passage such as Mark 13:24–37, at the end of Jesus's lengthy discourse on the destruction of the temple and the coming of the Son of Man. He tells his disciples that they will see the coming of the Son of Man in power and glory, and that he will gather his elect from the ends of the earth (vv. 24–27). These events are depicted as near and inevitable (vv. 28–31). Then, however, Jesus warns them against trying to predict the date of these occurrences:

> But about that day or hour no one knows, neither the angels in heaven, nor the Son, but only the Father. Beware, keep alert; for you do not know when the time will come. (Mark 13:32–33)

Jesus's followers are to stake their lives on the expectation of the coming kingdom of God, when God will restore Israel and establish justice. They are to "stay awake," however, not by gazing up into heaven or frittering away their time in fruitless calculations but by attending to the work that has been assigned to them by their master (Mark 13:34–37). That is the readiness that is required.

When Ernst Käsemann, in reaction against the demythologizing hermeneutic of his teacher Rudolf Bultmann, coined the maxim that "apocalyptic is the mother of Christian theology,"[3] he was identifying apocalyptic thought not only as historical background to the development of the NT but also as an

3. Ernst Käsemann, *New Testament Questions of Today*, trans. W. J. Montague and W. F. Bunge (London: SCM; Philadelphia: Fortress, 1969 [1965]), 137. Käsemann's fundamental insight on this point has been carried forward by the work of J. Christiaan Beker and J. Louis Martyn, both of whom should be counted among the influences for the position that I develop in this essay.

essential component of the kerygma. As I will argue in this essay, Käsemann was exactly correct in this description of the matter. The difficulty that has long plagued the church, however, is how to interpret the NT's apocalyptic hope in light of the fact that "all things continue as they were from the beginning of creation" (2 Pet 3:4b). Does the continuation of history without the parousia of the Lord, without the visible righting of all things, disconfirm the gospel? What account can we give, at the dawn of the third millennium since the incarnation, of the future hope that we continue to hold? Is the hope still credible? Or should the gospel proclamation be reformulated to deemphasize eschatological expectation? Should we Christians continue to honor and be instructed by our mother? Or must we regretfully disown her?

Three Unsatisfactory Strategies

A cursory survey of some strategies for dealing with this difficult hermeneutical problem shows that some of the solutions historically adopted by Christians are not real solutions: either they fail to resolve the problem or they settle the eschatological problem only by introducing fatal glitches elsewhere in the overall configuration of the theological system. In the latter case, the solution is more damaging than the problem it was designed to remedy. Let us consider three significant but unsatisfactory strategies for coping with the nonfulfillment of apocalyptic expectation.

The Johannine Option: Eternal Life Now

Already within the NT itself, we find evidence that Christians were grappling with the problem of reformulating their eschatological expectations in order to sustain the church into an extended temporal future. The clearest illustration of this development in the NT is to be found in the Gospel of John, which took its final form sometime late in the first century, after the death of the Beloved Disciple, the original witness to the community's tradition about Jesus (John 21:23). This Gospel is concerned to assure believers that even those who stand removed in time and place from Jesus are nonetheless able to be intimately united with him and to share his glory (17:20–26). Consequently, in the Fourth Gospel, future eschatology is emphatically deemphasized and overshadowed by an eschatology claiming eternal life as the *present* possession of those who believe in Jesus. Anyone who believes "has eternal life, and does not come under judgment, but has passed from death to life" (John 5:24; cf. 3:36). Jesus, having ascended to God, *is* the resurrection, and those who are one with him have already entered into his eternal life. That is why Jesus can say paradoxically to Martha, "I am the resurrection and the life. Those who believe in me, even though they die, will live, and everyone who lives and believes in me will never die" (John 11:25–26). In light of this bold claim, there is no need to look forward wistfully to "the resurrection on the last day" (11:24). In Jesus, the resurrection has engulfed the sphere of present temporality, and the future fades into relative insignificance, as does the reality of physical death.

The corollary of this conviction is that, in a real sense, judgment has already taken place whenever anyone hears the gospel and responds either in faith or in unbelief. "Those who believe in him are not condemned; but those who do not believe are condemned already, because they have not believed in the name of the only Son of God" (John 3:18). Nowhere in John do we hear of a final judgment that will hold any suspense or surprises (unlike, e.g., Matt. 25:31–46). Jesus's entry into the world polarizes humanity into believers and unbelievers, and their eternal destiny is already settled by that polarization, which separates those who love the light from those who love the darkness because their deeds are evil (John 3:19–21).

To be sure, we do find also in John's Gospel a few scattered expressions of the characteristic early Christian apocalyptic eschatology. For example, Jesus in one place declares that "the hour is coming when all who are in their graves will hear his voice and will come out—those who have done good, to the resurrection of life, and those have done evil, to the resurrection of condemnation" (John 5:28–29; see also 6:39, 40, 44, 54). Such passages stand out strikingly in a Gospel that otherwise proclaims judgment now and eternal life now.

Rudolf Bultmann hypothesized that the few future eschatological passages in John's Gospel were not originally part of the text; they must have been added later by an "ecclesiastical editor" who found John's radical realized eschatology unacceptable.[4] Bultmann's hypothesis is, however, pure speculation. The text of the Fourth Gospel as we have it includes these future-oriented apocalyptic passages as part of the canonical witness of John; there is no manuscript evidence for the existence of any text of John that lacks these passages. Furthermore, the First Letter of John, a later writing in the same Johannine community tradition, takes some care to give prominence to future eschatological themes, urging community members to abide in Jesus "so that when he is revealed we may have confidence and not be put to shame before him at his coming

4. Rudolf Bultmann, *The Gospel of John*, trans. George Beasley-Murray, R. W. N. Hoare, and John K. Riches (Philadelphia: Westminster, 1971 [1950]), 11, 219–20, 261–62.

(παρουσία)" (1 John 2:28; cf. 3:2–3; 4:17).[5] Raymond Brown has persuasively argued that 1 John should be read as an attempt to shape and clarify the church's reading of the Fourth Gospel, heading off heretical misreadings and showing how the teaching of the Gospel conforms to the broader church's teachings on eschatology, ethics, the humanity of Jesus, and other topics.[6]

Thus, the realized eschatology that is featured prominently in John's Gospel cannot stand on its own. Taken as a whole, the canonical Johannine texts do not supplant future eschatology with realized eschatology; instead, the future eschatology provides the temporal framework within which the realized eschatology must be understood: i.e., the eternal life that the believer experiences in the present *points forward to* a final consummation in the resurrection at the last day. When John is read this way, his eschatology is formally similar to the dialectical already/not yet eschatology found in Paul, albeit with a much stronger accent on the "already." To the extent that the "not yet" remains essential to John's vision, however, the realized eschatology must be read as poetic hyperbole that fails to resolve the difficulty of nonfulfillment.

On the other hand, if John is read as offering an unqualified eschatology of eternal life in the present, then the problem of nonfulfillment is solved, but at the high price of construing this Gospel as incipiently gnostic, unconcerned about the fate of God's created world, the physical body, and the suffering that we still experience in the present time. All things considered, the Fourth Gospel's depiction of Jesus as "the word made flesh" tells against such a reading; the Jesus who weeps at Lazarus's tomb (11:33–36) can hardly be a gnostic savior seeking to teach human beings how to transcend time and material existence.

Bultmann, drawing heavily on his reading of John, sought to demythologize apocalyptic eschatology, interpreting it as a primitive symbolic vocabulary that sought to bring to expression a deeper truth about humanity's existential situation before God: we are always confronted at every moment by the demand for decision and the possibility of authentic existence. Thus, in the Fourth Gospel—stripped of the "ecclesiastical editor's" future eschatological passages—Bultmann saw within the NT itself a precursor of his own demy-

5. In his *Theology of the New Testament*, vol. 2, trans. Kendrick Grobel (New York: Scribner, 1955 [1951]), 85, Bultmann also suggested that the same hypothetical ecclesiastical editor who was responsible for the apocalyptic insertions in the Fourth Gospel might have added these passages in 1 John as well.

6. Raymond E. Brown, *The Community of the Beloved Disciple* (New York: Paulist, 1979), 93–144.

thologizing program.[7] But this hermeneutical program is subject to some of the same objections enumerated in the previous paragraph: it posits such an exalted anthropology that it fails to account for the limitations and sufferings of human existence as we actually know it, which constantly falls short of the "authenticity" that Bultmann envisioned. Additionally, it has the fatal quasi-Marcionite flaw of producing a trimmed-down text that does away with (Jewish) apocalyptic eschatology in order to suit the requirements of a preconceived anti-apocalyptic program. Any ultimately satisfactory solution to the eschatological problem must attend to the form in which the canonical texts actually present themselves to us; it will not do merely to lop off pieces that fail to conform to our theological agenda.

The Jesus Seminar: Driving a Wedge between Jesus and the Gospels

In his programmatic address at the first meeting of the Jesus Seminar in 1985, Robert Funk pinpointed the NT's eschatology as one of the major difficulties that the Seminar must seek to overcome. The NT's canonical story of Jesus must be replaced by a new story, Funk proposed, because the NT's story of cosmic beginnings and endings has become incredible and therefore useless for modern people who have now seen the heavens through Galileo's telescope. The canonical Jesus is, of course, the Christ of the church's creed, who was raised from the dead and who will come again to judge the world. In order to construct a new Jesus who will be usable and marketable in our day, according to Funk, we must purge the story of such apocalyptic fantasies.[8]

Funk's initial concern with the untenability of apocalyptic traditions goes a long way toward explaining the Jesus Seminar's subsequent "discovery" of a noneschatological Jesus. According to *The Five Gospels*, the Seminar's summation of its findings, the real Jesus of history was entirely free of the influence of Jewish apocalyptic thought. Instead, "he had a poetic sense of time in which the future and the present merged, simply melted together, in the intensity of his vision."[9] Consequently, wherever the Gospels portray Jesus as using apocalyptic imagery, such passages are resolutely classified by the Seminar as creations of the early church, those pedestrian blunderers who "reverted, once

7. See particularly *Theology of the New Testament*, 2:75–92, "Faith as Eschatological Existence." On p. 85, Bultmann writes, "John has abandoned the old conception of Jesus' parousia held by the earliest church. The 'world' will see nothing of his coming again."

8. Robert W. Funk, "The Issue of Jesus," *Forum* 1.1 (1985): 7–12.

9. Robert W. Funk, Roy W. Hoover, et al., *The Five Gospels: The Search for the Authentic Words of Jesus* (New York: Macmillan, 1993), 137.

Jesus was not there to remind them," into their bad old Jewish apocalyptic ways of thinking and retrojected onto Jesus the naive apocalyptic ideas taught by John the Baptist.[10]

The production of an idealized noneschatological Jesus is facilitated by the Seminar's highly debatable methodological decision to treat Q and the Gospel of Thomas as the earliest sources for the Jesus tradition—with the proviso that the "Q" in question must be an expurgated "early layer" of Q with nearly all the apocalyptic sayings removed! This circular methodology produces just what it was designed to produce: a noneschatological Jesus, constructed by systematically isolating him from the apocalyptic matrix in which the synoptic evangelists have placed him.

Marcus Borg, whose own books on Jesus are more careful and much less polemical than Funk's work, has gone so far as to claim that there is now a new consensus among NT scholars in support of a noneschatological Jesus. In his book *Jesus: A New Vision*, he writes, "The majority of scholars no longer thinks that Jesus expected the end of the world in his generation."[11] Although this claim is of doubtful validity, it is certainly true that there have been a number of recent publications seeking to reconstruct Jesus along noneschatological lines, using methods that, to a greater or lesser extent, parallel Funk's argu-

10. Funk, Hoover, et al., *Five Gospels*, 4; cf. 137.

11. Marcus Borg, *Jesus: A New Vision* (San Francisco: Harper & Row, 1987), 14. Borg explains in a footnote (20n25) that this claim is based on a mail poll of members of the Jesus Seminar and participants in the Historical Jesus Section of the Society of Biblical Literature. The actual data are provided in his subsequent book, *Jesus in Contemporary Scholarship* (Valley Forge, PA: Trinity Press International, 1994), 59–60: the poll received thirty-nine responses from the membership of these two groups, twenty-three of whom answered that they did not think Jesus "expected the end of the world in his generation." Considering that the Society of Biblical Literature has several thousand members, readers may draw their own conclusions about the validity of this poll's sampling method. Perhaps even more crucial, however, is the wording of the question: the key phrase is "the end of the world." Although I would strongly maintain that Jesus was an apocalyptic prophet, I do not think he expected "the end of the world." What he expected was the resurrection of the dead and God's righteous final judgment. Thus, the wording of Borg's question blurs the issue. It should be noted, however, that *Jesus in Contemporary Scholarship* contains a helpful essay, "Jesus and Eschatology: Current Reflections" (69–96), in which Borg significantly qualifies his claims: he admits that "Jesus probably had some eschatological beliefs," that "Jesus was concerned about the future," and that Jesus "speaks in a time of crisis, issues indignant indictments of ruling elites, and warns passionately of coming catastrophe" (88–89). These clarifications bring Borg's picture of Jesus into closer proximity with the position I am advocating in the present essay.

ments in *The Five Gospels*.[12] The common denominator of these reconstructions is a Jesus who is an itinerant sage, a teacher of subversive wisdom and spirituality, more like a Cynic philosopher than an eschatological prophet. In some cases (Borg, Crossan), Jesus is also credited as the teacher of an alternative vision of social justice.

The difficulties with this portrayal of a noneschatological Jesus are both historical and theological in character. At the historical level, the method of these revisionist studies drives a wedge between Jesus and the authors who preserved our earliest traditions about him. This is a highly questionable historiographical procedure. As E. P. Sanders has observed, if Jesus was a follower of the apocalyptic prophet John the Baptist and left behind a group of followers whose writings burn with apocalyptic expectation, a heavy burden of proof lies with anyone who contends that Jesus himself did not share in this chain of apocalyptic thinking.[13] Borg's effort to refute this line of argument is unpersuasive.[14] In the present essay I cannot undertake a full discussion of these issues; a recent monograph by Dale C. Allison has undertaken an extended response to Borg and other champions of the "noneschatological Jesus" thesis.[15]

More to the point of our present concerns is the theological deficiency of this revisionist position. Its advocates—insofar as they have theological concerns—seem to presuppose that only the critically reconstructed Jesus of history is theologically valid and useful.[16] The function of the historical reconstruction is to challenge—or replace—the canonical image of the eschatological Jesus. This solves the problem of eschatological nonfulfillment by dissolving it, eliminating future eschatology from our construal of the gospel. But this strategy leaves us, alas, with no gospel at all. N. T. Wright, in an appreciative critique of Borg, poses the issue tellingly:

> Is Borg's Jesus really an eschatological figure or does he after all use the language of eschatology to express . . . the essentially timeless truth that God

12. In addition to Borg's work, see particularly Burton L. Mack, *A Myth of Innocence: Mark and Christian Origins* (Philadelphia: Fortress, 1988); and John Dominic Crossan, *The Historical Jesus: The Life of a Mediterranean Jewish Peasant* (San Francisco: HarperSanFrancisco, 1991).

13. E. P. Sanders, *Jesus and Judaism* (Philadelphia: Fortress, 1985), 91–95.

14. Borg, *Jesus in Contemporary Scholarship*, 76–80.

15. Dale C. Allison, *Jesus of Nazareth: Millenarian Prophet* (Minneapolis: Fortress, 1998).

16. Here again, Borg is a partial exception. His dichotomy between the "pre-Easter Jesus" and the "post-Easter Jesus" allows him to maintain a constructive place for the "Christ of faith" in his overall perspective.

> is always available to human beings, and requires compassion rather than exclusive and oppressive ways of life? In other words, does Borg's Jesus (like, say, Sanders') suppose that Israel's god was actually doing something climactic and unique, in and through which Israel's (and perhaps the world's) story would be brought to some kind of fulfilment?[17]

There is no promise here of a God who will come to rescue humanity from death and injustice, who offers hope beyond the grave. In place of such a hope, we are offered a handful of enigmatic aphorisms that might enable us to reexamine our lives, perhaps even to work for social change. If this strategy has any theological agenda, it is either Pelagian or softcore pantheist. Either way, the systematic consequences for theology are grave. If our lives and the fate of the human race are in our own hands, we are in deep trouble. As Paul says, if there is no resurrection of the dead, "we are of all people most to be pitied" (1 Cor 15:19). It is no accident that these new scholarly visions of a noneschatological Jesus have found their most enthusiastic reception in their natural sociological and theological home: a dwindling but affluent liberal Protestant church in North America seeking some way to reconnect with a kinder, gentler Jesus who will offer them new spiritual stimulation without threatening them with God's final judgment.

The other theological difficulty posed by this strategy is the devaluation of the canon of Scripture. The critique of the canon, in rescuing Jesus from the embarrassments of apocalyptic theology, erodes the foundation of the church's confession. This will not trouble the more aggressive revisionists (e.g., Funk and Mack), whose program has this end explicitly in view. I wonder, however, whether most Christians who find the more benign noneschatological constructions of Borg and Crossan attractive have fully thought through the consequences of this choice. Given the choice between Mark and Marcus Borg, or between John and John Dominic Crossan, as interpreters of dominical eschatology, whom shall we prefer?

N. T. Wright: Apocalyptic Eschatology Historicized

Finally, we must offer a brief comment on N. T. Wright's widely discussed proposals concerning the eschatological sayings of the Synoptic Gospels. Only the briefest sketch of Wright's ambitious project in *Jesus and the Victory of*

17. N. T. Wright, *Jesus and the Victory of God*, Christian Origins and the Question of God 2 (London: SPCK; Minneapolis: Fortress, 1996), 77.

God is possible here. Wright treats virtually all of the sayings traditions of the Synoptics as authentic material that goes back to Jesus of Nazareth, including the critically contested future Son of Man sayings and the parables that speak of a returning king or master. Thus, he will have no part of any strategy that excises the apocalyptic traditions from our picture of Jesus. Nor is he interested in a strategy of demythologizing that reads these materials as expressions of some timeless truth about God's relationship to the world. Instead, Wright mounts an extended argument that all the apocalyptic sayings in the synoptic tradition were spoken by Jesus as *symbolic descriptions of concrete events taking place in and through his own activity in the immediate historical setting of first-century Israel.* These sayings employ a symbolic shorthand well recognized in first-century Jewish culture to make claims about the salvation-historical significance of Jesus's own identity and mission.

The "synoptic apocalypse" passages (Mark 13 and parallels) are to be read not as predictions of the end of the world but as prophetic warnings of God's impending judgment and destruction of an unfaithful and unrepentant Jerusalem.[18] The parables of a returning king are not the early church's allegories about a future parousia; rather, Jesus told these stories as figurative portrayals of "the return of YHWH to Zion," which Jesus himself symbolically enacted in his climactic journey to Jerusalem.[19] When Jesus declares in his trial before the high priest that "you will see the Son of Man seated at the right hand of the Power and 'coming with the clouds of heaven'" (Mark 14:62), this is not a prophecy of a descent from heaven—a "second coming"—but rather a vision of exaltation and enthronement, as in Dan 7: Jesus foresees his own final vindication, as Israel's representative and King, at the right hand of God.[20]

The cumulative result of these exegetical proposals is that the apocalyptic prophecies of Jesus are, without remainder, seen to be fulfilled in Jesus's journey to Jerusalem, his death and resurrection, and, finally, the destruction of the temple by the Romans in 70 CE. Thus, at least with regard to these sayings, the problem of nonfulfillment is solved, for the world-transforming events to which the sayings point *had already taken place* by the time the Gospels were written. Thus, apocalyptic expectation has been both historicized and fulfilled.

18. Wright, *Jesus and the Victory of God*, 339–68.

19. See his chapter "The Return of the King," in Wright, *Jesus and the Victory of God*, 612–53.

20. Wright, *Jesus and the Victory of God*, 642–44.

It is not possible here to respond in detail to Wright's remarkable, comprehensive construal of Jesus's actions, teachings, and intentions. The proposal invites thorough exegetical scrutiny, text by text.[21] For the present I will merely record my response to one key point: with regard to Mark 14:62, Wright has converted me. Daniel 7:13–14 is without question a vision of ascent and enthronement of a human figure representing Israel's vindication and triumph over the kingdoms symbolized by the beasts in the preceding visions.[22] When, in Mark's story, Jesus quotes Daniel to claim this role for himself, the high priest quite understandably judges his words to be blasphemy, because Jesus is foretelling that he will share the divine throne with the Ancient of Days. The parallels in Matt 26:64 ("*from now on* you will see the Son of Man seated at the right hand of Power") and Luke 22:69 ("*from now on* the Son of Man will be seated at the right hand of the power of God") are even more clearly to be understood as references to enthronement rather than a future return from heaven to earth.

Whether the Jesus of history actually foretold such an exaltation for himself is a difficult question, but Wright tellingly observes that "we do not find Daniel 7 used in this way, with this christological import, in early Christianity outside the reported words of Jesus."[23] Indeed, where the allusion to Dan 7 turns up elsewhere in the NT (e.g., Acts 1:9–11; 1 Thess 4:16–17) it has clearly been reinterpreted to refer to Christ's descent on the clouds at his anticipated return. Thus, Wright has offered a serious case for taking Mark 14:62 and parallels as an authentic—if scandalous—saying of Jesus.

This reference to other NT passages that anticipate a return of Christ does, however, move the discussion forward to a very important point: Wright's novel interpretation of the synoptic apocalyptic sayings *does not intend to negate or circumvent the church's expectation of a future return of Christ, resurrection of the dead, and final judgment*. Despite the fact that he thinks Jesus meant something else when he uttered the words that we now find in the Synoptics, Wright does not want to debunk or demythologize future apocalyptic hope. Indeed, he acknowledges that elsewhere in the NT we do find an expectation of Christ's coming again. This point could easily escape readers of *Jesus and the Victory of God*, for it occupies no place in Wright's reconstruction of the

21. See the collection of responses to Wright's work in *Jesus and the Restoration of Israel: A Critical Assessment of N. T. Wright's* Jesus and the Victory of God, ed. Carey C. Newman (Downers Grove, IL: IVP Academic, 2009).

22. See N. T. Wright, *The New Testament and the People of God*, Christian Origins and the Question of God 1 (London: SPCK; Minneapolis: Fortress, 1991), 291–97.

23. Wright, *Jesus and the Victory of God*, 644.

historical Jesus; he mentions it only in passing.[24] Wright's position on this question is somewhat clearer in the first volume of his multivolume project, *The New Testament and the People of God.* Near the conclusion of that book, he discusses the hope of the early Christians and notes that they introduced several developments and innovations in relation to the Jewish eschatological tradition. One of these is, explicitly, "the expectation of the return of Jesus."[25] This expectation was a necessary innovation: "Precisely because Jesus' resurrection was the raising of one human being in the middle of the history of exile and misery, not the raising of all righteous human beings to bring the history of exile and misery to an end, there must be a further end yet in sight."[26] But Wright makes a careful distinction that must be observed in order to understand the theological import of the argument that he will make in his second volume: "It is vital to stress both that most of the texts normally drawn on in this connection [i.e., the return of Jesus] have nothing to do with the case, and that there are several others which still bear on it directly."[27] The only example of the latter category that Wright actually cites in this passage is Acts 1:10–11, but presumably he has in mind various Pauline texts as well. Thus, it would be a serious mistake to read Wright's historicizing interpretation of apocalyptic texts in *Jesus and the Victory of God* as a strategy for escaping the theological problems of unfulfilled apocalyptic hope.

Indeed, if anything, Wright's reading of the Jesus tradition cranks the tension between promise and present reality even higher; if Jesus has already enacted the return of YHWH to Zion, how can we possibly explain the persistence of suffering in the world? Wright sees this problem clearly and articulates it with characteristic eloquence: "Jesus interpreted his coming death, and the vindication he expected after that death, as the defeat of evil; but on the first Easter Monday evil still stalked the earth from Jerusalem to Gibralter and beyond, and stalks it still."[28] This means that, despite Wright's tendency to downplay the "delay of the parousia" as a problem for early Christian theology,[29] the urgency of our longing for final fulfillment can only be intensified by the foretaste of vindication that we have already been given. As Paul says,

24. E.g., Wright, *Jesus and the Victory of God*, 635.
25. Wright, *New Testament and the People of God*, 461.
26. Wright, *New Testament and the People of God*, 459.
27. Wright, *New Testament and the People of God*, 461.
28. Wright, *Jesus and the Victory of God*, 659.
29. E.g., Wright, *New Testament and the People of God*, 462–64.

> We know that the whole creation has been groaning in labor pains until now; and not only the creation, but we ourselves, who have the first fruits of the Spirit, groan inwardly while we wait for adoption, the redemption of our bodies. (Rom 8:22–23)

This theological problem—or, perhaps more accurately, this dimension of Christian experience—has not yet been adequately addressed by Wright's massive multivolume project, but it surely cries out to be dealt with in his future work.

Why We Need Apocalyptic Eschatology

We have surveyed three strategies for coping with the offense of the NT's apocalyptic theology: the Johannine tendency to envelop temporal eschatology in a timeless "vertical" eschatology of union with Christ; the revisionist dismissal of apocalyptic through isolating an idealized construction of Jesus from the canonical witnesses; and N. T. Wright's reading of the synoptic apocalyptic passages as symbolic references to events that have already occurred in the death and resurrection of Jesus. As we have seen, none of these strategies offers a satisfactory solution to the problem succinctly summarized by the author of the Letter to the Hebrews: "But now we do not yet see all things subjected to him" (Heb 2:8). History continues its grinding litany of human atrocities, and we see no compelling evidence that God is answering the prayer that Jesus taught us to pray: "May your kingdom come; may your will be done on earth, as it is in heaven" (Matt 6:10).

Consequently, as we begin a new millennium, the moment is propitious to recall that the preaching of the gospel—and the effort to comprehend theologically the gospel that we preach—cannot dispense with apocalyptic eschatology. The gospel is intelligible only within a narrative world shaped by biblical apocalyptic hope. Why is the NT's apocalyptic eschatology essential to Christian faith? The following enumeration of seven reasons is neither exhaustive nor fully developed, but it may serve as a starting place for further reflection.

(1) *The church needs apocalyptic eschatology to carry Israel's story forward.* Without a future-directed eschatological hope, we cannot affirm God's faithfulness to Israel, and the historical fate of the Jewish people becomes theologically unintelligible. The OT repeatedly narrates God's promise of faithfulness to Israel, pointing toward a future day in which "the Lord will vindicate his people, have compassion on his servants" (Deut 32:36). There will be a day, according to the prophetic promise, when God "will come to Zion as Redeemer"

(Isa 59:20) and gather the scattered exiles into a restored Israel where the glory of the Lord is manifest (60:1–4), and the people neither suffer violence nor inflict it (65:17–25). To be sure, the NT proclaims that these promises find their proleptic fulfillment in Jesus Christ and in the church as a prefiguration of the eschatological people of God, but the historical existence of the church is (only) a sign and anticipation of the full divine embracing (πρόσλημψις) of the eschatological Israel, including the empirical Jewish people who have—at least temporarily—refused the gospel (Rom 11:15).

To put the matter differently, without apocalyptic eschatology, Christian theology becomes inescapably supersessionist. If we do not believe that God will ultimately fulfill his promises by restoring Israel, then the OT can only be read in one of two ways: either it is merely an allegorical prefiguration of Christianity, or it is a primitive evolutionary stage now transcended by Christianity as a higher and purer religion. Either way, the outcome is a form of Christian theology that, when faced with Paul's plaintive question, "Has God rejected his people?" must answer, "Yes, as a matter of fact, he has." To give such an answer, however, is not only to reject Paul's anguished protestation to the contrary (Rom 9–11) but also to plunge our doctrine of God into an abyss of incoherence. If God can be faithless to Israel, then we are dealing with a fickle deity whose promises are not to be trusted.

God's apocalyptic deliverance of all Israel (Rom 11:26–27) is the mysterious missing piece of the puzzle in God's sovereign dealings with the world. Such a future is necessary in order to make sense of the past.

(2) *The church needs apocalyptic eschatology for interpreting the cross as a saving event for the world.* A similar point can be made about the cross as the climax of Israel's story. If Christian preaching is "to know nothing . . . except Jesus Christ, and him crucified" (1 Cor 2:2), we will find ourselves committed to telling an unfinished story, a story that requires an ending adumbrated, though not yet fully written, by the NT accounts of the resurrection. If we are to be faithful to the NT witnesses, we cannot interpret the death of Jesus solely as a propitiatory sacrifice for the forgiveness of the sins of individuals; the cross can be interpreted as an atoning event only if and when it is placed within the larger apocalyptic narrative of God's ultimate triumph over evil and death. In the event of the cross, God destroys the powers of the old order and inaugurates a new creation (Gal 6:14–16); yet, the syntax of this narrative requires the eschatological reservation ("not yet") and the future orientation of hope. The point is elegantly illustrated by Paul's careful formulation in 1 Cor 15:20–23, in which he insists that the resurrection of Jesus must be understood as the "first fruits" of the eschatological consummation:

> But in fact Christ *has been raised* from the dead, *the first fruits* of those who have died. For since death came through a human being, the resurrection of the dead *has* also *come* through a human being; for as all die in Adam, so all *will be* made alive in Christ. *But each in his own order: Christ the first fruits, then at his coming* (ἐν τῇ παρουσίᾳ αὐτοῦ) *those who belong to Christ.*

Without this promise, whose final fulfillment we do not yet see, the cross can only be construed as a defeat rather than a victory over the world.

(3) *The church needs apocalyptic eschatology for the gospel's political critique of pagan culture.* Without the claim that Jesus is the one to whom, ultimately, every knee will bow and every tongue confess (Phil 2:9–11), Christian theology loses its critical edge against pagan culture, accepts the politics of this world, and becomes spiritually otherworldly. "Render to Caesar the things that are Caesar's and to God the things that are God's" (Mark 12:17), rather than being heard in its original context as a challenge to apocalyptic discernment,[30] becomes domesticated into a maxim that cedes to Caesar sovereignty over the everyday world. But when we pray for the coming of the βασιλεία τοῦ Θεοῦ on earth as it is in heaven, we continually reaffirm the politically subversive vocation of the church as an anticipation of God's future, and we anticipate the day when we can truly sing, "The kingdom of the world has become the kingdom of our Lord and of his Christ" (Rev 11:15). As Oliver O'Donovan has observed, the Apocalypse of John bears witness to "that authority of truth and righteousness which our experience of political society on earth has consistently denied us," thereby "confronting a false political order with the foundation of a true one."[31] It is, therefore, no accident that the book of Revelation comes hermeneutically into focus when it is read as a political resistance document by communities of oppressed people, as in the civil rights movement in the United States or the struggle against apartheid in South Africa.[32] Understood in this way, Revelation becomes a diagnostic tool that enables us to recognize that Caesar's power is transient—and thereby to resist the seductions of materialism and violence in the world around us.

The Magnificat of Mary (Luke 1:46–55), though its verbs are conjugated prophetically in the aorist tense, is a profoundly apocalyptic text, envisioning

30. Ched Myers, *Binding the Strong Man: A Political Reading of Mark's Story of Jesus* (Maryknoll, NY: Orbis, 1988), 312.

31. Oliver O'Donovan, "The Political Thought of the Book of Revelation," *TynBul* 37 (1986): 90.

32. Schüssler Fiorenza, *Revelation*; Richard B. Hays, *The Moral Vision of the New Testament* (San Francisco: HarperSanFrancisco, 1996), 181–84.

God's eschatological reversal of the fortunes of the powerful and the lowly, God's help for the hungry and dismissal of the rich. A church trained by such imagery to see God's new world coming can never lapse into comfortable accommodation with the status quo in an unjust world.

(4) *The church needs apocalyptic eschatology to resist ecclesial complacency and triumphalism.* I have just said that a church trained by apocalyptic imagery cannot lapse into accommodation with the status quo, but of course that is a prescriptive remark rather than a descriptive one. In fact, the church can and does lapse into complacency. Where this is so—as we are reminded by the lectionary texts each Advent season—apocalyptic eschatology sounds a wakeup call. Thus, the critical cutting edge of apocalyptic challenges not only pagan idolatry but also ecclesial self-satisfaction. The numerous synoptic parables warning servants to remain alert and faithful in the absence of their master (e.g. Matt 24:45–25:30, placed significantly immediately following Matthew's "apocalypse" passage about the end of the age) stand as permanent reminders to the church in the time between the times that we must "be ready, for the Son of Man is coming at an unexpected hour" (Matt 24:44; cf. Mark 13:32–37). How are we to be ready? "Blessed is that slave whom his master will find at work when [his master] arrives" (Matt 24:46).

The letters to the seven churches in Rev 2:1–3:22 also illustrate this admonitory, corrective function of apocalyptic discourse. Words of comfort are spoken to communities that endure faithfully and keep God's word even though they have little power (e.g., 3:8), but the church at Laodicea, which perceives itself as rich and prosperous, is sternly warned of God's coming judgment: "because you are . . . neither cold nor hot, I am about to spit you out of my mouth" (3:16–17). Those who heed Christ's prophetic warning, however, will be granted the final reward of exaltation with Christ on his throne (v. 21). The looming reality of the final judgment serves to keep the church from grandiose perceptions of its own importance—for it is only a provisional servant of God's purposes in the time between the times—and also from becoming fat, sleepy, and abusive.[33]

(5) *The church needs apocalyptic eschatology in order to affirm the body.* This point may not be immediately obvious, because apocalyptic thought has so often been carelessly associated with "dualism" and annihilation of this worldly reality. In fact, however, where Christian theology has remained most closely in touch with its Jewish apocalyptic roots, it has most firmly insisted

33. For a treatment of the pastoral functions of apocalyptic judgment language, see David Kuck, *Judgment and Community Conflict: Paul's Use of Apocalyptic Judgment Language in 1 Corinthians 3:5–4:5*, NovTSup 66 (Leiden: Brill, 1992).

on the value and importance of embodied existence, in contrast to forms of Hellenized piety that regard the material realm as evil or inferior. The gospel proclaims the resurrection of the body, not the immortality of the disembodied soul. As Käsemann recognized, apocalyptic eschatology affirms the creator's final sovereignty over creation and his refusal to abandon it to decay. God is faithful to redeem what he has created. The alternative to the apocalyptic vision, then, is some form of Gnosticism that denies God's redemptive intention for creation and the body.

Paul had to drive this point home forcefully to some of the Corinthians who sought to accommodate the gospel to enlightened philosophical ideas about the transcendence of crass bodily existence. Paul insists, on the contrary, that the resurrection of the body is at the very heart of the gospel and that those who deny it are lost in futility (1 Cor 15:12–19). It may also follow that many of the Corinthians' moral problems were related to a perception that the body is of no consequence: sexual immorality (5:1–2; 6:12–20), rejection of sex within marriage (7:1–7), casual participation in eating idol meat (8:1–11:1), and excessive exaltation of certain spiritual gifts (12:1–14:40). Paul's final answer to these abuses is to reassert at great length the doctrine of the resurrection of the body (1 Cor 15), while taking care to explain that resurrection entails not merely an endorsement or continuation of embodied life as we know it but rather a transformation into a new embodied state beyond our limited powers of imagination (vv. 35–58).

Sadly, many Christians at the turn of the millennium have lost sight of the fundamental apocalyptic doctrine of the resurrection of the body. Those who continue to hope for some sort of postmortem existence more often imagine a disembodied salvation of the soul. In this circumstance, theology may need a millennial reminder of Justin Martyr's fierce advocacy of the doctrine of the resurrection. He observes sourly that there are "some who are called Christians . . . who say that there is no resurrection of the dead (ἀνάστασις νεκρῶν), and that their souls, when they die, are taken to heaven." He unhesitatingly labels such people as "godless, impious heretics," and declares that "I and others, who are right-minded Christians on all points, are assured that there will be a resurrection of the dead (σαρκὸς ἀνάστασιν)."[34] We may not need to emulate Justin's truculence, but the clarity of our theology would be well served by emulating his robust affirmation of the resurrection of the body.[35]

34. Justin Martyr, *Dialogue with Trypho* 80; English translation from *ANF* 1.

35. For further discussion, see Richard B. Hays, *First Corinthians*, IBC (Louisville: Westminster John Knox, 1997), 252–82.

(6) *The church needs apocalyptic eschatology to ground its mission.* In Acts 1, at the conclusion of the risen Lord's instruction of apostles, they ask him, "Lord, is this the time when you will restore the kingdom to Israel?" (Acts 1:6). This is not a stupid question. Jesus has been teaching them about this very thing (v. 4), and Luke has portrayed Jesus, from the beginning of his Gospel, as one who will fulfill Israel's hope (e.g., Luke 1:54–55, 68–75). The raising of the crucified Jesus from the grave could easily be understood as an apocalyptic sign that the final restoration of Israel was indeed at hand. Jesus's answer, however, without rejecting the premise of their question, makes it clear that they are not to speculate about the timing of the kingdom's coming and that he has business for them to attend to: they are to be his witnesses in an expanding mission that will extend to the ends of the earth (Acts 1:7–8). These words of commissioning are Jesus's last words, for he is immediately taken up into heaven, before the eyes of the gaping apostles. Luke, in a deft narrative stroke, reinforces Jesus's message by bringing onstage two angelic figures, who shatter the followers' reverie with a wry question and a piece of important information:

> "Men of Galilee, why do you stand looking up toward heaven? This Jesus, who has been taken up from you into heaven, will come in the same way as you saw him go into heaven." (1:11)

Just as Jesus did not reject the apostles' hope that perhaps the kingdom was at hand, so the angels reinforce the apocalyptic expectation of Jesus's coming again from heaven; just as Jesus redirected the apostles' attention away from speculation about the time of the restoration, so the angels implicitly redirect their attention from cloud gazing to the words just spoken by Jesus. They say, in effect, "Why are you standing there gawking? You've been given a job to do!"

This interplay of apocalyptic expectation and missional imperative is programmatic for Luke's second volume. The coming of the Holy Spirit, which will empower the mission (Acts 1:8), is itself an eschatological sign of "the last days" (2:17, quoting Joel 2:28), and the apostles' work of testifying everywhere as Jesus's witnesses is therefore to be carried out as a fulfillment of eschatological prophecy about the extension of God's sovereignty over the whole world; the Spirit is now to be poured out on "all flesh" (Acts 2:17), and all who call on the name of the Lord will be saved (vv. 21, 39). Yet Luke consistently focuses attention not on speculative timetables and scenarios but on the formation of the church as an eschatological community manifesting God's grace and power (2:41–47; 4:32–37).

Without the apocalyptic outpouring of the Spirit, the formation of such a community is impossible. The community's identity is given in and with its commission to serve as the instrument of God's proclamation to the world; the "great grace" that is upon them—as attested by the eradication of poverty through their practices of economic sharing (4:32–35)—is a proleptic sign of the "universal restoration" promised by the prophets (3:21).

Thus, in this Lukan portrayal, the mission of the church develops under the umbrella of apocalyptic eschatology. Even while Luke creates an extended interval for the expansion of the mission throughout the empire, the mission itself makes sense only as a part of the unfolding plan of God, which is interpreted in apocalyptic categories: the apostles' preaching of the resurrection offers the possibility of repentance in preparation for the day appointed for God's ultimate judgment (e.g., Acts 17:31).

Luke is hardly alone among NT writers in depicting the mission of the church as the outworking of God's apocalyptic design for judgment and redemption of the world (see, e.g., 2 Cor 5:11–6:2; Eph 3:7–13). Precisely to the degree that Luke is perceived to downplay apocalyptic expectation, the observations offered here become the more striking: the mission of the church is comprehensible in Luke-Acts only as an end-time phenomenon. Without this theological grounding, the mission loses both its rationale and its urgency. It is perhaps not too much to suggest that the liberal Protestant church's loss of a sense of missional urgency is directly correlated with the evaporation of its eschatological expectation.

(7) *The church needs apocalyptic eschatology to speak with integrity about suffering and death.* The NT's vision of a final resurrection of the dead enables us to tell the truth about the present, including its tragedies and injustices, without sentimental sugarcoating, without cynicism or despair. It allows us to name suffering and death as real and evil, but not final.

Too often, Christians use pious language about how those who have died have "gone to heaven" or "have gone to a better place" in order to deny the reality of death. Worse, the denial of death sometimes completely trumps the teaching of Scripture and tradition; I recently listened with horror at a Christian memorial service as a well-meaning family member of the deceased read an overtly pantheistic poem, in which the speaking persona of the dead person claimed to be present in various natural phenomena of wind and stars and sunsets and so forth, concluding with the cruelly deceitful affirmation, "I did not die."

Against all of this, the NT's apocalyptic eschatology offers a sturdy realism that acknowledges the reality of death, while looking to God ultimately to restore life and set all things right. In 1 Thess 4:13–18, Paul offers pastoral consolation concerning the deceased precisely by appealing to apocalyptic eschatology:

> But we do not want you to be uninformed, brothers and sisters, about those who have died, so that you may not grieve as others do who have no hope. For since we believe that Jesus died and rose again, even so, through Jesus, God will bring with him those who have died.

Paul continues his description of an apocalyptic scenario in which the Lord will descend from heaven with the sound of God's trumpet and the dead will rise and be caught up together with the living to be with the Lord forever. The striking thing is that Paul does not seek to comfort the grieving bereaved Thessalonians by telling them that their loved ones are already in heaven with Jesus. He acknowledges that the dead are dead and buried. The apocalyptic hope is that in the resurrection they will be reunited with the living in the new world brought into being at Christ's return. These are the words with which Christians are to "encourage one another" (1 Thess 4:18). These same considerations apply on a larger scale to Christian theology's reflection about the terrible tragedies that violent human cultures bring upon the world. In the face of mass murders, nonapocalyptic theology is singularly trivial and helpless. As Dale Allison writes,

> Jesus, the millenarian herald of judgment and salvation, says the only things worth saying. . . . If our wounds never heal, if the outrageous spectacle of a history filled with cataclysmic sadness is never undone, if there is nothing more for those who were slaughtered in the death camps or for six-year olds devoured by cancer, then let us eat and drink, for tomorrow we die. If in the end there is no good God to calm this sea of troubles, to raise the dead, and to give good news to the poor, then this is indeed a tale told by an idiot, signifying nothing.[36]

But an apocalyptically formed Christian faith knows how to confess that, while we groan along with a creation in bondage to decay, we wait eagerly for the redemption of our bodies. We hope for what we do not see and trust that the glory that is to be revealed will swallow up death and mourning and pain,

36. Allison, *Jesus of Nazareth*, 219.

when, in the new Jerusalem, God will wipe away every tear from our eyes (Rom 8:18–25; Rev 21:1–4).

The Hermeneutical Agenda: Apocalyptic Intratextuality

In the face of these formidable reasons why Christian theology requires apocalyptic eschatology, it might still be objected that some hermeneutical device is required to make apocalyptic thought intelligible for people in Western culture at the dawn of this new millennium. Two objections in particular are often raised against the viability of apocalyptic theology.

First, hasn't the passage of time disconfirmed the literal apocalyptic hopes of the NT writers? The answer is, simply, no. The NT itself already makes clear that the duration of the present age is uncertain and the date of Christ's return unknowable to mortal kind. It is therefore foolish presumption for us to turn the calendar page and declare, "It's been too long now; I guess he's not coming." This complaint was being voiced already by "scoffers" at the time of the writing of 2 Peter, probably the latest document in the NT canon (2 Pet 3:3–4). The answer given there (vv. 8–10) is a theologically profound one, alluding to the psalmist's doxological confession:

> For a thousand years in your sight
> are like yesterday when it is past,
> or like a watch in the night. (Ps 90:4)

Our mortal sense of temporality gives us no clue about God's timing, and we have no criteria to assess the appropriateness of the lag time between Christ's resurrection and parousia.

Second, hasn't science done away with the mythic cosmology presupposed by apocalyptic thought? This is where Wright's discussion of the character of apocalyptic language proves helpful.[37] As he rightly observes, such language was always poetic and metaphorical, from its OT origins onwards. The imagery used to articulate the apocalyptic hope must be interpreted with literary discernment, not in a flatfootedly literal way. This is not a matter of demythologizing the text for modern readers but of interpreting the text in accordance with the literary conventions of its own time. For instance, when Mark's Gospel

37. Wright, *New Testament and the People of God*, 280–338. See also G. B. Caird, *The Language and Imagery of the Bible* (London: Duckworth, 1980).

speaks of the sun and moon being darkened and the stars falling from the sky (Mark 13:24–25), these celestial portents should be read as figurative markers of cataclysmic *historical* events. Or again, Paul's poetic imagery of trumpets and clouds (1 Thess 4:13–18) draws on the iconographic vocabulary of biblical apocalyptic to depict the firm future hope that God will not abandon his creation, that God will make all things new. The images refer to real events in the future (i.e., the return of Christ, the resurrection of the dead), but the details of the description are imaginative constructions that should not be pressed literalistically.

When the NT writers describe the shape of the eschatological reality, they often exercise noteworthy restraint, hinting at images seen through a glass darkly. Here, for example, is 1 John on the character of our transformed future existence: "Beloved, we are God's children now; what we will be has not yet been revealed. What we do know is this: when he is revealed, we will be like him, for we will see him as he is" (1 John 3:2). Or again, here is Paul on the character of the "glory that is to be revealed": "Now hope that is seen is not hope. For who hopes for what he sees? But if we hope for what we do not see, we wait for it with patient endurance" (Rom 8:24–25). Such reverently restrained statements provide the interpretive lens through which we should read the more exuberant imagery of 1 Thess 4 or the book of Revelation. Apocalyptic theology holds open the question of the shape of the redeemed world, rather than prematurely foreclosing it.

With these caveats in place, I would suggest that the difficulty of reading apocalyptic texts has been vastly overstated by interpreters who seek to minimize the apocalyptic content of Christian proclamation. In fact, given the centrality of apocalyptic thought in the NT and the failure of demythologizing hermeneutical strategies, Christian theologians should press forward to a robust recovery of apocalyptic teaching and preaching. This recommendation is not a marketing strategy calculated to exploit millennium fever, which will, in any case, already have abated by the time this article appears in print. The recovery of unabashed apocalyptic theology is, rather, a recommendation pressed upon us by the character of the NT witnesses themselves, who steadily and adamantly construe the significance of Jesus's proclamation, as well as his death and resurrection, within apocalyptic categories.

What aspects of the apocalyptic narrative are indispensable anchor points for us as we look to a future disclosure of God's redemptive purpose for the world? I would suggest that the NT's story leads us to affirm, in a strong literal sense,[38] the ultimate glorification of Jesus Christ as Lord over all creation,

38. On the meaning of "literal sense," see Kathryn Greene-McCreight, *Ad Litteram: How*

the resurrection of the body, God's final judgment of all humanity, and "the life of the world to come" in true justice and peace. The echo of the Nicene Creed in that formulation is no accident. The church's credal heritage and its liturgy remind us again and again that the gospel is apocalyptic to the core. The Eucharistic liturgy condenses the gospel story into a threefold acclamation: "Christ has died, Christ is risen, Christ will come again." Any theology faithful to the NT witnesses must give balanced attention to all three moments of the story, two of which are indelibly apocalyptic in character.

What I am proposing here is an implication—not heretofore sufficiently noted—of George Lindbeck's salutary prescription that theology should be done as an "intratextual" enterprise.[39] If, as I have contended, the canonical NT is strongly apocalyptic in its interpretation of the story of Jesus, then to live and think within that story will necessarily draw the church into sharing its apocalyptic frame of reference. As we are formed by the story, we will learn to discern our own place as servants charged to watch expectantly in this time between the times.

Augustine, Calvin, and Barth Read the "Plain Sense" of Genesis 1–3, Issues in Systematic Theology 5 (New York: Peter Lang, 1999).

39. George A. Lindbeck, *The Nature of Doctrine: Religion and Theology in a Postliberal Age* (Philadelphia: Westminster, 1984), 112–38. Lindbeck writes, "Intratextual theology redescribes reality within the scriptural framework rather than translating Scripture into extrascriptural categories. It is the text, so to speak, which absorbs the world, rather than the world the text" (118).

Conclusion

A Hermeneutic of Trust

The Protestant Reformers of the sixteenth century proclaimed that God's word in Scripture must serve as the final judge of all human tradition and experience. Left to our own devices, we are capable of infinite self-deception, confusion, and evil. We therefore must turn to Scripture and submit ourselves to it, the Reformers insisted, to find our disorders rightly diagnosed and healed. Only through the biblical writers' testimony do we encounter the message of God's grace; only the revelation of Jesus Christ, disclosed uniquely and irreplaceably through the testimony of the evangelists and apostles, tells us the truth about the merciful God and our relationship to that God. Without this word which comes to us from outside ourselves, we are lost.

Clearly, the climate in which we read the Bible has changed drastically. Living as we do on this side of the Enlightenment, we cannot escape the intellectual impact of the great "masters of suspicion": Nietzsche, Marx, Freud, and more recently Foucault, along with other purveyors of "critical theory." These thinkers have sought to demystify language and to expose the ways in which our linguistic and cultural systems are constructed by ideologies that further the interests of those who hold power.

The Bible has not been exempt from such suspicious scrutiny. One need only consider the book display at the annual convention of the American Academy of Religion and the Society of Biblical Literature. Anyone who spends time browsing there will find the stalls flooded with books that apply a hermeneutic of suspicion to biblical texts. Some portray the apostolic witnesses less as revelatory witnesses to God's mercy than as oppressive promulgators of abusive images of God. For example, Elisabeth Schüssler Fiorenza writes that "a feminist

This essay was originally presented as a paper at the 1996 Annual Meeting of the Society of Biblical Literature in New Orleans.

critical hermeneutics of suspicion places a warning label on all biblical texts: *Caution! Could be dangerous to your health and survival.*"[1] I am not suggesting that suspicious interpreters categorically reject the Bible; most of them believe it can contain both liberating and oppressive messages. That is why they suggest that we must subject the Bible to ideological critique. Elsewhere Schüssler Fiorenza explains: "No biblical patriarchal text that perpetuates violence against women, children, or 'slaves' should be accorded the status of divine revelation if we do not want to turn the God of the Bible into a God of violence. That does not mean that we cannot preach . . . on the household code texts of the New Testament. It only means that we must preach them critically in order to unmask them as texts promoting patriarchal violence."[2]

The moral passion of such statements is to be welcomed. Sadly, our common history is marked by epidemic violence, including violence against women, children, and the powerless. Certainly this violence is to be condemned, and one might hope that interpreters of the Bible would have good grounds for proclaiming such condemnation. The difficulty in which we find ourselves, however, is this: If the Bible itself—the revelatory, identity-defining text of the Christian community—is portrayed as oppressive, on what basis do we know God or relate to God? A corollary question has crucial implications for biblical interpretation: If the Bible is dangerous, on what ground do we stand in conducting a critique of Scripture that will render it less harmful?

For Schüssler Fiorenza the answer to the latter question is clear: a feminist critical hermeneutic "does not appeal to the Bible as its primary source but begins with women's own experience and vision of liberation."[3] *Experience* (of a certain sort) is treated as unambiguously revelatory, and the Bible is critically scrutinized in its light. Regrettably, many practitioners of the hermeneutics of suspicion—and by no means only feminist interpreters—are remarkably credulous about the claims of experience. As a result, they endlessly critique the biblical texts but rarely get around to hearing Scripture's critique of us or hearing its message of grace.

While the hermeneutics of suspicion—rightly employed—occupies a proper place in any attempt to interpret the Bible for our time, I want to argue that a *hermeneutic of trust* is both necessary and primary. To get our bearings

1. Elisabeth Schüssler Fiorenza, "The Will to Choose or to Reject: Continuing Our Critical Work," in *Feminist Interpretation of the Bible*, ed. Letty M. Russell (Philadelphia: Westminster, 1985), 130.

2. Elisabeth Schüssler Fiorenza, *Bread Not Stone: The Challenge of Feminist Biblical Interpretation* (Boston: Beacon, 1984), 145.

3. Schüssler Fiorenza, *Bread Not Stone*, 88.

on the question of our fundamental attitude toward Scripture, I propose that we take our cue from the Reformers and return to Scripture itself.[4] If we attend carefully to Paul's treatment of trust and distrust in his letter to the Romans, the apostle may lead us to suspect our own suspicions.

This essay will proceed in four stages: (1) an examination of Paul's use of the term πίστις ("faith" or "trust") and its opposite, ἀπιστία (lit., "unfaith" or "distrust"), in Romans; (2) some observations about the relation between trust and atonement; (3) a discussion of Paul's *own* approach to Scripture interpretation as a model of the hermeneutic of trust; and (4) some theses about the practical implications of all this for our own practices of interpretation.

Ἀπιστία and Πίστις in Romans

According to Paul, those who stand in right relation to God are those who hear and trust what God has spoken. He laments Israel's tragic failure to do this. The name he gives that failure is ἀπιστία (Rom 3:3). The term refers both to the failure of the people of Israel to obey God's Torah and to their failure to trust God's covenant promises—and the two things are bound closely together. Their ἀπιστία has been brought into stark focus for Paul through their negative response to the proclaimed gospel of Jesus Christ. He addresses the problem explicitly in Rom 3:1–4: "Then what advantage has the Jew? Or what is the value of circumcision? Much, in every way. For in the first place the Jews were entrusted (ἐπιστεύθησαν) with the oracles of God. What if some were unfaithful (ἠπίστησαν)? Their ἀπιστία doesn't nullify the πίστις of God, does it? By no means!" Paul's wordplay highlights the contrast between human infidelity and God's fidelity: God's faithfulness to Israel (πίστις) is declared to Israel through the word of promise ("the oracles of God"). But Israel, failing to trust that word, is guilty of unfaithfulness—ἀπιστία. We might well translate the word here as "distrust" or "suspicion." Rather than trusting the scriptural oracles of God (which, in Paul's view, point to Christ and the church), they have slid away into unfaithfulness, just like the gentiles (cf. also 9:30–33). Nonetheless, their unfaithfulness cannot negate the faithfulness of the God who has embraced them through the covenant promise spoken to them.

4. The Reformers were not naive or credulous readers: they were acutely suspicious of the ecclesiastical institutions that controlled interpretation in their time; however, it was their conviction that only a fresh reading of Scripture under the guidance of the Holy Spirit gave them critical leverage against these institutions.

The paradoxical relation between Israel's unfaithfulness and the divine faithfulness creates the problem that Paul wrestles with throughout the letter. His reflections on these issues culminate in chapter 11, where the theme of Israel's ἀπιστία arises once again in his metaphor of the olive branches broken off the tree: "They were broken off because of their ἀπιστία but you stand only through πίστις. . . . But even these, if they do not persist in ἀπιστία, will be grafted in, for God has the power to graft them in again" (Rom 11:20, 23).

Earlier in the letter Paul depicted Abraham, in contrast to unfaithful Israel, as the figural type of trust in God:

> Hoping against hope, he trusted (ἐπίστευσεν) that he would become "the father of many nations," according to what was said, "So numerous shall your descendants be" [Gen 15:5]. He did not weaken in trust (πίστει) when he considered his own body, which was already as good as dead (for he was about a hundred years old), or when he considered the barrenness of Sarah's womb. No distrust (ἀπιστία) made him waver concerning the promise of God, but he grew strong in trust (πίστει) as he gave glory to God, being fully convinced that God was able to do what he had promised. (Rom 4:18–21)

This passage is particularly interesting because Abraham's πίστις is interpreted explicitly as his *trust* in God's promise despite its incongruence with Abraham's own *experience* of sterility and frustration. Abraham might have had good reason to exercise a hermeneutic of suspicion toward the divine word that had promised him numerous descendants, for all the empirical evidence—his experience—seemed to disconfirm God's word. Yet he did not: "no ἀπιστία," no suspicion, "made him waver." Abraham was not a simpleton who failed to see the tension between his experience and the word that God had spoken to him. He had to wrestle with doubts and—indeed—with the extinction of all human hope for normal progeny. This wrestling is clearer in the Genesis narrative, where Abraham openly questions God (see Gen 15:2–3; 16:1–16; 17:17–18; for Sarah's doubts see 18:12–15), than in Paul's brief summary. Nonetheless, according to Paul, Abraham discounted his own experience, rejected skepticism, and clung to the promise of God "who gives life to the dead and calls into existence the things that do not exist" (Rom 4:17); therefore, "it was reckoned to him as righteousness." Thus, Abraham becomes the prototype of the community of faith, which interprets all human experience through trust in God's word: in short, *Abraham exemplifies a hermeneutic of consent, a hermeneutic of trust*. (In this respect he is like

Mary, who asks suspiciously, "How can this be?" but in the end submits herself to the word of promise: "Let it be with me according to your word," Luke 1:34, 38.)

A trusting hermeneutic is essential for all who believe the word of the resurrection but still see the creation groaning in bondage to decay and do not yet see death made subject to God. The hermeneutics of trust turns out to be, on closer inspection, a hermeneutics of death and resurrection[5]—a way of seeing the whole world through the lens of the kerygma. Our reliance on God entails a death to common sense, and our trust is validated only by the resurrection.

Trust and Atonement

For Paul the theme of trust—πίστις—is also intimately related to the formation of right relations between God and humans. Another way of saying this is that for Paul the themes of trust and atonement are inseparable. But I must sound an important caveat here. We must not suppose that we can place ourselves in right relation to God through our own act of trust, as though faith were a meritorious work. Rather, Paul's argument is that covenant relationship is restored by God's initiative διὰ πίστεως Ἰησοῦ Χριστοῦ—through the faithfulness of Jesus Christ. Thus, for Paul trust and atonement are inextricably linked *in the person of Jesus Christ.*[6]

Paul's view of the relationship between trust and atonement is most compactly articulated in Rom 3. The argument goes like this:

1 Israel's ἀπιστία cannot nullify the faithfulness (πίστις) of God (3:3–6a).
2 Jews and Greeks alike are under the power of sin (vv. 9–18).
3 The law holds the whole world accountable to God but has no power to *justify* those who are under the power of sin—to set them in right relation to God (vv. 19–20).
4 Therefore God's justice has been manifested apart from the Law through

5. I owe this observation to N. T. Wright (conversation on November 17, 1996). See now also Richard B. Hays, "Reading Scripture in Light of the Resurrection," in *The Art of Reading Scripture*, ed. Ellen F. Davis and Richard B. Hays (Grand Rapids: Eerdmans, 2003), 216–38.

6. See Richard B. Hays, *The Faith of Jesus Christ: The Normative Substructure of Gal 3:1–4:11*, 2nd ed. (Grand Rapids: Eerdmans, 2002 [1983]).

> the faithfulness (πίστις) of Jesus Christ (vv. 21–22)—through his obedient, self-sacrificial death on the cross.[7]

Thus, according to Paul, God has overcome our ἀπιστία through a dramatic new act of πίστις—the πίστις of Jesus Christ, whom God "put forward" as a definitive demonstration (ἔνδειξις) of God's own covenant faithfulness (v. 25). That is the meaning of "the righteousness of God" (v. 21). Our relationship of trust with God is restored through the faith of Jesus Christ.

Those who receive this good news respond to it with trust. Their πίστις, which is prefigured in the OT story of Abraham, becomes shaped by the pattern of Jesus's own faith-obedience. That is part of what Paul means when he says that those whom God calls are to be "conformed to the image of his Son" (Rom 8:29), and when he calls upon his readers to model themselves upon Christ Jesus who emptied himself and became obedient even unto death on a cross (Phil 2:5–13).

Thus, atonement for Paul is not merely the forgiveness of sins through a vicarious blood sacrifice. Atonement also entails the *transformation* of God's people into the image of Jesus Christ, who is the embodiment of trust in God. Because Jesus was faithful, we are both called and enabled to trust.

Paul's Own Interpretative Practice

Paul's understanding of *trust* not only characterizes his view of atonement but also shapes his hermeneutical theory and practice. Israel, he says, failed to trust the oracles of God (Rom 3:2–3), but he is determined that this error not be repeated in the interpretative practices of the new community of faith that is constituted by the trust of Jesus. With his mind remade by the gospel, Paul goes back to Scripture and reads it anew through a hermeneutic of trust.

Rereading Scripture from this new perspective was no less challenging a task for him than trusting God's promise was for Abraham. The actual *experience* of Paul's missionary preaching had created a serious difficulty, both for Paul and for the new community. As Paula Fredriksen has expressed it, among those who believed the gospel, there were "too many Gentiles, too few Jews, and no end in sight."[8] If God's purpose was to overcome Israel's ἀπιστία, what

7. Cf. Rom 5:19: "through the obedience of one man the many were constituted δίκαιοι (righteous)."

8. Paula Fredriksen, "Judaism, the Circumcision of the Gentiles, and Apocalyptic Hope: Another Look at Galatians 1 and 2," *JTS* 42 (1991): 532–64.

had gone wrong? Why did Israel persist in ἀπιστία even when it heard the proclamation of the heralds of good news?

In light of this crisis, Paul was driven back to Scripture. The promises of God to Israel must be true, he reasoned, because "the gifts and the calling of God are irrevocable" (Rom 11:29). But how can this be true in light of his own *experience*? Jews refused to accept the good news, and God apparently had conferred grace upon those who had not even been seeking righteousness at all—the gentiles. Scripture must be true, but how can this situation be understood?

The problem comes to a head, of course, in Rom 9–11. "I say then, has God abandoned his people?" (11:1). Paul's answer is a ringing μὴ γένοιτο, "No way!" Trusting that God had not abandoned Israel, he wrestled with Scripture and found his way to a powerful new reading of God's promises.

Romans 9–11 is a powerful example of the hermeneutic of trust in action. In these chapters Paul achieves a transformative rereading of Scripture through the lens of the conviction he articulated earlier in 5:8: "God shows his love for us in that while we were yet sinners Christ died for us." This conviction, applied to the problem of Israel's ἀπιστία, leads Paul to discover in Scripture both the prefiguration of God's calling of the gentiles ("Those who were not my people, I will call 'my people,'" 9:25, quoting Hos 2:25 [2:23 in English translations]) and the prefiguration of his ultimate mercy on Israel ("'God has not abandoned his people,' whom he foreknew," Rom 11:2, quoting Ps 94:14).[9]

Thus, in Paul's fresh reading of Scripture the whole mysterious drama of God's election of Israel, Israel's hardening, the incorporation of gentiles in to the people of God, and Israel's ultimate restoration is displayed as foretold *in Scripture itself*—but this foretelling can be recognized only when Scripture is read through the hermeneutic of trust. God's oracles and promises are interpreted anew, in ways no one could have foreseen, in light of the *experience* of grace through the death and resurrection of Jesus, and the *experience* of the conversion of many gentiles. At the same time, the church's experience in Paul's own historical moment is reinterpreted in light of Scripture, which leads Paul to warn gentile believers against being wise in their own conceits (Rom 11:25a). Events are in God's hands. Gentiles have no reason to boast. This dialectical process through which experience is positively correlated with Scripture is possible only through the hermeneutics of trust.[10]

9. Or again: "The Deliverer will come from Zion; he will banish unfaithfulness from Jacob; and this will be my covenant with them when I take away their sins" (Rom 11:26–27, quoting Isa 59:20–21 and 27:9, while alluding also to Jer 31:33–34).

10. For a much fuller discussion of Paul's strategies as an interpreter of Scripture, see Richard B. Hays, *Echoes of Scripture in the Letters of Paul* (New Haven: Yale University Press,

Reading Scripture with a Hermeneutic of Trust

What consequences follow from this analysis of Paul's hermeneutics for *our* work as interpreters of the word? At least three things can be said.

(1) To read Scripture rightly we must *trust the God who speaks through Scripture*. As Schüssler Fiorenza rightly insists, this God is not a God of violence, not an abuser, not a deceiver. This God so passionately desires our safety and wholeness that he has given his own Son to die for us. "The one who did not spare his own Son but gave him up for us all, how will he not also graciously give us all things, along with him?" (Rom 8:32). Like Abraham, like Mary, like Jesus, like Paul, we stand before God with empty and open hands. That is the posture in which the reading of Scripture is rightly to be performed. Peter Stuhlmacher says something similar when he calls for a "hermeneutics of consent" (*Einverständnis*): a readiness to receive trustingly what a loving God desires to give us through the testimony of those who have preceded us in the faith.[11]

(2) What, then, of the hermeneutics of suspicion? Is all questioning to be excluded, all critical reading banished? Μὴ γένοιτο. Asking necessary and difficult questions is not to be equated with ἀπιστία. When we read Scripture through a hermeneutic of trust in God, we discover that *we should indeed be suspicious*: suspicious first of all of *ourselves*, because our own minds have been corrupted and shaped by the present evil age (Gal 1:4). Our minds must be transformed by grace, and that happens nowhere more powerfully than through reading Scripture receptively and trustingly with the aid of the Holy Spirit.

Reading receptively and trustingly does not mean accepting everything in the text at face value, as Paul's own critical sifting of the Torah demonstrates. Cases may arise in which we must acknowledge internal tensions within Scripture that require us to choose guidance from one biblical witness and to reject another. Because the witness of Scripture itself is neither simple nor univocal, the hermeneutics of trust is necessarily a matter of faithful struggle to hear and discern.[12] Consequently, we welcome the readings offered by feminists and

---

1989); and *The Conversion of the Imagination: Paul as Interpreter of Israel's Scripture* (Grand Rapids: Eerdmans, 2005).

11. Peter Stuhlmacher, *Historical Criticism and Theological Interpretation of Scripture*, trans. Roy A. Harrisville (Philadelphia: Fortress, 1977).

12. For an extended attempt to work out how Scripture might shape the community of faith, including situations in which we find internal tensions within the canon, see Richard B. Hays, *The Moral Vision of the New Testament: Community, Cross, New Creation* (San Francisco: HarperSanFrancisco, 1996).

other interpreters whose experience enables them to hear the biblical texts in new and challenging ways.

At the same time, we should be suspicious of the institutions that govern and shape interpretation. That means not only ecclesiastical institutions but also academic institutions. If our critical readings lead us away from trusting the grace of God in Jesus Christ, then something is amiss, and we would do well to interrogate the methods and presuppositions that have taught us to distance ourselves arrogantly or fearfully from the text and to miss Scripture's gracious word of promise.

(3) My concern that distrust may impede our reading of the Bible leads me to my final point. The real work of interpretation is to *hear the text*. We must consider how to read and teach Scripture in a way that opens up its message, a way that both models and fosters trust in God. So much of the ideological critique that currently dominates the academy fails to achieve these ends. Scripture is critiqued but never *interpreted*. The critic *exposes* but never *exposits*. Thus the word itself recedes into the background, and we are left talking only about the politics of interpretation, having lost the capacity to *perform* interpretations.

Many of us in the academy are weary of these tactics of critical evasion. And perhaps the tide is beginning to turn. Frank Lentricchia, who teaches English literature at Duke, has published a remarkable public recantation of his prior complicity with an approach to criticism that concentrates on literary *theory* and ignores *literature*. The piece, which appeared in *Lingua Franca*, was titled "Last Will and Testament of an Ex–Literary Critic."

Lentricchia, whose earlier work earned him the epithet "the Dirty Harry of literary theory," was the author of *Criticism and Social Change* (1983), which argued for reading all literature as "the most devious of rhetorical discourses (writing with political designs upon us all), either in opposition to or in complicity with the power in place."[13] But Lentricchia has grown impatient with having his own critical perspective parroted by graduate students who have no love of literature, no appreciation for the themes and content of great literature—indeed, who rarely read it at all because they are so enamored of "critical theory." So now Lentricchia repents publicly:

> Over the last ten years, I've pretty much stopped reading literary criticism, because most of it isn't literary. But criticism it is of a sort—the sort that

13. Frank Lentricchia, "Last Will and Testament of an Ex–Literary Critic," *Lingua Franca*, September/October (1996): 60.

> stems from the sense that one is morally superior to the writers that one is supposedly describing. This posture is assumed when those writers represent the major islands of Western literary tradition, the central cultural engine—so it goes—of racism, poverty, sexism, homophobia, and imperialism: a cesspool that literary critics would expose for mankind's benefit.... It is impossible, this much is clear, to exaggerate the heroic self-inflation of academic literary criticism.... The fundamental, if only implied, message of much literary criticism is self-righteous, and it takes this form: "T. S. Eliot is a homophobe and I am not. Therefore, I am a better person than Eliot. Imitate me, not Eliot." To which the proper response is: "But T. S. Eliot could really write, and you can't. Tell us truly, is there no filth in your soul?"[14]

Lentricchia's question, "Tell us truly, is there no filth in your soul?" reaches back, perhaps unwittingly, to the deeper roots from which the Western literary imagination springs—an imaginative tradition that owes much to Paul's hermeneutic of trust in God and suspicion of ourselves. Precisely because there is filth in our own souls we come to the text of Scripture, expecting to find the hidden things of our hearts laid bare and expecting to encounter there the God who loves us.

When I was an undergraduate at Yale University, students flocked to Professor Alvin Kernan's lecture courses on Shakespeare. Kernan's work predated the academy's current infatuation with ideological criticism. Even though it was the late 1960s and we were all living in an atmosphere charged with political suspicion and protest, none of this overtly impinged on Kernan's lectures. Kernan was not a flashy lecturer. What, then, was the draw?

He *loved* the texts. His teaching method—as I remember it—was simply to engage in reflective close readings of the Shakespeare tragedies and comedies, delineating their rich texture of image and metaphor and opening up their complex central themes—moral, philosophical, and religious. Often, Kernan would devote a significant part of his lecture time to reading the text aloud, not in any highly dramatic manner, but with sensitivity to the text's rhythms and semantic nuances. I would often sit in class thinking, "Oh! . . . I hadn't *heard* that in the text before." And I would leave the class pondering the problems Shakespeare addressed: love, betrayal, fidelity, sacrifice, death, and hope.

In Shakespeare's *Measure for Measure* the self-righteous villain Angelo pronounces a death sentence on Claudio, who is guilty of committing fornication. Claudio's sister Isabella comes to Angelo to plead for the life of her brother,

14. Lentricchia, "Last Will and Testament," 60.

but Angelo, who is trying to manipulate Isabella into bed with him, spurns her suit, saying,

> Your brother is a forfeit of the law,
> And you but waste your words.

Isabella's reply alludes to the great theme of Romans and calls upon the hypocritical judge Angelo to see his life anew in light of God's judgment and grace:

> Why, all the souls that were, were forfeit once;
> And He that might the vantage best have took
> Found out the remedy. How would you be
> If He, which is the top of judgment, should
> But judge you as you are? O, think on that;
> And mercy then will breathe within your lips,
> Like man new made.[15]

Isabella resists the oppressor by applying a hermeneutic of suspicion to his pose of righteousness and by appealing to a hermeneutic of trust in the biblical story of God's mercy. Isabella is a profound interpreter of Scripture. We should follow her example.

15. William Shakespeare, *Measure for Measure* 2.2.

Epilogue

Dark Fruition—Waiting in Hope

I am honored to be here tonight. And I am grateful to all of you who have come this evening to hear a few reflections from me on the occasion of my retirement from Duke Divinity School. Most of all, though, I am grateful to God for granting me a little more world and time to think back on what has been and to ponder what is yet to come. The keynote of all I have to say is gratitude. "This is the day that the Lord has made; let us rejoice and be glad in it" (Ps 118:24).

Most of you will know that three years ago I received a devastating diagnosis of pancreatic cancer and went on medical leave to undergo chemotherapy, radiation, and surgery. When I left the dean's office in July of 2015, I left in tears, with my hair falling out. I took up the tasks of reviewing my will and writing directions for my funeral service.

As I stand here tonight, I am unexpectedly able to look back on that night, that year of now done darkness. Three years ago, I could not have anticipated returning, this past spring, for a final, full, strenuous, joyful semester of teaching Introduction to New Testament Interpretation and Greek Exegesis of Romans. I could not have anticipated still being here tonight, three years later, apparently healed, chastened, and hopeful at age seventy, to continue the conversation I have shared with this community for more than a quarter of a century. And I certainly could not have anticipated the altered perception—and other changes in me—wrought by staring death in the face.

That altered perception is evocatively named by the twentieth-century poet John Hall Wheelock in his poem "Song on Reaching Seventy." Here is how he describes seeing the world anew from the perspective of an old man's awakened awareness of mortality:

Originally presented as my retirement lecture at Duke Divinity School, September 25, 2018.

How bitterly sweet and dear
All things have grown! How shall we bear the brunt,
The fury and the joy of every sound and sight,
Now almost cruelly fierce with all delight . . .
Oh, every sight and sound
Has meaning now! . . .
Oh, joy that is almost pain, pain that is joy,
Unimaginable to the younger man or boy—
Nothing is quite fulfilled,
Nothing is lost;
But all is multiplied till the heart almost
Aches with its burden . . . [1]

"All is multiplied." I find that to be so.

Tonight I want to revisit a few biblical texts that continue to resonate in my heart, until the heart almost aches with its burden. Many of you will have heard me speak about these texts before. But as I reread them at age seventy, I find that they speak again with deeper resonance, just as the final movement of a symphony gathers up and re-sounds themes from the earlier movements, in a grand recapitulation that transforms them into something new and revelatory.

A Grain of Wheat

The first text I want to revisit comes from the Gospel of John, at the very end of Jesus's public career. He recognizes that "the hour has come," and that his death and departure from the world are imminent. His friends—he calls them friends—do not understand what is about to happen; indeed, John repeatedly tells us that it was only later, after Jesus was raised from the dead, that his disciples remembered and understood (e.g., John 2:22; 12:16). Their understanding of the Scripture, and the word that Jesus had spoken, would later be illumined by the Spirit that Jesus promised to send (16:12–15). But that understanding—for them, as it is necessarily also for us—was always *retrospective*. It was always an act of reading backwards, always necessarily a matter of memory and belated recognition.

1. John Hall Wheelock, "Song on Reaching Seventy," in *This Blessed Earth: New and Selected Poems, 1927–1977* (New York: Charles Scribner's Sons, 1978), 56–57.

Jesus alone could see into the future and rightly interpret the death he was about to undergo. And so he explained it by a parable:

> Very truly, I tell you, unless a grain of wheat falls into the earth and dies, it remains a single grain; but if it dies, it bears much fruit. Those who love their life lose it, and those who hate their life in this world will keep it for eternal life. Whoever serves me must follow me, and where I am, there will my servant be also. (John 12:24–26)

This parable of Jesus resonates with chords that echo throughout the NT. Jesus's impending death is to be not futile but fruitful. Jesus himself is the Word sown into the good dark earth. *He* is the single grain that falls into the earth and dies, and so yields a rich harvest. *His* faithfulness—the faithfulness of Jesus Christ—unto death on a cross will become life-giving for others. Everything depends on *his* self-giving, not on our efforts or on our intelligence, not even on our faith.

But right along with that proclamation, he calls his hearers to follow after him; he challenges them to surrender their own lives, not to clutch them possessively. And he promises that those who follow will be *with* him, not only in death but also the life of the resurrection; they will be part of the rich harvest. That is the challenge, and the promise, that Dietrich Bonhoeffer echoed in *The Cost of Discipleship,* a book that influenced me powerfully when Judy and I first read it together, almost fifty years ago. Bonhoeffer wrote, "When Christ calls a man, he bids him come and die."[2] When I first read Bonhoeffer's words, in the heady days of the civil rights movement and the protests against the Vietnam War, they seemed to me a stirring call, noble and heroic. Now I hear them as a darker and richer mystery. "Whenever Christ calls us, his call leads us to death."

2. The phrase comes from the 1949 English translation: Dietrich Bonhoeffer, *The Cost of Discipleship*, trans. R. H. Fuller, rev. Irmgard Booth (London: SCM, 1949 [1937]). I have cited it here from the Macmillan Paperbacks edition (New York: Macmillan, 1963), 99. In preparing for this lecture, I went back for the first time to check the German original (1937), which actually reads, "Jeder Ruf Christi führt in den Tod," lit., "Every call of Christ leads into death" (cited here from the standard critical edition of Bonhoeffer's works: Dietrich Bonhoeffer, *Nachfolge*, ed. Eberhard Bethge et al., Dietrich Bonhoeffer Works 4 (Munich: Chr. Kaiser, 1989), 81. Fuller's widely cited translation was corrected in the more recent English translation of Bonhoeffer's works to read, "Whenever Christ calls us, his call leads us into death" (Dietrich Bonhoeffer, *Discipleship*, trans. Barbara Green and Reinhard Kraus, Dietrich Bonhoeffer Works 4 [Minneapolis: Fortress, 2003], 87).

The poet/priest Malcolm Guite has also heard that summons. Four years ago, he spent a few weeks here at Duke Divinity School as artist/theologian in residence. While he was here, he wrote a sonnet responding to Jesus's parable of the grain of wheat. Some of you may have seen it; a copy of it, written in beautiful calligraphy by Stephanie Gehring Ladd, now hangs on the wall of the Divinity School's cloister walk.

A Grain of Wheat

Oh, let me fall as grain to the good earth
And die away from all dry separation,
Die to my sole self, and find new birth
Within that very death, a dark fruition,
Deep in this crowded underground, to learn
The earthy otherness of every other,
To know that nothing is achieved alone
But only where these other fallen gather.
If I bear fruit and break through to bright air,
Then fall upon me with your freeing flail
To shuck this husk and leave me sheer and clear
As heaven-handled Hopkins, that my fall
May be more fruitful and my autumn still
A golden evening where your barns are full.[3]

As I have lived a little deeper into my autumn years, I have made Malcolm's sonnet my own prayer, my own response to Jesus's promise and summons.

When I now read backwards over the span of my life, I see Jesus's parable about the grain of wheat as a fitting bookend to the text that first brought me up short as a self-absorbed, intellectually pretentious nineteen-year-old sophomore—a text that stunned me into offering my life to Jesus. I encountered that text—or should I say it encountered me?—in the Gospel of Mark, while I was randomly opening a pew Bible in a darkened church in deep winter:

> "If any want to become my followers, let them deny themselves and take up their cross and follow me. For those who want to save their life will lose it, and those who lose their life for my sake, and the sake of the gospel, will save it." (Mark 8:34–35)

3. Malcolm Guite, *Parable and Paradox* (Norwich: Canterbury Press, 2016), 63.

How did I understand that as a nineteen-year-old? I understood it, very narrowly it now seems to me, as a call to surrender my proud attempts (fueled by a superficial reading of existentialist philosophy) to construct for myself the meaning of my own life. I heard it as a call to discover a new philosophical worldview through believing in Jesus, even though that worldview might appear irrational. Well . . . that was a starting place.

But now when I hear Jesus speak of the grain that must fall into the earth and die, I understand him to mean something that is both more literal and more radically transformative. It is not merely a matter of exchanging an inadequate self-understanding for a better one. It is a matter of letting go of life itself, of entering the mystery of death and resurrection. My own brush with literal death has deepened my conviction that our hope lies in our union with Christ and in the ultimate promise of resurrection of the body. That is what I mean by suggesting that Jesus's saying is more literal—for us, just as it was for him. He really was about to die. We too will die. And, as Jesus was raised from the dead, so too will we be raised with him.

But Jesus's saying about the grain is also more radically *transformative* than I understood at age nineteen. For those who follow Jesus, his pattern of death followed by fruit bearing becomes a typos, a pattern that remolds *everything* in the life we still live in this mortal flesh. Dying in order to bear fruit is not something that happens once at a moment of conversion. It happens over the span of a life.

Perhaps what I mean will be clearer if I mention some of the things to which I have been called to die. As I now look back on my life up to the summer of 2015, I am painfully aware of some of the insidious ways in which I have been able to use God's gifts and my positions of privilege to assert my critical superiority and my advantage over others. When I was an undergraduate at Yale in the 1960s, we students were told over and over by the university administration that Yale's mission with each new incoming class was to educate "a thousand male leaders" for the next generation. Yes, "male leaders," for my graduating class of 1970 was the last all-male undergraduate class at Yale. And those thousand male leaders were, in those days, overwhelmingly white male leaders. We all believed in civil rights and social equality, of course, but we also believed we were smarter than everybody else, that we were destined for success, and that we should be in the position of prescribing social order and passing enlightened judgment on everyone else's ideas and practices.

I'm afraid that same prideful attitude carried over into my later studies in theology. It is a bitter paradox that those of us in the academic world can use our knowledge of Scripture and theology to gain leverage over others, to compete and climb the ladder, to advance to professorships and named chairs, while subtly aggrandizing ourselves and putting others down. And I fear that the same thing can happen within the politics of the church.

In the time unexpectedly given to me for reflection over these past three years, I have more than once recalled T. S. Eliot's words about the pain of looking backward at one's life. He writes of:

> . . . the rending pain of re-enactment
> Of all that you have done, and been; the shame
> Of motives late revealed, and the awareness
> Of things ill done and done to others' harm
> Which once you took for exercise of virtue.[4]

None of this should come as a surprise to those who have really thought about Jesus's stern words of warning for the scribes and Pharisees who sit in named chairs (he calls it "the seat of Moses") and love the places of honor at banquets and love to be greeted with respect by people who call them "Professor" (Matt 23:1–7). Nor should any of this come as a surprise for those of us instructed by the apostle Paul, who looked back at his own advantages of birth and academic achievement and critical superiority and pronounced this judgment: "Whatever gains I had, these I have come to regard as loss because of Christ. . . . I want to know Christ and the power of his resurrection and the κοινωνία of his sufferings by becoming like him in his death, if somehow I may attain the resurrection from the dead" (Phil 3:7, 10–11).

What then? Am I saying that the rigorous study of Scripture and theology is pointless or wicked? As the apostle would say, Μὴ γένοιτο! But I *am* saying that the corrupting power of sin in human hearts is such that even the good gifts of scriptural and theological learning can be twisted into instruments of self-aggrandizement. Paul understood that in his bones. Those of us in places of privilege such as Duke Divinity School must constantly be aware of that danger and seek to be conformed to the life of the One good grain, the One who fell into the earth and died, in order to bear good fruit. For those of us who are scholars and teachers and pastors, the practice of falling into the dirt, into the earthly *humus*, corresponds, of course, to the cultivation of *humility*. Only if we fall into the dark earth can our labors of learning and teaching undergo a "dark fruition" and bear fruit in their turn.

4. T. S. Eliot, "Little Gidding," *Four Quartets*, in *The Complete Poems and Plays, 1909–1950* (New York: Harcourt, Brace & World, 1962), 142.

Hope for What We Do Not See: The Promise of New Creation

The work of cultivating fruit is a long process. Trees take years to grow. Fruit takes many months to ripen. This is not an easy message for us to hear. We live in a culture, including the culture of the university—perhaps *especially* the culture of the university—where we expect lightning-fast information, quickly measurable outcomes, immediate change, instant justice. But Scripture offers us a different narrative, a different account of human life and God's working in the world along a longer arc.

The second text I want to revisit tonight appears at one of the climactic points in Paul's extraordinarily complex Letter to the Romans. This is one of the texts that I have chosen to be read at my funeral—whenever that may be.

> We know that the whole creation has been groaning in labor pains until now; and not only the creation, but we ourselves, who have the first fruits of the Spirit, groan inwardly while we wait for adoption, the redemption of our bodies. [And please note, as I have told students for many years, Paul does not say "redemption *from* our bodies;" he says "the redemption *of* our bodies"—by which he surely means nothing other than the resurrection of the body.] For in hope we were saved. Now hope that is seen is not hope. For who hopes for what is seen? But if we hope for what we do not see, we wait for it with longsuffering endurance. (Rom 8:22–25)

"If we hope for what we do not see, we wait for it with *longsuffering endurance.*" Most English translations say "we wait for it with *patience.*" But that misses the connotative force of Paul's Greek word ὑπομονή. It means "longsuffering endurance." He is talking about the way in which the whole creation groans like a woman in labor. I was present with Judy for the birth of both of our children, and I don't think "patience" is the right word to describe her experience in labor. It was more like ὑπομονή: working hard in every muscle and nerve, hanging in there faithfully, enduring waves of pain, hoping to bring forth a child, hoping to bring forth life. That is a picture of Paul's vision of our life in Christ in the time between the times, already having the firstfruits of the Spirit, but not yet seeing the liberation of all creation from its bondage to death. We have not yet been made whole; we have not yet entered fully into the life of the resurrection.

That, I think, is what Malcolm Guite means to indicate when he prays that he might find "new birth / within that very death, a dark fruition." *A dark fruition.* That mysterious fruition occurs not only after the end of life, when our bodies are lowered into the grave, but also when in this life we die to ourselves—when we cease to clutch our prerogatives and achievements, when we find ourselves conformed to the self-giving of Jesus. That can feel like death, even the death of dreams we may have thought were in service of God.

As I leave behind a career of teaching and writing books and pouring my energies into building the institution of this divinity school for the past twenty-seven years, I say, as Paul said of his own labors, "I don't reckon myself to have got hold of it yet" (Phil 3:13a). What will become of those labors is in God's hands, not mine. But what I do know is this: the Lord is at work in me, still reshaping me into something I can't yet comprehend. I'm a little puzzled now when people ask me what I'm going to do in retirement. I don't know, exactly. After giving too many vague, waffly answers to that question, I finally settled on this reply: "I'm going to clean out my garage." But of course, that is a facetious and merely provisional answer. (And though I've been saying that for several months, I still haven't done it!) The truth is this: God is at work to do something beyond what I could ask or imagine; God is still at work to draw me into the life of the coming New Creation.

And I am confident that the same is true for the community of Duke Divinity School as a whole. It is no secret that the Divinity School has been through some difficult times in recent years. But if I may offer a word of encouragement as I depart from the faculty, I say that God has been at work through it all. Perhaps the community has been feeling the "freeing flail" that will "shuck this husk and leave [us] sheer and clear." Yet God is at work to draw this school, this whole heaven-handled community, more deeply into the life of the coming New Creation.

You probably guessed that I couldn't deliver a farewell lecture to the Divinity School without calling to mind one last time Paul's astonishing proclamation in 2 Cor 5:17: "If anyone is in Christ—New Creation! Everything old has passed away; see, everything has become new!" Those are the apocalyptic words engraved on the stone arch just outside the door of this chapel. We see them each time we walk in here, and they remind us again who we really are: God's children who have been brought from the old age of death into new life.

And yet, and yet . . . the same apostle tells the Romans soberly that we who have the firstfruits of the Spirit continue to groan in solidarity with the still-unredeemed creation. Our groaning is the more acute because we sense in our bones how wrenchingly painful is the tension between the suffering of the present age and the joy of the age to come, when God will set things right and wipe away every tear. In that tension, that paradox, lies our particular charism as followers of Jesus: we continue to pray that God's kingdom will come on earth as it is in heaven, and at the same time we proclaim the Lord's *death* . . . until he comes. And, make no mistake, that proclamation is found not only in our words but also in our lives—for, as the apostle insists, the message of New Creation is inextricably bound to the ministry of reconciliation. The community proclaims the New Creation to the world precisely insofar as it embodies reconciliation.

That My Fall May Be More Fruitful . . .

At this point, I have spoken about the cross and about New Creation, but I have not until just now spoken about the *first* of the three focal images that I proposed years ago in my book *The Moral Vision of the New Testament*: the image of *community*. I have deliberately left that one for last, because although I have spent much of my academic career *talking* about community, I have only belatedly begun to understand more deeply what it might mean to *live* it.

Malcom Guite's sonnet gently exhumes an insight that could all too easily lie buried in the Greek text of John 12. Jesus says, "Unless a grain of wheat falls into the earth and dies, it remains just a single grain." That's the New Revised Standard Version; most modern English translations make a similar, semantically justifiable, translation decision. But the Greek text carries an additional connotation. Here's what it says: "Unless a grain of wheat falls into the earth and dies, αὐτὸς μόνος μένει:" literally, "it remains *alone*." The King James Version rendered the phrase as "it abideth alone." That's a good translation; it not only catches the force of μόνος as "alone, solitary" but also highlights the Greek text's verbal link to Jesus's later contrasting invitation, in his farewell address to his disciples, the invitation to *abide* in him. Same verb in the Greek. (That observation, by the way, provokes me to make one last plea to those of you who are still students: don't leave this place without studying the biblical languages. They will enrich your imagination and your preaching.)

The first eight lines of Guite's sonnet highlight the way in which the death of the grain of wheat is a movement *away from* loneliness and *into* community. The poet prays, "Oh let me . . . die *away from all dry separation*, / Die *to my sole self*." Indeed the expression "sole self" deftly echoes John's Greek: αὐτὸς μόνος. And the praying voice of the sonnet envisions that the place of dark fruition is not a solitary dark tomb; instead, "deep in this *crowded* underground," alongside many other grains, the poet will learn "*the earthy otherness of every other*." It is precisely through learning that "earthy otherness," then, that he comes "to know that nothing is achieved alone / But only where these other fallen gather."

What better description could there be of the church? It is a place where "these other fallen gather," and where, like it or not, we rub up against the earthy otherness of every other. Whatever we achieve there, we will not achieve it alone, but only alongside other earthy creatures who gather to follow a Lord who humbled himself all the way to death on a cross.

For these past three years, I have had the unexpected blessing of falling into a small, ragged, vibrant church community that embraces people of different races, people who speak different languages and come from different cultures, people with disabilities, people with much education and people with little. We diverse and fallen folk gather to praise and pray and serve.[5] I am slowly learning not to think quite so much of my own erudition; I am slowly seeing that my academic culture's way of seeing and valuation is not necessarily the best or only way. To be sure, I don't reckon myself to have got hold of it yet. But for me it has felt like a breakthrough to bright air. For me, it has made this stage of improbable autumn life feel like a golden evening where God's barns may not yet be full—but where the fruits of the harvest are beginning to come in.

Recall that in Jesus's parable, the grain that falls into the earth and dies ultimately "bears much fruit." This is a figure for Jesus's own death. But in John's Gospel, Jesus has not yet finished talking about fruit. He comes back to that same theme of fruit bearing once again in his farewell discourse to the disciples, but now he reconfigures the metaphor into a picture of himself as the true vine (John 15:1–11).

I suspect that many of us gentile readers of John's Gospel fail to understand the force of Jesus's breathtaking imaginative portrayal of himself as the true vine. Our understanding of the whole NT, and of Jesus in particular, is impoverished if we fail to read the OT as our Scripture, if we fail to discern the unity of the whole scriptural story, from Genesis to Revelation. Throughout Israel's Scripture, the vine is consistently employed as a symbol for God's people Israel. In Ps 80, for example, there can be no doubt of the meaning of the vine imagery:

> You brought a vine out of Egypt;
>   you drove out the nations and planted it.
> You cleared the ground for it;
>   it took deep root and filled the land.
> The mountains were covered with its shade,
>   the mighty cedars with its branches;

5. I refer to CityWell United Methodist Church, Durham, North Carolina.

> It sent out its branches to the sea,
> and its shoots to the River. (Ps 80:8–11)

The psalm is clearly recalling Israel's exodus and the establishment of the kingdom in the promised land. But then the psalmist pours out a lament, because now the vine has been broken down and ravaged by enemies and wild beasts and fire. That lament leads into an urgent prayer for God to send help and deliverance:

> Turn again, O God of hosts;
> look down from heaven, and see;
> have regard for this vine,
> the stock that your right hand planted. (vv. 14–15)

And that prayer, in turn, morphs into a prayer for a *deliverer* who can give life:

> Let your hand be upon the one at your right hand,
> the one (lit., "son of man") whom you made strong for yourself.
> Then we will never turn back from you;
> give us life, and we will call on your name. (vv. 17–18)

I've been quoting the NRSV here. But, regrettably, in verse 17 the NRSV paraphrases the Hebrew text in a way that erases an intertextual link that is crucial for understanding John's interpretation of Jesus. The NRSV simply says, "the one whom you made strong." That's not exactly wrong, but it suppresses an important verbal echo. The Hebrew here speaks of a "son of man" (בֶּן אָדָם) who is at God's right hand as the hoped-for deliverer—and the Septuagint follows suit with a literal translation, υἱὸν ἀνθρώπου, "son of man." Why is this significant? Because John repeatedly uses the apocalyptic title "Son of Man" as a designation for Jesus—more than a dozen times in the Gospel.

What is my point? Just this: when Jesus in John's Gospel proclaims that he is the true vine, he is presenting himself as the surprising answer to the psalmist's prayer. In his death and resurrection, the vine Israel is given life again. He is *both* the hoped-for powerful Son of Man through whom God restores Israel *and* the revivified vine, the Israel that God is restoring.

What does all this have to do with *community*? The answer lies close at hand in John 15, for Jesus extends the metaphor to embrace his disciples. If he is the vine, he sings, then they are the branches whose life and fruitfulness depends on their organic union in and with him. They share in the hope of Israel. How? Because they receive life from him. Here is his word of promise:

> Just as the branch cannot bear fruit by itself unless it abides in the vine, neither can you unless you abide in me. I am the vine, you are the branches. Those who abide in me and I in them bear much fruit, because apart from me you can do nothing. (John 15:4–5)

We too rarely notice, I think, that the metaphor/image/parable of the vine and the branches implies that while the branches all depend on union with Jesus, their subsistence in him necessarily binds them all together organically in love as part of the one healthy, fruit-bearing plant. And what of the grapes that they are to yield? Grapes grow in clusters. Not single grapes on isolated branches.

That is why Jesus's metaphor of the vine grows organically into a forceful restatement of the commandment to love.

> This is my commandment, that you love one another as I have loved you. . . . You did not choose me, but I chose you. And I appointed you to go and bear fruit, fruit that will last. . . . I am giving you these commands so that you may love one another. (John 15:12, 16a, 17)

The whole purpose of Jesus's teaching, healing, death, and resurrection—the τέλος of the incarnation of the Word of God—is summed up here. Love one another, sacrificially and persistently, as Jesus has loved us.

So in the end, that is what I want to say to all of you here at Duke Divinity School. I have loved you—well, I've loved at least most of you most of the time. (I'm not Jesus, and I don't reckon myself to have got hold of it yet!) And I'm grateful for the love you have shown me and one another. In our life together as *community*, even in the midst of our groaning, we have tasted the firstfruits of the Spirit. That is why, even in a time of dark fruition, we wait in hope.

> May the God of hope fill you with all joy and peace . . . in harmony with one another . . . so that you may overflow in hope by the power of the Holy Spirit.

Bibliography

Alkier, Stefan. "Die Bibel im Dialog der Schriften und das Problem der Verstockung in Mk 4." Pages 1–22 in *Die Bibel im Dialog der Schriften: Konzepte intertextueller Bibellektüre*. Edited by Stefan Alkier and Richard B. Hays. Tübingen: Francke, 2005.

———. "Intertextuality and the Semiotics of Biblical Texts." Pages 3–21 in *Reading the Bible Intertextually*. Edited by Richard B. Hays, Stefan Alkier, and Leroy A. Huizenga. Waco: Baylor University Press, 2009.

Allison, Dale C., Jr. *The Intertextual Jesus: Scripture in Q*. Harrisburg, PA: Trinity Press International, 2000.

———. *Jesus of Nazareth: Millenarian Prophet*. Minneapolis: Fortress, 1998.

Anderson, Charles P. "Who Are the Heirs of the New Age in the Epistle to the Hebrews?" Pages 255–77 in *Apocalyptic and the New Testament: Essays in Honor of J. Louis Martyn*. Edited by Joel Marcus and Marion L. Soards. JSNTSup 24. Sheffield: JSOT Press, 1989.

Anderson, Gary A. "Joseph and the Passion of Our Lord." Pages 198–215 in *The Art of Reading Scripture*. Edited by Ellen F. Davis and Richard B. Hays. Grand Rapids: Eerdmans, 2003.

Aquinas, Thomas. "Selections from Thomas Aquinas' *Commentary on Romans*." Translated by Eugene F. Rogers Jr. Pages 320–37 in *The Theological Interpretation of Scripture: Classic and Contemporary Readings*. Edited by Stephen E. Fowl. Oxford: Blackwell, 1997.

Attridge, Harold W. *The Epistle to the Hebrews*. Hermeneia. Philadelphia: Fortress, 1989.

Auerbach, Erich. *Mimesis: Dargestellte Wirklichkeit in der abendländische Literatur*. Bern: Franke, 1946. ET: *Mimesis: The Representation of Reality in Western Literature*. Translated by Willard R. Trask. Princeton: Princeton University Press, 1953.

Avalos, Hector. "The Ideology of the Society of Biblical Literature and the Demise of an Academic Profession." *SBL Forum* 4.4. April 2006. http://www.sbl-site.org/publications/Article.aspx?Articleld=520.

Barclay, John. "Paul's Story: Theology as Testimony." Pages 133–56 in *Narrative*

Dynamics in Paul: A Critical Assessment. Edited by Bruce W. Longenecker. Louisville: Westminster John Knox, 2002.

———. Review of *A Rereading of Romans*, by Stanley K. Stowers. *JTS* 46 (1995): 646–51.

Barr, James. *The Semantics of Biblical Language*. Oxford: Oxford University Press, 1961.

Barth, Karl. *Church Dogmatics*. Vol. 2, *The Doctrine of God*. Part 2. Translated by G. W. Bromiley. Edinburgh: T & T Clark, 1957 (1942).

———. *Church Dogmatics*. Vol. 4, *The Doctrine of Reconciliation*. Part 1. Translated by G. W. Bromiley. Edinburgh: T & T Clark, 1956 (1953).

———. *Church Dogmatics*. Vol. 4, *The Doctrine of Reconciliation*. Part 2. Translated by G. W. Bromiley. Edinburgh: T & T Clark, 1958 (1955).

———. *The Epistle to the Romans*. 2nd ed. Translated by Edwyn C. Hoskins. Oxford: Oxford University Press, 1933 (1922).

Barth, Markus. "The Old Testament in Hebrews: An Essay in Biblical Hermeneutics." Pages 53–78, 263–73 in *Current Issues in New Testament Interpretation*. Edited by William Klassen and Graydon F. Snyder. New York: Harper, 1962.

Bartholomew, Craig G., and Mike W. Goheen. "Story and Biblical Theology." Pages 144–71 in *Out of Egypt: Biblical Theology and Biblical Interpretation*. Edited by Craig G. Bartholomew et al. Scripture and Hermeneutics Series 5. Grand Rapids: Zondervan, 2004.

Barton, Stephen. "The Hermeneutics of the Gospel Resurrection Narratives." Pages 45–57 in *Resurrection: Essays in Honour of Leslie Houlden*. Edited by Stephen Barton and Graham Stanton. London: SPCK, 1994.

Bassler, Jouette M., ed. *Pauline Theology*. Vol. 1: *Thessalonians, Philippians, Galatians, Philemon*. Minneapolis: Fortress, 1991.

Bateman, Herbert W. *Early Jewish Hermeneutics and Hebrews 1.5–13: The Impact of Early Jewish Exegesis on the Interpretation of a Significant New Testament Passage*. American University Studies 193. New York: Peter Lang, 1997.

Bauckham, Richard. *God Crucified: Monotheism and Christology in the New Testament*. Grand Rapids: Eerdmans, 1998.

———. "Life, Death, and the Afterlife in Second Temple Judaism." Pages 80–96 in *Life in the Face of Death: The Resurrection Message of the New Testament*. Edited by Richard N. Longenecker. Grand Rapids: Eerdmans, 2002.

———. "Reading Scripture as a Coherent Story." Pages 38–53 in *The Art of Reading Scripture*. Edited by Ellen F. Davis and Richard B. Hays. Grand Rapids: Eerdmans, 2003.

———. *The Theology of the Book of Revelation*. Cambridge: Cambridge University Press, 1993.

Baur, F. C. "Die Christuspartei in der korinthinischen Gemeinde, der Gegensatz des petrinischen und paulinischen Christenthums in der ältesten Kirche." *Tübinger Zeitschrift für Theologie* 5 (1831): 61–206.

Beale, G. K., and Benjamin L. Gladd. *Hidden but Now Revealed: A Biblical Theology of Mystery*. Downers Grove, IL: IVP Academic, 2014.

Beker, J. Christiaan. *Paul the Apostle: The Triumph of God in Life and Thought*. Philadelphia: Fortress, 1980.

Betz, Hans Dieter. *Galatians: A Commentary on Paul's Letter to the Churches in Galatia*. Hermeneia. Philadelphia: Fortress, 1979.

Blowers, Paul M. "The *Regula Fidei* and the Narrative Character of Early Christian Faith." *ProEccl* 6 (1997): 199–228.

Blumhofer, Christopher M. *The Gospel of John and the Future of Israel*. SNTSMS 177. Cambridge: Cambridge University Press, 2020.

Bockmuehl, Markus. *The Epistle to the Philippians*. BNTC. London: A & C Black, 1997.

———. *Seeing the Word: Refocusing New Testament Study*. Studies in Theological Interpretation. Grand Rapids: Baker Academic, 2006.

Bonhoeffer, Dietrich. *Nachfolge*. Edited by Eberhard Bethge et al. Dietrich Bonhoeffer Works 4. Munich: Chr. Kaiser, 1989 (1937). ET: *The Cost of Discipleship*. Translated by R. H. Fuller. Revised by Irmgard Booth. London: SCM, 1949. ET: *Discipleship*. Translated by Barbara Green and Reinhard Kraus. Dietrich Bonhoeffer Works 4. Minneapolis: Fortress, 2003.

Borg, Marcus J. *Jesus: A New Vision*. San Francisco: Harper & Row, 1987.

———. *Jesus in Contemporary Scholarship*. Valley Forge, PA: Trinity Press International, 1994.

Borg, Marcus J., and N. T. Wright. *The Meaning of Jesus: Two Visions*. San Francisco: HarperSanFrancisco, 1999.

Bornkamm, Günther. *Jesus of Nazareth*. Translated by Irene McLuskey and Fraser McLuskey. New York: Harper & Row, 1960 (1956).

Bovon, François. *Studies in Early Christianity*. WUNT 161. Tübingen: Mohr Siebeck, 2003.

Boyarin, Daniel. *Border Lines: The Partition of Judea-Christianity*. Philadelphia: University of Pennsylvania Press, 2004.

———. *A Radical Jew: Paul and the Politics of Identity*. Berkeley: University of California Press, 1994.

Breytenbach, Cilliers. *Versöhnung: Eine Studie zur paulinischen Soteriologie*. WMANT 60. Neukirchen: Neukirchener Verlag, 1989.

Brown, Raymond E. *The Community of the Beloved Disciple*. New York: Paulist, 1979.

———. *The Death of the Messiah: From Gethsemane to the Grave*. 2 vols. New York: Doubleday, 1994.

———. "The Gospel of Peter and Canonical Gospel Priority." *NTS* 33 (1987): 321–43.

Bruno, Christopher R. "The Deliverer from Zion: The Source(s) and Function of Paul's Citation in Romans 11:26–27." *TynBul* 59 (2008): 119–34.

Buckwalter, H. Douglas. *The Character and Purpose of Luke's Christology*. SNTSMS 89. Cambridge: Cambridge University Press, 1996.

Bultmann, Rudolf. *Das Evangelium des Johannes*. Göttingen: Vandenhoeck & Ruprecht, 1950. ET: *The Gospel of John*. Translated by George Beasley-Murray, R. W. N. Hoare, and John K. Riches. Philadelphia: Westminster, 1971.

———. "Neues Testament und Mythologie." Pages 15–48 in *Kerygma und Mythos*, vol. 1. Edited by Hans Werner Bartsch. Hamburg: Herbert Reich-Evangelischer Verlag, 1948. ET: "New Testament and Mythology." Pages 1–44 in *Kerygma and Myth: A Theological Debate*, vol. 1. Edited by Hans Werner Bartsch. Translated by R. H. Fuller. London: SPCK, 1953.

———. *Theologie des Neuen Testaments*. 3 vols. Tübingen: Mohr Siebeck, 1948–1953. ET: *Theology of the New Testament*. 2 vols. Translated by Kendrick Grobel. New York: Scribner, 1951–1955.

Byrne, Brendan. *"Sons of God"—"Seed of Abraham": A Study of the Idea of Sonship of God of All Christians in Paul against the Jewish Background*. AnBib 83. Rome: Biblical Institute Press, 1979.

Caird, G. B. "The Exegetical Method of the Epistle to the Hebrews." *CJT* 5 (1959): 44–51.

———. *The Language and Imagery of the Bible*. London: Duckworth, 1980.

———. *The Revelation of St. John the Divine*. HNTC. New York: Harper & Row, 1966.

Calvin, John. *The Epistles of Paul the Apostle to the Romans and to the Thessalonians*. Translated by R. Mackenzie. Calvin's Commentaries. Grand Rapids: Eerdmans, 1960.

———. *Institutes of the Christian Religion*. Edited by John T. McNeill. Translated by Ford L. Battles. LCC 20. Philadelphia: Westminster, 1960.

Campbell, Douglas A. *The Deliverance of God: An Apocalyptic Rereading of Justification in Paul*. Grand Rapids: Eerdmans, 2009.

———. *The Quest for Paul's Gospel*. London: T & T Clark, 2005.

———. "The Story of Jesus in Romans and Galatians." Pages 97–124 in *Narrative Dynamics in Paul: A Critical Assessment*. Edited by Bruce W. Longenecker. Louisville: Westminster John Knox, 2002.

Capes, David. *Old Testament Yahweh Texts in Paul's Christology*. WUNT 2/47. Tübingen: Mohr Siebeck, 1992.

Childs, Brevard S. *Biblical Theology of the Old and New Testaments: Theological Reflection on the Christian Bible*. Minneapolis: Fortress, 1992.

———. *The Struggle to Understand Isaiah as Christian Scripture*. Grand Rapids: Eerdmans, 2004.

Coakley, Sarah. *Powers and Submissions: Spirituality, Philosophy, and Gender*. Oxford: Blackwell, 2002.

Cohen, Shaye J. D. "The Significance of Yavneh: Pharisees, Rabbis, and the End of Jewish Sectarianism." *HUCA* 55 (1984): 27–53.

Cohn-Sherbok, D. M. "Jesus' Defence of the Resurrection of the Dead." *JSNT* 11 (1981): 64–73.

Collins, John J. *Daniel: A Commentary*. Hermeneia. Minneapolis: Fortress, 1993.

Cranfield, C. E. B. *The Epistle to the Romans*. 2 vols. ICC. Edinburgh: T & T Clark, 1975/1979.

Crossan, John Dominic. *The Cross That Spoke: The Origins of the Passion Narrative*. San Francisco: Harper & Row, 1988.

———. *The Historical Jesus: The Life of a Mediterranean Jewish Peasant*. San Francisco: HarperSanFrancisco, 1991.

Culpepper, R. Alan. *Anatomy of the Fourth Gospel: A Study in Literary Design*. Philadelphia: Fortress, 1986.

Dahl, Nils Alstrup. *Jesus in the Memory of the Early Church*. Minneapolis: Augsburg, 1976.

———. *Jesus the Christ: The Historical Origins of Christological Doctrine*. Edited by Donald H. Juel. Minneapolis: Fortress, 1991.

———. *Studies in Paul*. Minneapolis: Augsburg, 1977.

Daley, Brian E., SJ. "Is Patristic Exegesis Still Usable? Some Reflections on Early Christian Interpretation of the Psalms." Pages 69–88 in *The Art of Reading Scripture*. Edited by Ellen F. Davis and Richard B. Hays. Grand Rapids: Eerdmans, 2003.

Daniélou, Jean, SJ. *Sacramentum Futuri: Études sur les Origins des Typologie biblique*. Paris: Beauchesne, 1950. ET: *From Shadows to Reality: Studies in the Biblical Typology of the Fathers*. Translated by Wulstan Hibberd. London: Burns & Oates, 1960.

Davis, B. S. "The Meaning of *Proegraphē* in the Context of Galatians 3.1." *NTS* 45 (1999): 194–212.

Davis, Ellen F., and Richard B. Hays, eds. *The Art of Reading Scripture*. Grand Rapids: Eerdmans, 2003.

Dawson, John David. *Christian Figural Reading and the Fashioning of Identity*. Berkeley: University of California Press, 2002.

de Boer, Martinus C. "Paul, Theologian of God's Apocalypse." *Int* 56 (2002): 21–33.

Dodd, C. H. *According to the Scriptures: The Sub-structure of New Testament Theology*. London: Nisbet, 1952.

Donaldson, Terence L. *Paul and the Gentiles: Remapping the Apostle's Convictional World*. Minneapolis: Fortress, 1997.

Donfried, Karl P., ed. *The Romans Debate*. Rev. ed. Peabody, MA: Hendrickson, 1991 (1977).

Dreyfus, F. "L'argument scriptuaire de Jésus en faveur de le résurrection des morts (Marc XII, vv. 26–27)." *RB* 66 (1959): 213–24.

Drury, John. "Luke, Gospel of." Pages 410–13 in *A Dictionary of Biblical Interpretation*. Edited by R. J. Coggins and J. L. Houlden. London: SCM, 1990.

Dunn, James D. G. *Christology in the Making: A New Testament Inquiry into the Origins of the Doctrine of the Incarnation*. 2nd ed. London: SCM, 1989 (1980).

———. "Once More Pistis Christou." Pages 730–44 in *Society of Biblical Literature 1991 Seminar Papers*. Edited by Eugene H. Lovering. Atlanta: Scholars, 1991.

———. *Romans*. 2 vols. WBC 38. Dallas: Word, 1988.

———. *The Theology of Paul's Letter to the Galatians*. Cambridge: Cambridge University Press, 1993.

———. *The Theology of Paul the Apostle*. Grand Rapids: Eerdmans, 1998.

Eastman, Susan G. "Apocalypse and Incarnation: The Participatory Logic of Paul's Gospel." Pages 165–82 in *Apocalyptic and the Future of Theology*. Edited by Joshua B. Davis and Douglas Harink. Eugene, OR: Wipf & Stock, 2012.

———. "Israel and Divine Mercy in Galatians and Romans." Pages 147–70 in *Between Gospel and Election: Explorations in the Interpretation of Romans 9–11*. Edited by Florian Wilk and J. Ross Wagner. WUNT 257. Tübingen: Mohr Siebeck, 2010.

———. "Israel and the Mercy of God: A Re-reading of Galatians 6.16 and Romans 9–11." *NTS* 56 (2010): 367–95.

———. "Whose Apocalypse? The Identity of the Sons of God in Romans 8:19." *JBL* 121 (2002): 263–77.

Ehler, Bernhard. *Die Herrschaft des Gekreuzigten: Ernst Käsemanns Frage nach die Mitte der Schrift*. BZNW 46. Berlin: de Gruyter, 1986.

Ehrman, Bart D. *How Jesus Became God: The Exaltation of a Jewish Preacher from Galilee*. New York: HarperOne, 2014.

———. *Jesus, Interrupted: Revealing the Hidden Contradictions in the Bible (and Why We Don't Know about Them)*. New York: HarperCollins, 2009.

Eisenbaum, Pamela M. "Hebrews, Supersessionism and Jewish-Christian Relations." Paper presented at Annual Meeting of the Society of Biblical Literature. Philadelphia, Pennsylvania. 2005.

———. *The Jewish Heroes of Christian History: Hebrews 11 in Literary Context*. SBLDS 156. Atlanta: Scholars, 1997.

———. "Locating Hebrews within the Literary Landscape of Christian Origins." Pages 213–37 in *Hebrews: Contemporary Methods, New Insights*. Edited by Gabriella Gelardini. Leiden: Brill, 2005.

Engberg-Pedersen, Troels. *Paul and the Stoics*. Edinburgh: T & T Clark, 2000.

Enns, Peter. "The Interpretation of Psalm 95 in Hebrews 3.1–4.13." Pages 352–63 in *Early Christian Interpretation of the Scriptures of Israel: Investigations and Proposals*. Edited by Craig A. Evans and James A. Sanders. JSNTSup 148. Sheffield: Sheffield Academic Press, 1997.

Evans, C. F. *Saint Luke*. TPINTC. London: SCM, 1990.

Evans, C. Stephen. "Methodological Naturalism in Historical Biblical Scholarship." Pages 180–205 in *Jesus and the Restoration of Israel: A Critical Assessment of N. T. Wright's "Jesus and the Victory of God."* Edited by Carey C. Newman. Downers Grove, IL: IVP Academic, 1999.

Fee, Gordon D. *God's Empowering Presence: The Holy Spirit in the Letters of Paul*. Peabody, MA: Hendrickson, 1994.

Fish, Stanley E. *Self-Consuming Artifacts: The Experience of Seventeenth-Century Literature*. Berkeley: University of California Press, 1972.

Fishbane, Michael. *Text and Texture: Close Readings of Selected Biblical Texts*. New York: Schocken, 1979.

Fitzmyer, Joseph A. *The Acts of the Apostles*. AB 31. New York: Doubleday, 1998.

———. *Romans*. AB 33. New York: Doubleday, 1993.

Ford, David. *Barth and God's Story: Biblical Narrative and the Theological Method of Karl Barth in the "Church Dogmatics."* Frankfurt am Main: Lang, 1981.

Fowl, Stephen E. *The Story of Christ in the Ethics of Paul: An Analysis of the Function of the Hymnic Material in the Pauline Corpus*. JSNTSup 36. Sheffield: JSOT Press, 1990.

———, ed. *The Theological Interpretation of Scripture: Classic and Contemporary Readings*. Oxford: Blackwell, 1997.

Fox, Michael V. "Bible Scholarship and Faith-Based Study: My View." *SBL Forum* 4.2. February 2006. http://www.sbl-site.org/publications/Article.aspx?Articleld=490.

France, R. T. "The Writer of Hebrews as a Biblical Expositor." *TynBul* 47 (1996): 245–76.

Fredriksen, Paula. "Judaism, the Circumcision of the Gentiles, and Apocalyptic Hope: Another Look at Galatians 1 and 2." *JTS* 42 (1991): 532–64.

Frei, Hans W. *The Eclipse of Biblical Narrative: A Study in Eighteenth and Nineteenth Century Hermeneutics*. New Haven: Yale University Press, 1974.

———. *The Identity of Jesus Christ: The Hermeneutical Bases of Dogmatic Theology*. Philadelphia: Fortress, 1975.

Frye, Northrop. *Anatomy of Criticism*. Princeton: Princeton University Press, 1957.

———. *The Great Code: The Bible and Literature*. New York: Harcourt Brace Jovanovich, 1982.

Funk, Robert W. "The Coming Radical Reformation: Twenty-One Theses." Westar/Jesus Seminar website. www.westarinstitute.org/periodicals/21Theses/21Theses.html.

———. *Honest to Jesus: Jesus for a New Millennium*. San Francisco: HarperSanFrancisco, 1996.

———. "The Issue of Jesus." *Forum* 1, no. 1 (1985): 1–6.

Funk, Robert W., Roy W. Hoover, et al., eds. *The Five Gospels: The Search for the Authentic Words of Jesus*. New York: Macmillan, 1993.

Furnish, Victor P. *Jesus according to Paul*. Cambridge: Cambridge University Press, 1993.

Gadenz, Pablo T. *Called from the Jews and from the Gentiles: Pauline Ecclesiology in Romans 9–11*. WUNT 2/267. Tübingen: Mohr Siebeck, 2009.

Gager, John. *The Origins of Anti-Semitism*. Oxford: Oxford University Press, 1983.

Gaston, Lloyd. *Paul and the Torah*. Vancouver: University of British Columbia Press, 1987.

Gathercole, Simon. *The Composition of the Gospel of Thomas: Original Language and Influences*. Cambridge: Cambridge University Press, 2012.

———. Review of *Reading Backwards*, by Richard B. Hays. *Reformation 21*. August 2015. http://www.reformation21.org/articles/reading-backwards.php.

Gaventa, Beverly Roberts. "Galatians 1 and 2: Autobiography as Paradigm." *NovT* 28 (1986): 309–26.

———. "God Handed Them Over: Reading Romans 1:18–32 Apocalyptically." *ABR* 53 (2005): 42–53.

———. *Our Mother Saint Paul*. Louisville: Westminster John Knox, 2007.

———. "The Overthrown Enemy: Luke's Portrait of Paul." Pages 439–49 in *SBL Seminar Papers, 1985*. Edited by K. H. Richards. Atlanta: Scholars, 1985.

Gaventa, Beverly Roberts, and Richard B. Hays, eds. *Seeking the Identity of Jesus: A Pilgrimage*. Grand Rapids: Eerdmans, 2008.

Gelardini, Gabriella. "Hebrews, an Ancient Synagogue Homily for *Tisha Be-Av*: Its Function, Its Basis, Its Theological Interpretation." Pages 107–27 in *Hebrews: Contemporary Methods, New Insights*. Edited by Gabriella Gelardini. Leiden: Brill, 2005.

Genette, Gérard. *Narrative Discourse Revisited*. Oxford: Blackwell, 1980.

Gnilka, Joachim. *Das Matthäusevangelium*. Vol. 1, *Kommentar zu Kap 1,1–13,58*. 2nd ed. HThKNT 1/1. Freiburg: Herder, 1988.

Goodacre, Mark. *Thomas and the Gospels: The Case for Thomas' Familiarity with the Synoptics*. Grand Rapids: Eerdmans, 2012.

Goppelt, Leonhard. *Die typologische Deutung des Alten Testaments im Neuen.* Gütersloh: Bertelsmann, 1939. ET: *Typos: The Typological Interpretation of the Old Testament in the New.* Translated by Donald H. Madvig. Grand Rapids: Eerdmans, 1982.

Gorman, Michael J. *Cruciformity: Paul's Narrative Spirituality of the Cross.* Grand Rapids: Eerdmans, 2001.

———. *Inhabiting the Cruciform God: Kenosis, Justification, and Theosis in Paul's Narrative Soteriology.* Grand Rapids: Eerdmans, 2009.

Greene-McCreight, Kathryn. *Ad Litteram: How Augustine, Calvin, and Barth Read the "Plain Sense" of Genesis 1–3.* Issues in Systematic Theology 5. New York: Peter Lang, 1999.

Greer, Rowan A. *The Captain of Our Salvation: A Study in the Patristic Exegesis of Hebrews.* BGBE 15. Tübingen: Mohr Siebeck, 1973.

Grelot, Pierre. *Les Paroles de Jésus Christ.* Paris: Desclée, 1986.

Grieb, A. Katherine. *The Story of Romans.* Louisville: Westminster John Knox, 2003.

Guthrie, George H. "Hebrews' Use of the Old Testament: Recent Trends in Research." *Currents in Biblical Research* 1 (2003): 271–94.

Haacker, Klaus. "Das Bekenntnis des Paulus zur Hoffnung Israels nach der Apostelgeschichte des Lukas." *NTS* 31 (1985): 437–51.

Hafemann, Scott. "The Salvation of Israel in Romans 11:25–32: A Response to Krister Stendahl." *ExAud* 4 (1988): 38–58.

Harink, Douglas. *Paul among the Postliberals: Pauline Theology beyond Christendom and Modernity.* Grand Rapids: Brazos, 2003.

———. "Paul and Israel: An Apocalyptic Reading." *ProEccl* 16 (2007): 359–80.

Harnack, Adolf von. "Das Alte Testament in den Paulinischen Briefen und in den Paulinischen Gemeinden." *Sitzungsberichte der Preussischen Akademie der Wissenschaften: Philosophischhistorische Klasse* 12 (1928): 124–41.

Harvey, A. E. *Jesus and the Constraints of History.* Philadelphia: Westminster, 1982.

Hay, David M. *Glory at the Right Hand: Psalm 110 in Early Christianity.* SBLMS 18. Nashville: Abingdon, 1973.

———, ed. *Pauline Theology.* Vol. 2, *1 and 2 Corinthians.* Minneapolis: Fortress, 1993.

Hay, David M., and E. Elizabeth Johnson, eds. *Pauline Theology.* Vol. 3, *Romans.* Minneapolis: Fortress, 1995.

Hays, Richard B. "Die Befreiung Israels im lukanischen Doppelwerk: Intertextuelle Erzählung als kulturkritische Praxis." Pages 117–36 in *Die Bibel im Dialog der Schriften: Konzepte Intertextueller Bibellektüre.* Edited by Stefan Alkier and Richard B. Hays. Tübingen: Francke, 2005.

———. “Christology and Ethics in Galatians: The Law of Christ.” *CBQ* 49 (1987): 268–90.

———. “Christ Prays the Psalms: Paul’s Use of an Early Christian Exegetical Convention.” Pages 122–36 in *The Future of Christology: Essays in Honor of Leander E. Keck*. Edited by Abraham J. Malherbe and Wayne A. Meeks. Minneapolis: Fortress, 1993.

———. “Continuing to Read Scripture with the Evangelists: A Response.” *JTI* 11 (2017): 85–99.

———. *The Conversion of the Imagination: Paul as Interpreter of Israel’s Scripture*. Grand Rapids: Eerdmans, 2005.

———. “The Conversion of the Imagination: Scripture and Eschatology in 1 Corinthians.” *NTS* 45 (1999): 391–412.

———. *Echoes of Scripture in the Gospels*. Waco: Baylor University Press, 2016.

———. *Echoes of Scripture in the Letters of Paul*. New Haven: Yale University Press, 1989.

———. *The Faith of Jesus Christ: An Investigation of the Narrative Substructure of Galatians 3:1–4:11*. SBLDS 56. Chico, CA: Scholars, 1983. 2nd ed., The Biblical Resource Series. Grand Rapids: Eerdmans, 2002.

———. *First Corinthians*. IBC. Louisville: John Knox Press, 1997.

———. “Intertextuelle Pneumatologie: Die paulinische Rede vom Heiligen Geist.” *ZNT* 25 (2010): 30–37.

———. *The Moral Vision of the New Testament: Community, Cross, New Creation*. San Francisco: HarperSanFrancisco, 1996.

———. “ΠΙΣΤΙΣ and Pauline Christology: What Is at Stake?” Pages 714–29 in *Society of Biblical Literature 1991 Seminar Papers*, ed. Eugene H. Lovering. Atlanta: Scholars, 1991.

———. *Reading Backwards: Figural Christology and the Fourfold Gospel Witness*. Waco: Baylor University Press, 2014.

———. “Reading Scripture in Light of the Resurrection.” Pages 216–38 in *The Art of Reading Scripture*, ed. Ellen F. Davis and Richard B. Hays. Grand Rapids: Eerdmans, 2003.

———. Review of *A Rereading of Romans: Justice, Jews, and Gentiles*, by Stanley K. Stowers. *CRBR* 9 (1996): 27–44.

———. “What Is ‘Real Participation in Christ’? A Dialogue with E. P. Sanders on Pauline Soteriology.” Pages 336–51 in *Redefining First-Century Jewish and Christian Identities*, ed. Fabian E. Udoh et al. Notre Dame, IN: University of Notre Dame Press, 2008.

Hays, Richard B., Stefan Alkier, and Leroy A. Huizenga, eds. *Reading the Bible Intertextually*. Waco: Baylor University Press, 2009.

Holtz, Traugott. *Die Christologie der Apokalypse des Johannes*. TU 85. Berlin: Akademie-Verlag, 1962.

Horn, Friedrich W. *Das Angeld des Geistes: Studien zur paulinischen Pneumatologie*. FRLANT 154. Göttingen: Vandenhoeck & Ruprecht, 1992.

Horrell, David G. *Solidarity and Difference: A Contemporary Reading of Paul's Ethics*. London: T & T Clark, 2005.

Howard, George. "Hebrews and the Old Testament Quotations." *NovT* 10 (1968): 208–16.

———. "On the 'Faith of Christ.'" *HTR* 60 (1967): 459–65.

———. *Paul: Crisis in Galatia*. 2nd ed. SNTSMS 35. Cambridge: Cambridge University Press, 1990.

Huber, K. *Einer Gleich einem Menschensohn: Die Christusvisionen in Offb. 1,9–20 und Offb. 14,14–20 und die Christologie der Johannesoffenbarung*. NTAbh, new series, 51. Münster: Aschendorff, 2007.

Hughes, Graham. *Hebrews and Hermeneutics: The Epistle to the Hebrews as a New Testament Example of Biblical Interpretation*. SNTSMS 36. Cambridge: Cambridge University Press, 1979.

Hvalvik, Reidar. "A 'Sonderweg' for Israel: A Critical Examination of Current Interpretation of Romans 11.25–27." *JSNT* 38 (1990): 87–107.

Irenaeus of Lyons. *Against the Heresies*. Translated by Dominic J. Unger. Ancient Christian Writers. New York: Paulist, 1992.

Janzen, J. Gerald. "Resurrection and Hermeneutics: On Exodus 3:6 in Mark 12:26." *JSNT* 23 (1985): 43–58.

Jenson, Robert W. *Canon and Creed*. Interpretation Resources for the Use of Scripture in the Church. Louisville: Westminster John Knox, 2010.

———. "How the World Lost Its Story." *First Things* 36 (October 1993): 19–24.

———. "Scripture's Authority in the Church." Pages 27–37 in *The Art of Reading Scripture*. Edited by Ellen F. Davis and Richard B. Hays. Grand Rapids: Eerdmans, 2003.

Jewett, Robert. *Romans: A Commentary*. Hermeneia. Minneapolis: Fortress, 2007.

Johns, Loren L. *The Lamb Christology of the Apocalypse of John: An Investigation into Its Origin and Rhetorical Force*. WUNT 2/167. Tübingen: Mohr Siebeck, 2003.

Johnson, E. Elizabeth, and David M. Hay, eds. *Pauline Theology*. Vol. 4, *Looking Back, Pressing On*. SBL Symposium Series 4. Atlanta: Scholars, 1997.

Johnson, Luke Timothy. *The Creed: What Christians Believe and Why It Matters*. New York: Doubleday, 2003.

———. "Luke 24:1–11." *Int* 46 (1992): 57–61.

———. "A Marginal Mediterranean Jewish Peasant." *Commonweal* 119 (1992): 24–26.

———. *Reading Romans: A Literary and Theological Commentary*. Reading the New Testament. New York: Crossroad, 1997.

———. *The Real Jesus: The Misguided Quest for the Historical Jesus and the Truth of the Traditional Gospels*. San Francisco: HarperSanFrancisco, 1996.

———. "Romans 3:21–26 and the Faith of Jesus." *CBQ* 44 (1982): 77–90.

———. *Septuagintal Midrash in the Speeches of Acts*. The Père Marquette Lecture in Theology 2002. Milwaukee: Marquette University Press, 2002.

Johnson, Luke Timothy, and William S. Kurz. *The Future of Catholic Biblical Scholarship: A Constructive Conversation*. Grand Rapids: Eerdmans, 2002.

Jones, L. Gregory. "Embodying Scripture in the Community of Faith." Pages 143–59 in *The Art of Reading Scripture*. Edited by Ellen F. Davis and Richard B. Hays. Grand Rapids: Eerdmans, 2003.

Kähler, Martin. *The So-Called Historical Jesus and the Historic Biblical Christ*. Translated by Carl E. Braaten. Philadelphia: Fortress, 1964 (1896).

Käsemann, Ernst. *Commentary on Romans*. Translated by G. W. Bromiley. Grand Rapids: Eerdmans, 1980 (1973).

———. *Essays on New Testament Themes*. Translated by W. J. Montague. SBT 41. London: SCM, 1964 (1960).

———. *Exegetische Versuche und Besinnungen*. Vol. 2. Göttingen: Vandenhoeck & Ruprecht, 1964.

———. "Gottesgerechtigkeit bei Paulus." *ZTK* 58 (1961): 367–78.

———. *New Testament Questions of Today*. Translated by W. J. Montague and W. F. Bunge. London: SCM; Philadelphia: Fortress, 1969 (1965).

———. "Paul and Nascent Catholicism." *JTC* 3 (1967): 14–27.

———. *Paulinische Perspektiven*. Tübingen: Mohr Siebeck, 1969. ET: *Perspectives on Paul*. Translated by Margaret Kohl. Philadelphia: Fortress, 1971.

———. "Unity and Diversity in New Testament Ecclesiology." *NovT* 6 (1963): 290–97.

———. *Das wandernde Gottesvolk: Eine Untersuchung zum Hebräerbrief*. 2nd ed. FRLANT 55. Göttingen: Vandenhoeck & Ruprecht, 1957.

Keck, Leander E. "'Jesus' in Romans." *JBL* 108 (1989): 443–60.

———. "Paul and Apocalyptic Theology." *Int* 38 (1984): 229–41.

———. *Romans*. ANTC. Nashville: Abingdon, 2005.

———. *Who Is Jesus? History in Perfect Tense*. Columbia: University of South Carolina Press, 2000.

Keesmaat, Sylvia C. *Paul and His Story: (Re)Interpreting the Exodus Tradition*. JSNTSup 181. Sheffield: Sheffield Academic Press, 1999.

Kelly, J. N. D. *Early Christian Creeds*. 3rd ed. London: Longman, 1972 (1950).

Kermode, Frank. *The Genesis of Secrecy: On the Interpretation of Narrative*. Cambridge, MA: Harvard University Press, 1979.

Kingsbury, Jack Dean. *Matthew as Story*. Philadelphia: Fortress, 1982.

Kirk, J. R. Daniel. *Unlocking Romans: Resurrection and the Justification of God*. Grand Rapids: Eerdmans, 2008.

———. "Why Does the Deliverer Come ἐκ Σιών (Romans 11.26)?" *JSNT* 33 (2010): 81–99.

Kistemaker, Simon J. *The Psalm Citations in the Epistle to the Hebrews*. Amsterdam: Soest, 1961.

Klein, Günter. "Paul's Purpose in Writing the Epistle to the Romans." Pages 29–43 in *The Romans Debate*. Edited by Karl P. Donfried. Rev. ed. Peabody, MA: Hendrickson, 1991 (1977).

Koch, Dietrich A. *Die Schrift als Zeuge des Evangeliums*. BHT 69. Tübingen: Mohr Siebeck, 1986.

Koester, Craig. *Hebrews*. AB 36. New York: Doubleday, 2001.

Kuck, David. *Judgment and Community Conflict: Paul's Use of Apocalyptic Judgment Language in 1 Corinthians 3:5–4:5*. NovTSup 66. Leiden: Brill, 1992.

Kugel, James L., and Rowan A. Greer. *Early Biblical Interpretation*. Philadelphia: Westminster, 1986.

Lampe, Peter. "The Roman Christians of Romans 16." Pages 216–30 in *The Romans Debate*. Edited by Karl P. Donfried. Rev. ed. Peabody, MA: Hendrickson, 1991 (1977).

Lane, William L. "Living a Life in the Face of Death: The Witness of Hebrews." Pages 247–69 in *Life in the Face of Death: The Resurrection Message of the New Testament*. Edited by Richard N. Longenecker. Grand Rapids: Eerdmans, 1998.

Layton, Bentley. *The Gnostic Scriptures*. Garden City, NY: Doubleday, 1987.

Lehne, Susanne. *The New Covenant in Hebrews*. JSNTSup 44. Sheffield: JSOT Press, 1990.

Lentricchia, Frank. "Last Will and Testament of an Ex-Literary Critic." *Lingua Franca*, September/October 1996, 59–67.

Levenson, Jon D. *Resurrection and the Restoration of Israel: The Ultimate Victory of the God of Life*. New Haven: Yale University Press, 2006.

———. "Resurrection in the Torah? A Second Look." 2002 Palmer Lecture, Center of Theological Inquiry, Princeton. March 21, 2002.

Lieu, Judith. "'I Am a Christian': Martyrdom and the Beginning of 'Christian' Identity." Pages 211–32 in *Neither Jew nor Greek? Constructing Christian Identity*. Edinburgh: T & T Clark, 2003.

Lindbeck, George A. *The Church in a Postliberal Age*. Edited by James J. Buckley. Grand Rapids: Eerdmans, 2002.

———. "Confession and Community: An Israel-Like View of the Church." *The Christian Century* 107 (1990): 492–96.

———. *The Nature of Doctrine: Religion and Theology in a Postliberal Age*. Philadelphia: Westminster, 1984.

———. "The Story-Shaped Church: Critical Exegesis and Theological Interpretation." Pages 161–78 in *Scriptural Authority and Narrative Interpretation*. Edited by Garrett Green. Philadelphia: Fortress, 1987.

Longenecker, Bruce W., ed. *Narrative Dynamics in Paul: A Critical Assessment*. Louisville: Westminster John Knox, 2002.

Lüdemann, Gerd. *The Great Deception: And What Jesus Really Said and Did*. London: SCM, 1998.

———. *The Resurrection of Jesus: History, Experience, Theology*. Minneapolis: Fortress, 1994.

Luther, Martin. *Prefaces to the New Testament*. Edited by E. Theodore Bachmann. Luther's Works 35. Philadelphia: Fortress, 1960.

MacIntyre, Alasdair. *After Virtue: A Study in Moral Theory*. 2nd ed. Notre Dame, IN: University of Notre Dame Press, 1984.

Mack, Burton L. *A Myth of Innocence: Mark and Christian Origins*. Philadelphia: Fortress, 1988.

Mangina, Joseph L. *Revelation*. Brazos Theological Commentary on the Bible. Grand Rapids: Brazos, 2010.

Marshall, Christopher D. *Compassionate Justice: An Interdisciplinary Dialogue with Two Gospel Parables on Law, Crime, and Restorative Justice*. Theopolitical Visions 15. Eugene, OR: Cascade Books, 2012.

Martin, Dale B. *Slavery as Salvation: The Metaphor of Slavery in Pauline Christianity*. New Haven: Yale University Press, 1990.

Martyn, J. Louis. "De-apocalyticizing Paul: An Essay Focused on *Paul and the Stoics* by Troels Engberg-Pedersen." *JSNT* 86 (2002): 61–102.

———. Foreword to *The Bible and the Historian: Breaking the Silence about God in Biblical Studies*, by Paul S. Minear. Nashville: Abingdon, 2002.

———. *Galatians*. AB 33A. New York: Doubleday, 1997.

———. *Theological Issues in the Letters of Paul*. Nashville: Abingdon, 1997.

Matlock, R. Barry. *Unveiling the Apocalyptic Paul: Paul's Interpreters and the Rhetoric of Criticism*. JSNTSup 127. Sheffield: Sheffield Academic Press, 1996.

Meeks, Wayne A. *The First Urban Christians: The Social World of the Apostle Paul*. 2nd ed. New Haven: Yale University Press, 2003 (1983).

———. *The Origins of Christian Morality: The First Two Centuries*. New Haven: Yale University Press, 1993.

———. "Why Study the New Testament?" *NTS* 51 (2005): 155–70.

Meier, John P. *A Marginal Jew: Rethinking the Historical Jesus*. Vol. 1, *The Roots of the Problem and the Person*. ABRL. New York: Doubleday, 1991.

Meyer, Ben F. *The Aims of Jesus*. London: SCM, 1979.

Minear, Paul S. "Barth's Commentary on the Romans, 1922–1972, or Karl Barth vs. the Exegetes." Pages 8–29 in *Footnotes to a Theology: The Karl Barth Colloquium of 1972*. Edited by H. Martin Rumscheidt. Waterloo, ON: Corporation for the Publication of Academic Studies in Religion in Canada, 1974.

———. *Eyes of Faith: A Study in the Biblical Point of View*. Philadelphia: Westminster, 1946.

Moberly, R. W. L. *The Bible, Theology, and Faith: A Study of Abraham and Jesus*. Cambridge: Cambridge University Press, 2000.

———. "Living Dangerously: Genesis 22 and the Quest for Good Biblical Interpretation." Pages 181–97 in *The Art of Reading Scripture*. Edited by Ellen F. Davis and Richard B. Hays. Grand Rapids: Eerdmans, 2003.

Moessner, David P. "Luke's 'Plan of God' from the Greek Psalter: The Rhetorical Thrust of 'The Prophets and the Psalms' in Peter's Speech at Pentecost." Pages 223–38 in *Scripture and Traditions: Essays on Early Judaism and Christianity in Honor of Carl R. Holladay*. Edited by Patrick Gray and Gail R. O'Day. NovTSup 129. Leiden: Brill, 2008.

———. "Two Lords 'at the Right Hand'? The Psalms and an Intertextual Reading of Peter's Pentecost Speech (Acts 2.14–36)." Pages 15–32 in *Literary Studies in Luke-Acts: Essays in Honor of Joseph B. Tyson*. Edited by Richard P. Thompson and Thomas E. Phillips. Macon, GA: Mercer University Press, 1998.

Moffitt, David M. *Atonement and the Logic of Resurrection in the Epistle to the Hebrews*. NovTSup 141. Leiden: Brill, 2011.

Moore, Stephen D. *Literary Criticism and the Gospels: The Theoretical Challenge*. New Haven: Yale University Press, 1989.

Morales, Rodrigo J. *The Spirit and the Restoration of Israel: New Exodus and New Creation Motifs in Galatians*. WUNT 2/282. Tübingen: Mohr Siebeck, 2010.

———. "The Words of the Luminaries, the Curse of the Law, and the Outpouring of the Spirit in Gal 3,10–14." *ZNW* 100 (2009): 268–78.

Morgan, Robert. "Flesh Is Precious: The Significance of Luke 24.36–43." Pages 8–20 in *Resurrection: Essays in Honour of Leslie Houlden*. Edited by Stephen Barton and Graham Stanton. London: SPCK, 1994.

Moses, Robert Ewusie. *Practices of Power: Revisiting the Principalities and Powers in the Pauline Letters*. Minneapolis: Fortress, 2014.

Motyer, Stephen. "The Psalm-Quotations of Hebrews 1: A Hermeneutic Free Zone?" *TynBul* 50 (1999): 3–22.

Myers, Ched. *Binding the Strong Man: A Political Reading of Mark's Story of Jesus*. Maryknoll, NY: Orbis, 1988.

Newman, Carey C., ed. *Jesus and the Restoration of Israel: A Critical Assessment of N. T. Wright's "Jesus and the Victory of God."* Downers Grove, IL: IVP Academic, 1999.

Novenson, Matthew V. *Christ among the Messiahs: Christ Language in Paul and Messiah Language in Ancient Judaism*. Oxford: Oxford University Press, 2012.

———. "Paul's Former Occupation in *Ioudaismos*." In *Galatians and Christian Theology: Justification, the Gospel, and Ethics in Paul's Letter*. Edited by Mark W. Elliott et al. Grand Rapids: Baker Academic, 2014.

O'Donovan, Oliver. "The Political Thought of the Book of Revelation." *TynBul* 37, no. 1 (1986): 61–94.

———. *Resurrection and Moral Order: An Outline for Evangelical Ethics*. Rev. ed. Grand Rapids: Eerdmans, 1994.

Oakes, Peter. "Made Holy by the Holy Spirit: Holiness and Ecclesiology in Romans." Pages 167–83 in *Holiness and Ecclesiology in the New Testament*. Edited by Kent Brower and Andy Johnson. Grand Rapids: Eerdmans, 2007.

Origen. *Origen: Homilies on Genesis and Exodus*. Translated by Ronald E. Heine. FC 71. Washington, DC: Catholic University of America Press, 1982.

Painter, John. *Theology as Hermeneutics: Rudolf Bultmann's Interpretation of the History of Jesus*. Sheffield: Almond, 1987.

Pannenberg, Wolfhart. *Jesus: God and Man*. Translated by Lewis L. Wilkins and Duane A. Priebe. Philadelphia: Westminster, 1977 (1964).

Patterson, Stephen J. *The Gospel of Thomas and Jesus*. Sonoma, CA: Polebridge Press, 1993.

Pelikan, Jaroslav. *Acts*. Brazos Theological Commentary on the Bible. Grand Rapids: Brazos, 2005.

———. *Jesus through the Centuries: His Place in the History of Culture*. New Haven: Yale University Press, 1985.

Petersen, Norman R. *Rediscovering Paul: Philemon and the Sociology of Paul's Narrative World*. Philadelphia: Fortress, 1985.

Phillips, Zack C. "Filling Up the Word: The Fulfillment Citations in Matthew's Gospel." Ph.D. diss., Duke University, 2017.

Ploeg, Jean van der. "L'exégèse de l'Ancien Testament dans l'Epître aux Hébreux." *RB* 54 (1947): 187–228.

Powers, Daniel G. *Salvation through Participation: An Examination of the Notion of the Believers' Corporate Unity with Christ in Early Christian Soteriology*. CBET 29. Louvain: Peeters, 2001.

Rabens, Volker. "The Development of Pauline Pneumatology: A Response to F. W. Horn." *BZ* 43 (1999): 161–79.

———. *The Holy Spirit and Ethics in Paul: Transformation and Empowering for Religious-Ethical Life*. WUNT 2/283. Tübingen: Mohr Siebeck, 2010.

Radner, Ephraim. *Time and the Word: Figural Reading of the Christian Scriptures*. Grand Rapids: Eerdmans, 2016.

Räisänen, Heikki. *Beyond New Testament Theology: A Story and a Programme*. 2nd ed. London: SCM, 2000 (1990).

Ratzinger, Joseph. *Jesus of Nazareth: From the Baptism in the Jordan to the Transfiguration*. Translated by Adrian J. Walker. London: Bloomsbury, 2007.

———. *Jesus of Nazareth*. Part 2: *Holy Week: From the Entrance into Jerusalem to the Resurrection*. Translated by P. J. Whitmore. San Francisco: Ignatius, 2011.

Reno, R. R. "Biblical Theology and Theological Exegesis." Pages 385–408 in *Out of Egypt: Biblical Theology and Biblical Interpretation*. Edited by Craig Bartholomew et al. Scripture and Hermeneutics Series 5. Grand Rapids: Zondervan, 2004.

Rhoads, David, and Donald Michie. *Mark as Story: An Introduction to the Narrative of a Gospel*. Philadelphia: Fortress, 1982.

Riches, John K. *Jesus and the Transformation of Judaism*. New York: Seabury, 1982.

Roberts, Alastair. Review of *Echoes of Scripture in the Gospels*, by Richard B. Hays. *Themelios* 41 (2016): 517–18.

Robinson, James M. "History of Q Research." Pages xix–lxxi in *The Critical Edition of Q*. Edited by James M. Robinson, Paul Hoffman, and John S. Kloppenborg. Minneapolis: Fortress, 2000.

Rogers, T. J. "Hebrews and Biblical Theology." Pages 313–38 in *Out of Egypt: Biblical Theology and Biblical Interpretation*. Edited by Craig Bartholomew et al. Scripture and Hermeneutics Series 5. Grand Rapids: Zondervan, 2004.

Root, Michael. "The Narrative Structure of Soteriology." Pages 263–78 in *Why Narrative? Readings in Narrative Theology*. Edited by Stanley Hauerwas and L. Gregory Jones. Grand Rapids: Eerdmans, 1989.

Rowe, C. Kavin. *Early Narrative Christology: The Lord in the Gospel of Luke*. BZNW 139. Berlin: de Gruyter, 2006.

———. "For Future Generations: Worshipping Jesus and the Integration of the Theological Disciplines." *ProEccl* 17 (2008): 186–209.

———. "The Grammar of Life: The Areopagus Speech and Pagan Tradition." *NTS* 57 (2011): 31–50.

———. “Luke and the Trinity: An Essay in Ecclesial Biblical Theology.” *SJT* 56 (2003): 1–26.

———. “New Testament Theology: The Revival of a Discipline: A Review of Recent Contributions to the Field.” *JBL* 125 (2006): 393–410.

———. “Romans 10:13: What Is the Name of the Lord?” *HBT* 22 (2000): 135–73.

———. “The Trinity and the New Testament.” Paper presented at the 2009 Annual Meeting of the Society of Biblical Literature, Development of Early Trinitarian Theology Group.

Rowe, C. Kavin, and Richard B. Hays. “What Is a Theological Commentary?” *Pro-Eccl* 16 (2007): 26–32.

Sanders, E. P. *The Historical Figure of Jesus*. London: Allen Lane, 1993.

———. *Jesus and Judaism*. Philadelphia: Fortress, 1985.

———. *Paul and Palestinian Judaism: A Comparison of Patterns of Religion*. Philadelphia: Fortress, 1977.

———. *Paul, the Law, and the Jewish People*. Philadelphia: Fortress, 1983.

Sanders, E. P., and Margaret Davies. *Studying the Synoptic Gospels*. London: SCM; Philadelphia: Trinity Press International, 1989.

Sandys-Wunsch, John, and Laurence Eldredge. “J. P. Gabler and the Distinction between Biblical and Dogmatic Theology: Translation, Commentary, and Discussion of His Originality.” *SJT* 33 (1980): 133–58.

Savage, Thomas J. Review of *Echoes of Scripture in the Gospels*, by Richard B. Hays. *European Journal of Theology* 26 (2017): 180.

Schrage, Wolfgang. *The Ethics of the New Testament*. Translated by David E. Green. Philadelphia: Fortress, 1988 (1982).

Schröger, Friedrich. *Der Verfasser des Hebräerbriefes als Schriftausleger*. Biblische Untersuchungen 4. Regensburg: Pustet, 1968.

Schüssler Fiorenza, Elisabeth. *The Book of Revelation: Justice and Judgment*. Philadelphia: Fortress, 1985.

———. *Bread Not Stone: The Challenge of Feminist Biblical Interpretation*. Boston: Beacon, 1984.

———. *In Memory of Her: A Feminist Reconstruction of Christian Origins*. New York: Crossroad, 1983.

———. *Revelation: Vision of a Just World*. Minneapolis: Fortress, 1991.

———. “The Will to Choose or to Reject: Continuing Our Critical Work.” Pages 125–35 in *Feminist Interpretation of the Bible*. Edited by Letty M. Russell. Philadelphia: Westminster, 1985.

Schweitzer, Albert. *The Quest of the Historical Jesus*. Translated by W. Montgomery. New York: Macmillan, 1968 (1906).

Schlatter, Adolf. “The Theology of the New Testament and Dogmatics.” Pages 117–

66 in *The Nature of New Testament Theology: The Contribution of William Wrede and Adolf Schlatter*. Edited and translated by Robert Morgan. SBT 2/25. London: SCM, 1973.

Scott, James M. *Adoption as Sons of God: An Exegetical Investigation into the Background of υἱοθεσία in the Pauline Corpus*. WUNT 2/48. Tübingen: Mohr Siebeck, 1992.

Segal, Alan F. *Paul the Convert: The Apostolate and Apostasy of Saul the Pharisee*. New Haven: Yale University Press, 1990.

Seitz, Christopher R. *The Character of Christian Scripture: The Significance of a Two-Testament Bible*. Grand Rapids: Baker Academic, 2011.

———. *Figured Out: Typology and Providence in Christian Scripture*. Louisville: Westminster John Knox, 2001.

Shum, Shiu-Lun. *Paul's Use of Isaiah in Romans*. WUNT 2/156. Tübingen: Mohr Siebeck, 2002.

Slater, Thomas B. *Christ and Community: A Socio-Historical Study of the Christology of Revelation*. JSNTSup 178. Sheffield: Sheffield University Press, 1999.

Spong, John Shelby. *Resurrection: Myth or Reality? A Bishop's Search for the Origins of Christianity*. San Francisco: HarperSanFrancisco, 1994.

Stanley, Christopher D. "'The Redeemer Will Come ἐκ Σιων': Romans 11:26–27 Revisited." Pages 118–42 in *Paul and the Scriptures of Israel*. Edited by Craig A. Evans and James A. Sanders. JSNTSup 83/SSEJC 1. Sheffield: JSOT, 1993.

Stanton, Graham. *Jesus and Gospel*. Cambridge: Cambridge University Press, 2004.

Stendahl, Krister. "The Apostle Paul and the Introspective Conscience of the West." *HTR* 56 (1963): 62–77.

———. *Paul among Jews and Gentiles*. Philadelphia: Fortress, 1976.

Sternberg, Meir. *The Poetics of Biblical Narrative: Ideological Literature and the Drama of Reading*. Bloomington: University of Indiana Press, 1985.

Stowers, Stanley K. *The Diatribe and Paul's Letter to the Romans*. SBLDS 57. Chico, CA: Scholars, 1981.

———. *A Rereading of Romans: Justice, Jews, and Gentiles*. New Haven: Yale University Press, 1994.

Stuckenbruck, Loren T. *Angel Veneration and Christology: A Study in Early Judaism and in the Christology of the Apocalypse of John*. WUNT 2/70. Tübingen: Mohr Siebeck, 1995.

Stuhlmacher, Peter. *Biblische Theologie des Neuen Testaments*. 2 vols. Göttingen: Vandenhoeck & Ruprecht, 1992–1999.

———. *Historical Criticism and Theological Interpretation of Scripture*. Translated by R. A. Harrisville. Philadelphia: Fortress, 1977 (1975).

Thiessen, Matthew. "Hebrews and the End of the Exodus." *NovT* 49 (2007): 353–69.

Thomas, Kenneth J. "The Old Testament Citations in Hebrews." *NTS* 11 (1964–1965): 303–25.

Thompson, Alan J. *One Lord, One People: The Unity of the Church in Acts in Its Literary Setting*. LNTS 359. London: T & T Clark, 2008.

Thompson, Marianne Meye. "His Own Received Him Not." Pages 258–76 in *The Art of Reading Scripture*. Edited by Ellen F. Davis and Richard B. Hays. Grand Rapids: Eerdmans, 2003.

———. "*Jesus and the Victory of God* Meets the Gospel of John." Pages 21–38 in *Jesus, Paul, and the People of God: A Theological Dialogue with N. T. Wright*. Edited by Nicholas Perrin and Richard B. Hays. Downers Grove, IL: IVP Academic, 2011.

———. *The Promise of the Father: Jesus and God in the New Testament*. Louisville: Westminster John Knox, 2000.

Tönges, Elke. "The Epistle to the Hebrews as a 'Jesus-Midrash.'" Pages 89–105 in *Hebrews: Contemporary Methods—New Insights*. Edited by Gabriella Gelardini. Leiden: Brill, 2005.

Tonstad, Sigve K. *Revelation*. Paideia Commentaries on the New Testament. Grand Rapids: Baker Academic, 2019.

———. *Saving God's Reputation: The Theological Function of* Pistis Iesou *in the Cosmic Narratives of Revelation*. LNTS 337. London: Continuum, 2006.

Tuckett, Christopher M. "The Christology of Luke-Acts." Pages 133–64 in *The Unity of Luke-Acts*. Edited by Joseph Verheyden. Leuven: Leuven University Press, 1999.

———. "Thomas and the Synoptics." *NovT* 30 (1988): 132–57.

Van Harn, Roger E., ed. *Exploring and Proclaiming the Apostles' Creed*. Grand Rapids: Eerdmans, 2004.

Vanhoozer, Kevin J. *The Drama of Doctrine: A Canonical-Linguistic Approach to Christian Theology*. Louisville: Westminster John Knox, 2005.

Verhey, Alan. *The Great Reversal: Ethics and the New Testament*. Grand Rapids: Eerdmans, 1984.

Vielhauer, Philipp. "Zum 'Paulinismus' der Apostelgeschichte." *EvT* 10 (1950–1951): 1–15. ET: "On the 'Paulinism' of Acts." Pages 33–50 in *Studies in Luke-Acts*. Edited by Leander E. Keck and J. Louis Martyn. Nashville: Abingdon, 1966.

Wagner, J. Ross. *Heralds of the Good News: Isaiah and Paul "in Concert" in the Letter to the Romans*. NovTSup 101. Leiden: Brill, 2002.

Walters, Stanley D., ed. *Go Figure! Figuration in Biblical Interpretation*. Princeton Theological Monograph Series. Eugene, OR: Pickwick, 2008.

Watson, Francis. "Is There a Story in These Texts?" Pages 231–39 in *Narrative*

Dynamics in Paul: A Critical Assessment. Louisville: Westminster John Knox, 2002.

———. *Paul and the Hermeneutics of Faith*. London: T & T Clark, 2004.

———. *Paul, Judaism, and the Gentiles: Beyond the New Perspective*. Rev. ed. Grand Rapids: Eerdmans, 2007 (1986).

Wedderburn, A. J. M. *The Reasons for Romans*. Edinburgh: T & T Clark, 1988.

———. "Sawing Off the Branches: Theologizing Dangerously *Ad Hebraeos*." *JTS* 56 (2005): 393–414.

Wenham, David. *Paul: Follower of Jesus or Founder of Christianity?* Grand Rapids: Eerdmans, 1995.

Westerholm, Stephen. *Israel's Law and the Church's Faith: Paul and His Recent Interpreters*. Grand Rapids: Eerdmans, 1988.

Wilckens, Ulrich. *Der Brief an die Römer*. Vol. 2. EKKNT 6/2. Zurich: Benziger Verlag; Neukirchen-Vluyn: Neukirchener Verlag, 1980.

Wilk, Florian. *Die Bedeutung des Jesajabuches für Paulus*. FRLANT 179. Göttingen: Vandenhoeck & Ruprecht, 1998.

———. "Paulus als Nutzer, Interpret und Leser des Jesajabuches." Pages 93–116 in *Die Bibel im Dialog der Schriften: Konzepte intertextueller Bibellektüre*. Edited by Stefan Alkier and Richard B. Hays. Tübingen: Francke, 2005.

Williams, Sam K. "Again *Pistis Christou*." *CBQ* 49 (1987): 431–47.

Wills, Garry. *What Jesus Meant*. New York: Viking, 2006.

Winger, Michael. *By What Law? The Meaning of Νόμος in the Letters of Paul*. SBLDS 128. Atlanta: Scholars, 1992.

Witherington, Ben, III. *The Christology of Jesus*. Minneapolis: Fortress, 1990.

———. *The Jesus Quest: The Third Search for the Jew of Nazareth*. Downers Grove, IL: IVP, 1995.

———. *Paul's Narrative Thought World: The Tapestry of Tragedy and Triumph*. Louisville: Westminster John Knox, 1994.

———. Review of *Echoes of Scripture in the Gospels*, by Richard Hays. *Bible and Culture*. April 20, 2016. https://www.patheos.com/blogs/bibleandculture/2016/04/20/richard-hays-echoes-of-scripture-in-the-gospels-a-review/.

Wolmarans, Johannes L. P. "The Text and Translation of Hebrews 8.8." *ZNW* 75 (1984): 139–44.

Wolter, Michael. "Ein exegetischer und theologischer Blick auf Rom 11.25–32." *NTS* 64 (2018): 123–42.

Wrede, William. "The Task and Methods of 'New Testament Theology.'" In *The Nature of New Testament Theology: The Contribution of William Wrede and Adolf Schlatter*. Edited and translated by Robert Morgan. SBT 2/25. London: SCM, 1973.

Wright, N. T. "Christian Origins and the Resurrection of Jesus: The Resurrection of Jesus as a Historical Problem." *Sewanee Theological Review* 41 (1998): 107–23.

———. *The Climax of the Covenant: Christ and the Law in Pauline Theology*. Edinburgh: T & T Clark, 1991; Minneapolis: Fortress, 1992.

———. *Jesus and the Victory of God*. Christian Origins and the Question of God 2. London: SPCK; Minneapolis: Fortress, 1996.

———. "The Law in Romans 2." Pages 131–50 in *Paul and the Mosaic Law*. Edited by James D. G. Dunn. Tübingen: Mohr Siebeck, 1996.

———. "Messiahship in Galatians?" Pages 3–23 in *Galatians and Christian Theology: Justification, the Gospel, and Ethics in Paul's Letter*. Edited by Mark W. Elliott, Scott J. Hafemann, N. T. Wright, and John Frederick. Grand Rapids: Baker Academic, 2014.

———. *The New Testament and the People of God*. Christian Origins and the Question of God 1. London: SPCK; Minneapolis: Fortress, 1992.

———. *Paul and His Recent Interpreters: Some Contemporary Debates*. Minneapolis: Fortress, 2015.

———. *Paul and the Faithfulness of God*. Christian Origins and the Question of God 4. London: SPCK; Minneapolis: Fortress, 2013.

———. "Paul in Current Anglophone Scholarship." *ExpTim* 123 (2012): 367–81.

———. "Pictures, Stories, and the Cross: Where Do the Echoes Lead?" *JTI* 11 (2017): 49–68.

———. *The Resurrection of the Son of God*. Christian Origins and the Question of God 3. London: SPCK; Minneapolis: Fortress, 2003.

———. "Revelation and Christian Hope: Political Implications of the Revelation to John." Pages 105–24 in *Revelation and the Politics of Apocalyptic Interpretation*. Edited by Richard B. Hays and Stefan Alkier. Waco: Baylor University Press, 2012.

———. "Romans." Pages 393–770 in *Acts, Introduction to Epistolary Literature, Romans, 1 Corinthians*. Edited by Leander E. Keck. *NIB* 10. Nashville: Abingdon, 2002.

Yeago, David S. "The New Testament and the Nicene Dogma: A Contribution to the Recovery of Theological Exegesis." Pages 87–100 in *The Theological Interpretation of Scripture: Classic and Contemporary Readings*. Edited by Stephen E. Fowl. Oxford: Blackwell, 2001.

Index of Authors

Index of Subjects

Index of Ancient Sources

2 Corinthians

Galatians

Ephesians